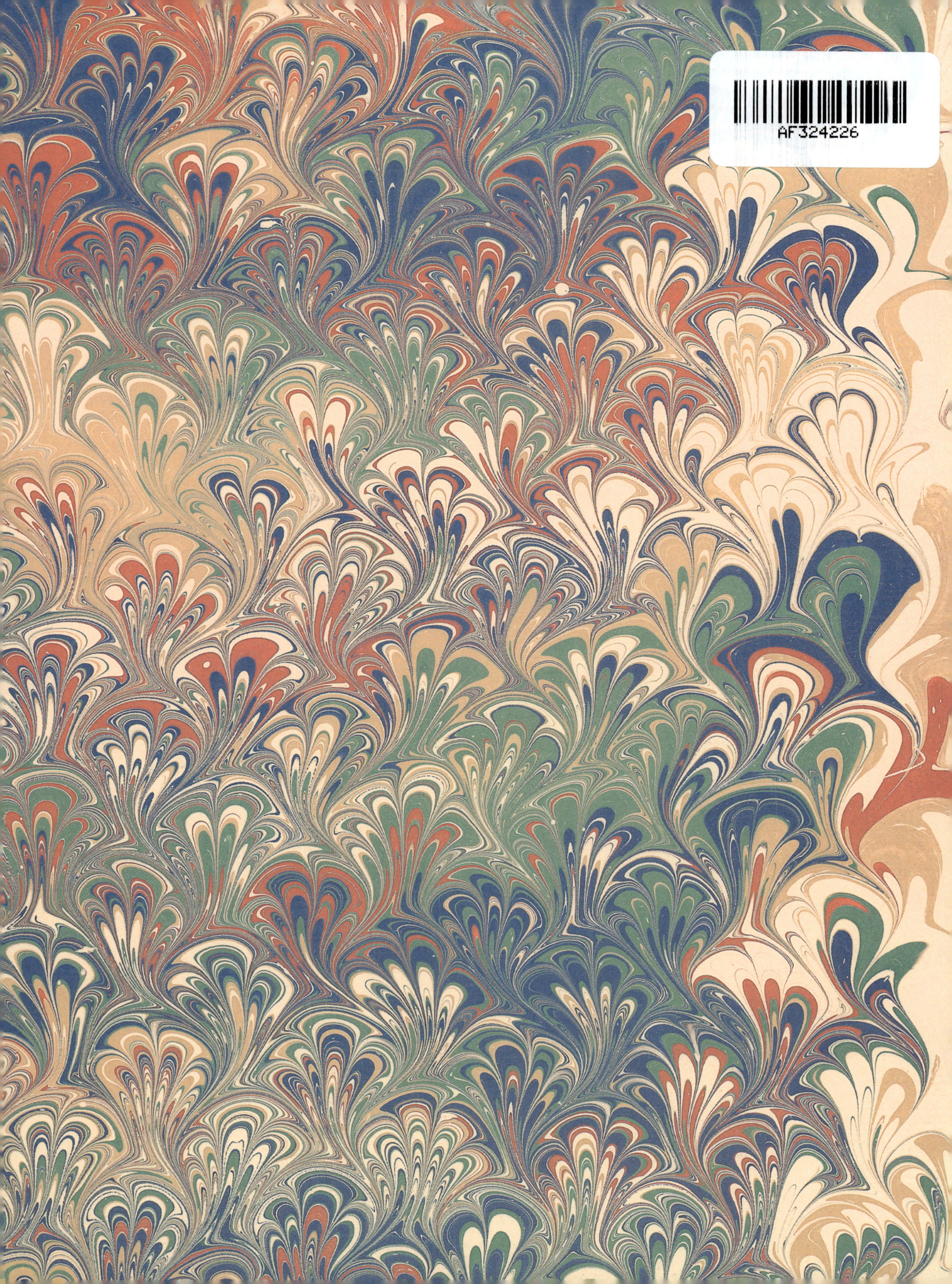
AF324226

Quest For Quimper

Barbara Walker & David Williamson

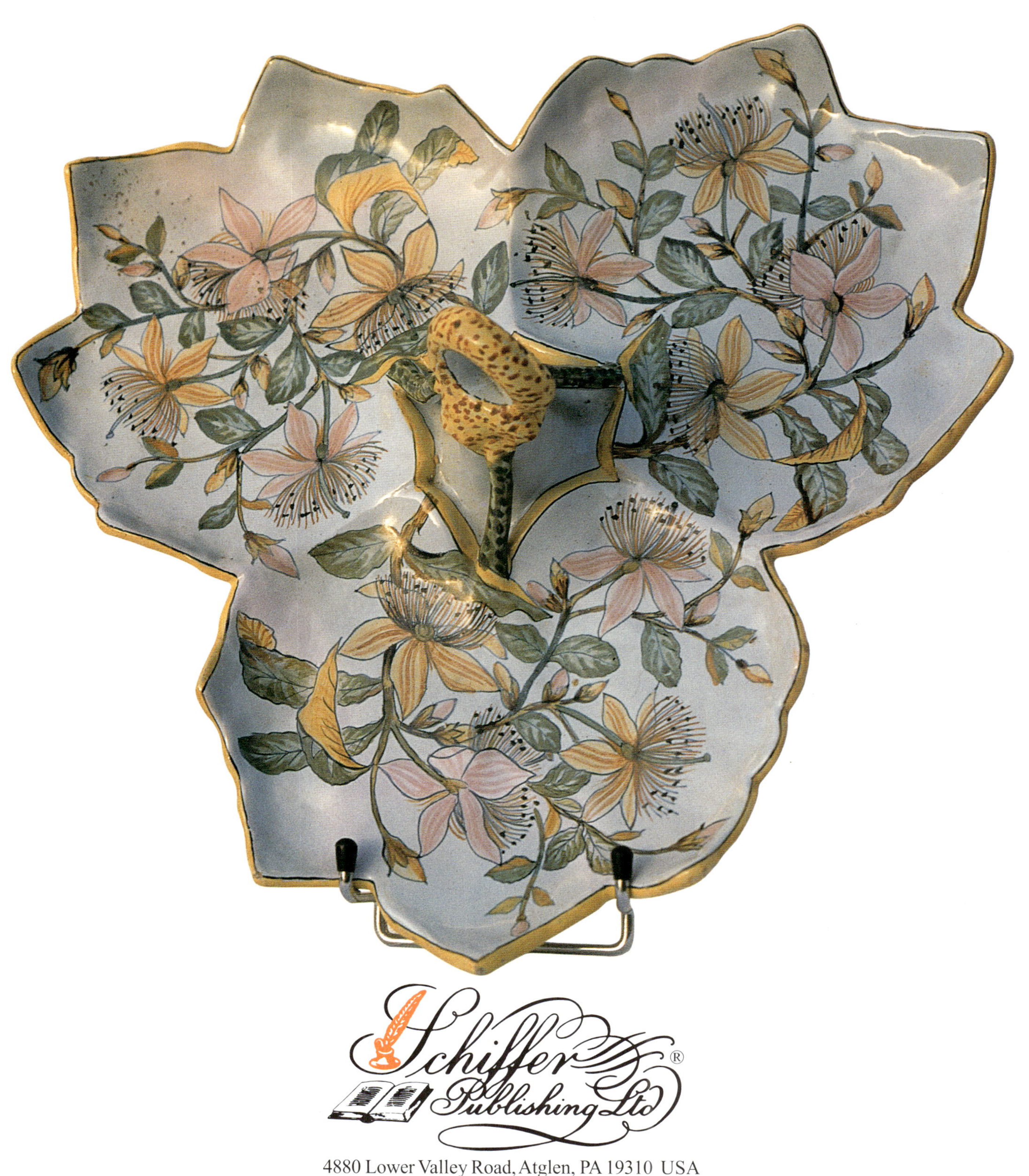

Schiffer Publishing Ltd

4880 Lower Valley Road, Atglen, PA 19310 USA

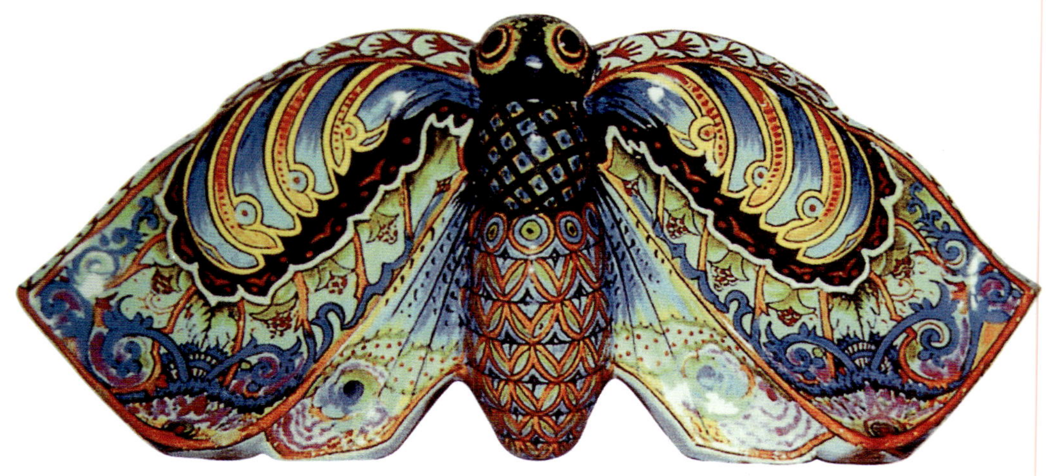

Copyright © 2002 by Barbara Walker & David Williamson
Library of Congress Control Number: 2001093576

Designed by "Sue"
Type set in Exotc350 DmBd BT©187
/Korinna BT

ISBN: 0-7643-1479-3
Printed in China
1 2 3 4

Published by Schiffer Publishing Ltd.
4880 Lower Valley Road
Atglen, PA 19310
Phone: (610) 593-1777; Fax: (610) 593-2002
E-mail: Schifferbk@aol.com
Please visit our web site catalog at **www.schifferbooks.com**
We are always looking for people to write books on new and related subjects. If you have an idea for a book please contact us at the above address.

This book may be purchased from the publisher.
Include $3.95 for shipping.
Please try your bookstore first.
You may write for a free catalog.

In Europe, Schiffer books are distributed by
Bushwood Books
6 Marksbury Ave.
Kew Gardens
Surrey TW9 4JF England
Phone: 44 (0) 20 8392-8585; Fax: 44 (0) 20 8392-9876
E-mail: Bushwd@aol.com
Free postage in the U.K., Europe; air mail at cost.

❧ Contents

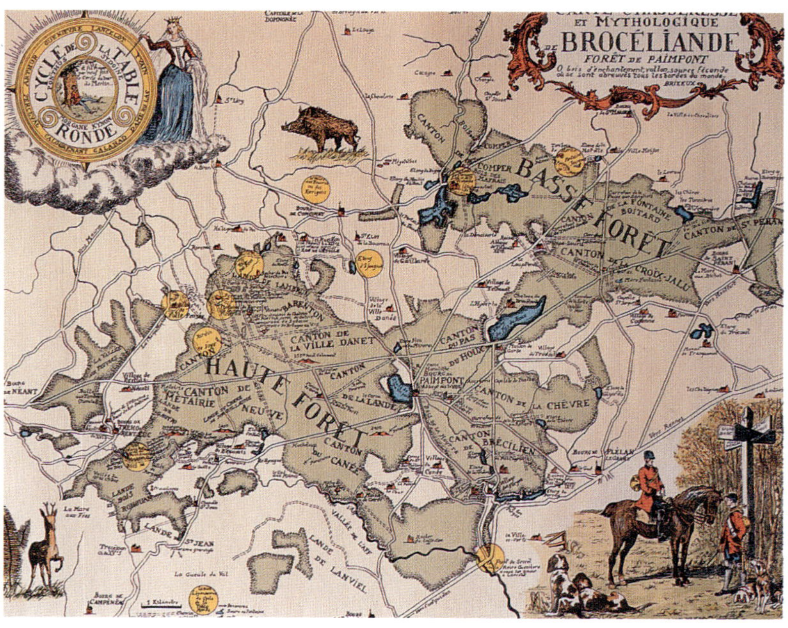

This map of early *Brocéliande* tells of mysterious places of enchantment where King Arthur, the Knights of the Round Table, and Merlin searched for the Holy Grail and eternal love. *Private Collection.*

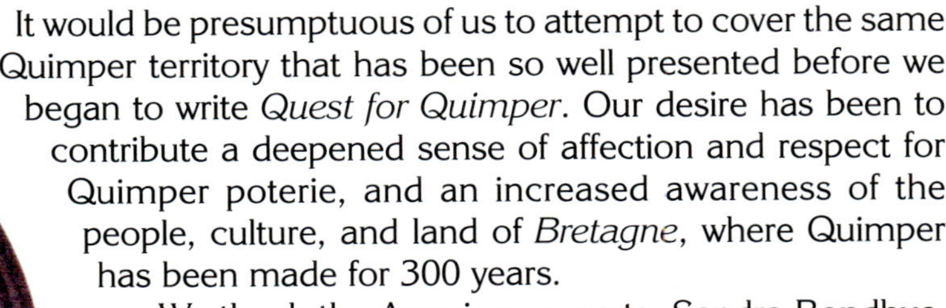

It would be presumptuous of us to attempt to cover the same Quimper territory that has been so well presented before we began to write *Quest for Quimper*. Our desire has been to contribute a deepened sense of affection and respect for Quimper poterie, and an increased awareness of the people, culture, and land of *Bretagne*, where Quimper has been made for 300 years.

We thank the American experts, Sandra Bondhus, Joan Datesman, Millicent Mali, Adela Meadows, and Ann Marie O'Neill for their research work and books. We are grateful to the Quimper writers and other experts in Brittany: Bernard-Jules Verlingue, Pierre-Jules Henriot, Laurent Cahn, Christian de la Hubaudière, Phillipe LeStum, Maurice Fouillen, André Cariou, Michel Roullot, J.R. Rotté, Marc Antoine Ruzette, Marjatta Taburet, Joseph Henriot, and many more. Also *Les Amis du Musée de la Faïence* bulletin and Millicent Mali's *Old Quimper Review* contributed immensely to our appreciation of Quimper poterie. A special note of thanks goes to Millicent Mali, Bernard Verlingue, and Lucy Williams for their continuing support and encouragement during the year we spent developing this work.

The contributors of Quimper examples to *Quest for Quimper* number over 50. Following are those who wanted their names in the acknowledgments only: Robert P. Carter, Jr., Valerie & Jerry DeVos, Gloria Ernst, Ann P. Griffin, Marilyn Levinson, Millicent S. Mali, David Schaff, Ltd., Yves and Claude Tréhu, Michael & Molly Williamson, William A. Rodgers, and Robert Zoll. Numerous other contributors are listed under photographs throughout the book. Thank you! And thank you also to those who contributed, but wished to remain anonymous.

All of the above have contributed to the documentation of the history and the personalities, as well as the faïence of Quimper. There are many, many others also who contributed to this body of knowledge, and we apologize for not having listed everyone. *Pardon!* We wish all a *bon voyage* to Brittany, whether in person, by book, or even by the Internet. We hope you enjoy the journey!

A wise young man said to us: *Every journey has an end...a goal is reached, a lesson learned, something accomplished. Writing a book is a journey, and all the effort, time, and experience are yours.* Thank you, Charlie. Your focus and assistance helped immeasurably.

Dedication

For Kathleen W. G. LaLonde, who knew how to travel and how to laugh at life's journey. Several years ago, my husband, David Williamson, and I, began to recount our visits to Brittany in search of Quimper poterie as a series of letters to Aunt Kay. This book grew out of those letters.

Barbara Walker

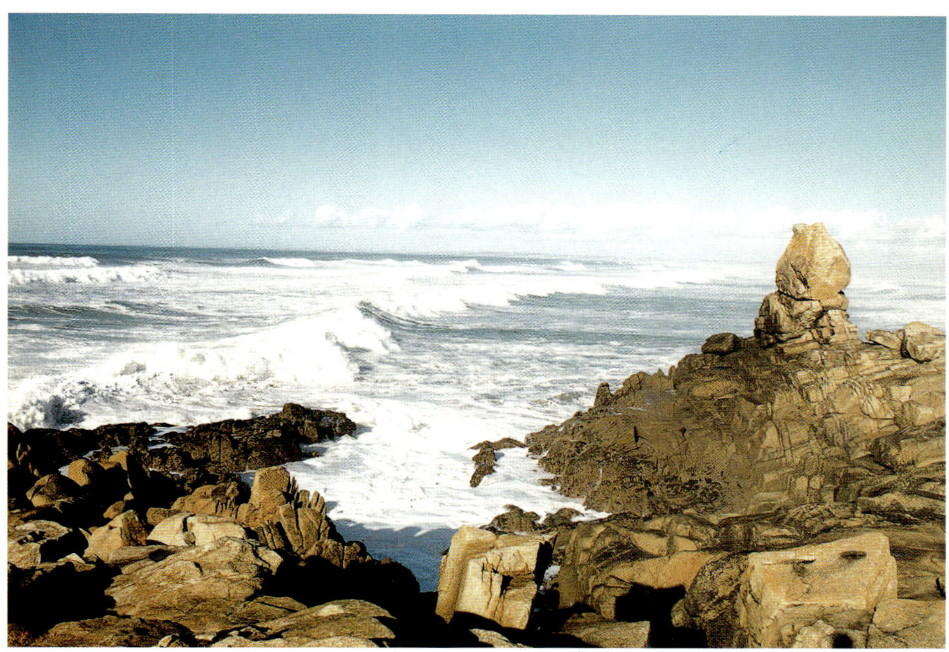

The ocean crashing at *La Torche* on the coast of *Pays Bigouden* stunned us with its might, even on a calm day. After seeing its power, we now envision the *triskele*, our logo, as the never-ending waves breaking on the rugged coast of Brittany.

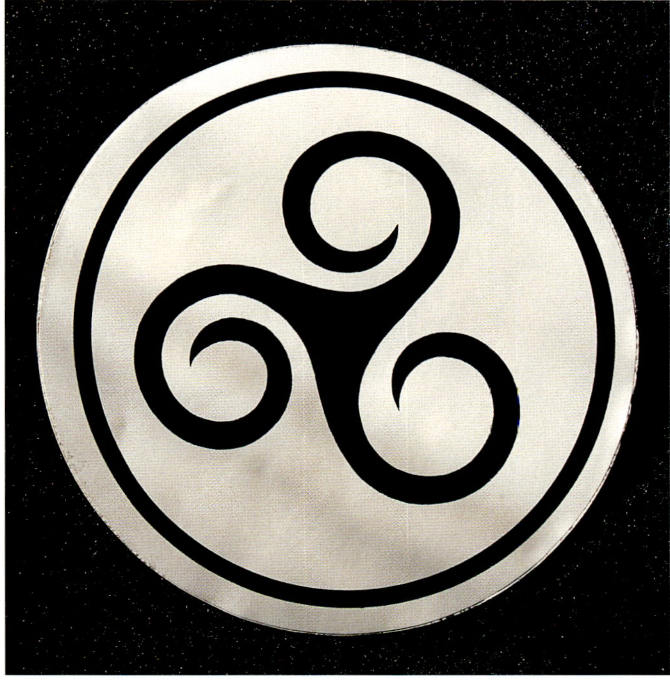

The simple *triskele* is a spiral with three arms radiating from its center, found on Celtic stonework and crosses. It also can be seen as representing the three aspects of nature required for making poterie: earth, water, and fire.

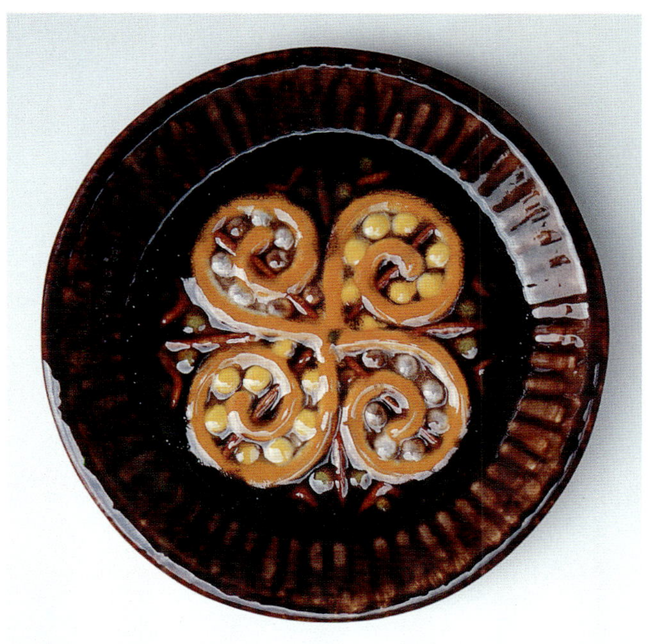

The evolution of the *triskele* from a simple spiral to a balanced, revolving circle can reflect humankind's growth in artistic expression. A version appears on René Quillivic's 10.5" charger for HB faïencerie, c. 1930. *Authors' Collection.*

✎ Foreword

Millicent S. Mali

In the last twenty-five to thirty years, the world of Quimper pottery collectors has been treated to a deluge of information on their favorite faience. Since 1976 when Marjatta Taburet's first booklet appeared in France, at least fifteen French and American authors have dealt with the history of the manufacture and the origins of the factories. Some books have told of artistic designs, be they from Marseilles, Nevers, or Rouen; or they have traced the development of new techniques as *coulage* or *à la poire*, or the creation of new formulae as in the production of *grès* ware and Odetta.

Through this information, the American collector has developed a love for the colorful pottery from Quimper, almost an addiction. Captivated by the little peasant figures, the assertive rooster and the handsome geometric patterns, collectors have zeroed in on the source. They come to Quimper, visit the factories and the museums, and feel they have reached Nirvana.

However, this book by Barbara Walker and her husband, David Williamson, takes the reader on a new tack. Here we are invitied to go along with the authors on their quest. The voyage becomes as important as the destination.

Over the years, as Barbara and David visit many sites throughout Brittany, they became aware of the folkways in each region. They discover aspects of the environment that characterize Breton culture and come to see how these influences show up in the art, the mystery, and the tradition that goes into the creation of Quimper faience.

Since 65 percent to 70 percent of the annual Quimper faience production is sold within the province of Brittany, it must follow that this product resonates with the Breton spirit.

In this book, Barbara Walker and David Williamson have given us access to a wider Breton experience and opened our appreciation for the larger picture. They have shared their encounters with Breton customs, architecture and prehistory, and shown us how this knowledge enriches our love for the pottery.

Welcome to Brittany! Welcome to the heart of Quimper faience!

✎ Authors' Note

A word on words: Poterie is the French word both for a piece of pottery and the place of manufacture. It has been used interchangeably with the French word *faïence*, the piece, and *faïencerie*, the place of manufacture.

Earthenware, faïence, and pottery also are synonymous, but to experts there are differences. Cox, in *The Book of Pottery and Porcelain*, explains that earthenware is used correctly to name pottery, whether glazed or unglazed, but excludes porcelains and stoneware. When earthenware is coated with a clear glaze, usually containing lead, it is called pottery, but if it is not glazed, it is called terra cotta. When it is coated with a stanniferous glaze, one containing tin oxide and lead, an opaque coating hides the color of the body of the piece, and it is called faïence, majolica, or delft, depending on the geographic locale. However, Cox warns against splitting hairs in the terminology, which has evolved over centuries in various locales and languages. (*Cox, pp. vii-viii and pp. xiii-xv*)

Pottery and faïence are used interchangeably by many American authors. The word faïence originates from the town of Faenza, Italy, where tin-enameled earthenware was produced in the 16th century. *(Cox, p. 354)* We chose to use the term poterie to cover the products of the Quimper faïenceries or poteries. We understand the experts' terminology, including that *grès* or stoneware differs from the technical definition of earthenware. For the sake of a general reference in this book, all of these terms come together under the heading of Quimper poterie. We have chosen to treat poterie, faïence, and faïencerie as English words, and not italicize them in the text, unless they're within a proper name.

❧ Introduction

Quimper poterie is a colorful record of the Breton people, their history, art, and spirit. Our passion for Quimper has taken us to Brittany more than a twelve times in the past dozen years on buying trips for our antiques business. We have learned about Breton customs, language, religious beliefs, and families, as well as a remarkable and humbling pre-history.

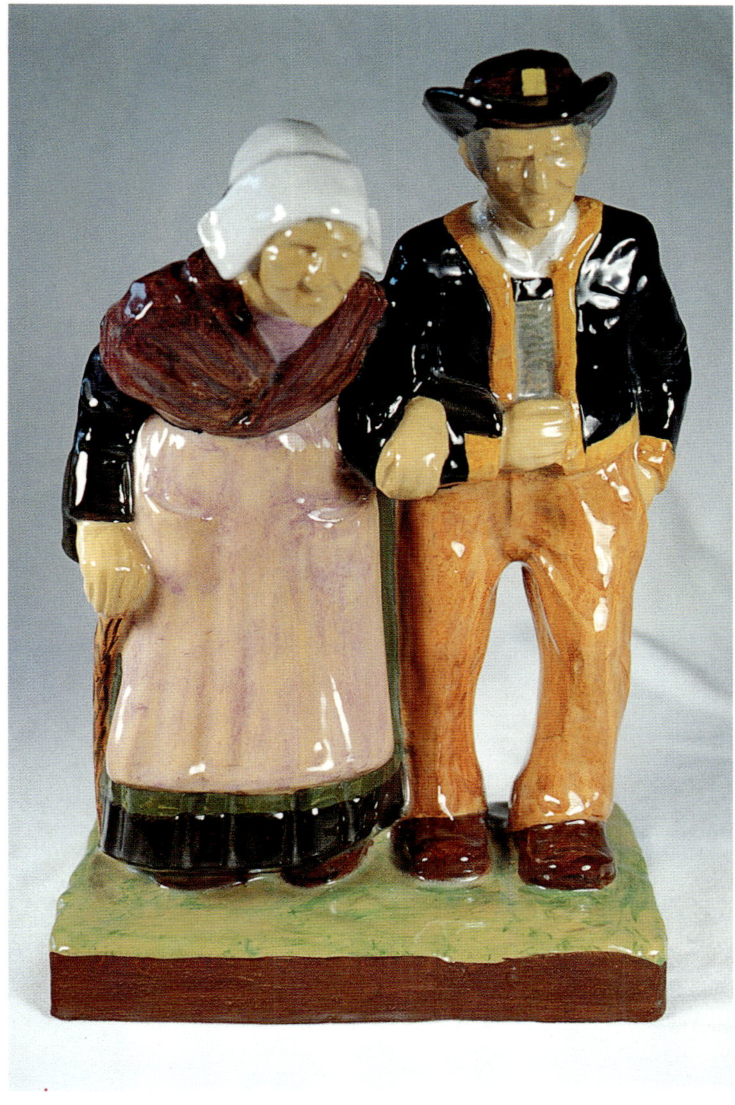

An elderly couple strolls through their golden years in this early-to-mid-20th century 12.75" tall faïence statue. It is signed with the town name, *Pornic*. Many souvenir wares were signed only with the name of the town or area where they were to be sold. *Courtesy of A.W. Styer.*

Below:
The *petit Breton* has captured the heart and imagination of people throughout the world, after first appearing on Quimper poterie in the 1860s. Legend has it the original *petit Breton* was based on a *pillou,* or itinerant goods hawker, from the *Monts d'Arrée*. This rendition on an 8" plate by Henriot is from the 1930s. *Authors' Collection.*

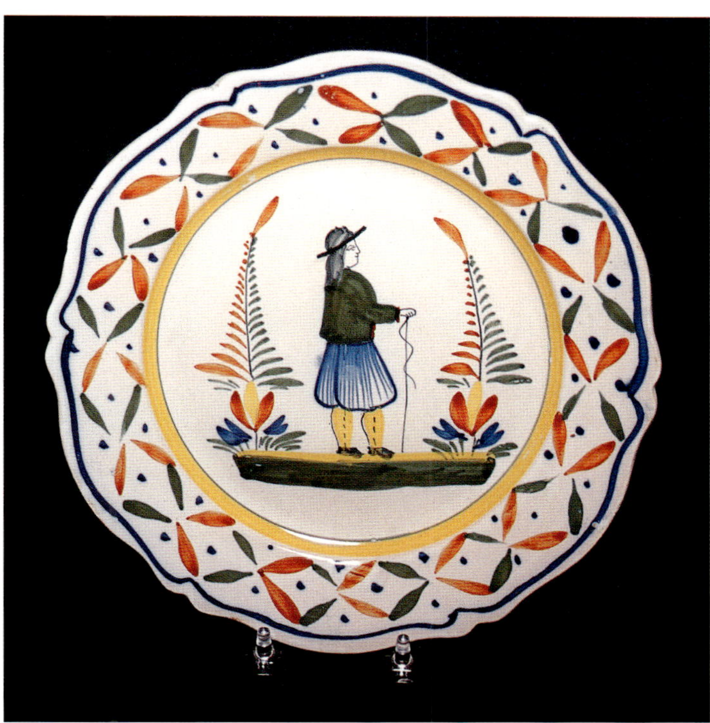

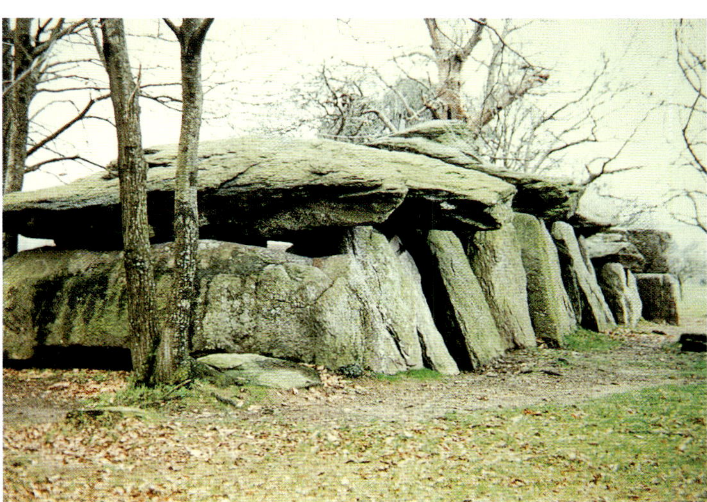

Prehistoric monuments abound in Brittany, including the famous *La Roche aux Fées*, or Fairies Rock, located about an hour's drive from Rennes, the capital of Brittany.

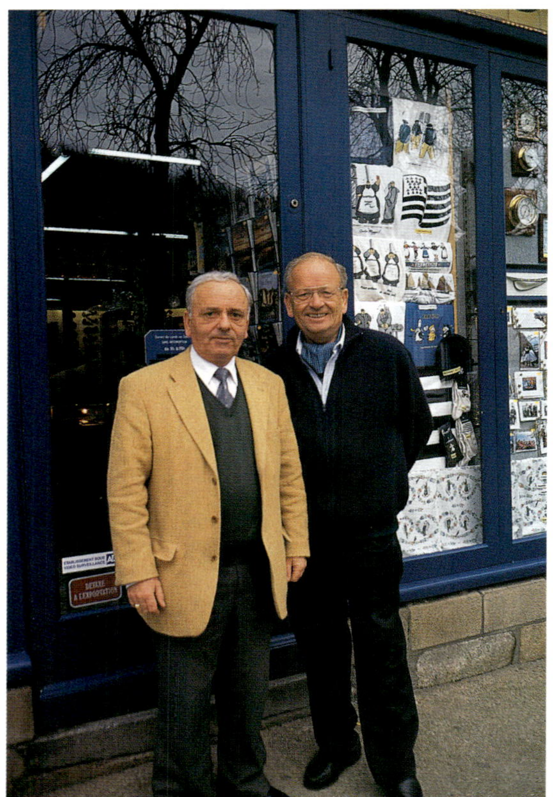

The Breton brothers, Jean-Claude (left) and Pierre (right), are known to most serious Quimper collectors. Their father, Alphonse Breton, began the family business in the city of Quimper in the 1930s and specialized in Quimper poterie. The tradition continues today with their grown children, Jean Claude's daughter, Gwénola, and Pierre's son, Michael, stepping into managerial positions at their respective stores.

We met a variety of merchants, faïencerie and museum directors, auctioneers, innkeepers, restaurateurs, and others on our quest, giving us a robust sense of *Bretagne*. We gained knowledge of her history, folklore, and present-day concerns through conversations and experiences with cordial Bretons, who were glad that we cared enough to slow down and see their land filled with history, a history that pre-dates our American experience.

The names Verlingue and Henriot are synonymous with the history of the *faïence de Quimper*. Left, Bernard Verlingue, whose grandfather finalized the purchase of the *HB/Grande Maison* faïencerie in 1917, and Pierre Henriot right, the great-grandson of the founder of the *Faïencerie d'Art Breton, Jules Henriot*.

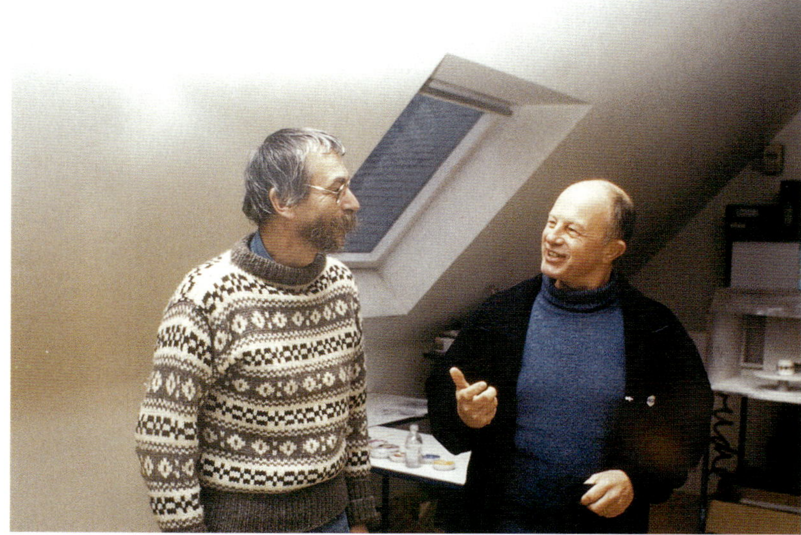

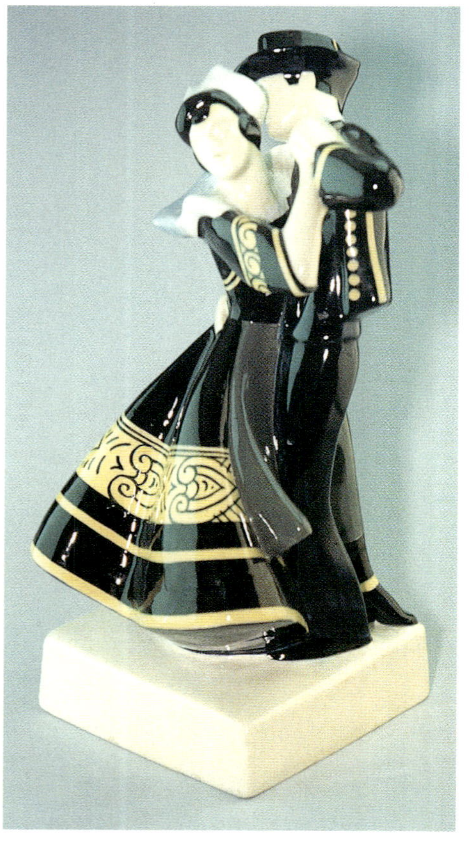

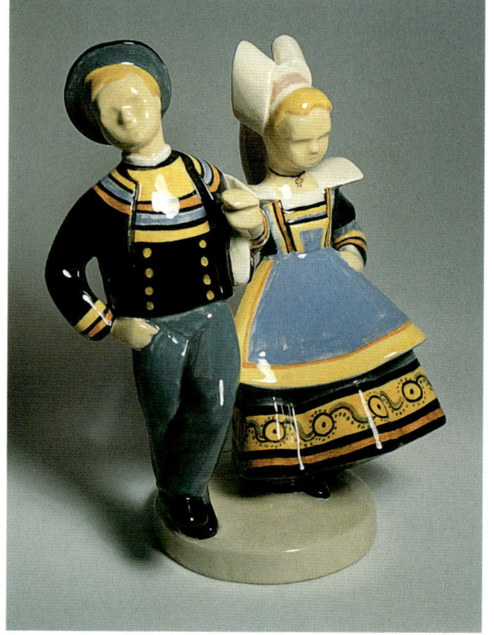

Micheau-Vernez also captured children dancing the *gavotte*. This sweet example is 9.25" tall, signed Henriot Quimper and from the 1940s. *Private Collection.*

Bretons swirl in ceramic to the music of Brittany played by *sonneurs*, the Breton musical duo of *biniou*, or bagpipe, and *bombarde*, an oboe-like instrument. Signed by Henriot artist R. Micheau-Vernez, the statue is 12.5", and from the 1930s. *Authors' Collection.*

Our first few trips were frenzied buying expeditions, racing to cover as much ground as we could. But our pace began to change, as we learned more of the culture surrounding Quimper. It still was essential to find wonderful examples to take home to our antiques gallery, but the real joy became the journey. Slowing our pace, we found even more Quimper poterie. Simultaneously, we began to see Brittany in all her beauty, culture, and history. Our most important discovery became *Bretagne*.

In the days when tourism was only for the few, those few knew how to open their eyes and learn from their journeys with the same care they put into getting pleasure out of them.
(Hélias, Images of Brittany, p.3.)

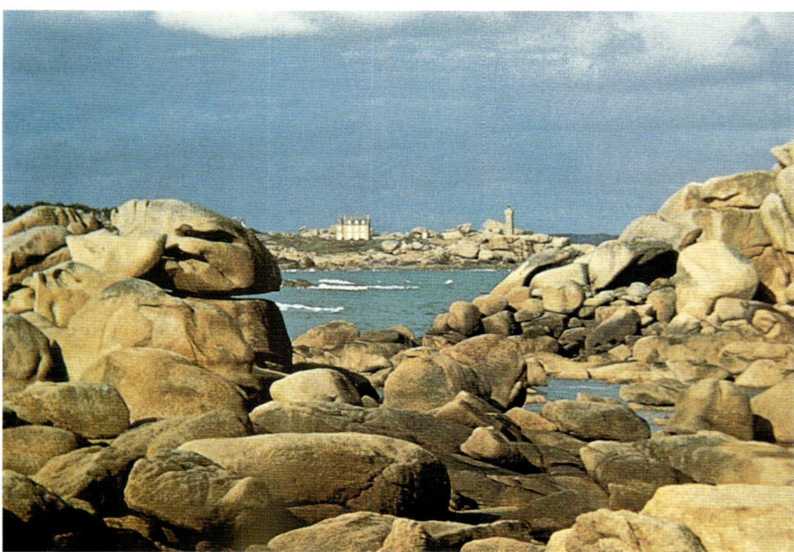

From the rocky northern coast of Armor …

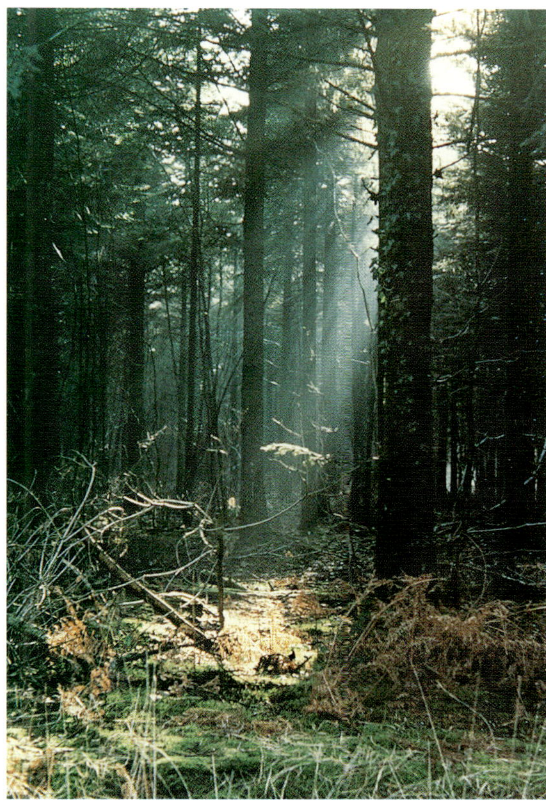

To the inland forests of Argoat …

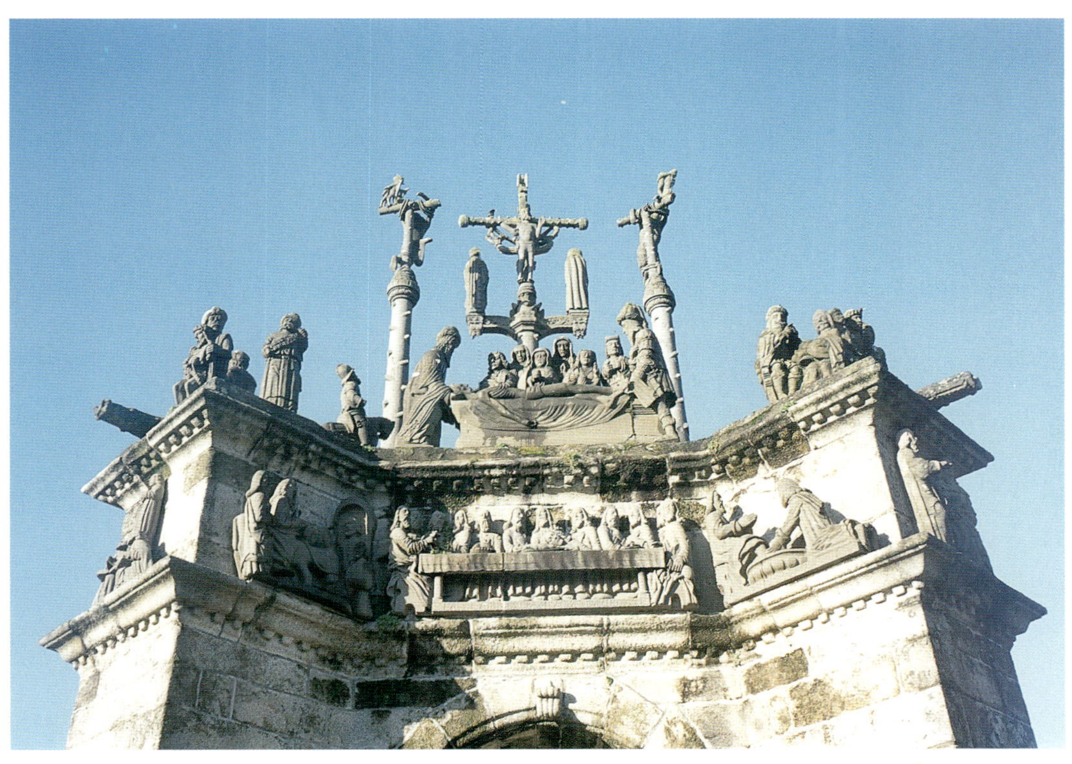

To parish closes like Pleyben … Brittany is a feast for the eyes.

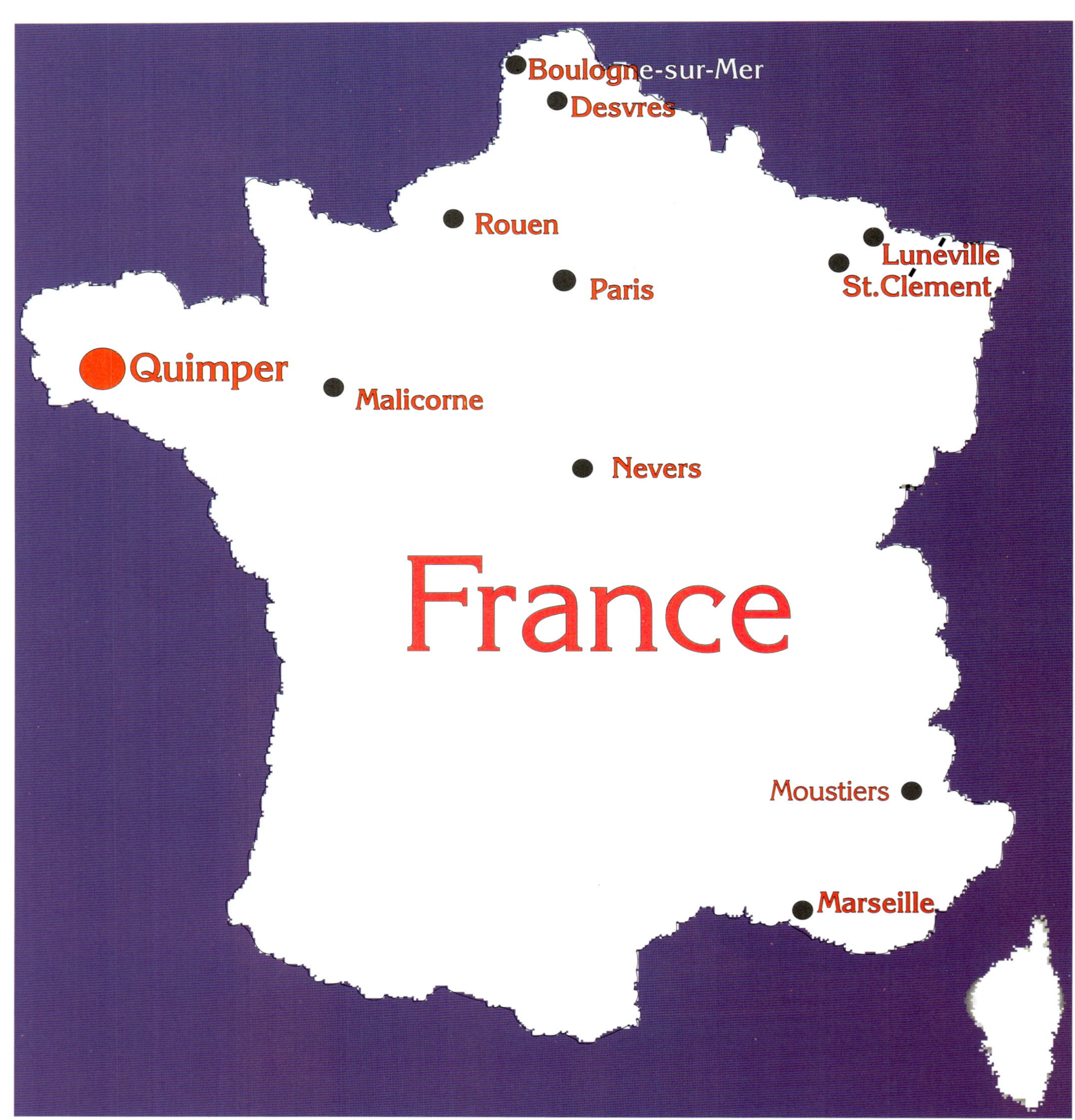

Boulogne-sur-Mer
Desvres
Rouen
Paris
Lunéville
St.Clement
Quimper
Malicorne
Nevers
France
Moustiers
Marseille

Part I The Road to Quimper
✤ Paris

Paris is called the most beautiful city in the world and we agree. The City of Lights also is a living museum. Works of art are everywhere, and at every turn of a corner is another historical building, sculpted gem, or intricately decorated bridge. Even everyday scenes take on an aura of glamour. Whether your bent is history, architecture, fine art or fine food, Paris has it all. Cosmopolitan, yet firmly rooted in the Old World, its many facets make Paris the city for lovers, artists, poets, and sightseers.

Paris belongs to the world. *(Carrick, Collector's Luck in France, p. ix.)*

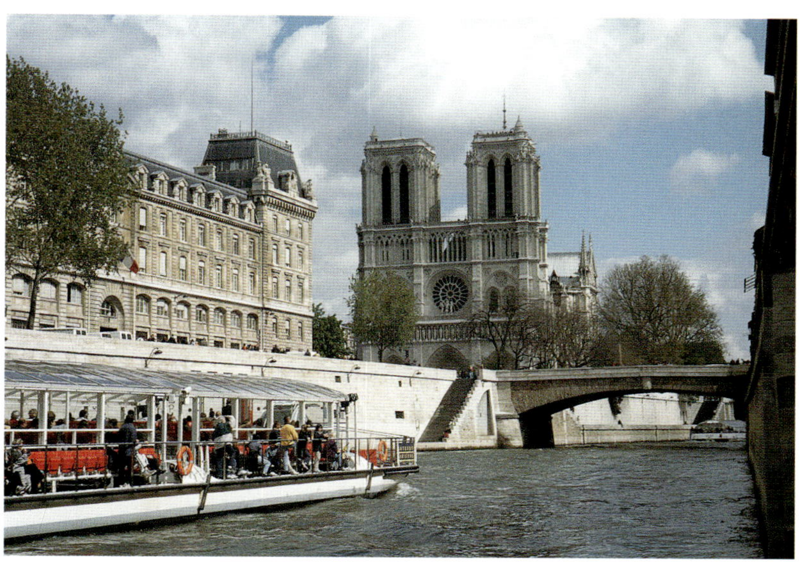

Ah, Paris… home to *Notre Dame* and the *bateaux-mouche* on the Seine.

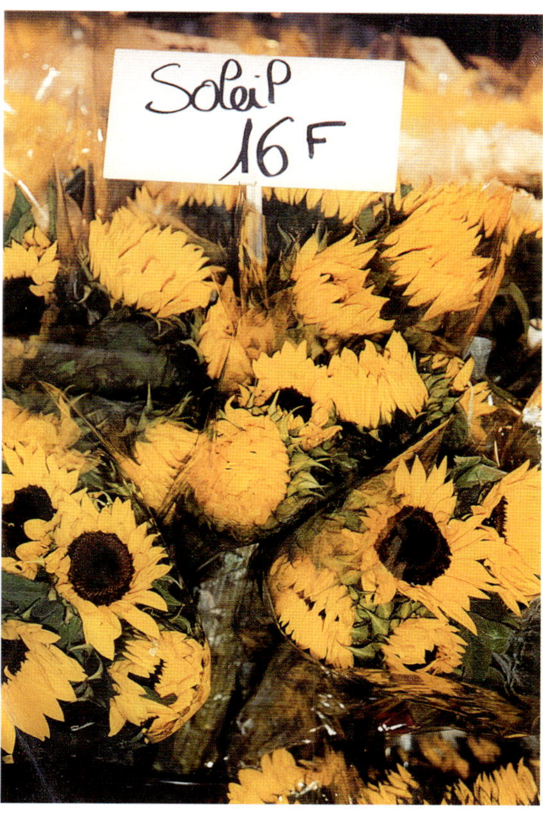

On every street corner throughout the city are scenes that shimmer with glamour and flowers.

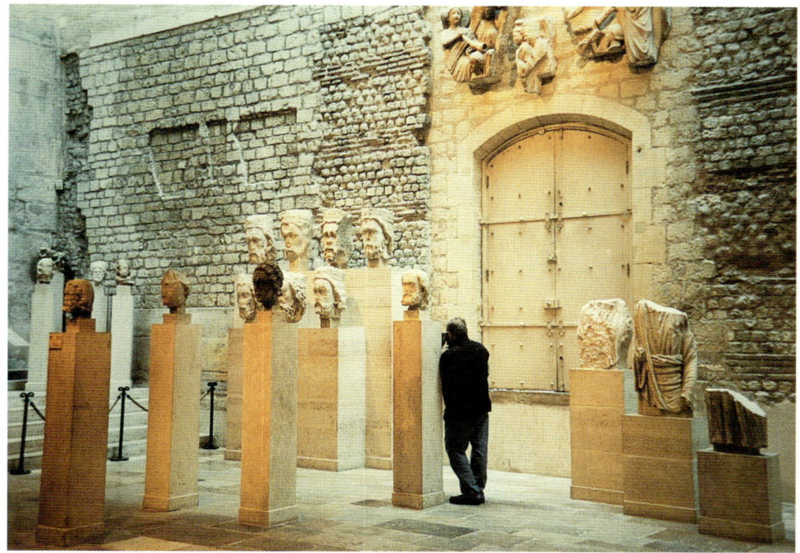

Museums, like the Louvre and Cluny, are part of the daily life of Paris.

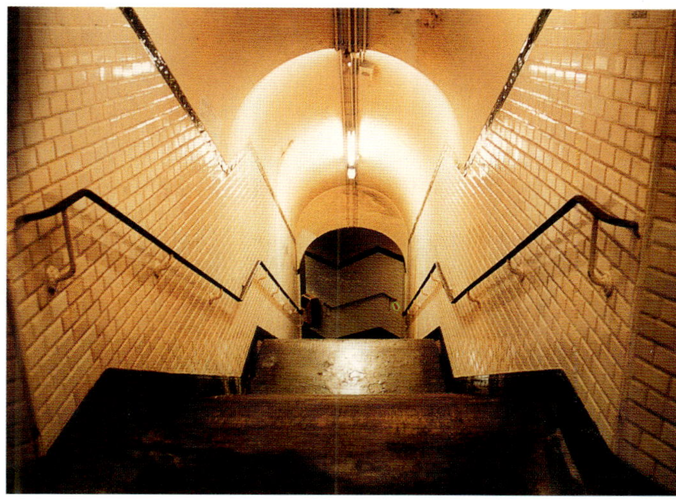

Even the Metro entrances can be a design in harmony.

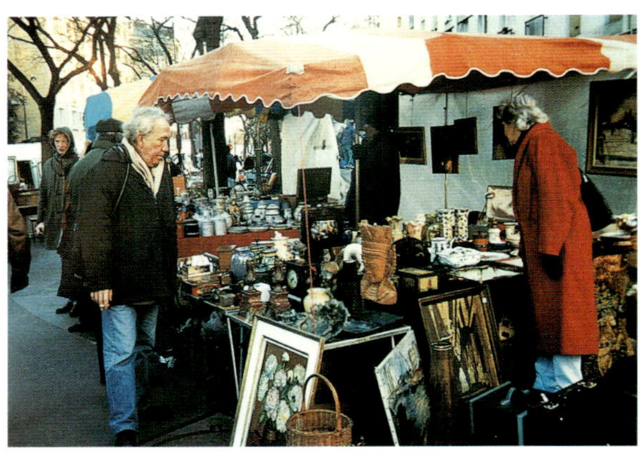

Vanves has fewer dealers than Clignancourt but offers an interesting assortment of faïence, art, and fabrics. Some goods are presented on tables, while others are on sidewalk blankets.

Paris put its Old World wares on display for sale at numerous antiques fairs and five major antiques markets, generally held on weekends. We began our pursuit of Quimper poterie in the antiques bazaars of Paris, and have developed some favorites.

Vanves

Imagine the street in front of your house was turned into a flea market every Saturday and Sunday for half the day. That is the scene along a six-block-long stretch in Vanves, starting around the corner from the Metro station. First-time visitors might have trouble finding it. But, as happens with so many outdoor markets, we quickly found the way by trailing the Vanves market's dedicated following. You'll find regular merchants, with an established pecking order, and several sell Quimper and related faïence artifacts. Instead of suggesting a specific starting point, we urge you to browse. There are treasures hiding in the myriad of merchandise spread out on sidewalk blankets and flimsy tables. Our best advice is to buy it when you see it, because it might be gone on your way back. Yes, it happened to us with a set of Plozévet furniture. Ouch!

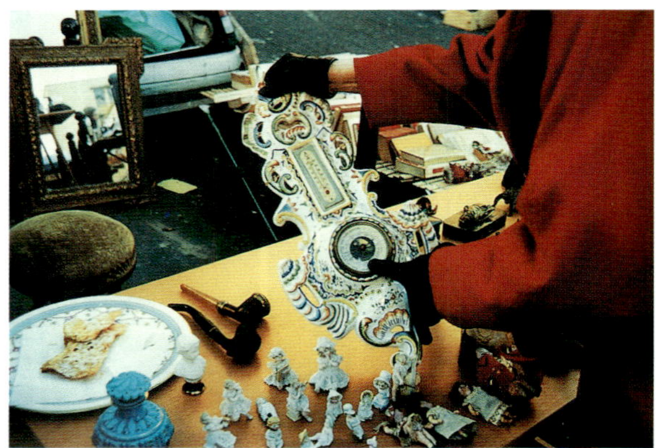

We suggest you look everything over carefully at any flea market before making your choice, and follow your instinct.

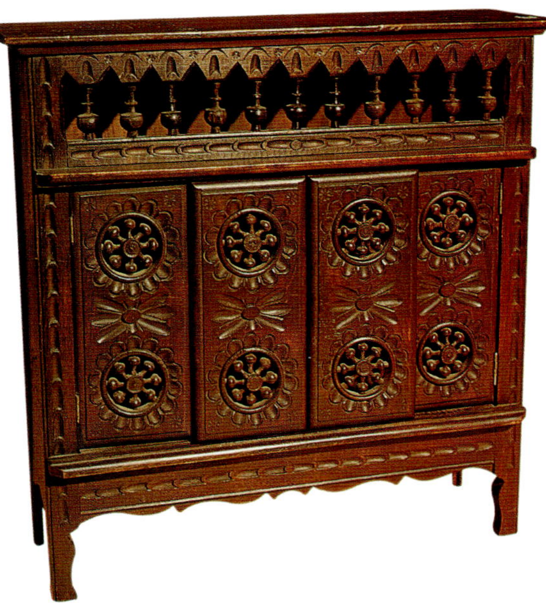

Doll furniture from Plozévet, a town about 35 kilometers west of Quimper, is prized by collectors. This example from the 1920s is a *lit clos,* or Breton enclosed bed. Plozévet doll furniture incorporates elements from full-sized Breton furniture, such as *fuseaux.*

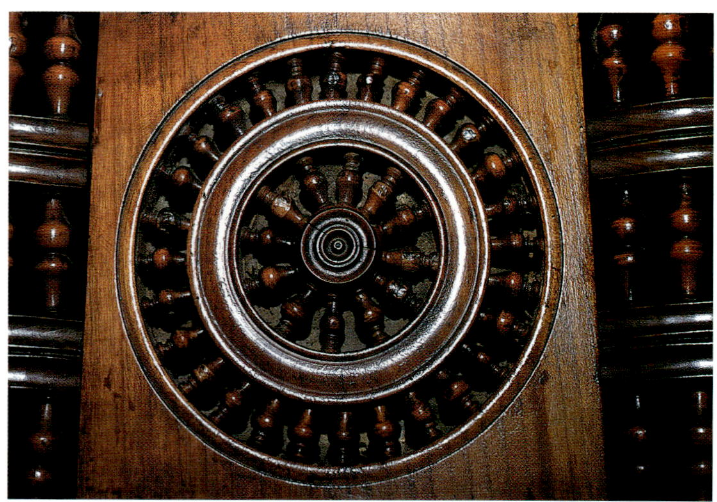

The décor element called *fuseaux* is a series of spindles set in a *rosace,* or circle. It is found on full-sized furniture of earlier days in Brittany.

We learned a valuable lesson in identifying fake Quimper at Vanves. A faïencerie outside of Paris is producing new Quimper-like items that look old, what we call, *made to fool*. This faïencerie, *Les Fils Duquenne*, or *Faïencerie d'Art de St. Germain, Reproduction de Fäiences Anciennes*, was identified by Millicent Mali. *(Mali, Old Quimper Review, October 1994.)*

We were caught in this fool's net when we unknowingly purchased a barber bowl, signed only with the word *quimper*. (Note the lower case *q*.) We paid the equivalent of $150 for it, and sold it soon after our return to the United States. After we discovered the true manufacturer, we contacted our purchaser and offered to buy back the barber bowl. The customer chose to keep it. The price of these fake Quimper barber bowls has fallen dramatically since, and in 2001 they were selling for a little over $50. Recently, a Vanves merchant assured us that a *Fils Duquenne* barber bowl was Quimper. Be aware and beware.

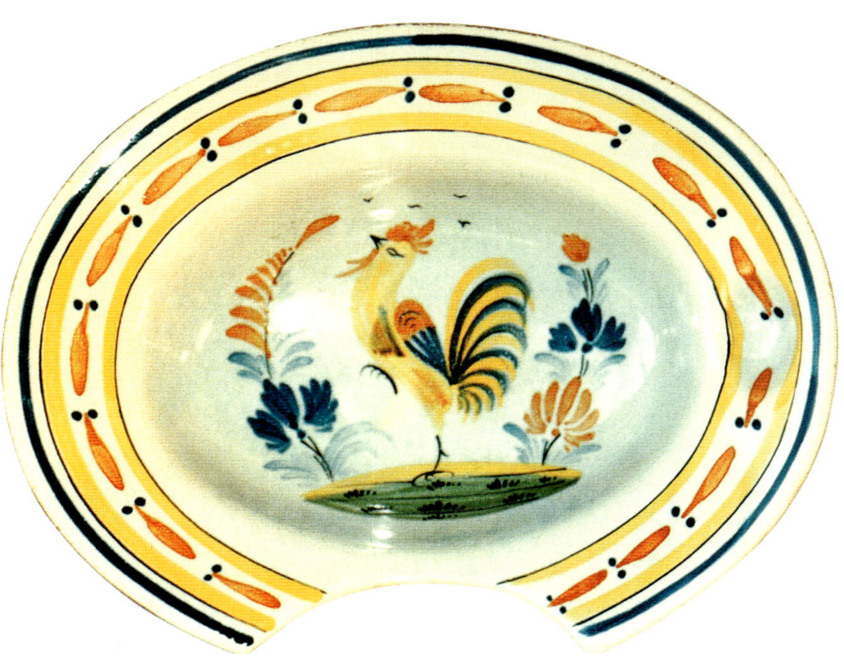

We were fooled by this barber bowl with a French *coq*. It looked like Quimper.

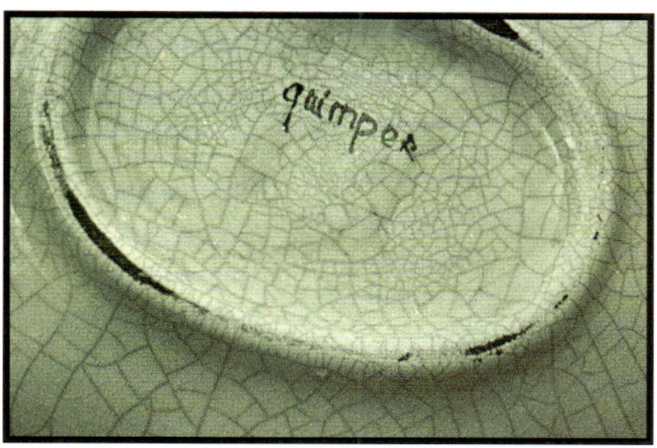

When we turned the barber bowl over, the signature of the *Les Fils Duquenne* factory read *quimper* only, with a lower case *q*.

Saint-Ouen, *Marché de Puces*, Clignancourt

This series of markets at Saint-Ouen, or *Marché de Puces*, is best known to most Americans by the name of the closest Metro stop, *Porte de Clignancourt*. Originally a settlement on the outskirts of Paris where hawkers sold their wares without interference from the police, this huge flea market has grown beyond the first merchants' wildest dreams.

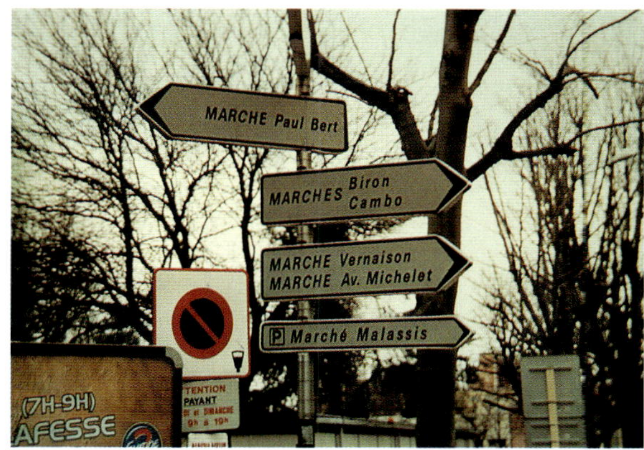

St. Ouen is a series of markets located at the end of a Metro line at *Porte de Clignancourt*.

If you're up for a physical challenge, try shopping all the markets at Clignancourt in one day. The first market most shoppers encounter is the quaintest. The Vernaison market's winding alleyways can confuse inattentive shoppers, sending you in a circle if you're not careful. And if you see something you want to come back to reconsider, mark your location well or you'll lose time trying to find the stall later. Then it's on to the adjacent markets at Clignancourt: Dauphine, Paul Bert, Biron, Serpette…the list goes on and on!

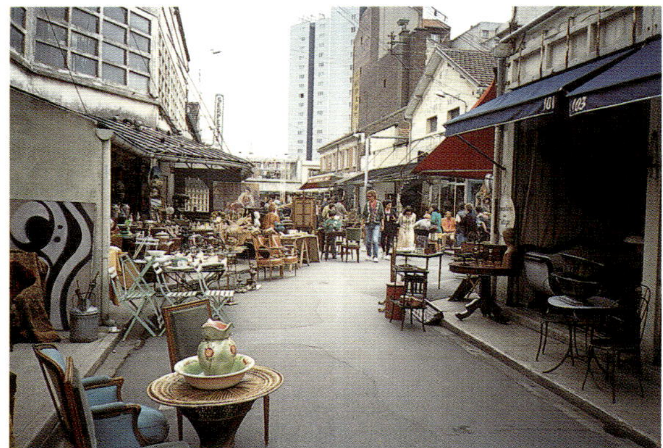

The market Vernaison has stalls along winding alleyways, which can become a labyrinth to the uninitiated.

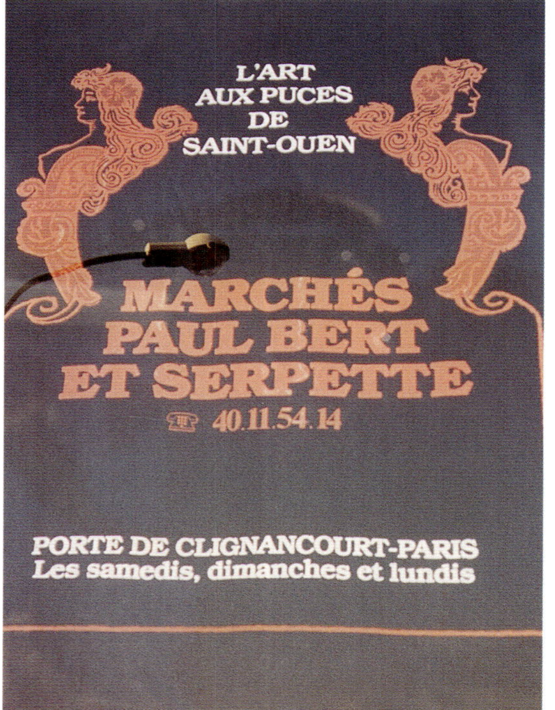

The many markets of Clignancourt can challenge the most inveterate Quimper shopper.

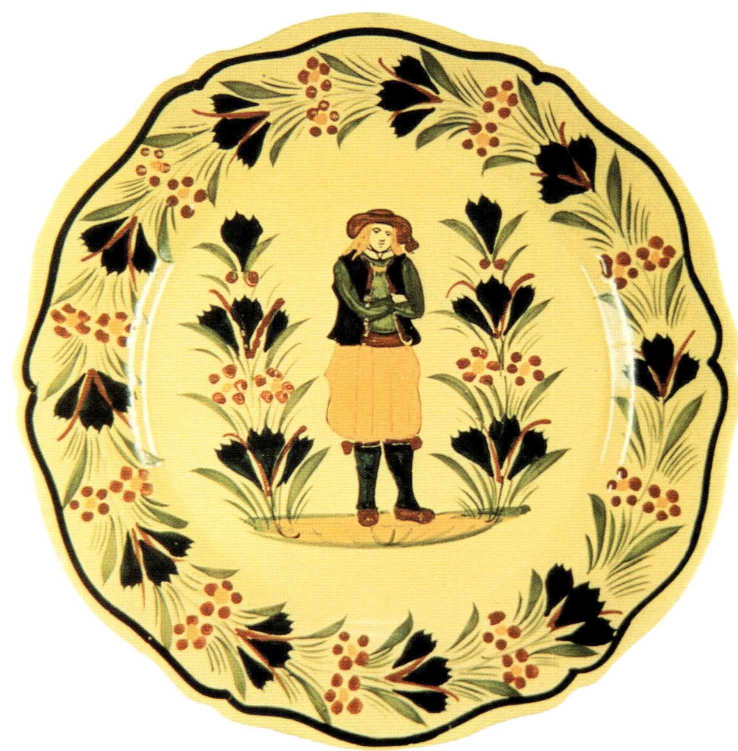

Some of the wonderful Quimper we bought in the markets of Clignancourt sold as soon as we got back to the United States. Sunny *décor soleil* plates are always popular. The Breton in mustard-colored *bragou-braz* stands with folded arms, full-faced to viewer. *Private Collection.*

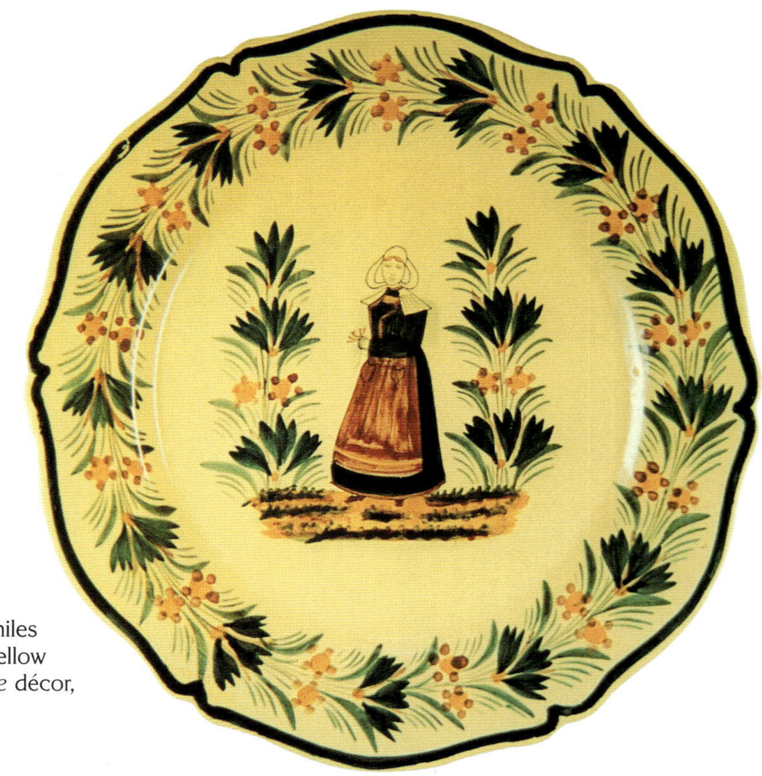

The Bretonne in a *coiffe* and collar from Thégonnec smiles demurely as she holds a posy. This pair of 9.5" sunny yellow plates from the 1930s are rendered in the *demi-fantasie* décor, and are signed Henriot Quimper. *Private Collection.*

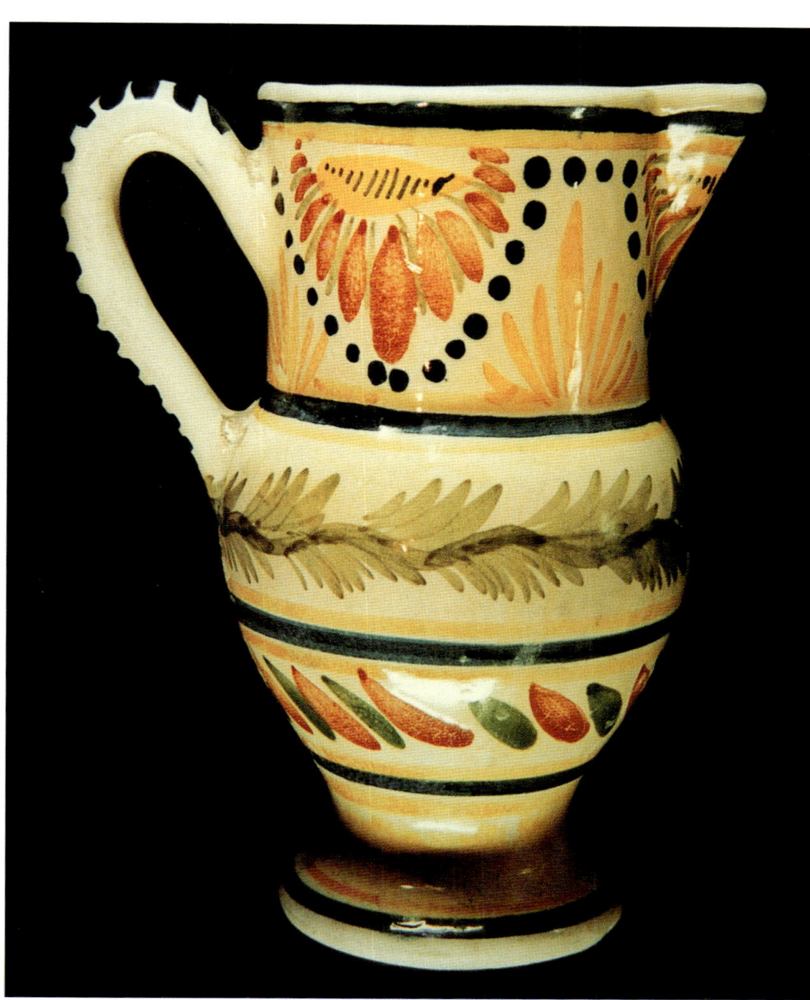

We found this 7.5" tall geometric pitcher by Henriot, c. 1930, in *Marché Serpette*. The dealer seemed disinterested in our business at first. We were just another Quimper-crazed American couple. *Private Collection.*

We have enjoyed the markets of Clignancourt in driving rains, during summer's heat and under the chill of winter. We have celebrated New Year's there with some of our favorite dealers. The Clignancourt dealers certainly know how to conduct business at any time of the year. It is not unusual to be greeted by a Sunday card game or mid-day meal set out on a folding table, replete with wine, linen napkins, and sometimes even a flower.

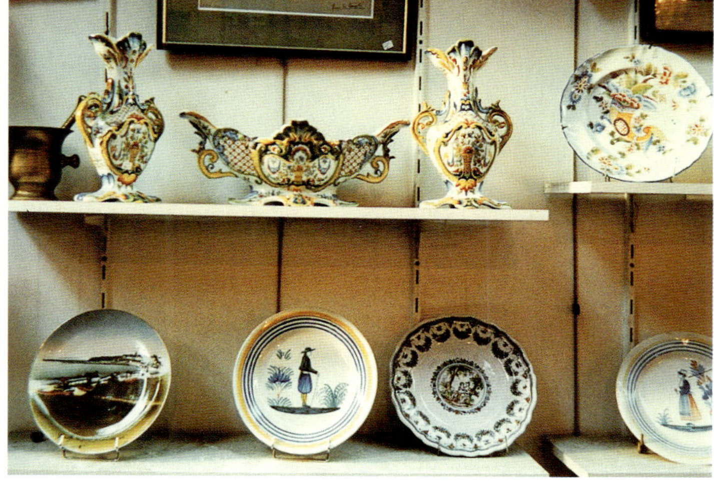

Don't give up; Quimper is everywhere.

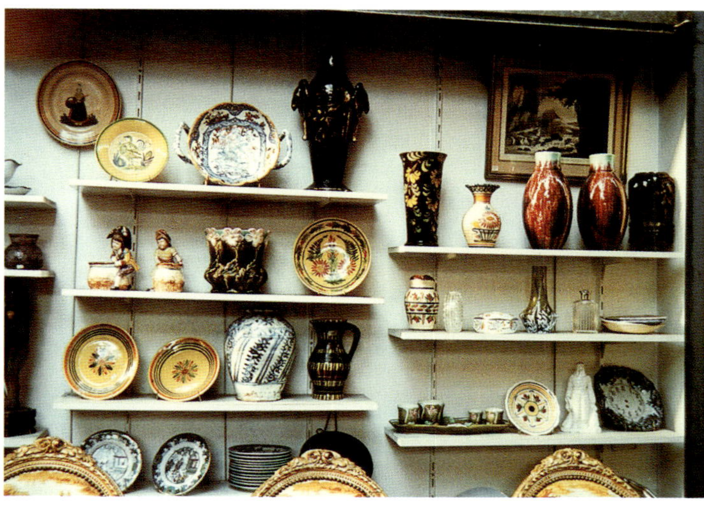

Just around another corner, more Quimper will find you.

New shops have been added since we first started shopping Clignancourt. We have seen some take root and grow; others fold up and are gone by the next time we visit. We know not to linger on the backmost streets of the markets, where sidewalk sellers hawk goods that may not have been given up voluntarily for resale. We keep our hands on our wallets and avoid the congested outermost alleyway on the way back to the Metro.

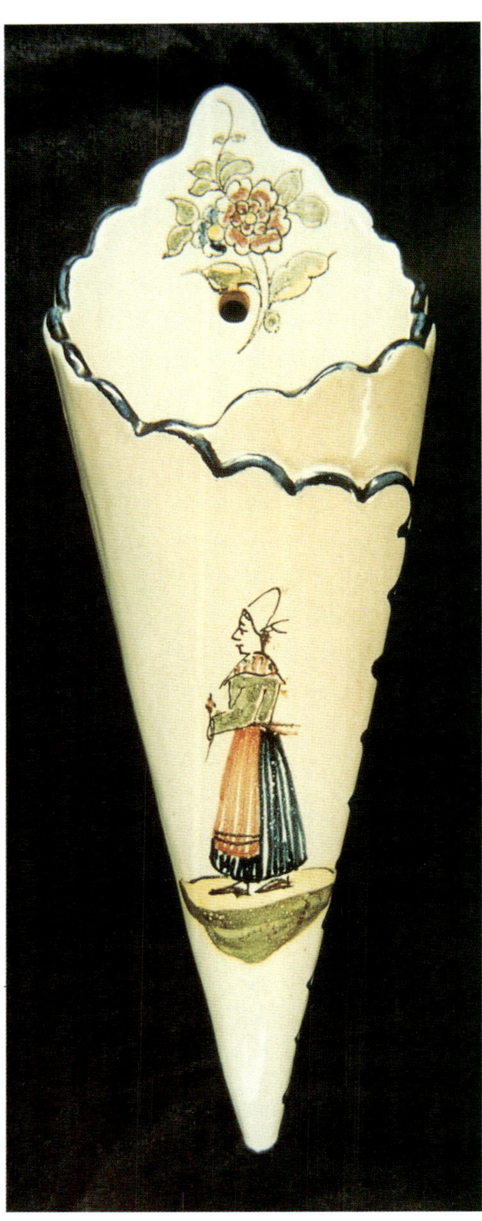

Not all of our purchases are Quimper. This 11" long wallpocket in the *cornet* or hornshape, is from the Malicorne faïencerie of Pouplard and is signed PBx. Many Quimper designs were adopted by the Pouplard faïencerie, which designed its signature to look similar to the Porquier-Beau faïencerie mark. *Private Collection.*

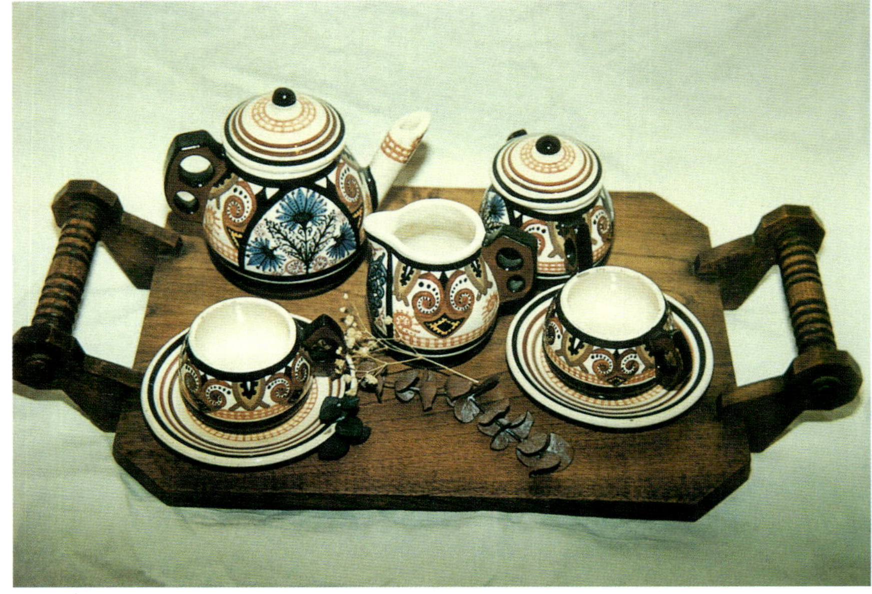

The Quimper artist Paul Fouillen was well-known for his Art Deco designs with a Celtic flair, as seen in this tea set with a wooden tray. Fouillen was *chef d'atelier* (workshop foreman) and designer for the HB faïencerie in the 1920s. This remarkable set was produced in his own faïencerie, which opened in 1929 on *Place Styvel* in Quimper. *Private Collection.*

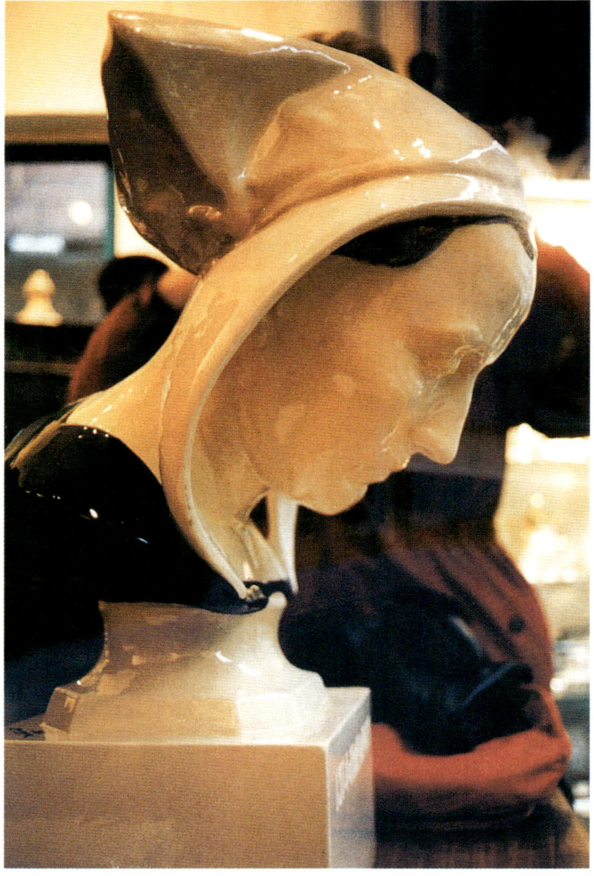

One of our favorite dealers at Clignancourt had this rendition of *Méditation* by the *HB/ Grande Maison* artist Jules-Charles LeBozec. In the *Musée Départemental Breton*, Quimper, we saw an earlier rendition of *Méditation*. LeBozec's wife posed for the artwork.

We also learned a most valuable lesson during one of our first excursions to Clignancourt. Our fondest and, at the same time, saddest finds there was an oil painting of what appeared to be the Breton or perhaps Dutch countryside. Women with white *coiffes* and a windmill made up the pastoral scene. The painting was pushed into a mismatched, ornate gilded frame, and was really too big for it. Our instincts told us to buy the painting, so we did. Our instincts, at least, turned out to be on the mark.

We brought the painting home and hung it in our antiques gallery with a price about three times what we paid, thinking we would pocket a tidy profit. Even at that price, it didn't last long. An art dealer came in and claimed interest in the frame, but agreed to take the painting and frame as a package. Even then, we had an uneasy feeling there was more we should know. The signature on the painting was distinctive, but we were novices and didn't know what or who it was. Remember this was more than a decade ago, and be kind in your thoughts! When we later realized we had sold an original Mathurin Méheut, we were crestfallen and embarrassed by our naiveté. Yes the painting bore the circled initials, MM, of the famous Breton artist and designer for the Henriot faïencerie. Many, many times we have regretted selling that painting.

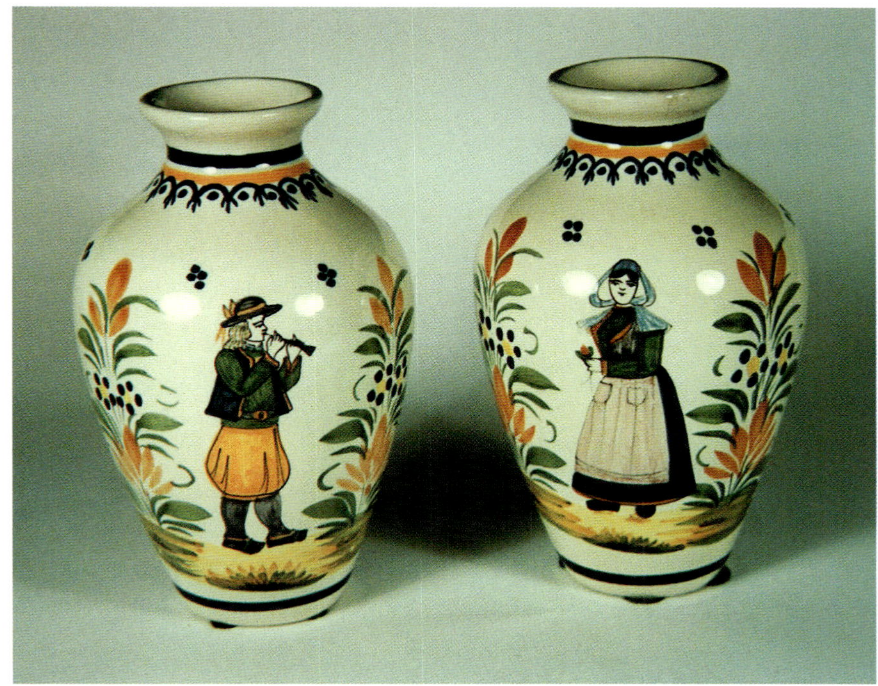

This wonderful matching pair of c. 1930 Henriot vases stands 8" high. Again, a Breton in mustard-colored *bragou-braz* (puffy pants) appears, but this time he plays the *bombarde*, an oboe-like instrument. On the other, a Bretonne demurely faces toward the viewer with a red posy in her hand, in the *coiffe* and collar of Thégonnec as seen on the *soleil* plates pictured previously. The same designs were used on a variety of faïence examples. *Private Collection.*

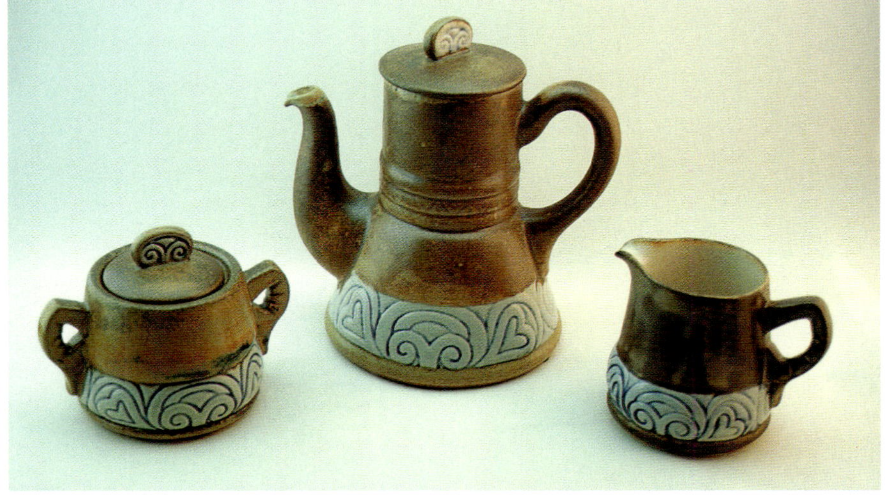

A type of *grès* poterie initiated in the early 1920s at the HB faïencerie is shown in this teapot, creamer, and sugar set. Celtic swirls around the base of each item feature heart and ram's horn designs. *Private Collection.*

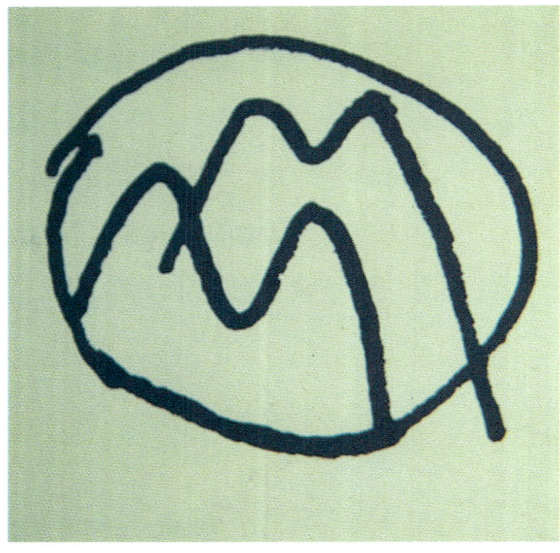

We discovered Quimper artist Mathurin Méheut's signature too late, but learned a valuable lesson.

Every time we return to Clignancourt, we make a pilgrimage to the stall in Vernaison where we bought the original Mathurin Méheut, in case there's another hidden among the piles of bric-a-brac and musty linens. Of course, there's not. But we have found many wonderful pieces of Quimper and related Breton items throughout all of the markets of Clignancourt. You certainly can say the advice, *Shop 'til you drop*, applies here!

Montparnasse

In Paris, we stay in the *6th Arrondissement* (an administrative division), not far from the train station, *Gare Montparnasse*, which takes travelers to points in western France. Conversely, this is the point of arrival for people coming to Paris from Brittany. Over the years, many who left home for opportunities in Paris stayed in the immediate area around the station, and an enclave of Breton-speaking people and shops emerged. It was on one of the narrow side streets near the station that we had a great Quimper-related experience.

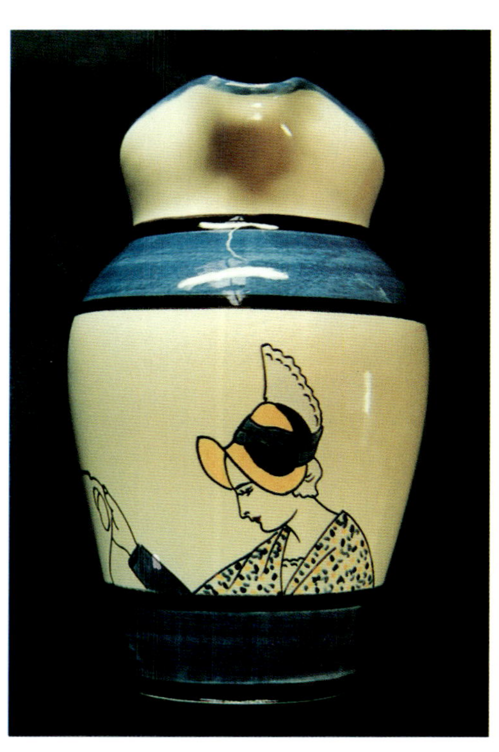

An 7.25" tall souvenir pitcher in bold modern movement colors caught our eye in one of the stalls in Vernaison. It was signed HB Quimper and *Néris-les-Bains*, a resort showing it was intended for the tourist market. *Courtesy of Joyce and William Sneddon.*

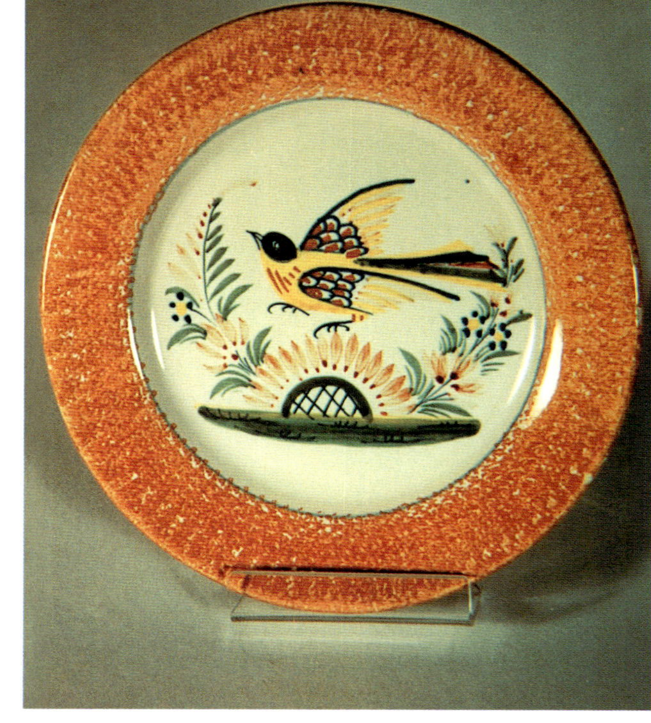

Orange-sponged rim treatment complements this 9" diameter Henriot plate from the second quarter of the 20th century. A colorful bird sits atop a *demi-fleur* and sings, *Wake-up everyone! Private Collection.*

The HB faïencerie made this stellar 11.5" long tray in geometric and *croisillon,* or lattice-work, from the mid-20th century. Reds, blues, browns, and yellow combine in an intricate design. *Private Collection.*

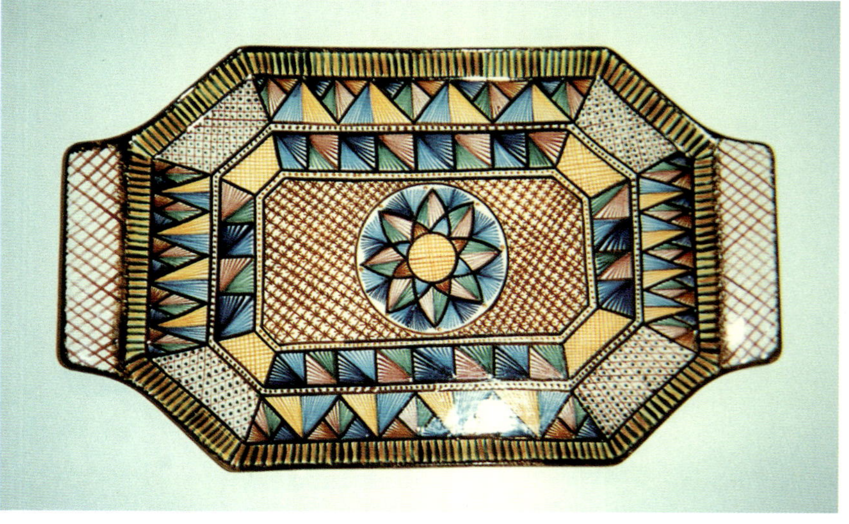

One afternoon, about three blocks from our hotel, we were startled to find a Parisian *pâtisserie* filled with Quimper poterie. Through the window displays of delicious pastries, we saw the poterie sitting on shelves high above the counters of breads, croissants, and candies. Entering, we inquired about the Quimper. The owner quickly came from the back of the shop, saying it was not for sale; it was her private collection. After chatting for a while, she told us she was from a small town near Brest, in northwestern Brittany. She then agreed to have some of her collection photographed. In fact, she brought other pieces of Quimper from the back room for us to see. It was a delightful encounter, and one that increased our understanding of the Breton connection with the *Gare Montparnasse* area. And it was all brought about by Quimper poterie.

A donut-shaped teapot from the first quarter of the 20th century, *petit Breton* plates by Henriot from the 1930s, and chargers in the *ivoire corbeille* and *fleuri* patterns from the 1950s, grace the shelves. *Courtesy of Boulangerie Littre, Paris.*

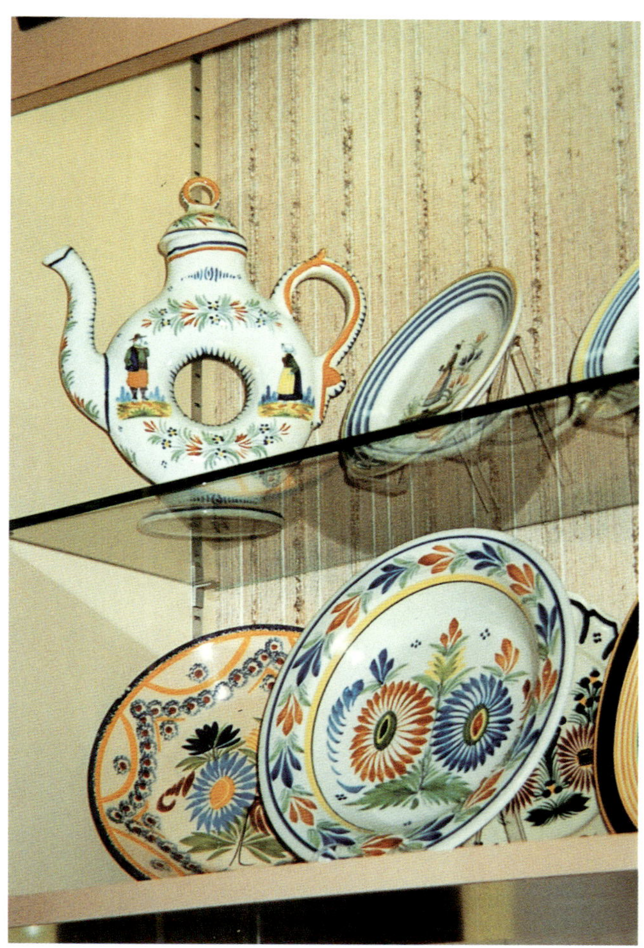

Inside the *Boulangerie Littre* store, Quimper and related Breton artifacts watch over the customers. A poster from Brest in western Brittany, Quimper plates, bowls, and pitchers accompany the candy display in this Breton-owned shop. *Courtesy of Boulangerie Littre, Paris.*

The shop owner brought several Quimper items from the back room to show us. The one she held most dear was a swan-handled basket in black and gold with *l'ajonc*, or gorse décor on the interior. *Courtesy of Boulangerie Littre, Paris.*

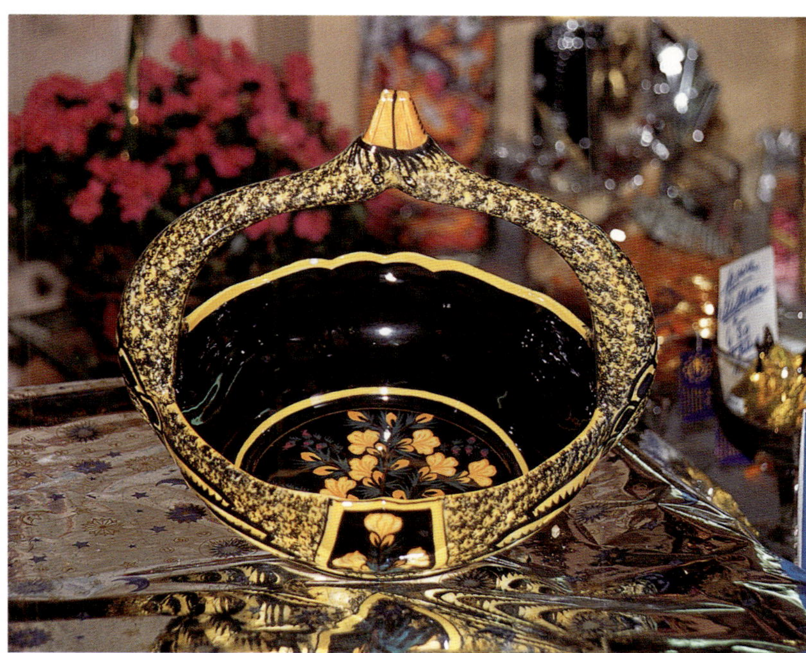

Still in Montparnasse, but two blocks in the other direction from our hotel, we spied a fabulous 16-inch-tall *broderie* décor vase designed by Paul Fouillen. The seller claimed it was intended as an anniversary piece, and the price steep. Besides, my husband doubted whether we could package and carry such a huge, fragile item on the airplane. We had been in this quandary before, and as a result passed up several large, wonderful Quimper items. This time, I persisted and we bought the vase. David, good husband that he is, found corrugated cardboard at a nearby department store and I bought a rectangular suitcase to carry on the flight. The vase was well prepared for its trans-Atlantic journey. When we went through airport security in Paris, the clerk laughed. She called a co-worker to see this strange suitcase filled with nothing but an oddly shaped, vague outline. We tried to explain it was a vase, *faïence de Quimper*. They shrugged and sent us on our way. The vase lasted in our antique gallery about three weeks, before we had to bid it *adieu*!

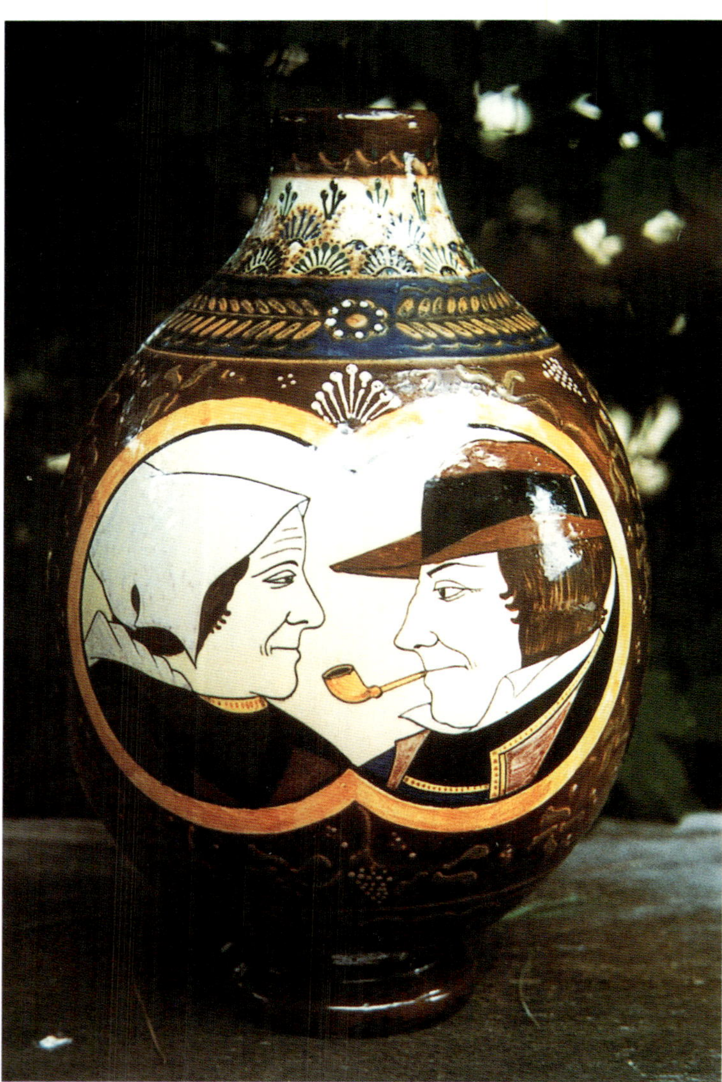

We had words about purchasing this 16" tall *broderie* vase, designed by Paul Fouillen while at the HB faïencerie in the 1920s. David finally agreed and found a way to package it safely for our trip home.

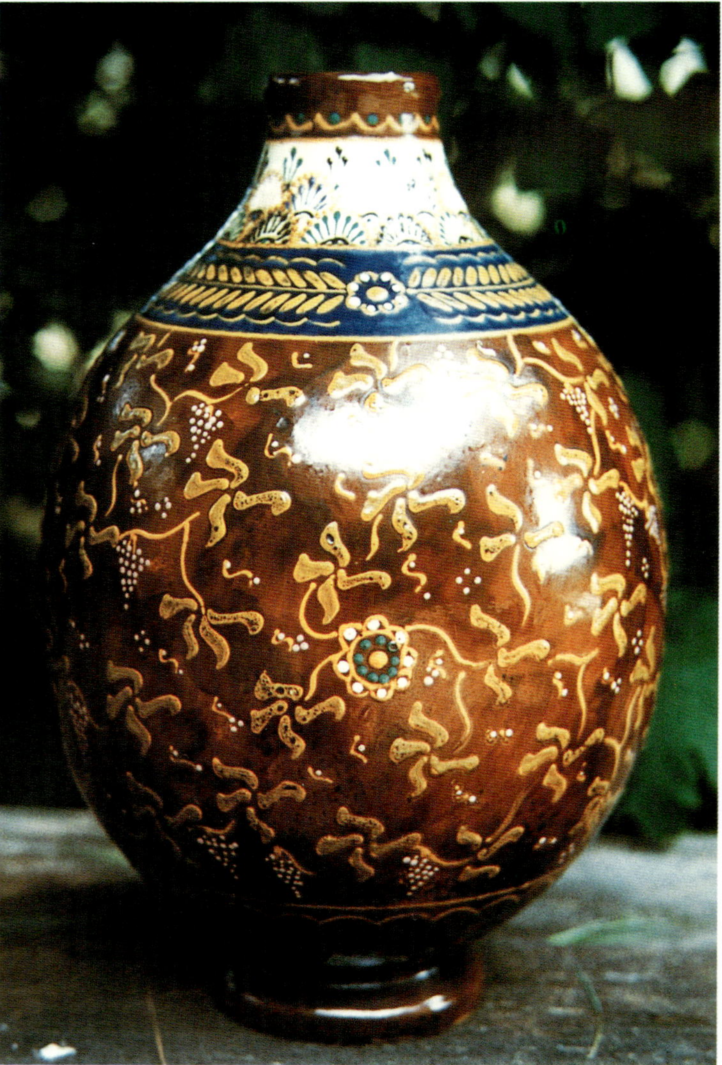

The seller claimed it was an anniversary vase, but the intricate *perlé* and *tubé* design, and the signature Fouillen portraits convinced us it was a winner. *Private Collection.*

❧ ON TO BRITTANY

The first time we left Paris for Brittany, we set the pattern for the next seven or so trips. From the *Gare Montparnasse*, the train station from which travelers depart for western France, we took the train to Rennes, the capital of *Bretagne*, about 360 kilometers west of Paris. We rented a car and stayed a few days, searching Rennes and environs for Quimper poterie. Then we headed further west toward the city of Quimper, which is about 200 kilometers from Rennes, stopping along the way at numerous small antique shops or *brocantes*. After the first trip, we altered our route slightly for at least part of the journey, as we became enchanted with the geography, history, and culture of the Brittany.

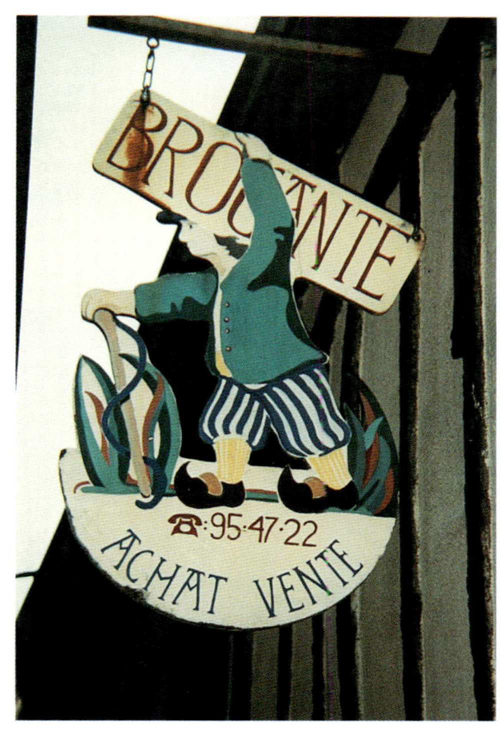

Many small antique shops, or *brocantes*, beckon throughout Brittany.

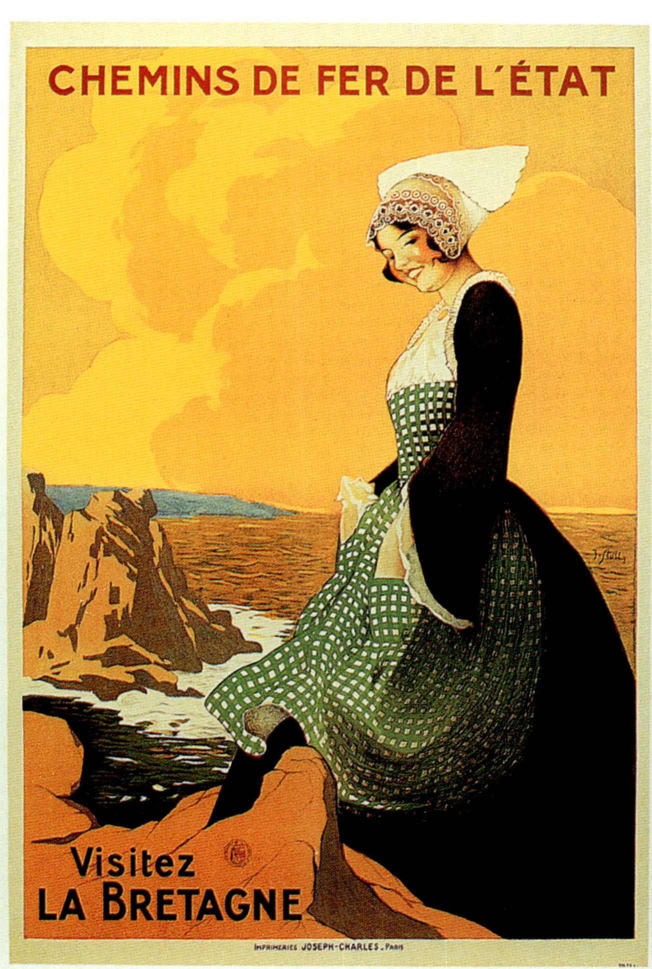

Posters beckon tourists to visit as the railroad opened the door to Brittany. *Private Collection.*

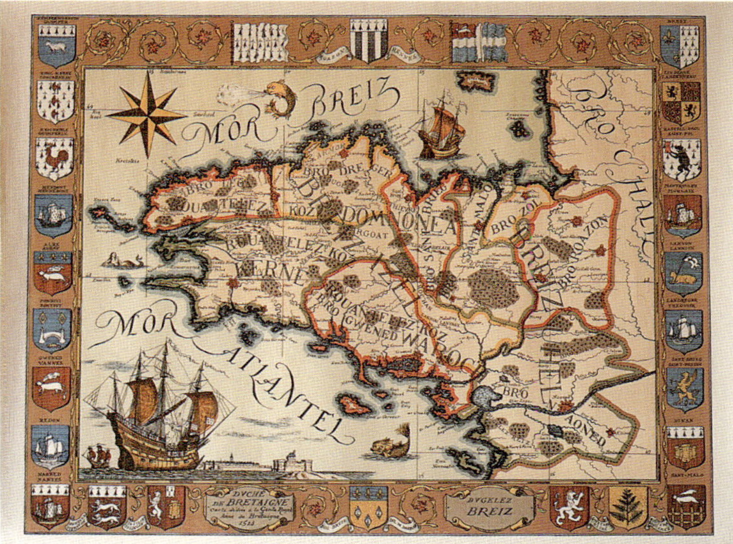

An early map of *Bretagne* shows Hélias' monster with a three-pointed tongue facing the setting sun. *Private Collection.*

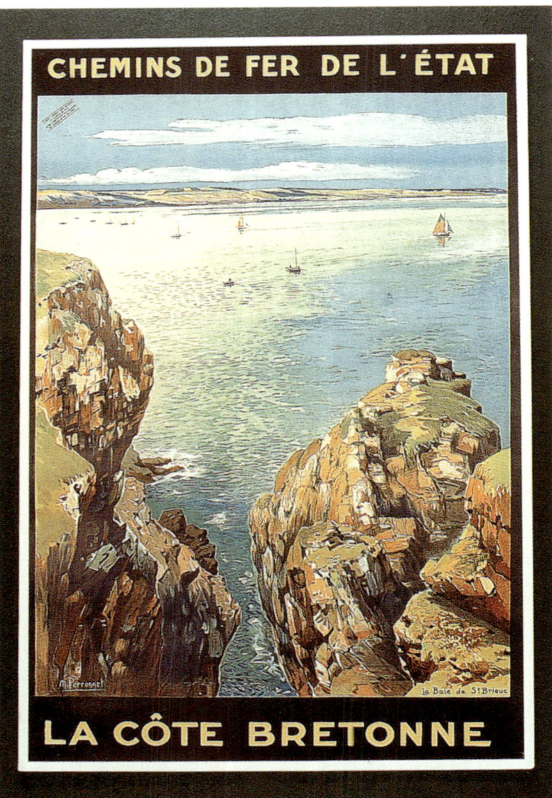

Other posters show the rugged coast of *Armor*, the ocean-facing land of Brittany. *Private Collection.*

Brittany is a large Atlantic province with four departments, similar to American states. The distinctive peninsula is described as resembling a monster with a three-pointed tongue, whose backbone guides the setting sun to its western bed off Europe. It is divided into eastern and western sections, known as Upper Brittany *(Haute Bretagne)* and Lower Brittany *(Basse Bretagne). Haute Bretagne,* or *Breiz-Uhel* in Breton, is further east and closer to Paris. The area is French speaking, and some think of it as the more sophisticated of the two. *Basse Bretagne,* or *Breiz-Izel*, is further west and seen as more isolated. This area retains colorful regional costumes, as well as the Breton language, *Brezoneg*, a Celtic language most closely related to Welsh and Cornish. *(Hélias, Images of Brittany, p. 3.)*

Brittany's four departments are: *Ille et Vilaine, Côtes d'Amor, Morbihan*, and *Finistère*. Each has its own distinct landscape, traditions, weather, and its own coastline, as well as inland areas. Also, the numerous villages within each department were isolated by the geography of *Armor* (the rugged coastline facing the Atlantic), and *Argoat* (a once heavily wooded interior, now a countryside dominated by thickets, cultivated fields, and plateaus with rock outcroppings).

The isolation created by the geography of Brittany led to specialized costumes, customs, and dialects. René Creston's book on the costumes of Brittany covers these differing modes of dress, and Jakez Hélias' book on the costumes of Brittany details the variety and evolution of head wear *(coiffe)* styles of many various villages in Brittany from the1800s to recent times.

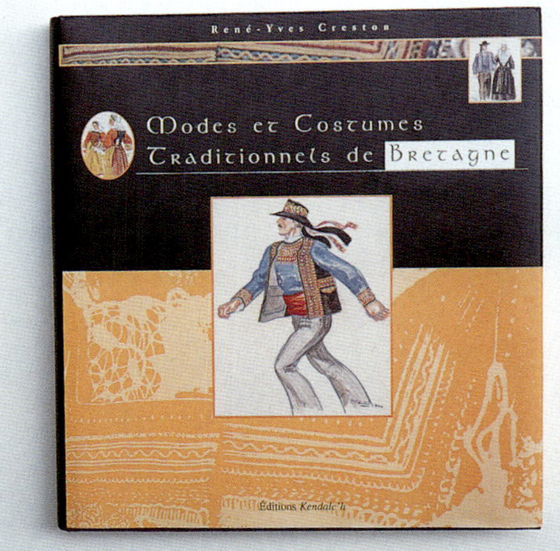

Quimper artist René Creston's reissued book contains over 300 pages of hand-drawn replicas of individualized costumes from villages and areas in Brittany. *Authors' Collection.*

The inland area of Brittany, known as *Argoat*, as viewed from the top of *Menez Bré.*

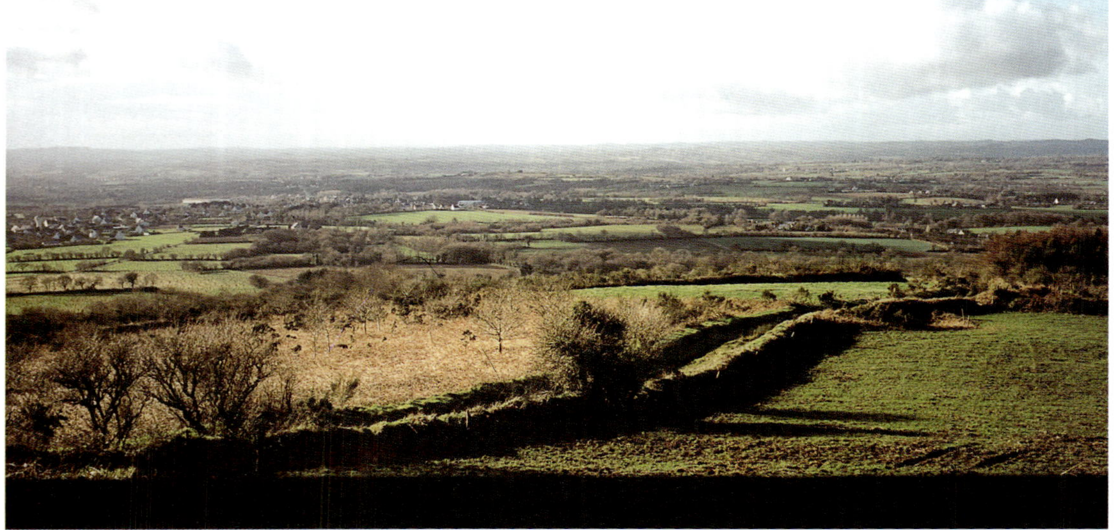

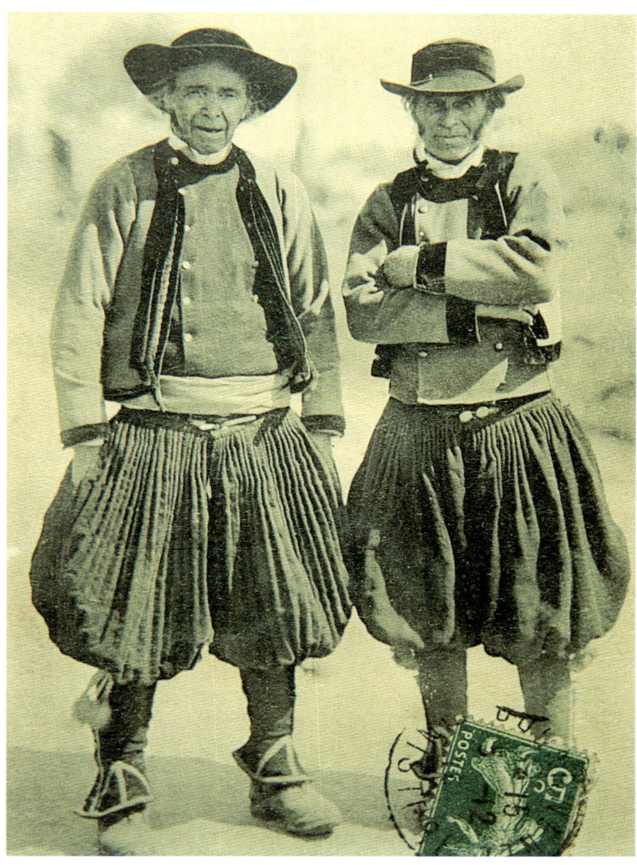

These gentlemen from *Finistère*, dressed in their best for a postcard called *Les Derniers Bragou-Braz,* or last of the *bragou-braz. Authors' Collection.*

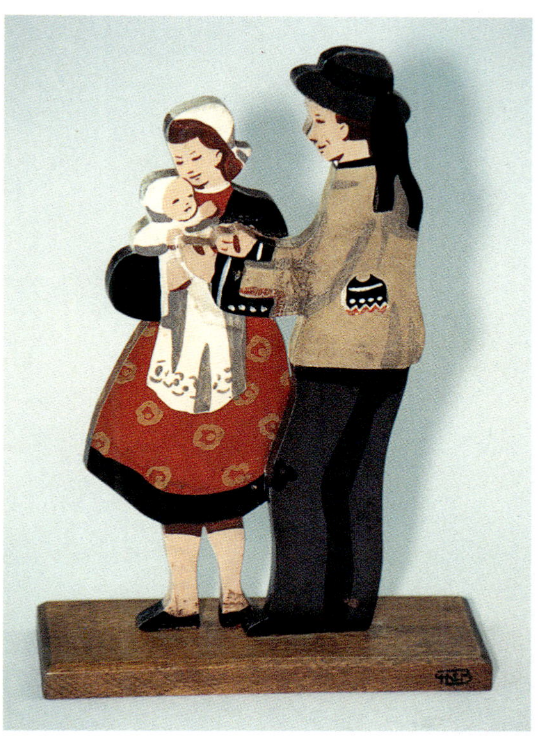

A couple with their baby is attired in the costume of Pontivy, a town in central Brittany about halfway between Rennes and Quimper. Pontivy was the childhood home of Paul Fouillen, well-known Quimper artist. Note the light-colored *chupen,* or jacket, and the long pants worn by the father from Pontivy. *Collection of Jen and Jeff Nowland.*

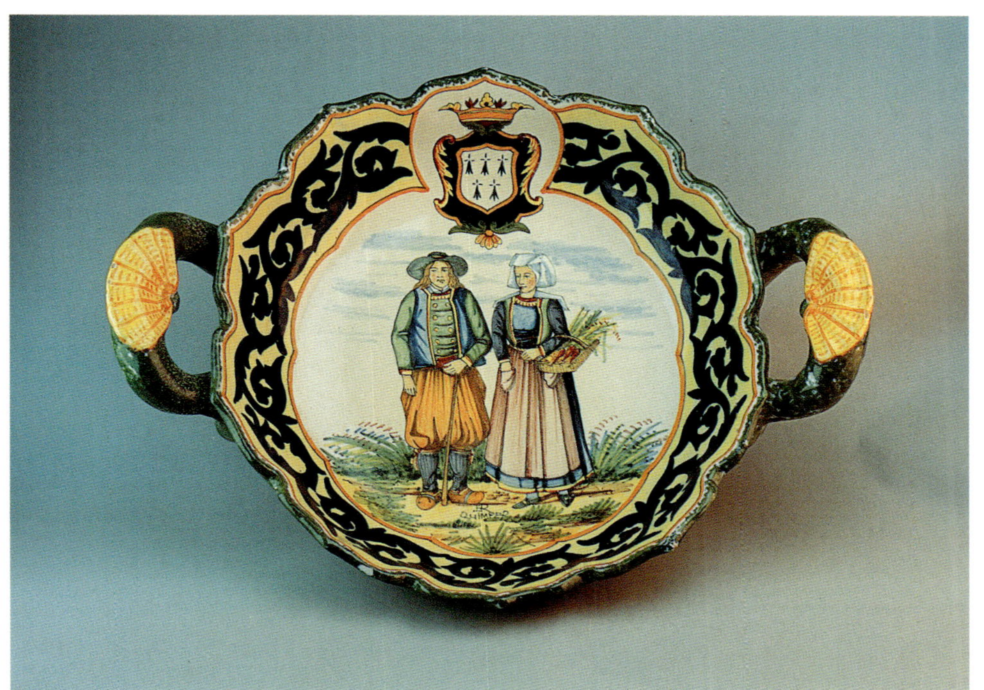

A *melonnière* by the Henriot faïencerie, c. 1900, features shell motifs on each sponged-handle, acanthus or scroll design, and the shield of *Bretagne,* in addition to a Breton couple in early costumes. He wears *bragou-braz* and she carries a basket of produce in this stellar rendition. Signed HR Quimper. *Private Collection.*

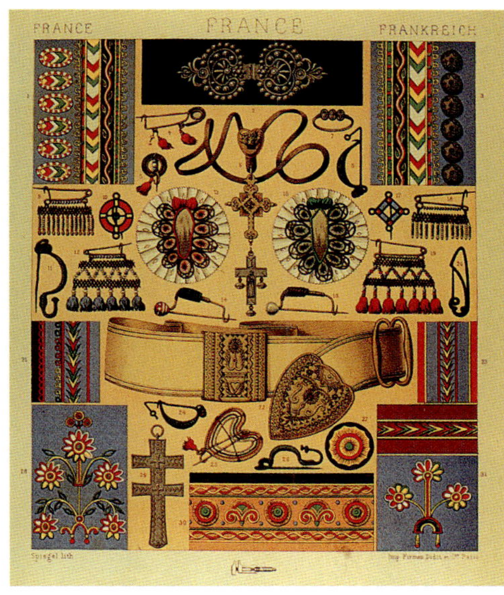

This print of embroideries and jewelry of the Breton peasant folk is from *Racinet's History of Costume,* dating from the 1880s. Illustrated are vest and cardigan embroidery patterns, the Cross of Ste. Jeanette, a belt buckle, and ornamental pins. *Authors' Collection.*

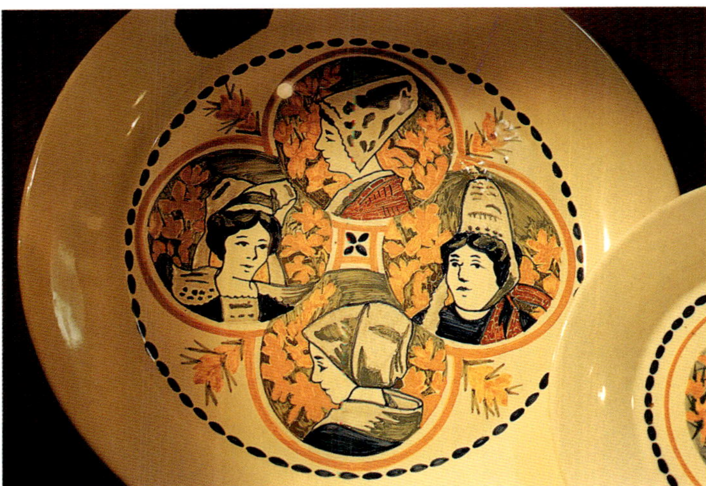

Plates in a series by HB faïencerie artist Alphonse Chanteau feature *coiffes* from various regions in Brittany. *Courtesy of Musée de la Faïence, Quimper.*

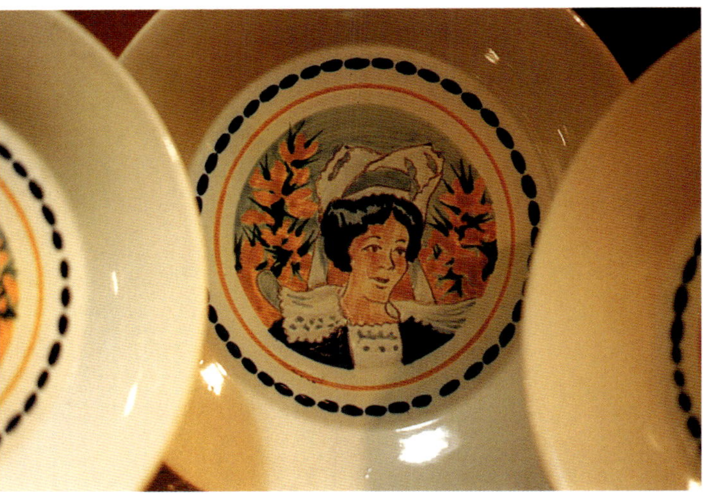

This HB plate by Chanteau features the *coiffe* from *Giz Fouenn*, an area encompassing the towns of Pont-Aven, Fouesnant, Elliant, Resporden, and Le Faouët, among others. *Courtesy of Musée de la Faïence, Quimper.*

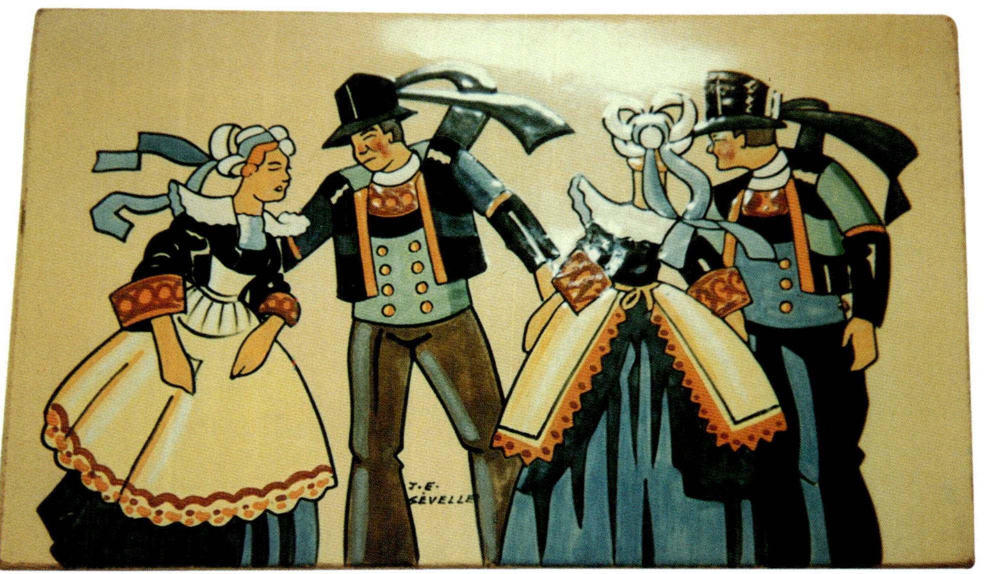

Quimper artist Jim-Emile Sévellec designed this tile for the Henriot faïencerie in the 1920s. It measures 9.25" long and features four dancers from the *Giz Fouenn* area. The costumes and *coiffes* sing with color and action. *Private Collection.*

A child-sized hat with buckle and two velvet ribbons comes from the area south and west of Quimper.

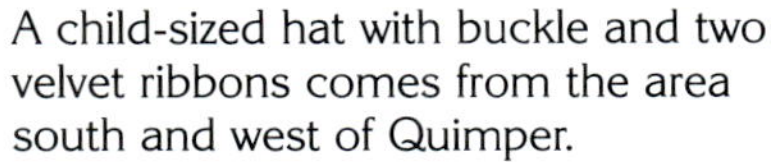

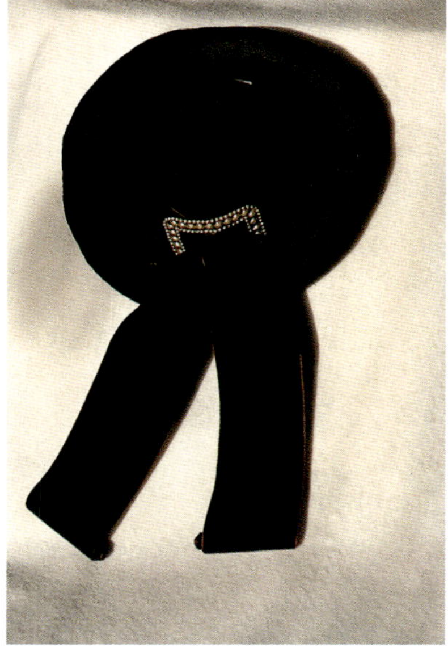

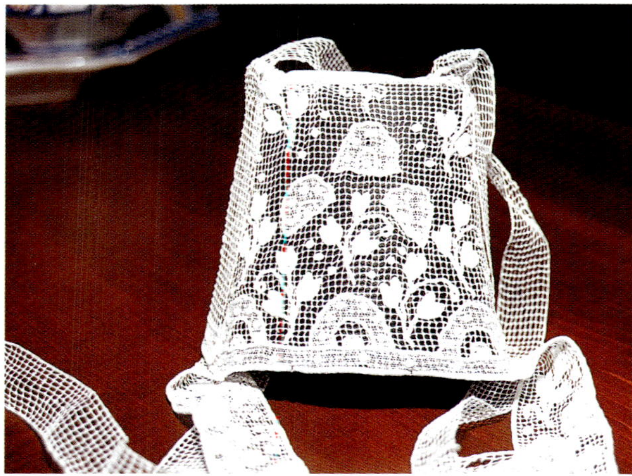

This *coiffe* from Le Juch, a town about 18 kilometers northwest of Quimper, is a reproduction of earlier models. *Authors' Collection.*

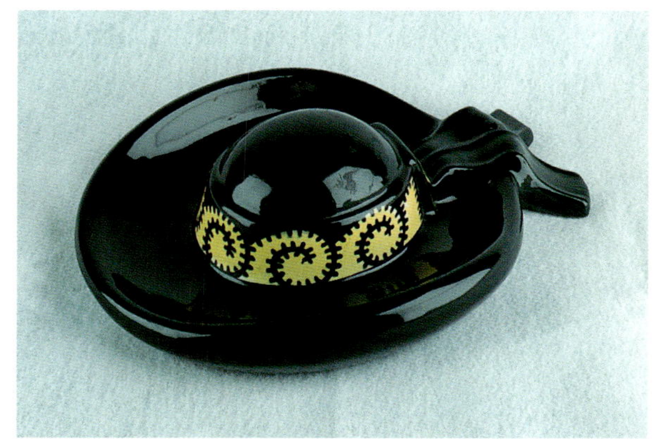

This time the hat is rendered in ceramic and shows Celtic swirls in lieu of a band of velvet. The diameter is 7" and it is signed C. Bernard Quimper.

Costumes can indicate the rank of the wearer. One story relates that the number of ribbons on a man's hat indicates his position in some Breton villages. Another tells that the height of the velvet on the wedding musicians' hats indicates the social standing of the couple. And still another relates how the number and width of the velvet stripes on a girl's skirt indicates the family's wealth. These costumes have been captured on Quimper poterie for over 100 years. *(Hélias, Horse of Pride, pp. 277-78; Hélias, Coiffes et Costumes de Bretagne, pp. 19-20; Mali, Old Quimper Review, March, 1990.)*

Granite dominates the Breton landscape, and is cited as an influence in forming the strong character of the Breton people. Geologists have determined the rock of Brittany is among the oldest in the earth's crust. Evidence indicates that 500 million to 600 million years ago, two of the tectonic plates covering the Earth collided, forcing a V-shaped mass of rock up through the ocean to create the area later known as France. These enormous outcroppings of rock became the two backbones of the Armorican massif. Most prominent after millennia of erosion are the parallel *Monts d'Arrée* in the north and *Montagnes Noires* in the south of Brittany, which in the past were as high as today's Alps. Remnants of their peaks are scattered throughout the Breton peninsula. On our journeys, we have been to the top of *Menez Hom* (1,075 ft), *Menez Bré* (990 ft.), and *Montagne St. Michel* (1,235 ft.), and we climbed the rocky path to the summit of one of Brittany's highest points, *Roc'h Trévezel* (1,260 ft.)

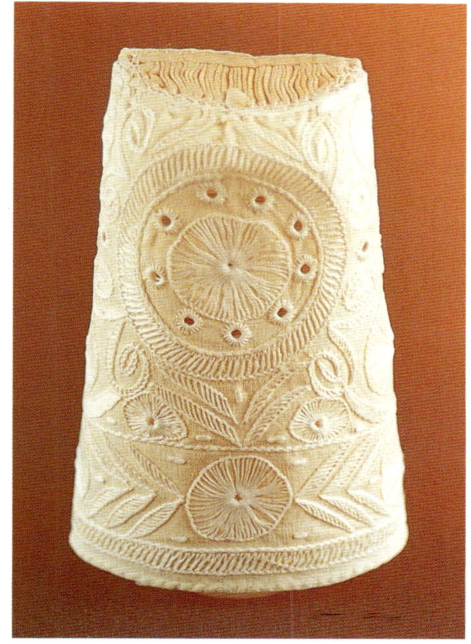

One of our favorite purchases in Brittany is this pre-1900, 5" tall *coiffe* from the *Pays Bigouden* area, south and west of Quimper. *Authors' Collection.*

Like the ancient rock, the people of Brittany have a remarkable staying power. The ocean, which surrounds the peninsula of Brittany on three sides, and the granite rock throughout, helped shape the stoic Breton character.

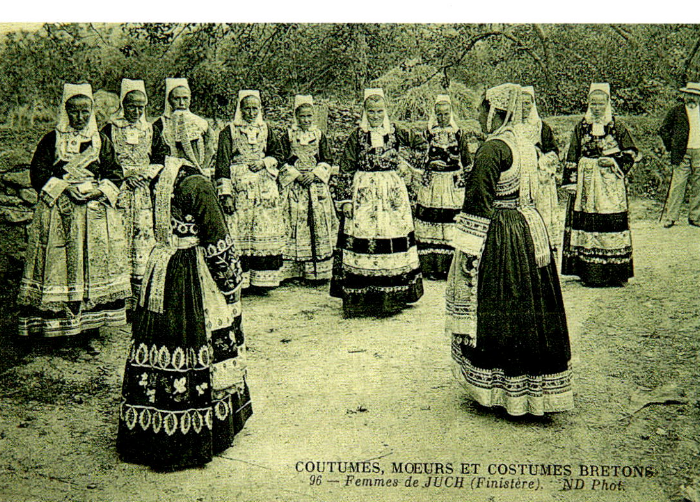

A group of young ladies from Le Juch are dressed in their holiday attire, including *coiffes*, on a turn-of-the-20th century postcard. *Authors' Collection.*

Right:
By the 1930s the *coiffe* from *Pays Bigouden* had grown to over 12" in height, as seen on this rendition of a *Bigoudène*, a woman from the area. Signed R. Micheau-Vernez, Henriot Quimper. *Courtesy of Claire and Jon Scarborough.*

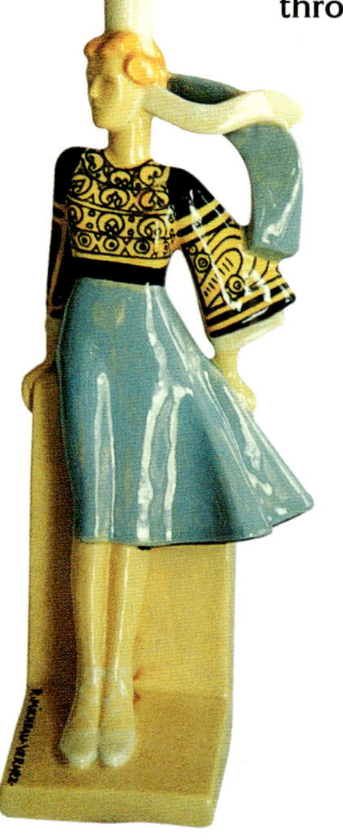

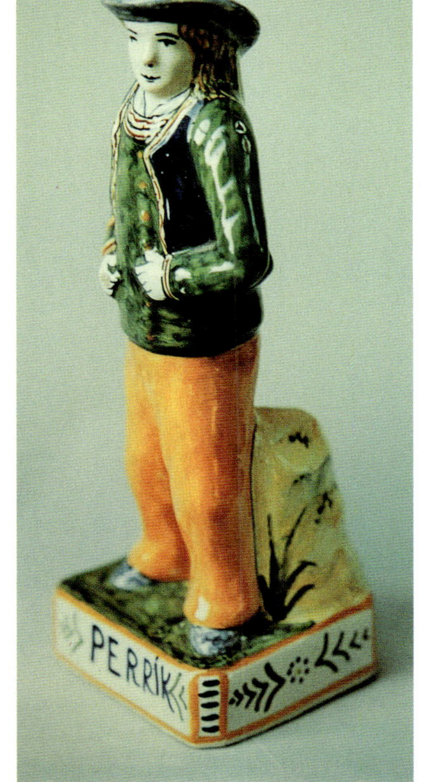

Bretons rendered in faïence were often shown standing by or leaning against the ever-present rocks of Brittany. This fellow's name is Perrick, he stands 8" high, and was made by the Henriot firm in the first quarter of the 20th century.

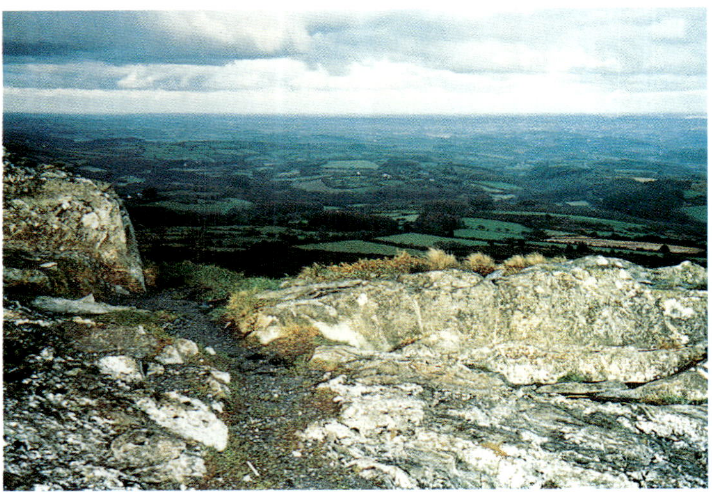

Was the view worth the 15-minute climb to the top of the 1,260-foot-high Roc'h Trévezel? YES!

Roc'h Trévezel

We found *Roc'h Trévezel* without planning it. Early one January morning we found the most direct route from Morlaix to Quimper was through the *Monts d'Arrée*. The road climbed and twisted around picturesque valleys. As with many of our discoveries in Brittany, *Trévezel* was one that we just happened by. The sunrise was so beautiful over the rugged Breton landscape we had to stop. It was then we saw the marker for *Roc'h Trévezel* and decided to climb to get a better view, and hopefully some great pictures from the top.

We scrambled up the rocky walk and laughed breathlessly as we raced to the top, not knowing it was one of the highest points in Brittany at about 1,260 feet. These mountains once stood 13,000 feet high, but time has worn them down so the remaining rock outcroppings are but remnants of their former glory.

The view was worth the 15-minute climb. To the north towards Morlaix is the *Léon* plateau with St. Pol-de-Léon, and beyond is the English Channel or *Manche*. To the south is *Montagne St. Michel,* which overlooks the *Youdic* marshes and a reservoir not far away, and beyond that stands the outline of the Noires Mountains. In legend, the *Youdic* marshes, or *Yeun Elez,* are called one of the entrances to hell, and witches and wild creatures are said to frequent the area after dark.

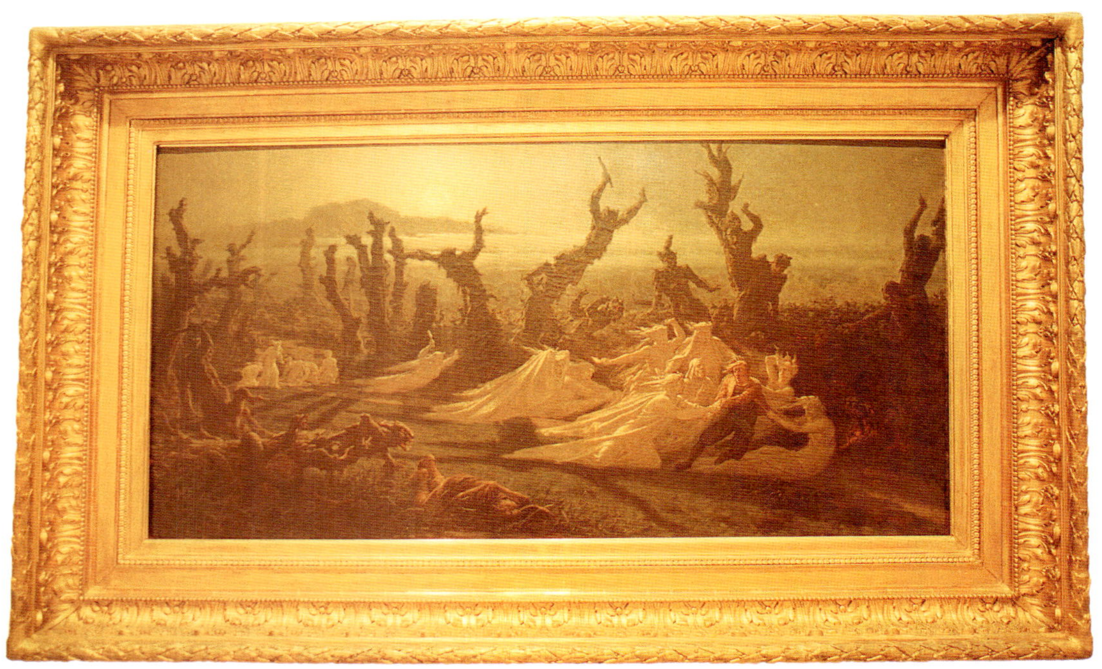

Yan Dargent's painting *Les Lavandières de la Nuit*, c. 1861, shows one of the legends popular in Breton folklore. All sorts of creatures awaited unsuspecting travelers on dark roads or bogs in Brittany. *Courtesy of the Musée des Beaux Arts, Quimper.*

Not much further south of *Roc'h Trévezel* is St. Michel Mountain. It is nearly as high as *Trévezel*, with a small chapel atop that overlooks the great peat bog *Yeun Elez*.

We also drove to the top of *St. Michel,* a few kilometers to the south, and were taken by the view. The uproar that greeted plans to build a nuclear power plant on the edge of the marsh across from *St. Michel* was typically Breton. One local wryly commented that if the nuclear reactor malfunctions, it really could become the entrance to the underworld. The prevailing feeling among the populace was that the Breton spirit and land would outlive all such contrivances. *(LeCunff, Wonderful Brittany, p. 14; Hélias, Images of Brittany, p. 38.)*

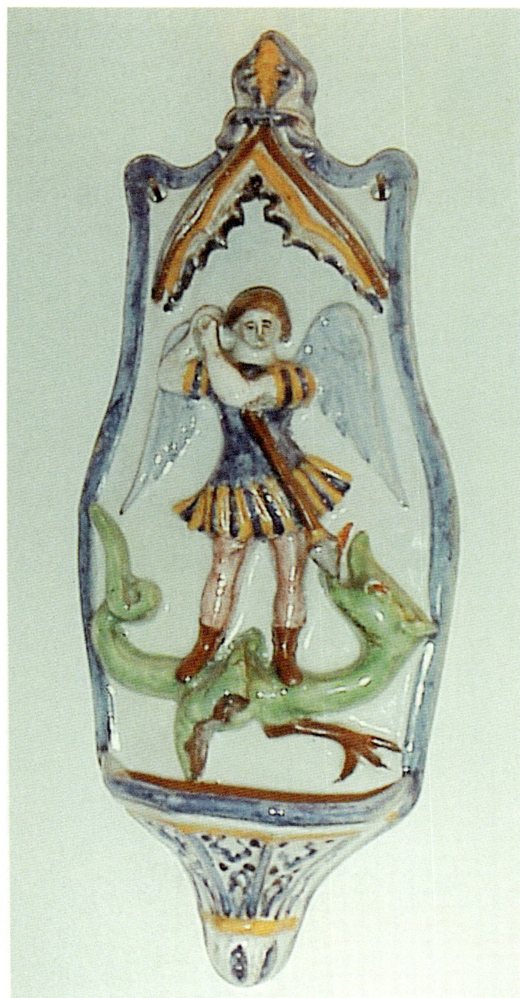

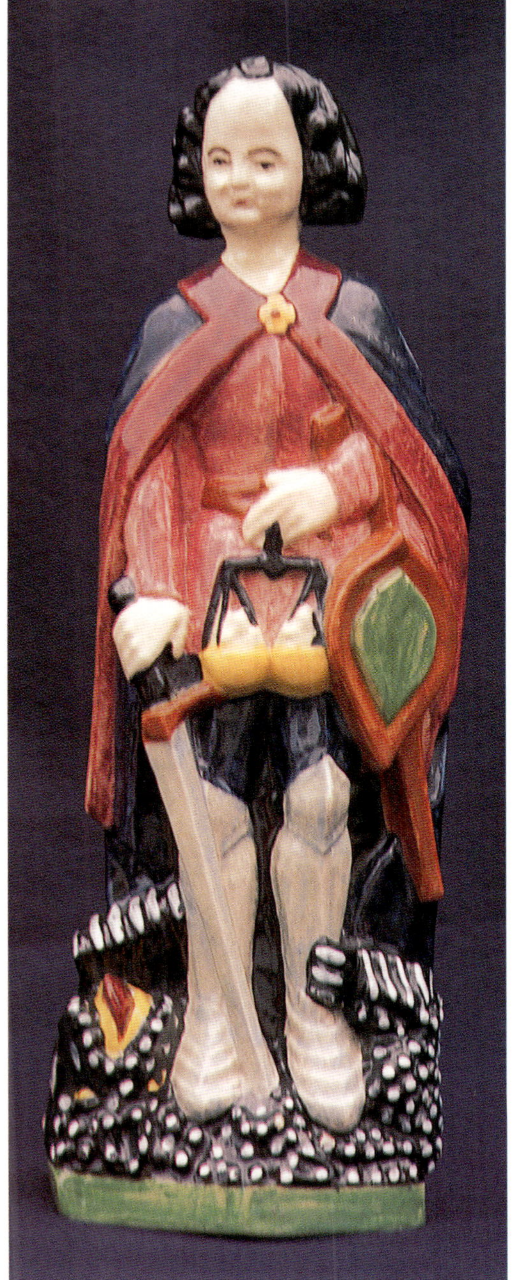

Left:
St. Michel appears on this faïence *bénitier,* slaying the ever-present, but soon-to-be dispatched dragon. The *bénitier* is *cul noir* (black back), is 13.25" long, and no maker's signature is present. *Courtesy of Lucy Williams.*

Right:
St. Michel is favored in Brittany for his dragon-slaying exploits, and this 13" tall rendition by Henriot, from the 1930s, highlights that reputation. The *aquarelle,* or watercolor model, for this version of St. Michel can be seen in *Cahn, p. 127. Private Collection.*

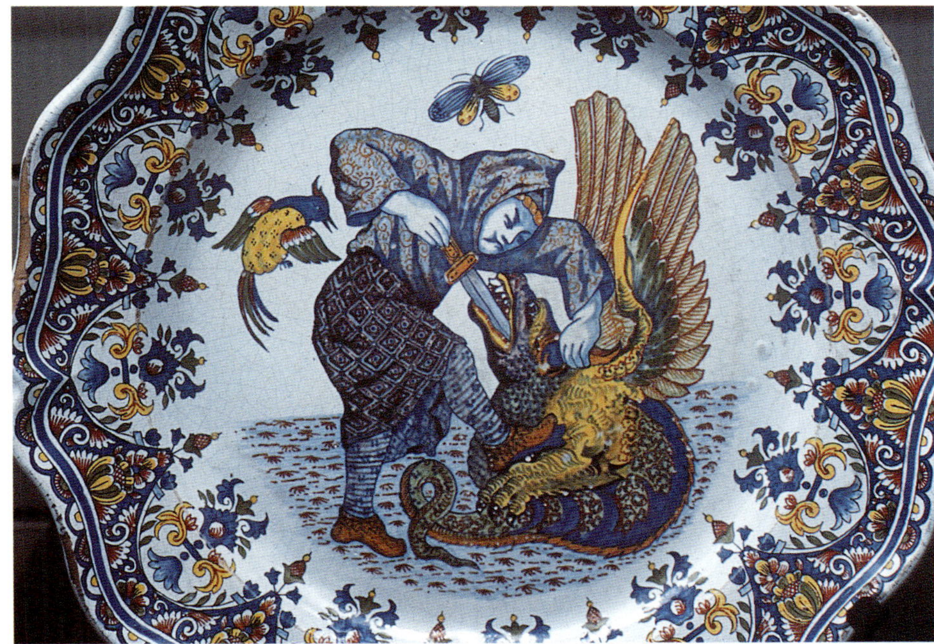

Another dragon bites the dust, but in style on this late 19th century Quimper faïence plate. An intricate Rouen border, a bird, and a butterfly surround the gruesome scene. *Courtesy of Musée Départemental Breton, Quimper.*

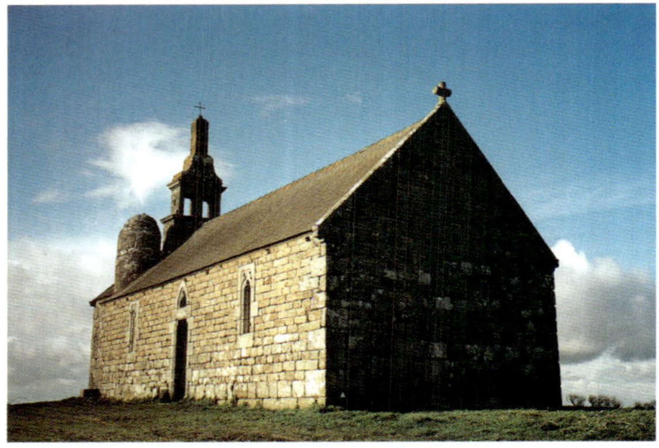

High locations with a command of the surrounding countryside were used as sites of worship by early people. *Menez Bré*, about 15 kilometers west of Guingamp, is one of those places sacred to early worshipers, including Druids, and later to Christians. *Menez Bré* is crested with a stone chapel.

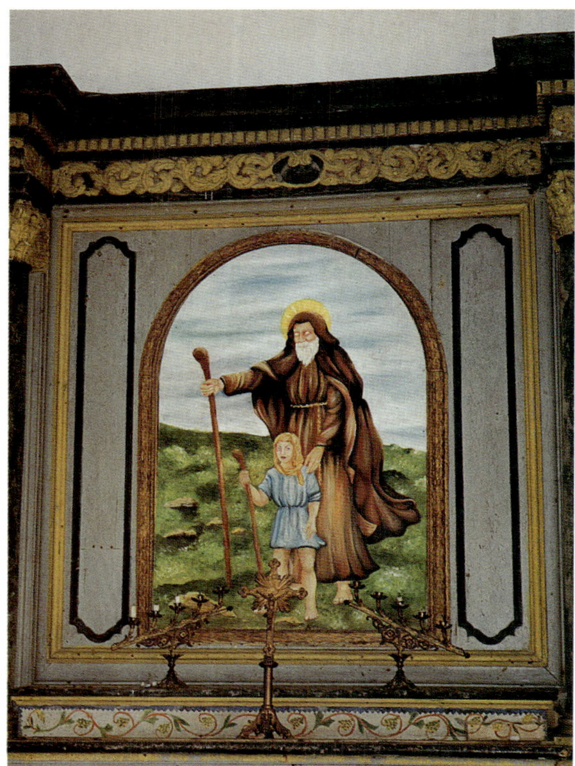

The small chapel on *Menez Bré* is dedicated to the blind St. Hervé, whose likeness is on the wall above the altar.

Right:
The legends of old Brittany live on, sometimes on faïence, as on this *légende Bretonne* plate designed by Alfred Beau. *Le Diable Trompé* is one of several Breton legends chronicled in Emile Souvestre's *Les Derniers Bretons*. As Beau's father-in-law, Souvestre influenced the painting of Breton cultural history on faïence. This 10" model is second period PB from the Henriot firm. *Courtesy of Lucy Williams*.

Menez Bré

Another experience with heights in Brittany was our journey to the top of *Menez Bré*. We were headed northwest to Morlaix from Rennes, and about 15 kilometers from Guingamp, there is a turn off the major highway, N 12, for *Menez Bré*. We wanted to retrace the steps of Frances Gostling, an early 20th century writer who fell in love with Brittany much as we have. She chronicled some of her experiences, and the description of the history and legends about *Menez Bré* captured our imagination.

As we approached, *Menez Bré* didn't appear to be a lofty peak. But it did rise high enough to give us a remarkable view. We drove up a gently curving, partially paved road around the mountain to near the top, where a small chapel stood. The view was stellar, from Cornouaille in the south to the English Channel to the north.

There is a small chapel dedicated to St. Hervé on the top of *Menez Bré*. We were fortunate to be there during a holiday season, and a young man let us in and explained some of its history. He pointed out a special circle within a cross on the tiled floor. Legend says, when a person stands in the circle as the sun comes through the door, he or she will be purified. The sun had already passed by the doorway for the day, so we weren't able to test the legend.

Mrs. Gostling's account was a bit more colorful. She said St. Hervé was the son of a Druid priestess and a Christian poet. He was blind, like most true bards, including his predecessor on *Menez Bré*, the wild old singer, Guenc'hlan. She described ceremonies she had read about that were held at the chapel hundreds of years ago. Incantations from the front porch had sent evil spirits flying from the sacred area. *(Gostling, The Bretons at Home, pp. 28-31.)*

It's difficult to understand Brittany without understanding the colorful legends that make up its past, since these legends remain vital today.

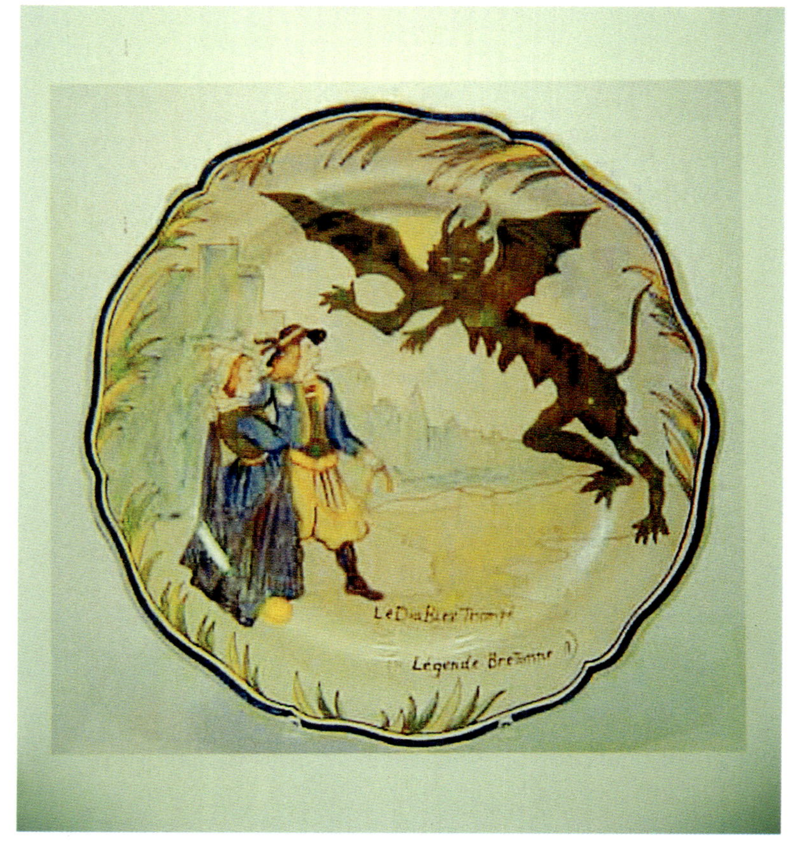

Coastal Brittany

Brittany is home to more than 3.5 million Bretons, most living on or near the 1,500 miles of coastline. It is isolated at the westernmost tip of Europe and surrounded by water on all but one-third of its perimeter, creating a mainly maritime, temperate climate similar to United States' Chesapeake Bay area. Much of the northern and western coasts are craggy and dramatic, lashed by strong winds and crashing waves, somewhat like the coast of Maine and Newfoundland. The southern coast near the Morbihan Gulf is sheltered and Mediterranean-like. Nearly all of the large towns, such as Morlaix, Roscoff, Vannes, and Quimper, lie at the head of bays, on harbors, gulfs, or river junctions. Water has played a dominant role in Breton life and, like the ancient rock, is seen as a major force in determining the people's character.

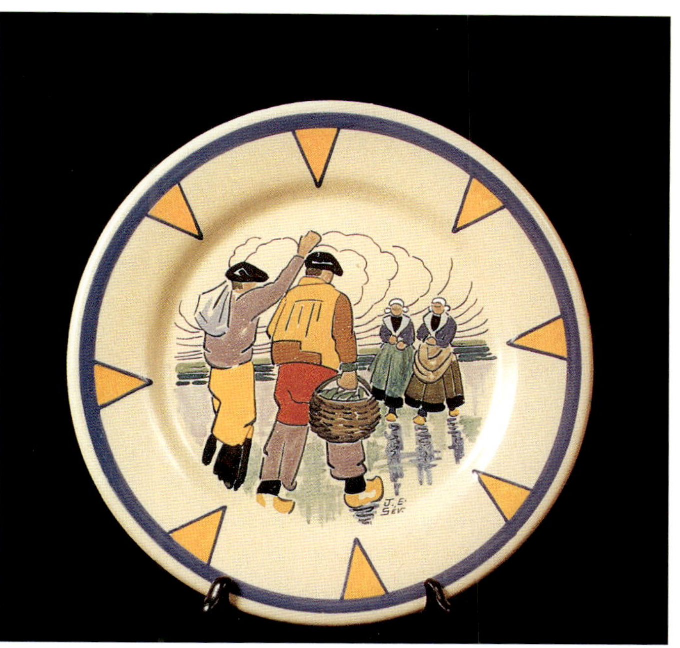

Jim-Emile Sévellec developed several designs of fisherman at work, and his *Service à la Mer* is a classic. The scene on this 9.75" Henriot plate from the 1930s shows *marins* waving to two Bretonnes as they walk across the shore. *Private Collection.*

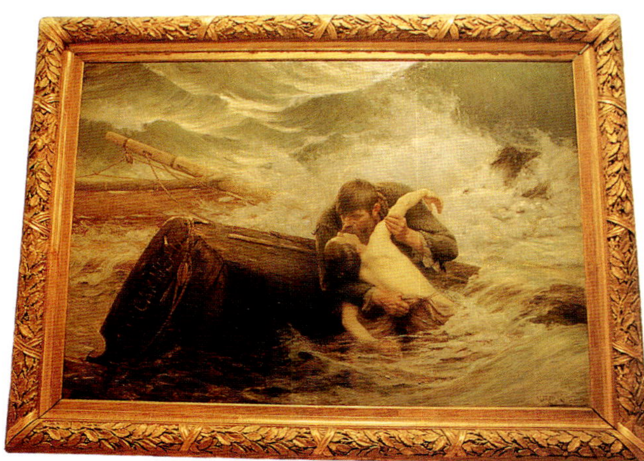

Steep rock walls and roiling waters characterize the northern and western coasts of Brittany. Many *marins*, or sailors, drowned in the treacherous waters along these shores. *Adieu!*, c.1892, by Alfred Guillou. *Courtesy of Musée des Beaux Arts, Quimper.*

HB produced this 18" long platter in the *décor riche* style, with *arabesque* or scrolling foliage border. It colorfully portrays a scene of young family saying goodbye to their Breton, as he leaves to make a living from the ocean. Signed HB Quimper, and the artist's signature (o.o.), an as-yet-undetermined HB painter. *Courtesy of Silvia and Gary Fritzhand.*

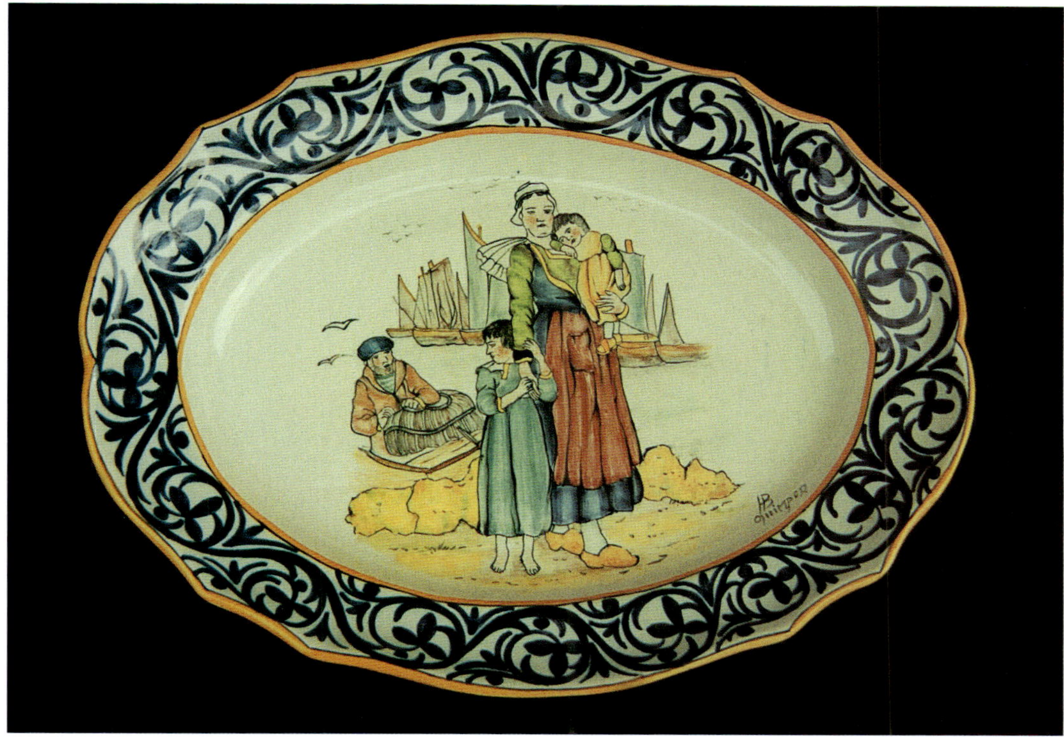

We have driven and explored many stretches of the Breton coast. On these journeys we have been overwhelmed by the might of the ocean at *Côte Sauvage* on the western coast of the Quiberon peninsula, and *Pointe du Raz*, west of Douarnenez, and awe-struck by the power and beauty of *Pointe de la Torche*, southwest of Quimper. In contrast, we also reveled in the balmy weather on the southern coast near Locmariaquier, grateful for its warmth on a sunny January afternoon.

Standing on the northern coast near St. Malo, covered by ocean spray, wind whipping across our faces, we pondered the strength of those who made their living on the water along the coast of Brittany. We reverently entered a chapel dedicated to those who never returned from the *mor* (Breton for ocean), and wondered at the fortitude of the Breton spirit, both of the mariners and of the families who waited for them on shore.

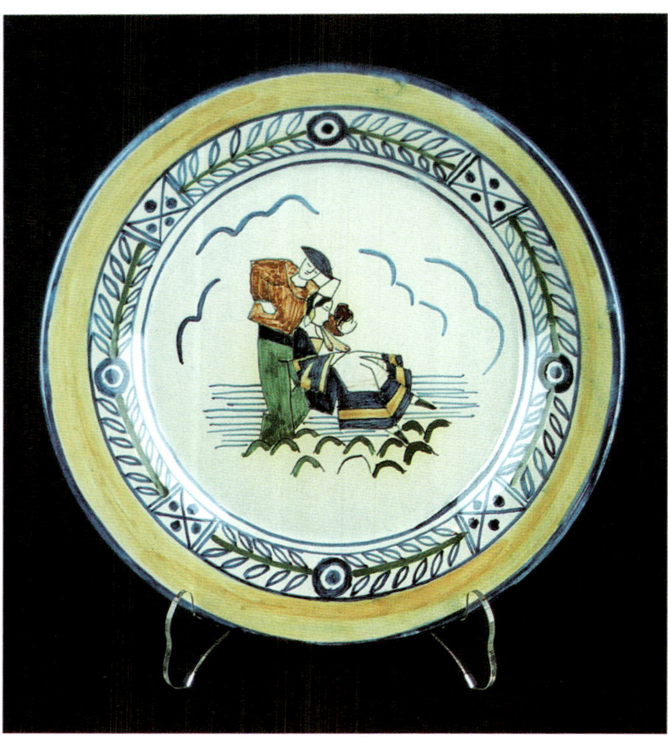

A sailor and his lady love cavort at the edge of the sea on this HB 8.75" plate from the 1920s or 1930s. Bernard Verlingue of the *Musée de la Faïence* identified the previously unknown originator of this sailor series. It is HB artist and designer Georges Brisson. *Private Collection.*

Another in the sailor series by Brisson appears on a well-designed teapot from the HB faïencerie, from the 1920s-1930s. Colorful Celtic swirls and design elements grace the panels of this highly regarded, 11" tall form. *Private Collection.*

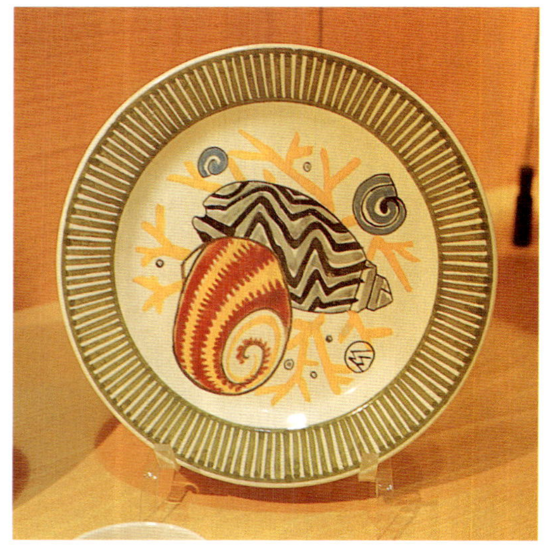

Mathurin Méheut, Henriot artist and designer, depicted fishing scenes and underwater creatures both on canvas and faïence. This colorful Henriot 9.75" plate is part of Méheut's *Service La Mer*, and was used on publicity brochures. *Courtesy of Musée de la Faïence, Quimper.*

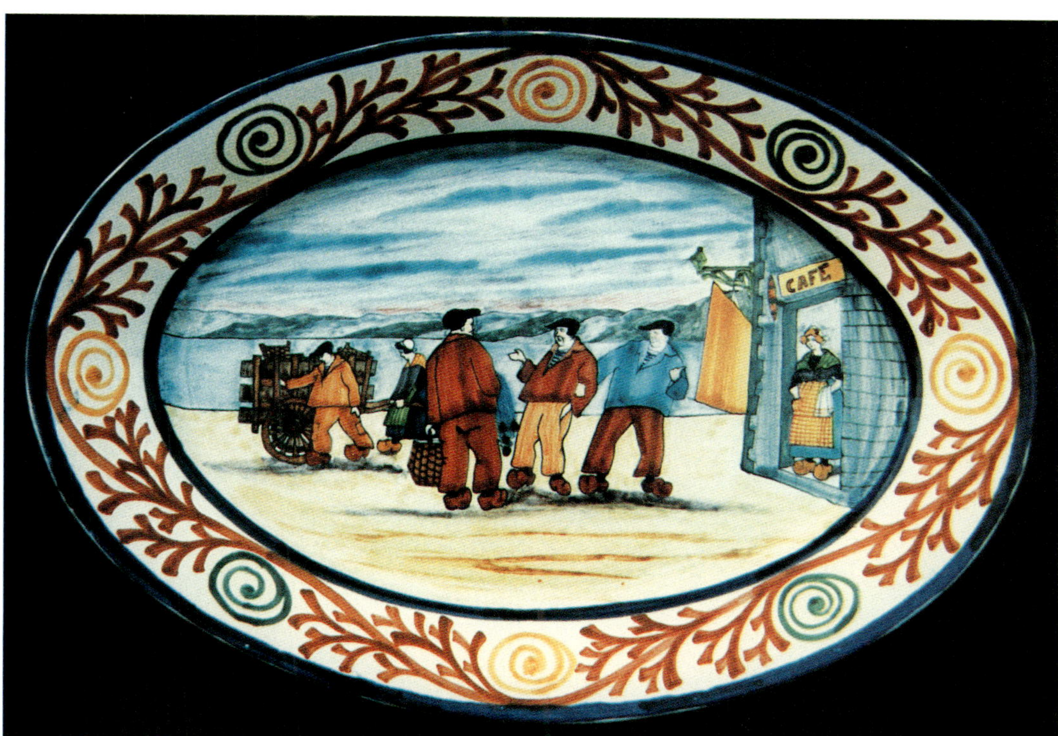

Paul Fouillen immortalized the fishermen's lifestyle in the *Pêcheur* and Port Series for the HB faïencerie. Items in the Port Series were executed as if they were paintings, and the borders were Celtic or nautical motifs. This port scene depicts three fellows chatting on the street. Two are headed to a café; a third seems to be disagreeing with them, while a Breton and a Bretonne push a cart in the background. A barmaid stands in the café door, hands in her apron pocket, blonde hair covered partially by a *coiffe*. The sky over the water and coast suggests sunset. Signed HB Quimper, 17" long. *(See Datesman, p. 7, for additional example.) Private Collection.*

After visiting these places it is easier to understand how the rugged geography and maritime occupations have influenced the Breton spirit and helped form the visions of Quimper artists, who understood the role the ocean played in the daily life in Brittany and celebrated the life of the sailors, or *marins*.

Few will dispute the challenging geography helped create a strong character in the people of Brittany. Physical isolation in small villages and towns helped maintain individualism, and the ocean tested Breton will, as it provided food and trade. Mysterious megalith monuments built by an unknown pre-Celtic race are scattered randomly across the peninsula, and helped color the Breton perspective with legends and myths. Strands of these myths were incorporated into Breton religion, and pre-history monuments can be seen as replicated in the parish closes of *Finistère*.

Pleyben

On our way to Quimper through the *Monts d'Arrée*, we came upon the well-known parish close of Pleyben, only about 25 kilometers northeast of our destination. A parish close or *enclos paroissial* is a phenomenon mainly in *Finistère*, particularly the Léon region. Originating in the 15th century as a way to either ward off the plague or as a thanksgiving for being spared, parish enclosures evolved over the centuries. The primary element is the church and cemetery within a walled area. The parish close grew to encompass a triumphal arch leading into the enclosed area, a highly decorated calvary, and an ossuary or charnel house. Breton calvaries often show several stages in the life of Christ carved in the solid granite of the region. Sometimes the characters are dressed in the Breton costumes of the carver's era, which gives the viewer a unique look at the biblical story.

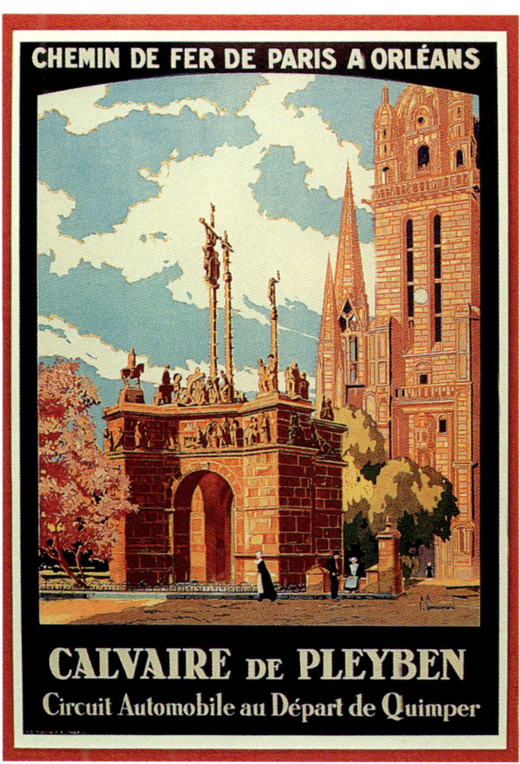

The *Calvaire* at Pleyben was immortalized on posters ... *Private Collection.*

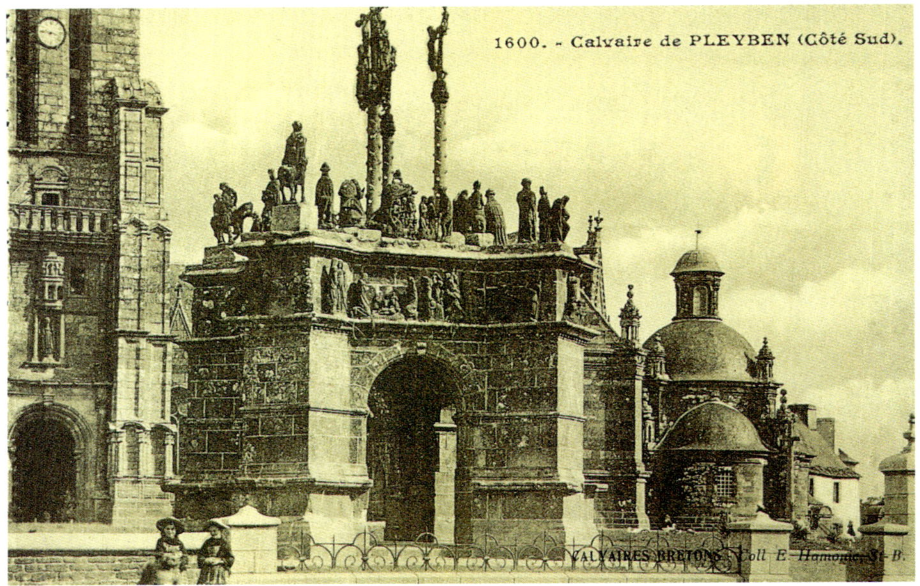

… And on postcards. *Authors' Collection.*

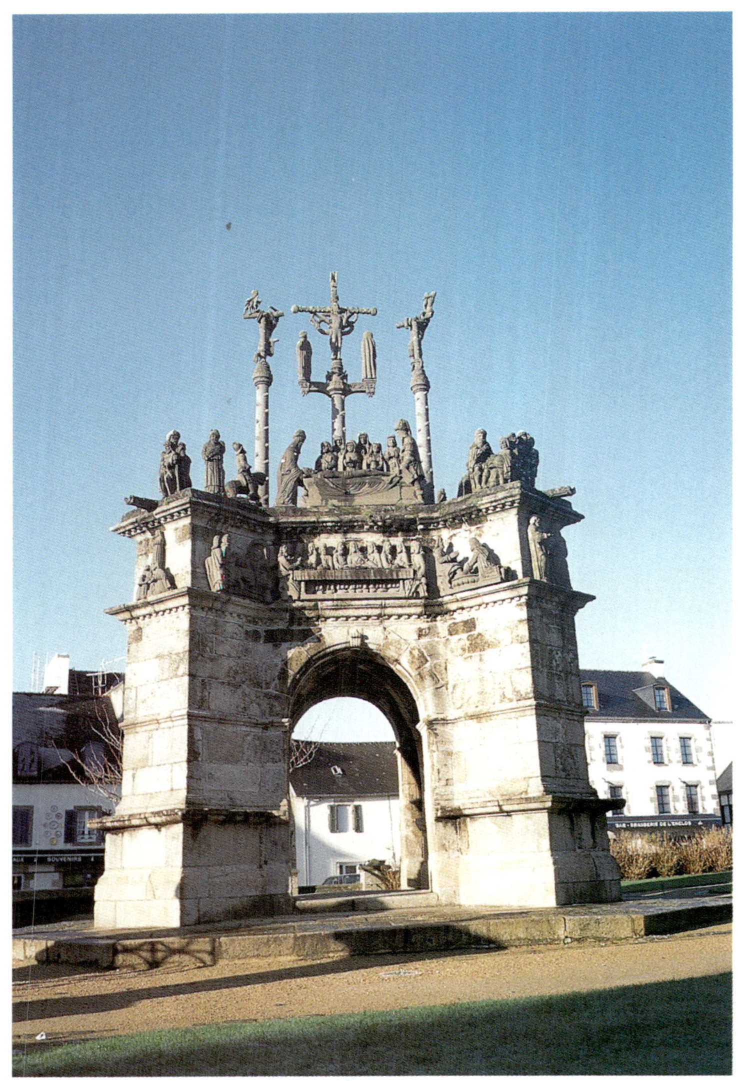

The calvary at Pleyben, constructed in the 16th century, contains about 180 figures in the various stages of the story of Christ. It was moved within the compound in 1738, and since then new scenes and repairs to various characters have been made. It is inspiring to walk around the calvary and view it against a brilliant blue Sunday morning sky.

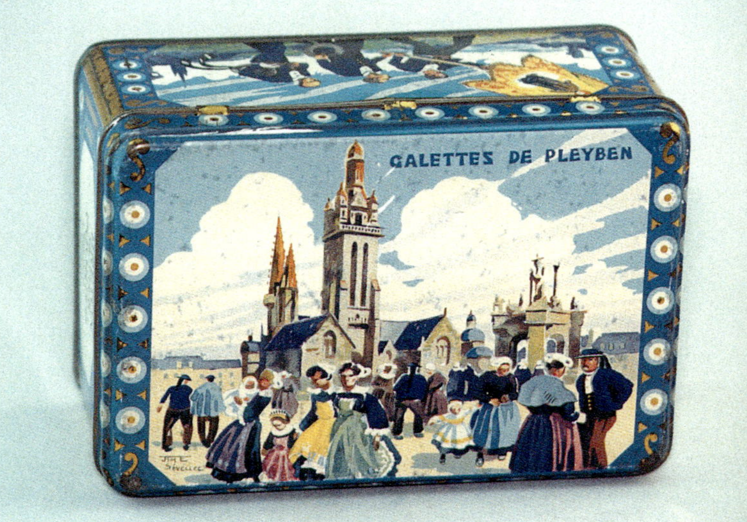

Pleyben also is known for its *galettes de Pleyben*. The famous cookies were sold in a 1930s tin decorated with a design by Jim-Emile Sévellec, featuring the famous parish close. *Private Collection.*

An element in Sévellec's design for the *galettes de Pleyben* shows banner carriers in the Breton breeze. *Private Collection.*

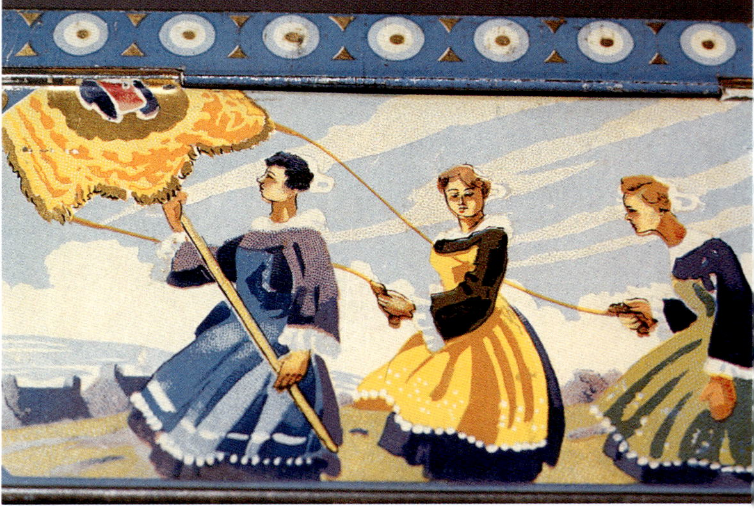

Hélias, the Breton author and philosopher, lamented the change that occurred in the parish closes when the cemeteries were moved from adjacent to the church to a site further away. The cemetery being next to the church kept the dead in constant contact with the living, who prayed at the graves as they left church services or stopped by after shopping in town, congregating and exchanging news. *(Hélias, The Horse of Pride, pp. 104-5.)*

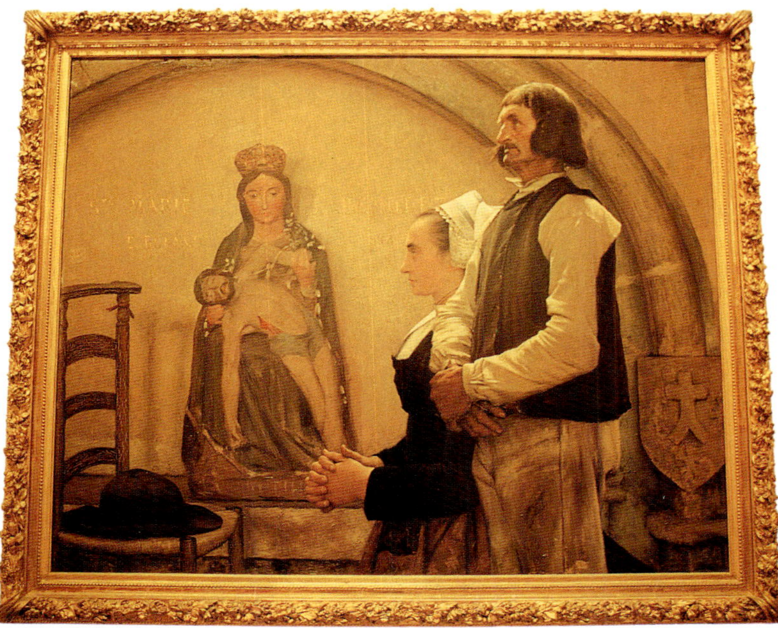

Bretons are known as a pious group, or at least as a people who give homage to forces larger than themselves. *Bretons en Prière*, c. 1898, by Jean-Eugene Buland. *Courtesy of Musée des Beaux Arts, Quimper.*

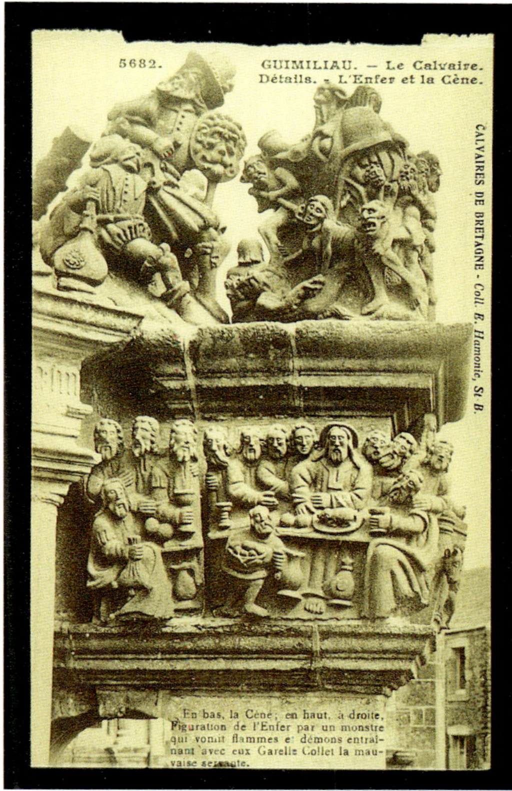

A rivalry evolved among Breton towns to build the most elaborate parish close. The triumphal arch and the calvary were the most easily observed and therefore became the focus for this art. Details from the calvary at Guimiliau on this vintage postcard illustrate the Passion story. Besides being beautiful, calvaries were teaching tools used by priests for the local populace. *Authors' Collection.*

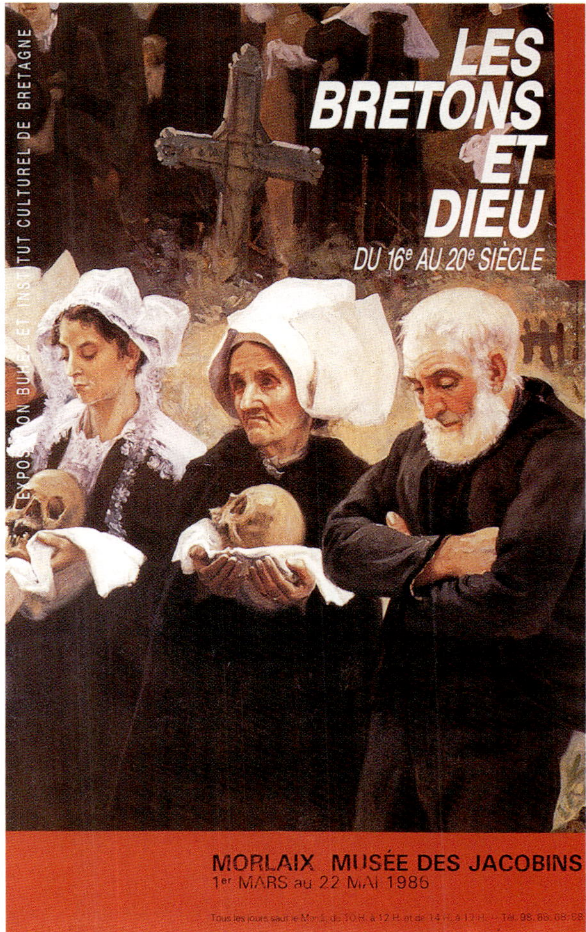

In 1986, the museum in Morlaix featured an exhibition of *Les Bretons et Dieu* (Bretons and God), from the 16th to the 20th century. This scene is from *La Transition des assements à l'ossuaire de Trégastel* by Georges Pollieux-Saint-Ange, 1896. *Courtesy of Musée des Jacobins, Morlaix.*

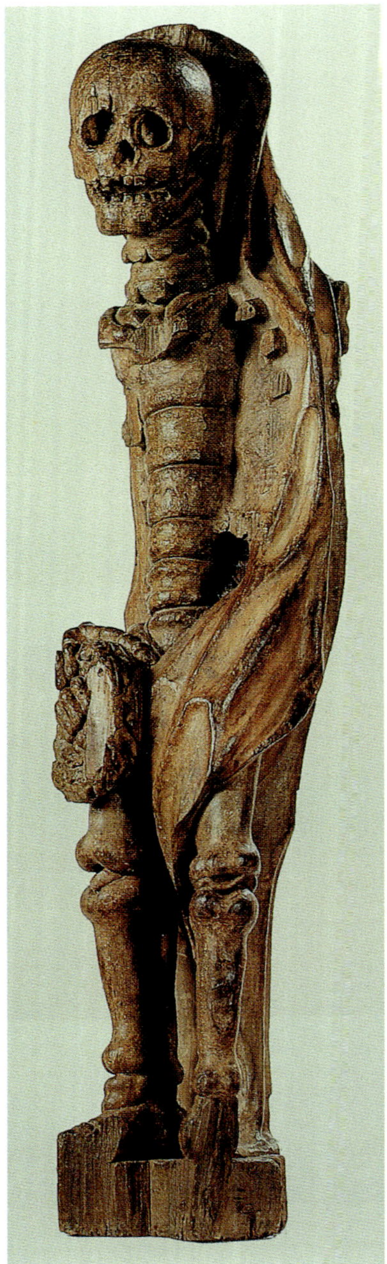

Some see the harsh geography and powerful ocean as creating a Breton personality in need of religion for protection from these natural forces. Others see the Bretons as stoically enduring their lot, with the help of innumerable saints and prayers. As Hélias saw it, Brittany is a land of dreams and legends and is slow to emerge from them. (*Hélias, Images of Brittany, p. 3.*)

Left:
Death, or *Ankou*, is always present on the minds of Bretons, according to some observers. Here *Ankou* is carved in oak. *Courtesy of Musée des Jacobins, Morlaix.*

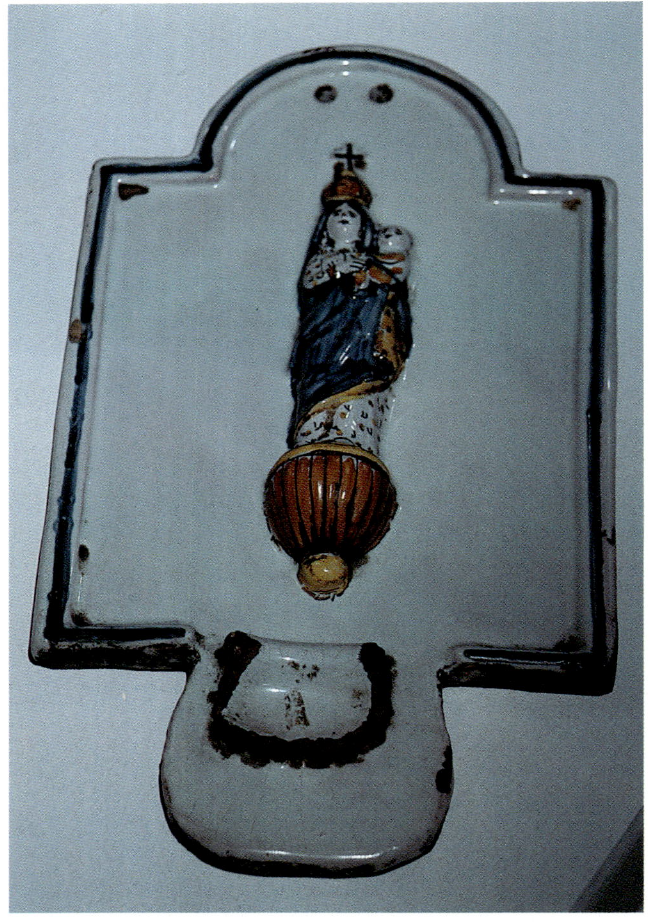

An early Quimper *bénitier*, or holy water font, from 1800s is on display in Morlaix. *Courtesy of Musée des Jacobins, Morlaix.*

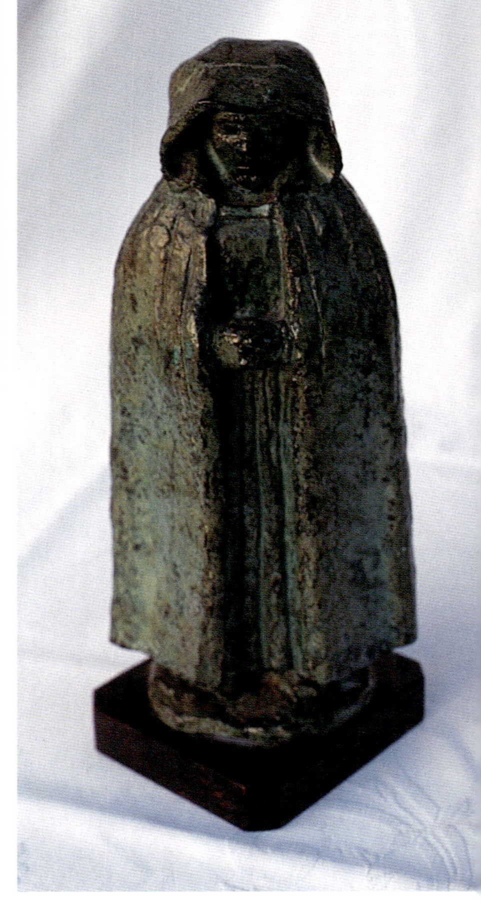

René Quillivic is the HB/Grande Maison artist who designed the *La Femme de Calvaire*. This rendition is 9.75" tall and executed in bronze. *Courtesy of Pierre Breton, Art de Cornouaille, Quimper.*

The first modern intrusion into the Breton reverie came with the railroad in 1863, which brought tourists and artists. During World War I and again during World War II, draftees *(conscrits)* left Brittany to join the battle. These Bretons were privy to a new, more complicated world, and the survivors brought it home with them. Quaint costumes began to disappear from everyday life, worn only for feast days and ceremonies such as weddings. French became more prevalent than Breton. Brittany began to lose the uniqueness her isolation had provided. Future generations would resurrect the memories of that other life, in the Celtic-Breton revivalist movements of the 20th century, and the numerous festivals celebrating the culture of an earlier life in Brittany. She would tell the world about herself, sometimes on Quimper poterie.

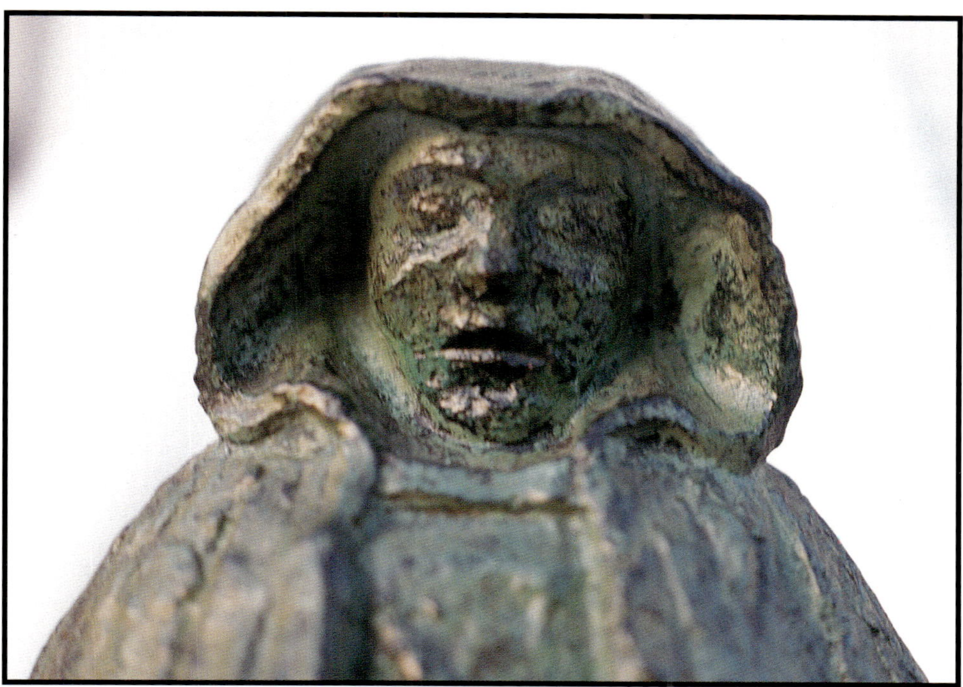

Also called the Prayer of a Poor Woman, the statuette detail captures the somber tone of the prayer. *Courtesy of Pierre Breton, Art de Cornouaille, Quimper.*

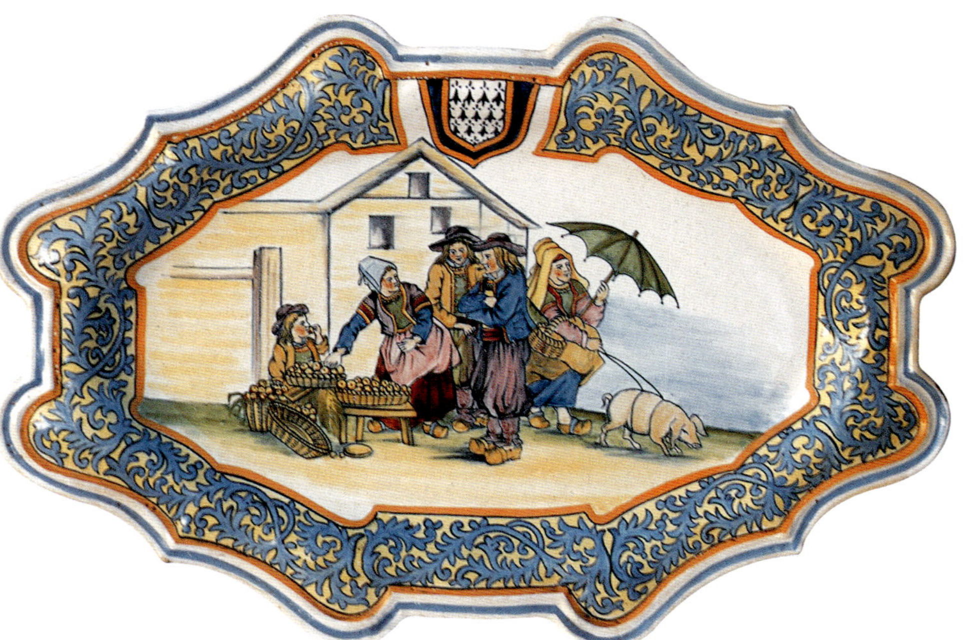

Quimper artists kept old *Bretagne* alive on faïence. Villagers crowd around a produce merchant on this Porquier-Beau *banêtte*, or two-handled tray. *Collection Pierre Breton, Art de Cornouaille, Quimper.*

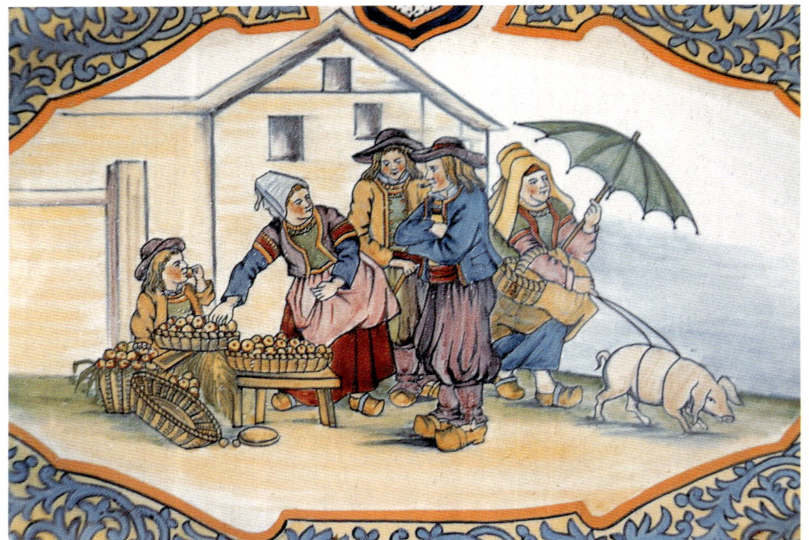

Left:
A closer look shows *coiffes, bragou-braz, sabots,* the wooden shoes of *Bretagne,* and even a pig on a leash, probably headed to market too! *Collection of Pierre Breton, Art de Cornouaille, Quimper.*

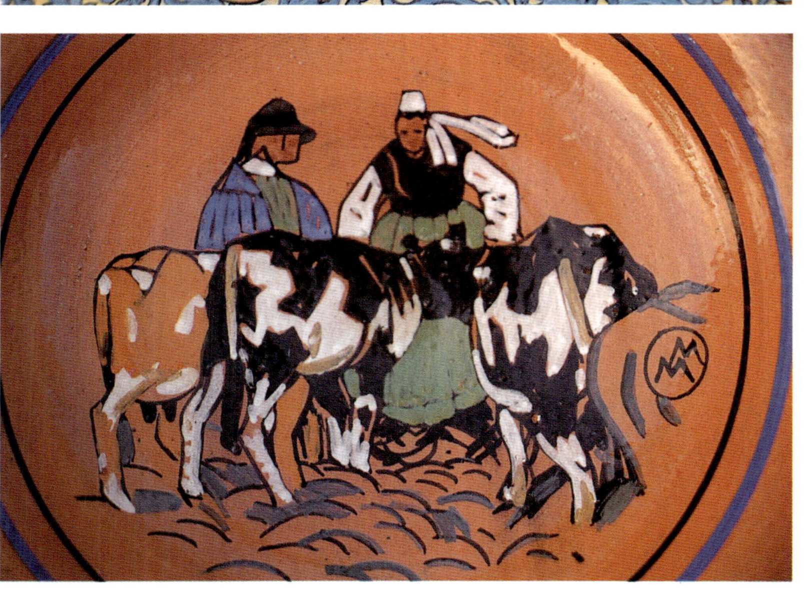

Mathurin Méheut gave a more modern look to village life in Brittany in this scene, where cows are being herded to market. Note the Méheut signature of MM in a circle on this 7.25" diameter Henriot bowl. *Collection of Pierre Breton, Art de Cornouaille, Quimper.*

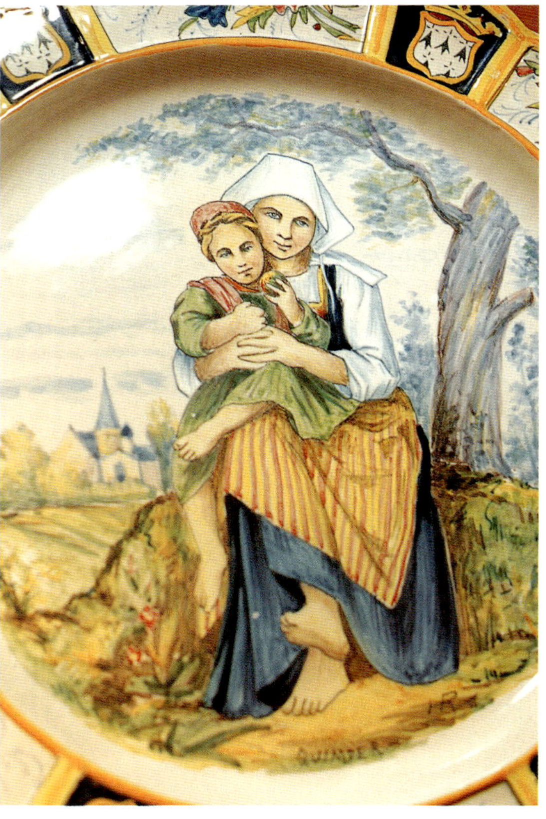

An Henriot artist captured a mother and child in a moment of Breton reverie on this early 20th century HR Quimper plate. Note the detailed visages, clothing, and scenery, all making this example stellar. *Courtesy of Musée de la Faïence, Quimper.*

Once upon a time, all of our routes through Brittany began at Rennes. This regional capital of *Bretagne* is a city of historic, artistic, and intellectual distinction. Located on the Vilaine River in the department of *Ille et Vilaine* west of Paris, Rennes is sophisticated, urbane, and home of two universities and a medical school.

After shopping the Paris markets, it's easy to hop the train from *Gare Montparnasse* to Rennes. We admire the French rail system and we buy our roundtrip tickets a day or two in advance at the station, to assure we have seats. Once we are past the new suburban housing developments, we are thrilled each time we see the Breton countryside unfold, with quaint, early stone farms, mistletoe hanging in clumps from old, tall trees, and large *manoirs* in the distance.

When we reach Rennes, we rent a car at the train station, which had a facelift in recent years. The physical improvements also marked an improvement in rental vehicle options. On a visit years ago, we became stranded when the one agency available at the time chose not to open on Sundays.

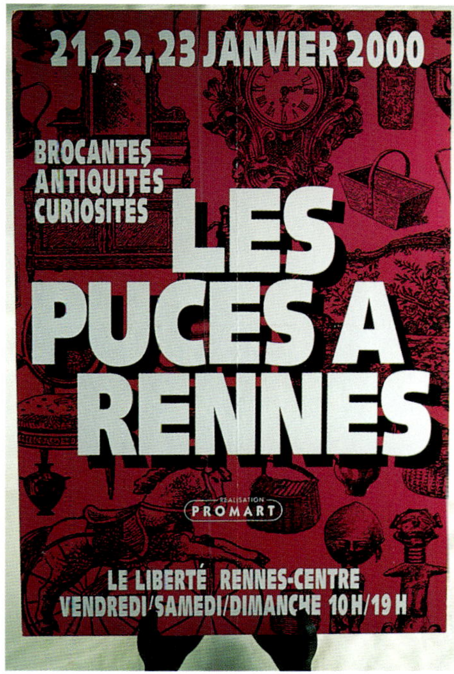

Rennes hosts a three-day flea market annually in January, about the time we usually visit.

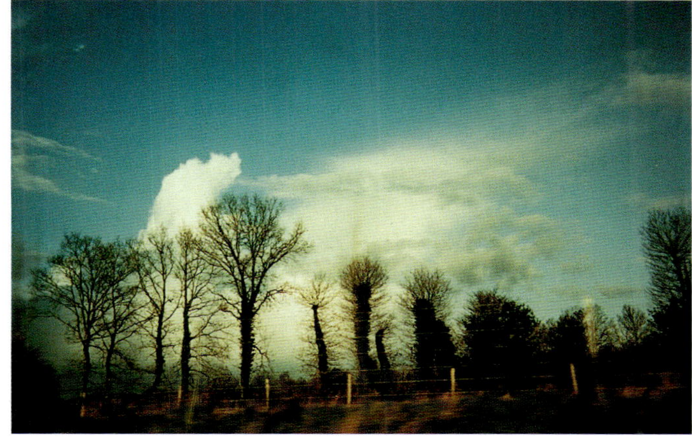

We were puzzled on our first trip to Rennes, when we saw rows of trees cut back nearly to the trunk. We later learned this tree-trimming method is called pollarding, which provides firewood for the winter and increases tree growth in the spring.

The edge on this 8.75" Henriot covered cheese dish is *dentillé*, or scalloped form. The lid carries out the theme with a painted scalloped effect surrounding the *petite Bretonne*. Note the handle with mistletoe décor, a Breton good luck sign, derived from Celtic or Druid beliefs. *Private Collection.*

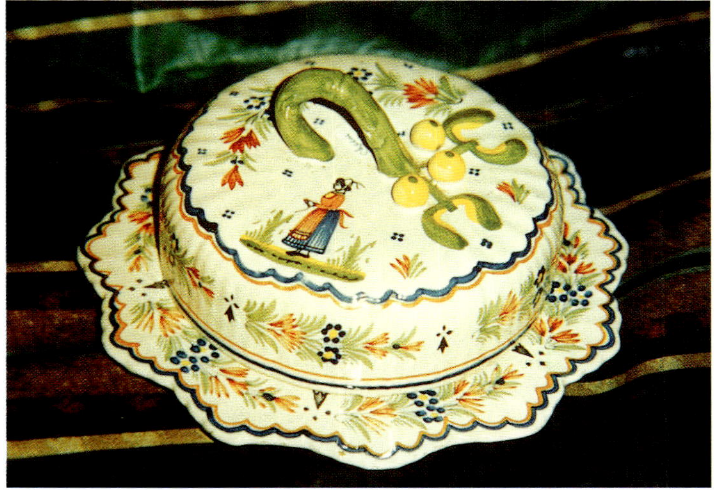

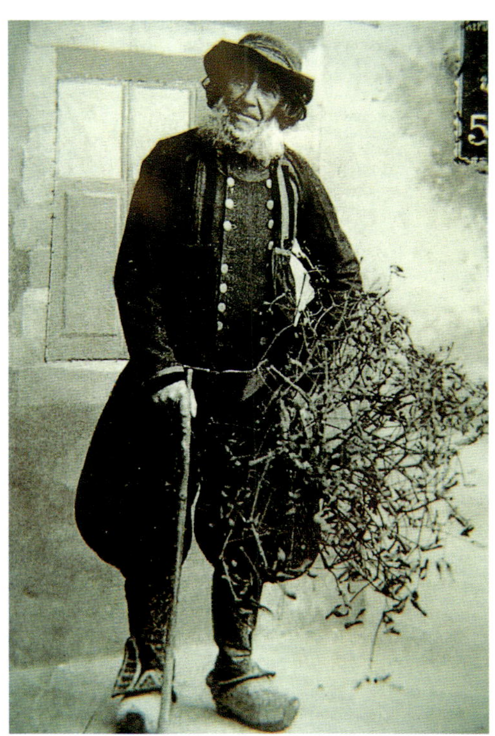

A vintage postcard shows a Breton mistletoe (*gui*) gatherer from the early 1900s. *Authors' Collection.*

We make Rennes our base as we shop for Quimper, first in the city and then in outlying areas within a day's roundtrip drive. We've found wonderful examples of Quimper in the shops close by the renovated *Palais de Justice* in Rennes. There is a *brocante* in St. Helier and one in a suburb, Chantepie, where we've found Quimper. We window-shop and sometimes purchase Quimper at the *Hôtel Le President*, on our way to one of our favorite restaurants.

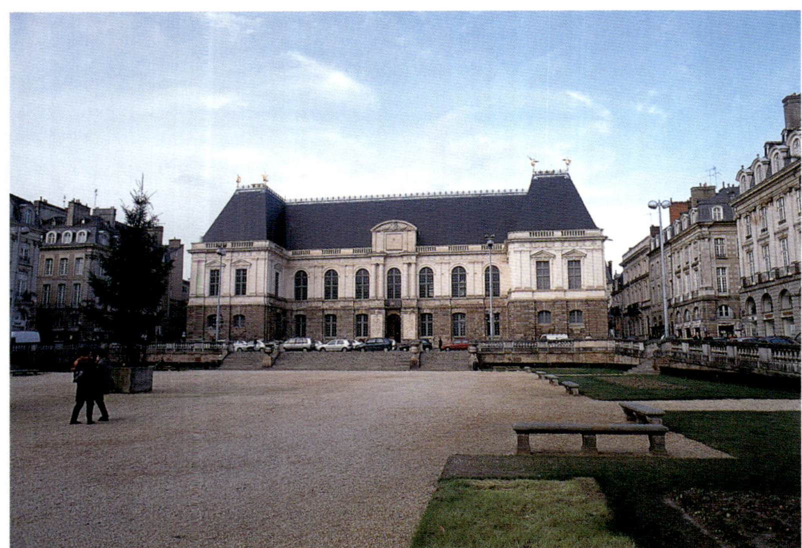

Left:
A renovated *Palais de Justice* was re-dedicated in 2000 by President Jacques Chirac. A 1994 fire severely damaged portions of the building, but it has been restored to its former glory.

Center Left:
An HB advertising sign was found in a shop close to the train station in Rennes. It measures 5.5" wide. *Courtesy of Elizabeth C. Ross.*

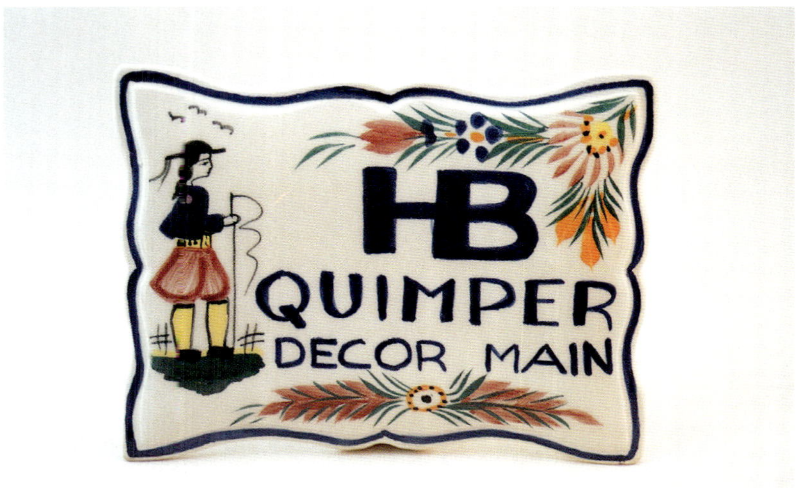

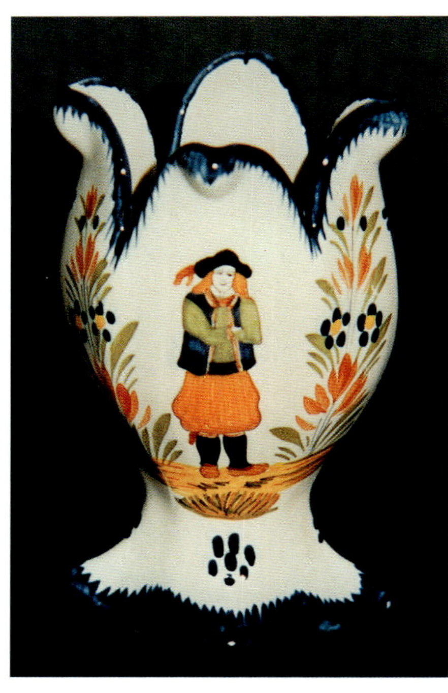

A c. 1930, 5" tall tulip-shaped vase by Henriot with a Breton in *bragou-braz* greeted us in a shop not far from the *Palais de Justice* in Rennes. *Private Collection.*

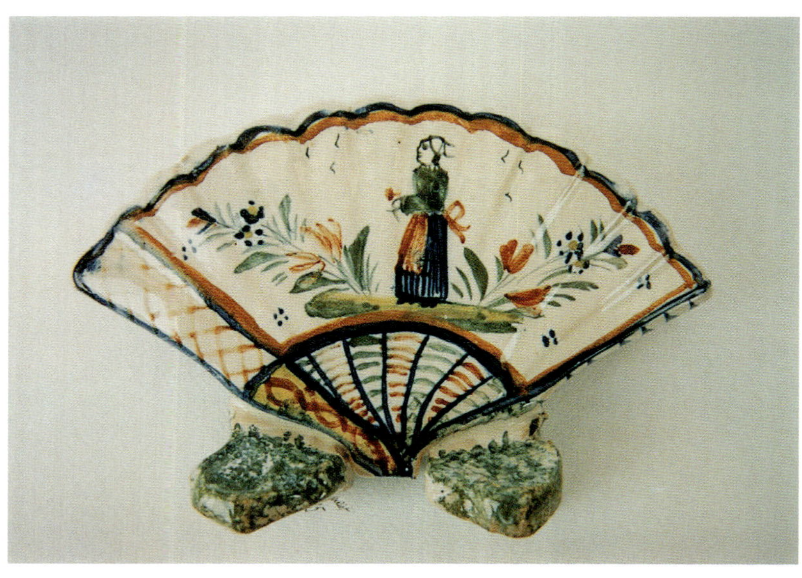

Left:
A fan-shaped (*éventail*) jardinière is a desirable form. This model by Henriot features sponged butterfly feet, *croisillon*, or lattice-work accents, and a demure Bretonne with a posy. We found this 5" tall by 8" wide example in the St. Helier section of Rennes. *Private Collection.*

When in Rennes, be sure to take in the medieval district of narrow winding streets and half-timbered houses, which survived a devastating 1720 fire. There is a magnificent formal garden in the city, *Jardin du Thabor*, on the site of a 16th century Benedictine Abbey. Take your time and enjoy this lovely spot. About two blocks away, in front of the *Palais St.-Georges*, is another beautiful formal garden. Perhaps you will uncover, as we did, an example of Quimper. Look closely beneath an arch on the left-hand side of this building. While taking the time to enjoy this sight on a recent trip, we discovered a sculpted memorial to France's fallen war heroes by L.H. Nicot, noted Quimper artist. We visited these gardens before but failed to notice this plaque. Finding this example of Quimper reminded us how important it is to us to slow down and enjoy the journey.

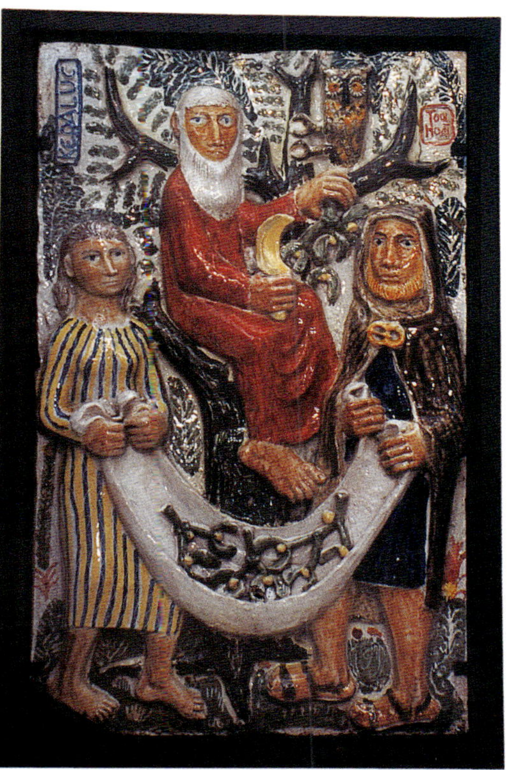

The *Keraluc* faïencerie created this bas-relief plaque showing early Breton mistletoe gatherers.

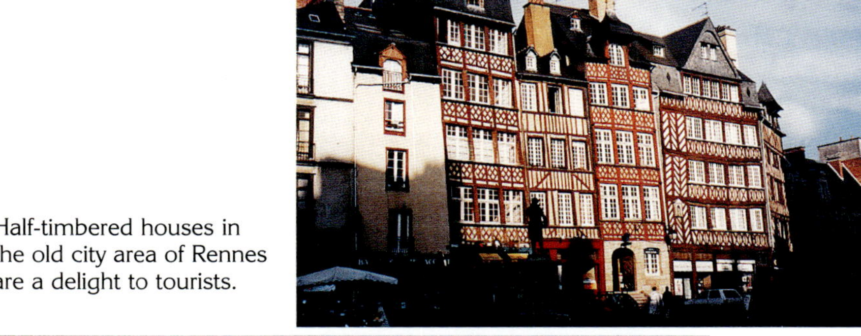

Half-timbered houses in the old city area of Rennes are a delight to tourists.

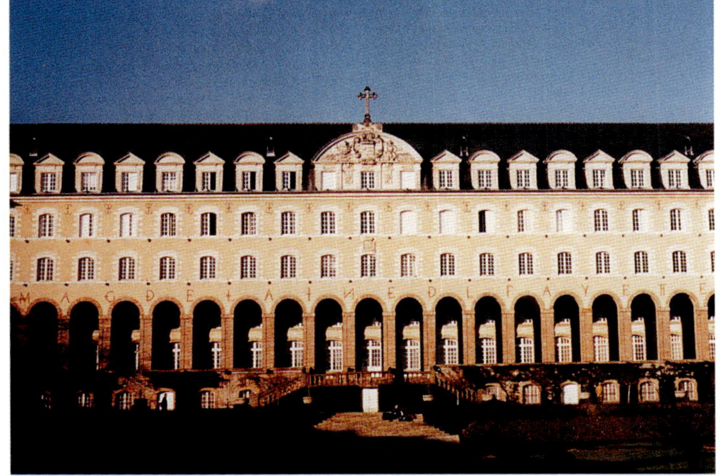

The *Palais St.-Georges*, two blocks from *Jardin du Thabor*, has a formal garden in front of its impressive building.

When we took a second look at *St.-Georges*, we found a Quimper treasure. This plaque commemorating Breton war losses, by Henriot artist L.H. Nicot, was waiting for us under an arch to the left of the building. We just had to slow our pace to find it.

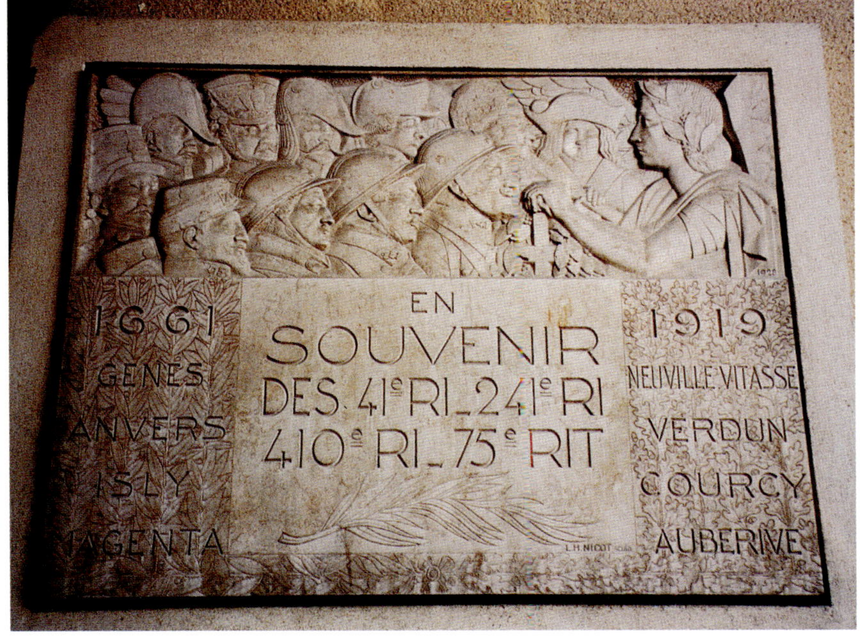

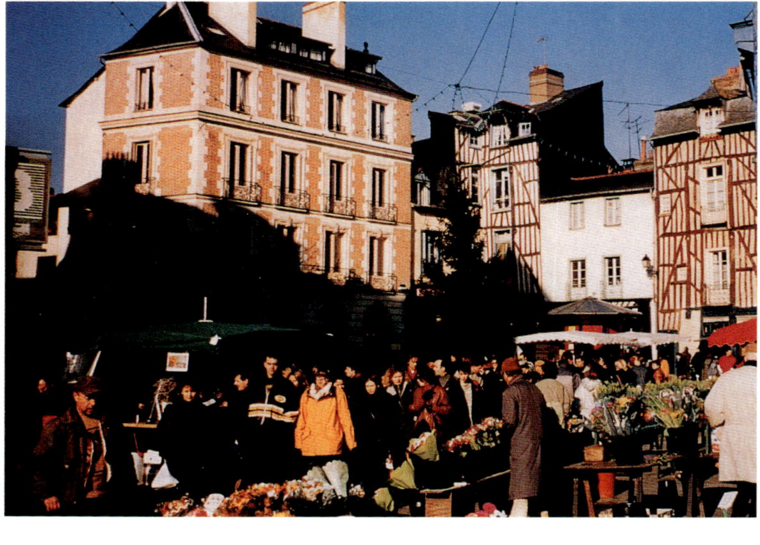

The Saturday market in Rennes has been held on the same site since the Middle Ages. The half-timbered houses have seen a lot of change since Du Guesclin jousted here.

In winter 2000-2001, the *Musée de Bretagne* at Rennes held an exhibit dedicated to *Ar Seiz Breur*, a Celtic-Breton cultural revivalist group. The initiators of *Ar Seiz Breur* were Quimper artists René and Suzanne Creston, and Jeanne Malivel.

Try to time your visit to Rennes to include the famed Saturday Market, which has been held in *La Place des Lices* since the Middle Ages. As a youth, the famed warrior Bertrand Du Guesclin gained respect from his family for performing bravely in a jousting tournament in this square in 1337, and Bretons still gather here regularly. The market provides a place where the flavor of country and city blend amid the half-timbered houses and cobblestone streets. We have enjoyed many bright, sunny Saturday mornings at the *Places des Lices*, eating local foods, buying cheeses and breads, and mingling with the crowd. Try the *galettes noir*, buckwheat pancakes filled with sausage, egg, and cheese, at one of the small *crêperies*. Be sure to browse the nearby shops where *triskeles* abound, along with books on menhirs, dolmens, and the myth of *Brocéliande* and King Arthur's search for the Holy Grail.

We recommend the *Musée de Bretagne* at Rennes, where we found displays of Breton furniture and costumes. Also, the pre-history, Gallo-Roman, and medieval era exhibits all reinforced our renewed sense of history. In the *Musée des Beaux Arts*, paintings and sculptures from the 14th century to the present day are on view, and a special display features Breton artists' paintings of Brittany. In 2001, there was a remarkable display about *Ar Seiz Breur* (Seven Brothers), the Celtic-Breton cultural revivalist group begun by Quimper artists.

Ar Seiz Breur

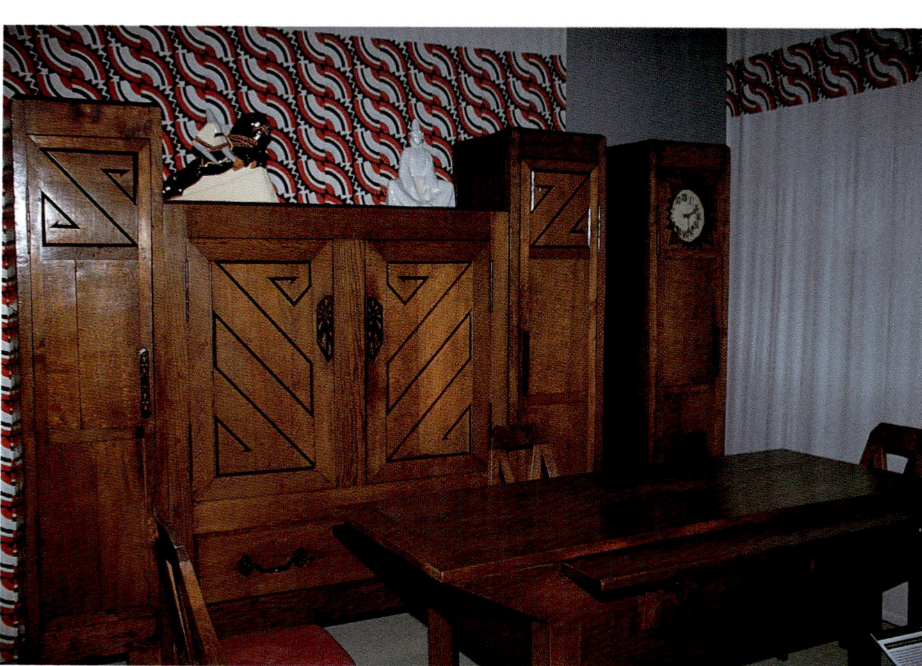

At the same time in 2001, the *Musée Départemental Breton* in Quimper displayed articles from *Ar Seiz Breur* members. Furniture designed in simplified, modern lines was graced with a statue (left) of *Nominoë sur son Cheval*, or Nominoë on his Horse, by Henriot artist and *Ar Seiz Breur* co-founder René-Yves Creston. A statue in *email blanc* of Jorg Robin's *Bigoudène Assise* (Seated Bigouden), designed for the HB faïencerie, is on the right.

An ardent group of Quimper artists dedicated to the renewal of the Celtic-Breton heritage joined together in 1923. Under the initial leadership of Jeanne Malivel and René and Suzanne Creston, this group became known as *Ar Seiz Breur*, or Seven Brothers. One story says it was named for the seven saints of early Brittany: Corentin, Pol, Tugdual, Malo, Brieuc, Patern, and Samson. Malivel had first conceived the idea for *Ar Seiz Breur* in 1917, as she sought to preserve the Celtic tradition in her own work. She and the Crestons recruited Pierre Abadie-Landel, Christian Lepart, Georges Sebilleau, and Jorg Robin. The group grew in size to over 30 members. They successfully introduced their aesthetic ideal to Quimper faïence, and to other applied and decorative arts as well. *(Rodallec, Trois Siècles de Faïences, p. 187.)*

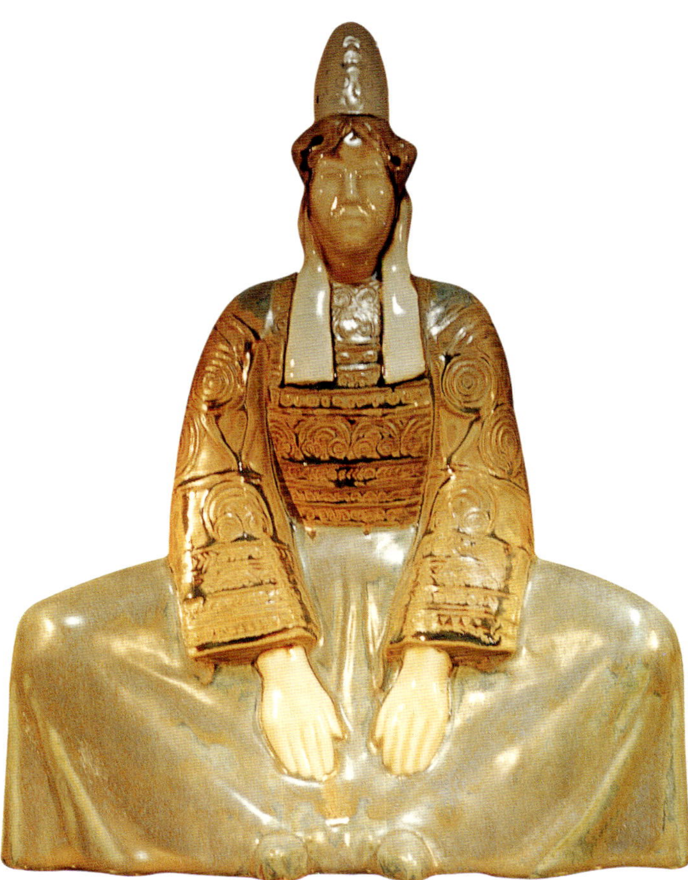

In the late 1920s, *Ar Seiz Breur* member Jorg Robin designed *Bigoudène Assise* in *grès*, 21.25" tall. This version resides in the *Musée de la Faïence* in Quimper. Robin's work was signed with the anagram Brion when the model was sold to *HB/Grande Maison. Courtesy of Musée de la Faïence, Quimper.*

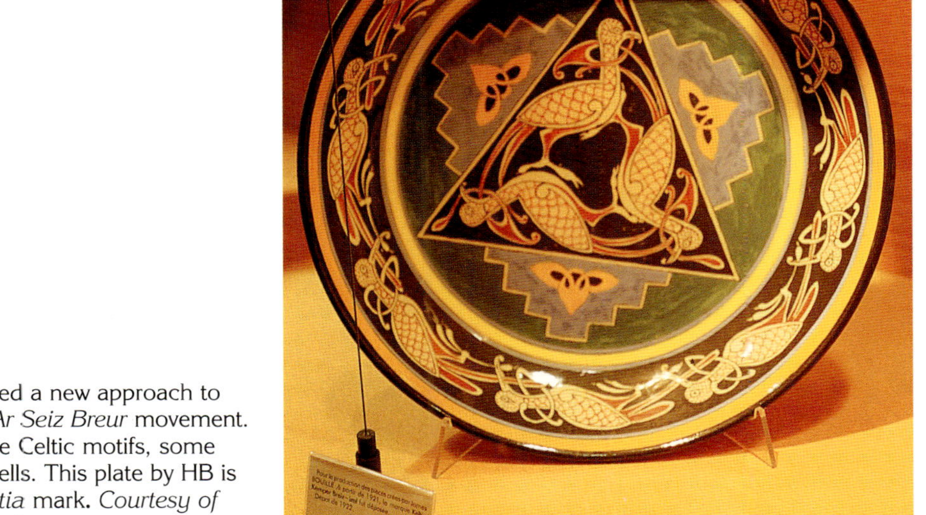

James Bouillé contributed a new approach to Quimper décor for the *Ar Seiz Breur* movement. He incorporated intricate Celtic motifs, some based on the Book of Kells. This plate by HB is signed also with the *Keltia* mark. *Courtesy of Musée de la Faïence, Quimper.*

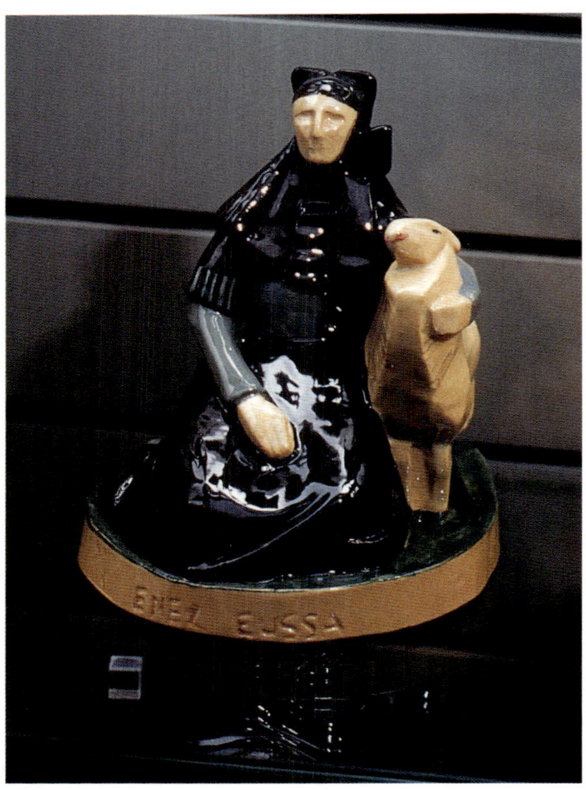

Ar Seiz Breur co-founder René-Yves Creston designed *Enez Eussa, Île d'Ouessant*, 7.5" tall, for the Henriot firm in 1930. The bold, angular form displays the new look for faïence figures. *Courtesy of Musée Départemental Breton, Quimper.*

Right:
Olivier Lapicque, the grandson of an original *Ar Seiz Breur* member, continues his family's tradition. His work appears on this *vase boule* by the *Faïence d'Art Breton (FAB). Courtesy of Faïence d'Art Breton, Quimper.*

The Breton display at the Paris 1925 *Exhibition Arts Décoratifs, Industriels, and Modernes* was planned by *Ar Seiz Breur*. The exhibit *Ti Breiz* (Breton House), featured furniture, paintings, fabrics, and ceramics with functional lines embellished by Celtic-Breton motifs. After the untimely deaths of Malivel and Robin in the 1920s, the group regenerated itself in time to participate in the 1937 *Exposition Internationale* in Paris. After World War II, *Ar Seiz Breur* dissolved, but individual artists continued to contribute their Celtic-Breton message to the art world. Today, Olivier Lapicque, the grandson of an original member of *Ar Seiz Breur*, Georges Sebilleau, carries forward the tradition. Lapicque works in ceramics, while his grandfather was a furniture designer. Lapicque, from Concarneau, has created various designs for *Faïencerie d'Art Breton* in Quimper. *(Couédic et Veillard, pp. 26-27, 79; Mali, Old Quimper Review, October 1999; Rotté, pp. 40-41.)*

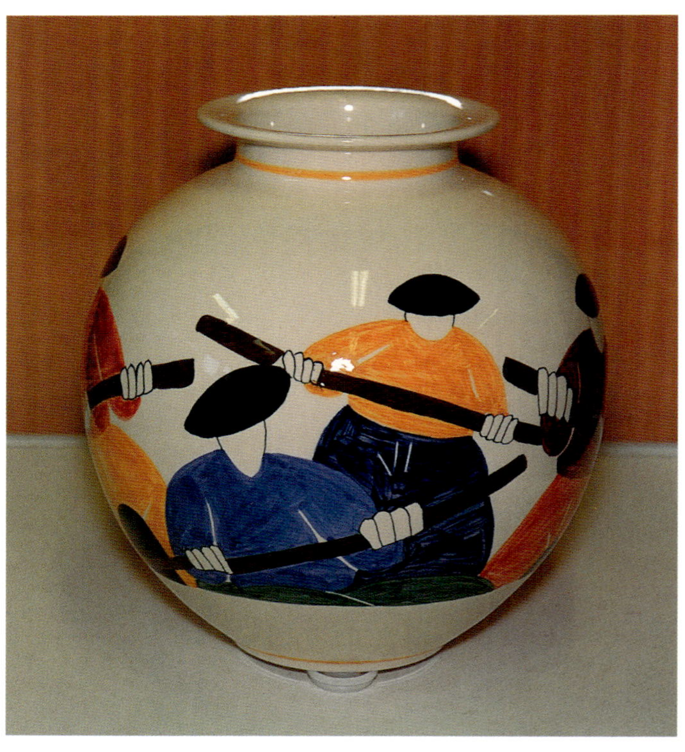

Day Trips from Rennes

Quimper poterie is abundant within a day's drive of Rennes and we enjoy the quest, which has included shopping trips from Rennes north to Dinan and St. Malo, west to Josselin, and south to Vannes, with many stops in between at both large and small establishments. We also treated ourselves to a day in *Brocéliande*, about 25 kilometers southwest of Rennes.

This map of early *Brocéliande* tells of mysterious places of enchantment where King Arthur, the Knights of the Round Table, and Merlin searched for the Holy Grail and eternal love. *Private Collection.*

Land of Arthur and Merlin, *Brocéliande*

We spent a glorious day in the *Fôret de Paimpont*, or the ancient *Brocéliande*. It was one of our most enjoyable searches for the heart of *Bretagne*. Located about 35 kilometers west of Rennes in central Brittany, or *Argoat*, this inland area is filled with thickets, pinelands, pools, and fields of gorse, broom, and heather. Our love of history and Brittany had us anxious to wander the back roads of this seeming forest primeval, lured by the legend of the sorcerer Merlin, King Arthur, and the Knights of the Round Table on their search for the Holy Grail. Other countries have claimed this bit of history, but a look at the English Cornwall and the Breton Cornouaille, named for it, show similar geography, including a rugged, wild coast and inland woods. To have it both ways, some believe Arthur was king of both *Grande* and *Petite Bretagne*.

As we left N24, the major highway heading west from Rennes, and drove into the forest, a feeling of reverence emerged. Quiet prevailed, and several times we stopped and walked totally absorbed by the silence. The forest originally covered a large part of inland Brittany and was estimated to extend for 140 square kilometers. Unfortunately, today it covers only about 70 square kilometers, due to cutting and clearing of timber over the past hundreds of years and a devastating fire in 1990. A reforestation program has taken root and nature's regenerative powers are slowly helping the deep, eerie forest reclaim its history.

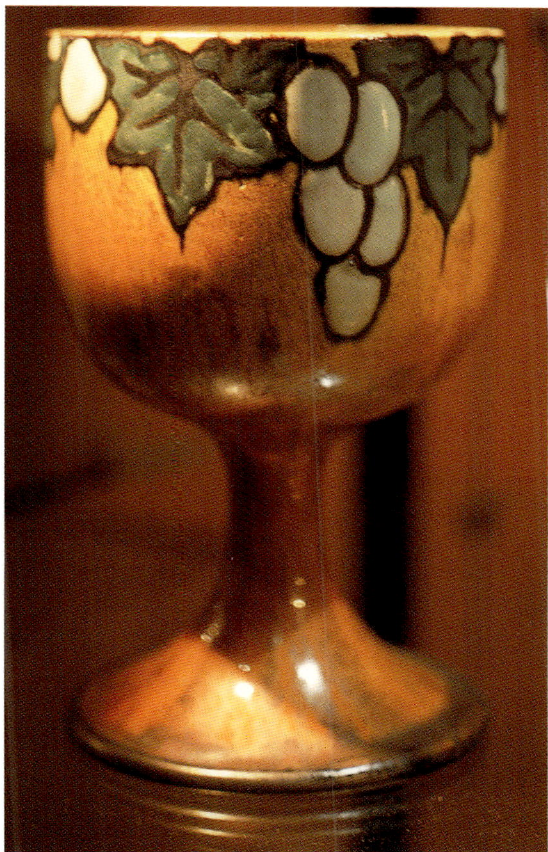

A *ciboire* (Greek goblet) by the HB faïencerie in the 1920s might be similar to the Holy Grail, the object of King Arthur's quest in *Brocéliande*. *Courtesy of Musée de la Faïence, Quimper.*

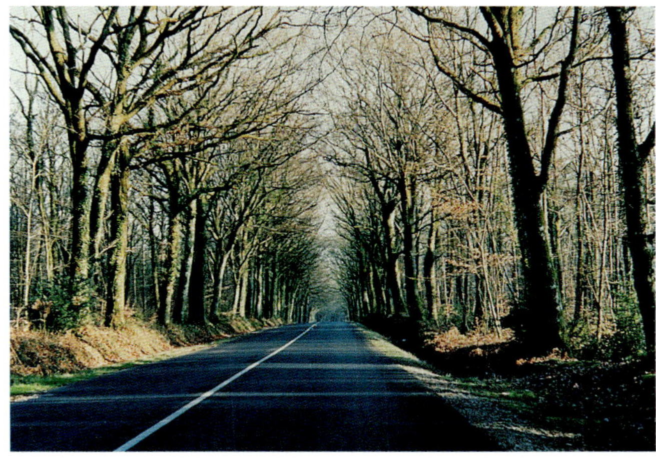

We left the major highway, N24, and took a charming road toward the *Fôret de Paimpont*, or *Brocéliande*. The deeper we drove into this forest primeval, the quieter and more serene it became.

We headed into the heart of the forest toward Paimpont, a market town dating from the French Revolution and located 16 kilometers from N24. The quaint lakeside village is dominated by a 6th century abbey, which now houses the mayor's office in one wing and the church, *Notre Dame de Paimpont*, in another. Ornate woodwork fills the church, making the legends of Christianity come alive. We left Paimpont and drove back into the forest, to search for places steeped in myth, magic, and solitude, imagining spells cast over long-ago visitors. We found the Valley of No Return, where Merlin was enchanted to remain, the Fairies Mirror, False Lover's Rock, and the Golden Tree.

In the heart of the forest, the 6th century abbey in Paimpont houses the town offices and the church, *Notre-Dame de Paimpont*.

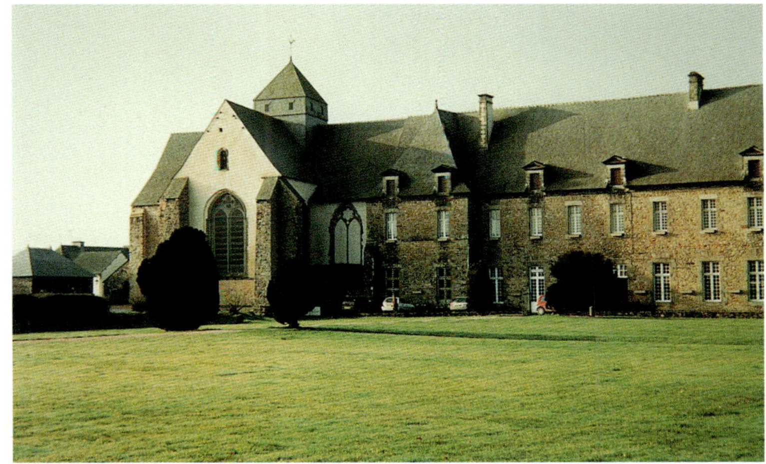

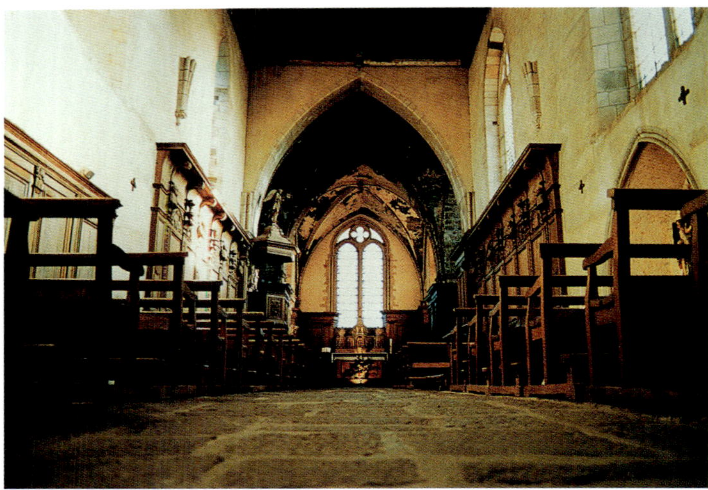

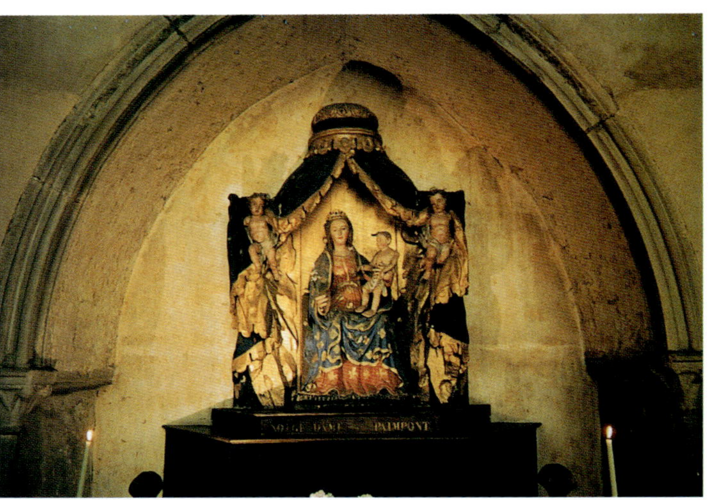

Notre-Dame de Paimpont is an interesting Breton church, known for its quiet setting and intricate woodwork. We visited on a day the church was empty, affording us an excellent view of the artistry within.

The statue of *Notre Dame of Paimpont* is deftly carved, painted and presented, in keeping with the craftsmanship of the entire church.

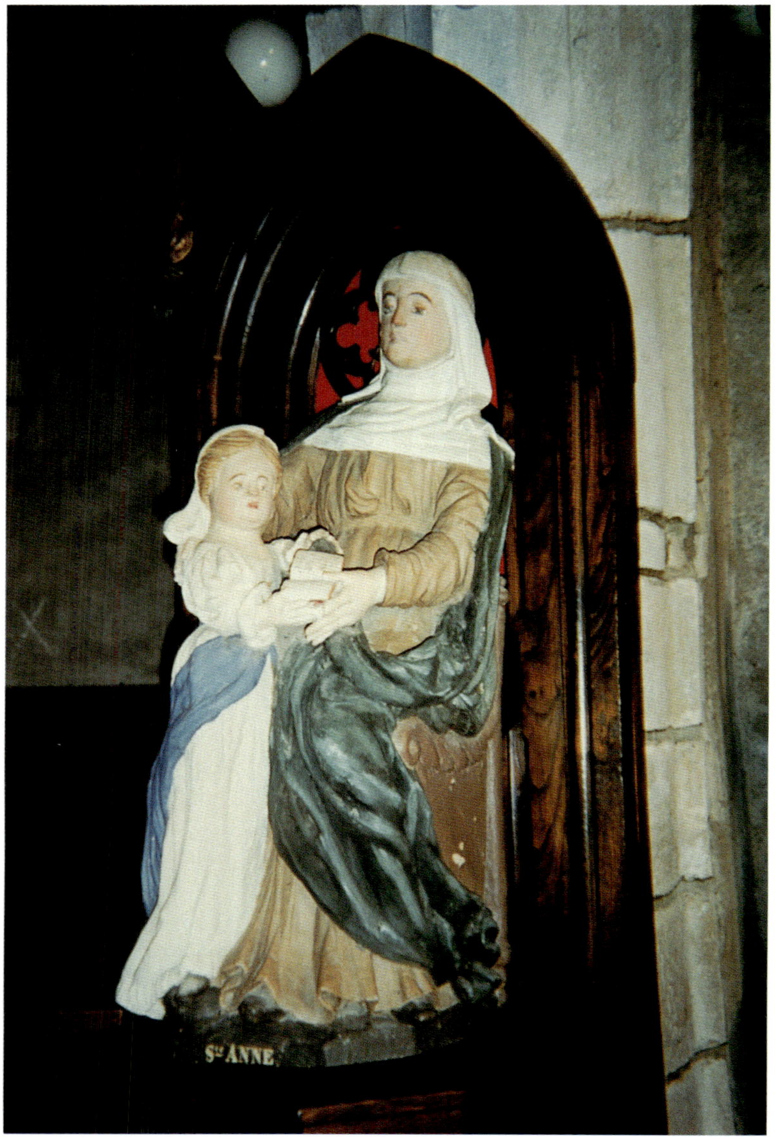

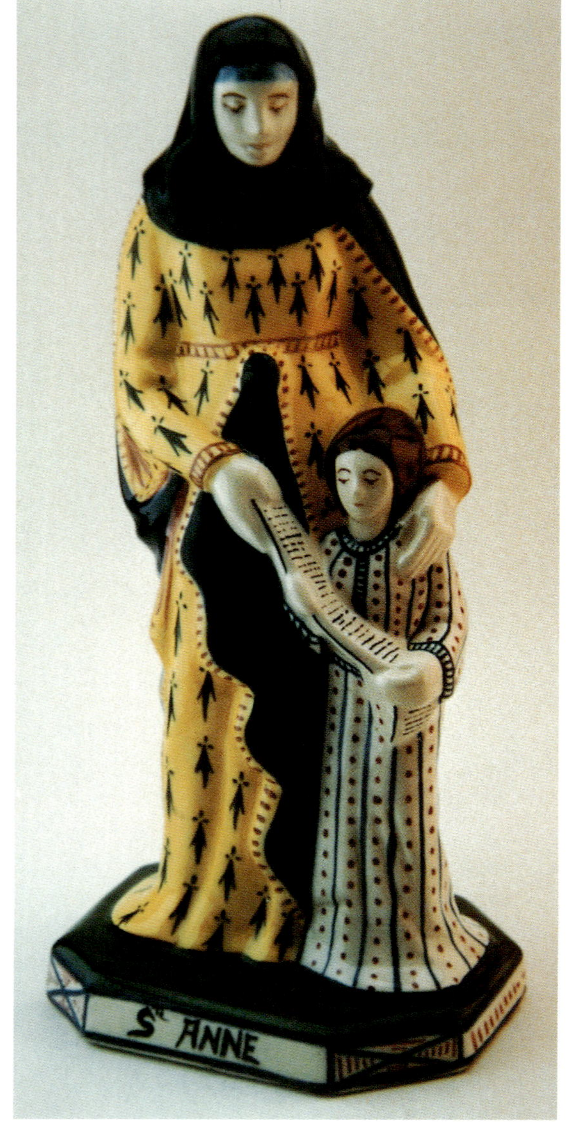

The patron Saint of Brittany is Saint Anne, the Virgin Mary's mother. Bretons believe Ste. Anne to be from Brittany. Here she appears with Mary as a child, just one of the many carved statues in the church at Paimpont.

The faïence version of Ste. Anne reading to the child Mary is Henriot, stands 14.5" tall, and is mid-20th century. *Private Collection.*

The Golden Tree, or *Arbre d'Or*, marks the spot where the devastating fire of 1990 came to an end. The memorial is stunning in its simplicity and uniqueness. Who else would have thought to paint a charred tree with gold, symbolizing where the fire stopped and *Bretagne* began to fight back? It is surrounded by small, upright rocks, which look like miniature menhirs. We theorize this was done to prevent intruders from taking pieces of this artwork. Many thanks are due its creator, François Davin, for a startling and moving sight.

On our drive around the roads of the Paimpont Forest we also found other sites related to the Arthurian myth. A late-January visit to Merlin's tomb revealed traces of candles and holly sprigs, perhaps evidence of vigil or a New Year's Druid rite. We heard during the high season in the summer months, the roads are clogged with tourists bent on instant insight into the myths and legends of Brittany. We recommend touring the Paimpont Forest in the low season, when the area is unencumbered by numerous sightseers.

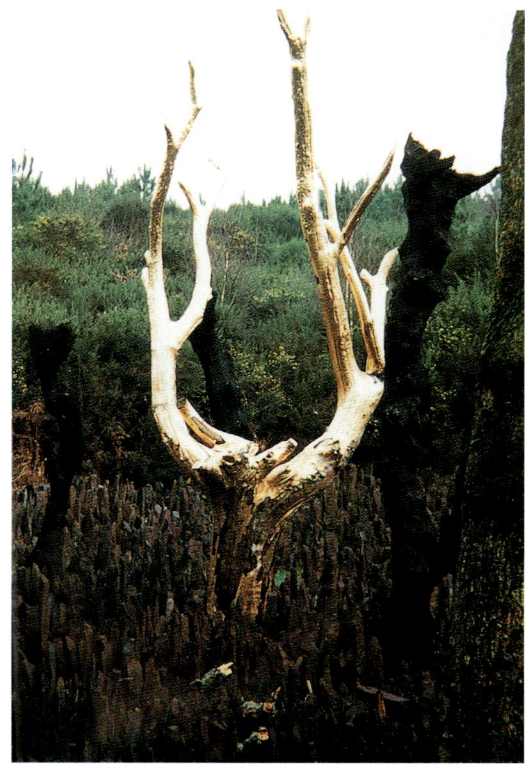

The Golden Tree, or *Arbre d'Or*, is an artwork by François Davin. It commemorates the point where the devastating 1990 Paimpont Forest fire was halted.

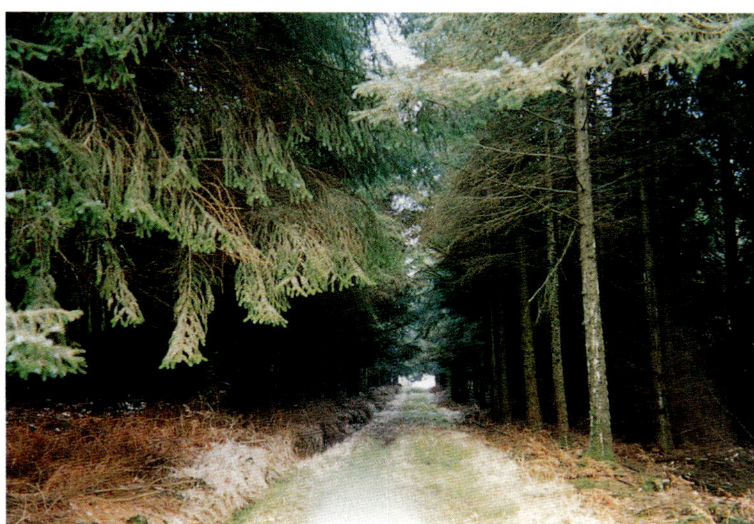

As we left the town of Paimpont and drove back into the forest, the more solitary and eerie it became.

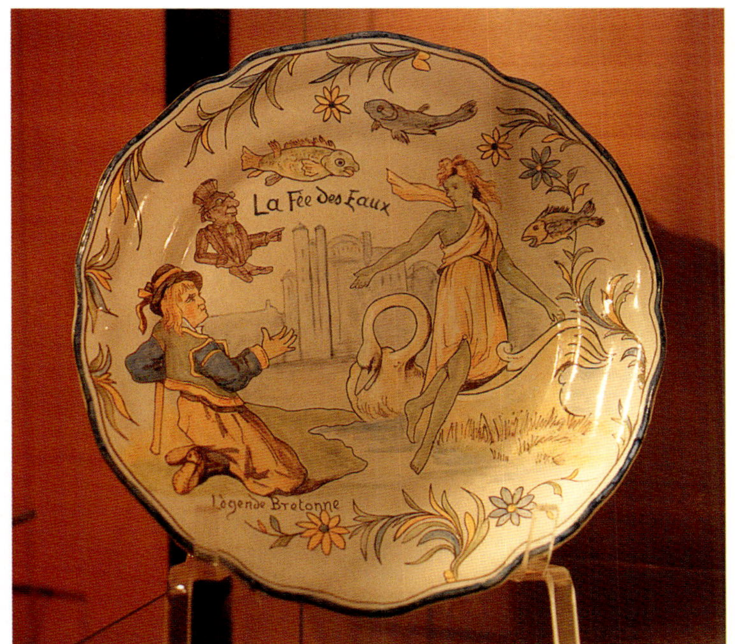

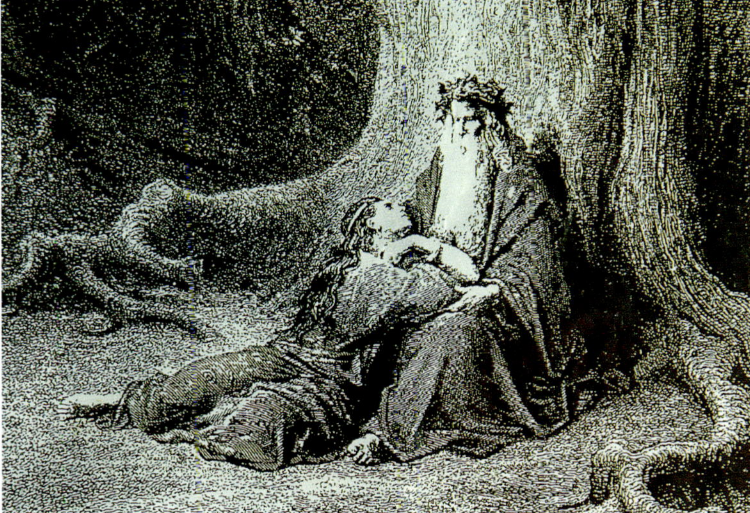

It was easy to imagine the magic of Merlin and the fairy Viviane in these deep woods, which used to cover 140 square kilometers of the inland, or *Argoat* area.

The solitary quiet of the forest made the myths and legends of Brittany come alive. The *légende Bretonne* work of Alfred Beau depicted on this 10" diameter plate is *La Fée des Eaux*, or The Water Fairy, is signed PB, and is from the last quarter of the 19th century. *Courtesy of Musée de la Faïence, Quimper.*

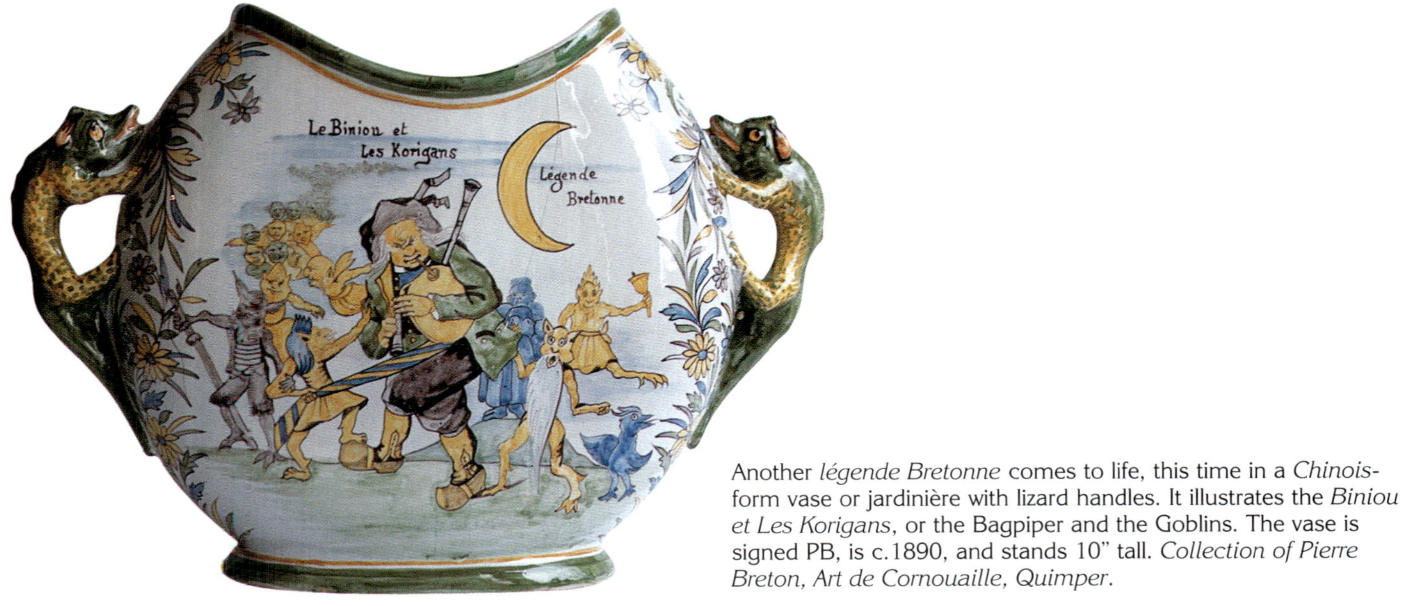

Another *légende Bretonne* comes to life, this time in a *Chinois*-form vase or jardinière with lizard handles. It illustrates the *Biniou et Les Korigans*, or the Bagpiper and the Goblins. The vase is signed PB, is c.1890, and stands 10" tall. *Collection of Pierre Breton, Art de Cornouaille, Quimper.*

Josselin

Josselin is about 70 kilometers southwest of Rennes, on N24, the same major highway that takes you by the Paimpont Forest. The small but historic town of Josselin is dominated by a castle, still owned and occupied by the descendents of the Rohan family. We were overwhelmed when we first caught sight of this structure on the banks of the Oust River. The exact date of its initial construction is not known, but it had been razed and rebuilt by 1370. The castle was razed again in 1488, as punishment for Rohan support of France against independent Brittany. When Anne of Brittany married and became Queen of France, she compensated the Rohan family, and the castle was rebuilt for a second time. During the rebuilding, Anne's emblem, the ermine, and the letter A were introduced as embellishments by the Rohan family in gratitude.

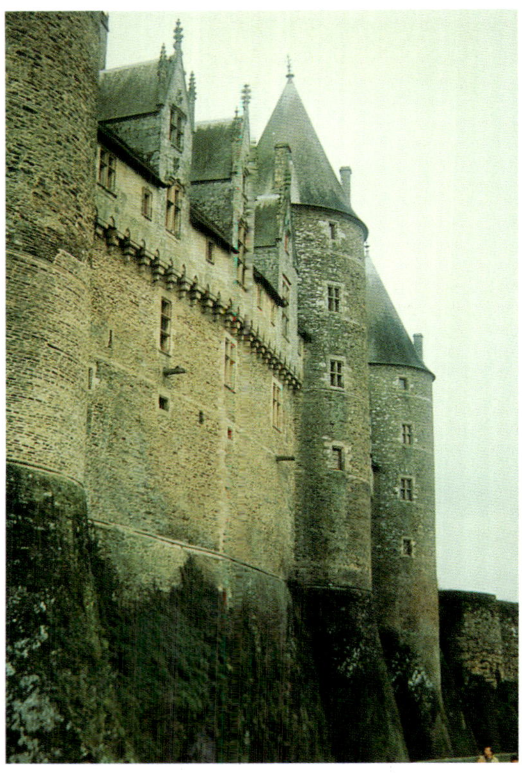

Rohan family descendents still reside in the castle at Josselin, which dominates the beautiful small town on the Oust River.

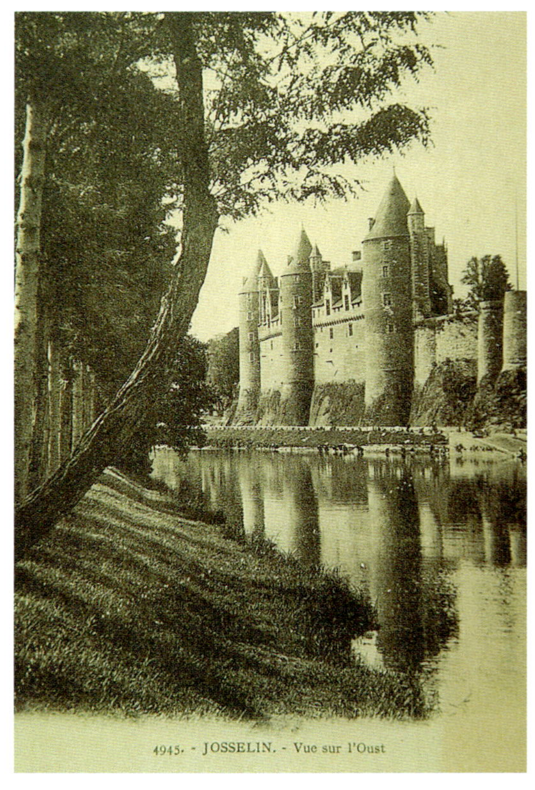

An early postcard also shows the significant role the castle plays in the town. *Authors' Collection.*

Josselin is the setting for many colorful legends and at least two shops selling Quimper. It's difficult to understand *Bretagne* and her people without paying homage to the history and the landscape that shaped them. The legend of *Notre Dame du Roncier* concerns the origin of the name of a Basilica built in Josselin over a thousand years ago, called Our Lady of the Brambles. The story tells of a peasant who found a glowing statue of the Virgin Mary in a bramble bush that mysteriously never lost its leaves. The peasant took the statue home, but the statue repeatedly disappeared from his home and reappeared in the bramble bush where he had found it. The peasant came to believe the Virgin wanted a chapel built on that spot. Legend says the first chapel was built of bramble branches, followed later by wood, then in the 12th century by stone, resulting in the Basilica's combination of styles and periods.

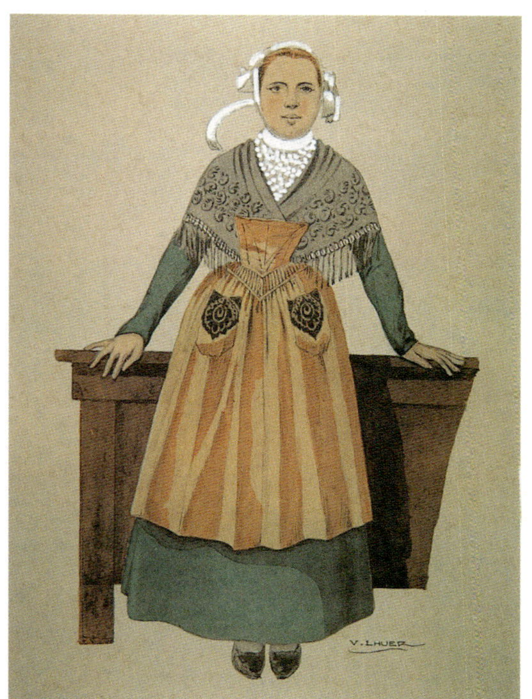

A 20th century print captures the *coiffe* and costume of Josselin, c. 1920. *Private Collection.*

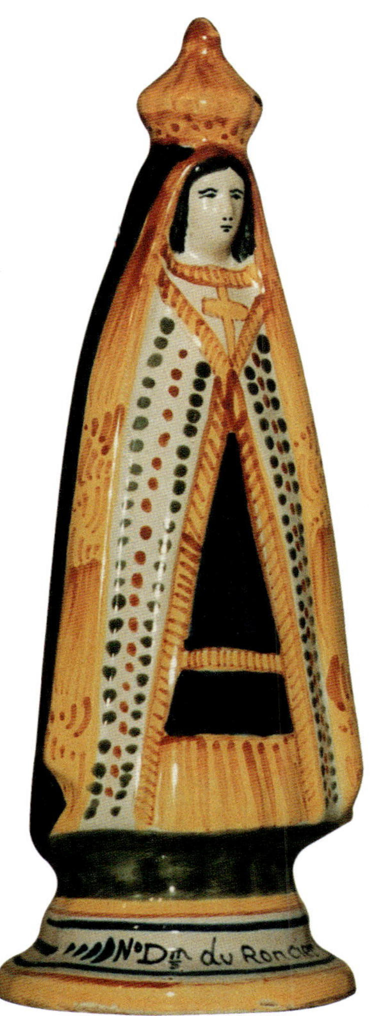

Our Lady of the Brambles, or *Notre Dame du Roncier*, is rendered in faïence by Henriot in this 8.25" tall version from the second quarter of the 20th century. *Private Collection.*

Another colorful legend surrounding the Basilica of *Notre Dame du Roncier* gave rise to a religious event held every September since 1728. According to local lore, the barker's *pardon* commemorates how the women of Josselin were punished for refusing to help the Virgin, who had disguised herself as a poor woman. Their punishment was to bark like dogs, unless they kissed the holy relics in the Basilica every Whitsunday. Bretons continue to attend this annual gathering, which strangely enough also is believed to cure epilepsy.

We found two shops in Josselin selling Quimper and purchased several pieces. One merchant was very pleased to share with us the names of other American buyers who frequent her *brocante*. It was interesting to know other Americans were there before us. We had this experience more than once in Brittany, and hoped that the others were enjoying the journey as much as we were.

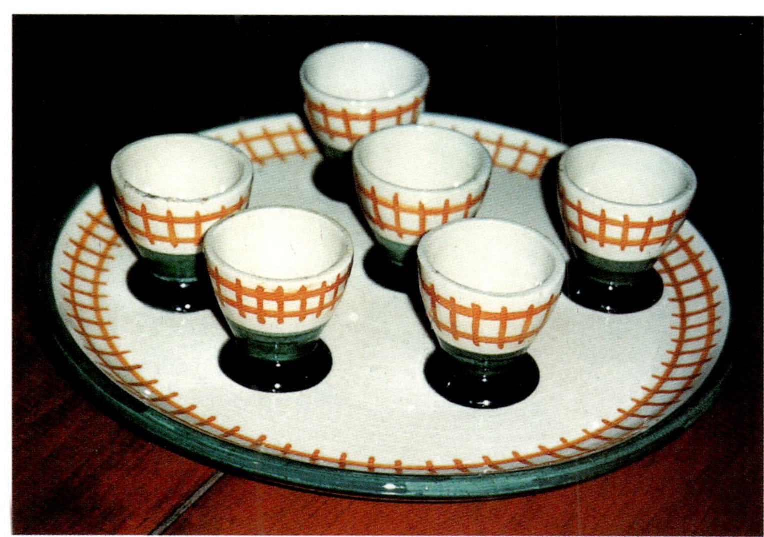

Six egg cups and matching plate were designed by the Quimper artist, André Galland. The plate is 9.75" in diameter and the cups are 2" tall. The signature is Henriot Quimper, with artist's initials, ag, in lower case. Sometimes his *chiffre*, or monogram, appears as AG. *Authors' Collection.*

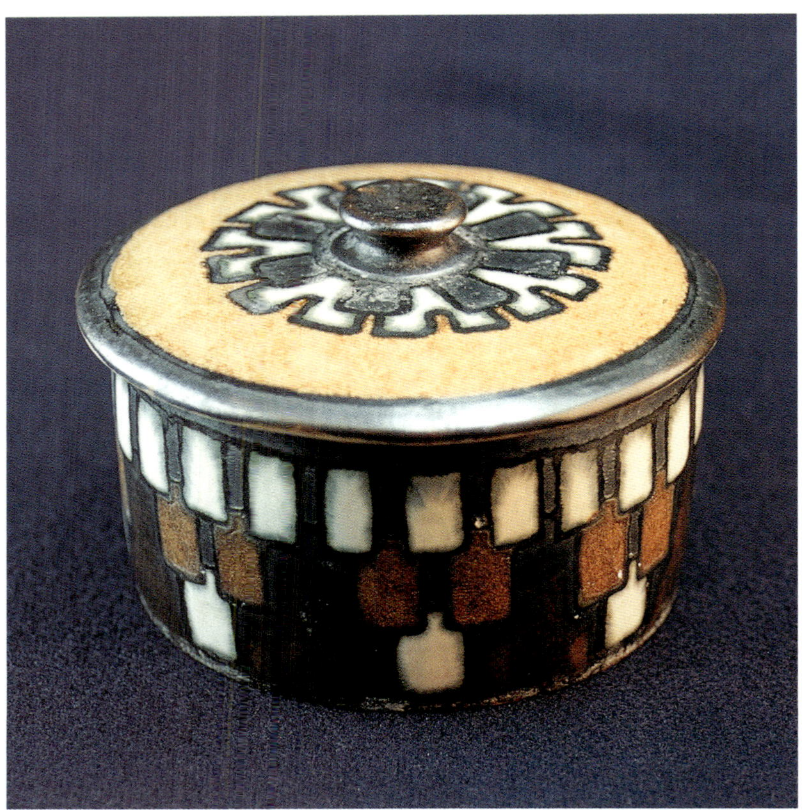

An Odetta *bonbonniere*, a candy dish with a lid, has tan, brown, white, and black coloration. It measures 4.5" in diameter and is signed HB, Odetta, #302-1302. *Private Collection.*

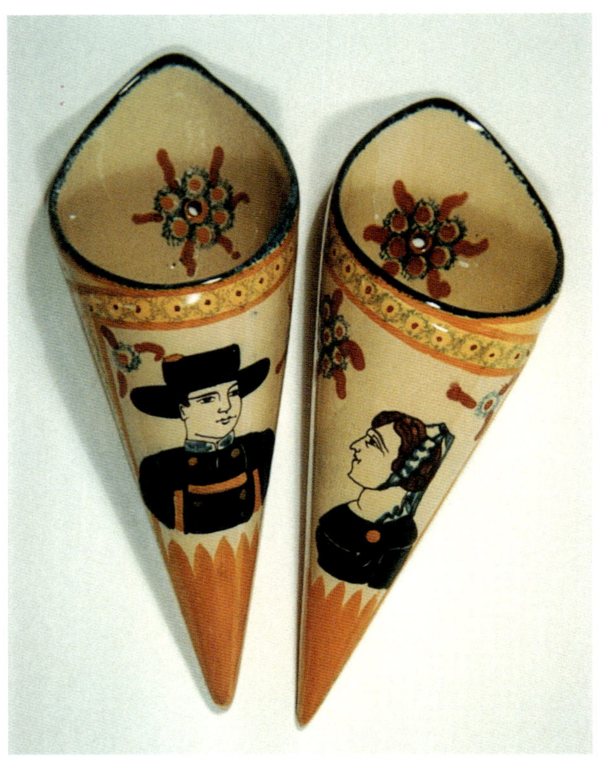

Décor *ivoire corbeille* graces this pair of 9.75" long HQ wallpockets. Mustard, black, blue, and magenta are the predominant colors on the *cornet* (horn-shaped) vases designed to hang on the wall. *Private Collection.*

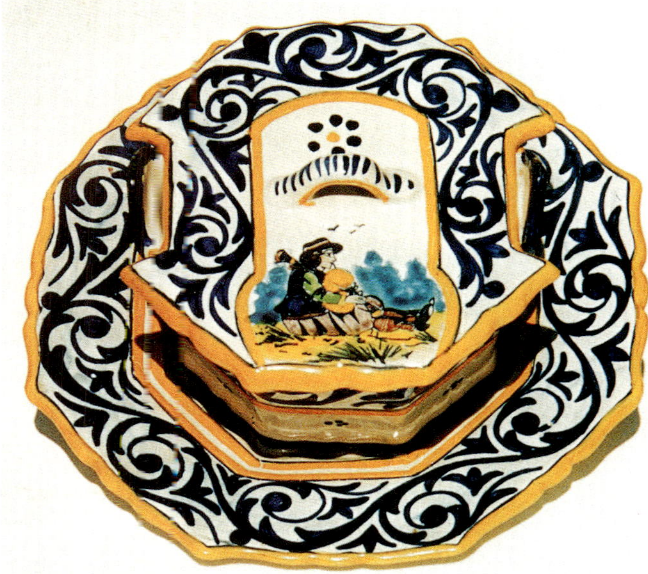

The HB faïencerie manufactured this 1920s-1930s butter dish in the *décor riche* motif, with acanthus or scrolling foliage border. The Breton is sitting in the countryside playing the *biniou* (bagpipe), a familiar scene. *Private Collection.*

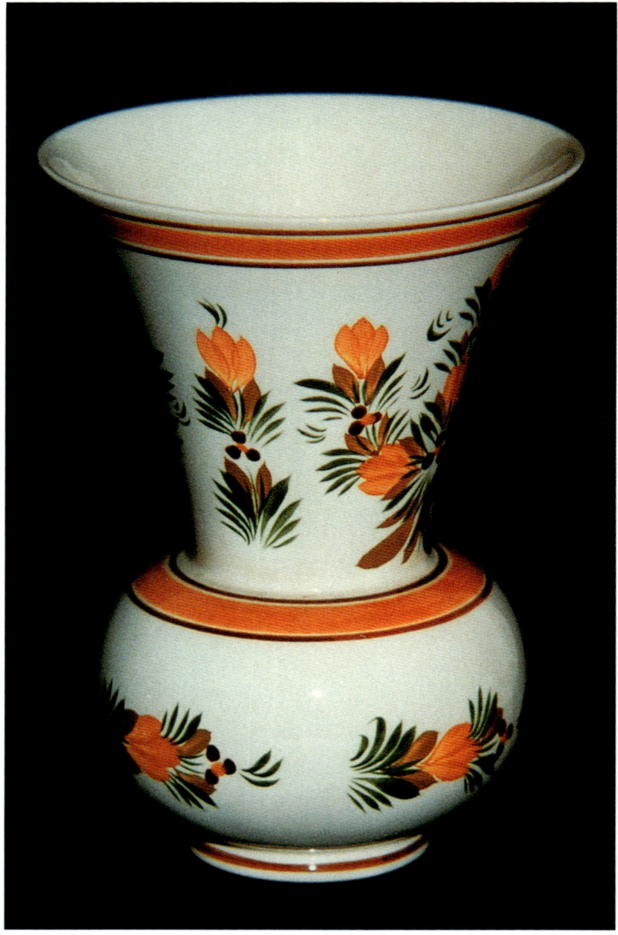

Gorse blossoms, or *l'ajonc*, decorate this 9.75" tall vase purchased in a *brocante* in Josselin. It is from the 1960s, but quickly found a home in the United States, despite its fairly recent vintage.

Breton Resistance Museum

Less than 20 kilometers southeast of Josselin is the town of Saint Marcel, home to a museum dedicated to the Breton Resistance Movement of World War II. We were amazed to learn about the intricate network of operatives engaged in subverting the German occupation forces in Brittany. The underground protected escaped prisoners and downed Allied pilots, committed sabotage, and prepared for the Allied invasion to retake their homeland. Some people thought the history of the Breton separatism movement would encourage Nazi allegiance in Brittany, but this museum set the record straight.

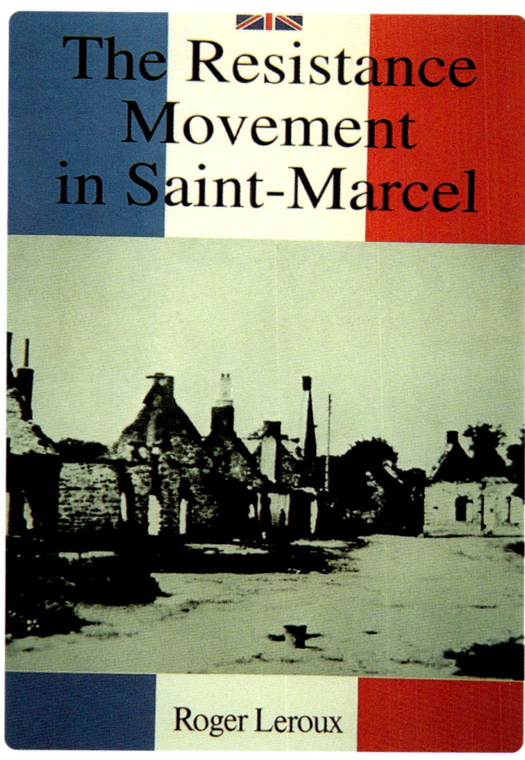

Not far from Josselin is the Breton Resistance Museum in Saint Marcel. We were impressed with the information presented about Breton activities to undermine the German occupation forces in Brittany during World War II.

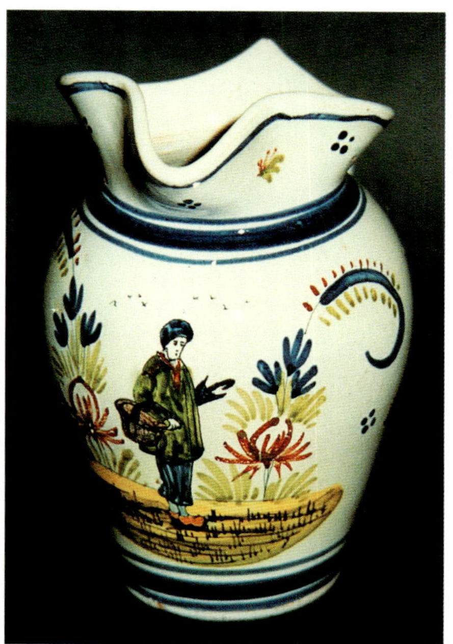

In a small shop between Josselin and St. Marcel, we found this HB *décor riche* vase with a Bretonne on her way to market. The merchant told us the vase belonged to her grandmother and was made before World War II. The handles had disappeared but the repair was barely discernable. The vase stood 8.5" tall and came home with us. Guess we're vulnerable to grandmother stories! *Private Collection.*

We later discovered the mark, which looks like a transposed L connected to a D, represented the Leroy-Dubois factory in Malicorne, from 1899 to 1918. *Private Collection.*

It was getting dark when we passed a *brocante* on our way back to Rennes from St. Marcel. David backed up the car, and we went in the shop and found this great-looking pitcher with a *tricorne* (three-cornered hat-like) rim in a design we'd not seen. *Private Collection.*

We knew the factories at Quimper made special poterie items for the occupying forces during World War II, to commemorate the German victory in Brittany. To us it was odd to see Quimper items with German slogans celebrating events like *Kriegsweihnacht, 1943* (Christmas, 1943). Later we learned the Quimper faïenceries provided jobs for many Breton males, protecting them from being sent to forced labor camps.

An anecdote shared by Bernard Verlingue, grandson of the first Verlingue to own a Quimper faïencerie, told of an unintended over-shipment of coal for the HB faïencerie kilns by the Germans. (Coal was how the Germans paid for the commemorative wares they ordered from the faïenceries.) When the Henriot faïencerie director saw 20 loads instead of the usual 2 loads being delivered, he called the director at HB and requested half of the coal, which was done. Small victories can win big battles, and nothing sustains like a good laugh at an opponent's error.

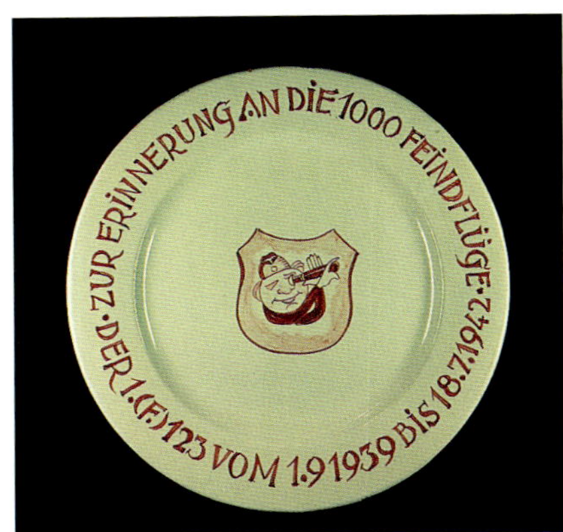

A plate commissioned for the German occupying forces commemorated the 1000th air raid (observed) by the 1.F.123 VOM (air raid observation units) from September 1, 1939, to July 18, 1942. It measures 11" diameter and was made by the Henriot faïencerie. *Authors' Collection.*

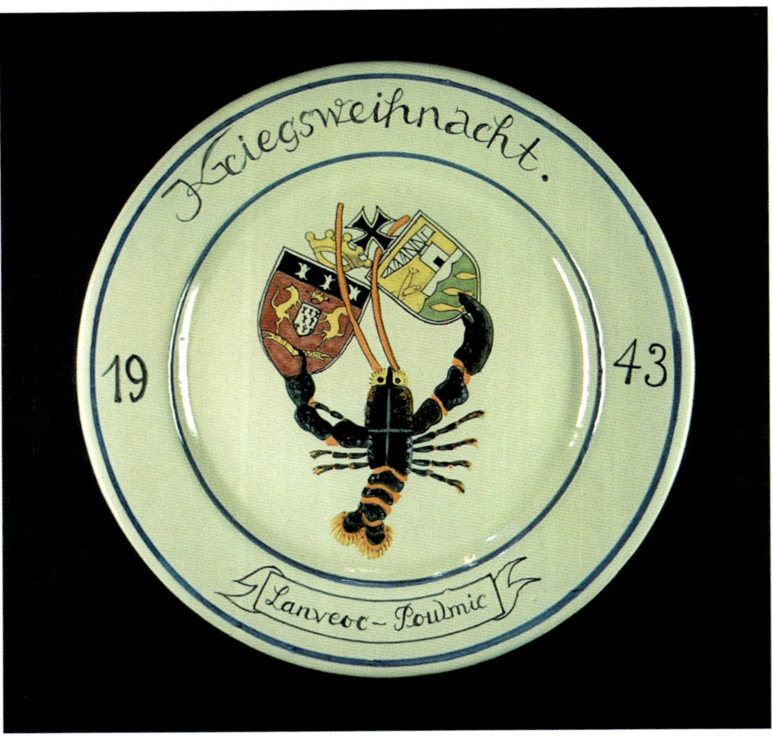

A 9.5" commemorative plate made by Henriot for the German submarine unit based at *Presqu'île de Quiberon* reads: *Wartime Christmas, 1943.* The lobster or crawfish holds a shield of Brittany topped by a crown in one claw, and a shield of the German submarine service topped by the German Iron Cross in the other. The German occupying forces commissioned similar items, and payment was made to the faïenceries with shipments of coal. *Private Collection.*

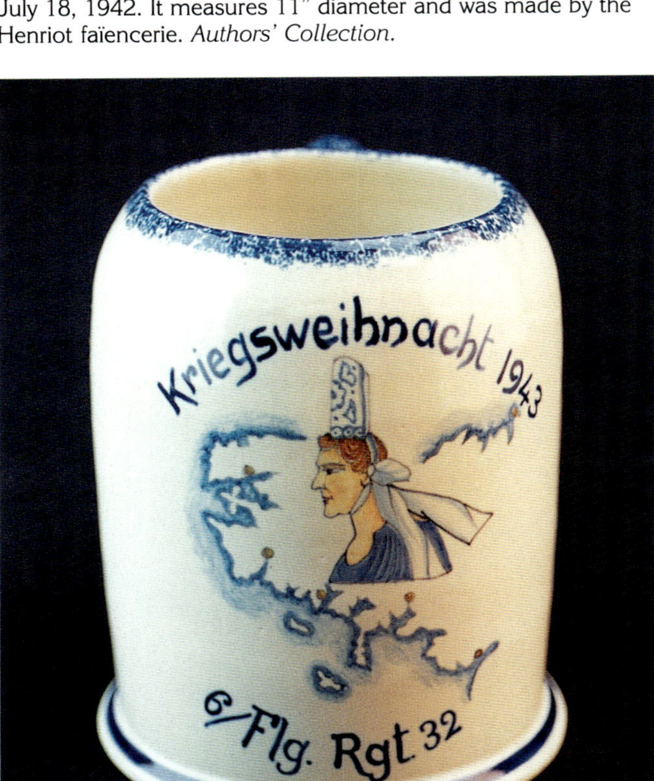

Another commissioned piece, a 5" tall mug by Henriot, reads: *Wartime Christmas, 1943.* It was made for the 6th *Kampfgeschwader* (combat squadron), 32nd regiment. The female figure is a *Bigoudène*, as identified by her tall *coiffe. Courtesy of Carter Yeatman.*

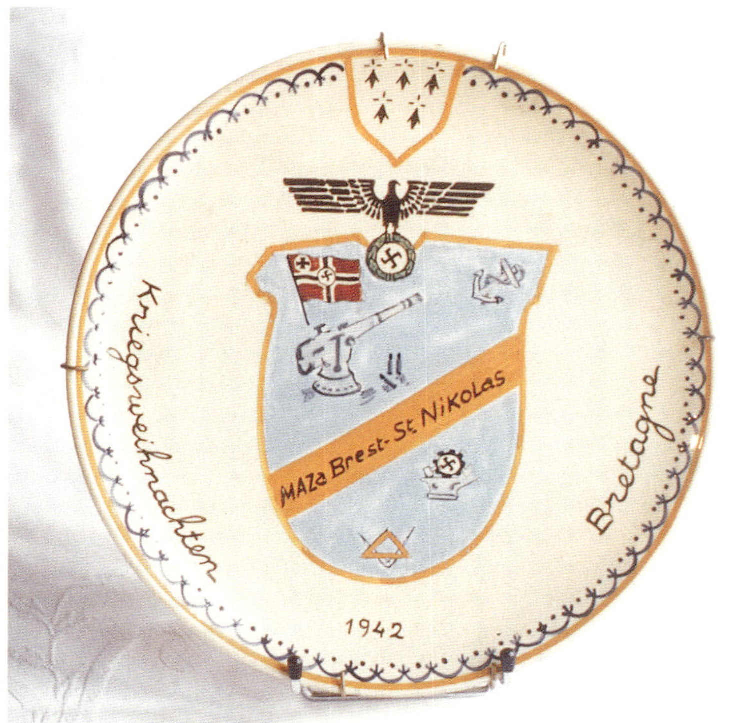

Another Henriot plate was made for the occupying forces in Brest during Christmas, 1942. It features the shield of Brittany at the top, and a central shield with an anti-aircraft gun, German flag, and engineering implements, topped by a German insignia. *Collection of Pierre Breton, Art de Cornouaille, Quimper.*

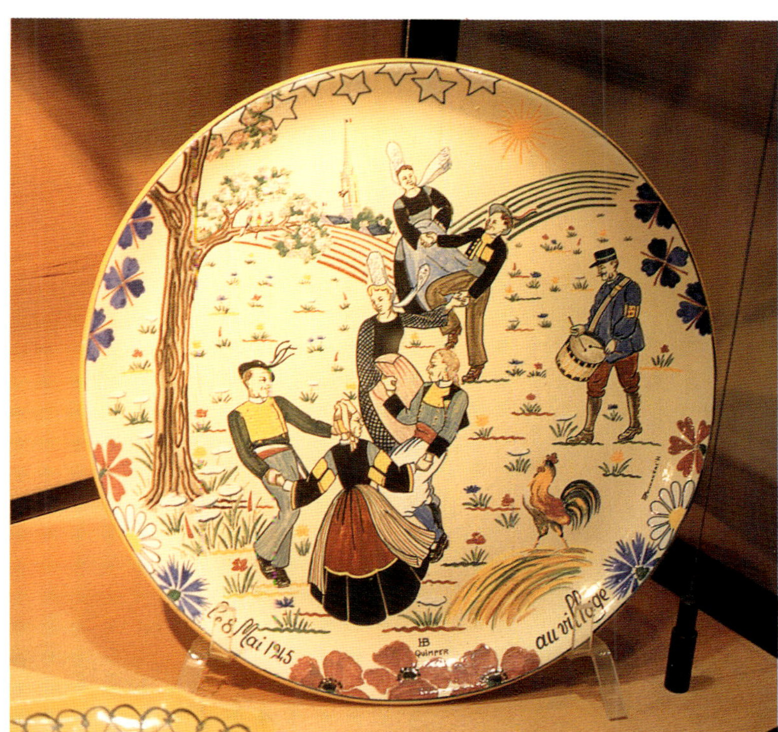

Liberation from Germany was celebrated in many ways. HB faïencerie artist and *atelier* director Raymonde Pennaneac'h designed this charger showing Bretons in their village dancing for joy. White stars representing the United States and a rooster, a French national emblem, are additional elements. *Courtesy of Musée de la Faïence, Quimper.*

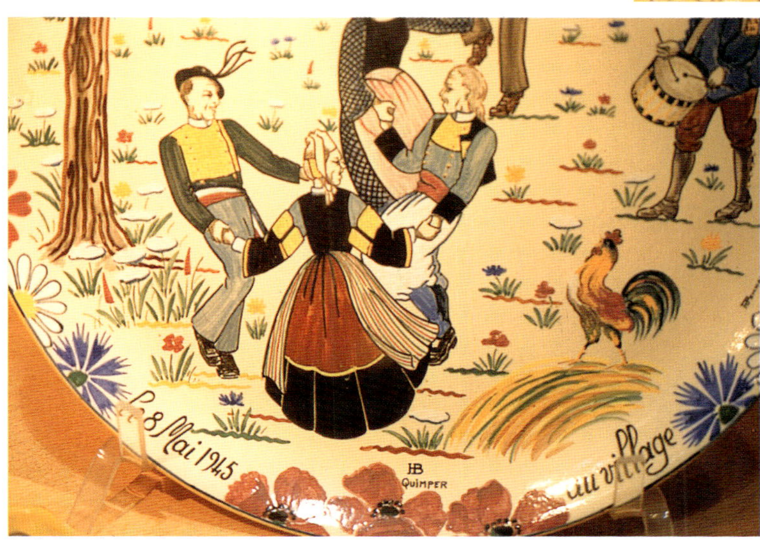

The date *Mai 1945* and *Au Village* explain this liberation celebration work by Raymonde Pennaneac'h. *Courtesy of Musée de la Faïence, Quimper.*

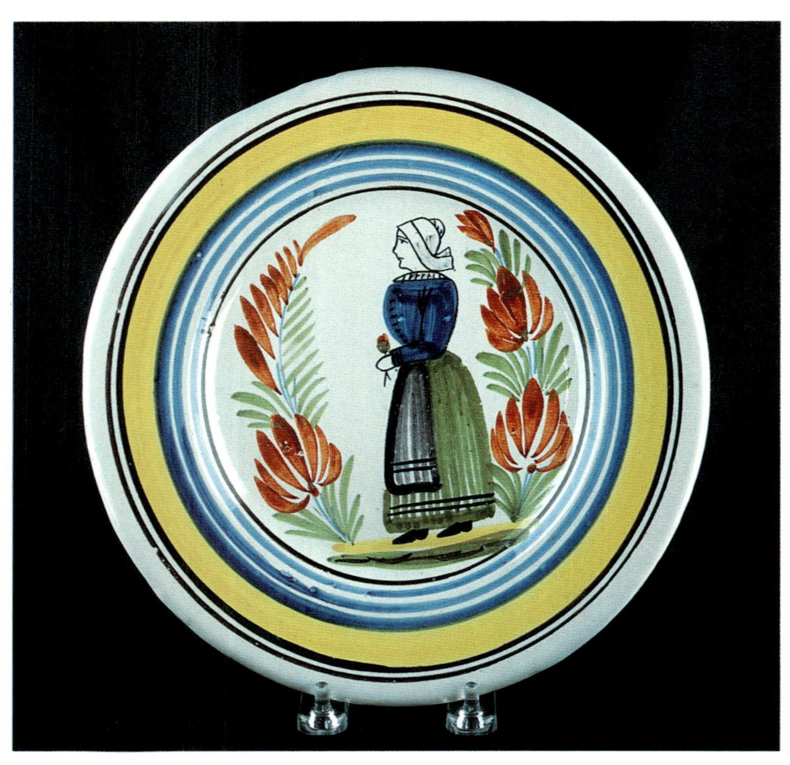

The memorial to those who lost their lives in World War II from Châteauneuf de Faou.

We saw many memorials to the fallen Bretons of World War II but the most memorable was in Châteauneuf du Faou, a beautiful small town about 40 kilometers northeast of Quimper. We stopped briefly one gray Sunday morning to buy some bread and cheese in the center of town. While there, we took a stroll. On an outside wall of the church was a memorial to local victims of World War II. It was in the form of a cross, made up of 36 square tiles. In the center of each tile was a picture, with the person's name above it and the birth and death date beneath. In front of the cross of tiles was a bust on a granite pillar. It was Abbé Cadiou, the *curé* (priest) of Châteauneuf. It was on this spot on August 6, 1944, that the Germans shot Cadiou.

Vannes

Vannes is on the Gulf of Morbihan in southern Brittany about 55 kilometers south of Josselin, or about 115 kilometers southwest of Rennes. We found three shops selling Quimper and one has continued to be a source for us over the years. The shop is located in the heart of the old town, and is run by a husband and wife who are friendly and accommodating. Some of the wonderful Quimper items purchased from them include a gigantic fish-shaped platter and early *petit Breton* plates. On a recent trip we just missed an Henriot Quimper *garniture de cheminée*, a clock flanked by two matching vases, which sold the day before our arrival.

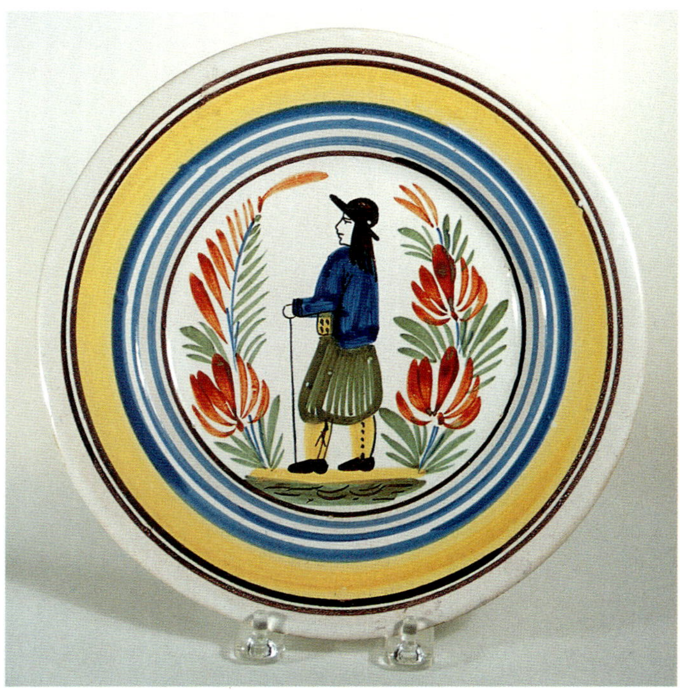

The *petit Breton* motif has been used on Quimper poterie for over 140 years. This 8.25" diameter plate is unsigned, but most likely is HB or AP. This fellow and his mate were purchased in Vannes. *Private Collection.*

The mate, a *petite Bretonne* plate, exhibits lumpy glaze over reddish clay and pontil marks on the back where it sat in the wood fired kiln. These qualities, plus the painting and detail, all point to turn-of-the-20th century production. *Private Collection.*

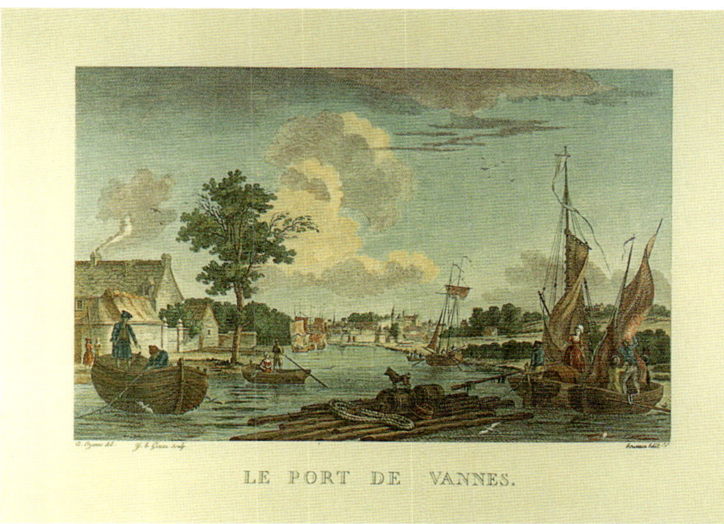

The city of Vannes sits at the head of the Gulf of Morbihan
in southern Brittany. It is named for the *Veneti*, a tribe of
Celtic warriors who valiantly fought against Caesar's
invasion in 56 B.C., but lost.

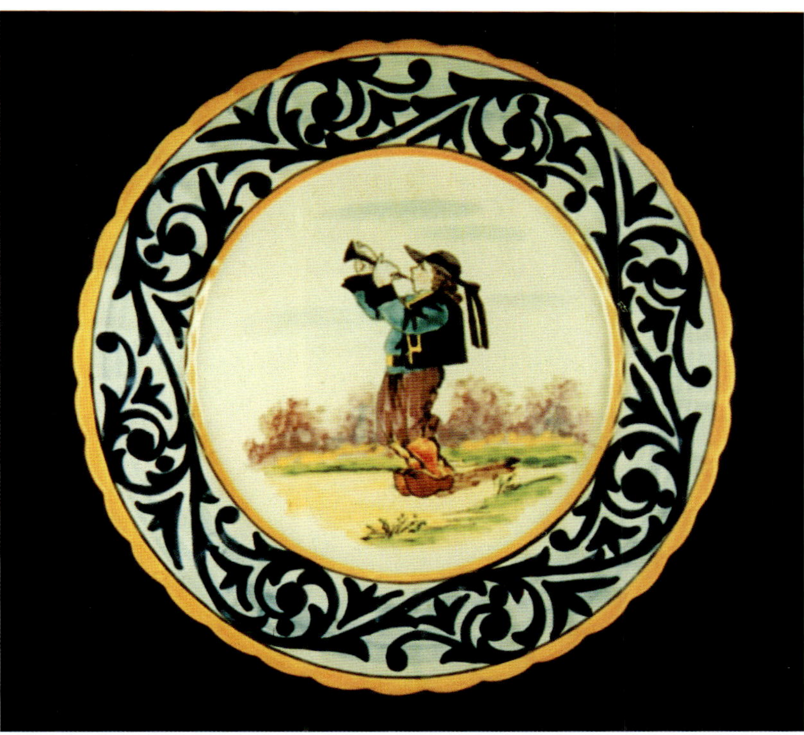

In contrast, the following *petit Breton* plates, also purchased in
Vannes, are of later vintage. The *décor riche* border highlights
this happy Breton playing the *bombarde* (Breton oboe-like horn).
Private Collection.

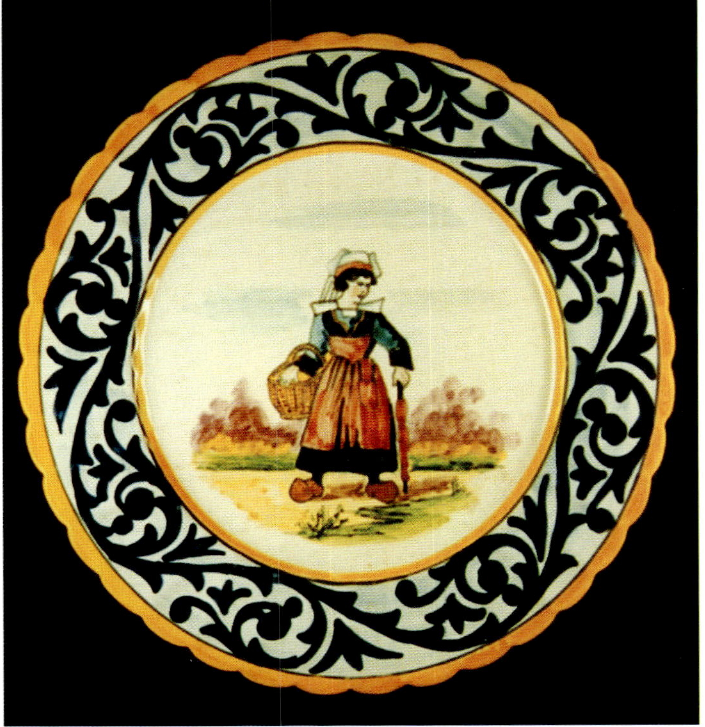

His mate is a Bretonne on her way to market with a *parapluie*, or
umbrella. Both are from the HB faïencerie, from the 1920s
1930s, and measure 9.75" diameter. *Private Collection.*

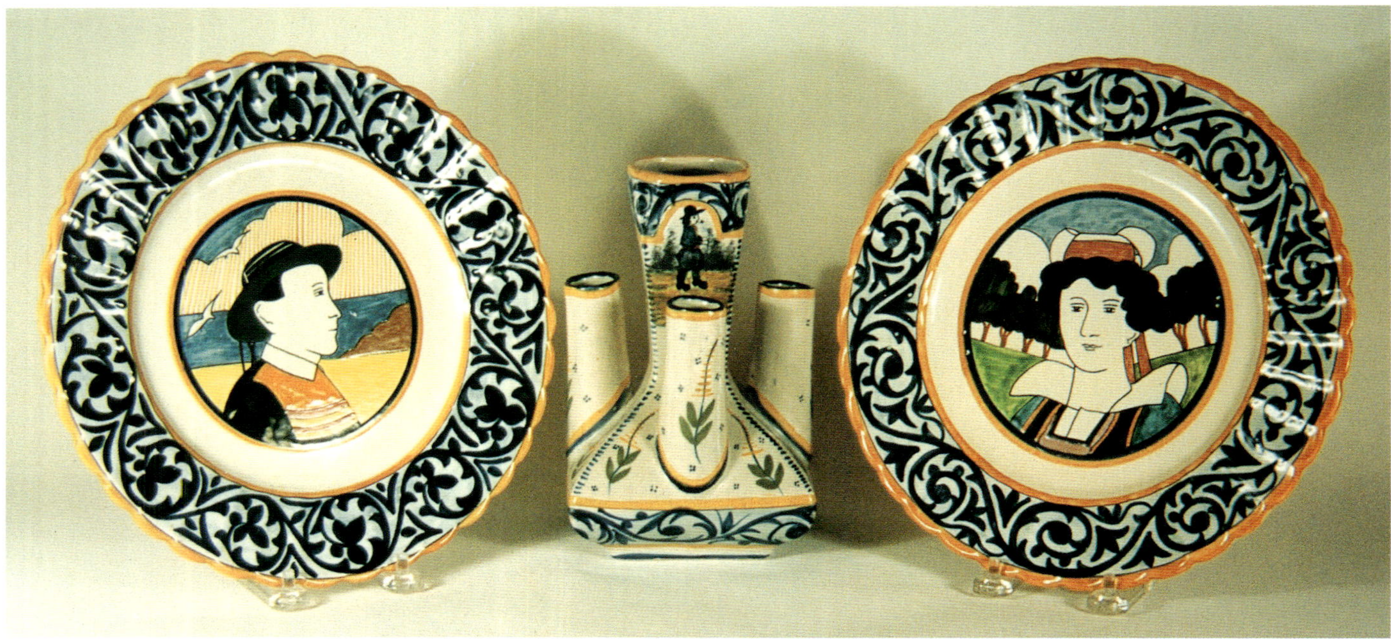

Another pair of *décor riche* plates, this time portraits of Bretons, also were purchased in Vannes. The faïencerie is *HB/Grande Maison*, and the pair dates from the 1930s. In between the two plates is a *tulipière* vase, *HB/Grande Maison*, that we found in the United States. *Private Collection.*

This large and colorful fish-shaped platter measures 18.5" long. How did we get this one home from Vannes? Very carefully! *Private Collection.*

The first time we entered Vannes, we were immediately taken with the harbor on the edge of the old town. Vannes sits at the head of the Morbihan Gulf and canal-like waterways bring sailboats right into the *Place Maréchal Joffre*, where outdoor cafes set tables for mariners and visitors like us. Directly behind is the 16th century *Porte St. Vincent*, which took us into the old town. The city was named for the tribe of Celtic warriors from the area, the Veneti, who defied Caesar before being defeated in 56 B.C. It also was the home of Nominoé, who founded Breton unity in 845 A.D.

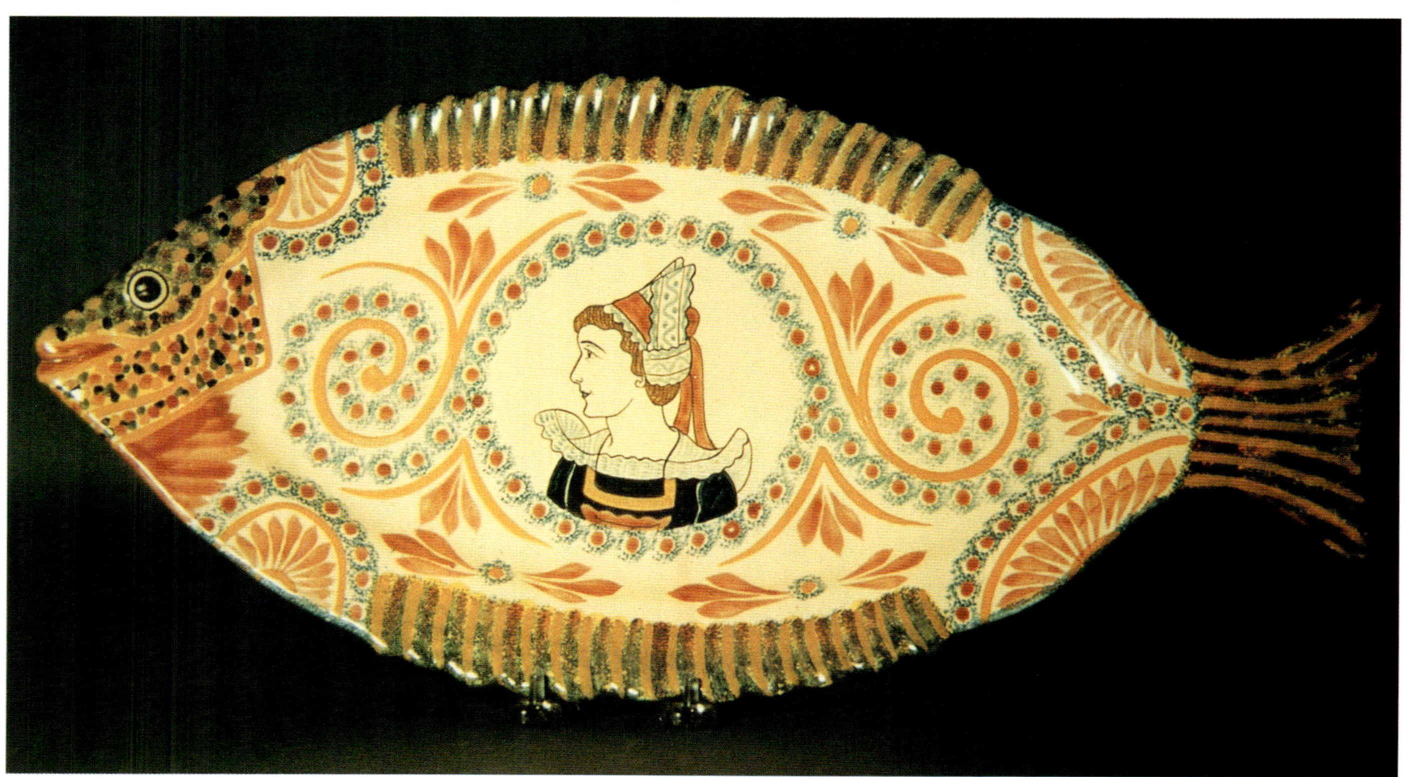

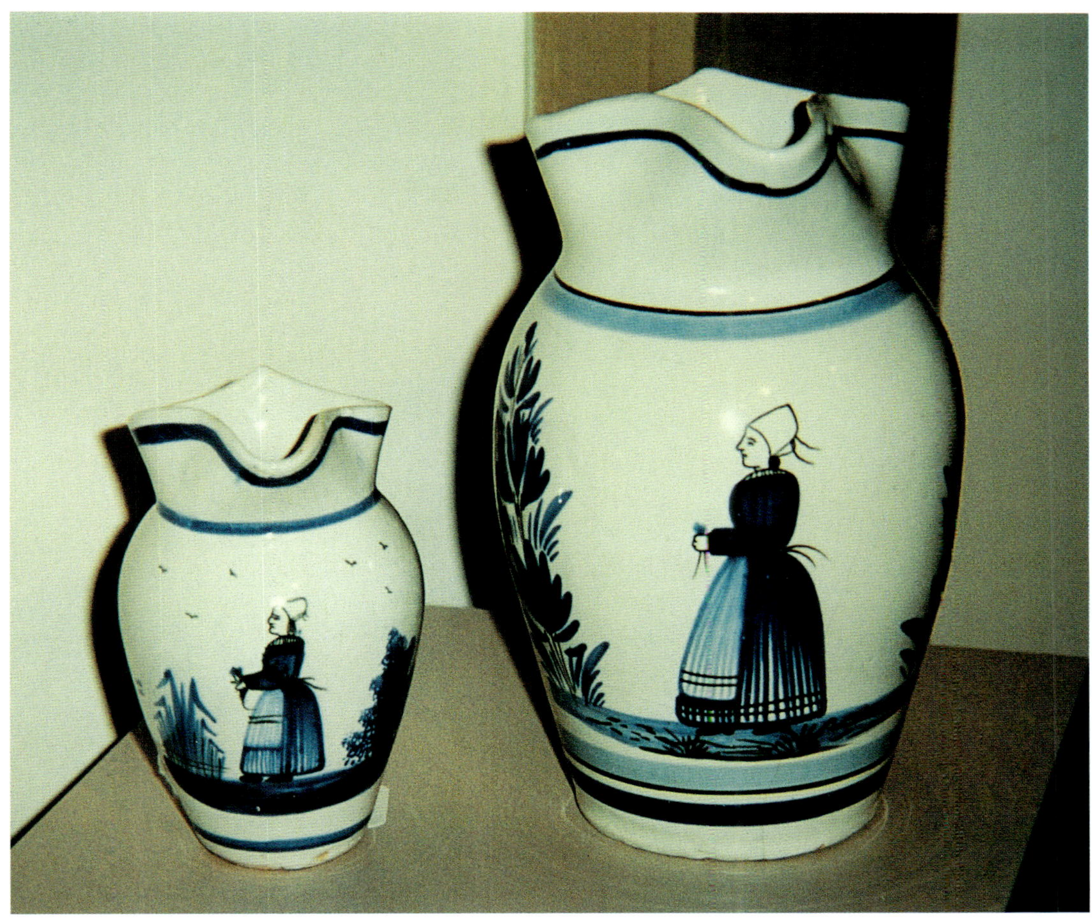

We found these two HB pitchers in another Vannes shop. They are painted in the *camäieu* technique, where only one color in varying shades is used. The pitchers have *tricorne* rims and stand 4.75" and 8.25" tall respectively. They are 1920s-1930s. *Private Collection.*

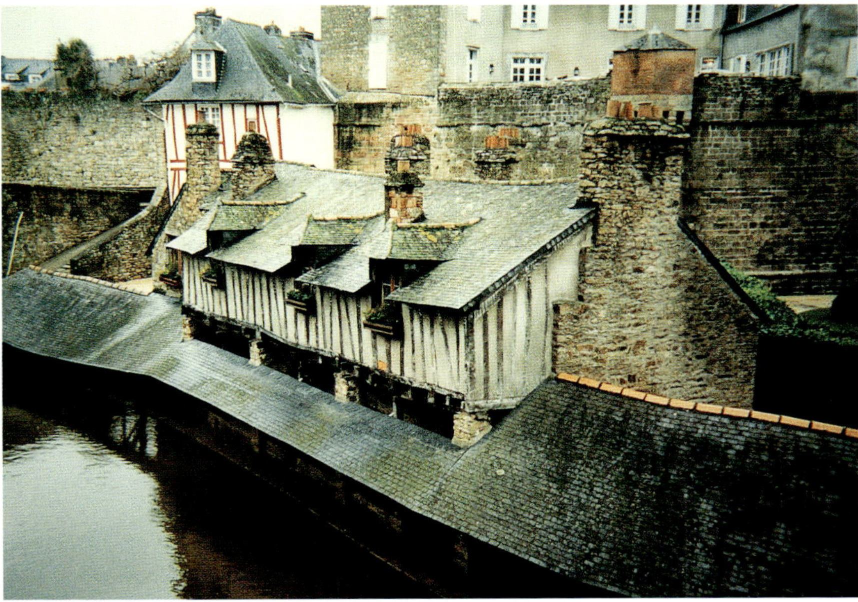

The sights in Vannes everyone wants to see are the communal washhouse at the ramparts …

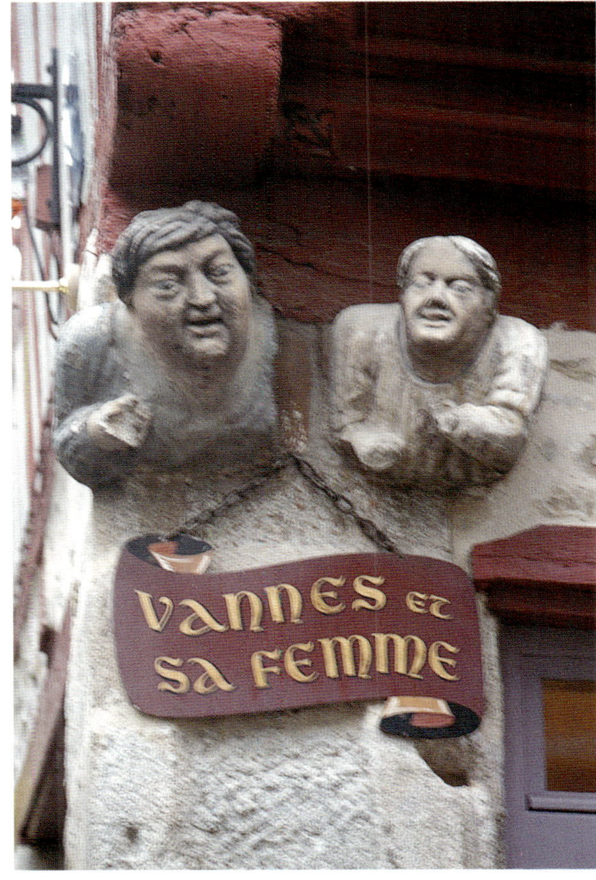

… And the other well-known sight, the carved figureheads of Old Vannes and his wife.

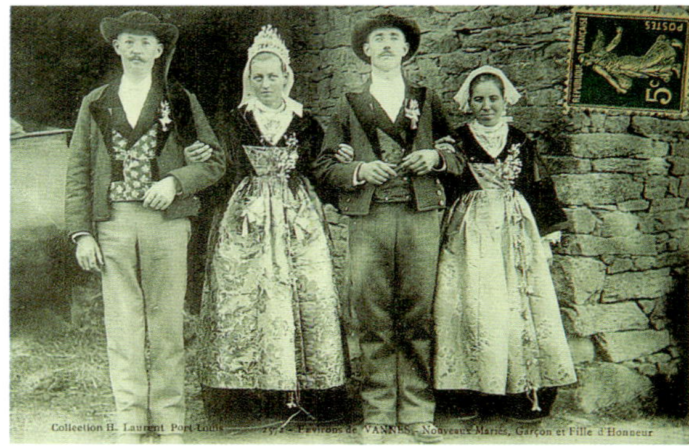

Natives of Vannes turned out in their *fête* (festival) costumes to be photographed for this turn-of-the-20th century postcard. *Authors' Collection*.

The sights in Vannes everyone looks for are the communal washhouse, the ramparts, and old Vannes and his wife, all very popular with photographers. Another charming stop in Vannes is the *Musée des Beaux Arts*, which featured Jules Noël and Henri Moret, local painters inspired by Brittany's scenes and history.

Dinan

Dinan is located in the opposite direction from Vannes, about 50 kilometers northwest of Rennes. Dinan is one of oldest fortified towns in the region. The city sits 280 feet above the estuary of the Rance River, surrounded by ramparts, and boasts half-timbered houses, cobbled streets, and an impressive 14th century castle.

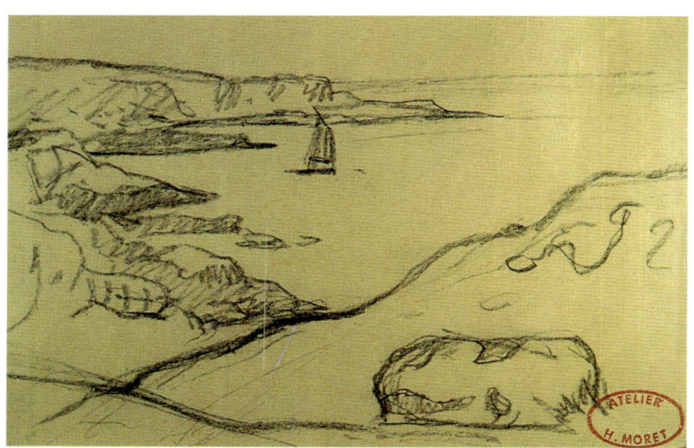

Henri Moret lived in the Vannes area, where his work is featured in the city museum. This piece is entitled *Harbor in Finistère*, c. 1900, measures 6" x 8", is pencil on paper, and estate stamped. *Private Collection*.

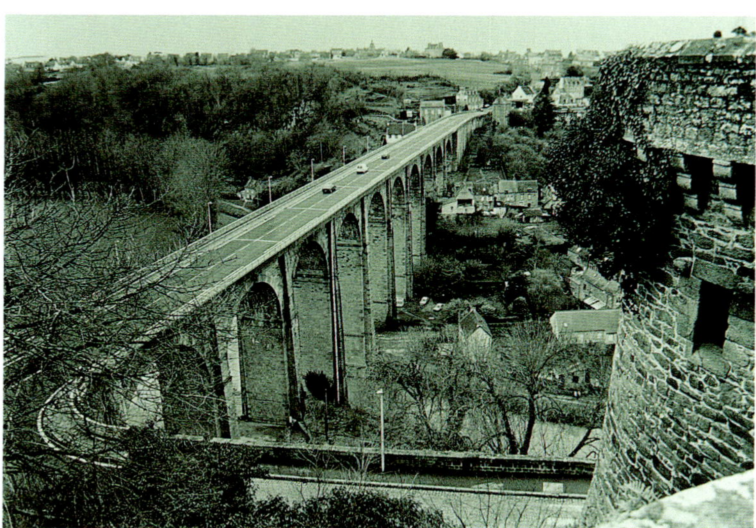

A recent photograph shows how travelers from the east must cross a viaduct over the Rance Valley (elevation 280 feet), to reach the plateau where Dinan is situated.

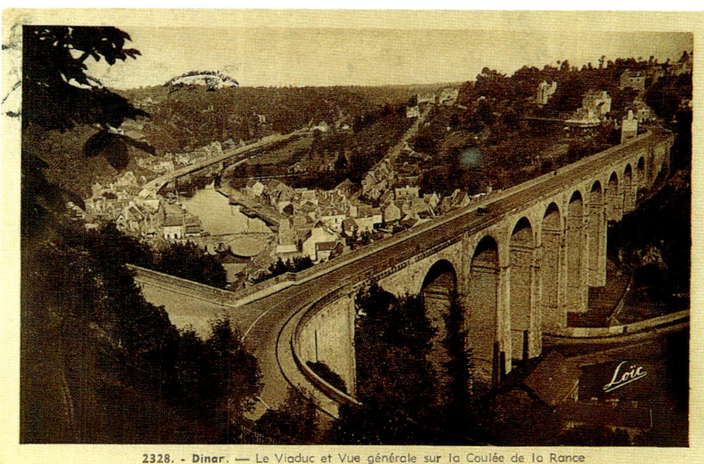

A turn-of-the-20th century postcard shows a similar view of the viaduct. *Authors' Collection*.

Another view of the viaduct is shown in this etching from the mid-1800s. *Authors' Collection*.

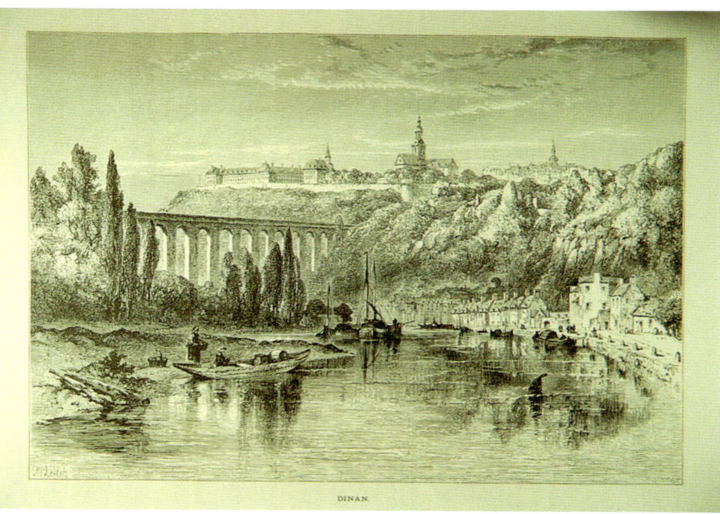

Today, the *Place Du Guesclin* is home to weekly markets and we arrived in time to enjoy one of these affairs. There were colorful tents filled with textiles, produce, and clothing. In medieval times, fairs were held here and in the nearby *Place de Champs*. At *Place de Champs*, Du Guesclin defeated Canterbury over the unknightly capture and ransom of Du Guesclin's brother, Olivier, during the 1359 siege of Dinan. Du Guesclin's heroics so impressed Tiphaine Raguenel, a re-fined and educated Dinan native, that she later married him.

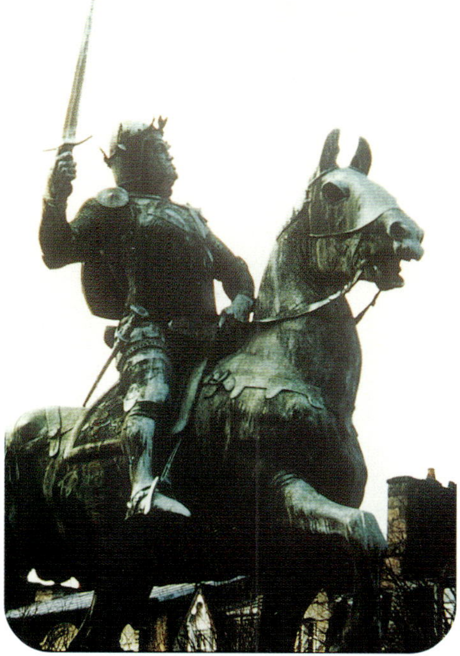

A statue of Bertrand Du Guesclin, the 14th century Breton warrior, dominates the central square in Dinan. Du Guesclin was born in *La Motte-Broons,* a few kilometers from Dinan. When he died in 1380, his heart was buried at *St. Sauveur* church in Dinan. His legacy lives on.

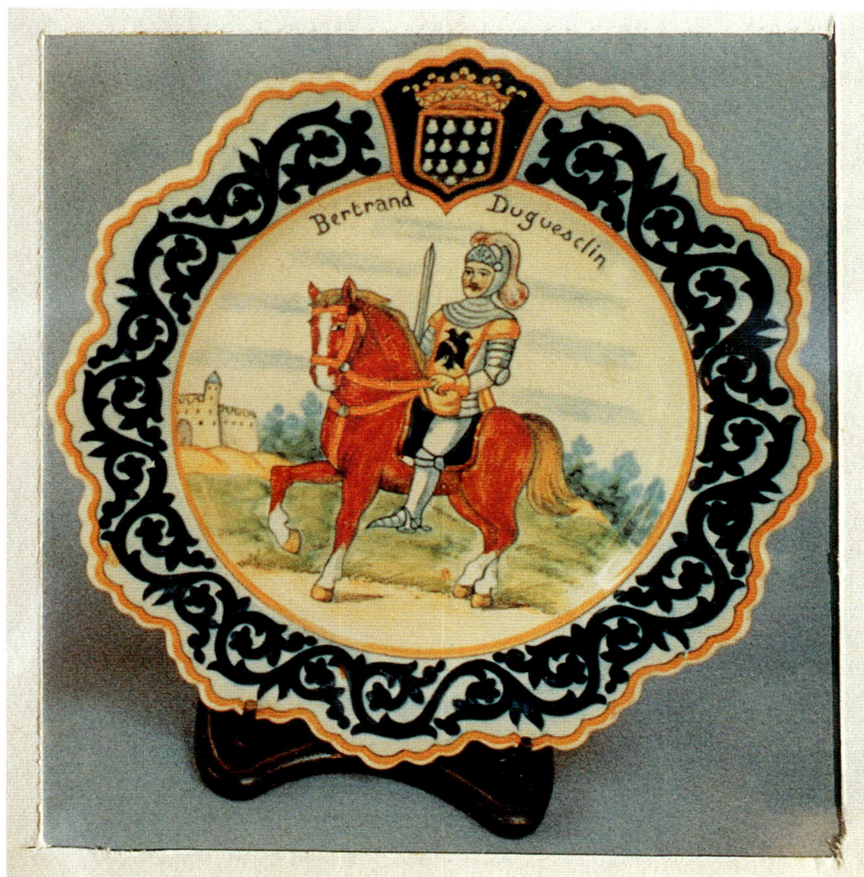

Du Guesclin still rides his charger, but this time on faïence. This flattering rendition of the famous Breton does not match descriptions of him, but perhaps the Henriot artists were kind. The 10" diameter plate, from the 1920s, is framed by a *dentillé* edge. (For a discussion of rim styles, see *Mali, Old Quimper Review, March 2001.*) *Private Collection.*

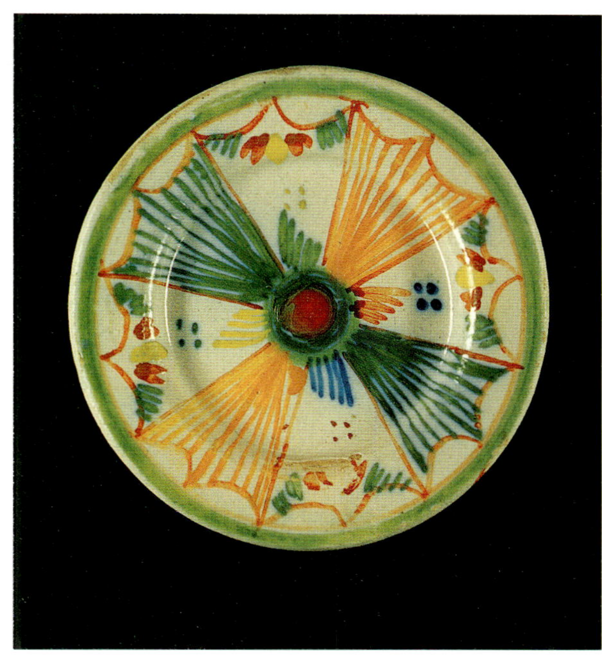

Henriot made this 3" doll plate in the 1920s. It is bold and colorful. *Private Collection.*

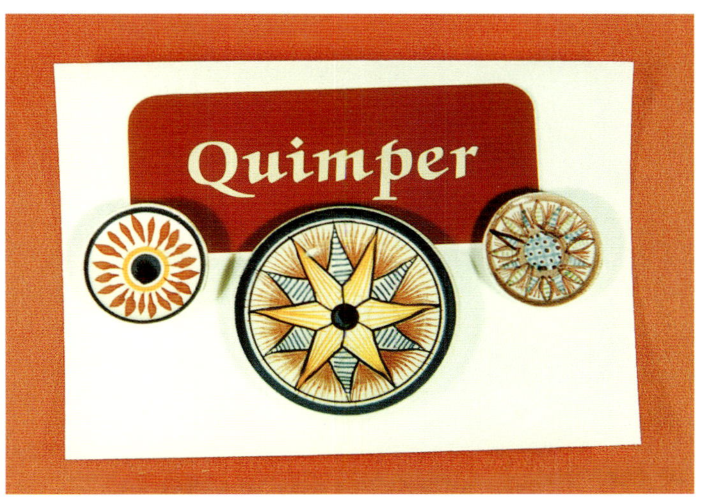

We found a great shop in Dinan where we purchased an assortment of doll plates, varying in size from 1.75" to 3" in diameter. There is some confusion in the Quimper collecting community about doll plates versus butter pats. These examples in colorful geometric designs are doll plates. *Private Collection.*

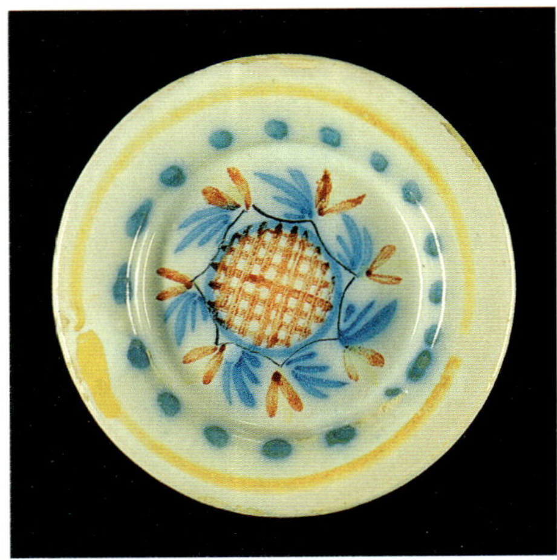

Another Henriot 3" doll plate from the 1920s has muted colors and a *croisillon* center, which some call the tennis ball motif. *Private Collection.*

Right:
Another gem was waiting for us on the trip from Dinan to St. Malo. Henriot manufactured this bell with a Bretonne figural handle. The bell stands 4.5" high, and the Bretonne wears a mustard-colored apron and white *coiffe*. *Private Collection.*

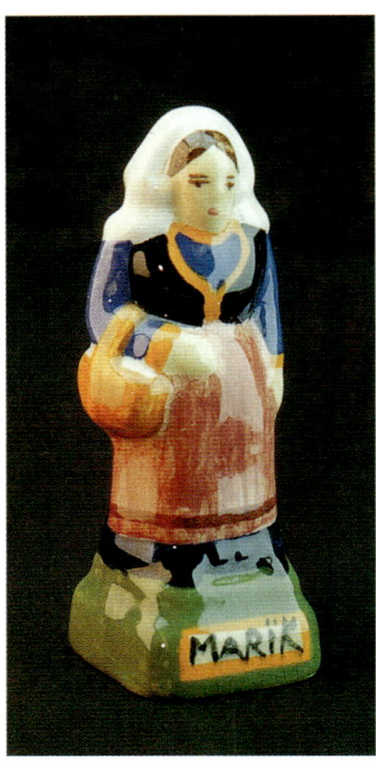

Right:
Henriot is the manufacturer of this mid-20th century 3.75" statue entitled Marik. She carries a market basket on one arm and is attired in blues and rose colors, with a white *coiffe*. We found her in a shop near Dinan, and had to bring her home with us. *Authors' Collection.*

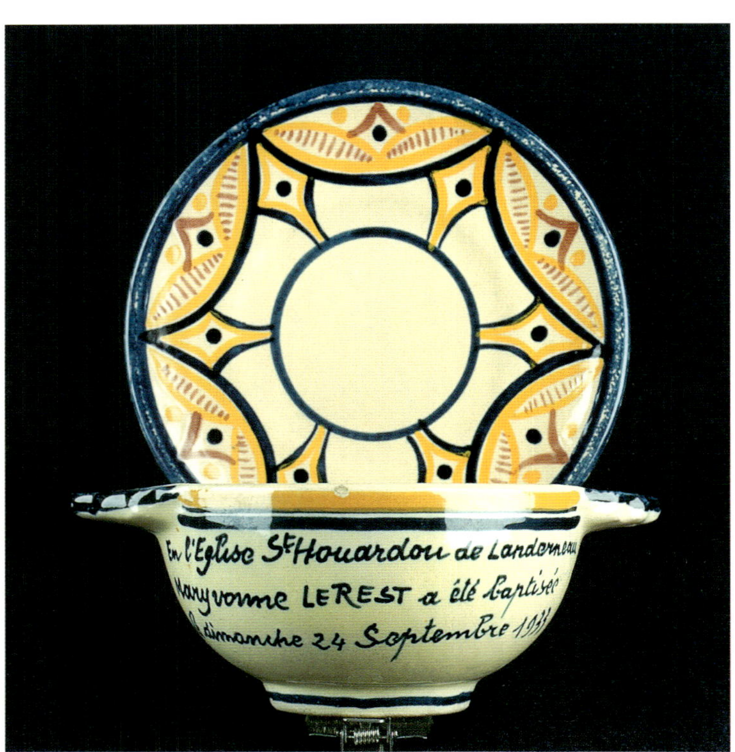

The Henriot factory produced this commemorative porringer with ears, or *bol à oreilles*, and matching under plate. The occasion was the baptism of Maryvonne LeRest at the church St. Houardoude, in Landerneau, on September 24, 1933. *Authors' Collection.*

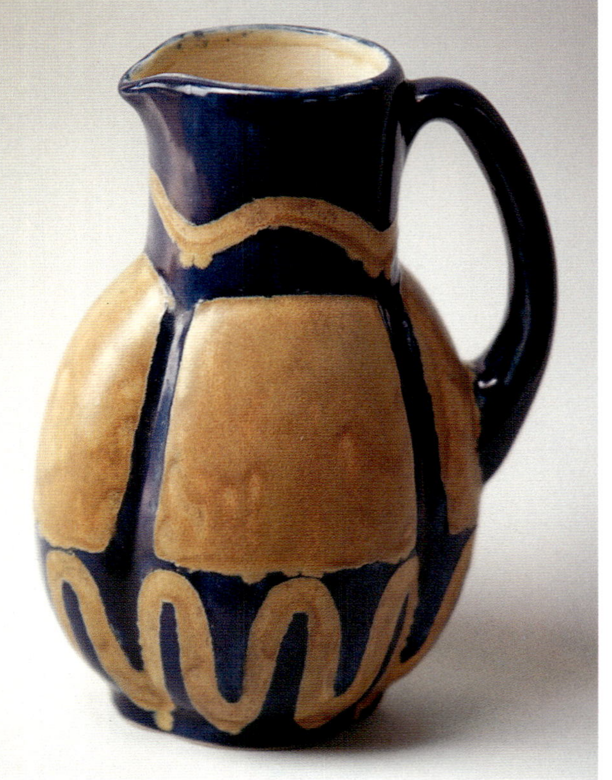

We also found this 9.75" tall HB Quimper Odetta cider pitcher on the way to St. Malo. It is stunning in gold and cobalt blue and is form #206 and décor #1087 in the Odetta catalogue from the *Musée de la Faïence*, Quimper. *Private Collection.*

St. Malo

St. Malo is about 25 kilometers northeast of Dinan, on the coast of the *Manche*, or English Channel. It was here that Du Guesclin built a home for his wife, Tiphaine, while he was commander of the St. Malo garrison in 1365.

Many historic figures have hailed from St. Malo including explorer Jacques Cartier, who discovered the entrance to the St. Lawrence River; privateer Robert Surcoff, who became extraordinarily rich as a *corsair*, and the writer/poet François-René de Chateaubriand, who spent part of his youth not far from the port of St. Malo.

The town was named for the Welsh monk Malo, who in the 6th century converted the local peasants to Christianity and became their bishop. The original settlement was open to attack by invaders, so the inhabitants moved to a close-by island. This became the site of today's St. Malo. The island was a fortress for the bishops who resided there, and in fact became so independent that the phrase, *Ni Francais, ni Breton, Malouins suis,* (neither French or Breton, but from Malo) was the city motto.

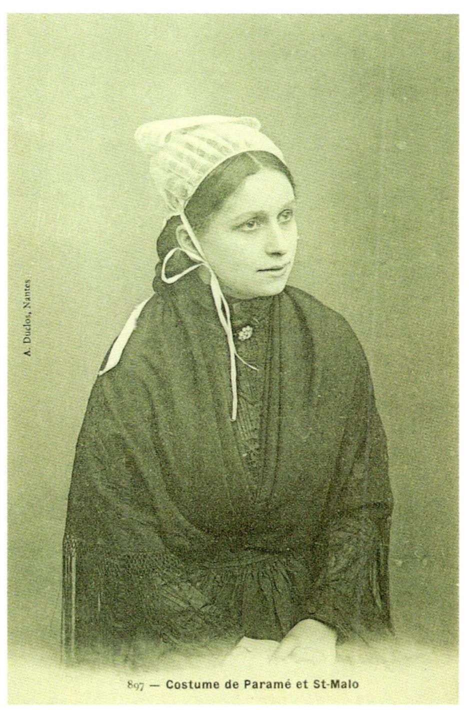

After World War II, much of St. Malo, including the ramparts, was successfully rebuilt in its original style.

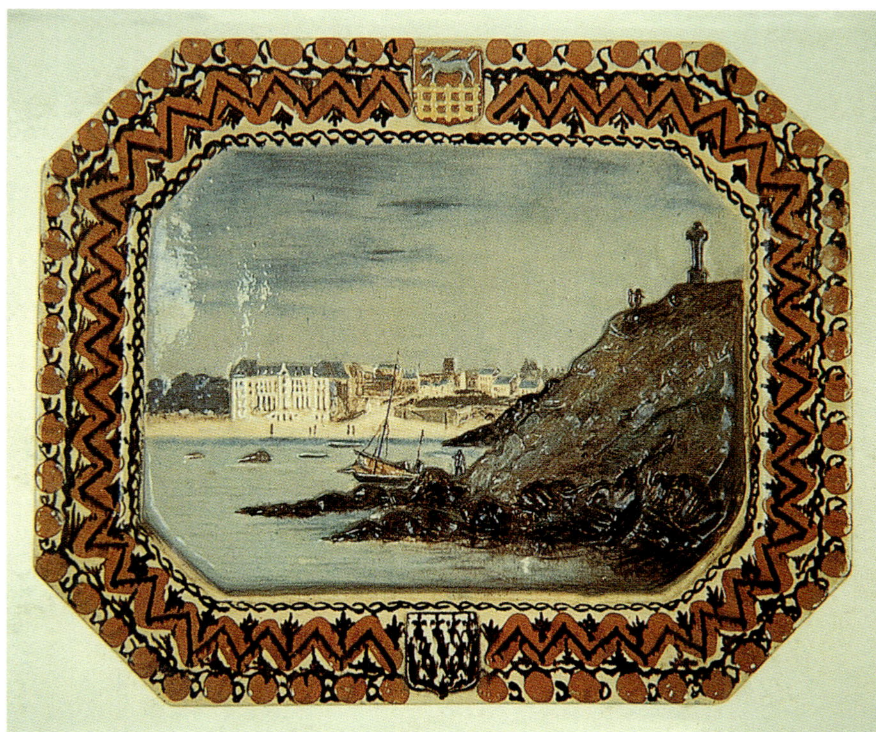

Alfred Beau captured the port at St. Malo in relief on this octagonal platter measuring 18.25" long and 15" wide. The armorial of St. Malo is in the top center of the *aile*, or rim, and the armorial of Brittany is on the bottom center *aile*. *Courtesy of Oriot & Dupont, Morlaix.*

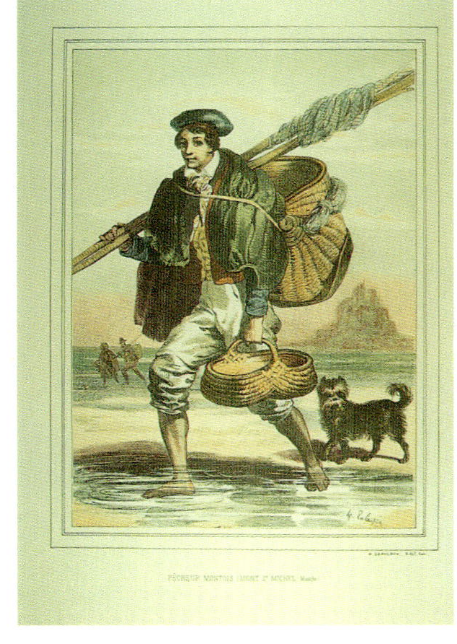

A young lady from St. Malo appears in this turn-of-the-20th century postcard. *Authors' Collection.*

A St. Malo *marin* from St. Malo is captured in a Lalaisse print documenting the costumes of an earlier era in Brittany. *Authors' Collection.*

We enjoyed walking the ramparts of this island fortress, despite the wind and rain of a soggy January afternoon. And we especially remember with regret a piece of Quimper we did not buy, at the shop not far from the statue of Robert Surcoff. It was a gorgeous tureen, and the price was right. What held us back? We hesitated, and decided not to buy it because it was extraordinarily large. Of course we could have done it, but we were young and naïve, or at least naïve. Ah, those pieces of Quimper poterie we did not buy haunt us all sometimes!

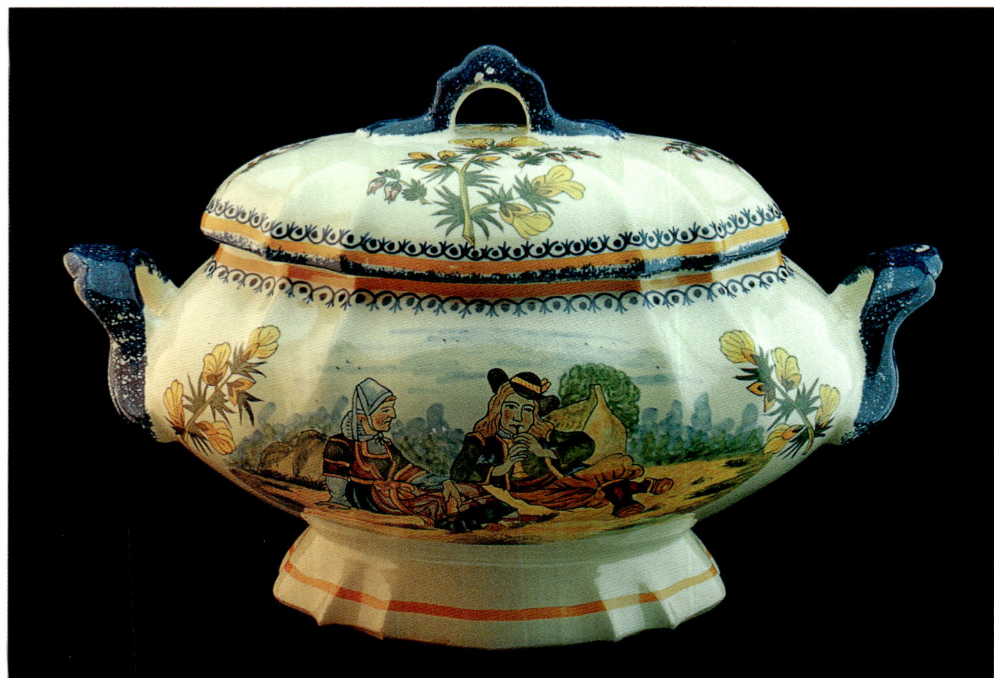

This Henriot tureen features a *Bretonne* relaxing in the countryside, as her Breton plays the *bombarde*. It has sponged handles, *l'ajonc* and *bruyère* (Breton gorse and heather) accents, dark-blue, scallop-and-dot borders, and well-painted scenes. The form and the artistry are superb. The tureen is second quarter of the 20th century, and measures an impressive 15" long and 10" high. *Courtesy of J. Cameron and Kathleen Yorkston.*

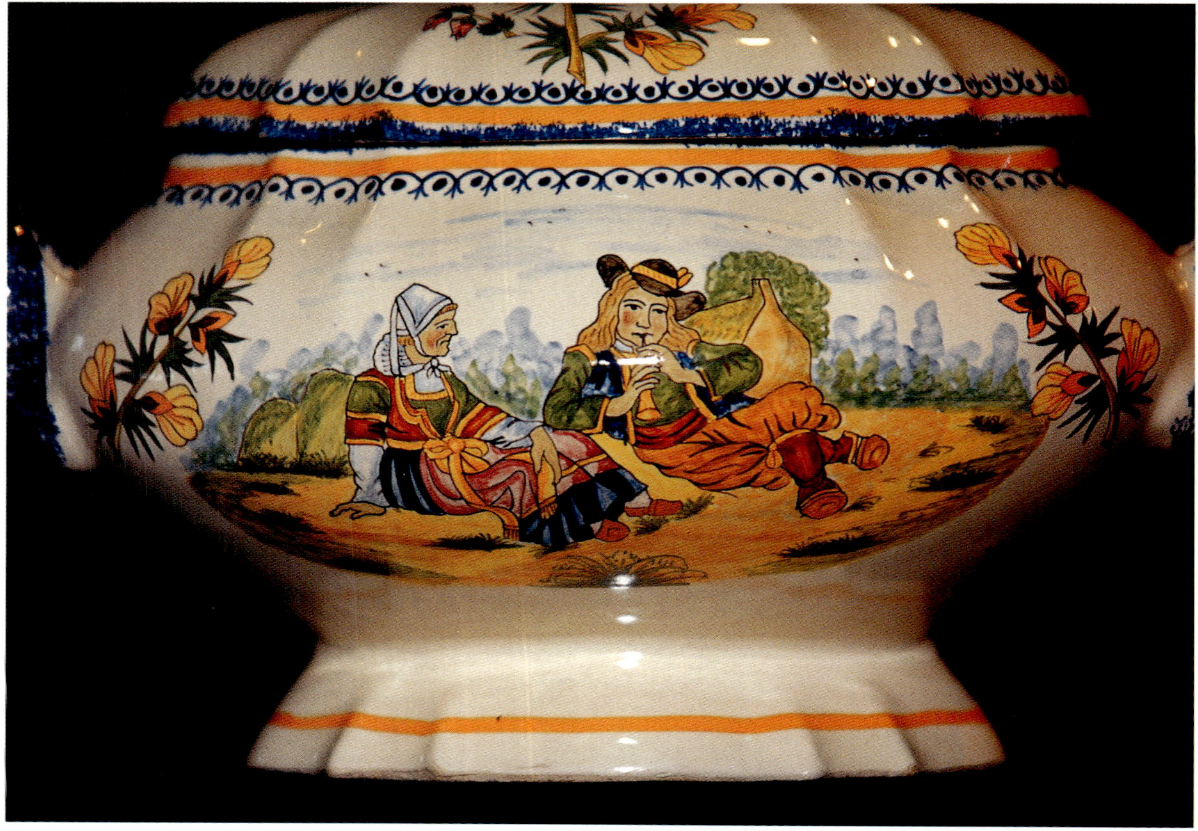

A close-up view of the Bretons on the tureen shows a happy life in Brittany, as well as the shaped form of the tureen's body and lid and the excellent attention to detail. *Courtesy of J. Cameron and Kathleen Yorkston.*

Château de Quintin

One glorious day trip from Rennes is to Quintin, about 20 kilometers southwest from St. Brieuc. The *Château*, which has been in the Bagneau family since the 12th century, became known to Quimper collectors because of a fabulous display of Porquier-Beau faïence. Annual exhibitions have been held at the *Château* since 1987, but the Porquier-Beau faïence exhibit was the first one held over for another season. The catalogue of the exhibit, *Faïence de Quimper, Porquier-Beau, 1875-1905, Exposition 1998-1999, Château de Quintin*, is highly prized in the Quimper community.

Fairies Rock or *La Roche-aux-Fées*

We often take breaks from our shopping quests to explore local landmarks and legends. In the process, we learn more about the people who created and inspired Quimper poterie. We also learn about ourselves, and our special kinship with this land. One of our most memorable – and mystical – experiences took place when we decided to visit *La Roche-aux-Fées*, a significant megalithic site dating back between 4,000 and 5,000 years.

The Fairies Rock was not easy to find, at least for us, even though it's only about 25 kilometers southeast of Rennes. To get there we drove main roads to narrow farm lanes, but then became lost. The day was chilly but mostly clear. When we finally found the site there were no others about. We left our car at a parking area, where the multilingual signs explained what we were about to see. We trudged up a slight rise to a grove of trees. In the middle of this oasis of oaks and chestnuts we saw an array of huge stones.

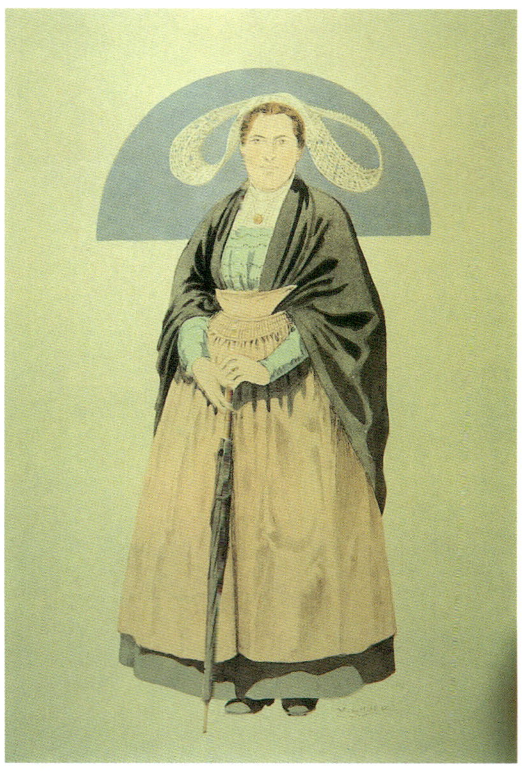

The dress and *coiffe* from the town of Quintin are shown in this early 20th century print. *Private Collection.*

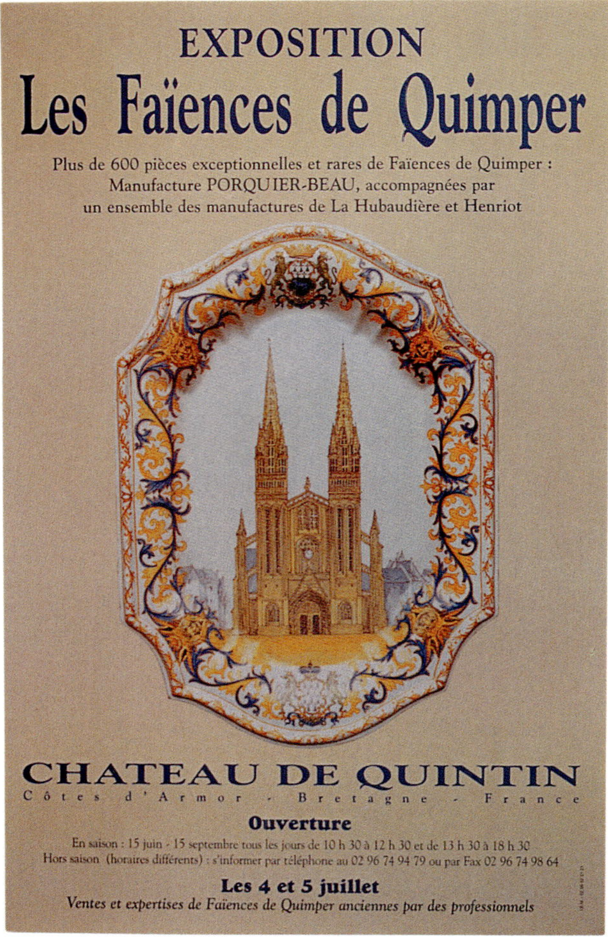

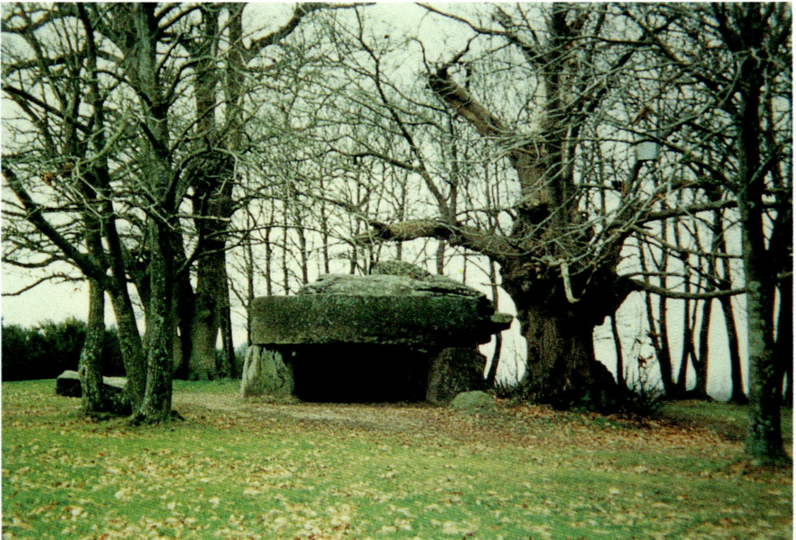

Fairies Rock, or *La Roche-aux-Fées*, is an impressive megalithic monument between 4,000 and 5,000 years old. It was built by unidentified ancestors, who obviously had remarkable engineering skills.

Left:
The poster commemorating the Alfred Beau exhibit was a gift from the Bagneau family. St. Corentin Cathedral in Quimper, rendered in faïence by Beau is the central element of the poster. *Authors' Collection.*

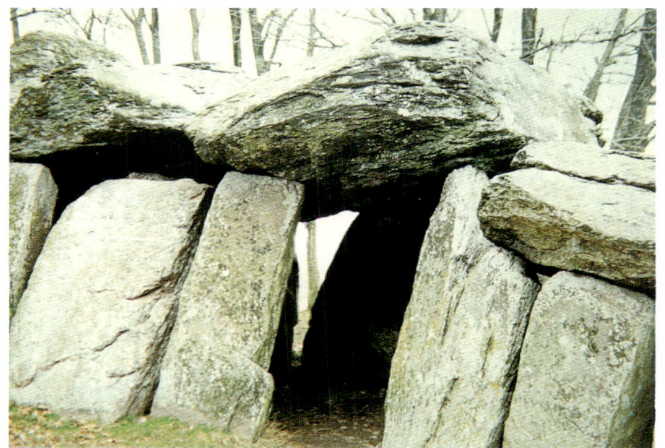

The grand entrance to *La Roche* contains stones weighing 30 to 40 tons each. The site was used for burials and probably for religious ceremonies as well. Earlier researchers suggested priests even might have lived within the monument.

We counted the stones in separate directions, as the legend dictates. When David stooped to walk inside the structure to count again, he was overwhelmed by an eerie sensation.

This megalithic monument stands as testimony to prehistoric man's engineering skills. The stones at *La Roche* are arranged like a hallway measuring nearly 70 feet long. The entrance, called a trilithon, contains a horizontal squared-off slab of rock atop two vertical stone pillars. All three stones weigh at least 30-40 tons each, and were toted here from several kilometers away. The entrance faces approximately toward the rising sun at winter solstice. A low-ceilinged passage leads from the grand entrance to a vast high chamber, which is divided into four sections constructed with 40 or so large stones.

One *La Roche* legend says a couple can guarantee good fortune if they count the same number of stones while circling the perimeter in opposite directions. A Breton would walk to the right and his mate to the left. When they both completed the circle, if the number counted by each matched, they had a bright future. If they were off by more than two they could be in for a rough time.

David and I tried the count. David retraced his steps to be sure of the number, stooping slightly to maneuver inside through the standing stones and into the heart of the structure. Immediately a sensation swept over him, like being compressed from head to toe and insulated from all sound, as if in a pressurized cocoon. He was suddenly seized by a fear the stones might collapse, but dismissed this thought as ridiculous. Why would they collapse after having rested in the same position for more than 5,000 years?

Once outside the chamber, David's eerie feeling disappeared. But he also didn't reenter to see if the sensation would recur. Was this the work of fairies or of ghosts entombed there? Or was it merely his first claustrophobic experience?

Steve Smith, another American Quimper merchant, later told us about a legend concerning a secret sequence of steps designed by Celtic priests. He suggested David might have walked this sequence, inadvertently triggering a connection to *another* world! Whatever it was, David always will remember the eerie feeling and our visit to *La Roche-aux-Fées*.

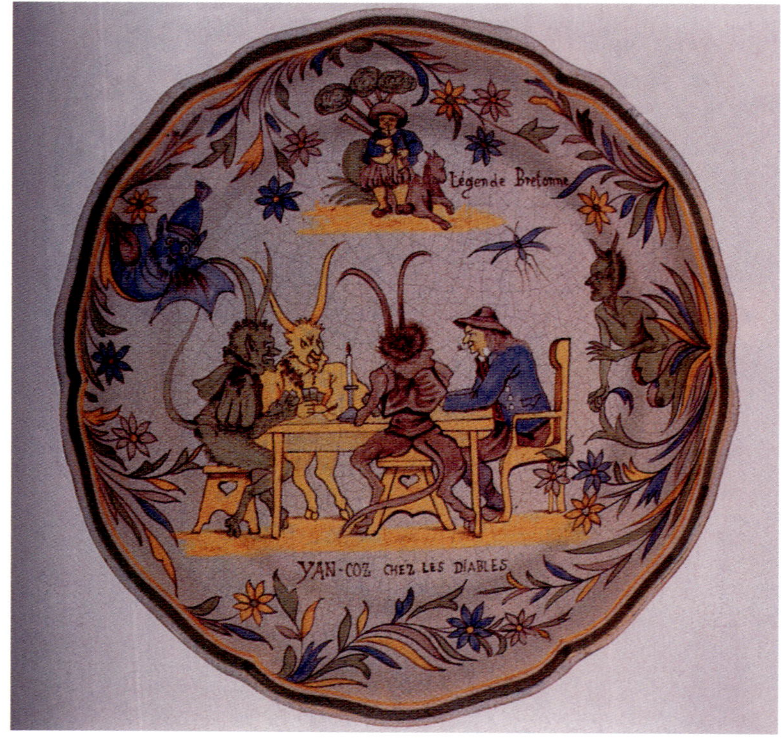

Were the fairies or *korigans* playing tricks on David or just playing cards, as seen on this Porquier-Beau *légende Bretonne* plate, *Yan Coz Chez Les Diables* (Old Jean Among the Devils), by Alfred Beau. The story is derived from a book written by Beau's father-in-law, Emile Souvestre, *Le Dernier Breton*. Legends live on in Brittany! *Courtesy of Oriot & Dupont.*

Morlaix tends to be underrated by tourist guides and Quimper seekers. Perhaps we are giving away one of our secrets, but we consistently have found many fine pieces of Quimper poterie in the Morlaix area. Located in the *Léon* region of *Bretagne,* Morlaix is the home of a renowned Quimper poterie auction, which in itself is an excellent reason for any faïence lover to visit! Of course, we are always looking for Quimper in shops along our journey, but we've been especially successful in and around Morlaix.

And we also found Morlaix enchanting, on a more personal level, and a wonderful source of much Quimper-related history.

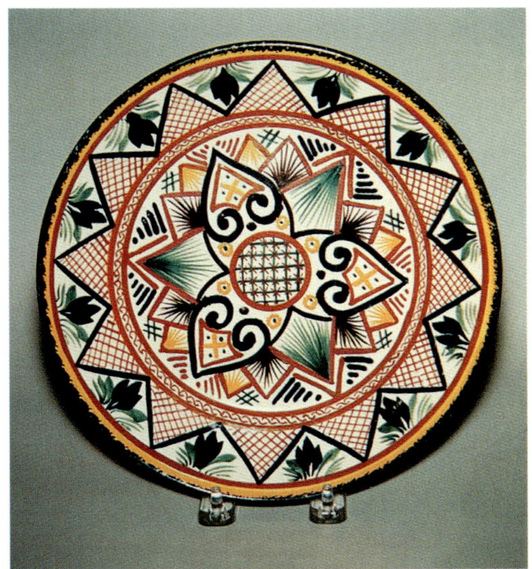

In Mortaix we purchased an *HB/ Grande Maison* 9" diameter geometric plate from the second quarter of the 20th century. The Celtic motif on the plate is stellar and crisp, containing hearts and *croisillon* décor. The plate is bordered with yellow and red bands and a sponged-blue edge. Interspersed throughout are flowers in dark-blue and green, executed in the famous *à la touche* technique. *Authors' Collection.*

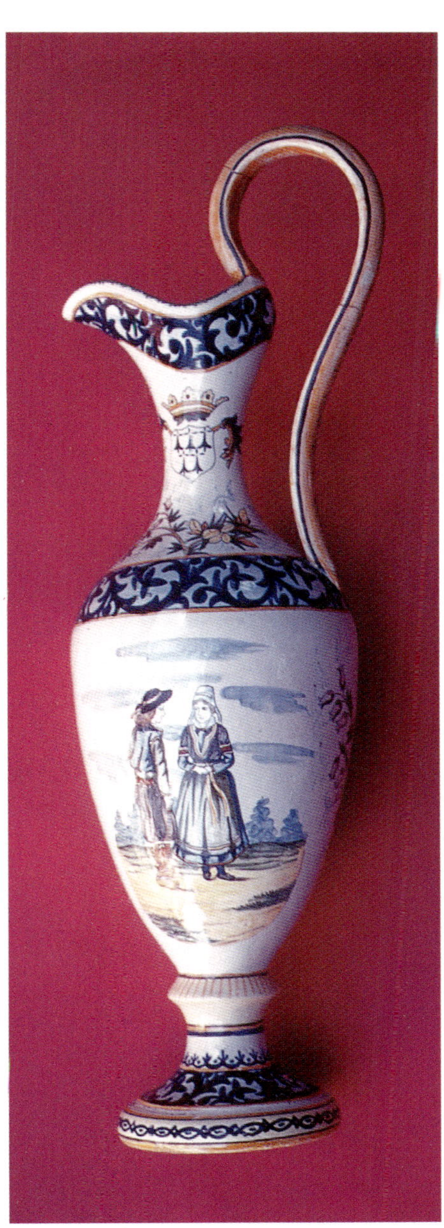

We also purchased an Henriot ewer from the 1930s. A full 18" tall, it has a stately presence wherever displayed. The décor features a sweet Bretonne turned to face the viewer, and a Breton gazing lovingly at her, with the armorial of *Bretagne* above them. *Private Collection.*

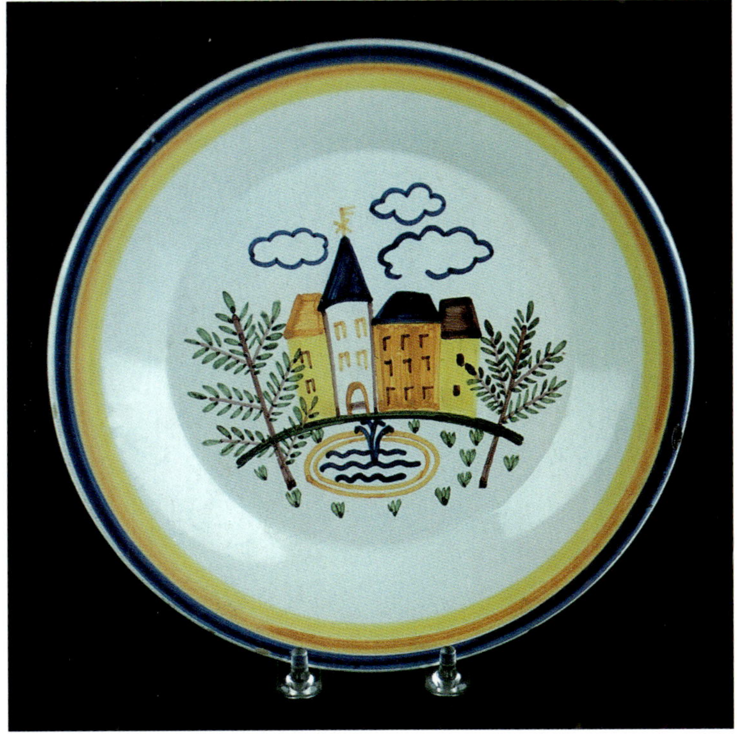

A unique *manoir* décor 8.5" diameter plate also was purchased in Morlaix. It is *HB/Grande Maison* and has a pre-World War II artists' signature called Morse Code-like by some experts. *Authors' Collection.*

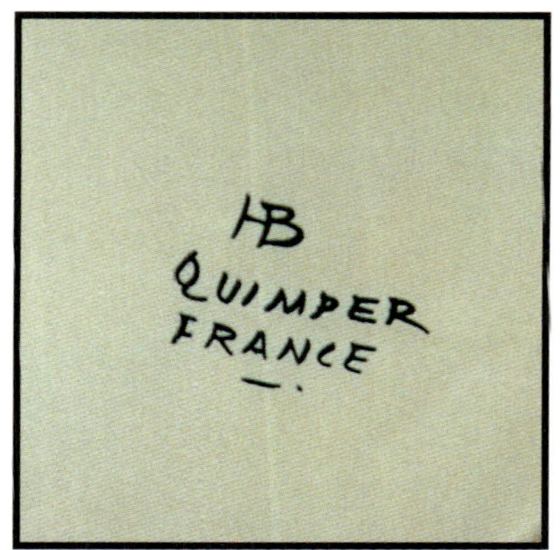

This HB signature, dash dot (-.), represents Monsieur Chapalain. A list of some HB and Henriot artists' signatures from the 1920-1930s and post-World War II is found in *Taburet, p. 216.*

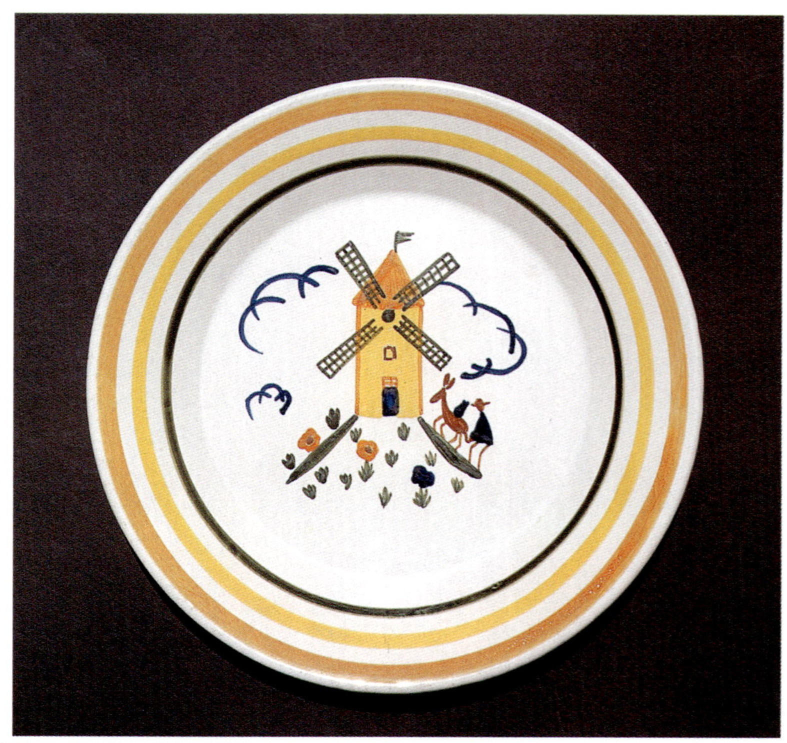

Another unique *HB/Grande Maison* design is reminiscent of Don Quixote, with a windmill and donkey motif. The plate is 8.5" diameter, signed with the 1920s-1930s HB signature of Morse Code-like marks, and was purchased at the same *brocante* in Morlaix as the *manoir* plate. *Authors' Collection.*

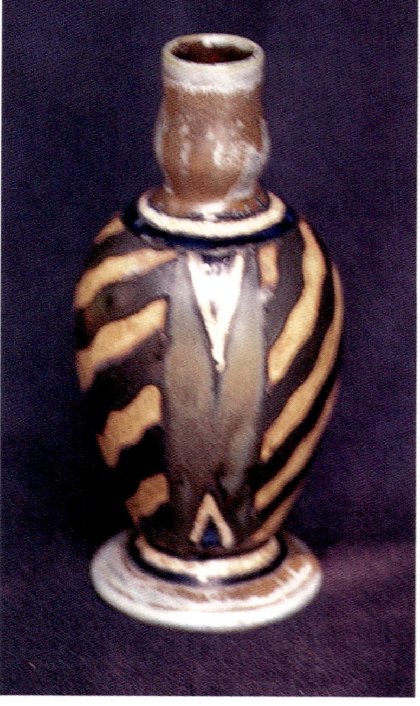

The *manoir* décor was an early design, as seen on these 18th century Quimper examples. *Courtesy of the Musée Départemental Breton, Quimper.*

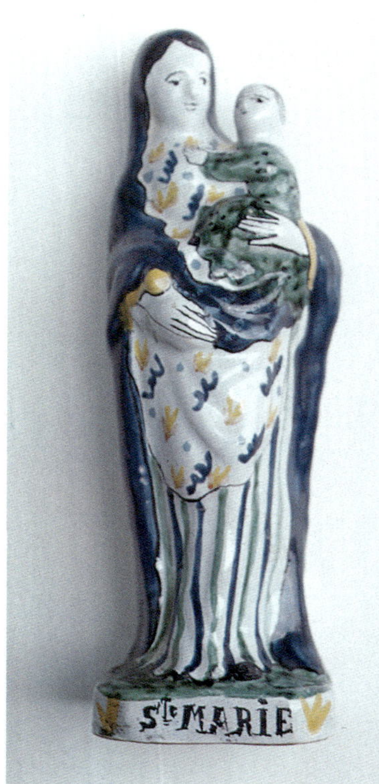

We purchased this 19th century, unsigned 9.5" tall *Vierge* in Morlaix, near the Oriot & Dupont auction house. The Virgin has a sweet countenance, and early design elements, including the *trou*, or hole, pierced in the back to protect against explosion when the clay is fired. The décor on her robe is similar to that found in *Cahn, pp. 37 and 44,* but the seller labeled the statue Malicorne. *Authors' Collection.*

Another gem we found in Morlaix is this 7.5" tall Odetta vase, signed HB Quimper, Odetta, #99-1280. The numbers on Odetta examples were cataloged in a 1999 publication by *L'Association des Amis du Musée de la Faïence.* In the book, the vase is described as having a narrow neck *(col étroit)* and a geometric décor. *Private Collection.*

The most prominent landmark in Morlaix, which lies in the valley of the Dossen (or Morlaix) River, is the railroad viaduct built in the 1860s linking Paris and Brest. The railroad opened Brittany for tourist excursions and forever changed the way people did business and traveled in the area. The towering viaduct magnificently dominates the view, rising 190 feet above the rooftops of the half-timbered houses in Morlaix.

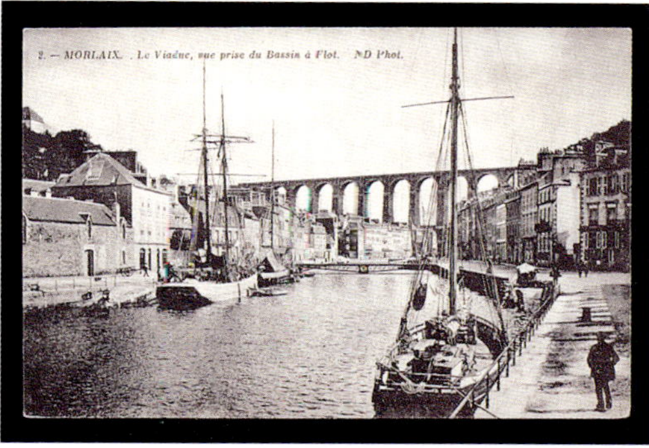
An early postcard of the viaduct and quay at Morlaix shows the quaint charm of the old town. *Authors' Collection.*

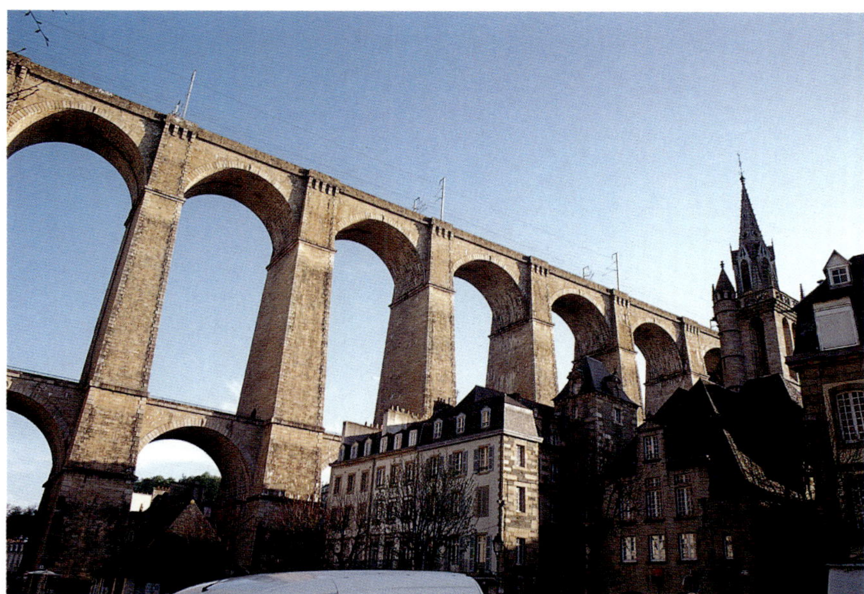
The 19th century viaduct dominates the old town and surrounding area. The railroad viaduct brought tourists and commerce to Brittany and opened doors to another world for her inhabitants.

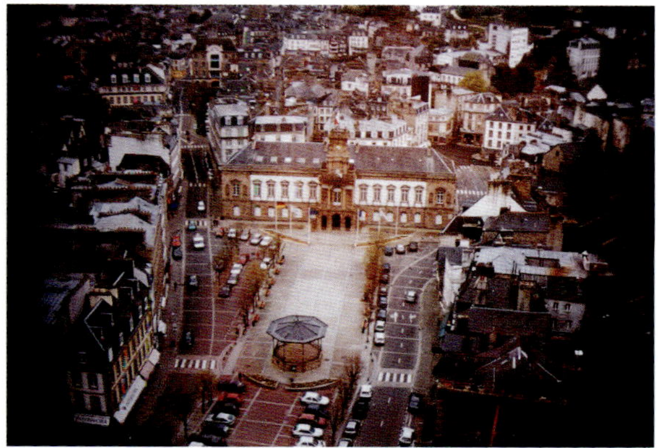
We took photos of the center of old town Morlaix as we sailed across the famous 19th century viaduct on France's high-speed train.

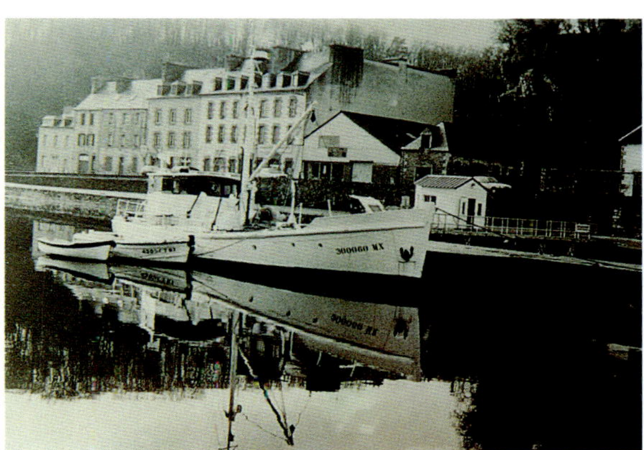
A recent black-and-white photograph captures the enduring spirit of Morlaix's quay.

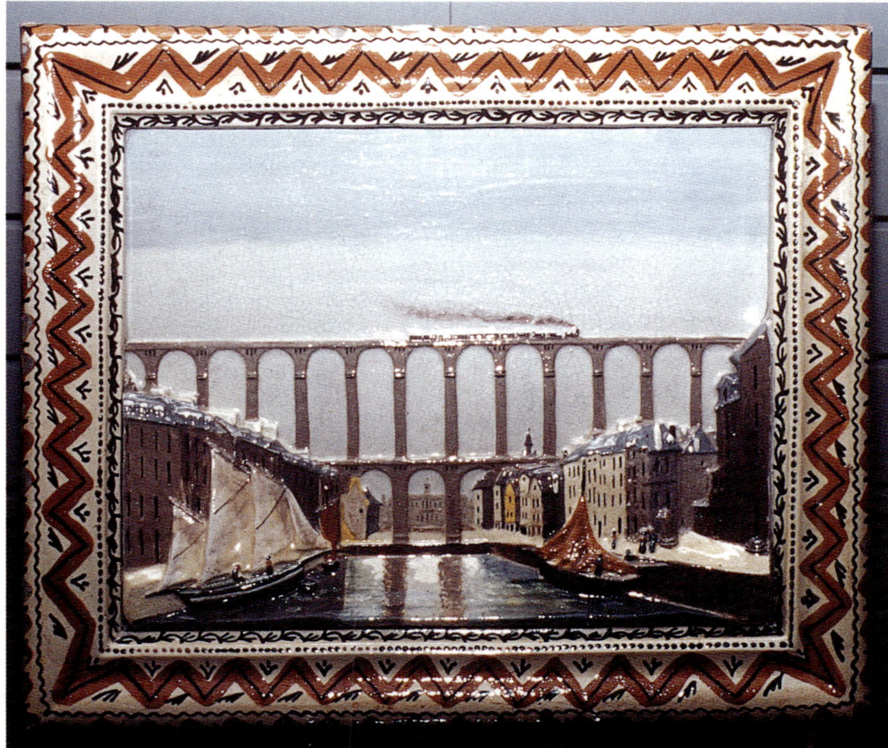
The Morlaix viaduct was rendered in *terre vernissée* by native-son Alfred Beau for the Porquier-Beau faïencerie. It measures 18" wide and is from the 1890s. *Courtesy of Musée Départemental Breton, Quimper.*

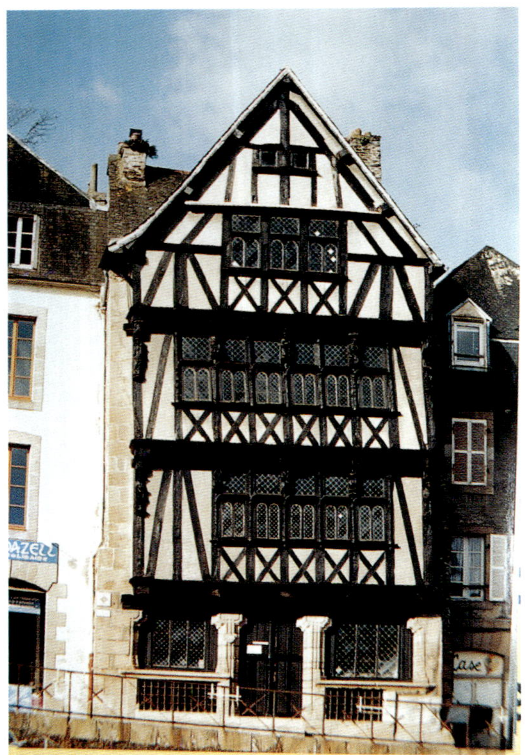

You also will find the *Maison de la Reine Anne*, or Queen Anne House, a sterling example of a Renaissance-era skylight house, in Morlaix. The interior of the *Maison* boasts an exceptional carved oak staircase; religious figures adorn the newel post and landings. Most remarkable is the single oak post that forms the spine of the thirty-six foot high spiral staircase. Legend says an oak log was immersed in the salt water of the quay so the sweet sap would leach out, making the wood more resistant to termite infestation. That's why it has survived for five hundred years, providing us a first-hand glimpse of what existed half a millennium ago.

Queen Anne, the Bretonne who became Queen of France but never forgot her homeland, stayed in this house in 1505 when it was relatively new. She was on a pilgrimage to churches in Brittany to give thanks for her husband King Louis XII's recovery from a serious illness. The town showered her with gifts, including a tame ermine with a diamond-studded collar. The ermine was the emblem of Queen Anne, and the Bretons revered her as their *Duchesse en sabots* because of her allegiance to her native *Bretagne*.

Morlaix is the home of the *Maison de la Reine Anne*, a three-story residence where Queen Anne stayed in 1505. It belonged to a wealthy merchant and is an example of a *lanterne,* or skylight house, with an open interior courtyard and skylight roof.

On entering the Queen Anne house, it seems as if the upper floors stopped halfway between the front and back of the house. This was a clever construction feature, which allowed light from the skylight to illuminate the entire inside of the back of the house from rooftop to the floor below. An early print of the interior of a *lanterne* house in Morlaix shows how the roof skylight brightened the interior, a bonus in the days before electricity. *Private Collection.*

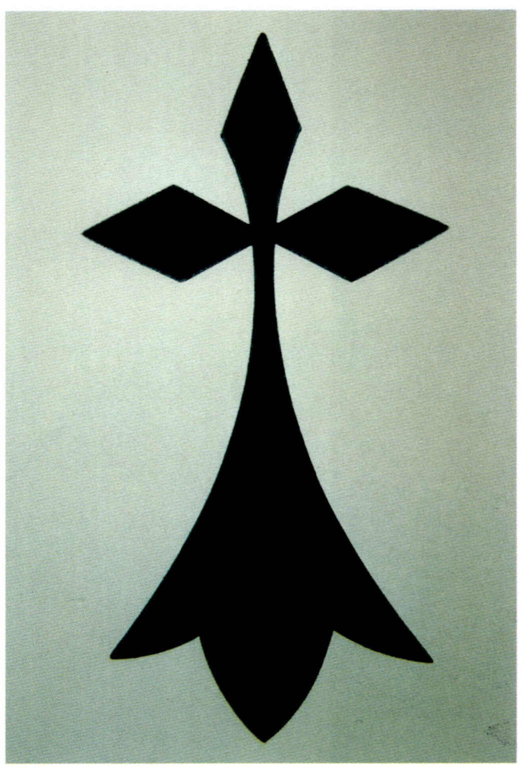

Right:
The ermine and ermine-tail were emblems of Queen Anne. The ermine-tail often is found as accent decoration on Quimper poterie and other French faïence.

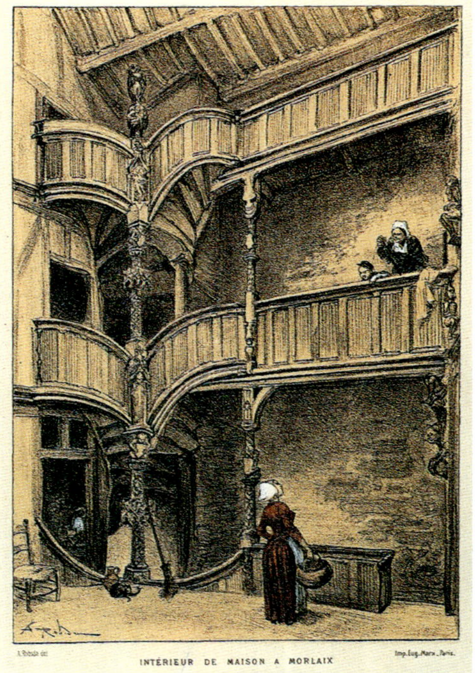

Left: The *cygne,* or swan, with an arrow-pierced breast, was the armorial of Claude, Anne's daughter. Center: The ermine was Queen Anne's emblem. Right: The *porc-epic,* or porcupine, was the emblem of King Louis XII, Anne's second husband. Note the scattered ermine-tail accents. These early 20th century plates are unmarked but mostly likely from Blois. *Private Collection.*

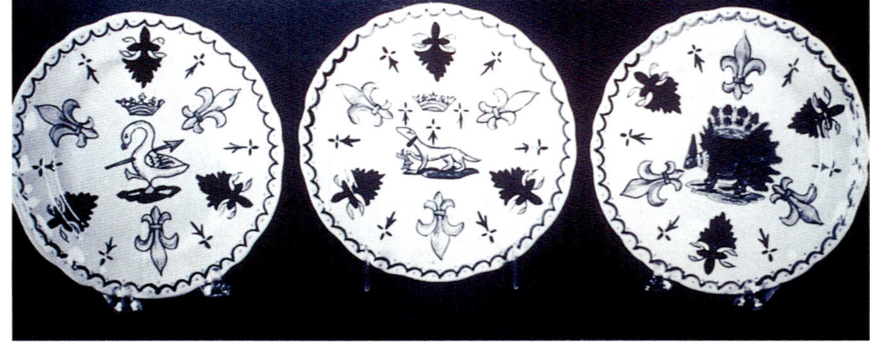

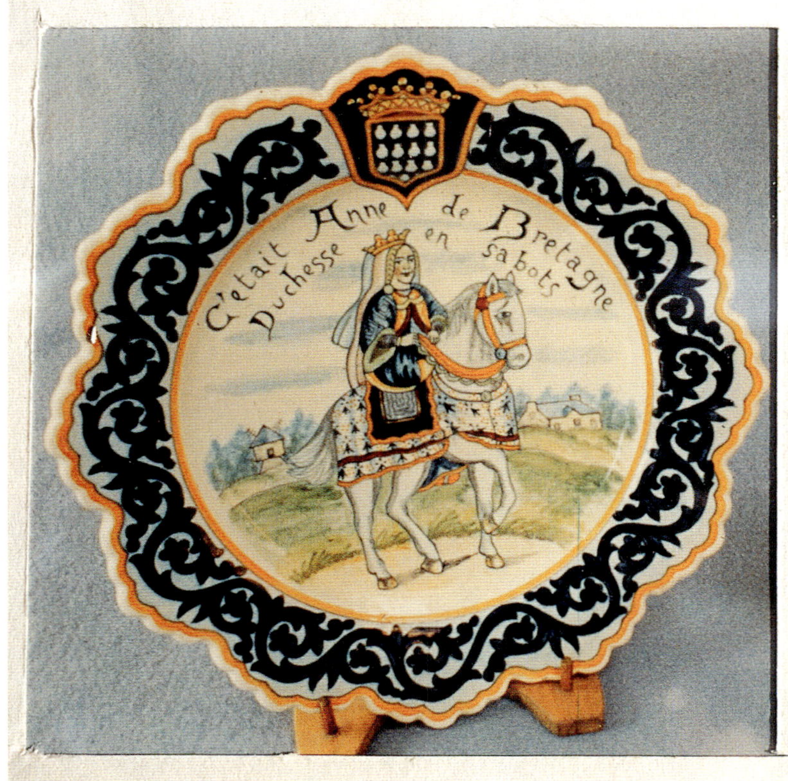

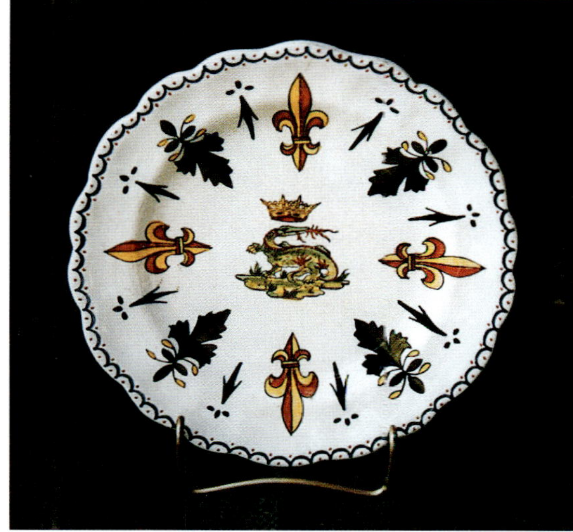

The salamander was the armorial of François of Angoulême, who became King François I. He was husband to Claude, Queen Anne's daughter. This 7.5" diameter plate is most likely from Blois, early 20th century period. The ermine-tail accents appear again. *Private Collection.*

The Bretonne who became Queen of France is shown on this c. 1930, 10" diameter HQ plate with a *dentillé* edge. The plate calls Queen Anne *Duchesse en sabots,* or the Duchess who wore the wooden shoes of Brittany. Anne, the oldest daughter of François II, the last Duke of Brittany, became Queen of France in 1491 when she married King Charles VIII. After his untimely death in 1498, she wed Charles' successor, Louis XII. *Private Collection.*

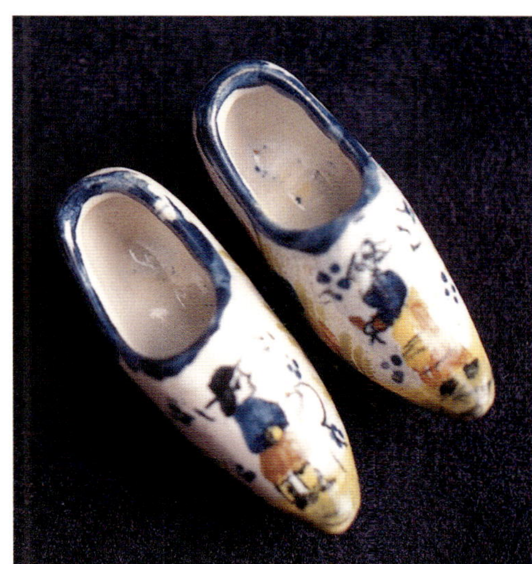

HB/*Grande Maison* faïence *sabots* from the 1920-1930s are only 2.5" long. Because of their very small size, they were intended as souvenir items. Some larger sabot forms were used as salts. *Authors' Collection.*

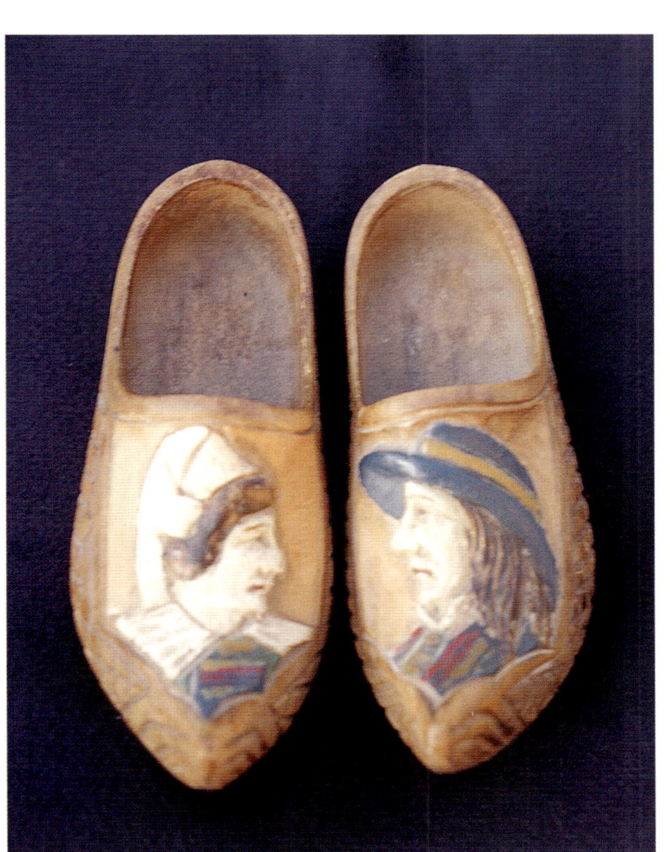

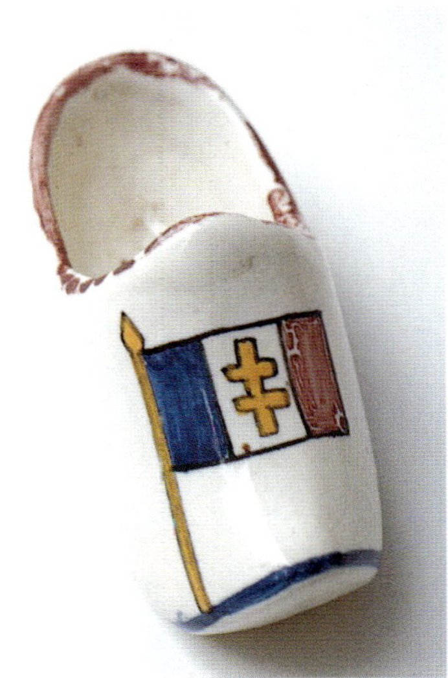

Left:
Many varieties of *sabots* are made as souvenirs for tourists. Some are marked with the town's name, as is this 10" long pair, which reads, *August, 1937, Hennebont* (a town about 60 kilometers southeast of Quimper). *Authors' Collection.*

Right:
A 2.5" long *sabot* with the *Croix de Lorraine,* or Cross of Lorraine, by Henriot is a souvenir from the World War II era. *(For additional examples of Croix de Lorraine, see Taburet, p. 173). Authors' Collection.*

Morlaix is embraced by quaint alleyways called *venelles,* which wind up the steep hills on either side of the old town; picturesque quays are arrayed before colorful houses and the cigar factory. *St. Mélaine* is a 15th century church tucked beneath the viaduct in the center of Morlaix. Across the street are the *Place des Otages,* the town hall, and the Visitors Center. A ceramic tile map on the outside of the Visitors Center caught our attention. It was signed by noted Quimper artist J.E. Sévellec.

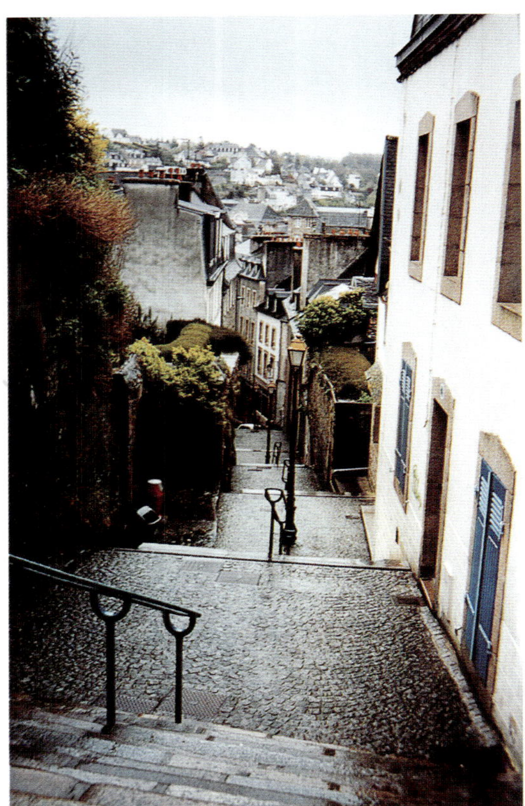

Morlaix is known for its quaint *venelles,* side streets that wind up either side of the town.

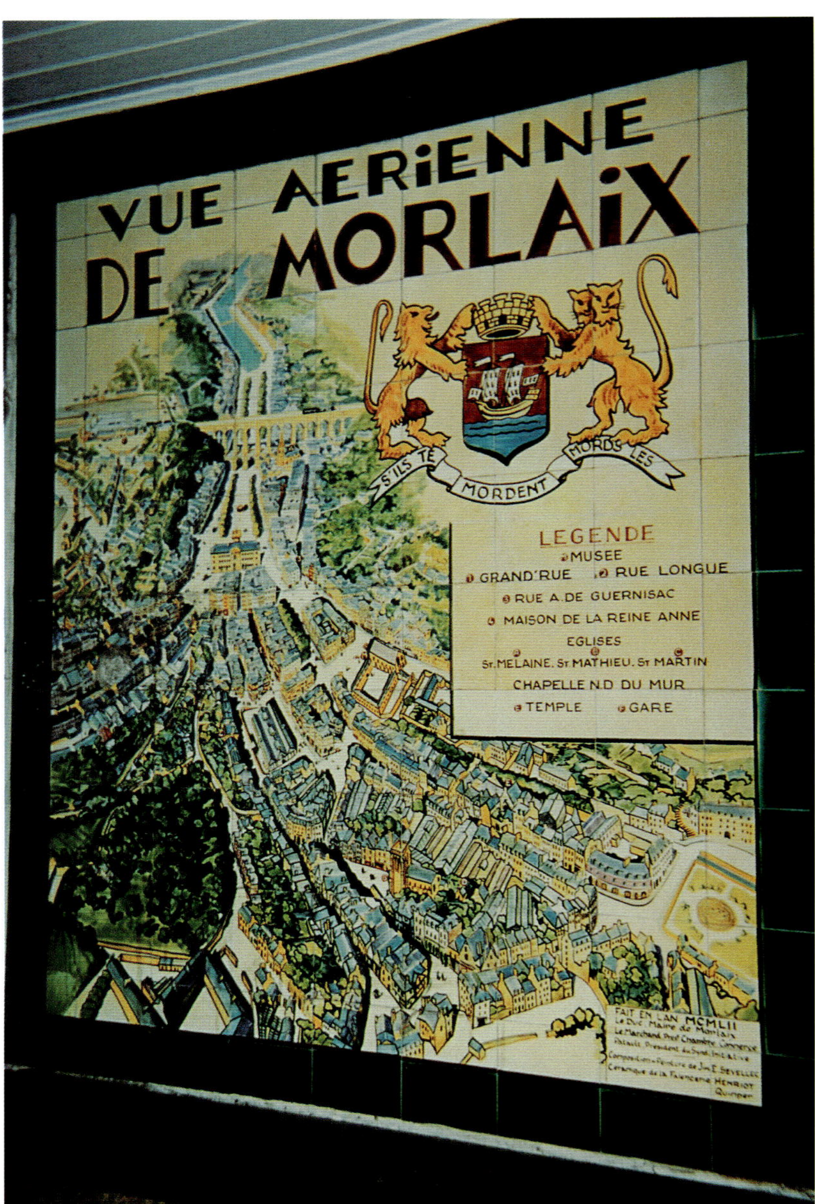

On our journey, we have found that if we keep our senses open to the local ambience some very special scenes and moments emerge. These unexpected experiences are abundant in Brittany, such as finding Quimper artist Jim-Emile Sévellec's ceramic tile aerial map of Morlaix.

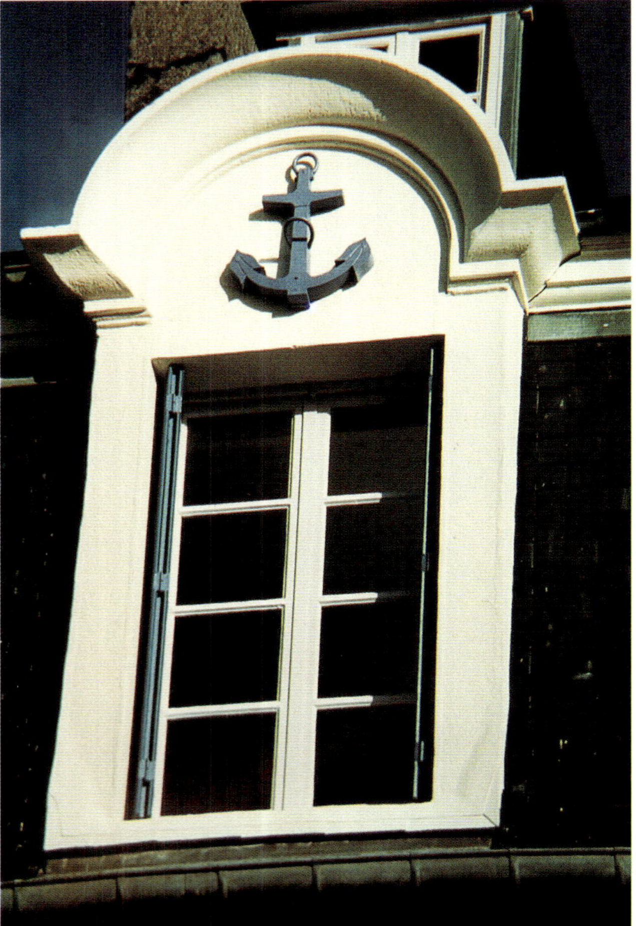

Morlaix's quays are a photographer's heaven, as are the colorful buildings and windows facing the harbor.

Jim-Emile Sévellec created many unique and wonderful pieces of poterie during his career at the Henriot firm. He was a talented painter, illustrator, and sculptor; his *Village Breton,* a depiction of a religious festival in a small town, often is considered as one of his finest accomplishments. We were delighted to find Sevellec's ceramic *Vue Arienne de Morlaix,* or Aerial View of Morlaix, and a companion tile scene of the Bay of Morlaix at the Visitors Center, as well as a series of pastoral Breton scenes in tile by Sévellec. Seeing these made us look forward all the more to seeing the map in Camaret, the town on of his birth, and the map in Penmarc'h.

Sévellec's Breton tile scenes show churches, this one in Roscoff …

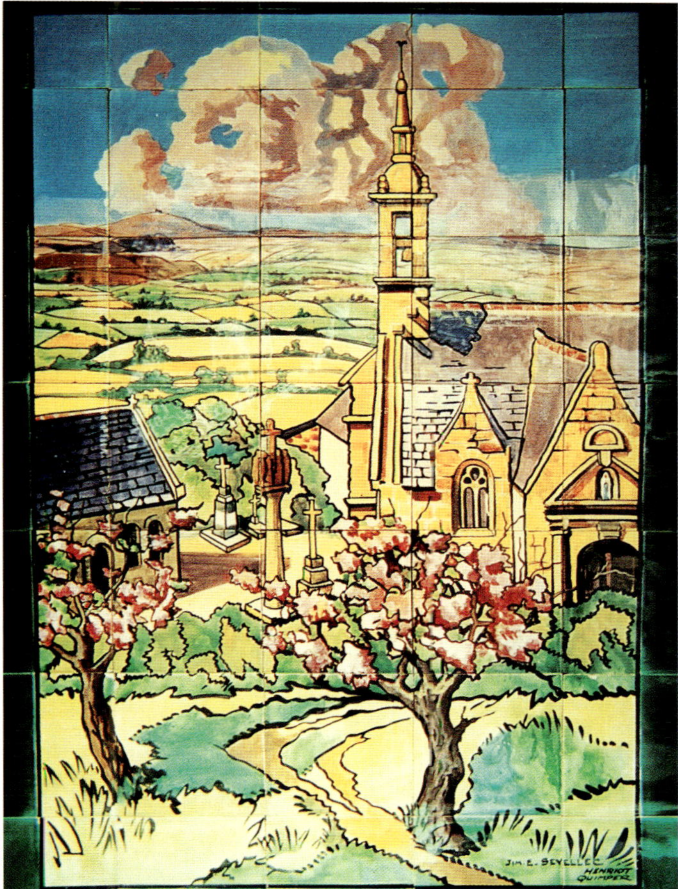

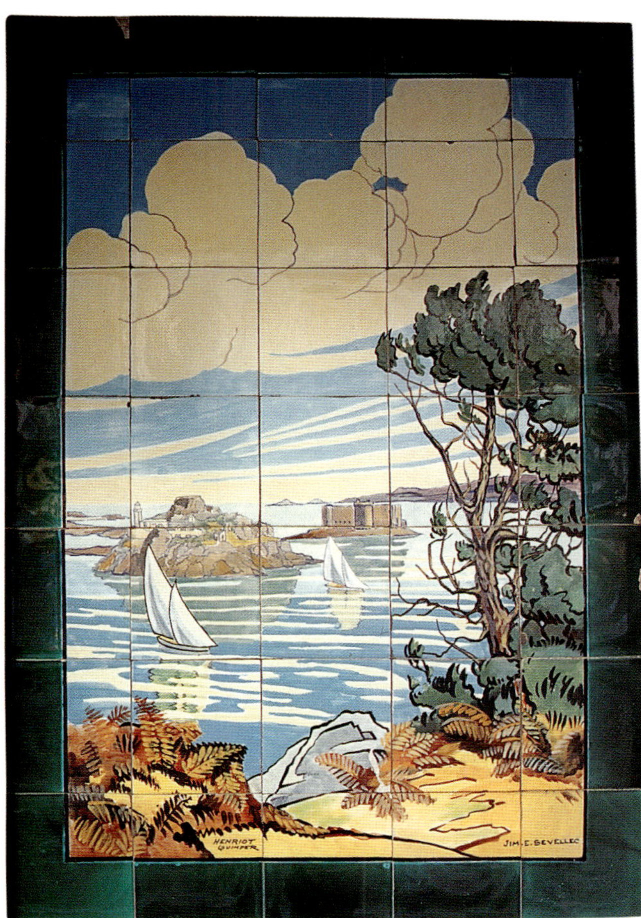

Sévellec tiles abound at the Visitors Center in Morlaix. This view of Morlaix Bay is charming.

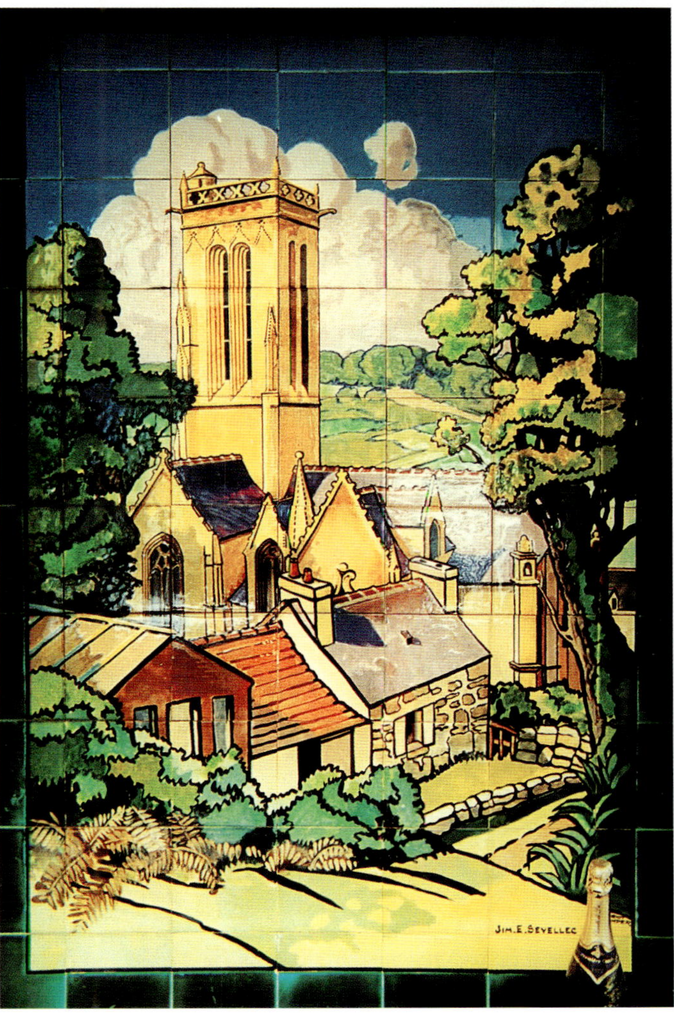

… And the other church perhaps is the Cathedral in St. Pol-de-Léon.

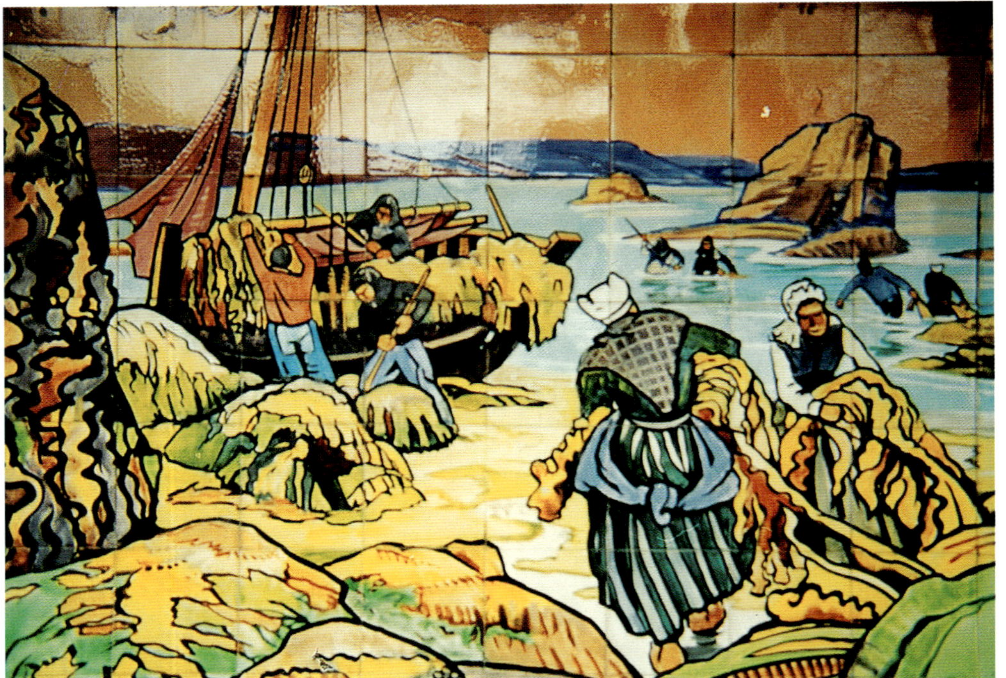

Sévellec also depicted fishermen and women on the tiles in Morlaix …

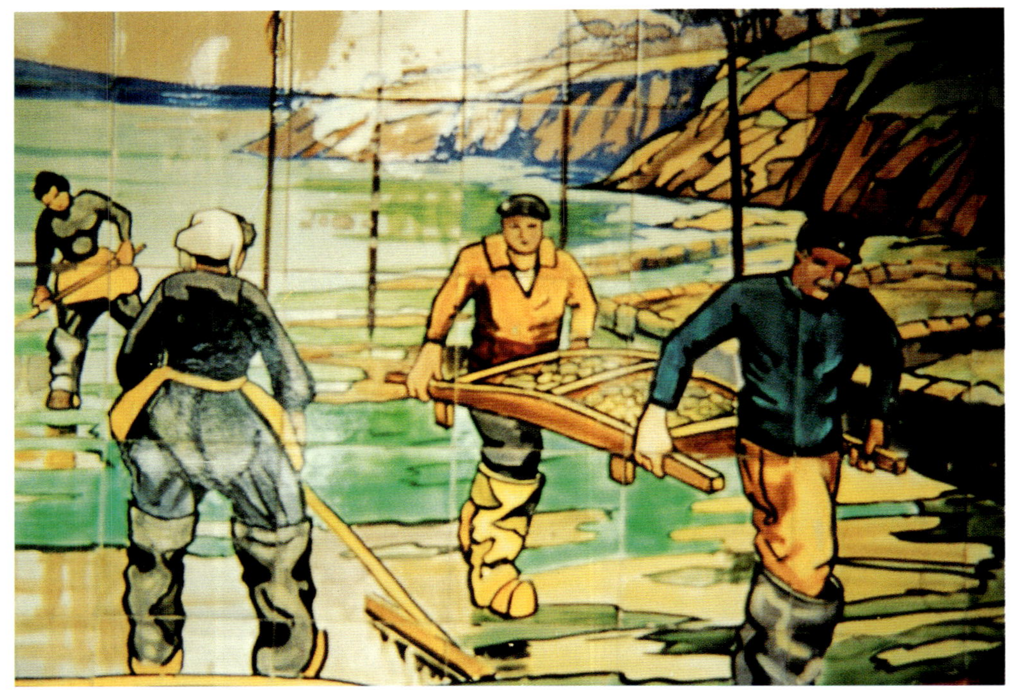

… And all of Sévellec's tiles were waiting for us about a block from our hotel!

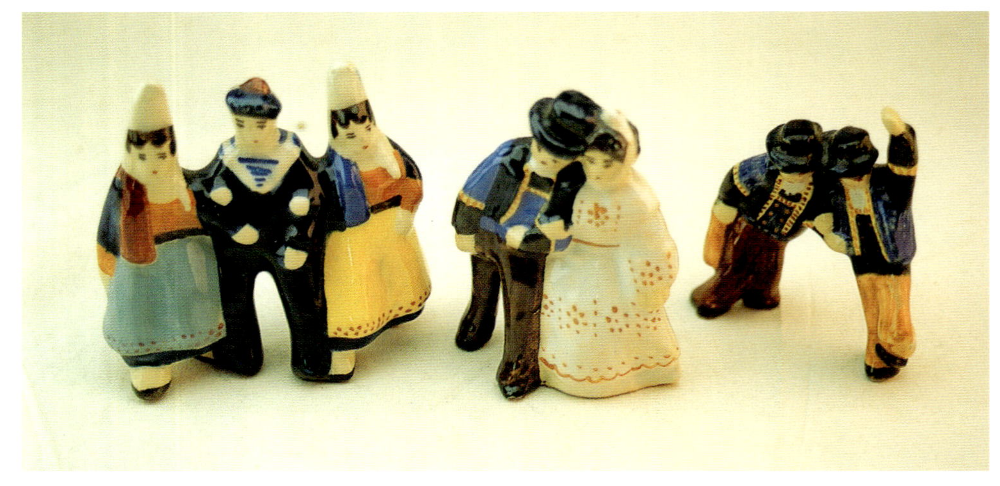

Sévellec's talent for designing figurines is evident in the many local characters he developed for his well-known *Village Breton*, considered by many to be one of his finest accomplishments. The Henriot figures of the bride and groom are 3.5" tall. The other participants are a *marin*, or sailor, with two Bretonnes, and two chaps who imbibed a bit too much. *Collection of Nancy Wyman.*

The original Sévellec map designs of Camaret, Morlaix, and Penmarc'h were translated into large ceramic works by Henri Le Phuez. Most designers did not do the actual work or décor painting, leaving it to the technicians at the faïencerie or in the workshops, called *ateliers*. Henri Le Phuez was the *Chef d'Atelier, Fantaisie Décor* for the Henriot firm from 1946 to 1977. Artists who specifically requested his services for painting or for bringing their creations to reality were Jim-Emile Sévellec, R. Micheau-Vernez, and Mathurin Méheut, among others. (*Roullot, Les Amis du Musée de la Faïence, Bulletin #4, 1996.*)

A particularly poignant story about Le Phuez concerns one of the large-scale maps he created. Le Phuez's rendering of the map designed by Adolphe-Jean Lachaud of *La Cornouaille* once graced the bus station in Quimper. It was to be saved from destruction as the old station came down for the new, but sadly it was demolished in June 1992. The destruction of this valuable piece of Quimper history generated a call for *patrimoine,* the preservation of the inheritance of Quimper ceramics. It is a lesson for us all. (*Mali, Old Quimper Review, October 1992.*)

Famous Morlaisiens

The famed naval officer Cornic, who began his life at sea at age 8 on a *corsair* (privateer), was from Morlaix, as was the author, Charles-Emile Souvestre. Edouard Corbière moved to Morlaix in the early 1840s, and his son, Edward-Joachim, whose pen name was Tristan Corbière, was born there in 1845. But the most widely known Morlaisien in Quimper collector circles is Alfred Beau.

Alfred Léopold Pascal Beau was born in Morlaix in July 1829. In 1863, he had a photography studio at 49 Rue de Bourret, and often incorporated this new artistic technique in creating paintings and ceramic works by using some of his photographs as models. He was skilled in sketching, watercolors, and oils, as well as ceramic décor, and was influenced by Michel Bouquet, the noted painter and ceramicist who had an *atelier* near Roscoff. Beau joined the Porquier firm, forming a partnership with the widow of Clet-Adolphe Porquier in the early 1870s, which continued until the middle 1890s. Also, Beau served as the Director of the *Musée des Beaux Arts* in Quimper from 1878 until his death in 1907. (*Les Amis du Musée de la Faïence, Bulletin #5*, and *Château de Quintin Exposition Catalogue, p. 4.*)

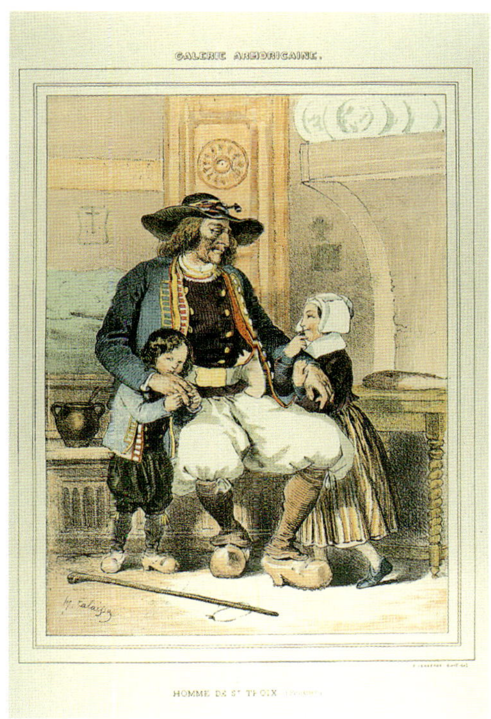

Alfred Beau's rendition of the Breton peasants was influenced by Lalaisse's *Galerie Armoricaine,* which featured costumes native to various villages throughout Brittany. This illustration by Lalaisse is *Homme de St. Thoix,* a gentleman of St. Thoix with children. *Authors' Collection.*

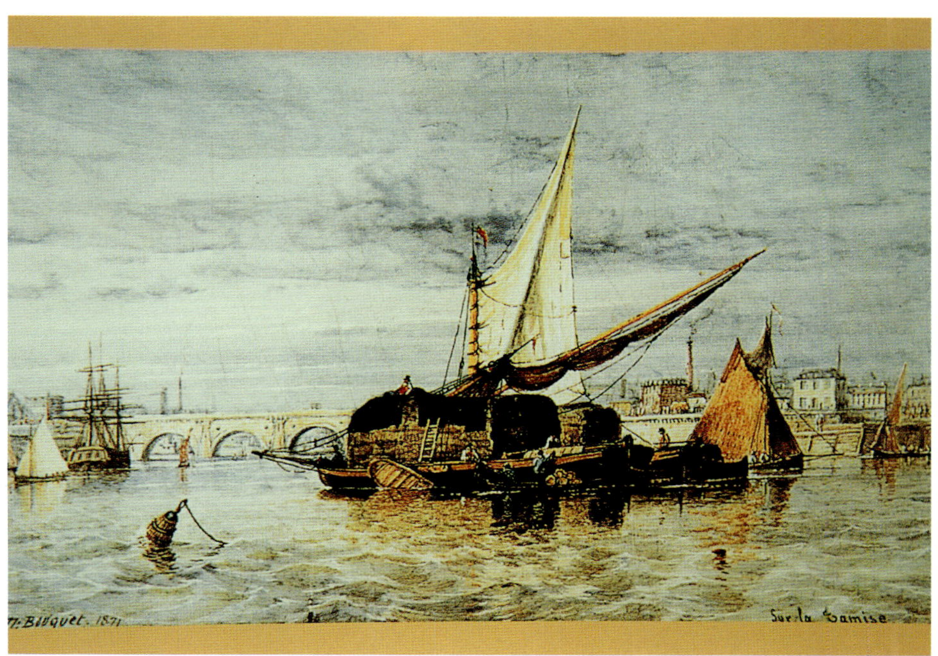

Left:
The artist Michel Bouquet is thought to have influenced Alfred Beau. Bouquet's technique is shown in this scene entitled *Sur la Tamise,* which was painted on faïence by Bouquet in 1871. *Courtesy of Thierry & Lannon, Douarnenez and Brest.*

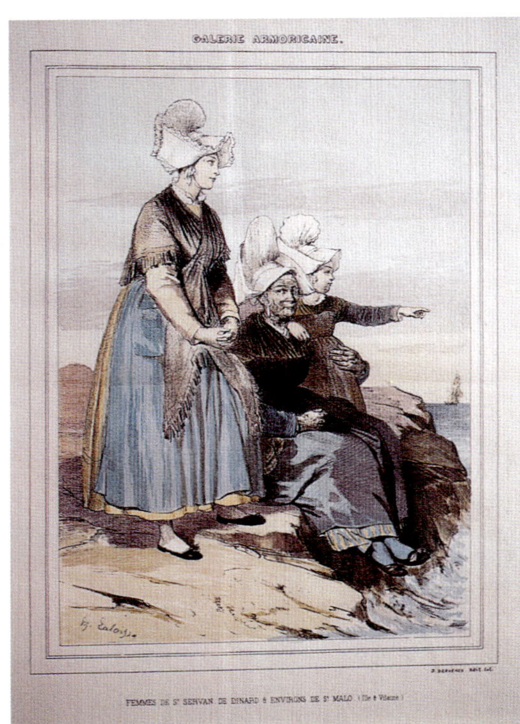

The Romantic era was reflected in the subject and treatment of paintings and other artworks in France. Here, Lalaisse presents a romanticized look at the *Femmes de St. Servan, de Dinard & Environs de St. Malo,* three generations of women from the northern coast of Brittany. *Authors' Collection.*

Alfred Beau was instrumental in promoting the Breton people as a colorful and charming folk in faïence. Beau's interest in preserving the peasant heritage of *Bretagne* was inspired by his father-in-law, Emile Souvestre's *Les Derniers Bretons* and *Foyer Breton.* Also credited among Beau's influences are Olivier Perrin's *Galerie Bretonne,* and its reissue, *Breiz-Izel,* and François Hippolyte Lalaisse's *Galerie Armoricaine. (Mali, pp. 38-40.)*

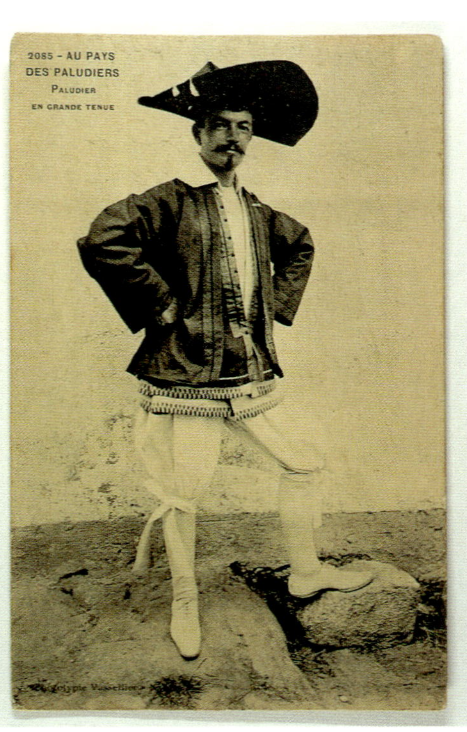

Right:
The same costume is echoed in a late 19th century postcard. The town (*bourg*) of Batz is on the Guérande peninsula, southwest of Vannes. Area salt marshes were harvested for their bounty by *paludiers,* who certainly dressed with flair. *Authors' Collection.*

This Beau rendition, based on Lalaisse's work, shows life in Brittany more than 100 years ago, when begging was part of the fabric of life for those less fortunate. A woman and child from Quéménéven are shown begging on this 9.25" diameter plate, signed PB. Note the border décor is green acanthus, or scrolling foliage, on a yellow background. Many color combinations appear on *décor riche* works in this period. *Collection of Pierre Breton, Art de Cornouaille, Quimper.*

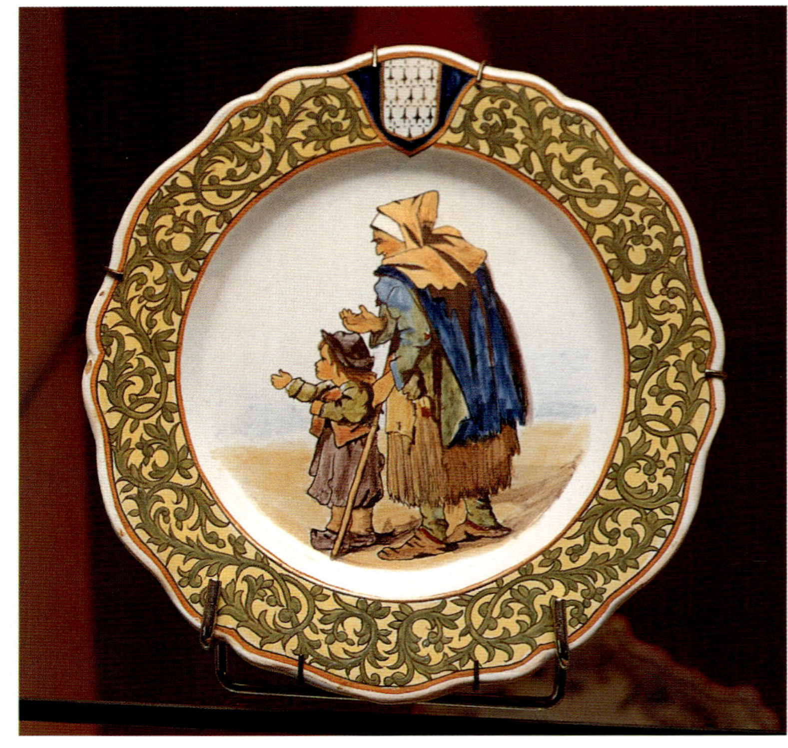

The *fête* costume from Batz, not to be confused with the *Île de Batz,* is seen in the *Galerie Armoricaine* print by Lalaisse. *Authors' Collection.*

Primarily a designer for the Porquier faïencerie, he created *scènes Bretonnes* and *légendes Bretonnes*, in keeping with the Romantic era's idealization of the past. His efforts immortalized in faïence the distinctive dress, customs, and culture of the different regions, villages and towns of earlier times in *Bretagne*. Beau's contributions to the subject matter and quality of renditions on Quimper faïence are stellar. Additional Beau works on display at the *Manoir Kérazan* may be seen in the Chapter *Environs de Quimper*.

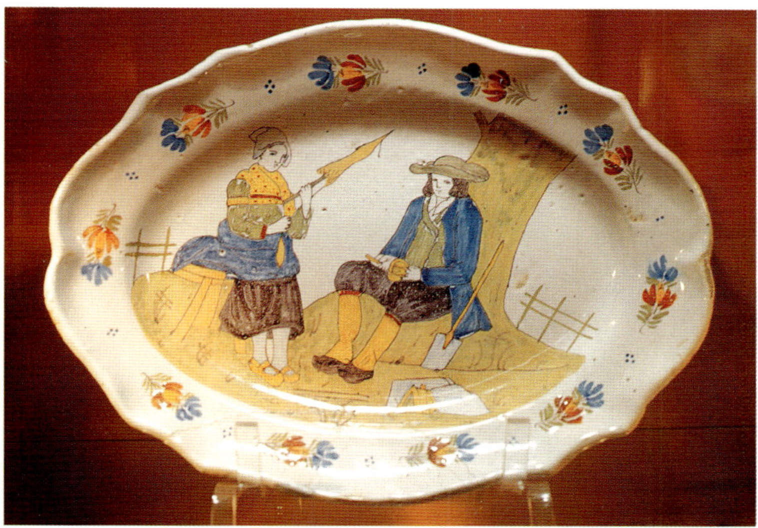

Alfred Beau's designs were a much more sophisticated approach to the original *petit Breton* motif, which often is the novice's introduction to Quimper poterie. In contrast, the rendition of the subject matter on this early Breton scene platter by the HB faïencerie is naïve in execution. *Courtesy of Musée de la Faïence, Quimper.*

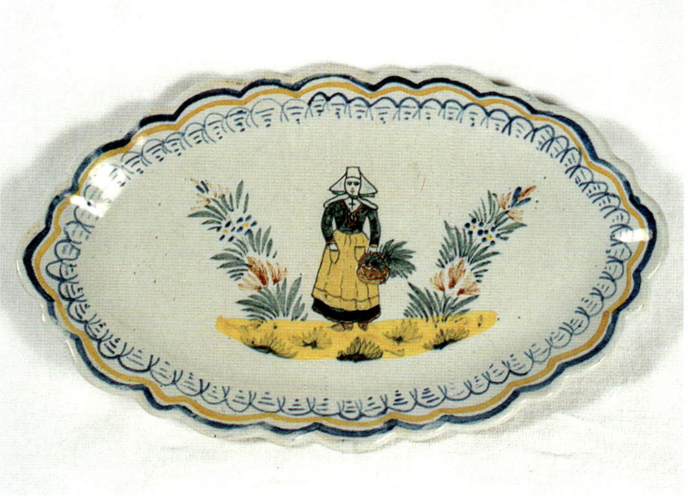

Henriot is the maker of this c. 1900 platter, signed HR, which features a sweet Bretonne. While it is very attractive with many unique accents, it doesn't have the detailed touch of Beau's *scènes Bretonnes*. But it is lovely, n'est-ce pas? *Courtesy of A. W. Styer.*

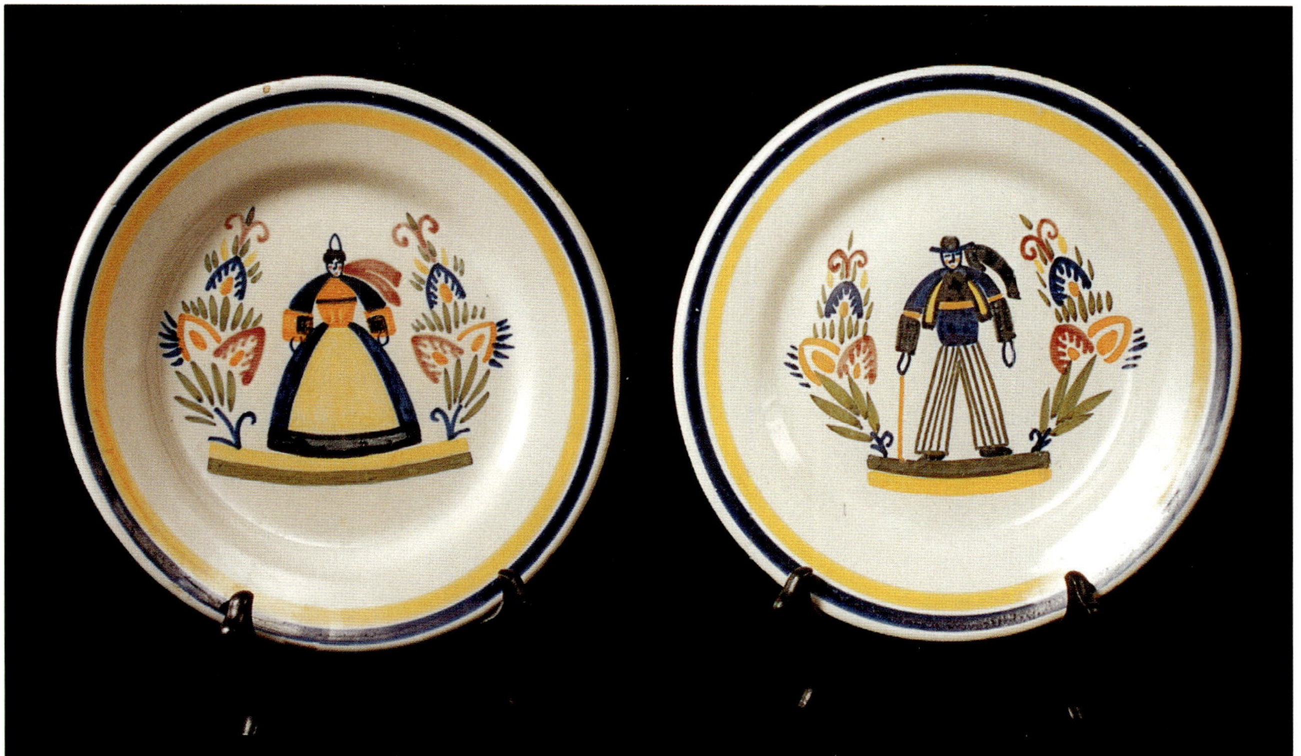

Art Deco influences are seen in these two 8.25" plates by Henriot, which are part of a dessert set from the 1930s. The *petit Breton* graduated into the modern age, with angular, clean lines and bold styling. *Private Collection.*

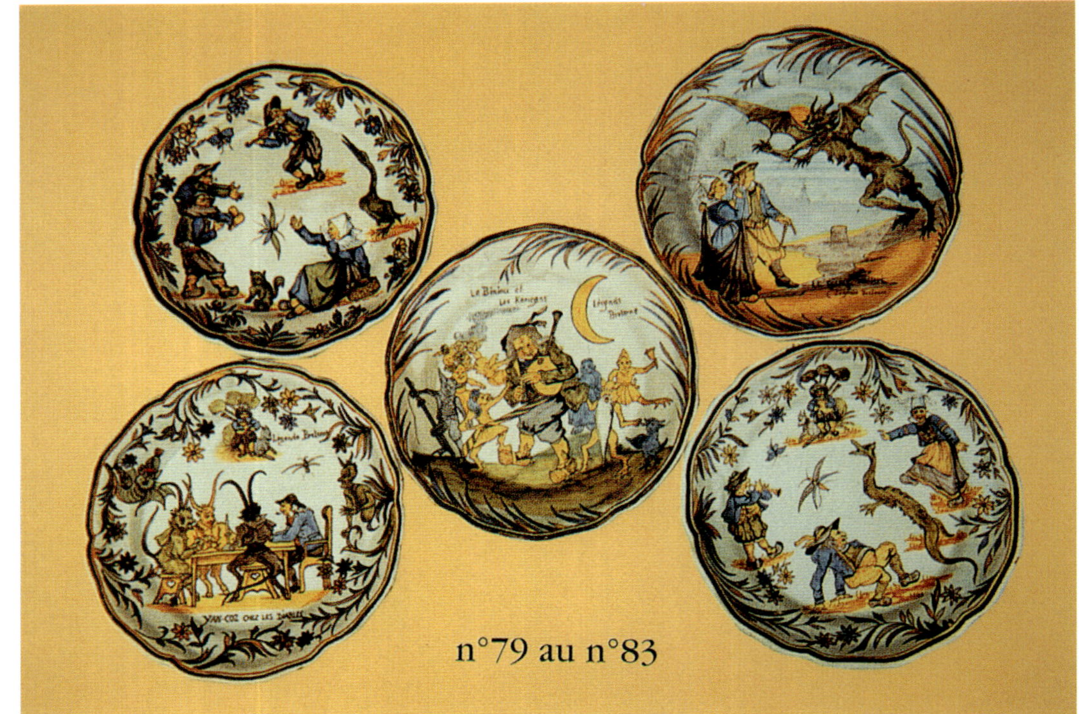

Beau's *légendes Bretonnes* portrayals reflected the *Dernier Breton* stories of his father-in-law, Souvestre. Among the legend plates here: *Le Biniou et les Korigans*, or The Bagpiper and the Goblins; *Yan Coz chez les Diables*, or Old Jean among the Devils; and *Le Diable Trompé*, or the Devil Deceives. *Courtesy of Thierry & Lannon, Douarnenez & Brest.*

Musée des Jacobins

About two blocks from the Queen Anne House is the *Musée des Jacobins*. We spent more time in this museum, absorbing its beauty, than the total time one person suggested for the entire town! Our visit was delightful, as we explored the paintings, sculptures, furniture, and other Breton memorabilia. We chatted with a curator who gave first-hand information about the history of the museum, as well as the town and its cultural heritage and historical figures.

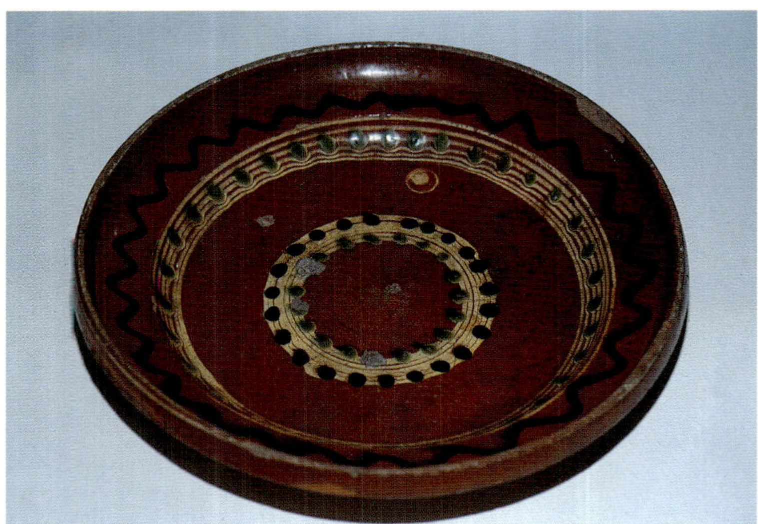
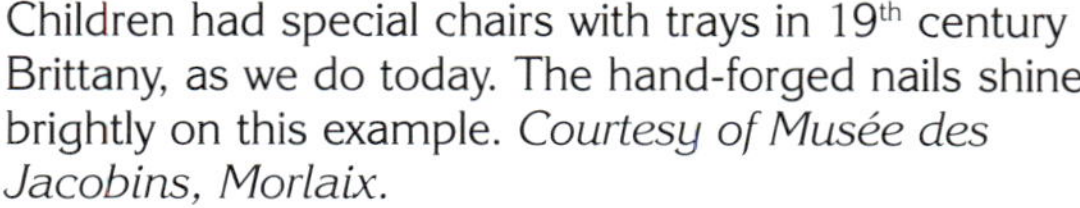

A 19th century unsigned earthenware bowl of Quimper manufacture has yellow, black and dark-green slip décor (*engobe*) over the clay-colored base. *Courtesy of Musée des Jacobins, Morlaix.*

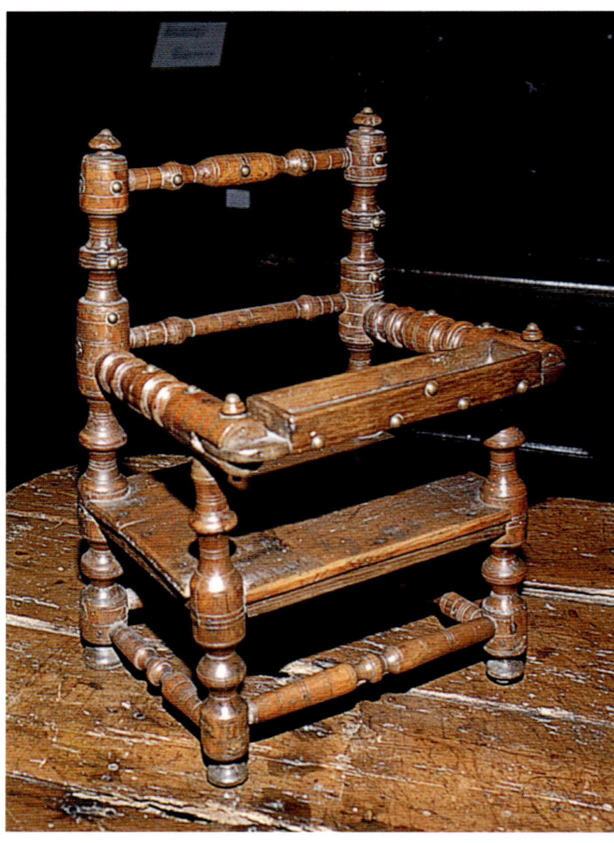

Children had special chairs with trays in 19th century Brittany, as we do today. The hand-forged nails shine brightly on this example. *Courtesy of Musée des Jacobins, Morlaix.*

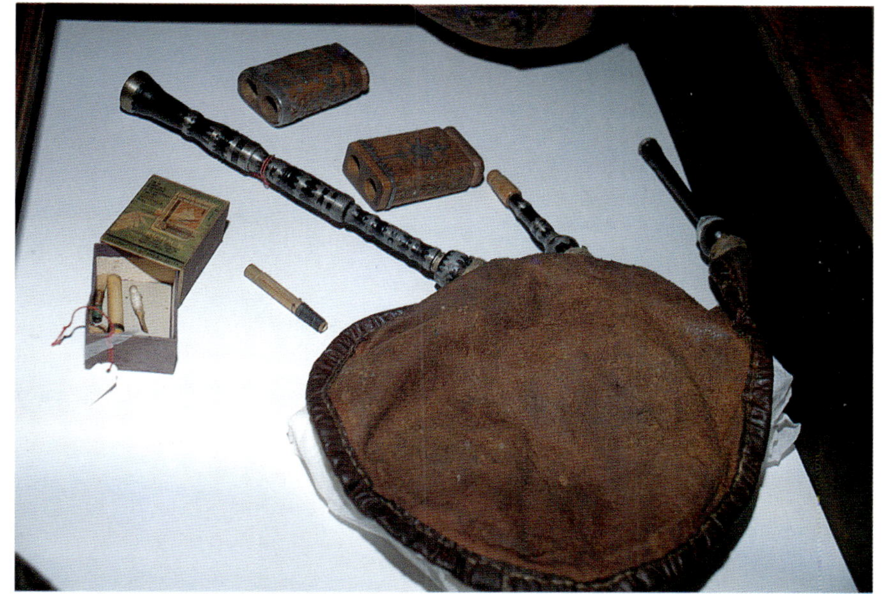

This was our first look at an early *biniou*, the Breton bagpipe, after seeing so many renditions of *biniou* players on Quimper faïence. *Courtesy of Musée des Jacobins, Morlaix.*

Housed in a 13th century Church of the Jacobins adjacent to an ancient convent, the *Musée* has a magnificent 15th century *rosace*, or rose window. There are fabulous Breton paintings, both old and modern, as well as local archeological items, life-sized wooden religious sculptures, and 17th century furniture from the *Léonais* region. We were enchanted by works from Courbet and Monet, as well as scenes of Brittany by Morlaisiens Le Guennec, Penther, Pascal, and Puyo.

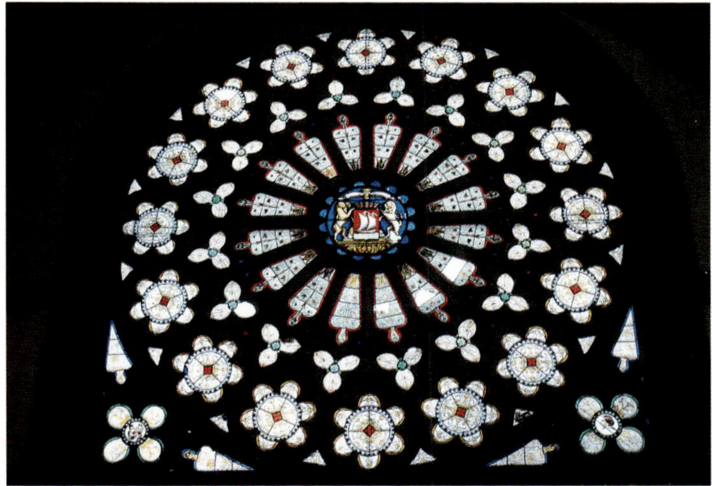

The *Musée des Jacobins'* remarkable rose window, which has survived from the 15th century, was covered with wood to protect it from bombing and gunfire during World War II.

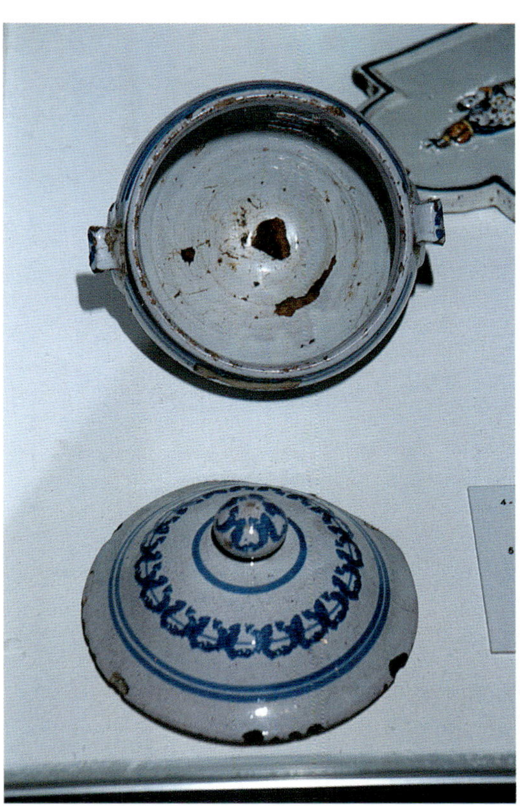

A mid-19th century Quimper *petite soupière* (small covered soup tureen) resides at the museum in Morlaix. *Courtesy of Musée des Jacobins, Morlaix.*

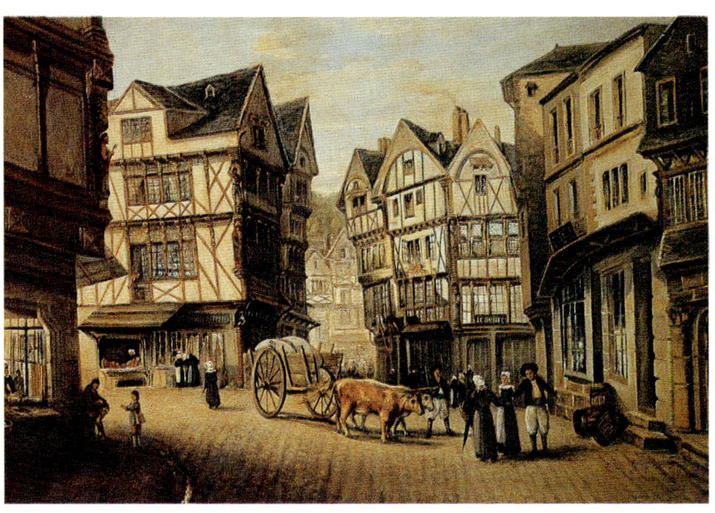

Local painter Edmond Puyo rendered a charming early scene of Morlaix in 1815. Puyo is one of many local artists whose works are displayed in the museum. *Courtesy of Musée des Jacobins, Morlaix.*

Also, there were Quimper items and even a *biniou,* the Breton bagpipe. Most important to us was a remarkable settee done in the *pyrogravé* technique by Paul Fouillen. Again, by taking time to look more closely at Brittany, we found more Quimper and related items that we would have missed.

Paul Maurice Fouillen, Quimper artist of unique talent, worked for the HB faïencerie during the 1920s. While at HB, Fouillen served first as a decorator, then as *atelier* director. He created several distinct décors, and his designs for the *grès* ware art poterie, Odetta, were an important contribution to the positive reception received by the HB display at the 1925 *Arts Décoratifs Exposition* in Paris. Fouillen moved into his own studio on *Place Styvel* in 1929, and made woodenware and other objects decorated with the pyrogravure technique. After World War II, Fouillen added electric kilns and made faïence and *grès* products in modern motifs.

During the artistic revolution of the 1890s, French artist Henri Riviére experimented with colored woodcuts of Breton scenes. (LePaul, p. 136.) Quimper poterie artists most certainly were influenced by the innovations of the Post-Impressionists of Pont-Aven and other coastal towns in Brittany. Perhaps Fouillen and Ar Seiz Breur artists were taken with Riviére's work.

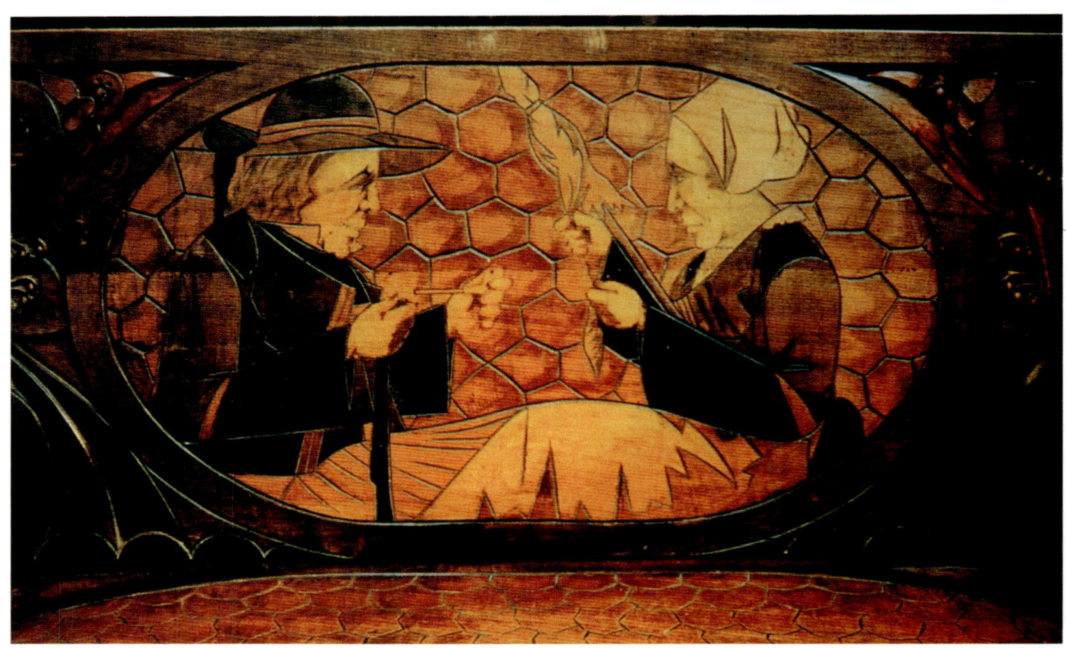

An excellent example of Fouillen's *décor pyrogravé* greeted us on the second floor of the *Musée des Jacobins.* Furniture with the *décor pyrogravé,* such as *salle á mangers,* or dining room sets, and armoires, chairs, and benches, like the one in the museum, are highly prized by collectors. (For additional examples, see *M. Fouillen et al, p. 53.) Courtesy of Musée des Jacobins, Morlaix.*

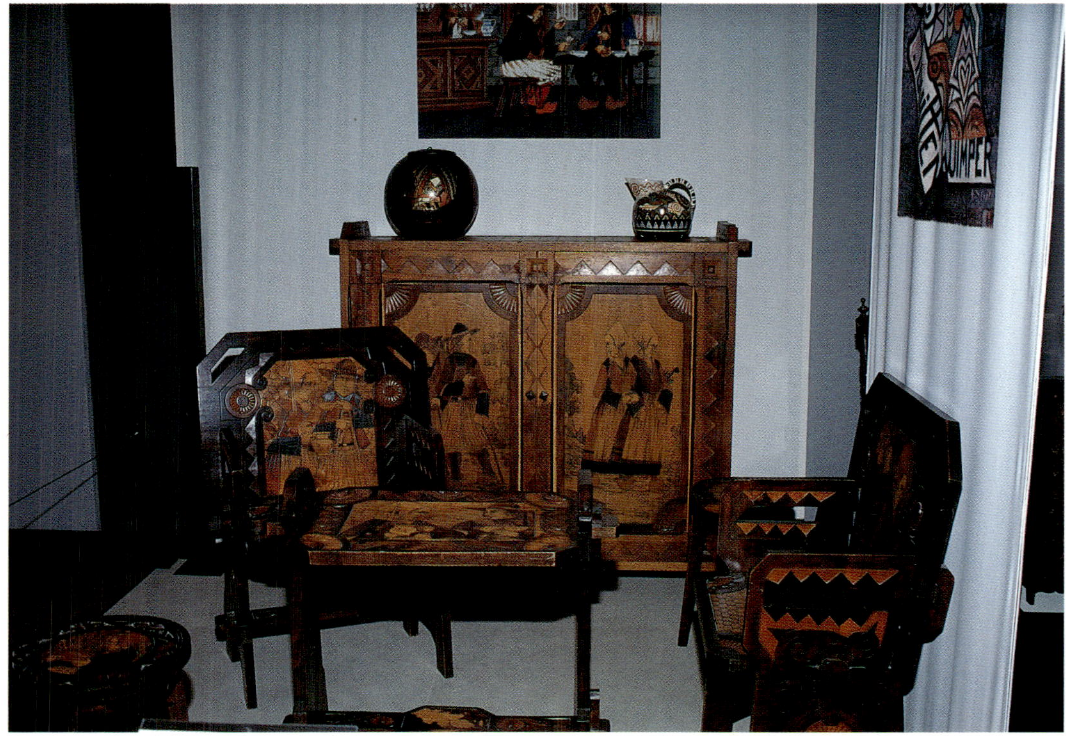

The *Musée Départemental Breton* displayed an entire room of Fouillen's *pyrogravé* furniture in the winter of 2001. A Paul Fouillen pitcher and vase are on the *pyrogravé décor* buffet. *Courtesy of Musée Départemental Breton, Quimper.*

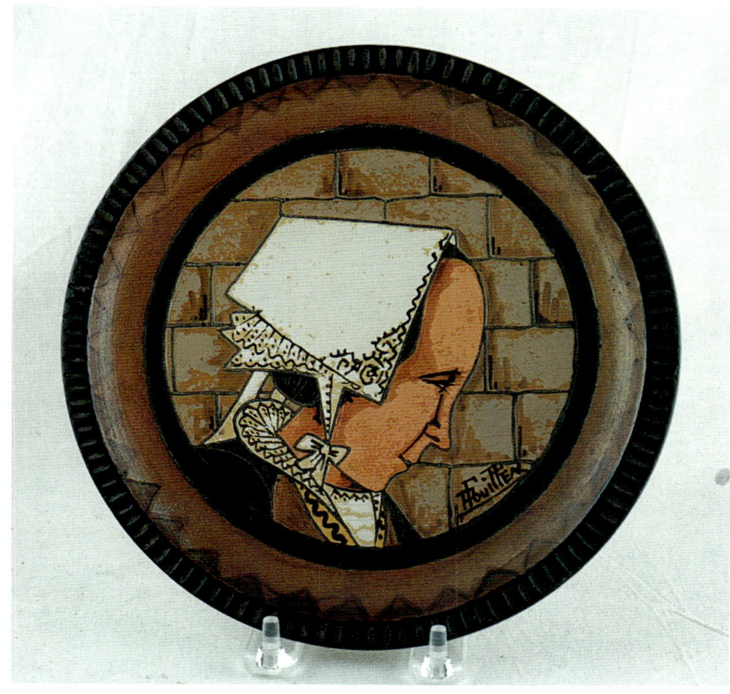

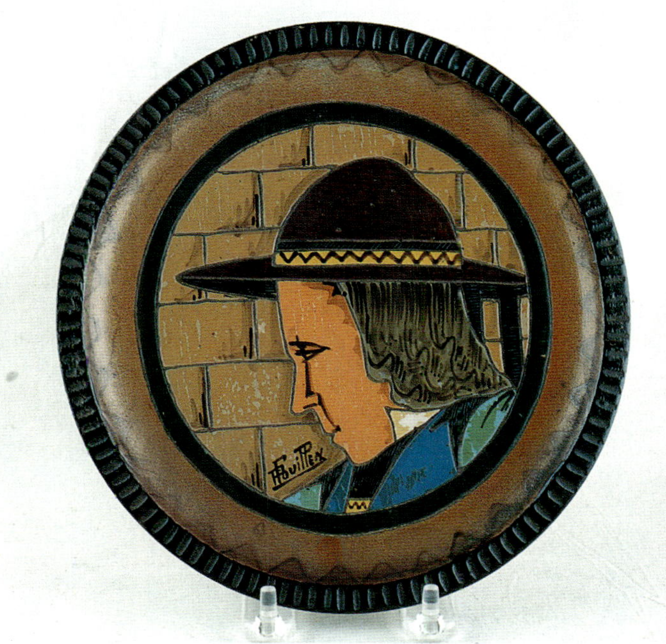

The Bretonne's mate also shows the Paul Fouillen touch. Influences from the Book of Kells and Breton embroidery work merged with Art Deco design elements in Fouillen's work, and brought a more modern look to the *petit Breton*. *Private Collection.*

Fouillen's touch on this 8" diameter *pyrogravé* plate is everywhere, from the tilted, profiled head, to the stone wall background, and of course, the signature, PFouillen. *Private Collection.*

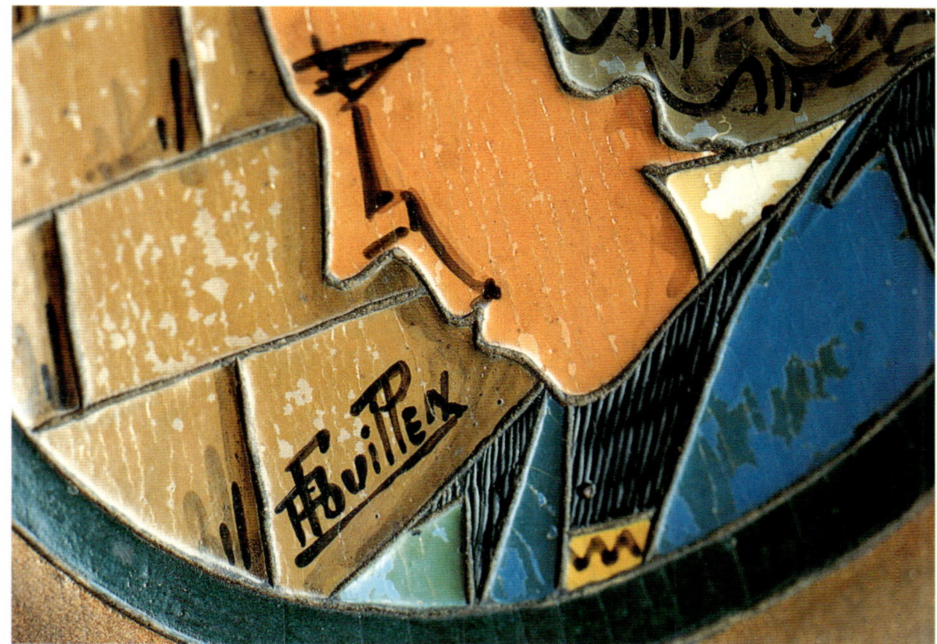

A close look at the PFouillen signature on the front of the *pyrogravé* plates. *Private Collection.*

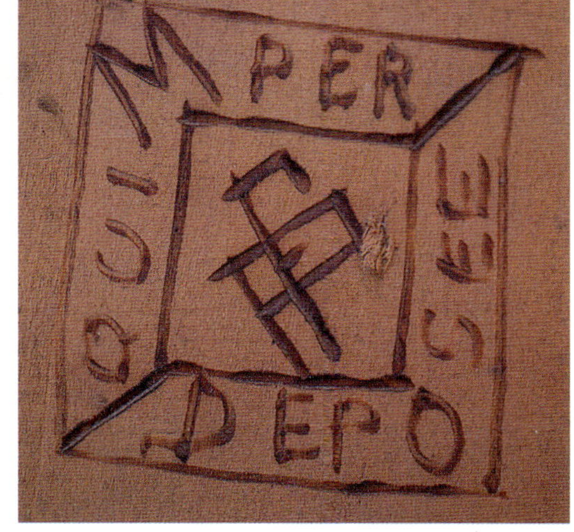

The PFouillen stamp was used on the back of the woodenware manufactured in his own *atelier* on *Place Styvel. Private Collection.*

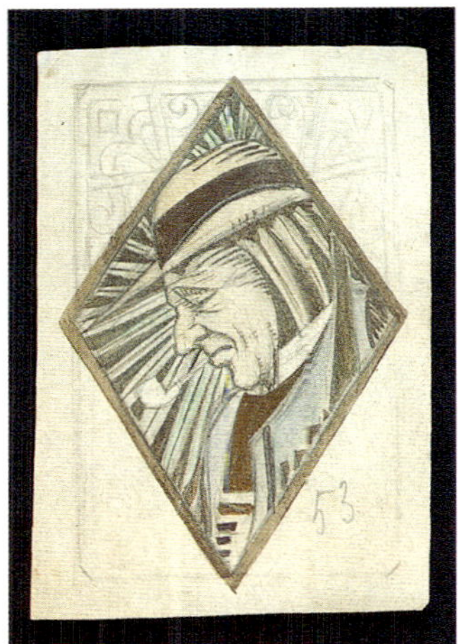

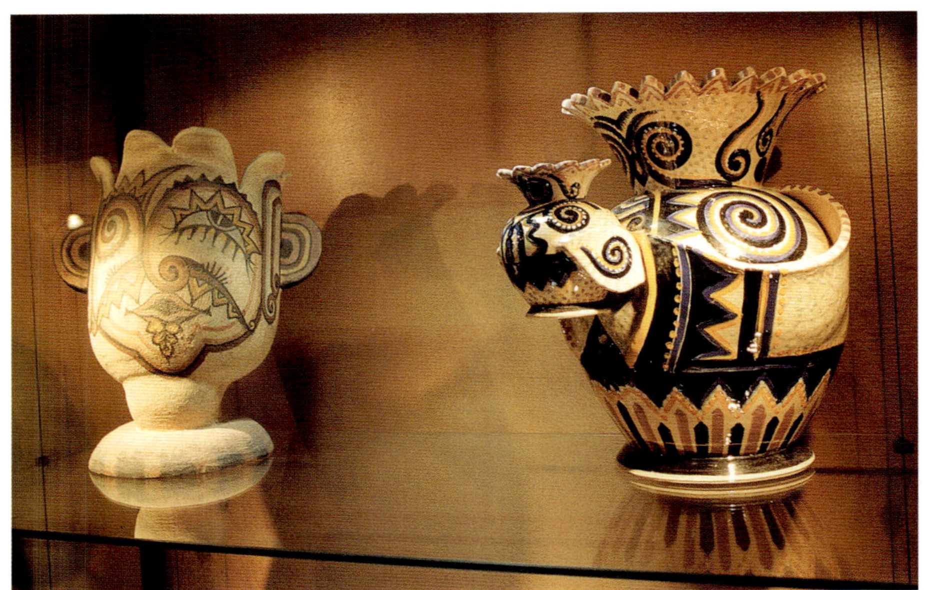

Fouillen did this 7" long sketch in pencil and pen between 1922 and 1929, according to his son, Maurice Fouillen. The sketch demonstrates the angular lines and tilted-head pose for which Paul Fouillen is famous. *Courtesy of Carter Yeatman.*

Zoomorphic and anthropomorphic forms were Fouillen's 1950s specialty. *Courtesy of the Musée de la Faïence, Quimper.*

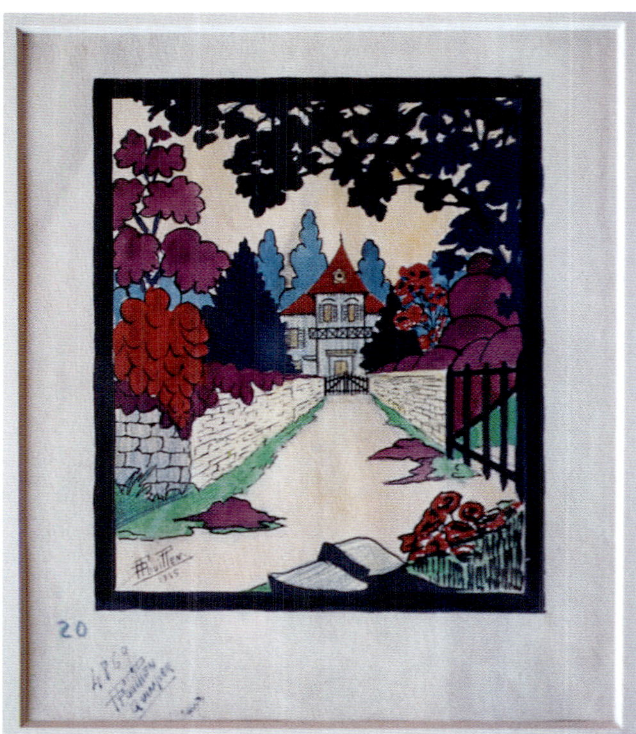

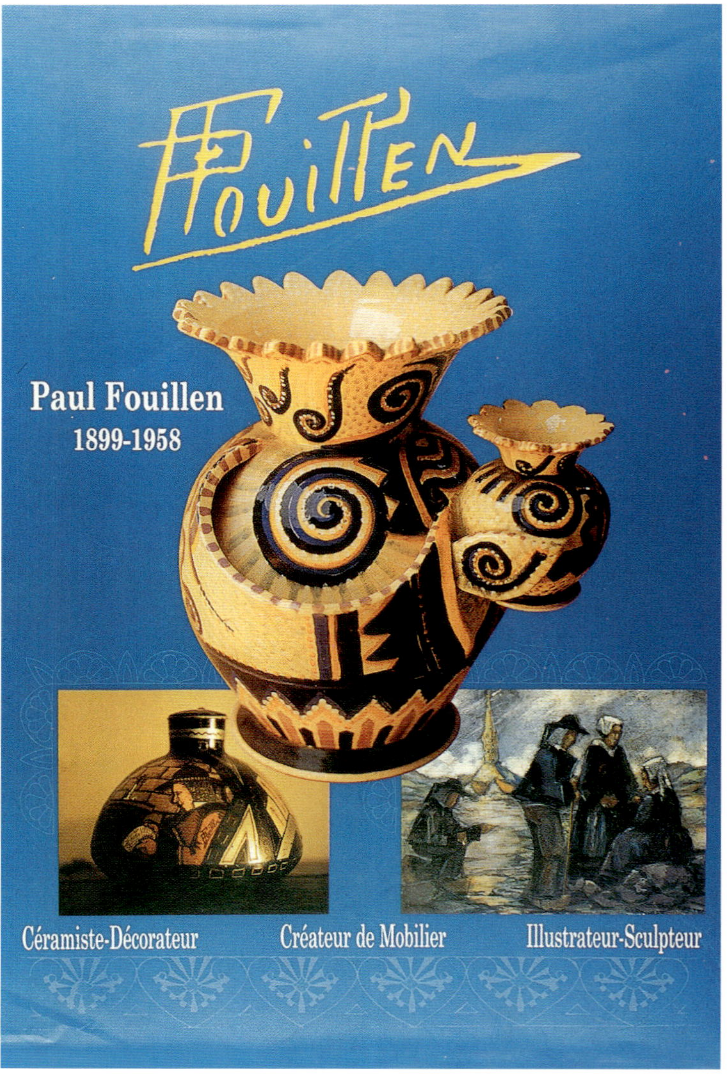

Another Fouillen artwork is in bold colors and lines of the Art Deco period, while focusing on the warm thoughts of a comfortable home. It measures 5" by 6", and is signed PFouillen, 1925. *Authors' Collection.*

The 100th Anniversary of Fouillen's birth was celebrated in 1999 with the publication of the book, *PFouillen*, written by his son, Maurice, with Sévère and Theallet. One of the final pages has the quote: *Le Triskele, la Flamme, et le Coeur … L'esprit Fouillen,* above a plate with a *triskele* design by Paul Fouillen. The Celtic-Breton *triskele* spins on. (Fouillen, Sévère, Theallet, p. 136.)

Our visit to the *Musée* was further enhanced by works from Quimper artist, pupil and friend of Mathurin Méheut, Yvonne Jean-Haffen. An exhibition featuring her work entitled *Finistère* was held in 1997, and the catalogue introduced us to the range of her genius. Before our visit to Morlaix we knew Yvonne Jean-Haffen for her *Potiers Bretons*, a remarkable depiction of the steps for making Quimper poterie. The work stands nearly 6 feet high and won a gold medal while part of the Henriot display at the 1937 *Exhibition Universelle* in Paris. It now resides at *Le Musée de la Faïence* in Quimper and can be seen in the Chapter *On to Quimper.*

The Morlaix Auction Action

When in Morlaix we frequent the *Hôtel d'Europe,* built in the 1890s. It is *the* place to stay if you want to be in the center of the old town and close to the auction house. It has ornately carved paneling in the lobby and marvelous ambience overall. Many attendees of the Oriot & Dupont Auction, formerly Boscher & Oriot, meet in the restaurant adjacent to the hotel prior to the sale.

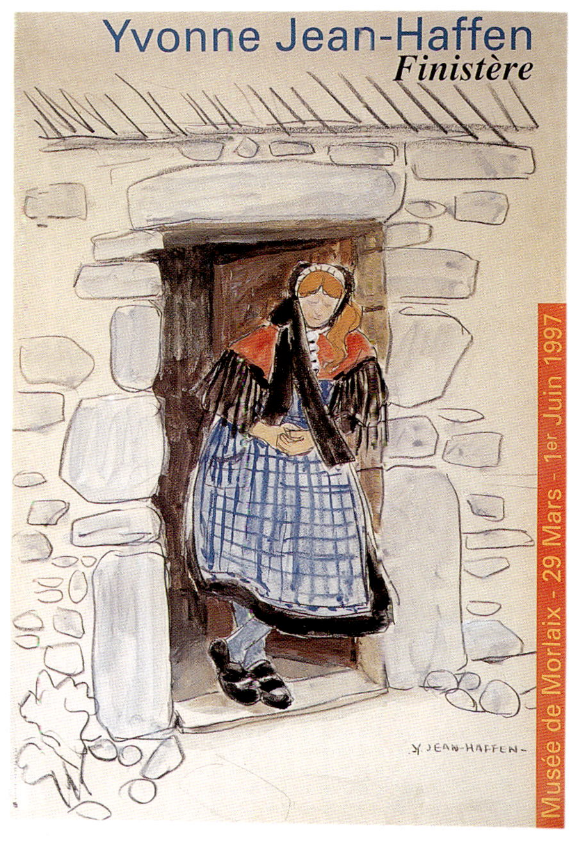

Yvonne Jean-Haffen, a pupil and friend of artist Mathurin Méheut, had a retrospective of her paintings at the *Musée des Jacobins* in 1999. *Courtesy of Musée des Jacobins, Morlaix.*

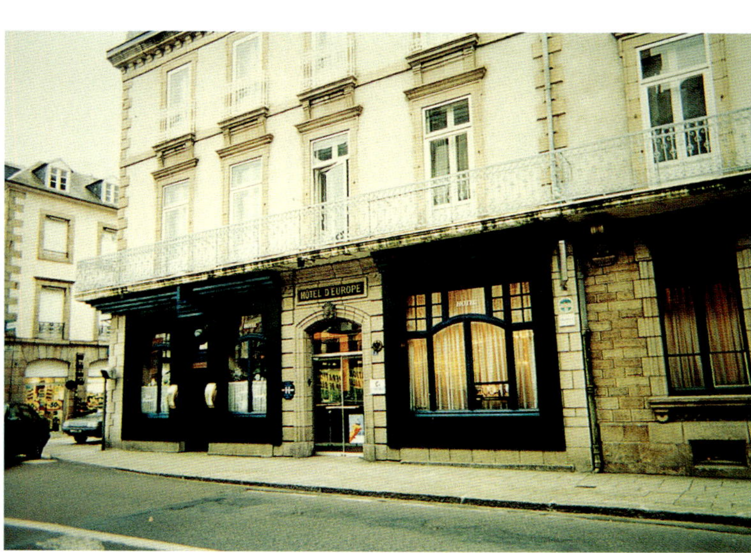

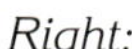

The *Hôtel d'Europe* and an adjoining restaurant are in the heart of old town Morlaix, and within five minutes of the auction house of Oriot & Dupont. Both the accommodations and repast are superb. *Courtesy of Hôtel d'Europe, Morlaix.*

Right:
A restaurant connected to the *Hôtel d'Europe* surprised us with two large paintings by Louis Garin, noted *HB/Grande Maison* artist of the 1920s-1930s. *Courtesy of Hôtel d'Europe, Morlaix.*

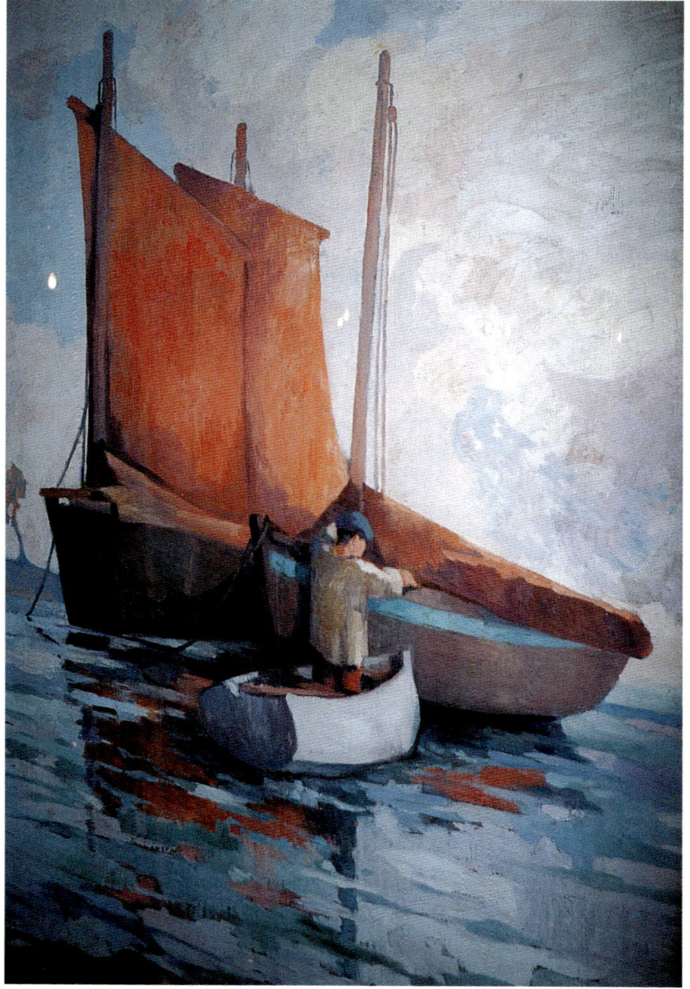

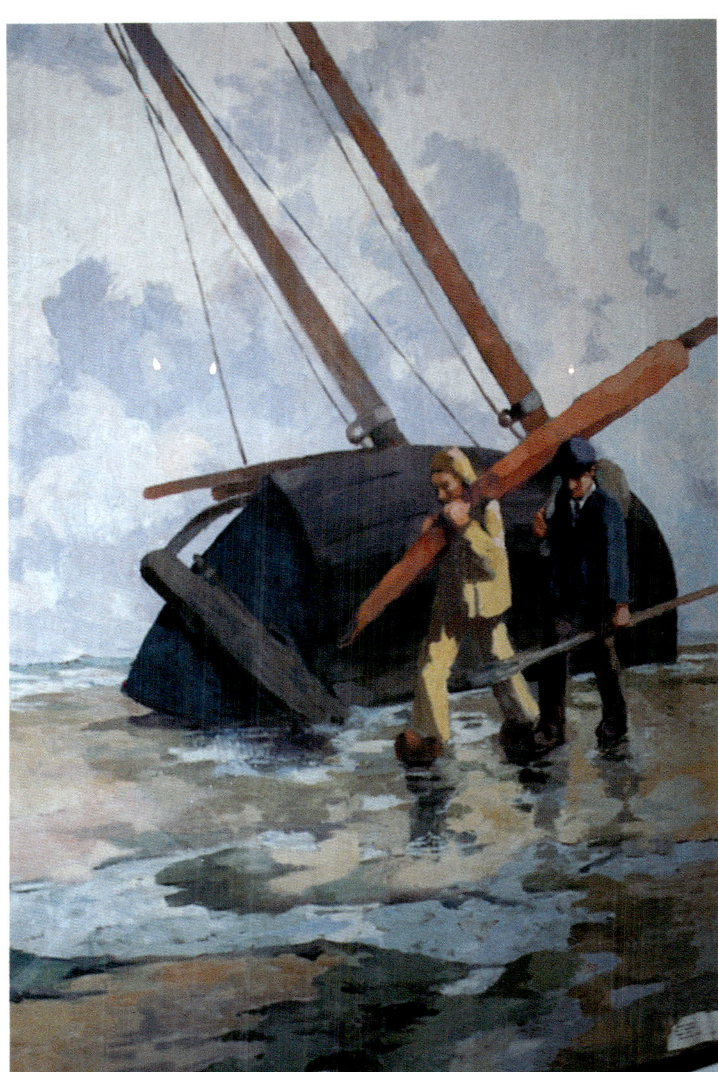

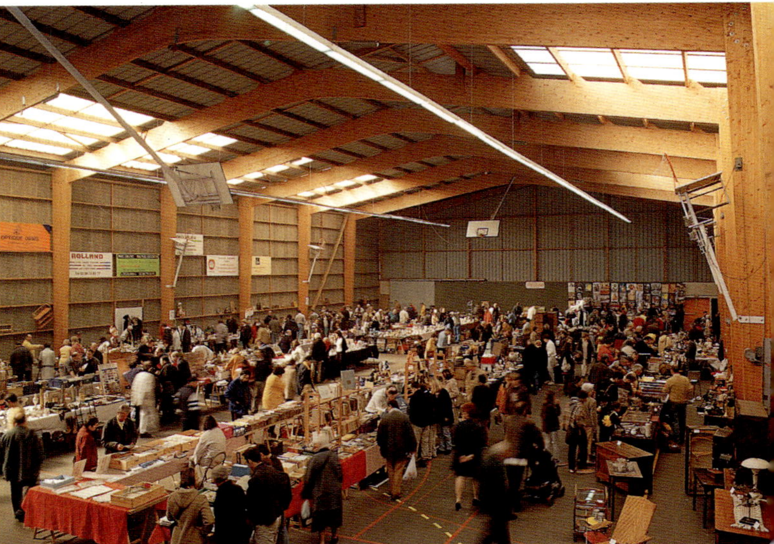

The same weekend as the Quimper auction of Easter 2000, a flea
market and an antiques show were held within 25 kilometers of
Morlaix. Plouigneau was a crowded bazaar with over 100 vendors set
up in a community center.

The auction house, located at 37-39 Rue de Paris, is a five-minute
walk from the town hall and the *Hôtel d'Europe.* A stranger could pass
by the plain wooden doors with battleship gray paint and never know it
was there. The construction is typically French, a storefront *façade* with
a large door to allow vehicle entry to a concealed courtyard, which has
been covered over to make a hall.

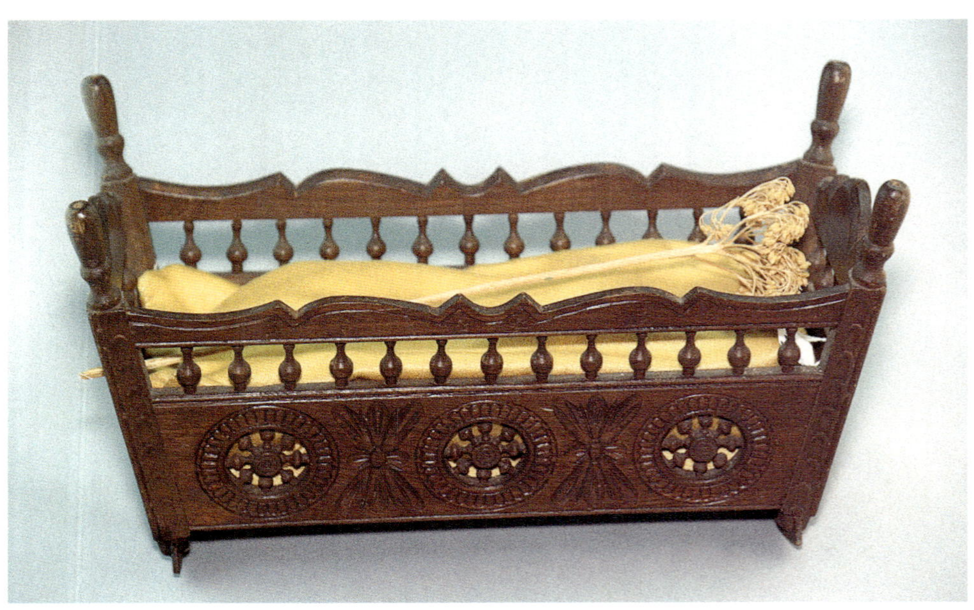

We purchased a Plozévet doll cradle
from the 1920s at the flea market in
Plouigneau. Plozévet is a town about
35 kilometers west of Quimper, where
doll and child-sized Breton furniture
was made beginning in the late 1800s.
The doll cradle is 14" long. *Authors'
Collection.*

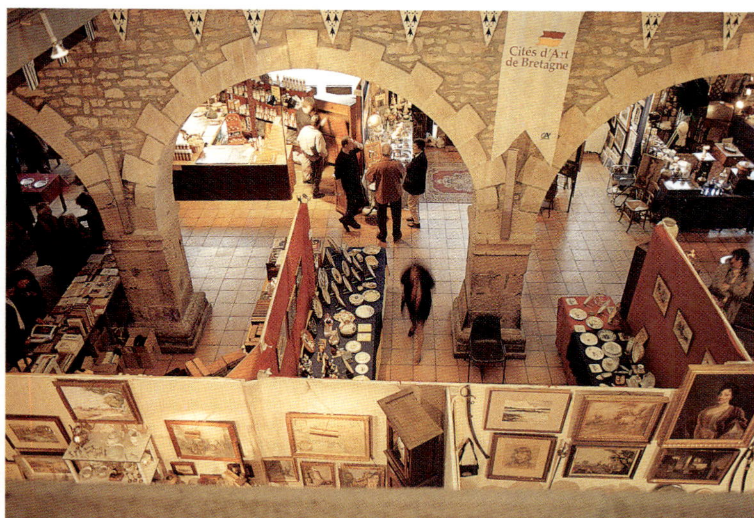

In Guerlesquin, the antiques fair was a smaller but more upscale affair, with wine and cheese served to patrons as they browsed. Several dealers specializing in Quimper displayed some exceptional wares.

Right:
We purchased an unsigned 13.5" diameter AP or HB charger at the Guerlesquin antiques fair from husband and wife Parisian dealers. Note the treatment of the flowers as blue-sponged circles, and the design of the Breton, determining factors in defining this as an early example. *(Bondhus, p. 34, and Verlingue, p. 31.) Private Collection.*

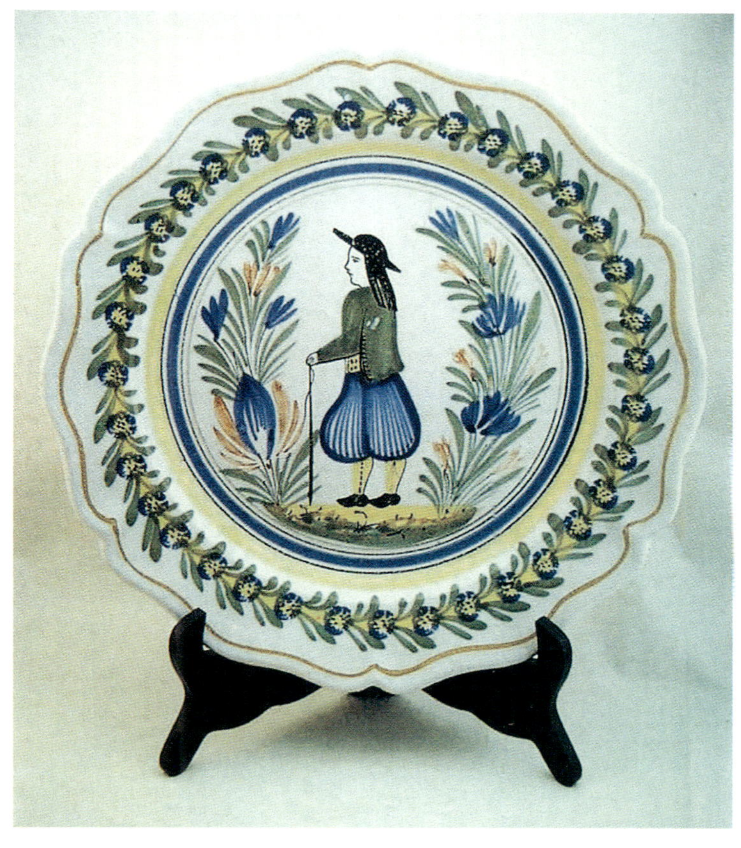

In addition to the regular scheduled auctions at Oriot & Dupont, special auctions of Quimper poterie have been held three times a year. These Quimper auctions usually offer an estate collection, as well as various consignment pieces, and they bring customers from throughout France, the rest of Europe, England, and the United States.

We decided to attend the *Vente de Pâques,* or Easter auction in 2000, which featured items from the estate of Robert Henriot, who with his brother, Joseph, was co-director of the Henriot establishment from 1927-1959. R. Henriot's widow, Marie-Paule Leberre, was over 100 when she died, and two of her estate's 21 listings were to bring the highest bids of the day.

The rare *Lampadaire de Salon,* decorated in the *Italo-Nivernais* style, brought 62,000F (nearly $9,000), or 22,000F higher than predicted. The *Grand Tête de Soudanaise* by Emile Monier brought 58,000F (over $8,200), or 28,000F more than expected. The exchange rate was about 7 French francs per U.S. dollar at the time, and the prices do not reflect the nearly 11 percent buyer's premium charged by the auction house.

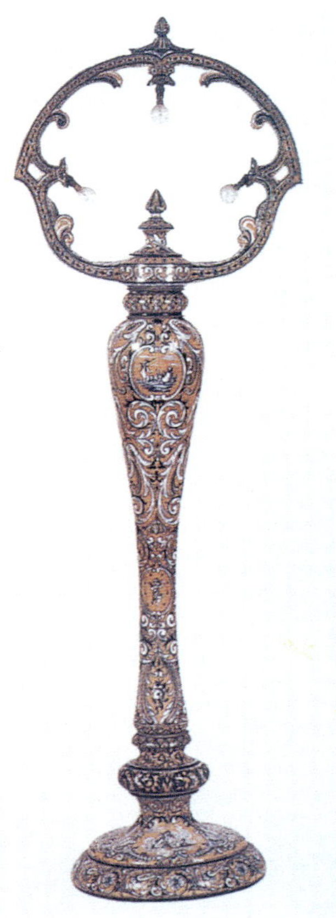

Right:
The Henriot *Lampadaire de Salon,* in the *Italo-Nivernais* style, was from the Robert Henriot estate and brought the highest price of the day, 62,000F, or nearly $9,000, with the exchange rate of about 7 French francs to the U.S. dollar at the time. It stands 75" high and is second quarter of the 20th century. *(See similar example in Bondhus, p. 192.) Courtesy of Oriot & Dupont, Morlaix.*

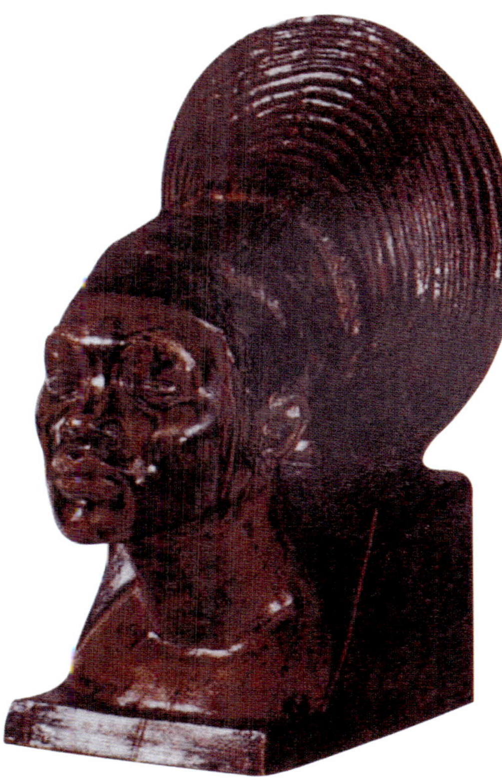

Le Grand Tête de Soudanaise, 18.25" tall, by Emile Monier, brought the second-highest price at the auction, at 58,000F, or over $8,000, not including the buyer's premium. We had just seen an example of this *Tête* made for the 1931 Colonial Exposition, at the *Musée de la Faïence* in Quimper. (See *Trois Siècles de Faïences*, p. 153 and *Rotté and Verlingue*, p. 28.) *Courtesy of Oriot & Dupont, Morlaix.*

A 9.75" x 6" catalogue, partially in color, described in detail each of the 249 Quimper lots and was mailed to interested parties about a month prior to the auction. It also was available for 50F during the previews, which were held for three days prior to the sale. Descriptions of the listings were accurate, clear, and concise, being authored by Michel Roullot, Quimper expert and noted author. As with important auctions, each item carried a range of expected value.

The time allotted for Quimper was about 3 hours, before going on to the silver and furniture items. The auctioneers were assisted by nine people who held items, labeled them with the buyer's number, ran for payments, worked the telephones, and recorded sales on computers. The auction has the reputation for selling high-dollar Quimper, and it certainly deserves it. Most lots went higher than expected. If they did not, either auctioneer would pronounce, *un cadeau,* a gift! Only 12 of the 249 Quimper lots did not sell.

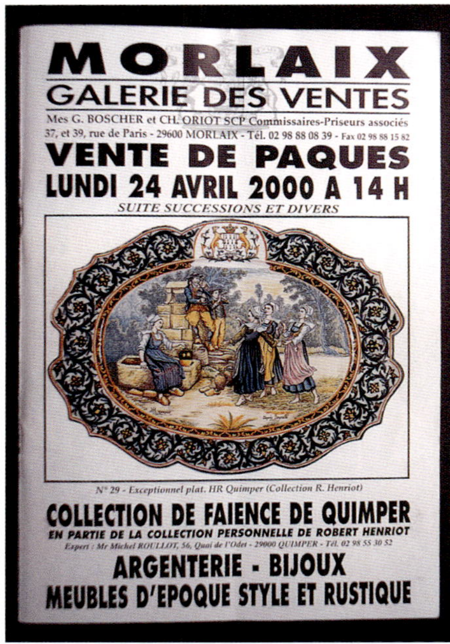

The Morlaix auction of Oriot & Dupont is known for selling quality faïence at healthy prices. Several special auctions presenting Quimper from estates and private sources are held each year and are closely watched by Quimper collectors and dealers. *Courtesy of Oriot & Dupont, Morlaix.*

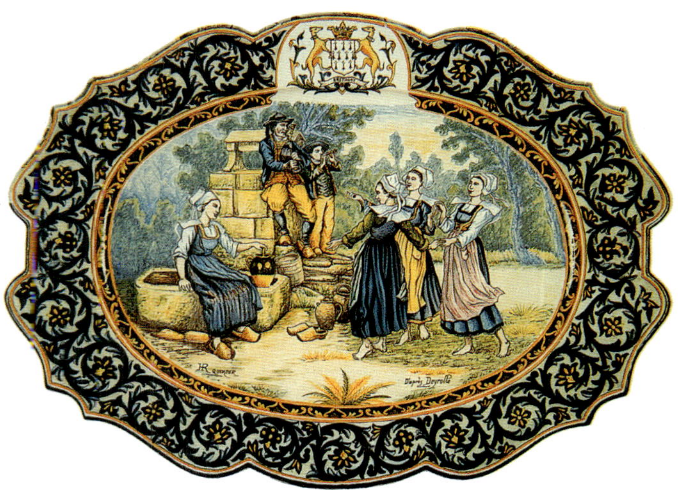

The Henriot platter featured on the cover of the 2000 *Vente de Pâques* auction in Morlaix brought 36,000F, or $5,538, not including buyer's premium. It was part of the R. Henriot collection, was 26" long, and signed HR Quimper, *Après Deyrolle*. The scene shows young Bretonnes dancing at a well. *Courtesy of Oriot & Dupont, Morlaix.*

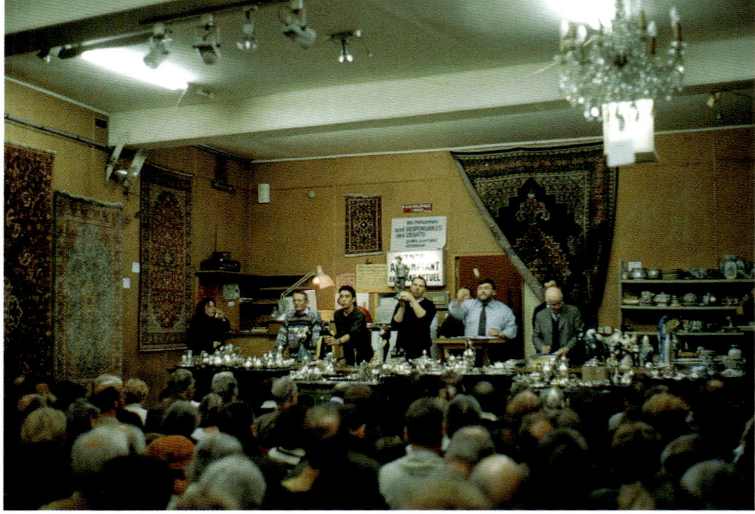

The auction hall was crowded and warm, the reserved seats filled early, and the balance stood in the back. Nine people assisted the auctioneers by holding items, giving out numbers and collecting money or checks from winning bidders, taking telephone bids, processing left bids, and tallying sales. Auction rules required buyers to pay for the first item won with French francs or a guaranteed check drawn on a French bank.

A French auction differs from most in the states in that the winning bidder must pay for the item right away. The Morlaix auction has combined the French method with the American, and the first item won is paid for by the buyer immediately in French francs or with a signed check drawn on a French bank. The winner then is given a large plastic card with the number corresponding to the catalogue item won, using it to bid for the remainder of the sale. The buyer then settles the total of all purchases before receiving the merchandise.

Space was limited, with preferred seating in front. About 150 wooden folding chairs were set in two sections and allocated by ticket. The catalogue advised attendees to reserve seats early for good reason. The small hall was jammed, and the back of the room and aisles filled with another 150 people. Proceedings began exactly at the appointed time as one auctioneer took control, cleared the runner's aisles, and forced the standees to the rear of the hall.

Successful bidding at an auction might be classified as an art or science, but more accurately it is a matter of positioning. The obvious, frequent buyers take the front rows of reserved seats in full view of the auctioneer, and know each other well. Cagier buyers mingle and lurk in the back of the hall, popping up from time to time to counter the seated bidders, driving the prices higher, and winning some items for themselves or the customers they represent.

We decided to use the left bid avenue to avoid possible confusion in bidding in French. Our bids were above the high estimates, but each Quimper item we selected went for much more than the predicted high bid, as did the majority of the lots that day. When we felt we understood the bidding, we began to participate from the floor. We bought a pitcher early in the sale, by the Henriot artist known only as POL. We were asked to produce French francs, but we only could come up with American dollars, disrupting the flow of the sale. It was a tense few moments while we handed our passports and $100 to the runner. The auctioneer paced behind the podium, but all was set straight and the sale continued.

One memorable point involved telephone bidding. Three phones were in use behind the podium and the auctioneer turned his back to the audience periodically and conducted the bidding from phone to phone to phone. At the conclusion of one of these sessions, he turned again to face the room and slammed down the gavel. The crowd responded with amazement at the price the two statues by Berthe Savigny brought — 10,000F, or over $1,400 each — instead of the predicted high of 1,500F. Savigny was the featured artist at *Le Musée de la Faïence* in Quimper at the time, so perhaps it should have been expected.

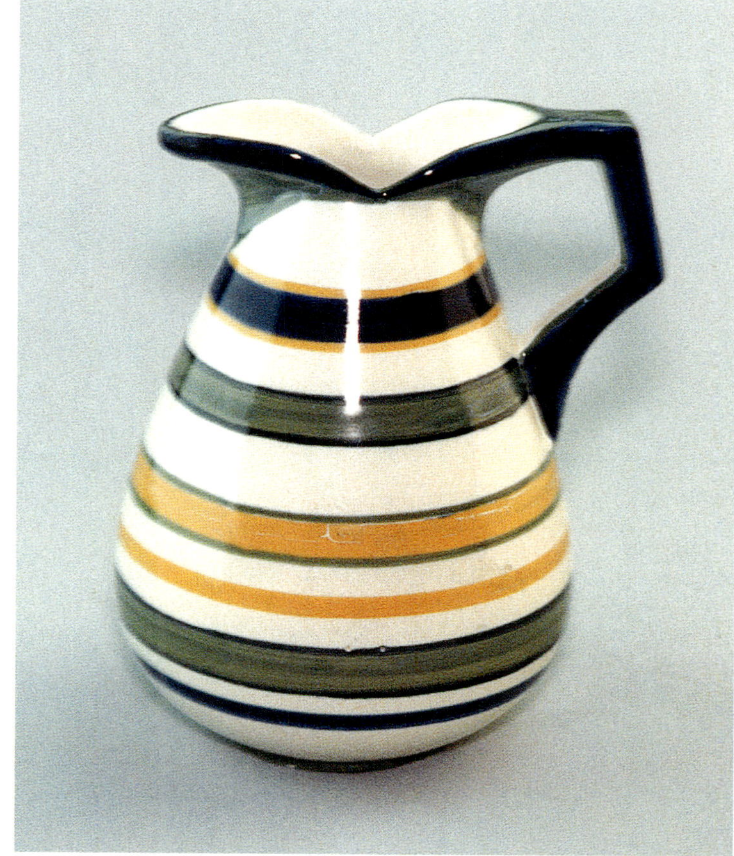

The Henriot artist, known only as POL, designed this modern-looking pitcher in the 1930s. The pitcher is 5.5" tall. *Authors' Collection.*

Right:
Savigny's *bébé* figurines strike a chord in most everyone, and her success with this genre is undeniable. This example in *grès* is 4.5" tall. *Private Collection.*

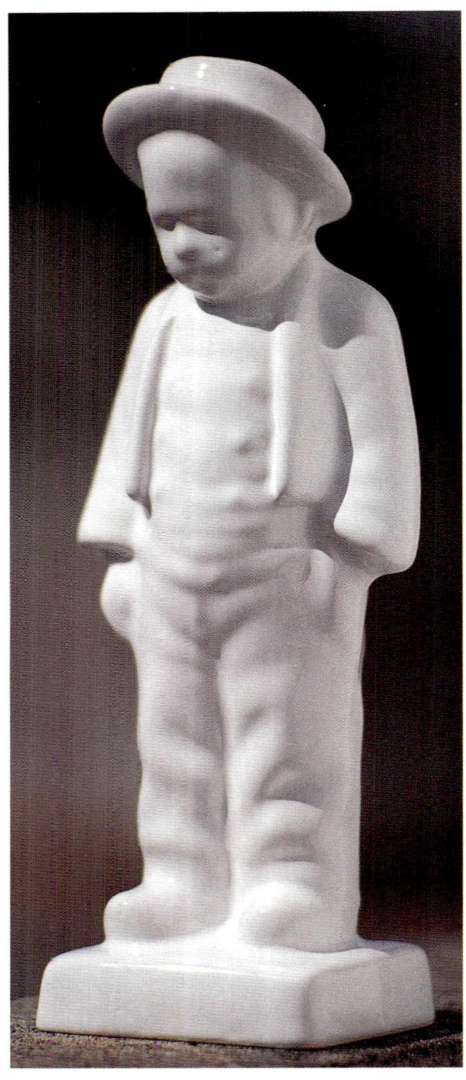

Savigny's touch is apparent with this rendition of an 8" tall *Jeune Bigouden* in *email blanc*, or white finish. *Private Collection.*

Berthe Savigny is known for her sweet renditions of Breton children in faïence and *grès*. The retrospective of her work at the *Musée de la Faïence* showed her talents included works in oil on wood, ivory, porcelain, silk, canvas, and pencil and watercolors on paper. Her sketches on menus were particularly whimsical. She was born into a family of artists in July 1882 at Quimper and lived in Pont-l'Abbe, Concarneau, and Pont-Aven. A recent count shows 70 different models of the famous *bébé* in various materials. Savigny's figurines strike a chord in most everyone, and her success with this genre is undeniable. *(Trognée and Verlingue, Berthe Savigny, p.17.)*

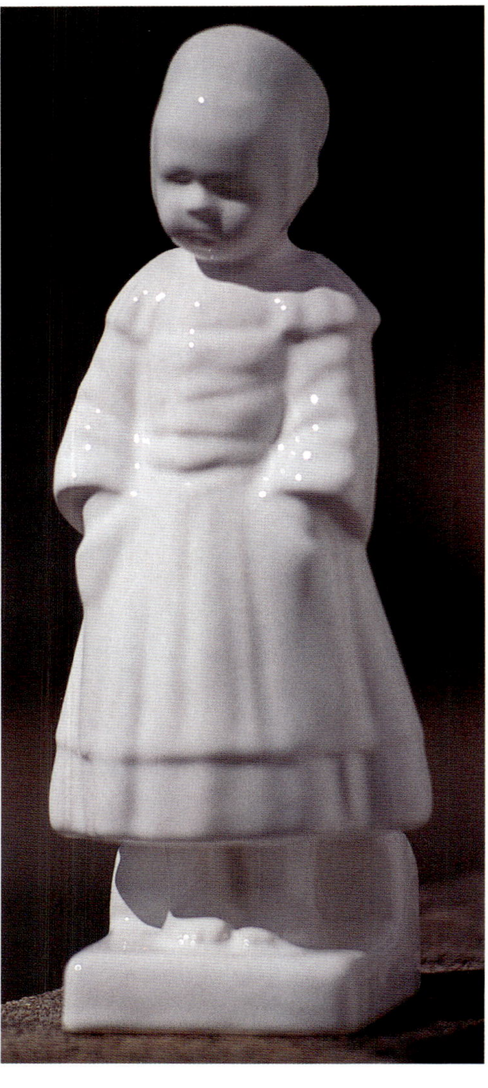

Another *email blanc* or *faïence blanche* Savigny example, perhaps the sister of the *Jeune Bigouden*. Both examples are HB/Henriot re-editions, and date 1984 or later. *Private Collection.*

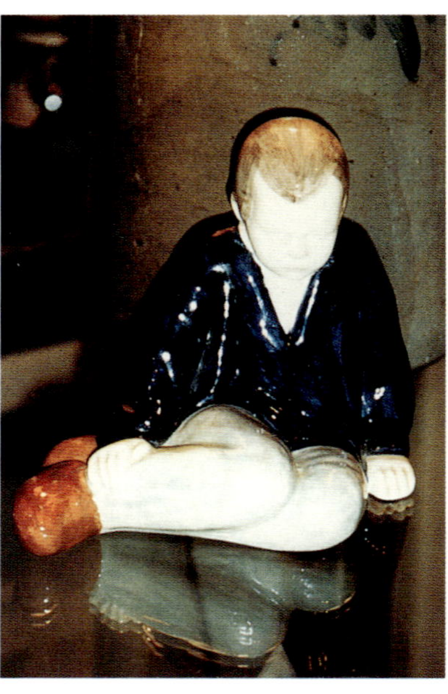

Savigny stikes again with a rendition of a *Jeune Garçon*, c. 1930, 5.5" tall for the HB faïencerie. *Private Collection.*

More amazing were the prices two statues by René Quillivic realized. His *Garçonnet Bigouden* had an estimated high price of 10,000F, or $1,429, and instead brought 27,000F, or $3,857. The other, *Fillette en Riche Costume Bigouden,* also known as *Jeune Bigouden au Doigt dans la Bouche,* was estimated to bring 5,000F, or $714, and instead brought 19,000F, or $2,714, from a phone bidder. Many of the statues went to phone bidders, including one by the artist R. Micheau-Vernez, *Groupe de Trois Danseurs en Costume de Pont Aven,* for 12,000F, or $1,714, above its estimated high by more than $200. One statue in *terre cuit* (terra cotta) by Mathurin Méheut, *Homme Portant des Raies,* realized 22,000F or $3,142, rather than the 6,000F or $857 predicted.

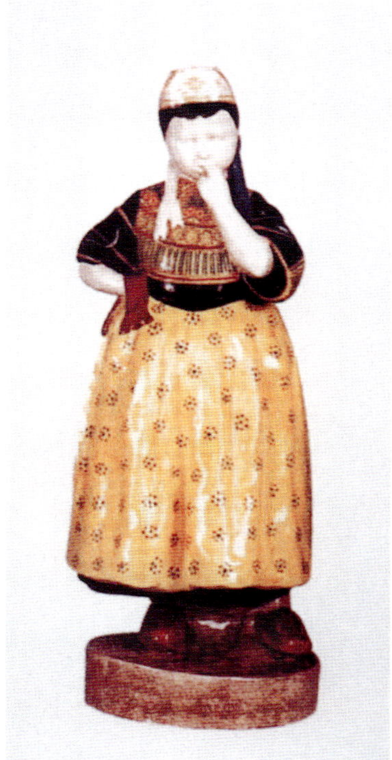

Left:
Quillivic's other figure, *Fillette en Riche Costume Bigouden* went to a telephone bidder. It achieved 19,000F, or nearly $3,000 more than the high estimate. Signed HB Quimper, Quillivic, and it stands 20" tall. (For an example in *email blanc,* see *Trois Siècles de Faïences, p. 167.*) *Courtesy of the Oriot & Dupont, Morlaix.*

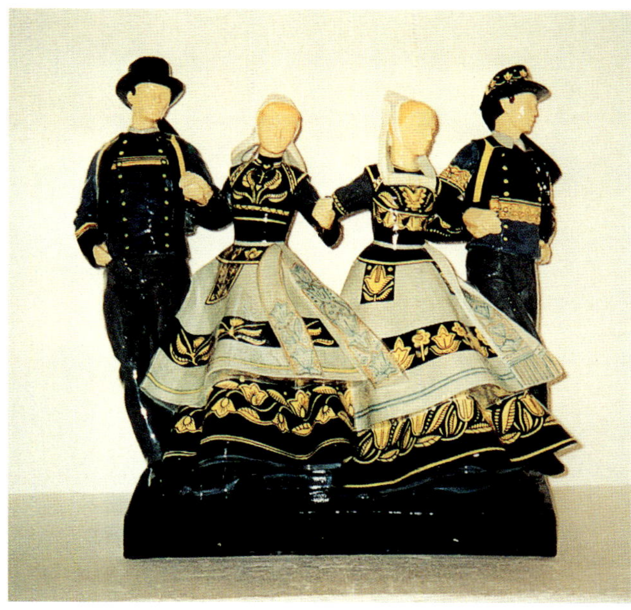

R. Micheau-Vernez is known for his dancers from *Pays Bigouden.* This 17.5" tall *Groupe de Trois Danseurs en Costume de Pont-Aven* brought 12,000F, or more than $1,700, not including buyer's premium. *Courtesy of Oriot & Dupont, Morlaix.*

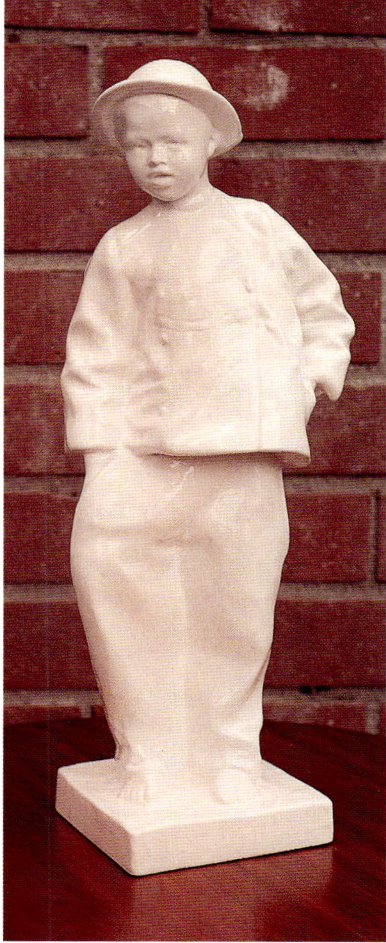

René Quillivic's figures are highly popular in France and elsewhere. His 19" tall *Garçonnet Bigouden* sold in the hall for 27,000F, or 17,000F more than the high estimate, not including buyer's premium. That was nearly $4,000. It was signed HB Quimper, Quillivic, 45/200, 1907. The model pictured is post-1984 and in *email blanc.* (For an earlier model, see *Trois Siècles de Faïences, p. 162.*) *Courtesy of Jeff and Ezat Williamson.*

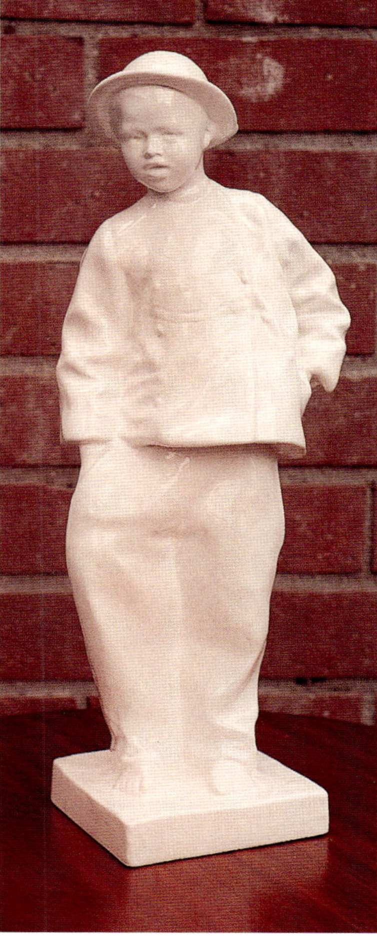

A similar but larger group of Micheau-Vernez dancers was displayed at the museum in Morlaix. They seem to sway gracefully to music unheard by us. *Courtesy of Musée des Jacobins, Morlaix.*

The previous Quimper poterie sale at Morlaix brought some extraordinary prices for Porquier-Beau botanical plates; it had been the talk of all the dealers on our trip soon after that sale. So the audience was primed when the bidding began on *les assiettes de la serie botanique.*

This time there were ten plates, a *pichet à cidre*, and two jardinières in *décor botanique*. The cider pitcher brought 9,000F, or $1,285, the jardinière with the lizard handles brought 21,000F, or $3,000, and the other brought 13,500F, or $1,928. The prices realized for the plates ranged from a high of 17,000F, or $2,428, to a low of 8,500F, or $1,214. The total for the 10 plates was 139,500F, or $19,928, with an average of 13,950F, or $1,992 per plate. In addition, the buyers had to pay a nearly 11 percent premium to the auction house on each purchase.

The Porquier-Beau (PB) botanical items sold for the following amounts. Left to right, **Row 1:** PB plate *botanique* with flowering branch. Estimated: 4,000F. Realized: 13,000F, or $1,857. PB plate with border of *arabesque* rim décor with *Bretagne* armorial, and center featuring a young Breton with a scythe. Estimate: 6,000F. Realized: 11,000F. or $1,571. PB plate *botanique* with flowering branch. Estimate: 5,000F. Realized: 16,000F, or $2,285. **Rows 2 & 4:** Set of four PB *porte menu* in the style of miniature plates. Damage to two supports. Estimate: 4,000F. Realized: 17,000F, or $2,428. **Row 3:** PB Quimper plate, *légende Bretonne*, inscription: *Jean Rouge-Gorg.* Estimate: 4,000F. Realized: 12,000F, or $1,714. PB plate *botanique, sans* mark, with a branch and three butterflies. Estimate: 6,000F. Realized: 17,000F, or $2,428. PB Quimper plate,. *légende Bretonne*, inscription: *Yan Coz chez les diables.* Estimate: 4,000F. Realized: 5,000F, or $714. **Row 5:** PB plate *botanique* with blossoming branch and butterfly. Estimate: 5,000F. Realized: 14,5000F, or $2,071. PB plate with border of arabesque and armorial of *Bretagne*, and center featuring a Bretonne with a donkey and milk containers. Estimate: 6,000F. Realized: 10,500F, or $1,500. PB plate *botanique* with flowering vines. Estimate: 5,000F. Realized: 16,000F, or $2,285. **Row 6:** Pair of 4" long AP wallpockets, cornucopia shaped with a Breton and Bretonne. Estimate: 800F. Realized: 2,200F, or $314. **Row 7:** PB plate *botantique* with flowering branch and butterfly. Estimate: 5,000F. Realized: 10,500F, or $1,500. PB *calotte*, or soup plate, with the center décor, *au cochon ailé*, or winged pig. Estimate: 6,000F. Realized: 9,000F, or $1,357. PB plate *botanique* with forget-me-nots. Estimate: 5,000F. Realized: 13,000F, or $1,857. None of these prices include the nearly 11 percent buyer's premium. *Courtesy of Oriot & Dupont, Morlaix.*

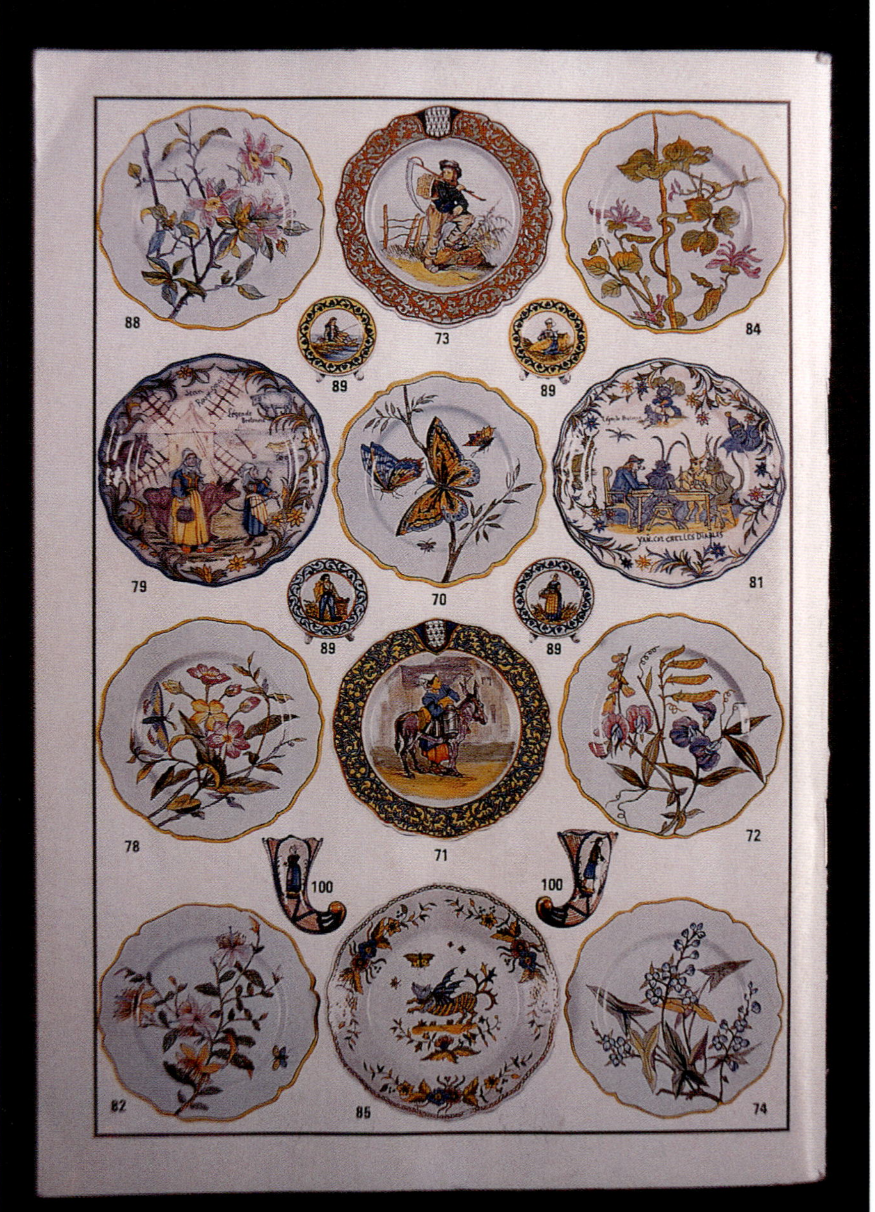

Excitement rippled through the crowd again when a group of 37 *secouettes*, or snuffs, came up for sale. They were to be sold consecutively and the bidding began with determination. Most of the action took place between competing bidders in the first row, on either side of the podium. It was as if the audience was watching a tennis match as the spectators' heads turned back and forth to catch the action.

Of the 37 *secouettes*, eight were bought in-house. The total for the 29 that did sell was 261,750F, or $37,392. This was an average of 9,025F, or $1,289 per *secouette*, excluding buyer's premium.

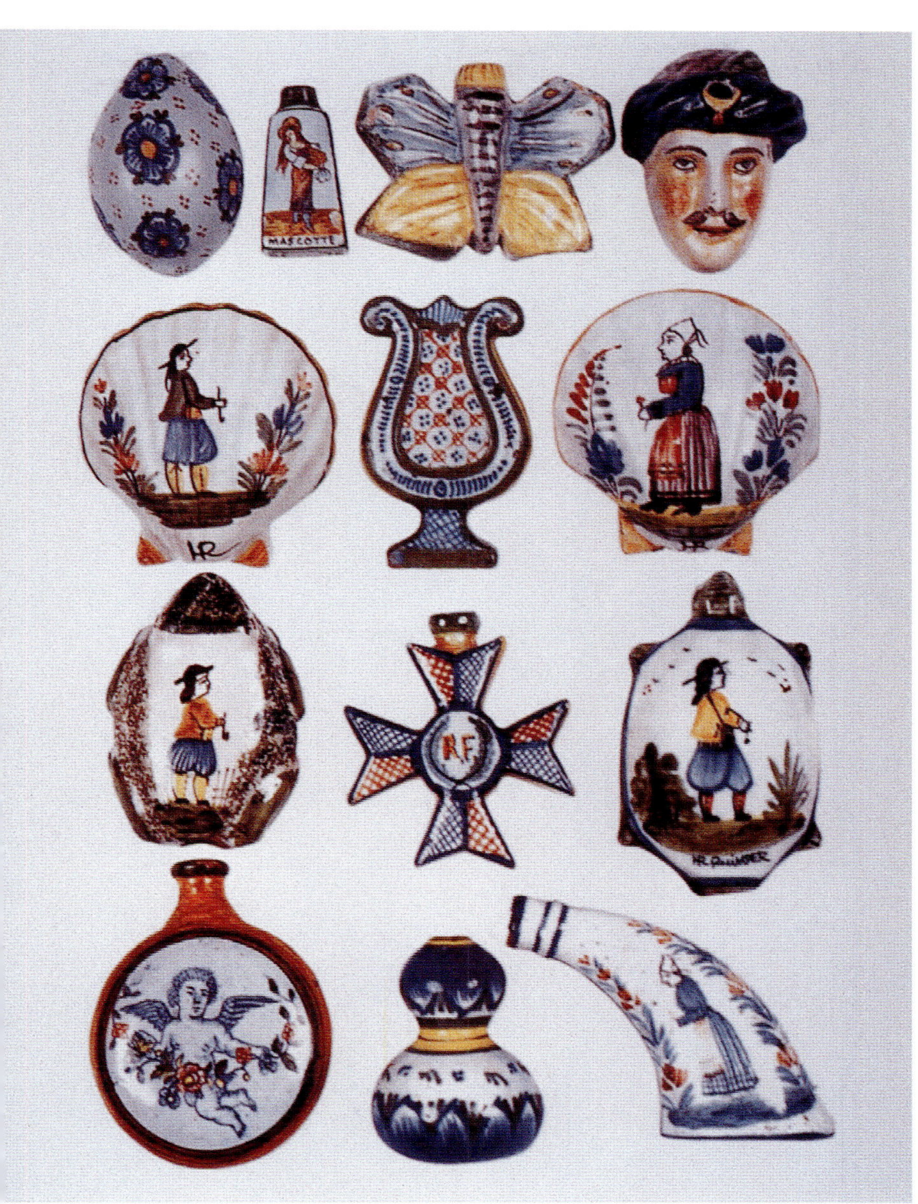

The *secouettes*, or snuffs, pictured here sold for the following amounts. Left to right, **Row 1:** Rare *secouette* in shell-shape, decorated with flowers. Quimper *sans* mark. Estimate: 12,000F. Realized: 16,000F, or $2,285. *Secouette* in the shape of a small bottle decorated with a woman and the inscription, *Mascotte*; Quimper *sans* mark. Estimate: 4,000F. Realized: 10,000F, or $1,428. *Secouette* in the shape of a butterfly, HR mark. Estimate: 9,000F. Realized: 9,500F or $1,357. Curious *secouette* in the shape of an Oriental man in a turban. Origin undetermined. Estimate: 5,000F. Realized: 19,000F, or $2,714, the highest *secouette* price of the sale. **Row 2:** Two *secouettes* in the shape of scallop shells, decorated with a male and female. HR mark. Estimate: 12,000F for the pair. Realized: 11,500F, or $1,642, for the pair (one of the few *secouette* lots which sold under-estimate). *Secouette* in the shape of a lyre. Quimper *sans* mark. PB 19th century. Estimate: 12,000F. Realized: 18,000F, or $2,571. **Row 3:** *Secouette* in the shape of a frog, decorated with a Breton; HB mark, 19th century. Estimate: 9,000F. Realized: 10,500F, or $1,500. Rare *secouette* in the form of a *Croix d'Honneur*, with the initials RF in the center. PB, 19th century. Small amount of enamel missing. Estimate: 12,000F. Realized: 14,000F, or $2,000. *Secouette* in the shape of a turtle, decorated with a *petit Breton* carrying a pipe. HR mark. Estimate: 9,000F; no sale. **Row 4:** *Secouette* in the shape of a flask, decorated with a rare motif of an angel holding a garland of flowers. Quimper *sans* mark. Estimate: 6,000F. Realized: 12,000F, or $1,714. *Secouette* in the shape of a gourd. PB, 19th century. Estimate: 10,000F. Realized: 10,000F, or $1,500. Rare *secouette* in the shape of a powder horn decorated with a Bretonne and flowers. HR mark. Some damage. Estimate: 10,000F. Realized: 11,000F, or $1,571. Again, prices do not reflect the nearly 11 percent buyer's premium. *Courtesy of Oriot & Dupont, Morlaix.*

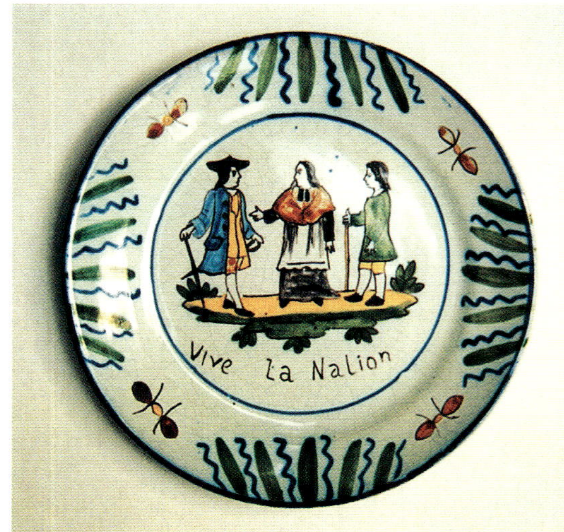

A 9.5" *décor revolutionnaire* plate was one of the last faïence items sold. The plate, which reads *Ma vie est à ma Patrie*, or My Life is for my Country, was described as probably Desvres, and realized 1000F, or about $140. *Private Collection.*

The predicted high sale amount for all the Quimper poterie lots was 916,303F, or $132,032, including the buyer's premium. In actuality, the auction house took in 1,635,702F, or $235,764, with the premium, nearly twice the expected amount.

The lessons we learned from our experience with the Morlaix auction are: Arrive on time, reserve a seat (if you don't want to stand for over two hours); and bring lots of cash in francs, or a check drawn on a French Bank. It was a great experience, although we did not come away with as much merchandise as we had hoped. That's the price of learning as you go. We did buy two commemorative plates *décor revolutionnaire*, in addition to the *pichet dessin moderne* by POL. Will we go back? Yes. Will we try other Quimper auctions too, such as the ones held by Thierry & Lannon at Douarnenez and Brest? Yes, because you never can find too much Quimper.

A second 9.5" *décor revolutionnaire* plate was offered, again probably Desvres. This one reads *Vive la Nation*, or Long Live the Nation, and realized the same amount as the other revolutionary motif plate. *Private Collection.*

St. Pol-de-Léon

The seven original bishoprics in Brittany are: Dol for Samson, St. Malo for Malo, St. Brieuc for Brieg, Treguier for Tugdal, St. Pol for Pol Aurelian, Quimper for Korentin, and Vannes for Patern. A *Tro Breiz* or *Tour de Bretagne* was made by the faithful to visit the seven tombs in the seven dioceses. All social classes blended together as they made their pilgrimage on foot, averaging about 12 miles a day on the nearly 315-mile circuit. (Ganachaud, *Les Traditions Bretonnes*, p. 7.)

About 15 kilometers northwest of Morlaix is St. Pol-de-Léon, named for St. Paul the Aurelian. St. Pol was a Welsh monk who came to Brittany in the 6th century, along with many other missionaries who left Britain and Ireland when the Anglo-Saxons invaded. The Celtic Monastic Schools in Ireland and Wales were considered the best in Europe, and there are many legendary tales chronicling the voyages of monks who carried religious teachings abroad from there. These voyages brought St. Pol and six other monks to Brittany, where they became the founding bishops of the first seven dioceses in Brittany. (Pennick, *The Celtic Cross*, p. 18.)

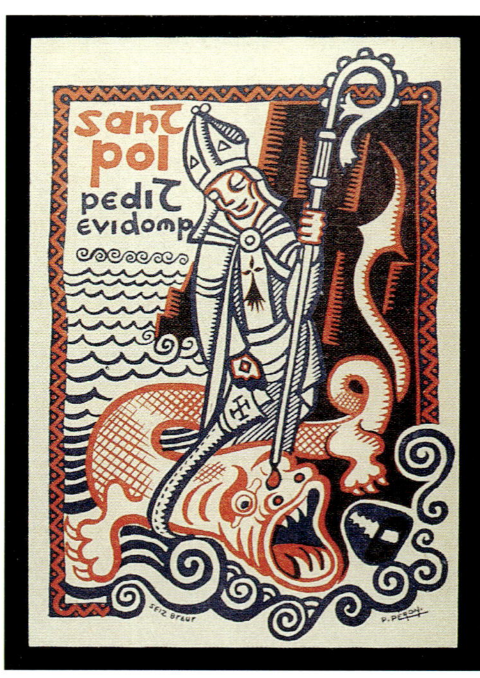

St. Pol is shown slaying the dragon in this stylized wood print. *Private collection.*

The St. Pol bell is a popular subject among faïence makers, and is unusual in design. The handle usually is shaped like the head of a fish. Legend tells us that Paul asked King Mark of Cornwall if he could take one of the seven bells used to call his religious order to meals on his journey. He was denied. When Paul reached Brittany, a fisherman brought him a large fish. In its mouth was a bell similar to the one he left behind, which he saw as a sign that he was on a just mission.

By the Middle Ages, the town and bishopric named for St. Paul had become the religious center for northern *Finistère*. The Cathedral of St. Pol-de-Léon, where his remains lie in a gilt reliquary, and the Kreisker Chapel were the center of the life in the town. From the top of the Kreisker chapel – a 169-step climb – the view inland goes south to the Arrée Mountains, and north to Roscoff, and the *Île de Batz,* where St. Pol lived his final years.

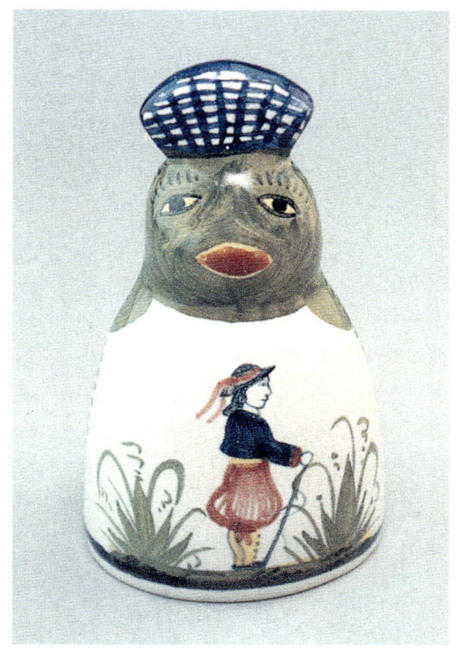

An Internet auction described this St. Pol bell as *having a chicken face.* It is signed Henriot Quimper and stands 4" tall. *Private Collection.*

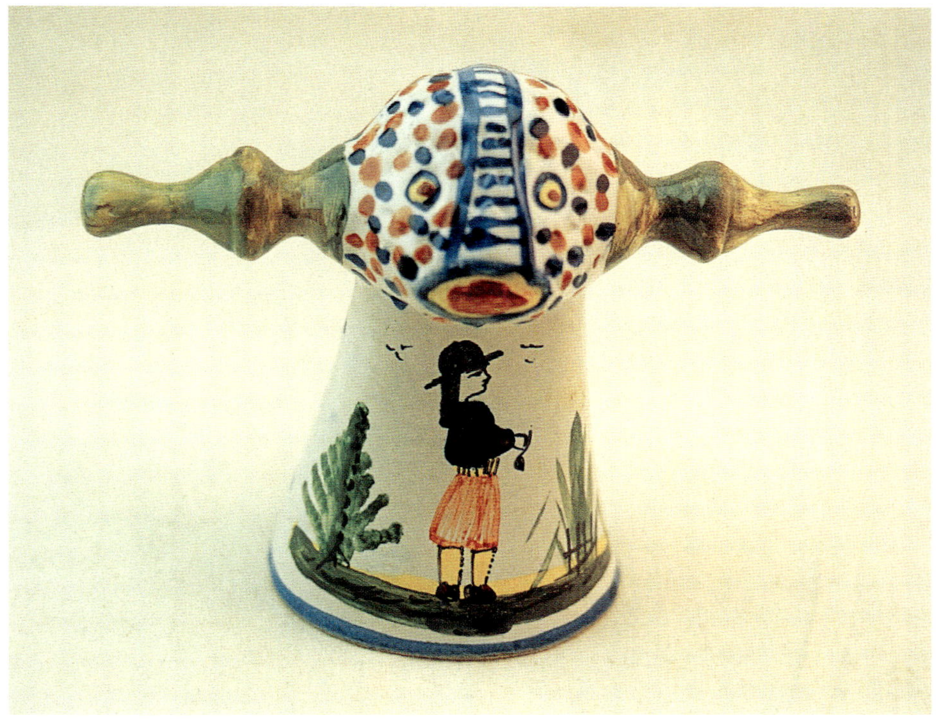

St. Pol's bell, with the features of a fish's face as the handle, has been popular with visitors to the region. This version is signed HB Quimper, is second quarter of the 20th century, and is 4" tall. *Collection of Nancy Wyman.*

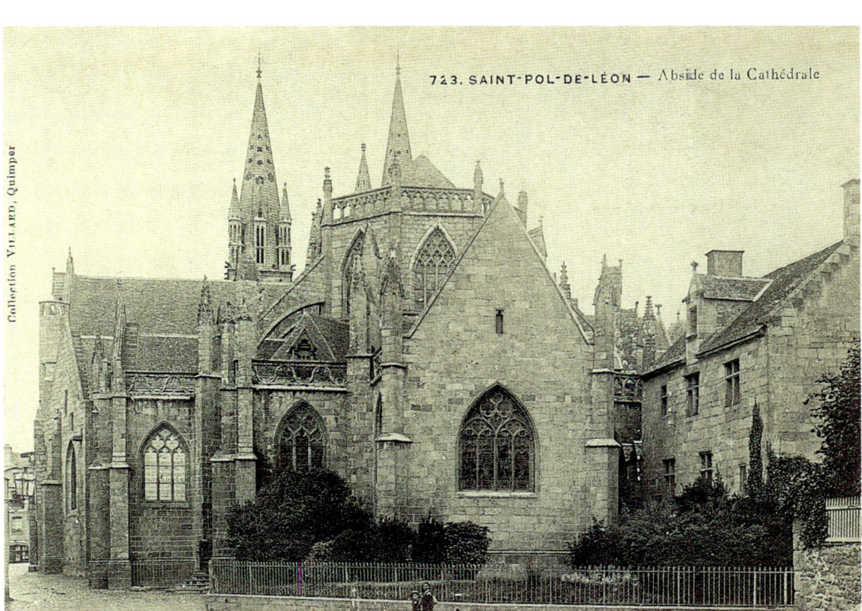

A turn-of-the-20th century postcard features the Cathedral at St. Pol-de-Léon. *Authors' Collection.*

On one of our trips to this town we had the good fortune to witness a procession to the St. Pol-de-Léon Cathedral, the capital of the diocese, honoring the end of the Catholic Church's Jubilee 2000. Banners waved in the misty afternoon breeze and hymns of praise wafted from the open doors of the church, as the representatives from diocese parishes made their way up the street to the Cathedral's main entrance on the square.

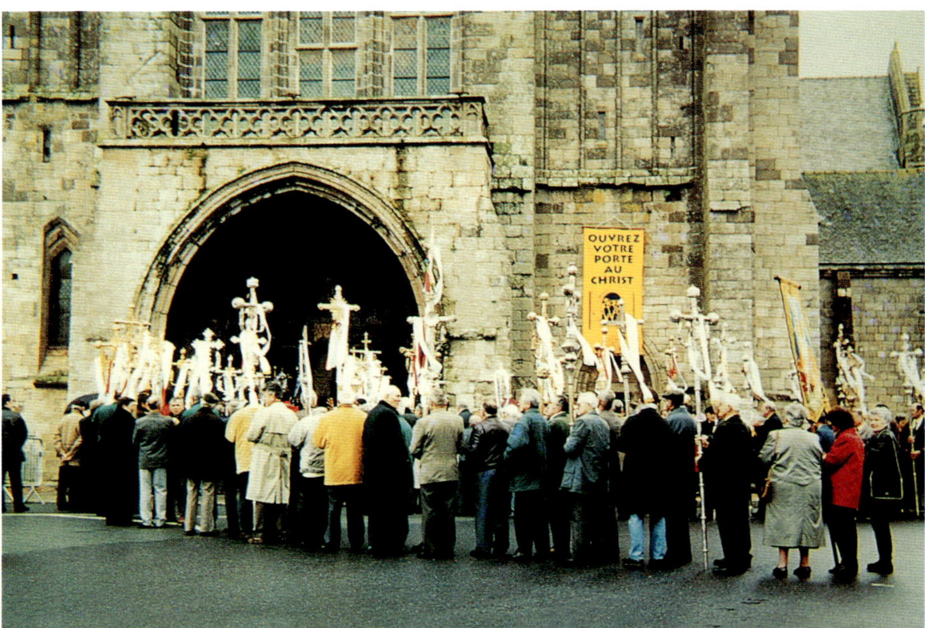

Right:
Eighty-three crosses and banners were carried by Bretons on a Sunday afternoon marking the end of the Jubilee 2000.

Below left:
Over 2,500 participated in the Jubilee celebration. The banner of St. Pol was carried proudly to the hometown Cathedral.

Below right:
Among the marchers were *Quimpérois*, people of Quimper, carrying the banner of St. Corentin, filled with colorful and intricate needlework.

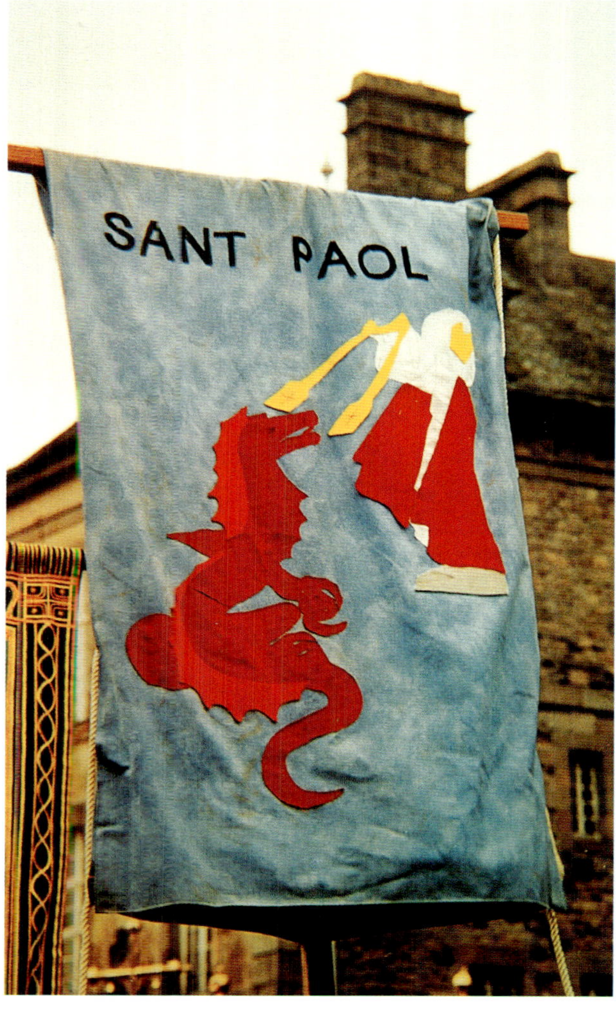

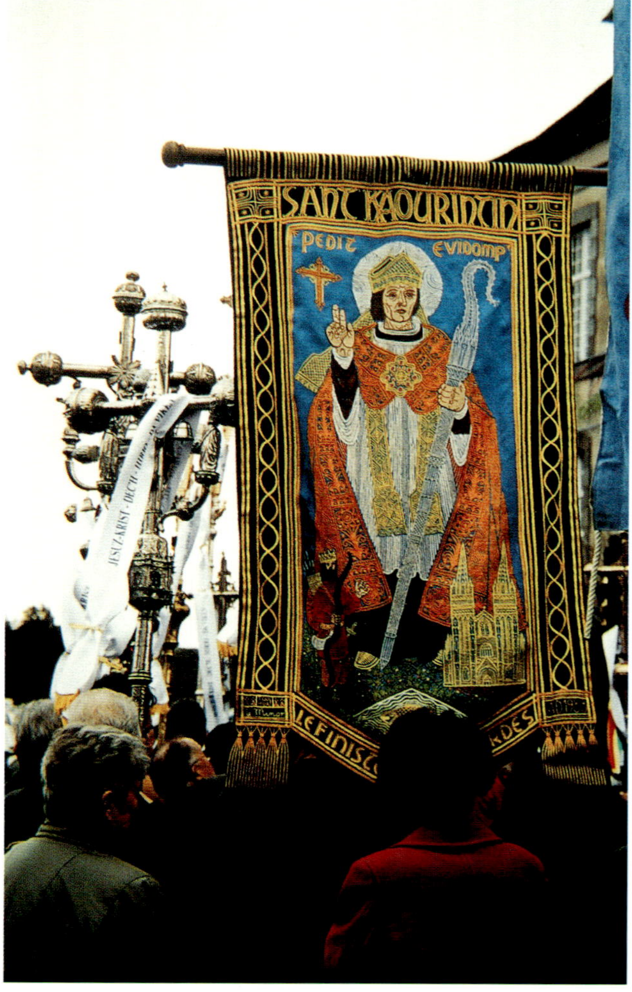

Quimper collectors interested in history should not miss the cemetery at the southern end of the town in St. Pol-de-Léon. The First World War devastated the populace of Brittany. Countless war memorials pepper the province, honoring fallen *conscrits*, or draftees. During this traumatic period, one tenth of France's population was killed or missing in action, a total of about 1.4 million persons. Nearly three million more were wounded.

In the far corner of the immaculately groomed cemetery there is a small chapel devoted to St. Peter, illuminated by modern stained glass windows. At the end of a nearby alleyway of trimmed shrubs stands the magnificent World War I Memorial by Quimper artist René Quillivic. The groundskeepers were glad to share what they knew about it. Originally, they said, there only had been a semicircular wall decorated in bas-relief. Now the Quillivic memorial stands encircled by this wall. The drive to commemorate the fallen Bretons brought about numerous memorials, and this is one of the most impressive ones.

Quillivic: Par mon essence d'artiste et d'homme du people, j'ai un droit de regard sur la Bretagne car tout ce qui s'y passé vibre dans ma coeur en joies et douleurs. **Essentially, as an artist and a man of the people, all things *Bretagne* thrill me, joys and sorrows.** *(Rotté and Verlingue, p. 42.)*

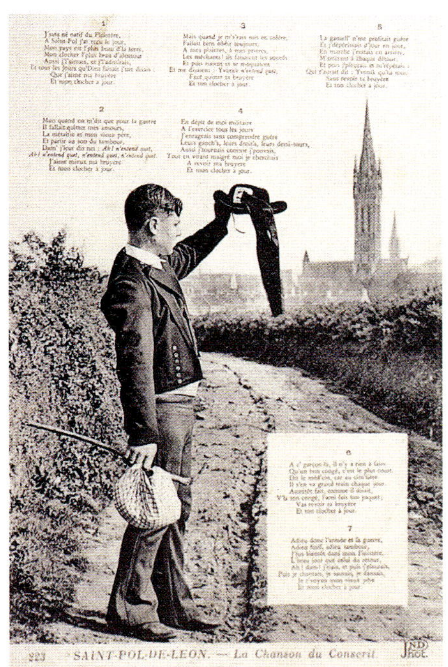

A 1918 postcard shows a young man from St. Pol-de-Léon bidding farewell to his town, with the verses of *La Chanson de Conscrit* (Song of the Draftee) printed across the card. *Authors' Collection.*

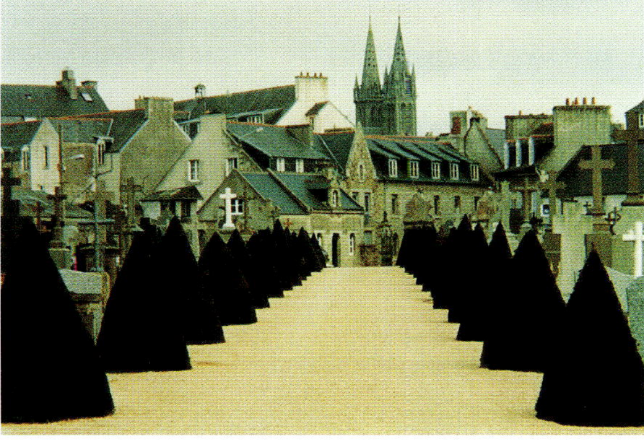

René Quillivic's sculpted tribute to Breton losses in World War I was placed in front of an earlier semi-circular wall in the St. Pol-de-Léon cemetery. It is approached though an alleyway of neatly trimmed shrubs.

Right:
Quillivic was commissioned to create important works throughout Brittany, including numerous memorials to those killed in combat.

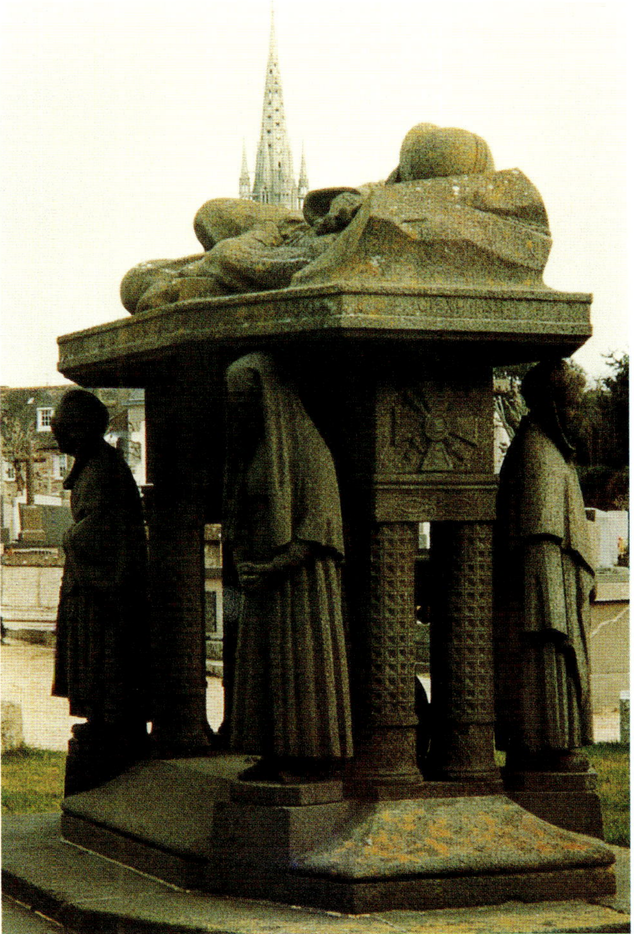

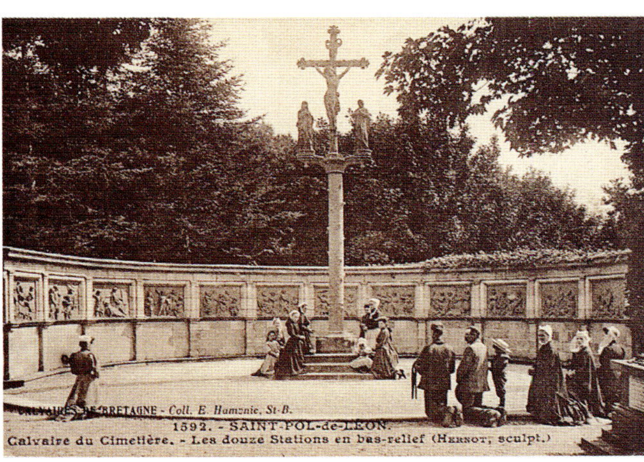

A pre-World War I postcard shows the cemetery in St. Pol-de-Léon prior to the Quillivic memorial. *Authors' Collection.*

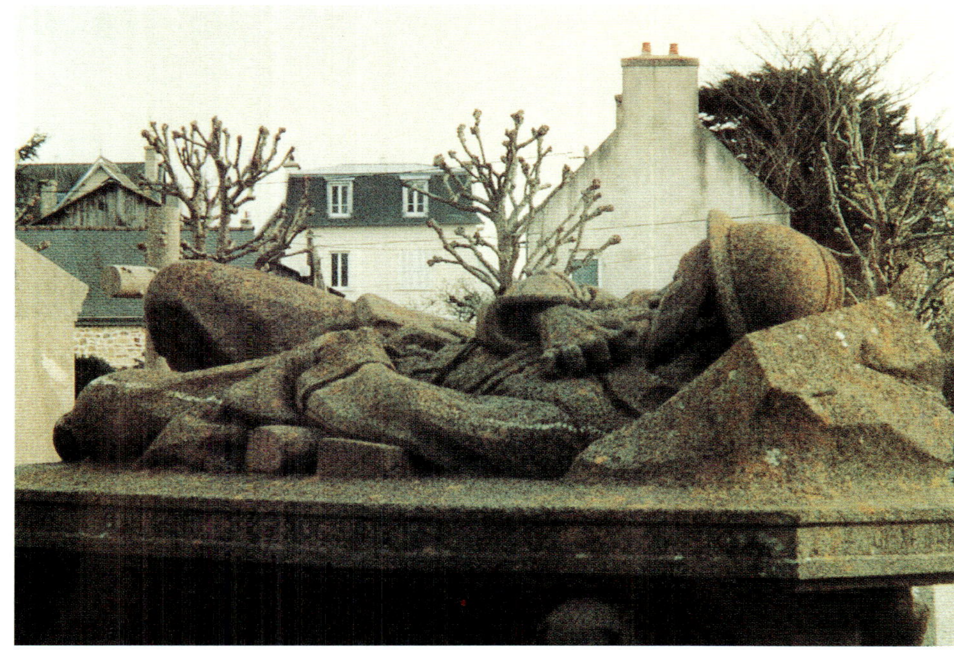

The monument stands as testimony to the depth of feeling generated in Breton hearts for the loss of their kin.

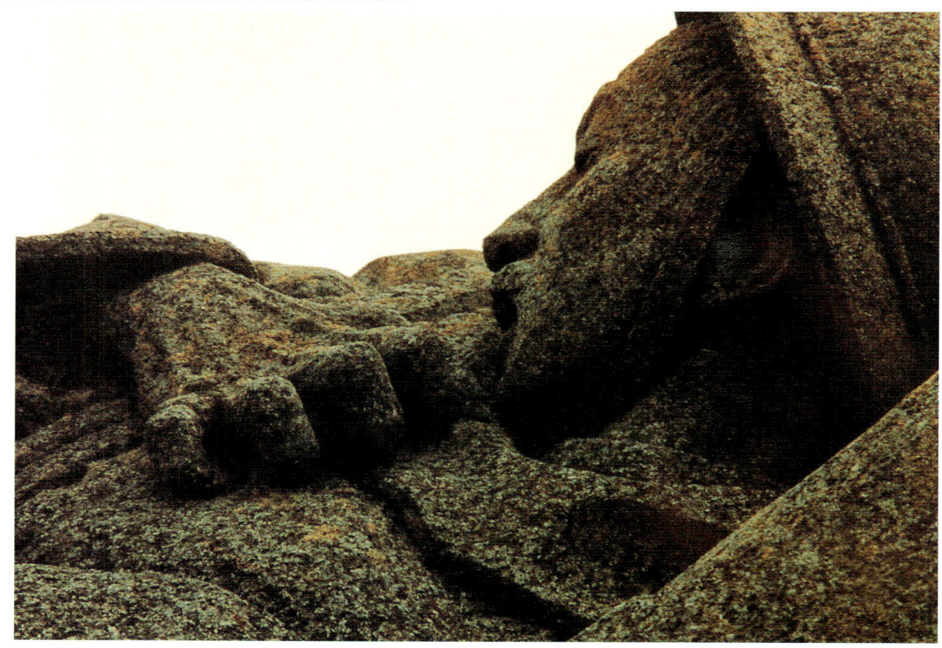

Quillivic's rendition of a fallen brother speaks a thousand words of tribute.

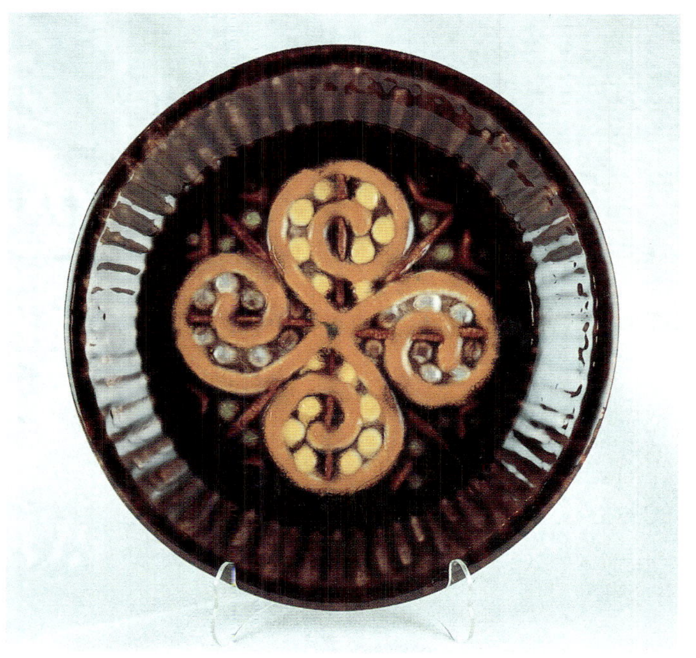

The Quimper artist and designer René Quillivic was born in 1879 at Plouhinec to a family of fishermen, leaving that profession after a near-fatal storm at sea. He apprenticed to a cabinetmaker, learning to carve decorative motifs, and went on to the *École des Beaux Arts* in Paris while continuing with woodworking to sustain himself. In the early 1920s, Quillivic was offered his own *atelier* by the HB faïencerie in Quimper.

René Quillivic already was a sculptor of note before being hired by Jules Verlingue. He brought a new look to *HB/Grande Maison* faïence. A richer color palette and Celtic motifs were Quillivic innovations. The plate measures 10.5" diameter and is signed HB Quimper, Quillivic. (*For a similar example, see Rotté and Verlingue, p. 25.) Authors' Collection.*

Sculptures decorating the various pavilions at the Paris *Exposition Universelle* in 1900 had a significant impact on Quillivic. Later, while at HB, he developed models for statues, which won wide recognition. These statues included *Jeune Fille de Plouhinec*, *Les Deux Fumeuses*, *Garçonette Bigouden*, and *Fillette en Costume Riche Bigouden*. The latter two brought rich returns at the Morlaix April 2000 auction. The statues, and many others, were in addition to the many large commissioned war memorials he designed for numerous towns in Brittany.

Roscoff

Just five kilometers north of St. Pol-de-Léon is Roscoff, and close by is *Île de Batz*. Roscoff is a picturesque port once known for its *corsairs*, but it's known now as an export site for Brittany's produce, a pleasure boat harbor, and as a Mecca for those seeking sea cures. A deepwater port was installed in the 1960s and the subsequent export of artichokes, cauliflower, potatoes, and onions have renewed earlier Celtic ties with Ireland and England.

We arrived for the first time in Roscoff on a beautiful late January afternoon, as the sun was beginning to set. A fish *criée* (auction) was being held and the pier overflowed from the day's catch of shellfish and crustaceans. Despite the cold air, we walked along the pier with the others toward the *Chapelle de Ste. Barbe,* which sits on a hill across the harbor. The tiny chapel was stark on a winter's day against the sky, but in summer it's surrounded by a lovely garden. Any time of the year it provides a splendid view of the town, *Île de Batz,* and the ports, and is itself a gem to enjoy. We vowed to find out more about this startling sentinel, and we later did.

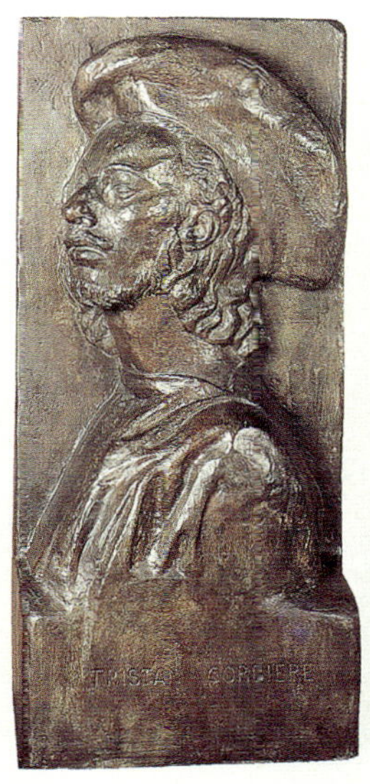

Roscoff, buccaneer's lair, old corsair's den, sleep your granite sleep above cellars haunted by the tide. Tristan Corbière. *Courtesy of Musée des Jacobins, Morlaix.*

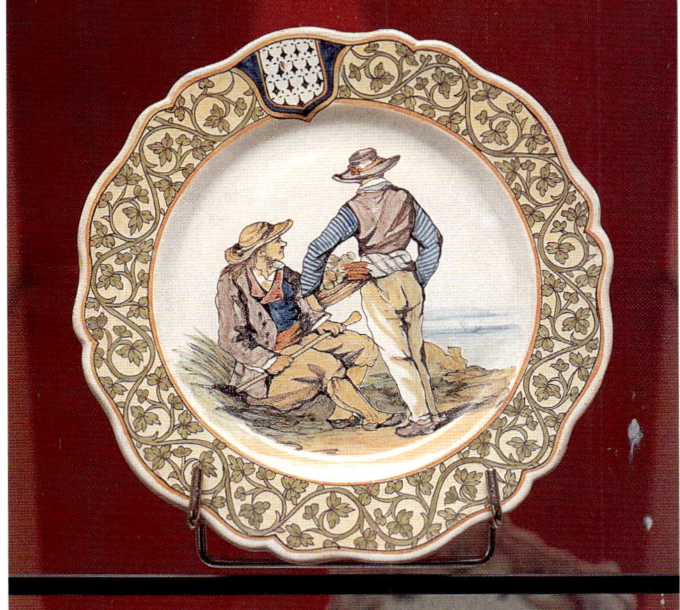

This 1880s *scène Bretonne* shows Alfred Beau's rendition of two gentlemen, one from Carantec, the other from Roscoff, towns about 15 to 20 kilometers northwest of Morlaix. The plate is signed PB, and is 9.25" diameter. The work is based on a print of Lalaisse. *(See Château de Quintin Exposition Catalogue, p. 95.) Collection of Pierre Breton, Art de Cornouaille, Quimper.*

A vintage poster shows the skyline of the port of Roscoff on the northern coast of Brittany. *Private Collection.*

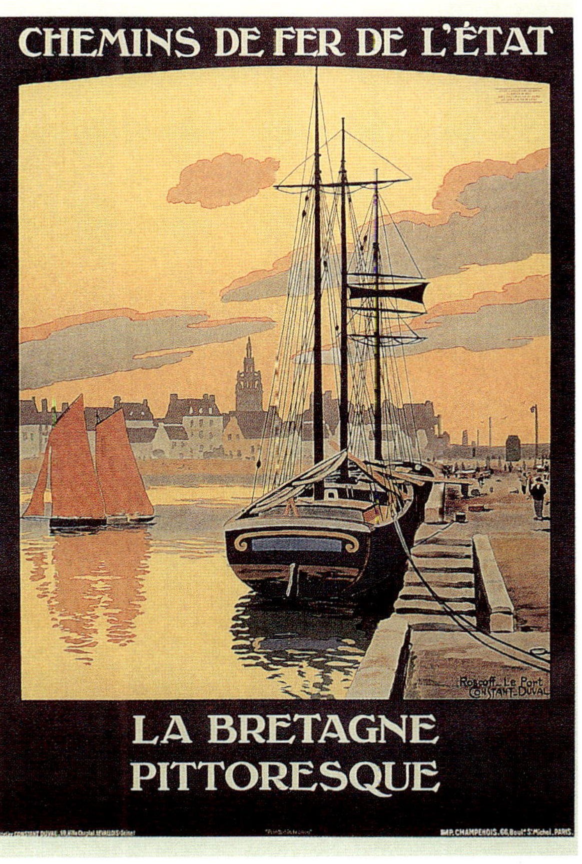

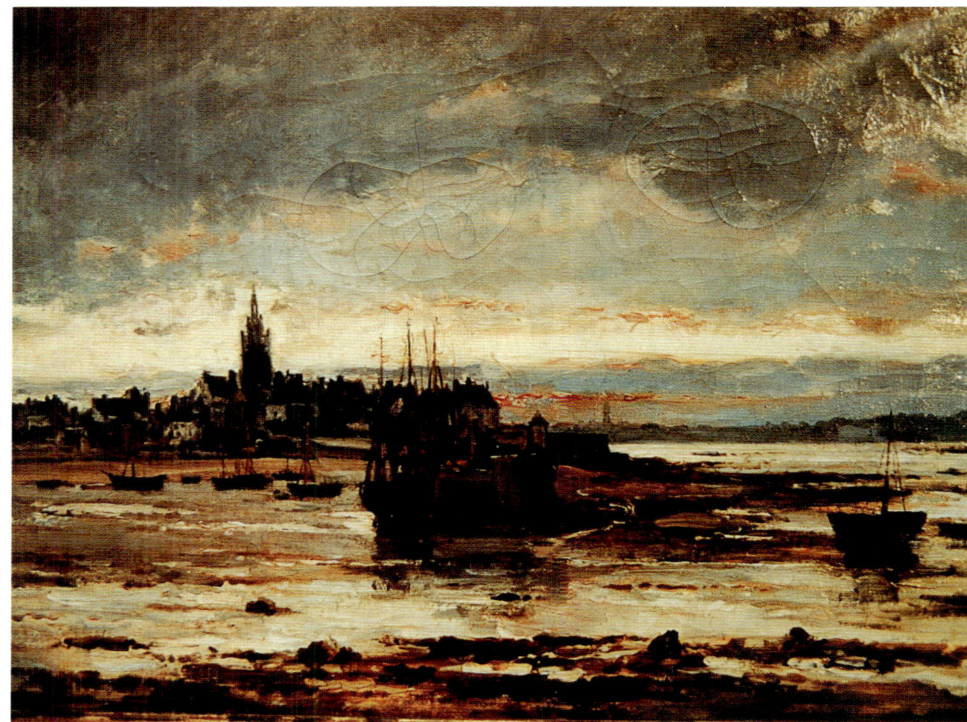

The skyline in Roscoff is memorable in any age. It was captured in oils by Venier in this 19th century painting. *Courtesy of Musée des Jacobins, Morlaix.*

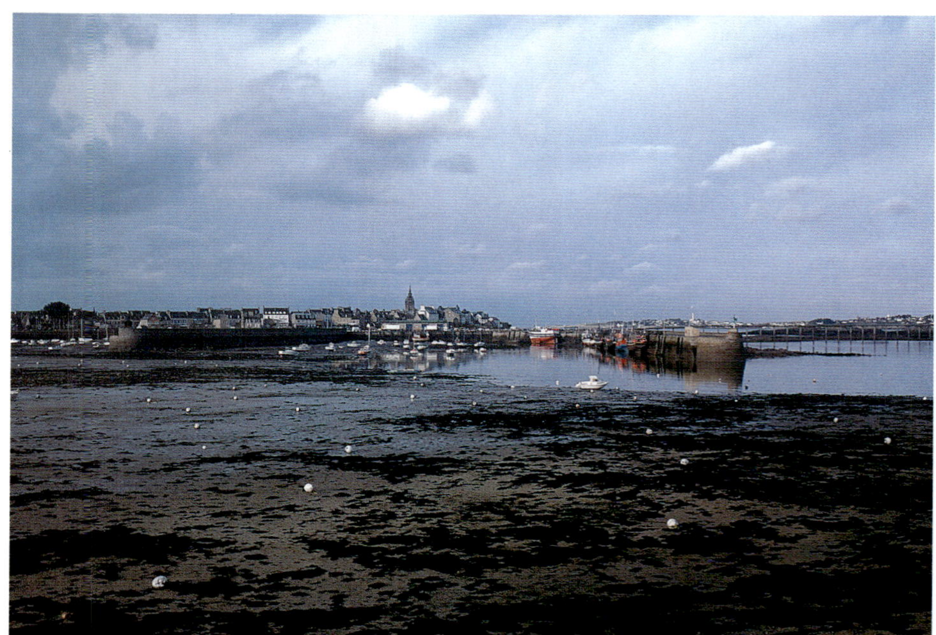

We captured a similar view of Roscoff on film at low tide on a sunny January morning over 100 years later.

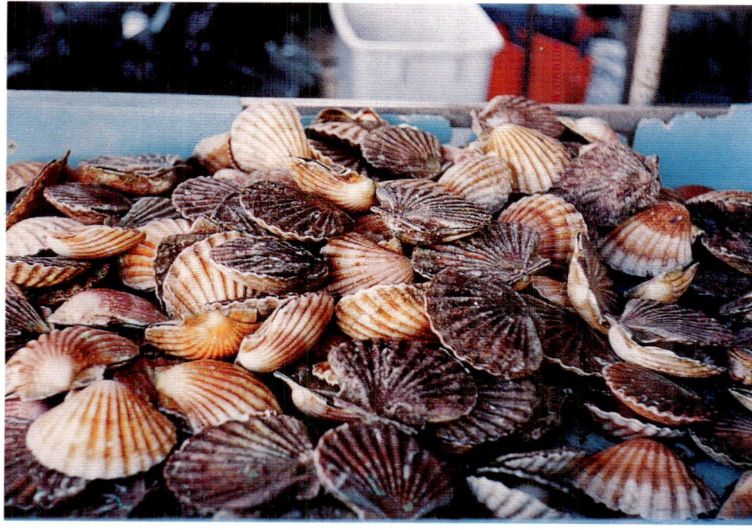

In Roscoff, a fish *criée* (auction) was taking place on the pier. It's a twice-a-day event in the many fishing ports of Brittany, as buyers vie for the best fish at the lowest price. The night's catch is sold at 6:30 a.m. and the day's catch at 4:30 p.m.

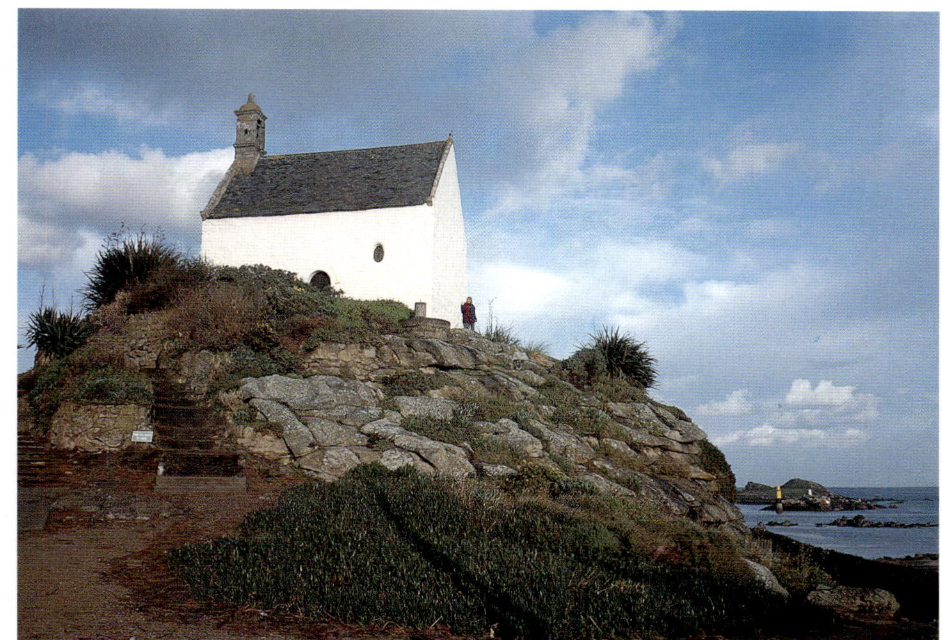

Left:
Ste. Barbe's chapel stands like a sentinel over the harbor at Roscoff. It was a landmark for *marins* returning from ocean voyages. The sun and clouds cast a lyrical spell over *Chapelle de Ste. Barbe* on this January Sunday morning.

Below:
Ste. Barbe was a young Bretonne who upon converting to Christianity was imprisoned in a tower by her father. As the legend relates, he killed her and then was struck dead by lightning. Ste. Barbe is shown here in faïence standing next to a miniature tower. Other forms show her holding a miniature tower. *(For examples, see Cahn, pp. 84, 94, 112, 129.) Private Collection.*

We enjoyed the spectacle as the sun set, and thought of Mathurin Méheut, who studied marine life here. In the early 1900s Méheut was a visitor to Roscoff and the nearby *Île de Batz* biology stations, while on a magazine assignment for *Art et Décoration.* He became enchanted by the marine life, and the local seaweed harvesters and fishermen, and returned to the region many times throughout his life. *(Mali, Old Quimper Review, October 1996.)*

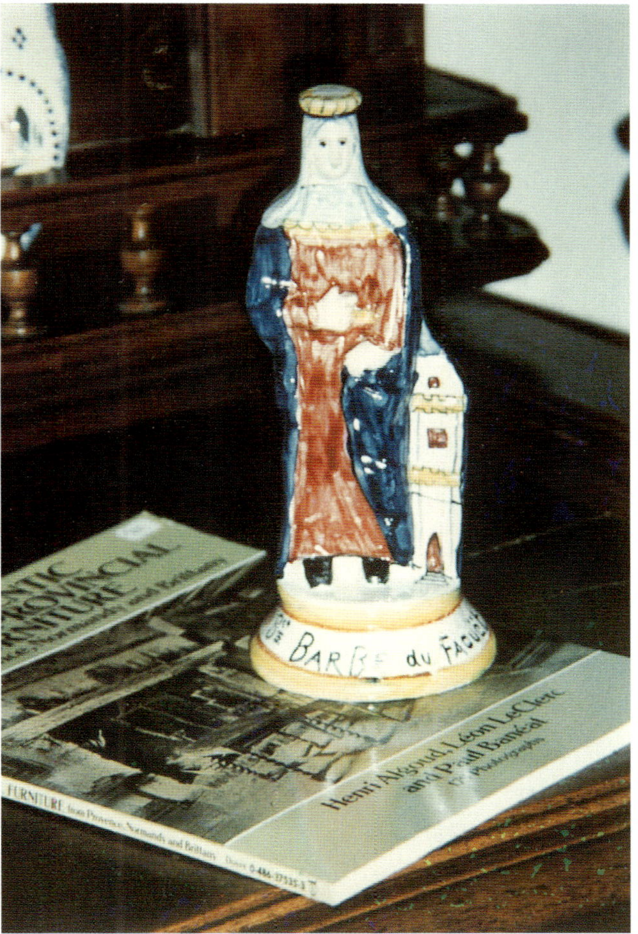

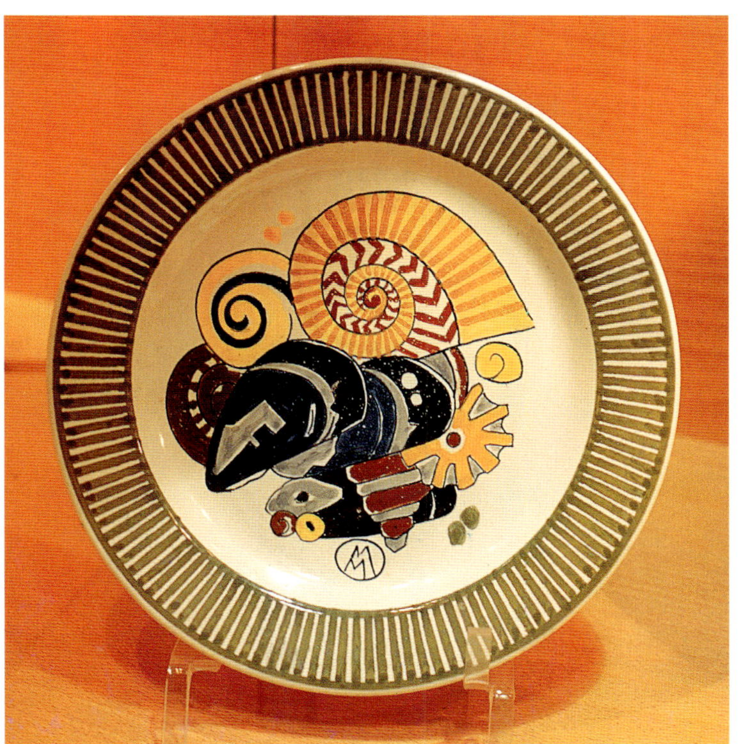

Marine life became the focus of ceramic works done by Mathurin Méheut for the Henriot faïencerie. The *La Mer* dinner service featured underwater life motifs. This plate from the series measures 9.75" diameter, is bold and colorful, and contains his *chiffre*, MM, in a circle. *Courtesy of Musée de la Faïence, Quimper.*

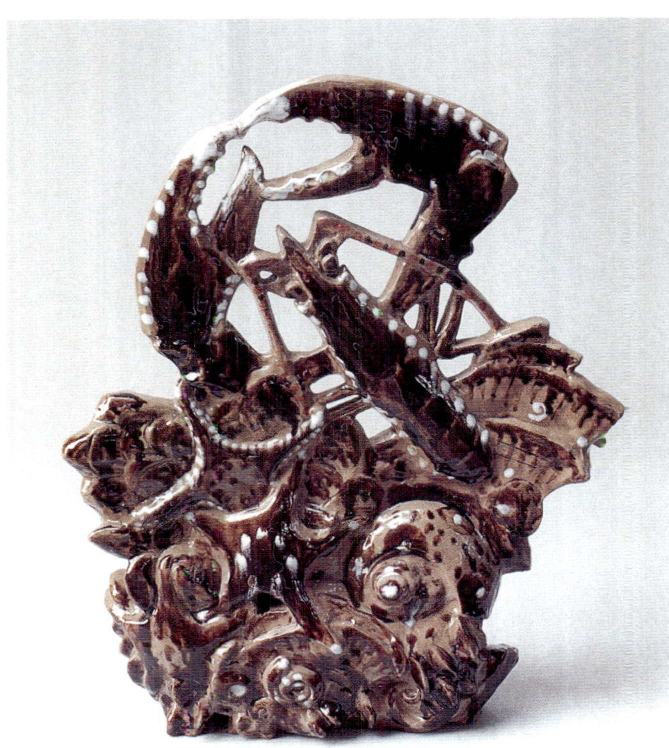

As a result of his fascination with the sea, Méheut became a well-respected marine life painter and designed many sea-related items in faïence for the Henriot factory. Méheut's contributions included the table service designed in the early 1920s entitled *La Mer,* which featured various underwater life forms, and a remarkable sculpture, *Crustacés et Mollusques,* from the 1930s, which is nearly 21" high. *(See Trois Siècles de Faïences, p.150.)*

The church Notre Dame de Kroaz-Batz with its eye-catching late-Renaissance tiered belfry is another landmark in Roscoff. In addition to the usual Passion scenes, the church is decorated with carved galleons and cannon, reflecting the town's seaside heritage. In the 1500s and 1600s, the *corsairs* (pirates) who made Roscoff their home donated amply to the church – when they weren't running raids on Channel shipping.

A remarkable sculpture, 20.5" tall, was designed by Mathurin Méheut between 1930 and 1940, and features crustaceans and mollusks. Méheut observed these creatures on his many trips to the northern coast of Brittany, a place he loved. Another example of this mold may be seen at *Le Musée de la Faïence* in Quimper, and in *Trois Siècles de Faïences, p. 151. Private Collection.*

Île de Batz

Île de Batz, pronounced *ba*, is a short boat ride from Roscoff across what can be a treacherous tidal race. The island is only about 4 kilometers long and 1 kilometer wide, but has numerous small beaches. It boasts a lighthouse with 200 steps, and the ruins of a monastery said to have been built by St. Pol.

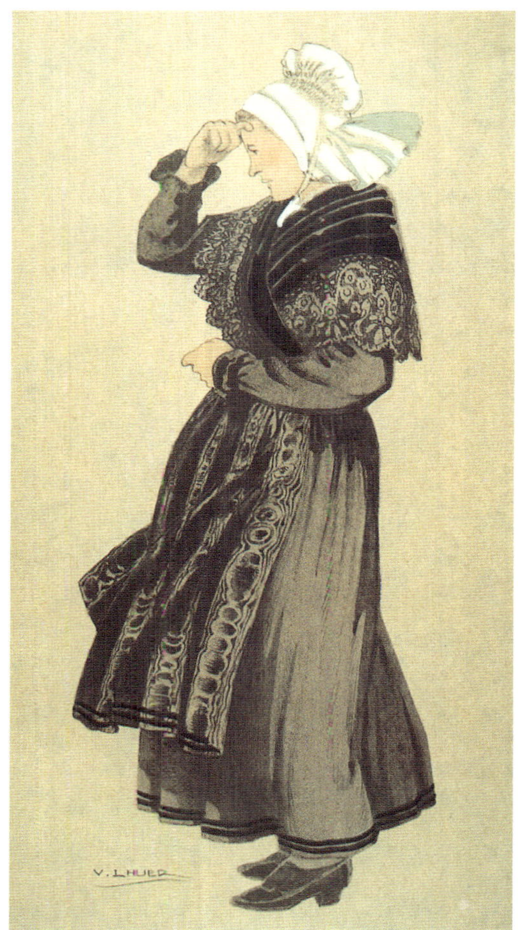

A woman from the *Île de Batz* is shown in regional dress in this 19th century print. *Private Collection.*

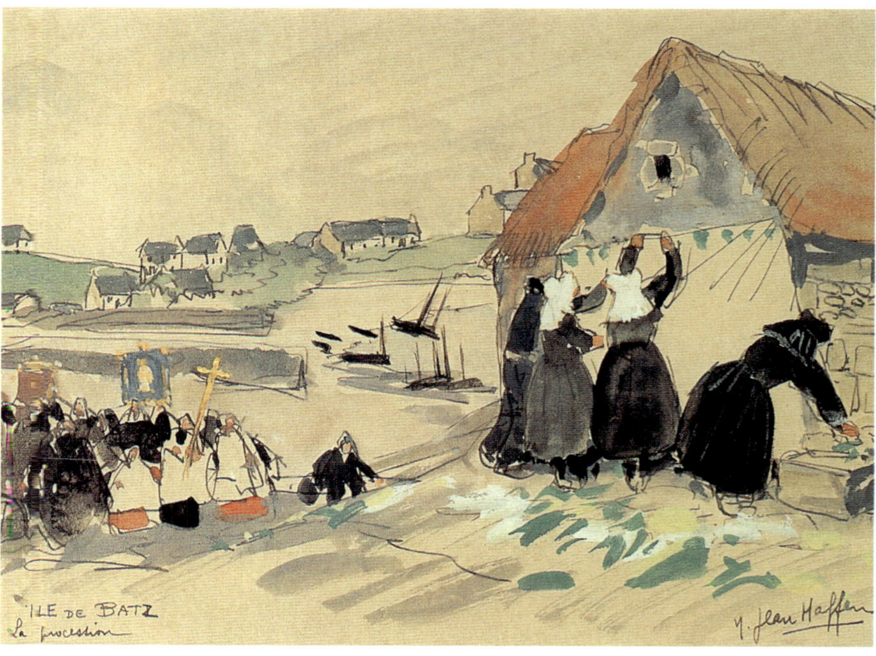

Méheut pupil and friend Yvonne Jean-Haffen painted this scene from the *Île de Batz,* showing a religious procession and costumes of the women from the island. *Courtesy of Musée des Jacobins, Morlaix.*

Legend tells that St. Pol conquered a dragon on the island by wrapping a stole around its neck and hurling it into the sea, akin to the St. Armel legend. A statue of St. Pol resides in the island *Chapelle de Sainte-Anne*, and the *Kroaz Paol*, Breton for Cross of St. Paul, which was torn down during the French Revolution, is affixed to a nearby dolmen. St. Pol, known as the Bishop who wanted to remain a monk, lived out his life of a reported 104 years on the island! Batz today is a serene location with no motorized vehicles, a mild climate, and perhaps a touch of Eden. *(Hillion and Mingant, Île de Batz, pp. 11-13.)*

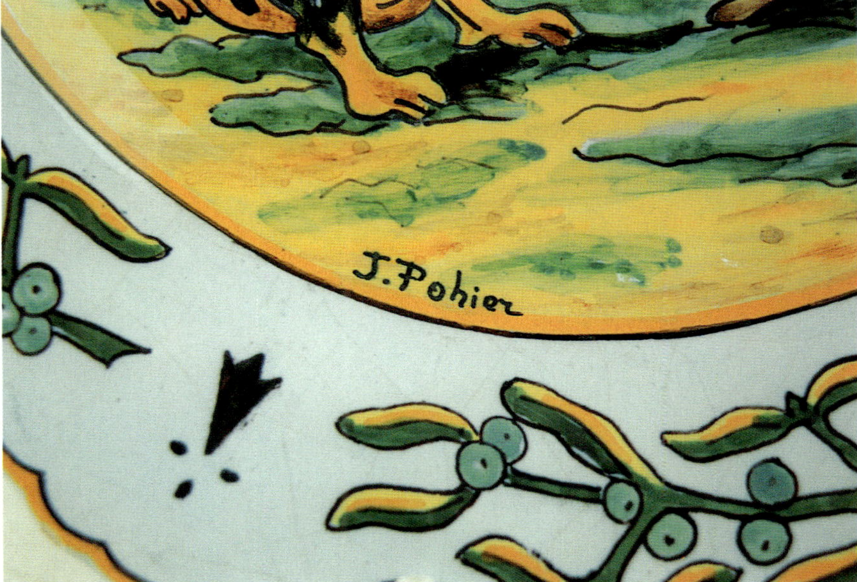

One legend about St. Pol recounts his domination of a dragon on *Île de Batz*. He captured the creature by throwing his shawl around its neck and casting it into the sea, in a place called the *Trou de Serpent*. This 10" Henriot plate is signed HR and J. Pohier. It shows St. Armel, a contemporary of St. Pol, conquering a dragon in the same manner. *Private Collection.*

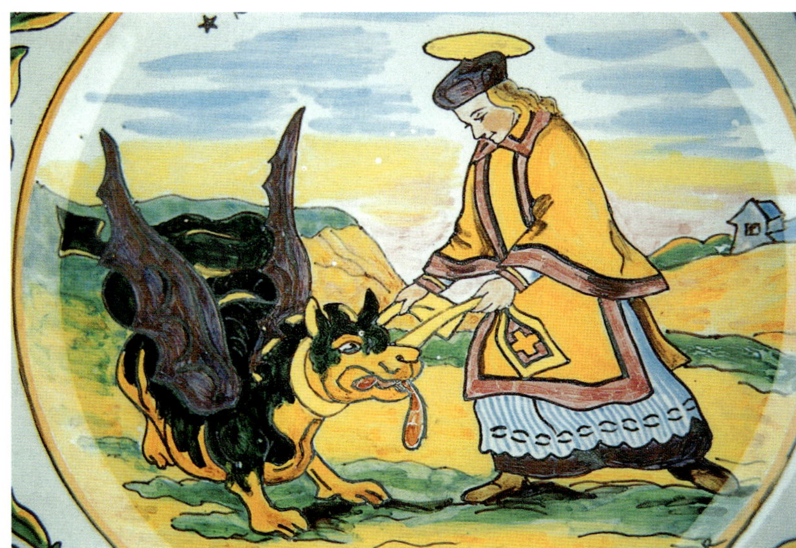
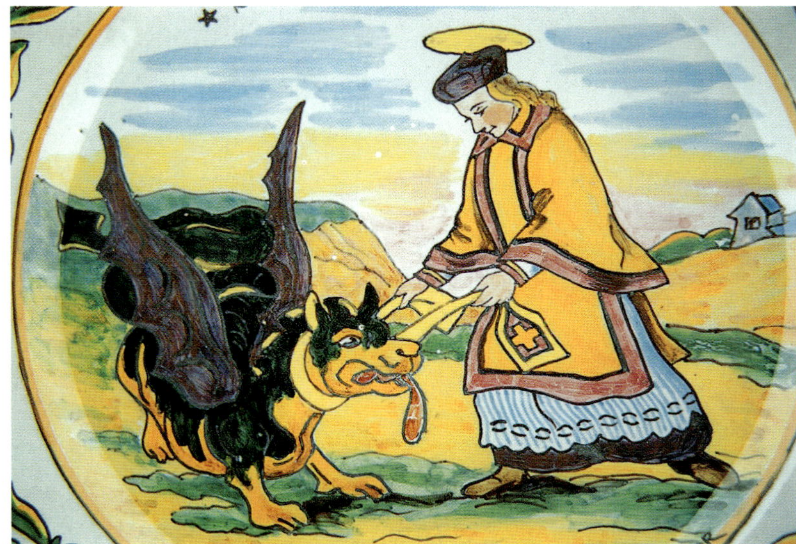

A close-up view of St. Armel capturing a dragon with his shawl shows the detailed painting done by Pohier. *Private Collection.*

The St. Armel plate is signed by the artist, J. (Jacques) Pohier, and is one in a series on the saints of Brittany executed by Pohier from the first decade of the 20th century. *(Meadows, p. 117.)* Additional examples are in the Chapters *Environs de Quimper* and *Quimper Sampler A to Z.*

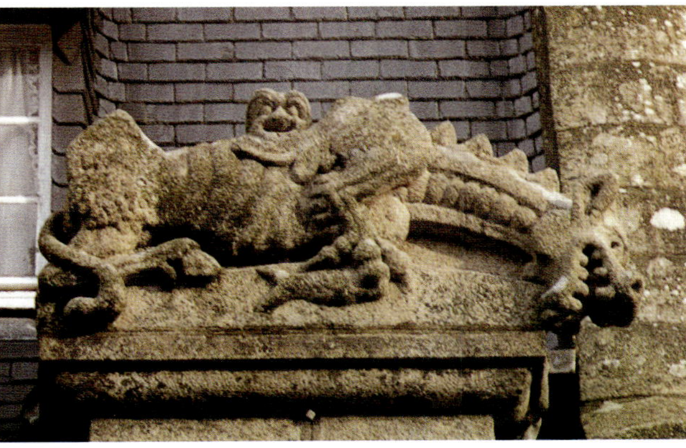

Be it legend, myth, or reality, there are no dragons today in Brittany – except those captured by artists on faïence, or as building adornments. This one is in Roscoff.

Barnenez

One day we were shopping for Quimper poterie northeast of Morlaix, when we passed a marker for a pre-history monument. Making note, we made our way back there later in the day. After our first impressive look at pre-history in Brittany at Carnac on the southern coast, we rarely pass up the opportunity to wonder at the megalithic sites scattered throughout Brittany.

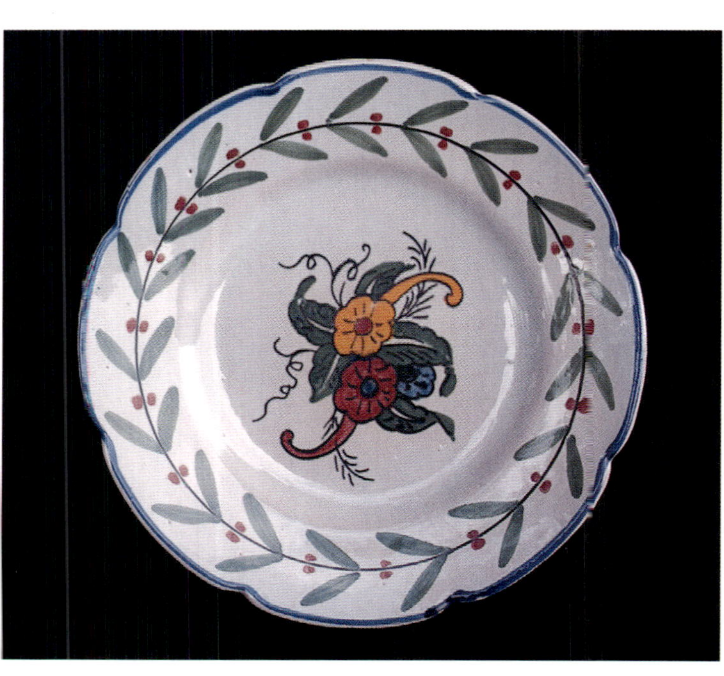

We found this Boulogne-sur-Mer 10.5" diameter plate with a floral design in St. Martin's, a suburb of Morlaix, on one of our day shopping trips. *Authors' Collection.*

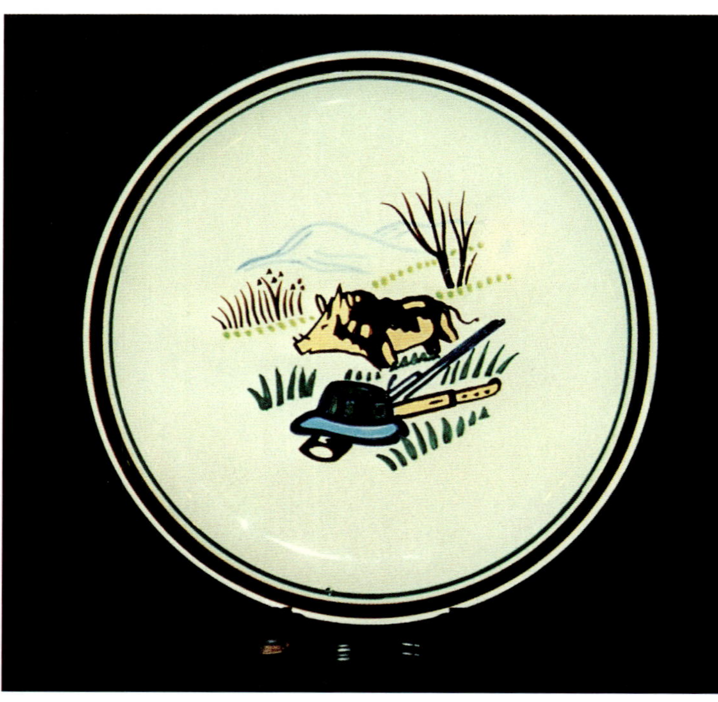

Another find was this hunt scene plate by Adolphe-Jean LaChaud. It is part of a set called *Chase* he designed for the HB faïencerie. *Private Collection.*

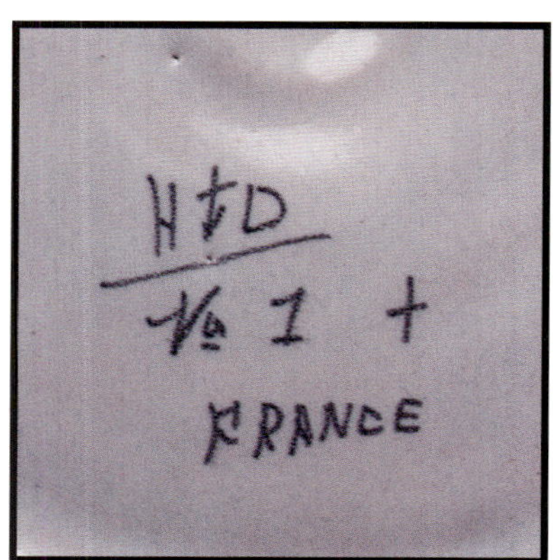

The signature on the Boulogne plate shows it was manufactured after Jules Verlingue sold his business to Henri Delcourt in 1917. The HD signature replaced the VJ signature used by Verlingue. *(Correspondence with Bernard Verlingue, April 2001.)*

We also found this *panier fleuri* (basket of flowers) plate on a day shopping trip from Morlaix. It was unsigned, but early, so we bought it. *Private Collection.*

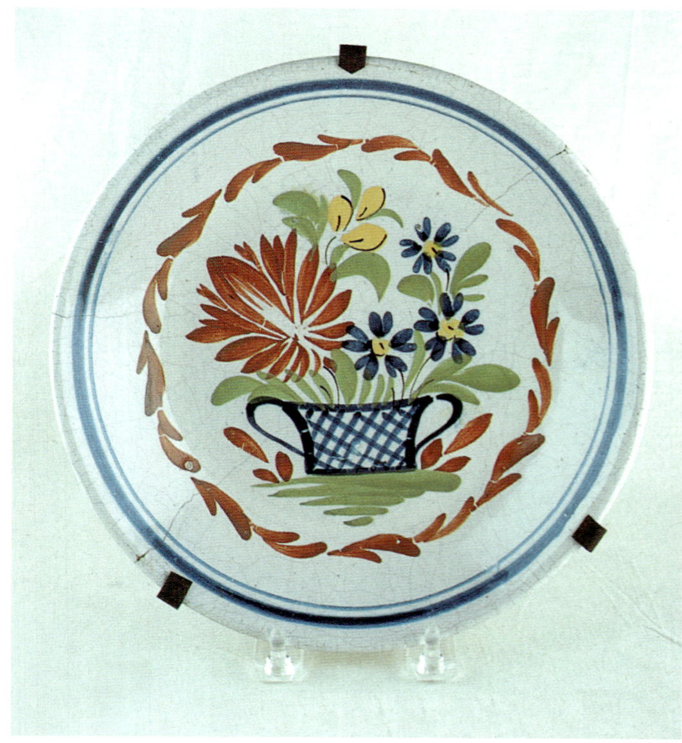

If you have any interest in archaeology or prehistory, as we do, make time to visit *Le Grand Cairn de Barnenez*. Barnenez, an estimated 6,000 years old, is acknowledged as one of the best prehistoric sites in northern Brittany. It is located about 16 kilometers northeast of Morlaix, and consists of two cairns. The second section, in lighter colored stone, was designed to tightly blend into the first. It was added about 200 years after the first section, which is dated 4200 B.C. Barnenez was used by a still unknown people as a burial site until about 2000 B.C., according to carbon dating.

Cairn: Pile of stones surrounding one or more burial tombs.
Dolmen: Megalithic monuments built of stone slabs and thought to be burial sites.
Megalith: Prehistoric monuments made of very large stones.
Menhir: Single, upright stone placed alone or in lines, alignments.
Tumulus: An artificial mound, built of stones, earth, or a combination of the two. It may cover dolmens. *(Briard, Megaliths of Brittany, p. 2)*

The Barnenez Cairn was saved from destruction, the fate of too many megalithic sites in Brittany and elsewhere.

During the 1950s, when the site was considered an uninteresting pile of rubble, it was opened as a quarry. This unfortunately was the fate of more than one megalithic burial site in Brittany. Several of the 11 burial chambers were exposed, showing the extent and importance of the cairn, and restoration began. Barnenez opened to the public in 1968.

Some of the burial chambers were constructed in the hive or oven style, and others were in the flat-granite-slab style. There are 12 to14 tons of small stones piled in this 270-foot-long structure. Engravings can be found on some chamber walls and pottery remnants are scattered about, especially in the terrace area, which is considered a ceremonial site. Earliest examples of pottery from Brittany date back to about 3000 B.C. and show an advanced stage of development. The pottery usually was linked to megalithic religion, and most Neolithic sites, such as mounds and passage graves, provide pottery fragments. *(Giot, Brittany, pp. 28-30.)*

Our exploration of Barnenez served as a journey of discovery, in many ways. Poring over these ruins, we came to realize that more than 5,000 years ago – more than 3,000 years before Christ – humans had a culture in this area that could not be denied. They built structures and had rituals, such as burying their dead, which set them apart from most other forms of life. It is often said that the mysterious stones at Carnac, Barnenez, *La Roche-aux-Fées*, and other areas in Brittany, France, and throughout the world, stand on the landscape, asking us to examine who we are and prodding us to ponder how we evolved. It is easy to see why some people argue that the early people who constructed these monuments should be recognized for their sophisticated civilization, and that we, in fact, are really no different than they.

The Grand Cairn is a National Monument, and has been a protected site since its discovery in the 1950s.

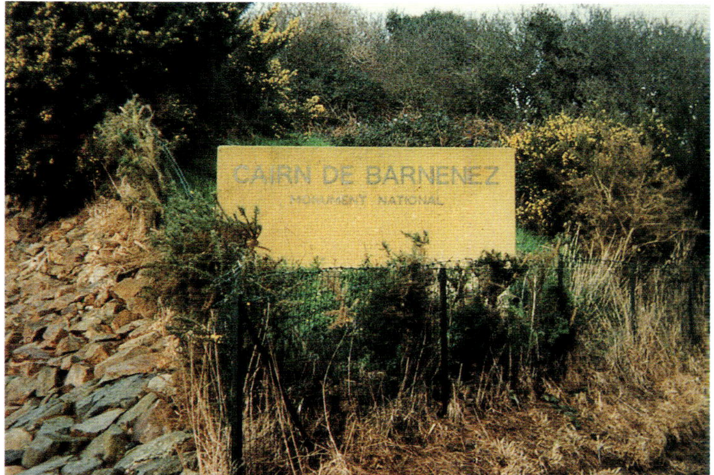

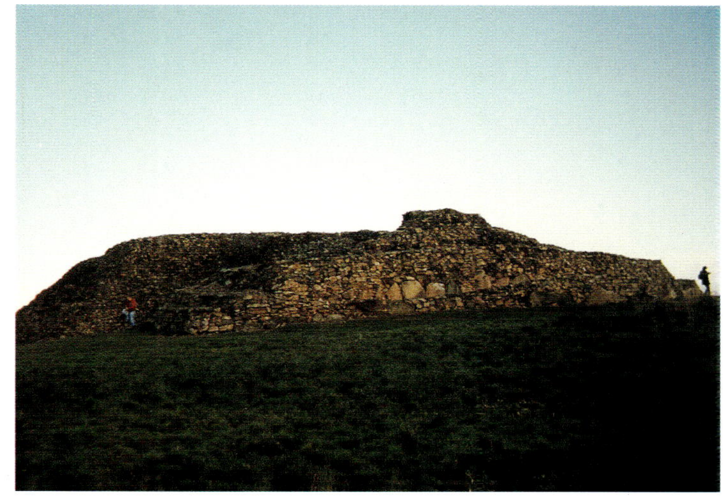

The sheer size of the cairn at Barnenez overwhelms the viewer. Clearly it took great effort and time by the Neolithic people to build it.

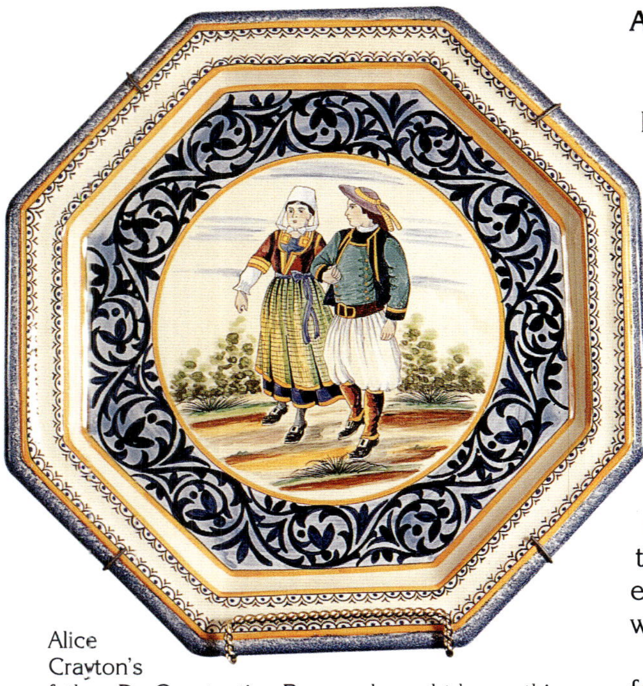

Alice Crayton's father, Dr. Constantine Roscoe, brought home this *HB/Grande Maison* 15.25" diameter octagonal *plat*, or large serving plate, from his World War II stay in the Morlaix area. He purchased the *plat* at the faïencerie in Quimper, before heading to another assignment in Belgium. *Collection of Alice and Mike Crayton.*

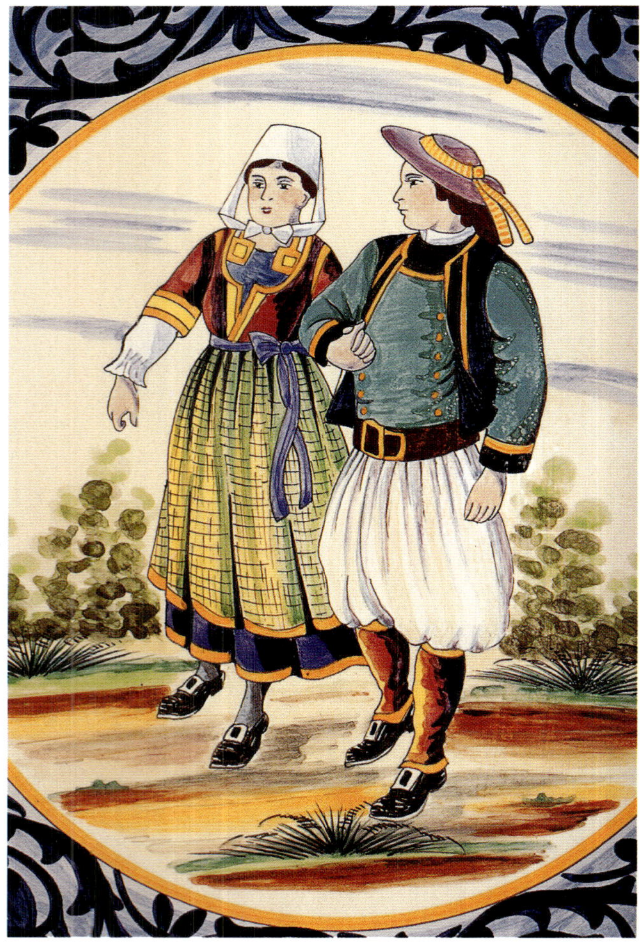

Alice Roscoe Crayton

We met Alice Roscoe Crayton when she came into our rural Pennsylvania antiques gallery to look at Quimper. She is one of seven Roscoe children, and always fancied the Quimperware her parents purchased in France during World War II. Alice's quest for Quimper brought her into contact with us, and she shared with us the story of how her family's interest in Quimper began.

It started with Alice's parents, who met in Brittany during World War II, soon after the June 1944 invasion of Normandy. Her father, Dr. Constantine Roscoe, a Thomas Jefferson Medical School graduate, and her mother, Virginia Van Dyke Roscoe, a registered nurse from Michigan, were assigned to a hospital in the Morlaix area. They recall that it was similar to a M*A*S*H unit. There were constant air raids, a lot of time spent waiting for the injured, then sudden rushes of incoming wounded. Her parents married in Belgium, where they had been transferred to assist with the wounded after the Battle of the Bulge.

Before leaving Brittany, Alice's father recalls visiting the Quimper factories and buying poterie. Some was for Virginia and him, and some he sent home to his parents in Pittsburgh, where his father was a Byzantine Catholic priest. He carried one item, an octagonal plate, through the rest of the war. When he came home, he gave the Quimper plate to a friend and classmate of his uncle's, Dr. Norman Macneil. When Dr. Macneil passed away, he willed the plate back to Alice's father.

When Alice and Michael Crayton were married, her parents gave them the collection of Quimper accumulated in France, including the octagonal plate. Alice was the only one of the seven children who had expressed interest in the Quimper, and she fondly recalls drinking her coffee from the *soleil* (yellow) mugs every morning before school. Alice and Mike treasure their wedding gift and have it prominently displayed in their home. In 1983, when they were traveling in France, they even made a special trip to Brittany, to retrace Alice's father's steps as he purchased Quimper so long ago. Since then they have purchased more Quimper pieces to add to their lovely collection. Alice and Mike's two daughters, Virginia and Madeline, both are very interested in Quimper, so the collection will be cherished into the future.

The plate features a Breton couple walking in the countryside, and perhaps reflects Alice's parents' meeting during WW II in Brittany. It is signed HB Quimper (...+), the type of signature used by the HB faïencerie artists in the 1920s-1930's. This signature belongs to Mlle. Péron. *(Taburet, p. 216.)*

৬ ON TO QUIMPER

For us, all roads in Brittany lead to Quimper. Leaving Rennes heading west to Quimper, we've taken northern routes through Morlaix, central routes through Mur-Bretagne and the Guerledan Lake area, and southern routes through Vannes. Each trip has been memorable and taught us about Brittany and her people. We traveled differently than some merchants who rush from sale to sale on their quest for Quimper, but we are grateful we take the longer way.

Quimper is named for the Breton word *kemper*, meaning meeting place or confluence, in this case where the rivers Odet and Steir converge. Many Americans struggle with the pronunciation of Quimper. A Breton acquaintance living in the United States told us what we found to be the simplest pronunciation on one of our early quests for Quimper. Think of *camp*(ing) outside in the *air*; thus, *camp-air*, and you can say it easily.

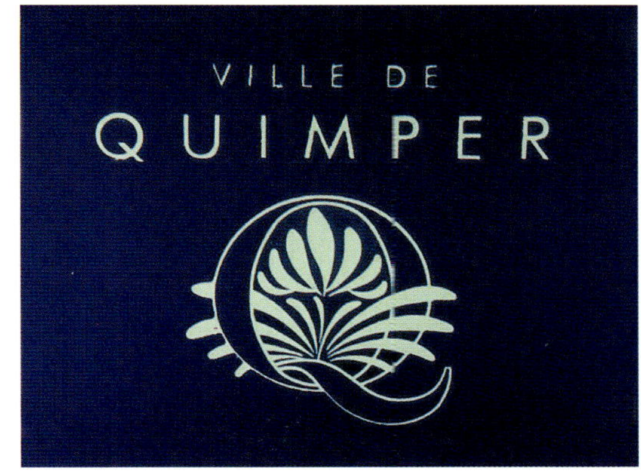

Quimper is known as the *Ville d'Art et d'Histoire*. The city is full of art, history, and spirit all waiting for the visitor.

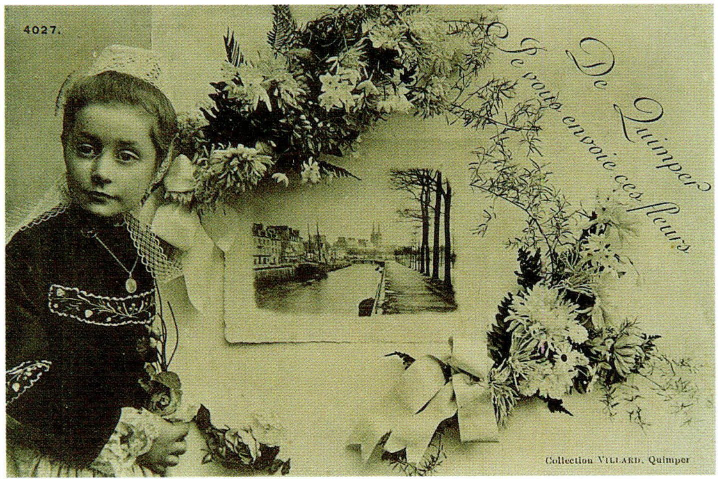

A vintage postcard shows a young Bretonne, flowers, and a photograph of the port of Quimper from Locmaria. Quimper is also called the city of flowers. *Authors' Collection.*

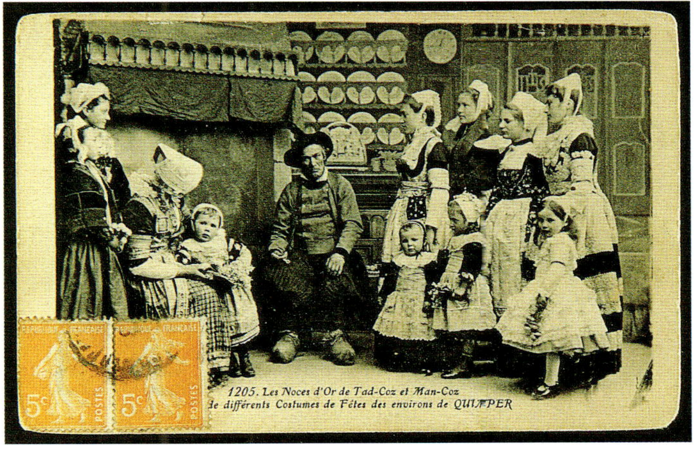

An early postcard shows a Breton home with the family gathered in their finery. Note the Quimper poterie in the plate racks and the costumes of a bygone era. *Authors' Collection.*

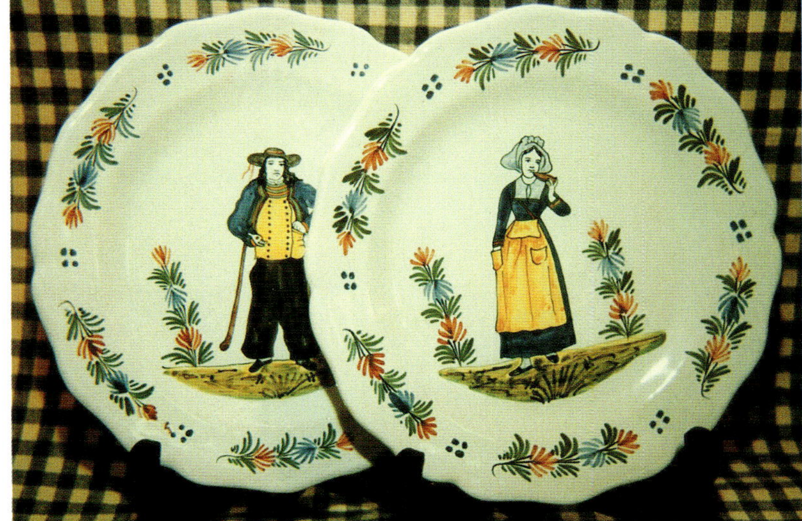

Earlier times are reflected on these 9.5" naïve-style unsigned plates most likely from the HB faïencerie, turn-of-the-20th century. The Breton is dressed in long pants and carries a walking stick. The Bretonne wears a yellow apron and appears to be eating some bread. *À la touche* floral sprays are on either side of the Bretons, and the border floral garlands are interspersed with a blue four-dot design. *Private Collection.*

Another Bretonne appears on a 11" long *biniou*-shaped wallpocket by the *HB/Grande Maison*. She is walking in the *campagne* (countryside) and carries a *cruche* (jug). Idealized Bretons in costumes of an earlier time are not walking on the streets of Quimper today, as some collectors may like to imagine! *Private Collection.*

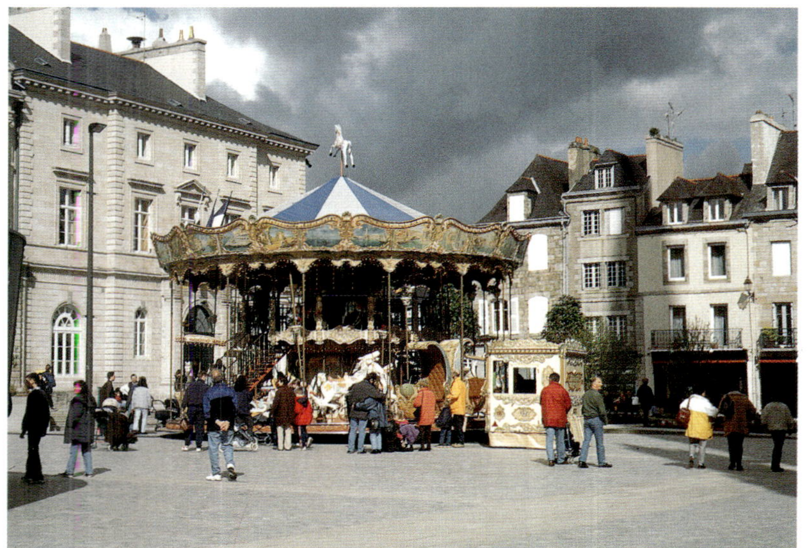

The Cathedral Square in Quimper hosts markets and festivals, and has for centuries.

The first time we entered Quimper, it was dusk and rush hour. We were shocked, naively having expected a quaint town, not a thriving urban center. Where were the *petits Bretons* from the plates, vases, and wallpockets? Quimper's population used to be around 16,000. Then in 1960, the mayor of Quimper proposed and achieved the consolidation of three smaller towns with Quimper. A later mayor brought in three additional small towns, so by 2001 the population was over 65,000. Most *Quimpérois* live in housing outside the historic district, not where most Americans visualize as *vieux*, or old Quimper. *(J. Datesman, Quimper Club International Newsletter, Spring 2000.)*

Years of searching for Quimper in the United States and months of planning the trip made the wait until the next day difficult. Here we were finally in the home of Quimper poterie, and excitedly, we went over our agenda. Our search for the history, art, and spirit of Quimper was about to begin. And we found these qualities in the museums, the faïenceries, and the people of Quimper. Our *triskele* spins on!

Cultural History in Quimper

Quimper is known throughout Brittany, France, and the Quimper collecting community for the largest folk festival, *La Fête de Cornouaille*, held annually in July. For a week prior to the last Sunday of the month, parades of regional costumes, theatrical performances, and musical events fill the town. *Bretons* and *Bretonnes* in native attire from many individual towns in *Finistère* mingle with the thousands of tourists, as Quimper reflects on its cultural heritage. Some people denigrate folk festivals as childish, naïve, and a foolish longing for the past, but the Breton author Jakez Hélias saw folklore as timeless and a protest against the future.

The value of our civilization has been acknowledged (through folk festivals in honor of our) *culture*. which prior to World War II almost no one, not even the antiques dealers, would have dared to grace with that word. (*Hélias, Horse of Pride, p. 337.*)

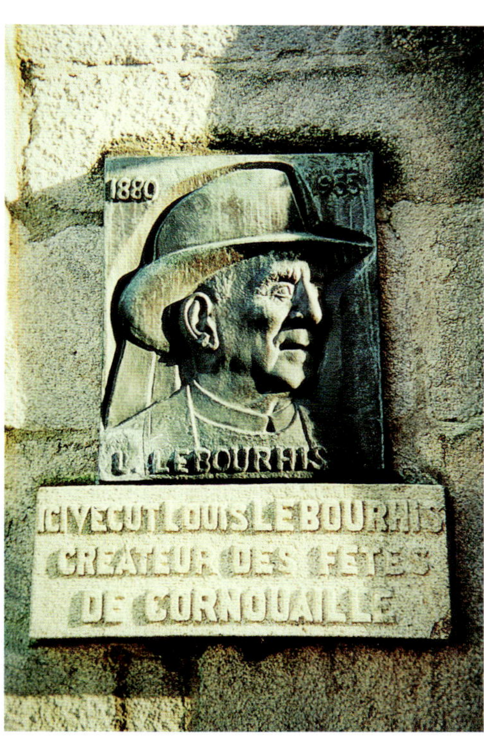

Not far from the center of the historic district, we found a plaque commemorating the founder of the annual festival in Quimper. Louis Le Bourhis is credited with initiating the *Fête de Cornouaille* held each July.

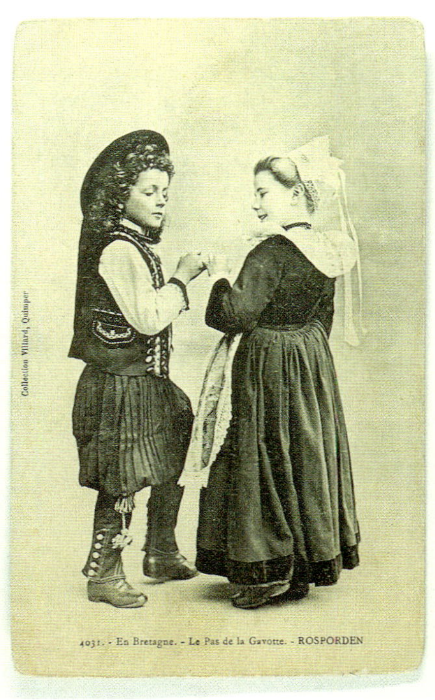

Costumes like these on children from Rosporden, a small town about 25 kilometers southeast of Quimper, are seen at the annual festival. *Fête* participants parade and dance variations of the *gavotte*, the energetic Breton dance. *Authors' Collection.*

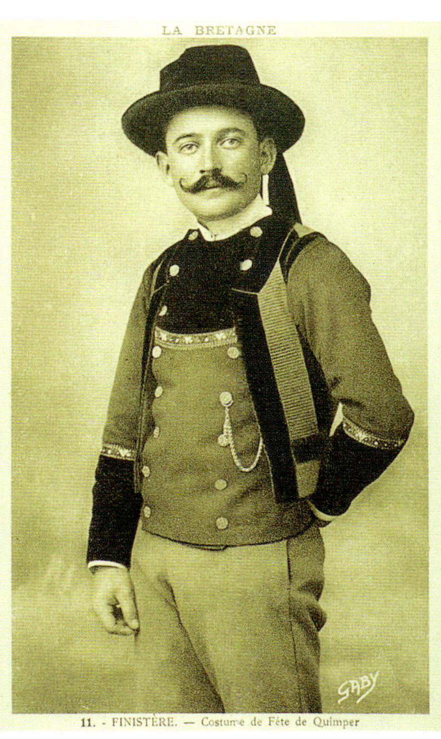

A Quimper gentleman's *fête* costume is featured on this early 20th century postcard. *Authors' Collection.*

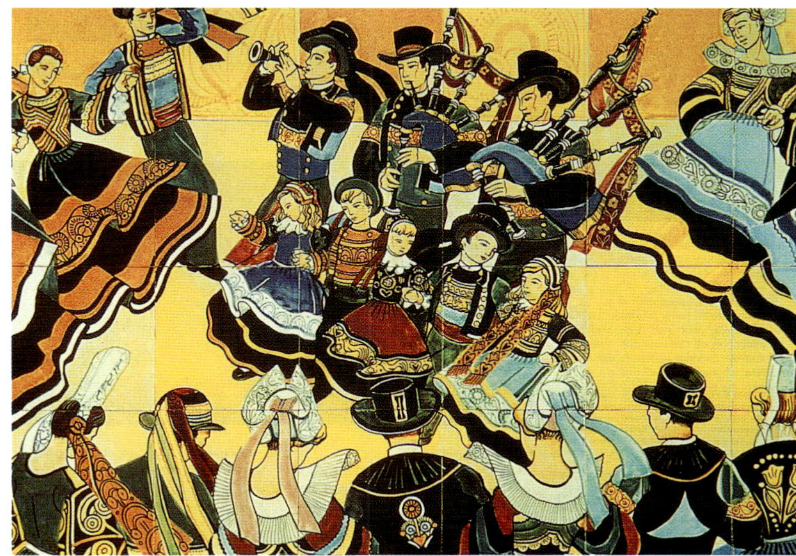

Colorful festival dancers are captured on tile mural by Henriot artist R. Micheau-Vernez. The action is exciting and the *biniou* and *bombarde* practically can be heard from this art on display at Quimper's train station.

On our first full day in Quimper we enthusiastically set out early in the morning with a full agenda. We found the tall, half-timbered medieval houses on *Rue Kéréon*, which leads to the Gothic *Cathédral de Saint Corentin*, the *Musée des Beaux Arts*, with its wealth of Breton works, the *Musée Départemental Breton*, with a compelling display of Quimper poterie, costumes, and furniture. But first we had to wend our way through the triple-lane conduits around the old city, and as novices to Quimper, we hampered the other drivers who didn't care we had come thousands of miles just to visit the home of the famous Quimper faïence.

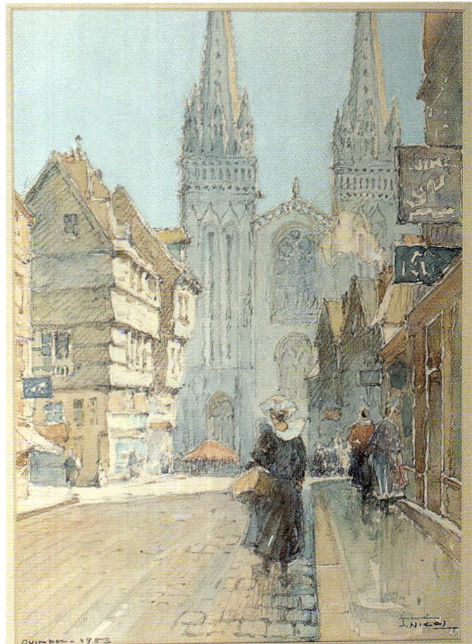

This watercolor view shows the *Cathédral de St. Corentin* from *Rue Kéréon*. *Courtesy of A.W. Styer.*

Right:
An early *chemin de fer*, or railroad poster, advertises Breton attractions. This view of St. Corentin from the *Rue Kéréon* is from a slightly different angle than the watercolor. *Private Collection.*

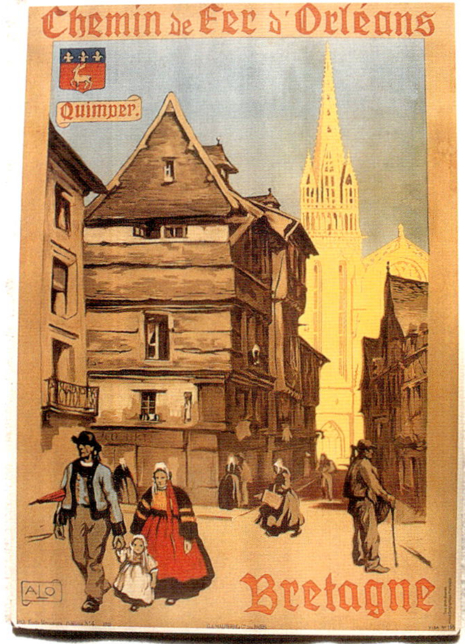

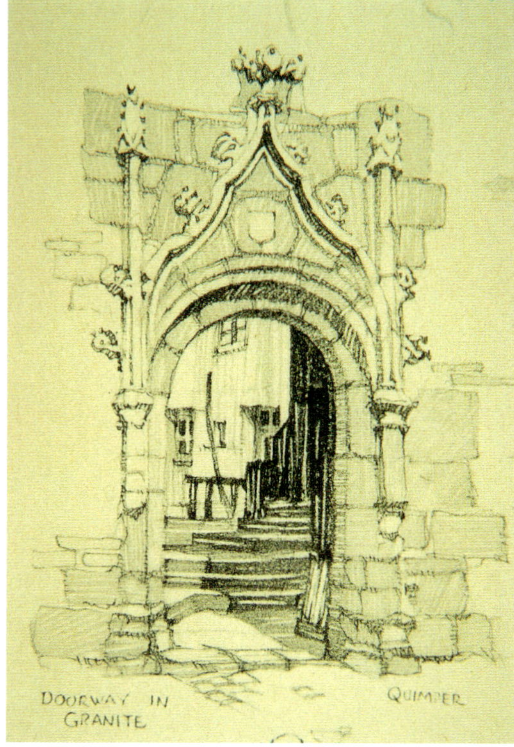

A granite doorway in old Quimper is captured in this sketch from a late-19th century book on Breton architecture. *Authors' Collection.*

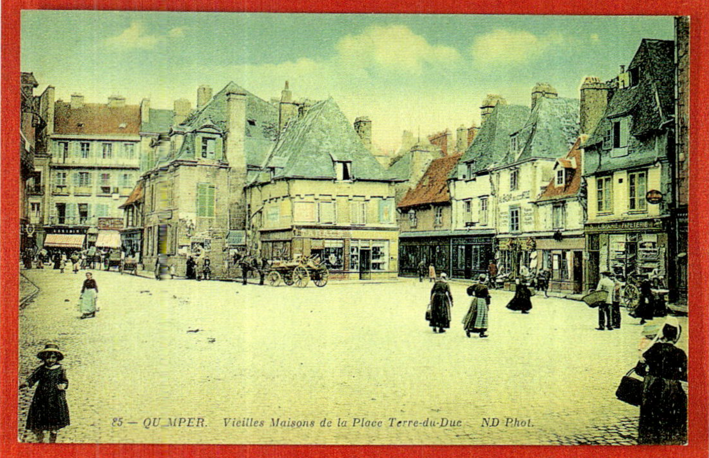

This turn-of-the-century colorized postcard of Quimper's famous *Place Terre-au-Duc* shows the old half-timbered houses surrounding the square where the *Duc de Bretagne* market was held.

Right:
An interior scene of a tea room in Quimper on this vintage postcard shows fabulously carved period Breton furniture and Quimper, of course. Berthe Savigny figurines decorate the walls along with Quimper plates. Quimper also is in the plate racks, on shelves, and on tables. A large faïence statue of *Notre Dame de Locmaria* stands watch over all, along with a painting of a view of Quimper from *Rue Kéréon. Authors' Collection.*

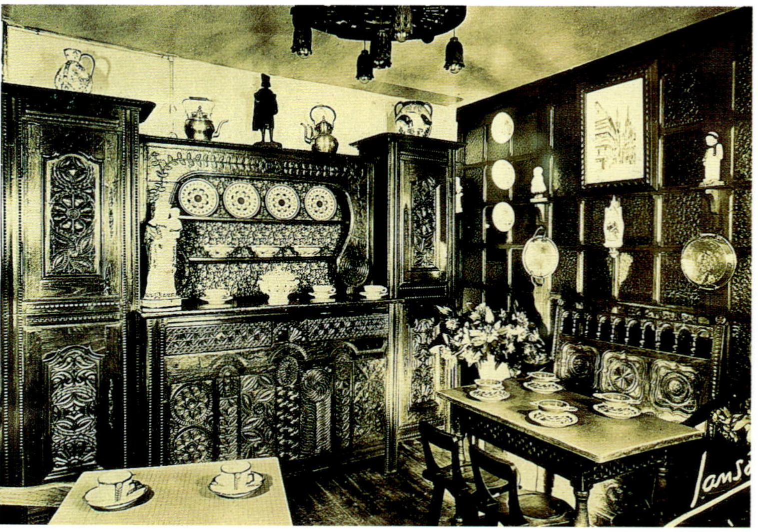

The jewel of the historical section of Quimper is *Cathédral de Saint Corentin*, named for the hermit who according to legend fed Gradlon, King of Cornouaille, and his followers from a single fish. Gradlon then invited Corentin to live in Quimper, where he became one of the seven founding bishops of Brittany. The Cathedral is on the seven stops of the *Tour de Bretagne*, *Tro Breiz* in Breton, or circuit of the bishoprics walked by the faithful.

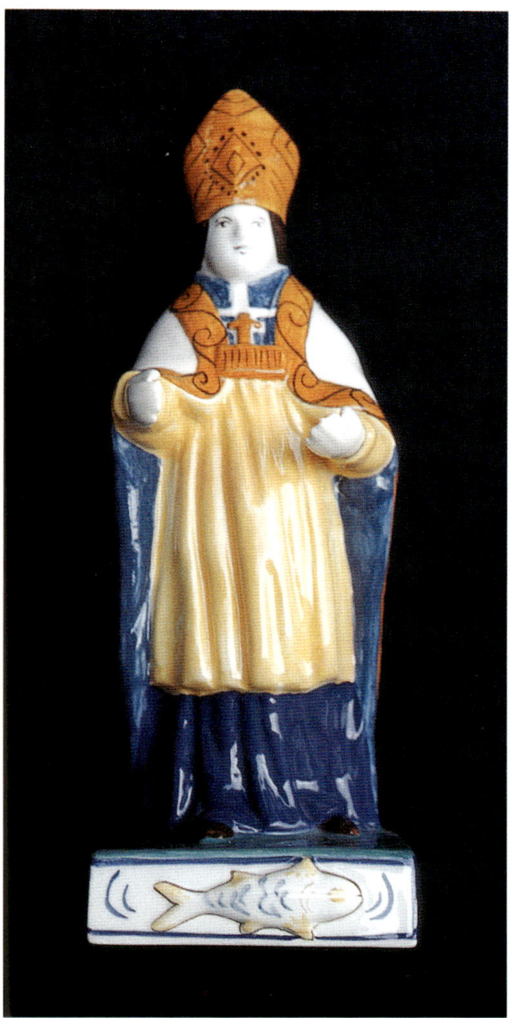

Right:
St. Corentin in faïence signed HB/Henriot, is a 9.5" tall recent version of the saint for whom the Cathedral is named. Note the fish on the base, representing the legend of a regenerating fish St. Corentin used to feed Gradlon and his followers. *Authors' Collection.*

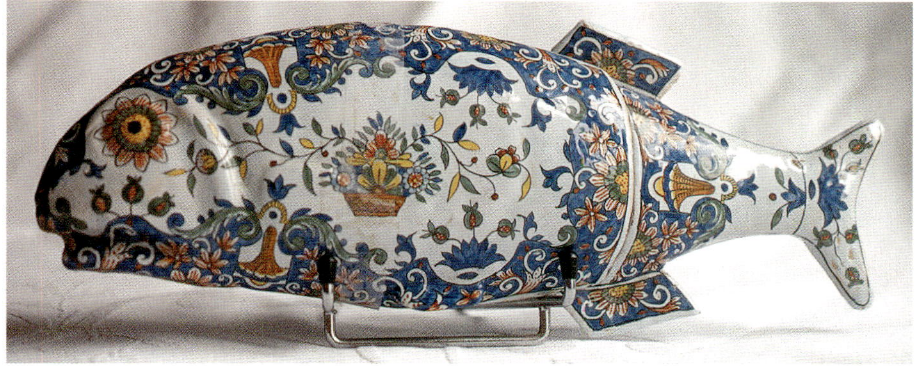

St. Corentin's fish by Porquier-Beau is 11.75" long and comes apart in the middle to form a holder for precious items. *Collection of Pierre Breton, Art de Cornouaille, Quimper.*

The Cathedral is a matter of pride to the people of Quimper. On our first visit to the city, Pierre Breton, a well-known Quimper merchant, took us on a guided tour of what is acknowledged to be the most complete Gothic cathedral in Brittany. Local granite was used to build the church, which was begun in the mid-thirteenth century, and completed about 1515. Pierre showed us how the mid-13th century chancel is out of alignment with its 15th century nave. Between the slender twin spires, added in the mid-1800s, the statue of King Gradlon astride his horse overlooks the *Place de la Cathédral* and passing Bretons. The Cathedral dominates the skyline for miles around, especially when it is viewed from Mount Frugy, which gives a stellar view of the city of Quimper for those willing to climb to the top.

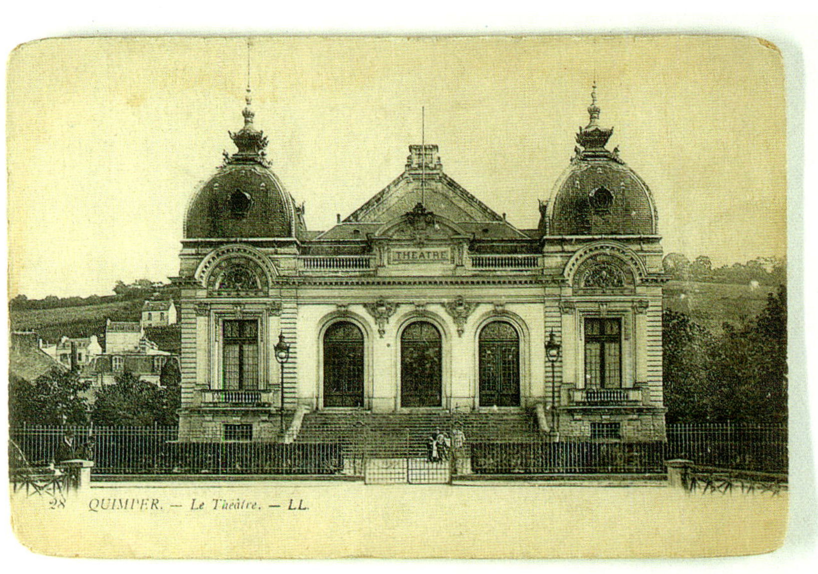

The theater in Quimper sits along the quay of the Odet River and is seen here on a postcard from the 1930s. It has been renamed for the artist/writer from Quimper, Max Jacob, as has a nearby bridge. Jacob loved his native Quimper, and he called it *Sweet Quimper, the nest of my childhood,* in *Quimper Yesterday and Today.* He studied literature and art in Paris and became friends with luminaries such as Picasso. *Authors' Collection.*

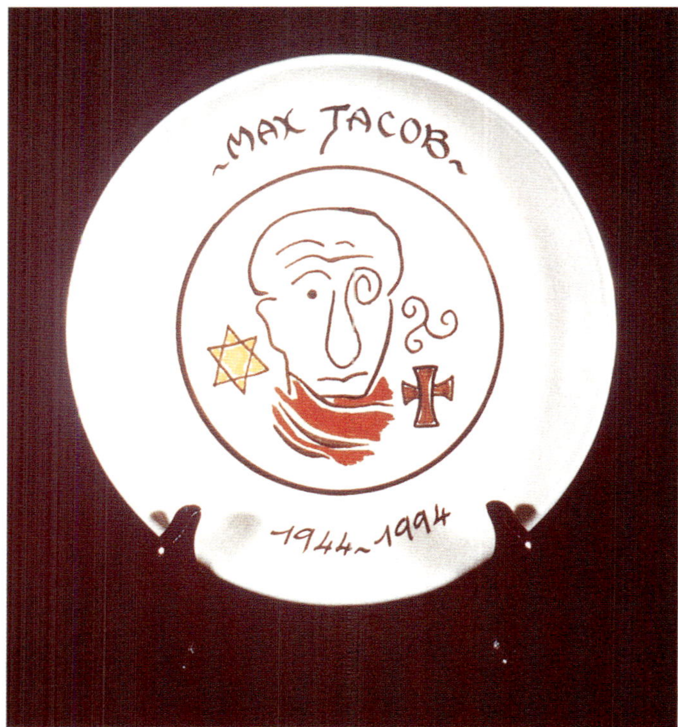

Max Jacob was imprisoned in a German detention camp, where he died in 1944. This commemorative plate signed HB/Henriot was produced in a limited edition, and is #19 of 50. The commemoration celebration was sponsored by the *Musée des Beaux Arts* in Quimper and the Picasso Museum in Paris. The plate is in honor of the 50-year anniversary of Max Jacob's death. *Private Collection.*

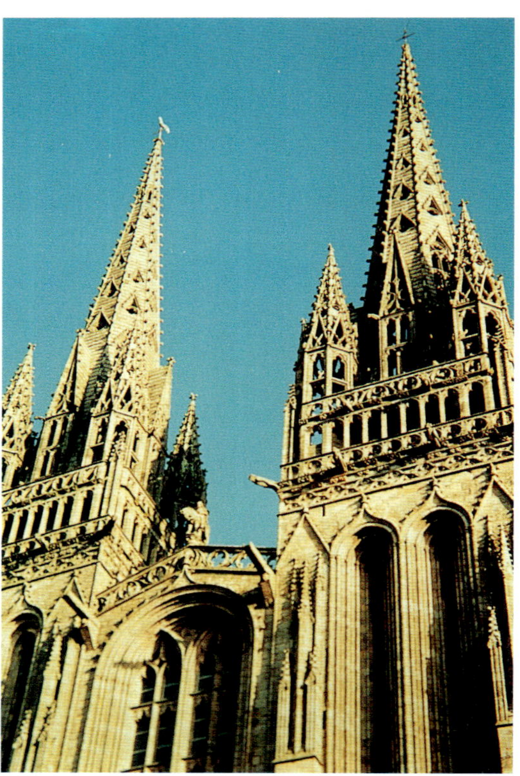

Gradlon, the King of Cornouaille, rides his stone steed between the twin spires of the *Cathédral de St. Corentin* on a glorious sunny day in Quimper.

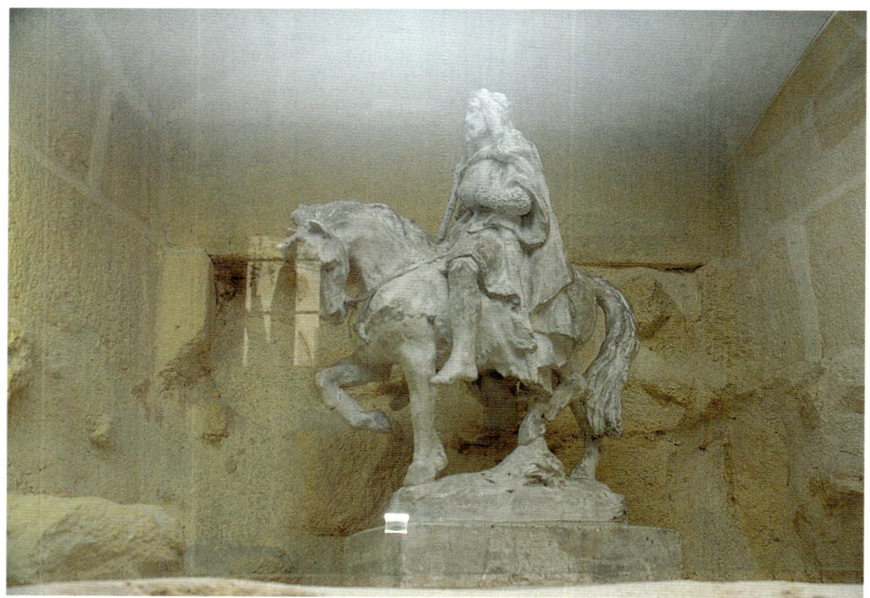

This early statue of King Gradlon on his steed resides behind a glass enclosure inside the *Musée Départemental Breton. Courtesy of Musée Départemental Breton, Quimper.*

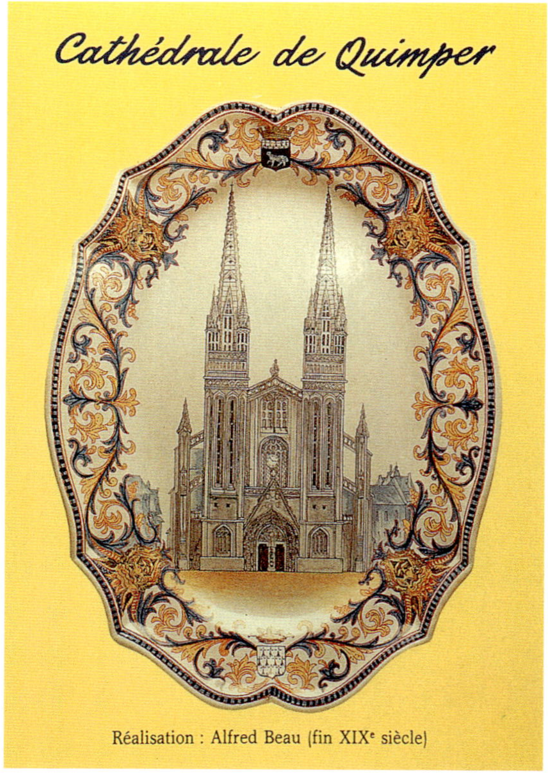

A Porquier-Beau large oval platter of St. Corentin Cathedral, designed by Alfred Beau, makes a stunning poster commemorating the church, which dates from the 13th century. *Private Collection.*

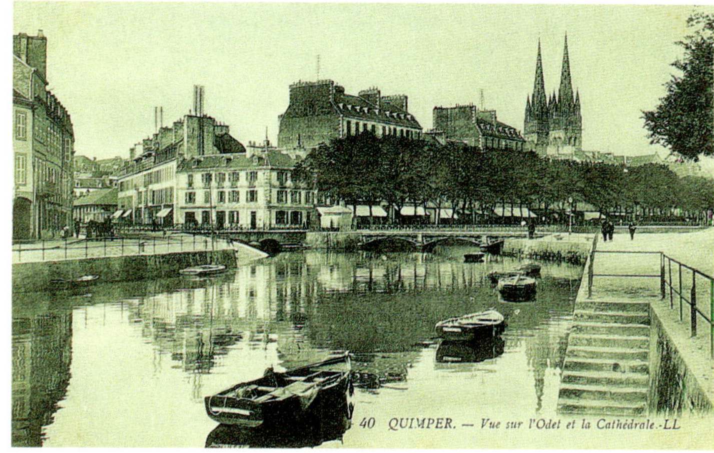

The twin spires of St. Corentin, added in the mid-1800s, are visible from the quay along the Odet River on this vintage postcard. *Authors' Collection.*

Next to the Cathedral is the former Bishop's Palace, a magnificent 16th century building that houses the *Musée Départemental Breton*. On our first trip to Quimper we discovered the wealth of Quimper poterie on display there. We were so taken by the collection we didn't want to leave for the obligatory lunch break from noon until 2 p.m. It was the first time we'd seen so much Quimper in one place, and our heads were reeling over the superb examples on display. (The *Musée de la Faïence, Jules Verlingue* had not opened yet.) In addition to the display of poterie, the *Musée Départemental Breton* collection includes historical regional costumes and furniture, as well as archeological findings showing the beginnings of the town. It also houses the sculpted monument of *Troilus de Mondragon*, c. 1540, which Jakez Hélias set out to see on one of his first visits to Quimper. The museum is overseen by the *conservateur*, Monsieur Philippe Le Stum, who is also the author of an excellent book, *Arts Populaire de Bretagne.*

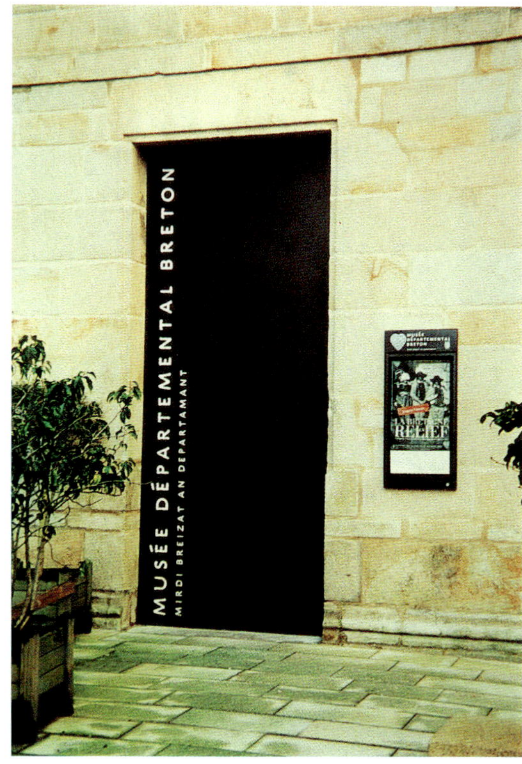

The *Musée Départemental Breton* stands next to St. Corentin Cathedral, and once was home to the Bishops of Quimper.

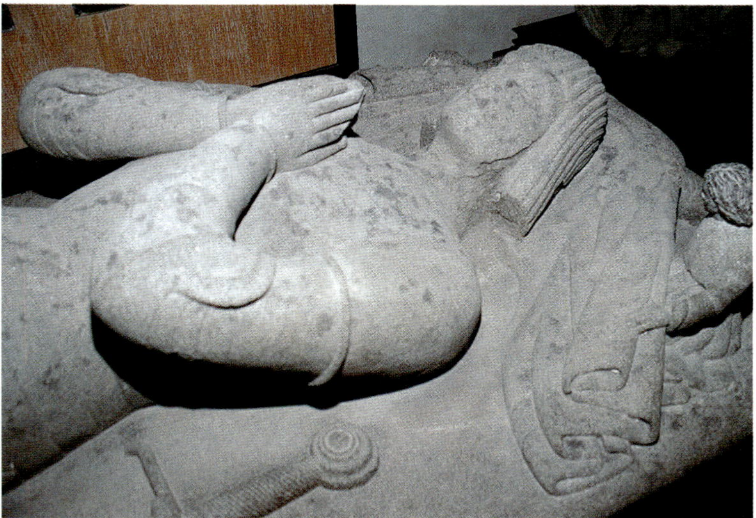

One of the first things we asked to see on a visit to the *Musée* was the *Tombeau de Troilus de Mondragon*, c. 1540. We read that as a young boy, Jakez Hélias paid a visit to what he called *the stone knight* on his initial trip to Quimper. *Courtesy of Musée Départemental Breton, Quimper.*

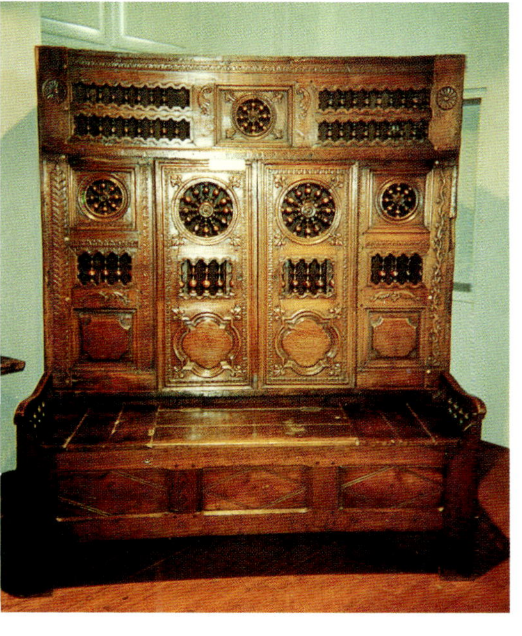

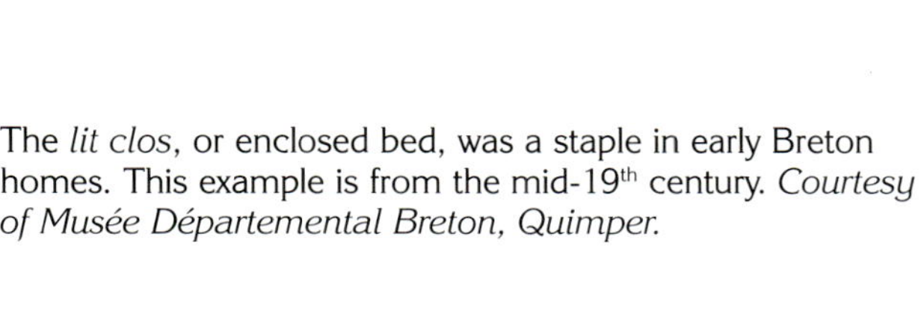

The *lit clos*, or enclosed bed, was a staple in early Breton homes. This example is from the mid-19th century. *Courtesy of Musée Départemental Breton, Quimper.*

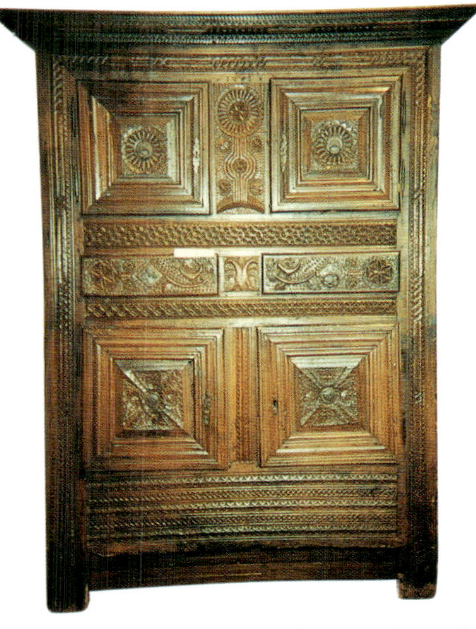

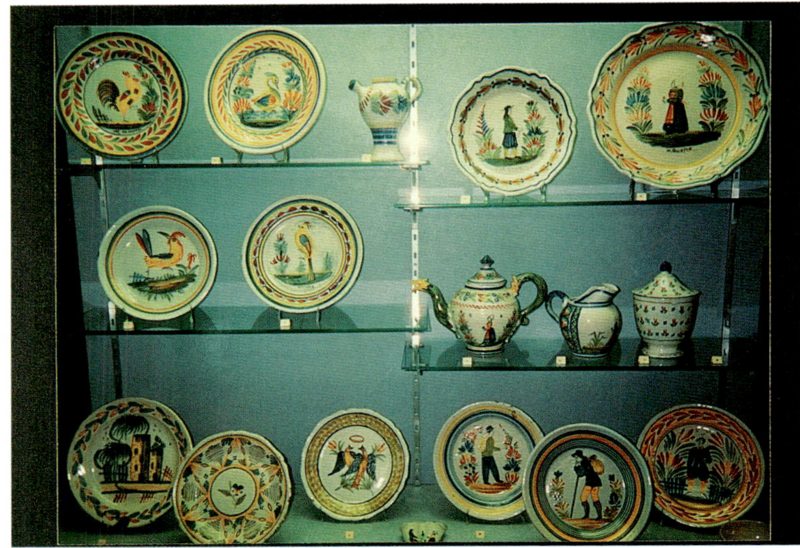

In *Horse of Pride*, Hélias tells of his mother polishing the furniture until the light from the evening fire was brilliantly reflected on it. This linen press from *Finistère* is c. 1825. *Courtesy of Musée Départemental Breton, Quimper.*

We were delighted to find a wide selection of Quimper poterie in the *Musée Départemental Breton* on our first visit to Quimper years ago. A potpourri of 19th century Quimper awaited us. There were several plates with bird motifs, a *biberon* (infant feeding bottle), plates with variations of the *petit Breton*, a *manoir* example, another with two *colombes* (turtle doves) with a wedding ring – signifying marriage – and a dragon-handled teapot. *Courtesy of Musée Départemental Breton, Quimper.*

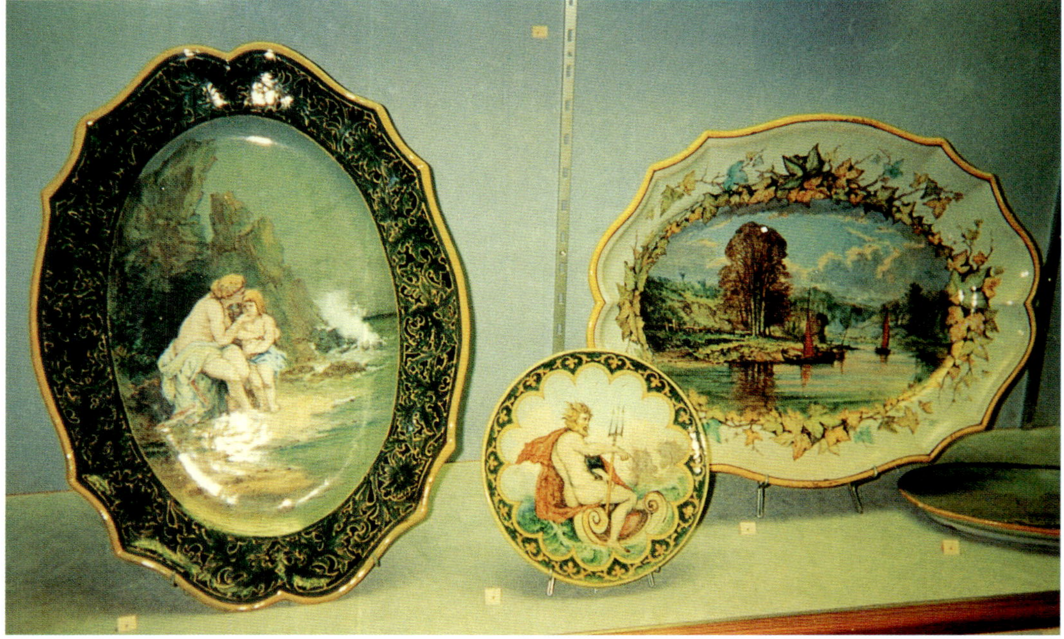

These Alfred Beau examples are stellar. The platter on the left is *Le Bain* (The Bath), dated 1893, is nearly 21" high, and is signed Alf. Beau. The smaller plate in the center also is by Alfred Beau, features Neptune and is dated 1880. The platter on the right, also signed Alf. Beau, is entitled *Bateaux de Pêche les Voiles au Sec* (Fishing Boats with Dry Sails), and is from the 1870s. *Courtesy of Musée Départemental Breton, Quimper.*

Right:
A closer look at Beau's Neptune plate shows the exquisite detail and color. *Courtesy of Musée Départemental Breton, Quimper.*

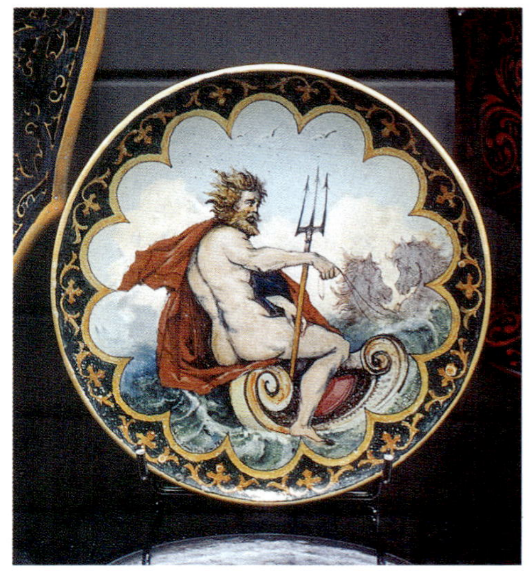

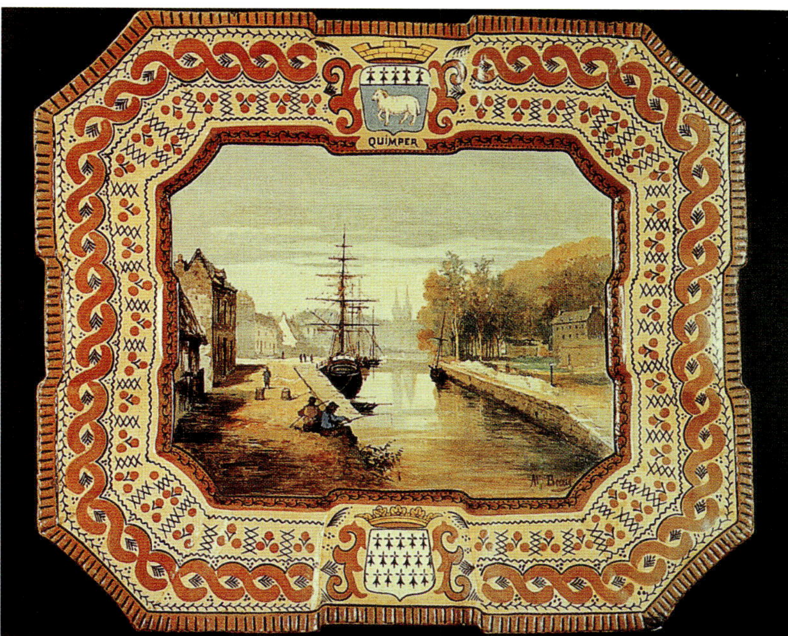

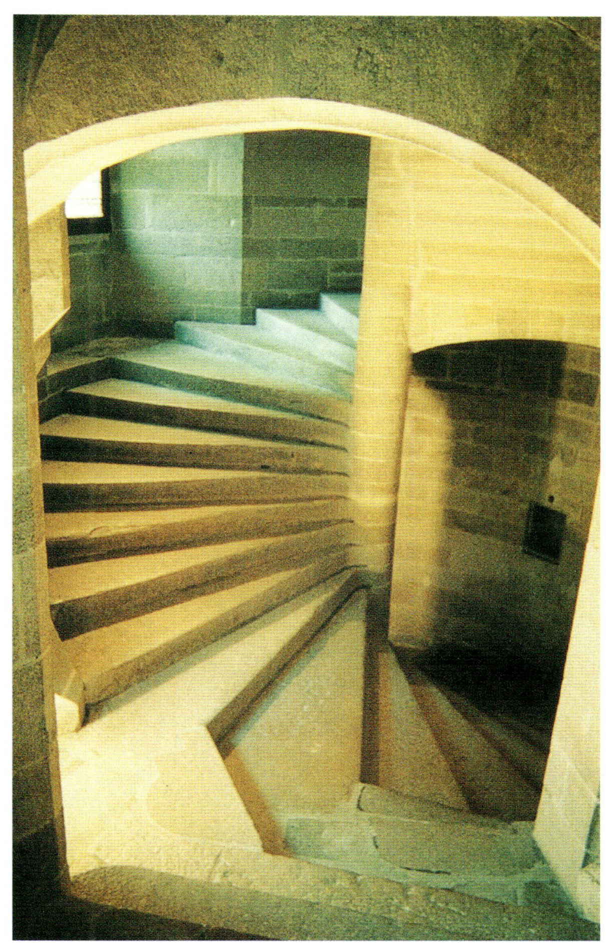

The Port of Quimper at Locmaria was one of Beau's creations featured on a *terre vernissée* 21.25" long Porquier-Beau plaque or platter. It has the armorial of the city of Quimper at the top center and the armorial of *Bretagne* at the bottom center. *Courtesy of Musée Départemental Breton, Quimper.*

Rohan Tower steps in the *Musée/ Départemental Breton* are an artwork.

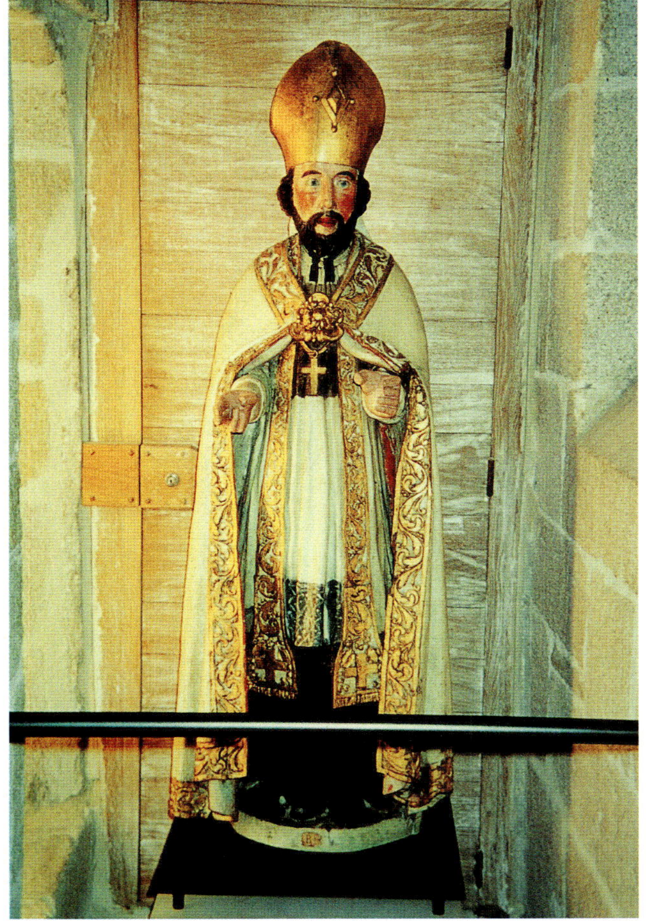

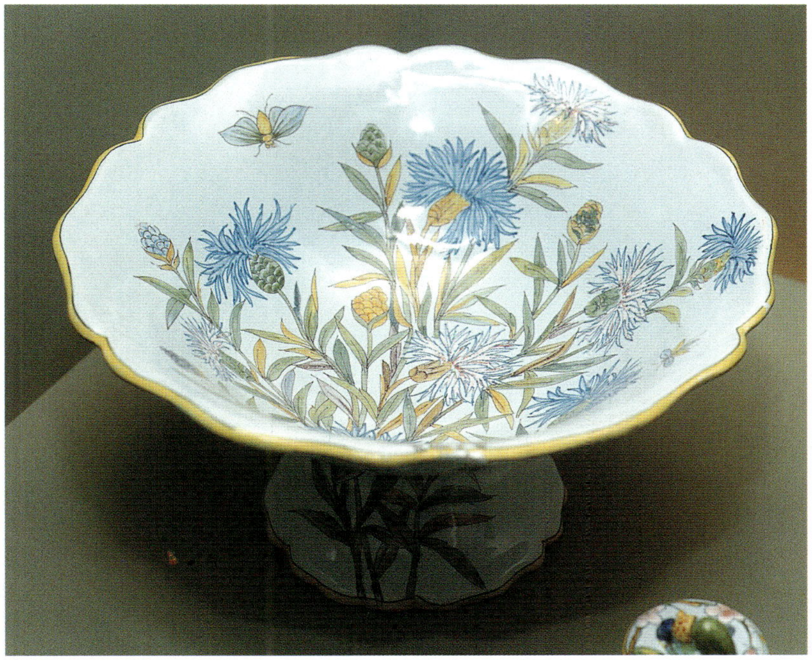

As we rounded a corner, a wooden statue named *St. Évêque* greeted us. Some observers suggest this is a rendition of St. Corentin, since *évêque* means bishop in French. The oak statue is dated 12th century. *Courtesy of Musée Départemental Breton, Quimper.*

Alfred Beau's *botanique* design on this Porquier-Beau footed compote is delicate and pastel in color. The attention to detail shows a much more sophisticated approach to rendering a floral motif than earlier Quimper works. *Courtesy of the Musée Départemental Breton, Quimper.*

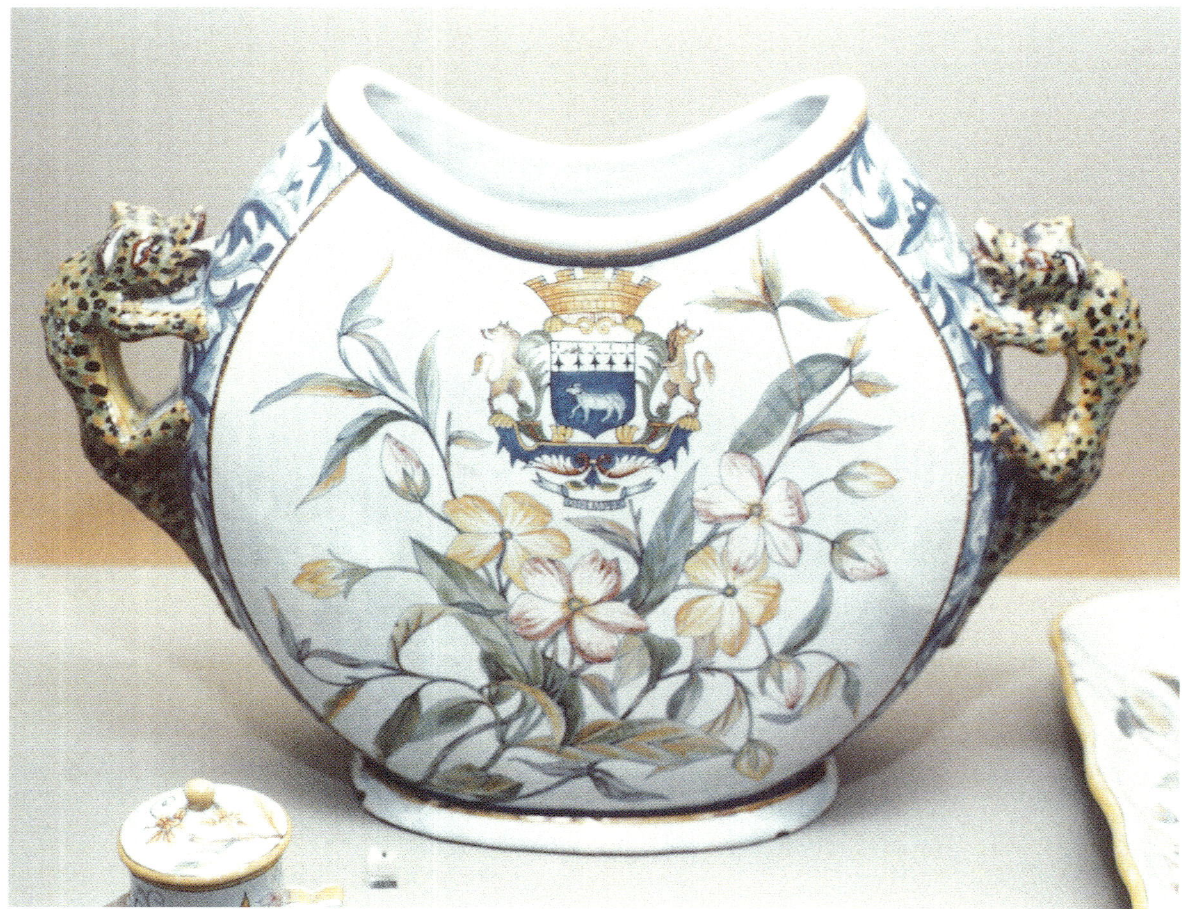

Delicately rendered botanicals grace this *chinois*-form vase, which also is called a moon jardinière, designed by Alfred Beau. The lizard handles are done with a playful coloration of black spots on a yellow ground, and the armorial of the city of Quimper is integrated into this Porquier-Beau work from the last quarter of the 19th century. *Courtesy of Musée Départemental Breton.*

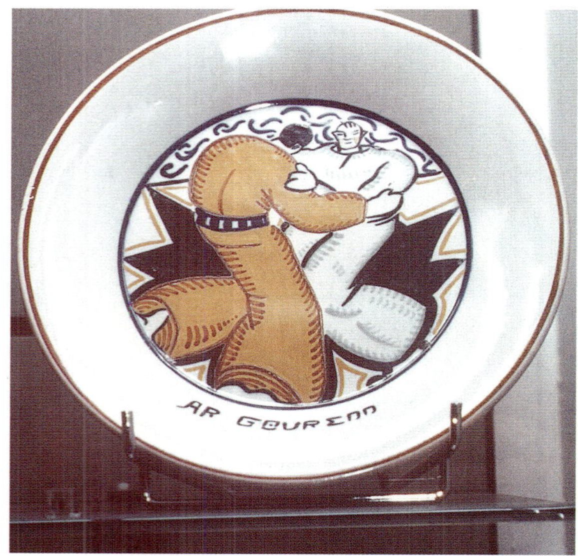

Pierre Abadie-Landel, an *Ar Seiz Breur* member, designed this stylized 9.5" plate for the HB faïencerie in the mid-1920s. The title in Breton, *Ar Gourenn*, or *La Lutte Breton* in French, means the struggle or fight. Perhaps it represents Brittany's struggle to regain her Celtic-Breton identity, after years of absorbing French manners, language, and ideas. *Courtesy of Musée Départemental Breton, Quimper.*

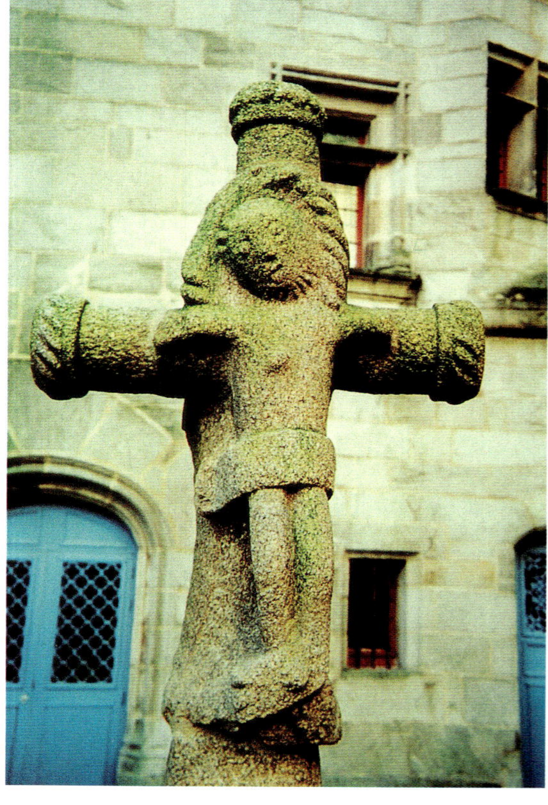

As we left the *Musée Départemental Breton,* an early stone cross awaited us in the courtyard. Reminders are everywhere that the history of the Breton people is much older than our American experience.

Across the square from the Cathedral stands the *Musée des Beaux Arts*, another extraordinarily well-appointed museum. Its first *conservateur* was Alfred Beau, and today's *conservateur* is Monsieur André Cariou. The *Trois Siècles* or 300th Anniversary celebration of poterie production in Quimper was held in the *Musée des Beaux Arts*, and the historically important books cataloging the Quimper poterie display were developed under Monsieur Cariou's direction. The museum is a grand setting, creatively displaying a collection of paintings from the 16th through the 20th century. It also has an active outreach program for youths and adults in the Quimper area.

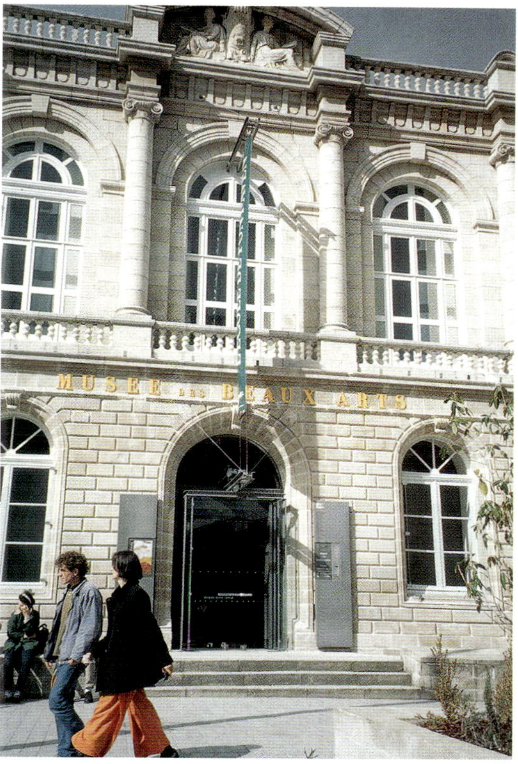

The *Musée des Beaux Arts*, the *Musée Départemental Breton*, and St. Corentin Cathedral all are within a few yards of each other around Cathedral Square.

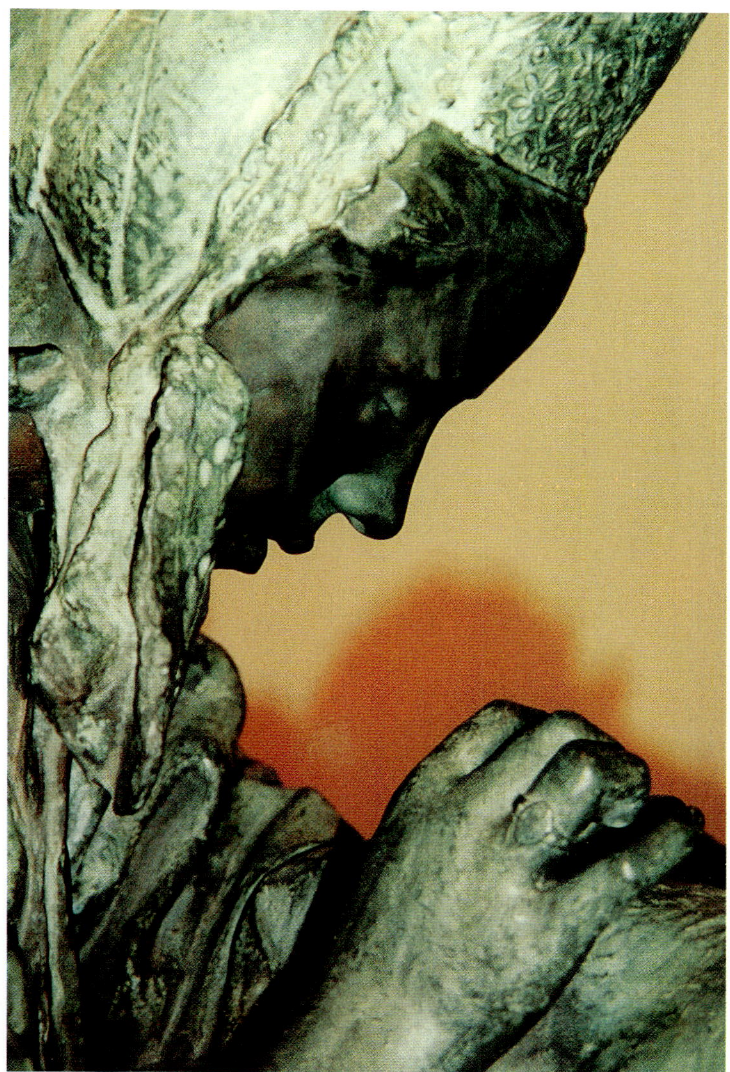

On our first visit years ago, we were taken with the large bronze sculpture by René Quillivic entitled *Brodeuse de Pont-l'Abbé*, or the Embroiderer of Pont-l'Abbé, dated 1907. *Courtesy of Musée des Beaux Arts, Quimper.*

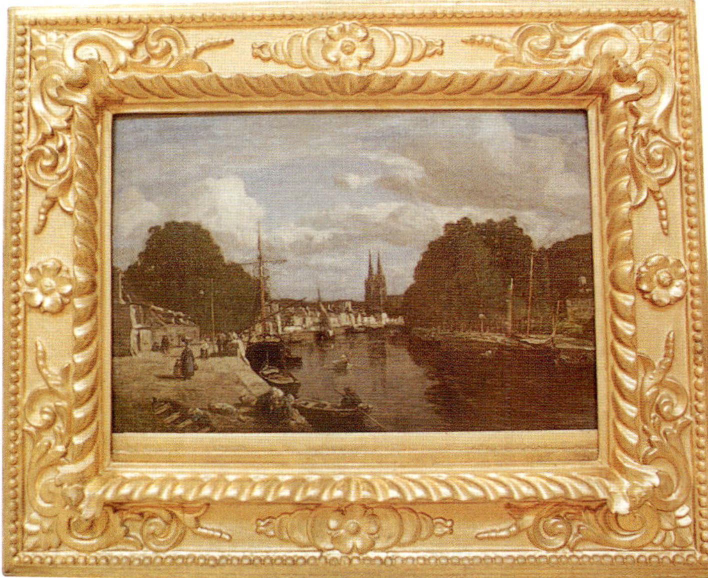

Right:
A recent visit to the museum allowed us to compare views of the Port of Quimper in a variety of mediums. The painting by Eugene Boudin, entitled *Vue du Port de Quimper*, 1858, resides at the museum. *Courtesy of Musée des Beaux Arts, Quimper.*

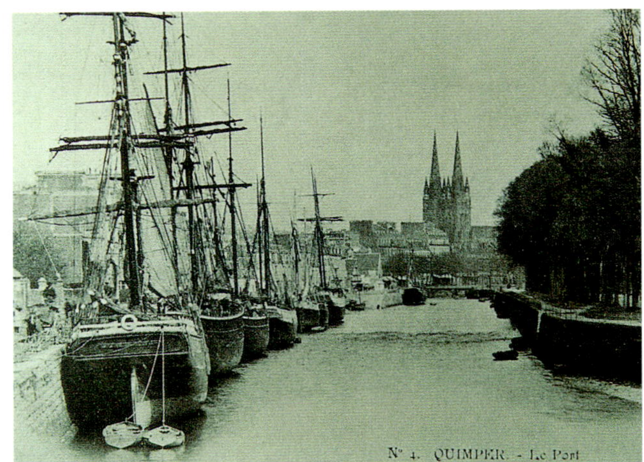

A vintage postcard shows a similar view in black and white. *Authors' Collection.*

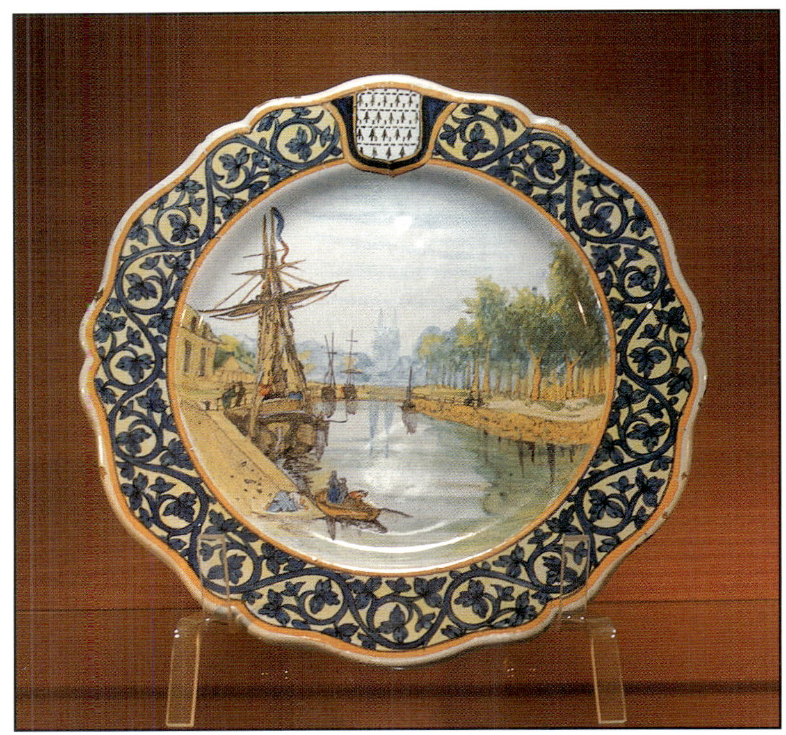

A 10" faïence plate by Porquier-Beau from the 1880s displays a view of the Port of Quimper from the same perspective. *Courtesy of Musée de la Faïence, Quimper.*

A similar view of the port appears on a Porquier-Beau *terre vernissée* platter, entitled *Port of Quimper*, also from the 1880s. This one contains black smoke, perhaps from a faïencerie kiln. *Courtesy of Musée de la Faïence, Quimper.*

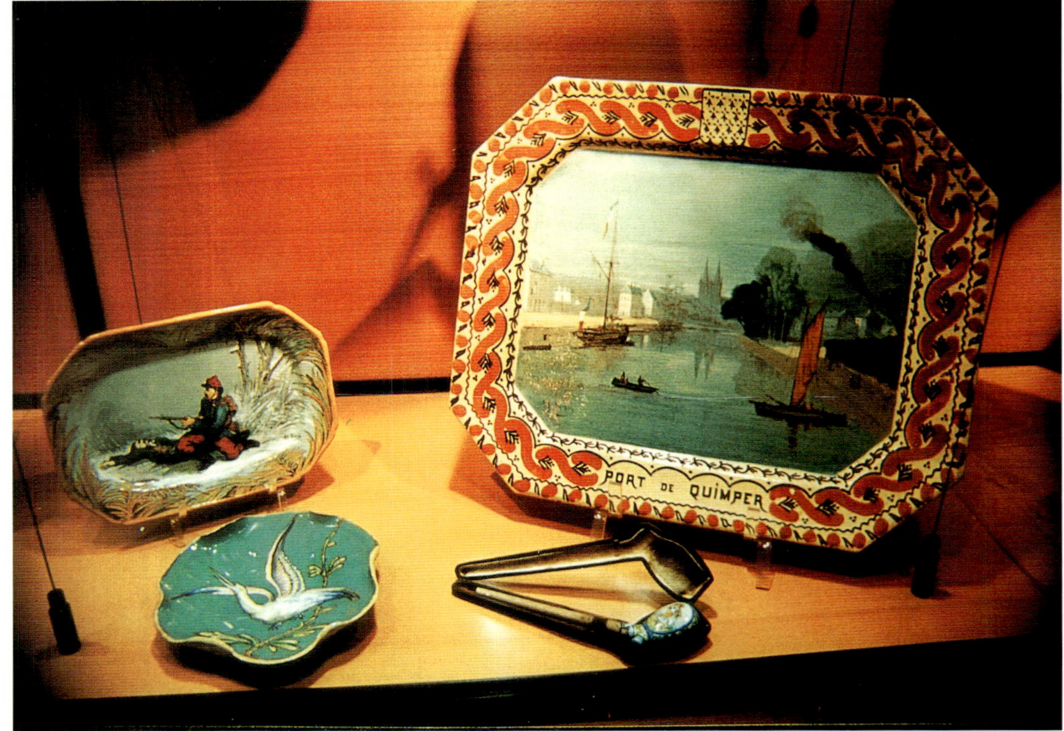

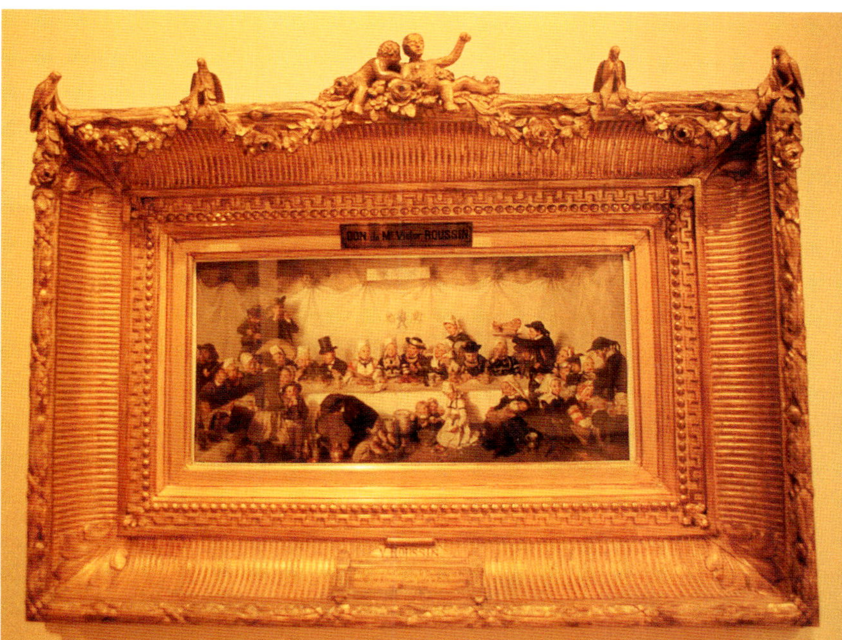

A popular painting at the *Musée des Beaux Arts* is entitled *Les Noces de Corentin Le Guerveur et d'Anne-Marie Kernivel,* by Victor Roussin, 1880. It illustrates a marriage banquet of the 19th century in *Finistère. Courtesy of Musée des Beaux Arts, Quimper.*

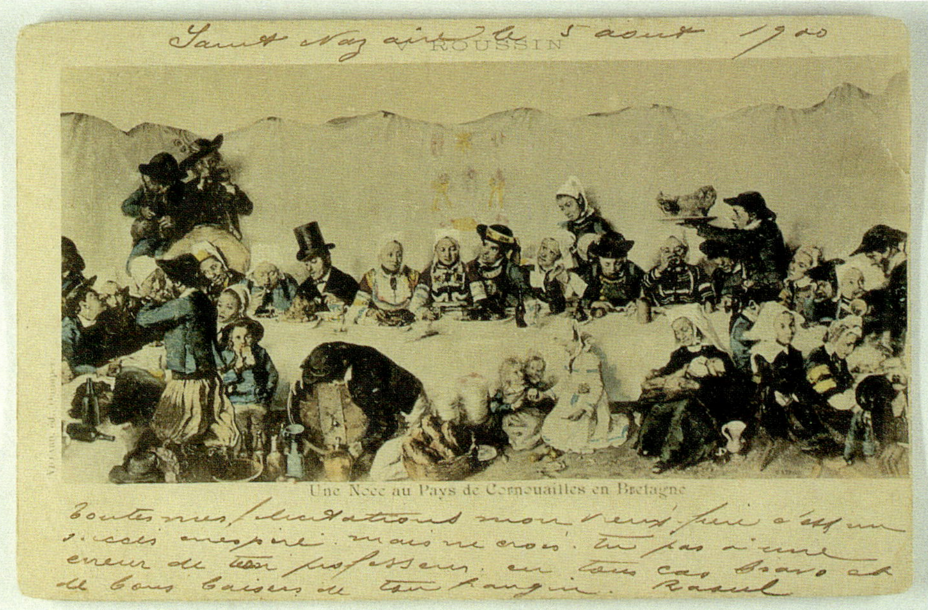

The popularity of the *Les Noces* painting is seen in its reproduction on a turn-of-the-century postcard. *Authors' Collection.*

This couple posed in wedding finery for an early postcard entitled *Maries de Cornouaille.* The bride's dress is termed *broderica d'or,* or gold embroidered. *Authors' Collection.*

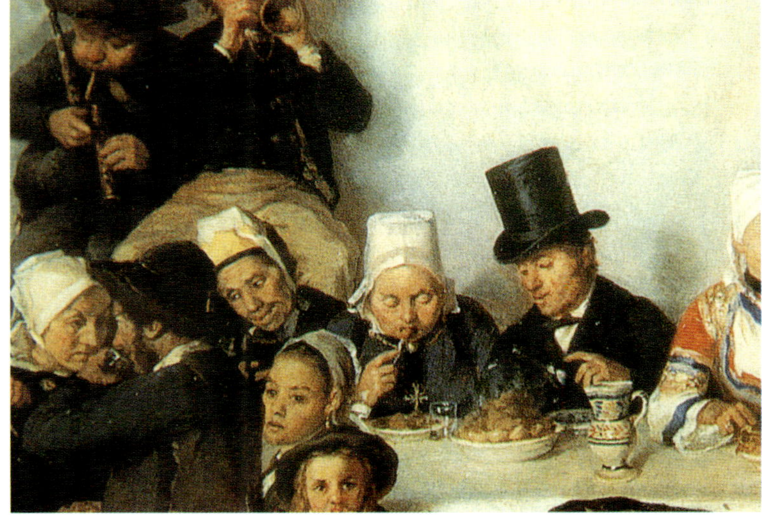

A close-up view of a portion of the painting shows a Quimper pitcher on the banquet table, while the wedding party enjoys its repast.

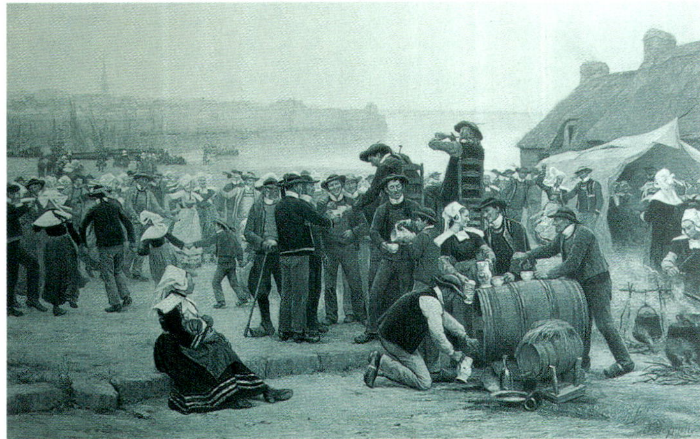

A *Wedding Party in Brittany* is the title of this Théophile Deyrolle print. The cider is drawn from large casks into Quimper pitchers and served in Quimper cider cups. The background looks very much like the harbor at Concarneau, where Deyrolle founded his famous art school. *Authors' Collection.*

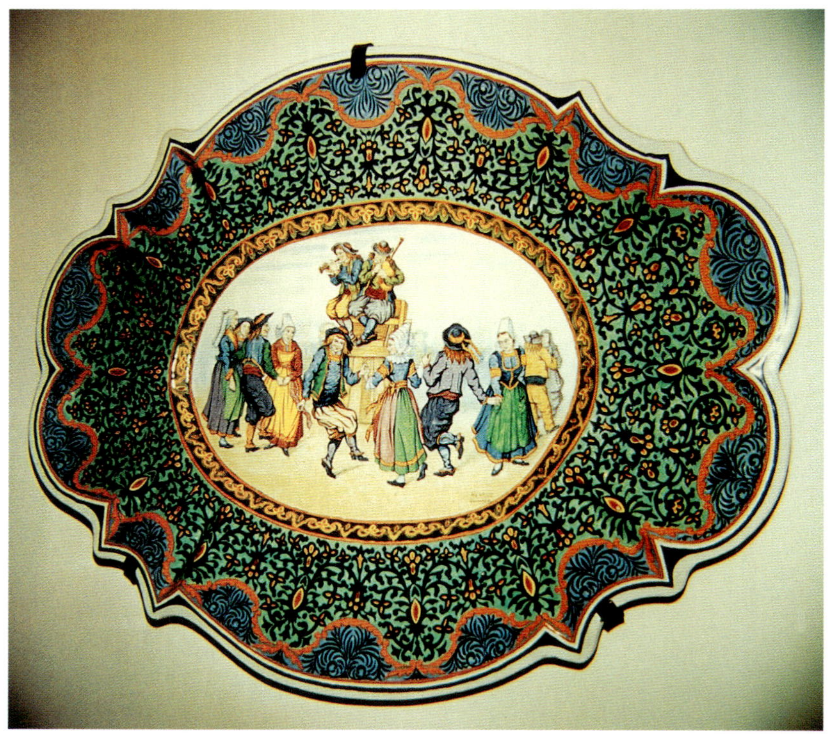

In this wedding reception scene on a large faïence platter by Henriot, the *sonneurs* are seated on chairs high above the crowd. The border design is spectacular in color and execution. *Courtesy of Musée de la Faïence, Quimper.*

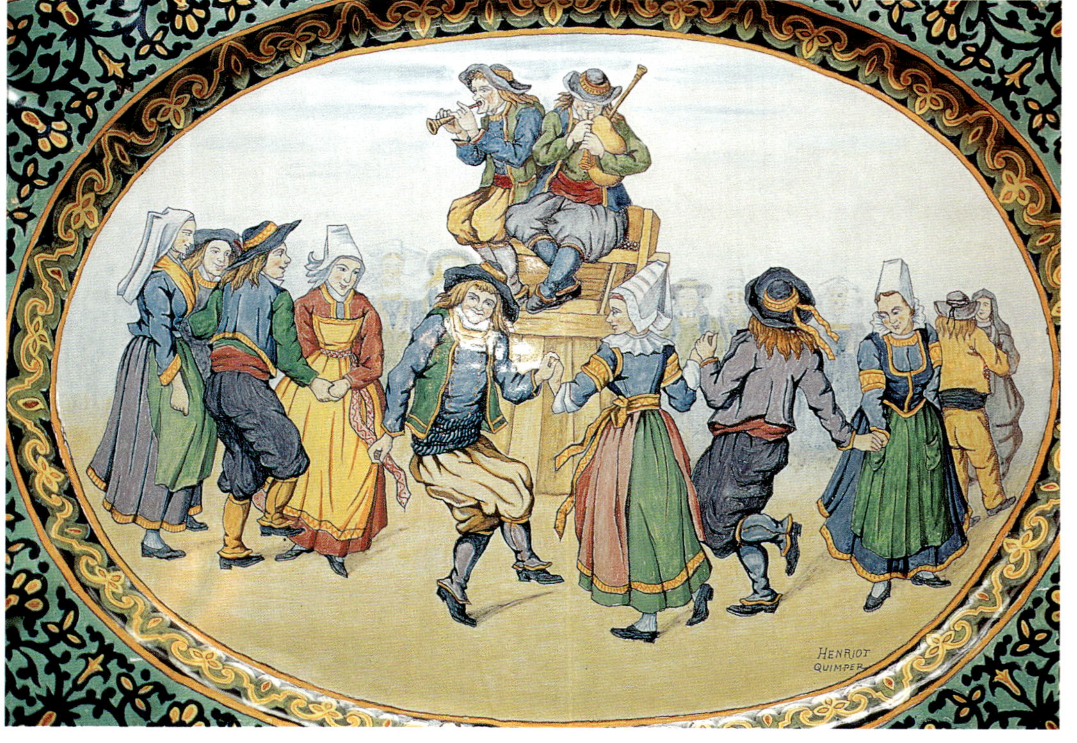

A closer look at the festivities shows couples joyfully dancing a local version of the *gavotte* to the Breton musical duo. The platter is signed Henriot Quimper, and dates post-1922. *Courtesy of Musée de la Faïence, Quimper.*

Present Major Quimper Faïenceries

The heart of our mission and our quest for Quimper lies in the city's faïenceries. To appreciate the beauty and meaning of Quimper poterie, one must learn of the landscape and people of *Bretagne*. But to become truly knowledgeable of Quimper faïence and how its artistic excellence is created and has evolved, one must explore and come to understand the history of the faïenceries of Quimper. Much has happened, particularly over the past 20 years. Quimper poterie production nearly ceased, and was rescued by a consortium of interested parties. This was followed by a revival of old names and famous families coming together to create a new business venture.

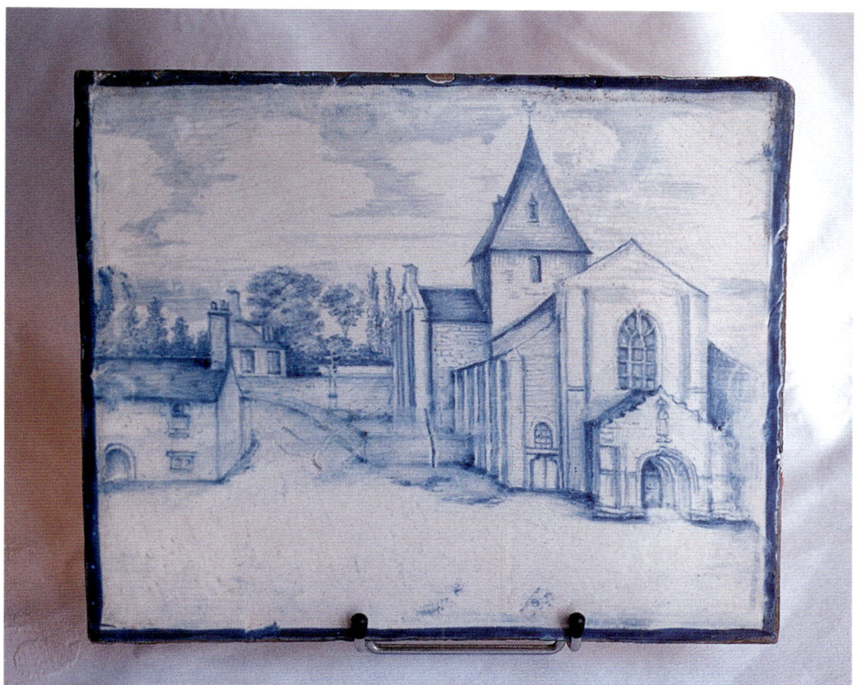

A faïence plaque or tile, decorated in *camaïeu bleu* features the church of Locmaria in the foreground. Also shown is the de la Hubaudière faïencerie. The tile measures 10.25" by 12.5" and is unsigned, but thought to be from the Porquier firm in the 1850s. *Courtesy of Pierre Breton, Art de Cornouaille, Quimper.*

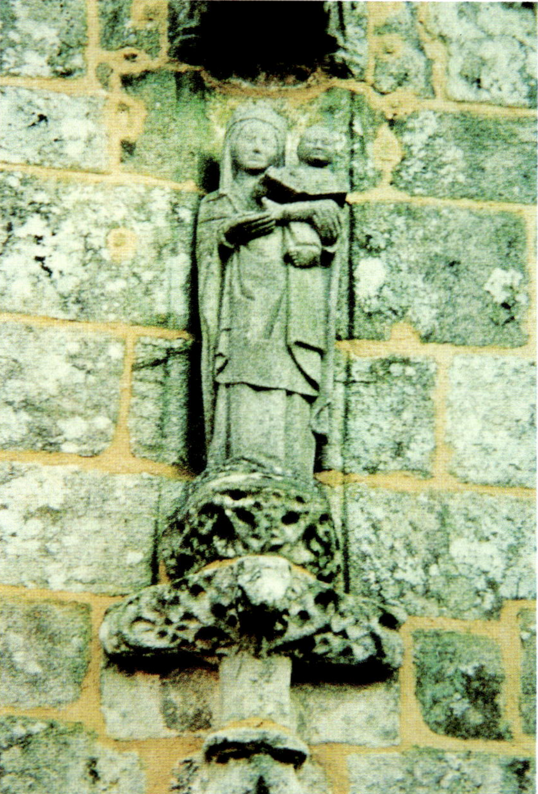

Notre Dame de Locmaria rendered in stone looks down from the church at those of us scurrying by, perhaps on our way to purchase Quimper poterie.

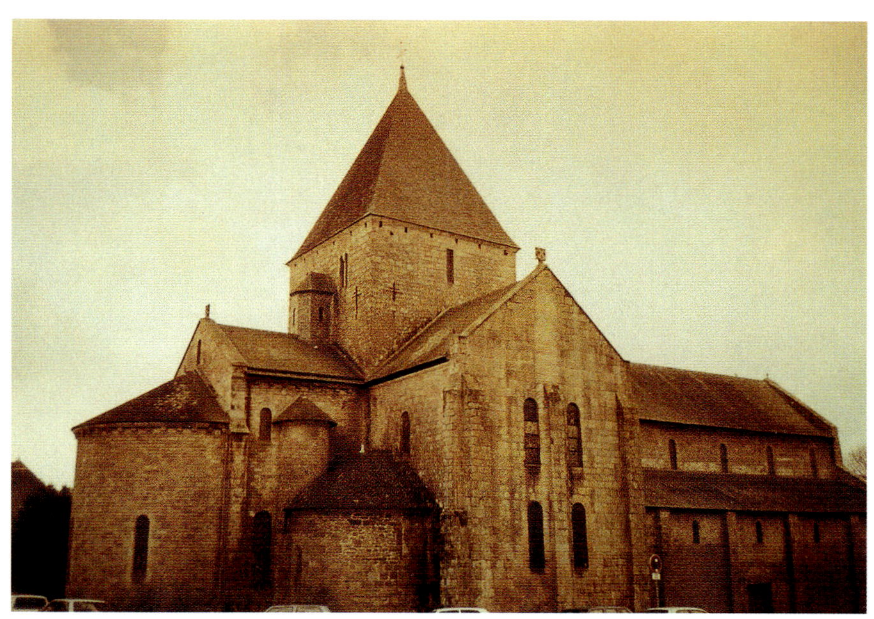

The Quimper faïenceries settled in the Locmaria section of the town, near the *Eglise de Locmaria*. Locmaria was called the *berceau*, or cradle, of Quimper.

HB/Henriot: *Société Nouvelle des Faïenceries de Quimper.*
One of the most significant events in the recent history of Quimper faïenceries occurred in February 1984, when collectors banded together to save *Les Faïenceries de Quimper* factory from closing permanently. Twenty-five or so investors headed by Paul and Sarah Janssens, an American couple known for importing Quimper to the United States, formed Quimper Faïence, Inc., and bought the troubled business.

The *Société Nouvelle des Faïenceries de Quimper,* better known as HB/Henriot, is close to the Odet River in the Locmaria section of Quimper. The scene on this HB/Henriot cookie tin is reminiscent of port scenes captured on faïence and in oils. *Private Collection.*

Right:
The *Société's* building on *Rue Haute* is decorated with the works of Quimper artists.

The Janssens' plan for renewing the faïence industry in Quimper was deemed the most viable by the Court in Quimper overseeing the bankruptcy proceedings. By March 1984, the *Société Nouvelle des Faïenceries de Quimper/* HB/Henriot opened for business, keeping alive the lengthy history of faïence production in Quimper.

The new faïencerie remained in the same building and more than 50 people were employed, including many former HB and Henriot employees. Pierre Henriot was appointed Director General and Bernard Verlingue, son of the previous owner, was appointed Technical Director, familiar positions for both. Staff benefits were updated to include options such as profit sharing and early retirement packages, and business began again.

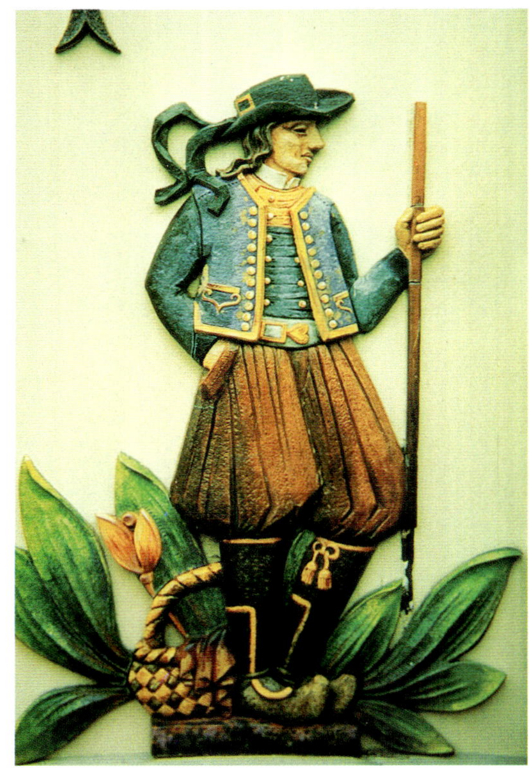
On either side of the HB/Henriot establishment front door are Breton figures …

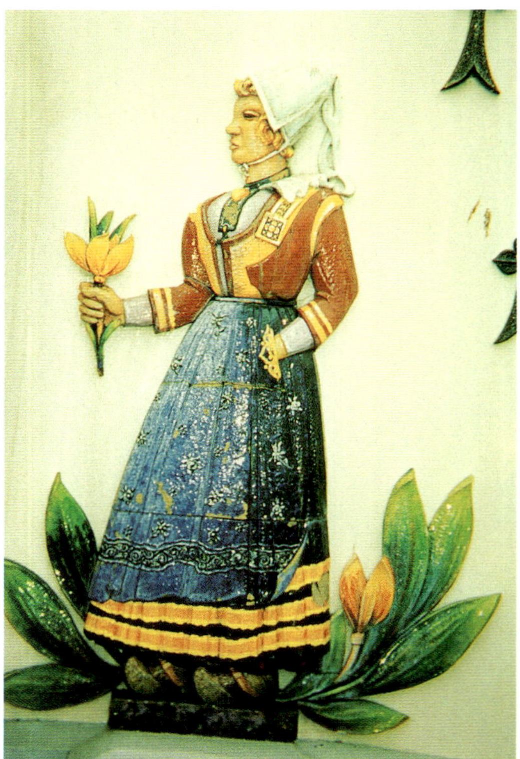
… Both the Breton and Bretonne are bas-relief poterie designed by HB artist Georges Renaud.

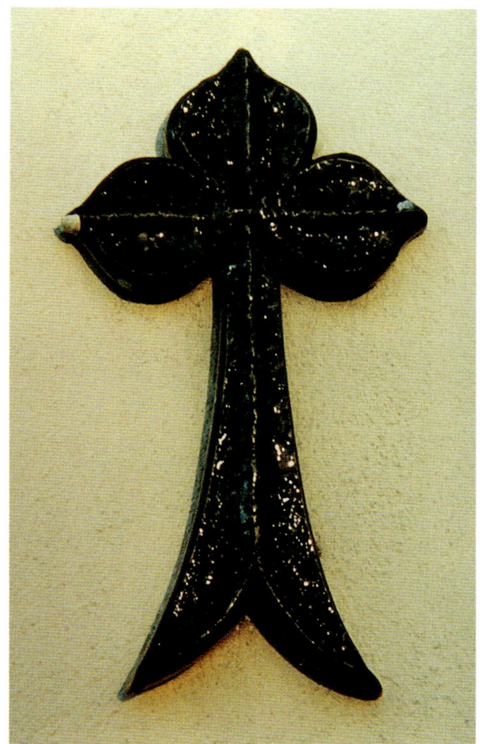

Even the iron ermine-tails, a symbol of *Bretagne*, add an important dimension to the *Société's* building.

… And one for the Breton. The two are seated in the countryside; he smokes a pipe and she has a basket of apples. *Décor riche* borders complement the scenes. The blue sky of Quimper and a modern building across the highway are reflected in the lobby's glass doors.

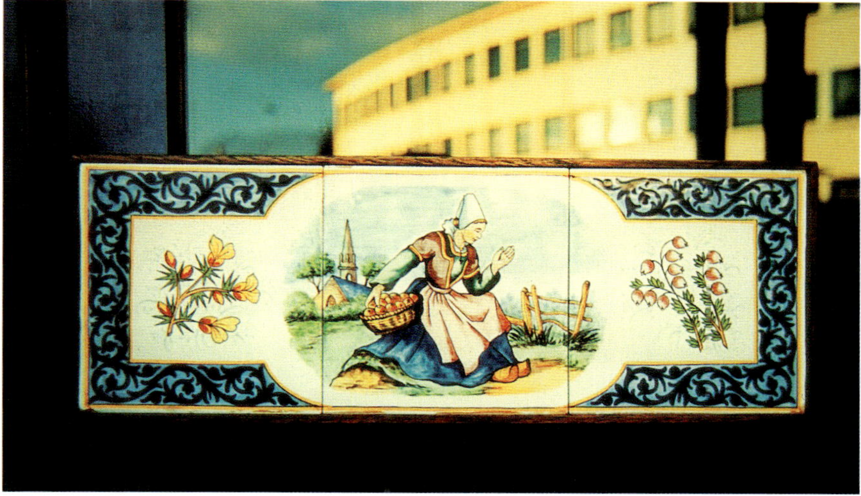

Quimper tile door pulls, decorated with *l'ajonc* and *bruyère* accents, are an extraordinary delight at the faïencerie's entrance. One for the Bretonne …

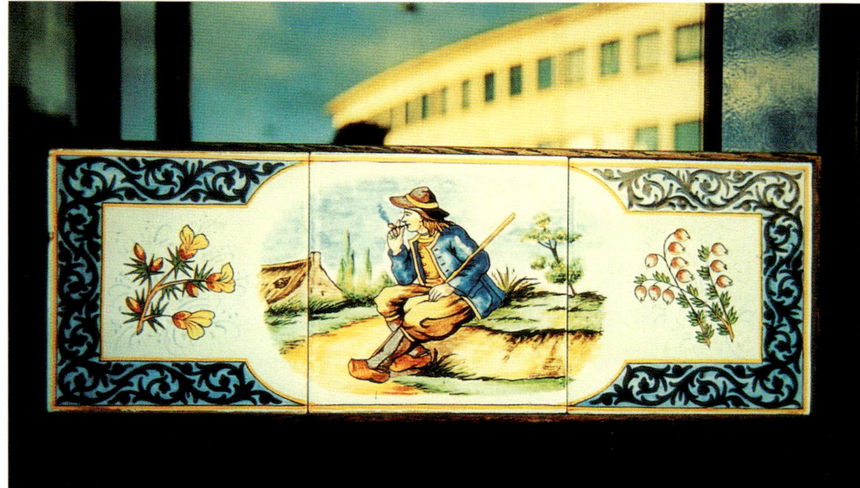

The top priority was improving the financial management of the factory. This meant modernizing the production methods, while maintaining the individually hand-painted products that so delight the buying public. New lines and items were introduced to meet modern standards and modern needs. Sales promotion emphasized the history of the Quimper product, as well as the artistic talent represented in the finished work. These innovations, along with an active marketing plan, set the faïencerie on a course toward financial health.

Across the street is another faïence outlet building. It is decorated with a scene from Jim-Emile Sévellec's, *Service à Mer*, a set of dishes featuring various scenes from the *marins'* life on the coast of Brittany.

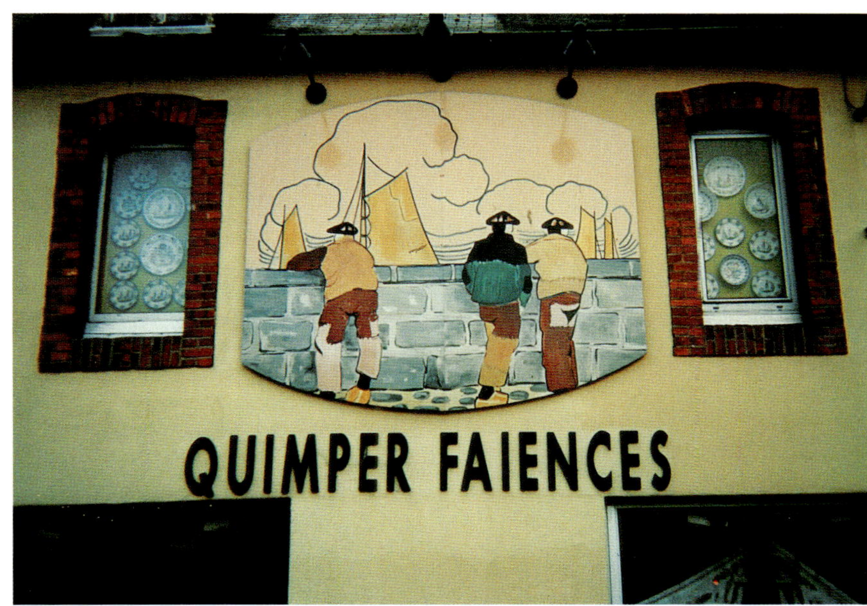

One new marketing concept was to develop company-owned stores to sell Quimperware. This included strategic locations in Paris, and in the United States in Stonington, Connecticut, and Old Town Alexandria, Virginia. An outlet store was added to the faïencerie itself in 1994, where top of the line as well as seconds were available for retail customers. Sarah Janssens headed these efforts, as well as creating a mail order business.

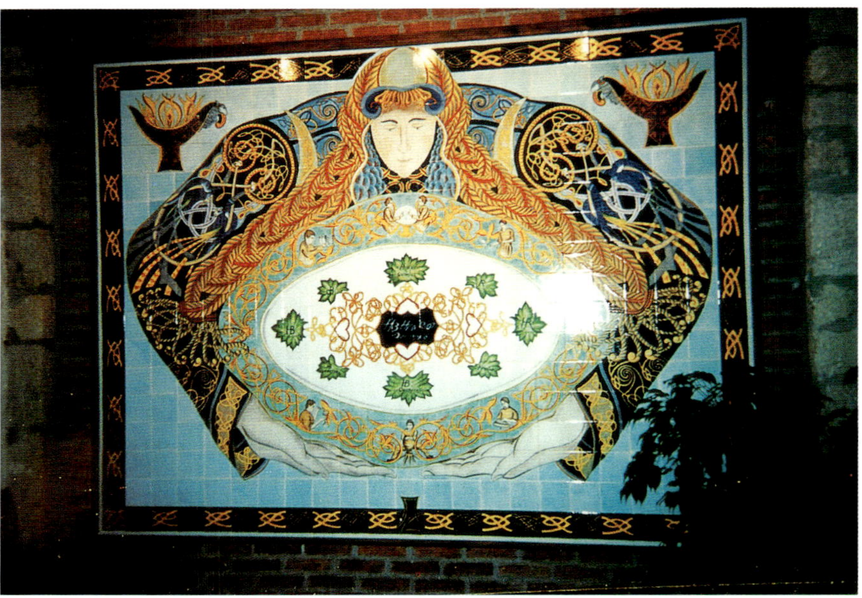

An HB/Henriot tile mural in the entrance greets visitors to the *Société's* outlet shop. Various faïencerie marks are on the leaves, which form a circle in the center of the design.

Another important factor in the faïencerie's renewal has been positive publicity. The 300th Anniversary of continuous faïence production in Quimper celebrated in 1990 created the perfect promotional opportunity. Faïencerie personnel and volunteers played a key role in planning and promoting the faïence exhibition held at the *Musée des Beaux Arts* for the *Trois Siècles de Faïences*.

By the mid-1990s, the *Société* had achieved financial good health. Nearly 10 years after the *Les Faïenceries de Quimper* factory temporarily closed, both the gross income and the number of employees had more than doubled. In 1993, the *Société* took over the failing *Keraluc/Stylform* faïenceries and incorporated its staff into the HB/Henriot team. We all are grateful for the continuation of the faïence tradition in Quimper. The investors who refused to let that tradition pass away are worthy of accolades. *(Jehl, Les Faïences de Quimper, pp. 19-24; Mali, French Faïence, pp. 49-50; Mali, Old Quimper Review, July 1990.)*

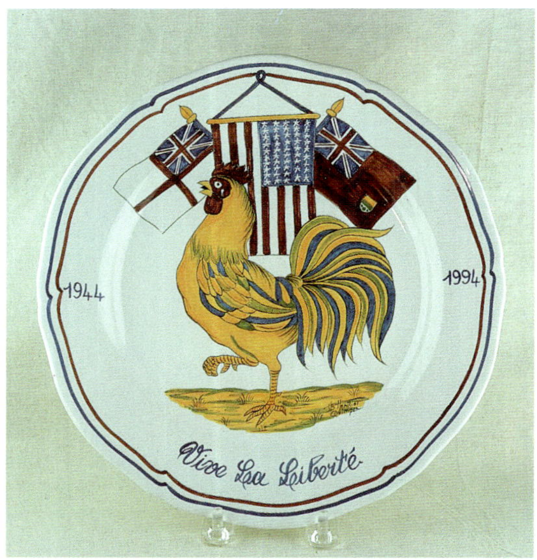

A new *Société Nouvelle des Faïenceries de Quimper* plate with a strutting rooster, the dates 1944 and 1994, and *Vive La Liberté*, commemorates the liberation of France during World War II. *Private Collection.*

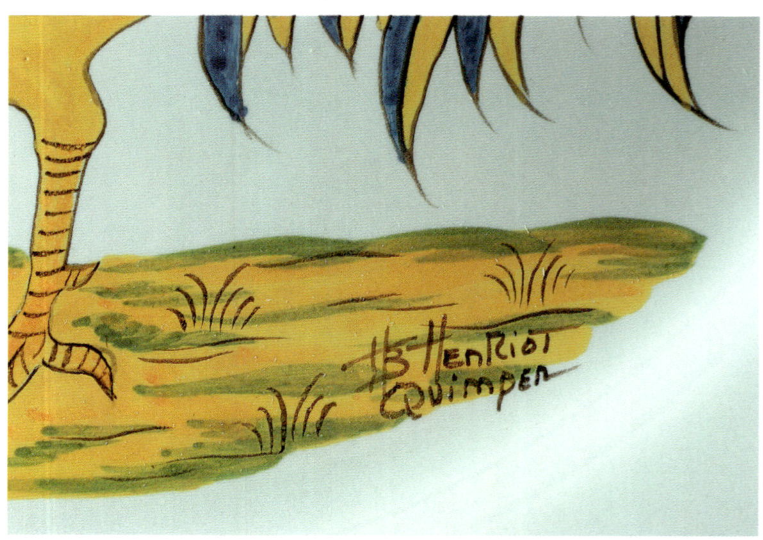

A close look shows the mark of the combined HB and Henriot faïenceries.

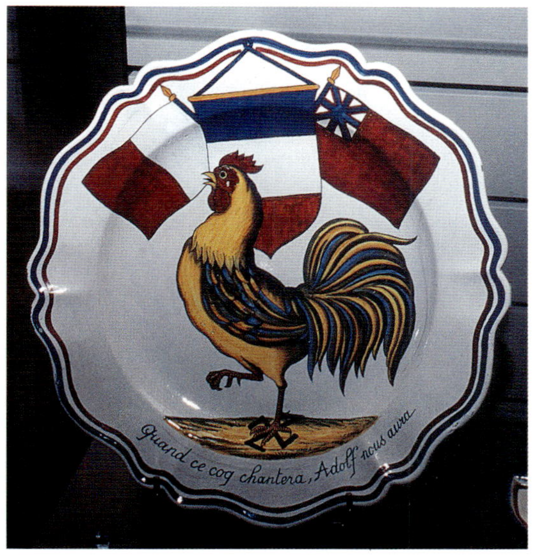

An earlier version of the rooster plate from the 1940s, resides in the *Musée Départemental Breton. Courtesy of Musée Départemental Breton.*

Faïencerie d'Art Breton. During this renaissance of the 1990s, another faïencerie emerged in Quimper. It began in August 1994, when the *Faïencerie d'Art Breton* was born anew. Pierre-Jules Henriot is the director of this faïencerie, which has deep roots in Quimper. Pierre's great-grandfather, Jules Henriot, was first to use this historic name. Jules Henriot became deeply involved in the family faïence business after his father's death in 1884, and subsequently changed its name to *Faïencerie d'Art Breton, Jules Henriot.* Today, the name reminds us of this family's commitment to faïence production in Quimper for many generations.

Pierre Henriot described the opening of the new faïencerie as similar to the creation of life. In August 1994, four factions met to discuss the initiation of a new faïencerie, one linked to several famous families with generations invested in Quimper faïence. Those parties were: Pierre and Jean-Claude Breton, sons of Alphonse Breton, well-known marketer of Quimper faïence; Jean-Yves Verlingue, former owner of the previous *Les Faïenceries de Quimper,* and his son, Bernard; Daniel Rivard, owner of the Montgolfier faïencerie in Daumeray, and Pierre-Jules Henriot.

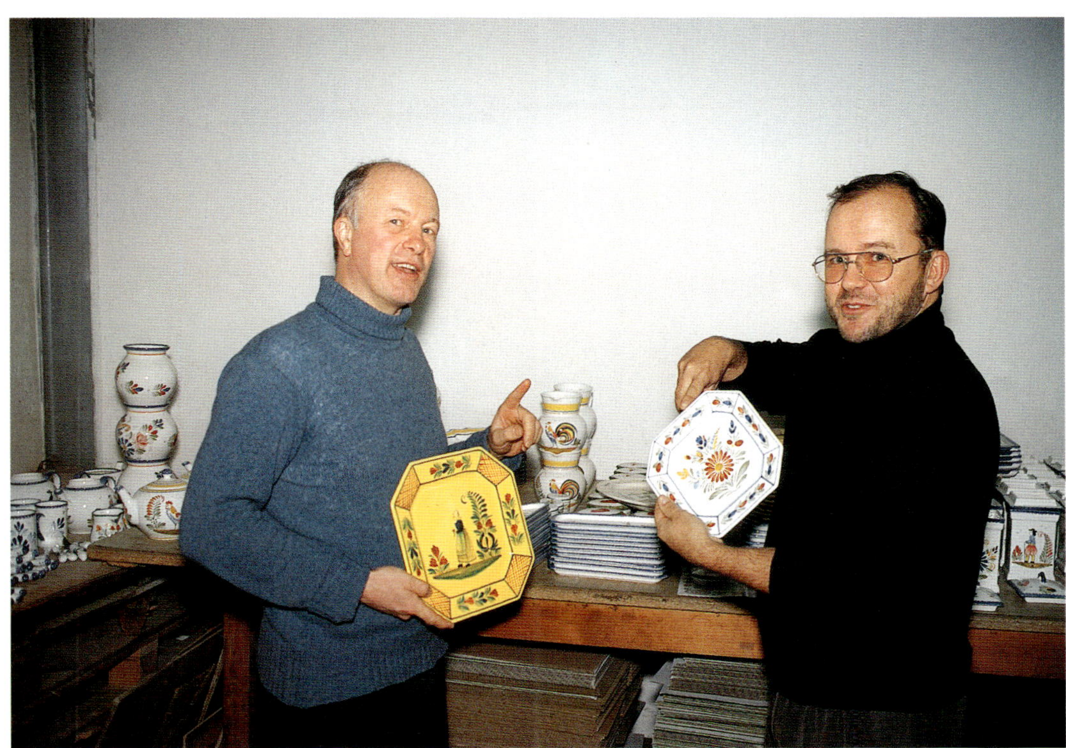

Pierre Henriot, a direct descendant of the Henriot faïencerie family, is the director of *FAB.* His younger brother, Philippe, is the sales director. *Courtesy of Faïenceries d'Art Breton.*

Three weeks later, on September 9, without kilns, factory, or employees, the group announced it was opening a new faïencerie under the name *Faïencerie d'Art Breton, (FAB)*. The newspapers were filled with the story the next day. Pierre recalls those early days, and how a friend of his father and Jean-Claude Breton provided *FAB* with its first home when he offered part of his building at 50 Rue de Locronan, Quimper. This kind gentleman was Bernard Lannaud, the inventor of the smallest car in the world, the *La Naudal*. Later *FAB* developed a commemorative plate featuring this auto and its inventor.

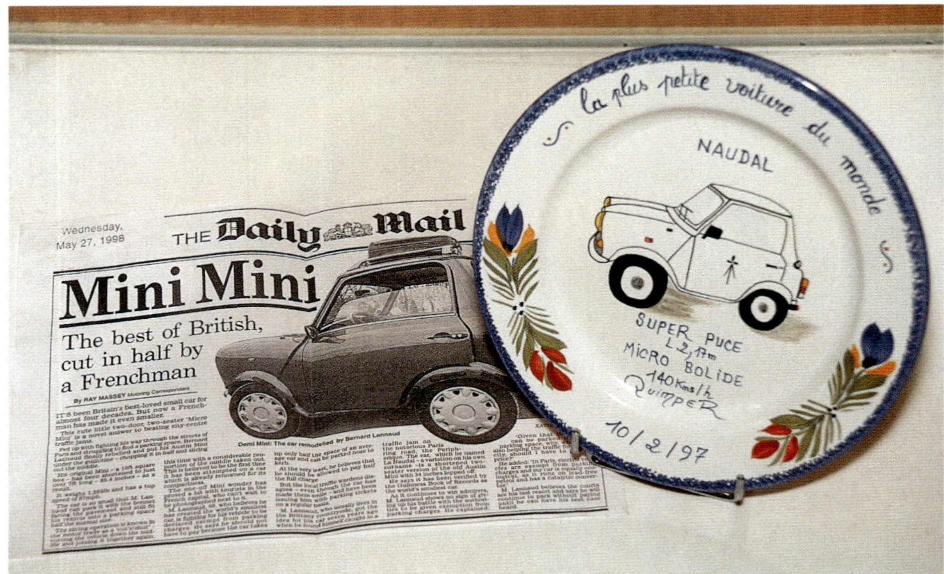

FAB opened in October 1994, in quarters donated by Bernard Lannaud, a friend of the faïencerie founders. The name of mini-car, *Naudal*, was an anagram of the inventor's name. *La plus petite voiture du monde* (the smallest car in the world) was commemorated on a limited edition *FAB* plate in 1997. *Courtesy of Faïenceries d'Art Breton.*

On October 14, 1994, the new company's By-Laws were signed. By November 1, *FAB* began operations with a staff of four, plus director Pierre Henriot. On December 8, *FAB's* first faïence was produced, beating the self-imposed deadline of December 24, 1994. Philippe Henriot, Pierre's brother, joined the firm in 1996, and today the faïencerie employs 19 people, distributing *FAB* faïence throughout Europe and in the USA.

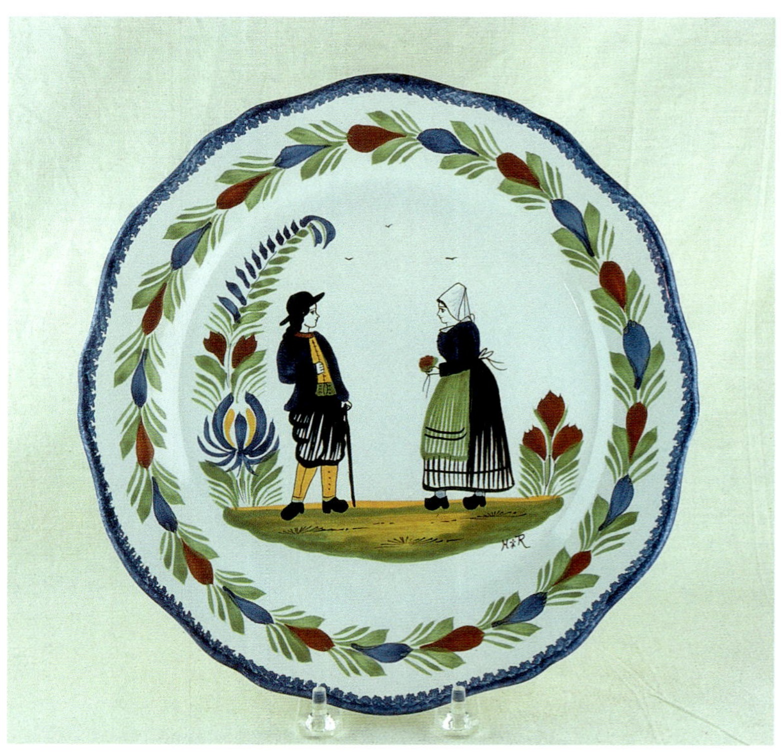

The *petit Breton* design at FAB is based on early prints of Perrin and Lalaisse, 19th century artists who documented the costumes of Brittany. *Courtesy of Faïenceries d'Art Breton.*

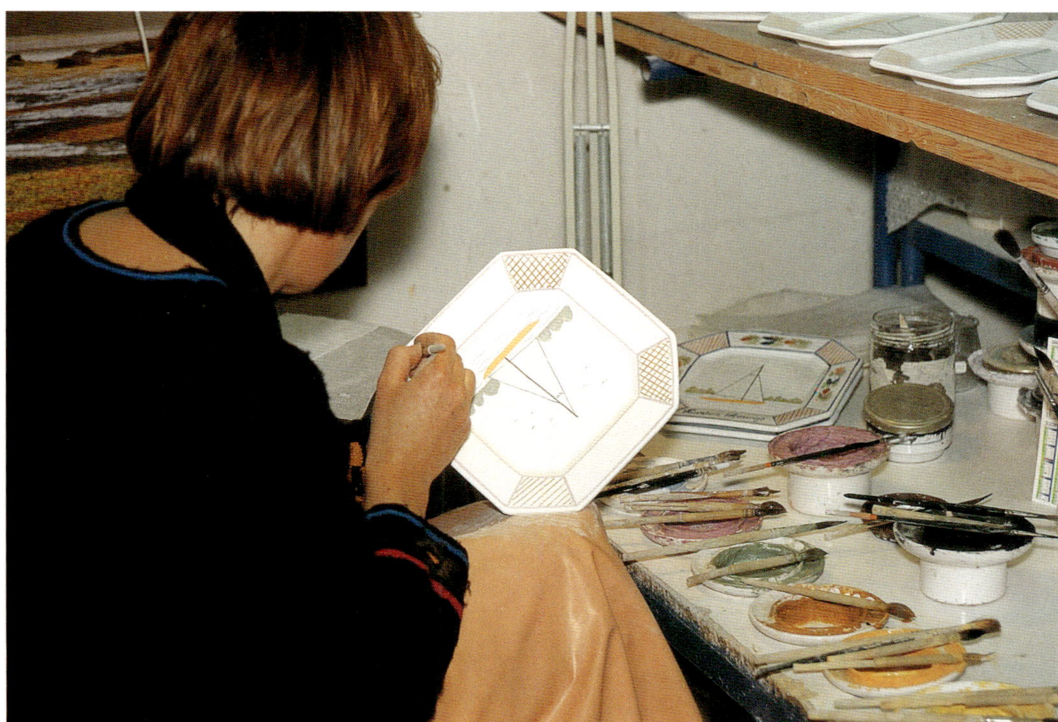

FAB artists employ the same hand-painting techniques used by earlier faïenceries in Quimper. This particular design is a special order for Bluff Gardens, *FAB*'s American distributor in Harbor Springs, Michigan. *Courtesy of Faïenceries d'Art Breton.*

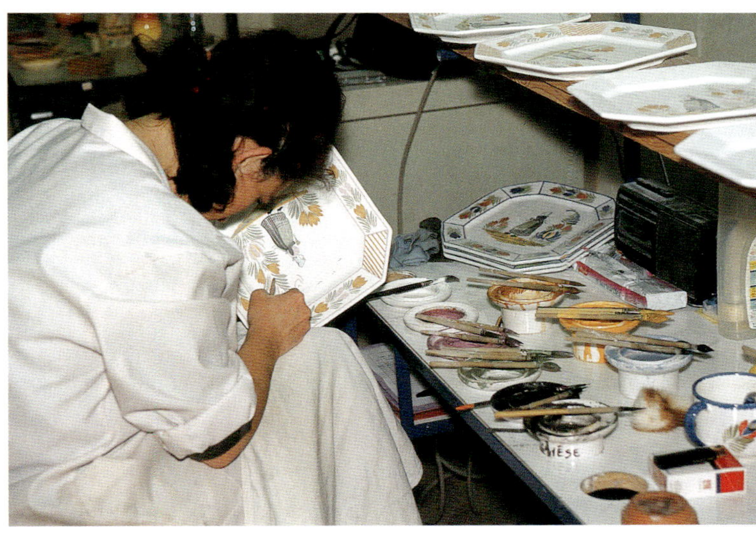

The *à la touche* stroke, accomplished with a quick wrist action, is used by *FAB* artists. It has been a Quimper faïence technique in painting since the late 1700s. *Courtesy of Faïenceries d'Art Breton.*

In the Quimper tradition, all *FAB* products are hand-painted using the *à la touche* technique, but the *petits Bretons* vary from other faïenceries' renditions. Also, *FAB* designs reflect earlier motifs inspired by the 19th century artists Perrin and Lalaisse, and all are executed with the time-honored *coups de pinceau*, or wrist-snapping motion. More importantly, *FAB* has encouraged artists to develop designs for the future, while honoring the past. *FAB* sponsors these artists' work in special events and promotions. One such artist is Patrice Cudennec of St. Brieuc, whose work has been displayed in France, Germany, Belgium, Great Britain, and the USA, where it received rave reviews. Cudennec's work has been rendered on faïence in limited edition works by *FAB*.

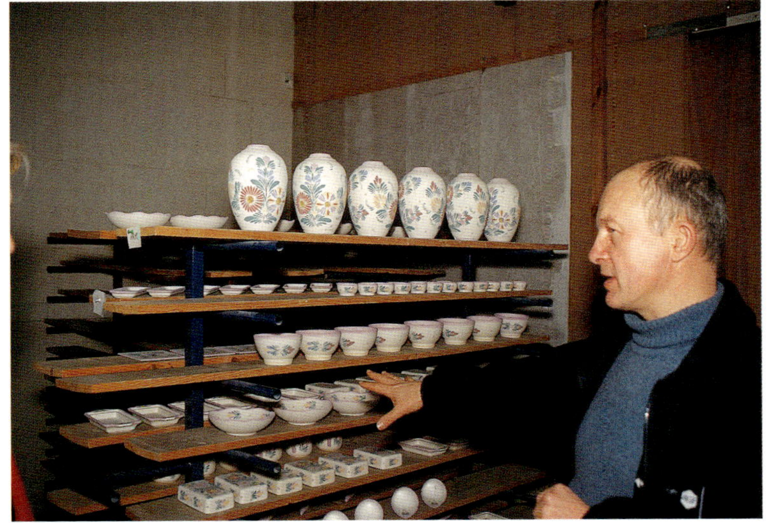

Pierre Henriot personally explained the various steps in the faïence production at *FAB*. *Courtesy of Faïenceries d'Art Breton.*

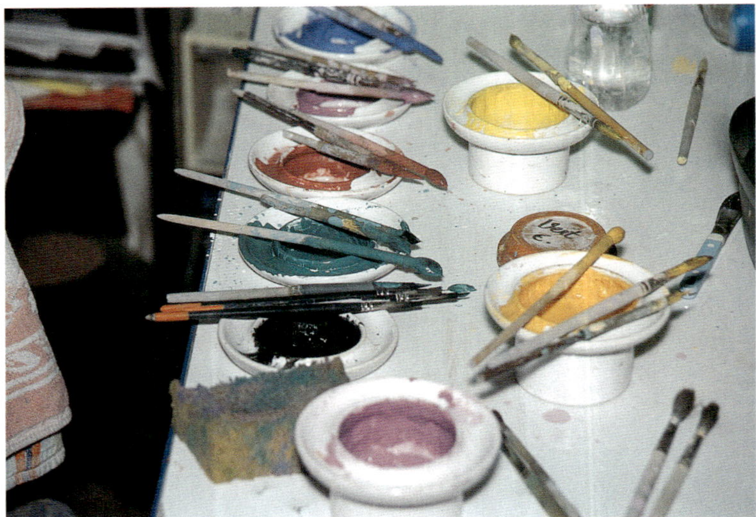

Artists' colors are a different hue before the painted product is fired in the *FAB* kiln. *Courtesy of Faïenceries d'Art Breton.*

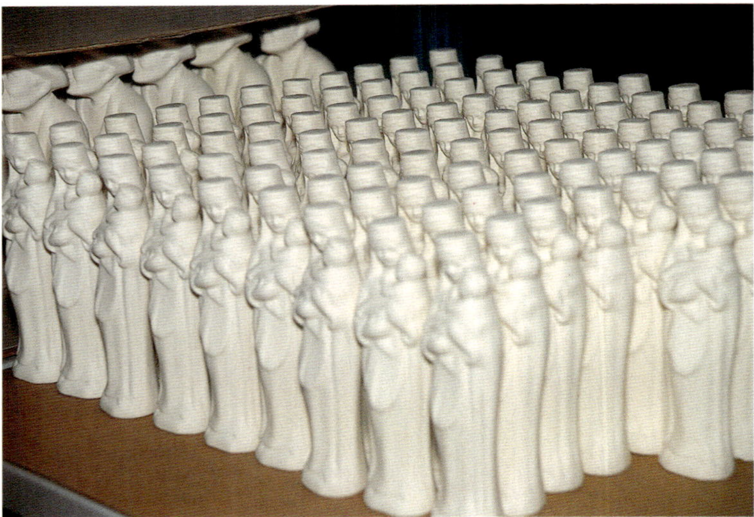

Pierre Henriot also told about the variety of sources for the molds used at *FAB*. The Montgolfier faïencerie, whose owner Daniel Rivard is one founder of *FAB*, is the primary supplier. *Courtesy of Faïenceries d'Art Breton.*

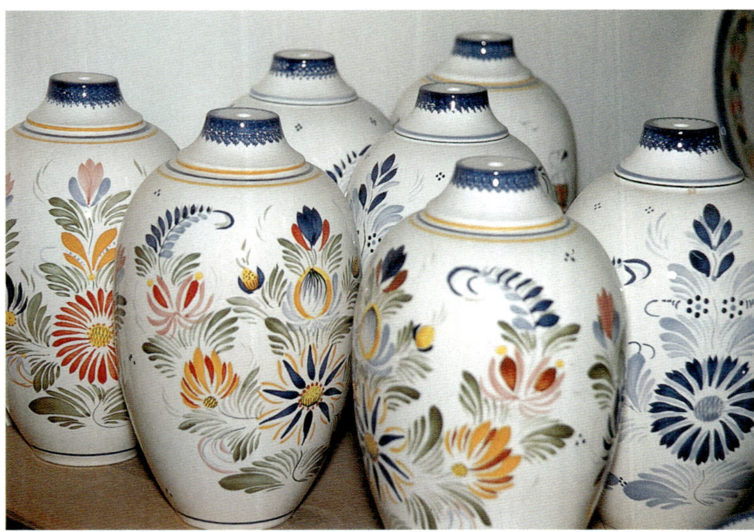

A group of completed vases stands ready for shipment to one of many *FAB* customers. *Courtesy of Faïenceries d'Art Breton.*

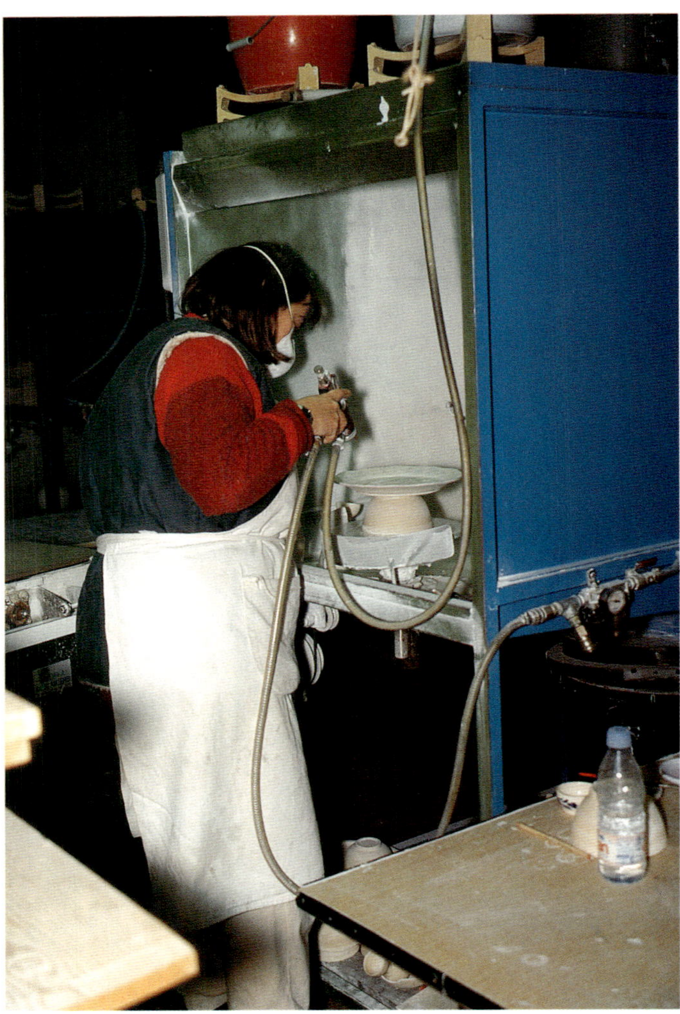

Each step is handled with precision, in keeping with *FAB's* concern for quality control. *Courtesy of Faïenceries d'Art Breton.*

World-known artist Patrice Cudennec created a series of designs for production on *FAB* faïence, which have been well-received. They are modern while retaining the essential Breton spirit. *Courtesy of Faïenceries d'Art Breton.*

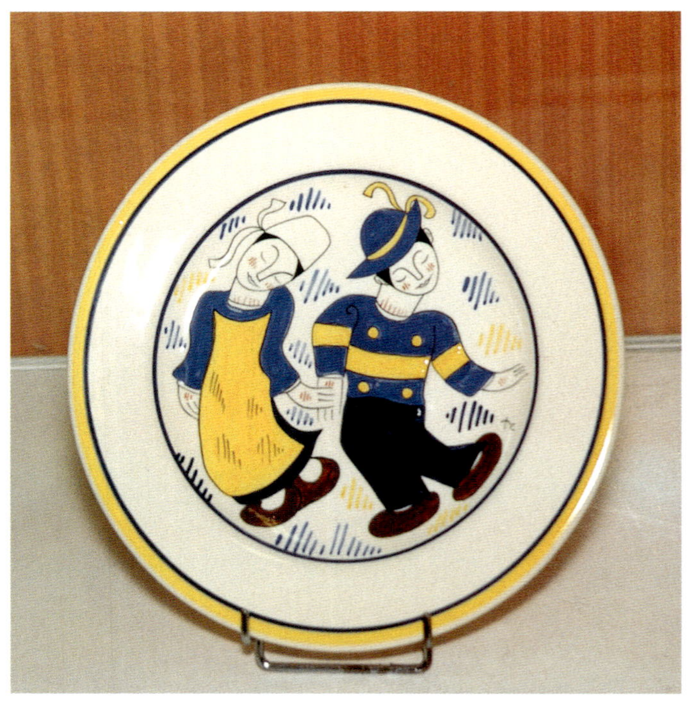

Other artists who have collaborated with *FAB* include Alexander Goudie, a Scotsman; Jeanne Leveque, from Auray; and Olivier Lapicque, from Concarneau, grandson of Gaston Sebilleau, a member of *Ar Seiz Breur*, the Breton cultural revivalist organization of the 1920s and 1930s. (*Mali, Old Quimper Review, October 1999.*)

In addition to the *FAB* mark, *Faïencerie d'Art Breton* has registered another mark directly linked to the past. Pierre Henriot related the history of the battle of the marks between *HB/Grande Maison* and the *Faïencerie d'Art Breton, Jules Henriot*. In 1922, HB won a court case claiming the Henriot signature, HR, resembled the HB signature used by the *Grande Maison*, thereby confusing the purchasing public. (A similar suit was filed years earlier by the *Porquier* establishment against the Malicorne faïencerie of *Pouplard*, which signed its name either with a backwards P and a B and then PBx, both close to the PB signature of *Porquier-Beau* faïencerie.)

The decision in favor of the *HB/Grande Maison* prevented the use of the HR mark, but the court's ruling stated that HR could be used if another mark was inserted between the two initials. Pierre explained that the H and R stood for the last name of his great-grandfather Henriot and the maiden name of his great-grandmother, Riou. Rather than follow the court's instruction to separate the letters, the mark was changed in 1922 to HenRiot, thereby maintaining the H and R of his family's lineage.

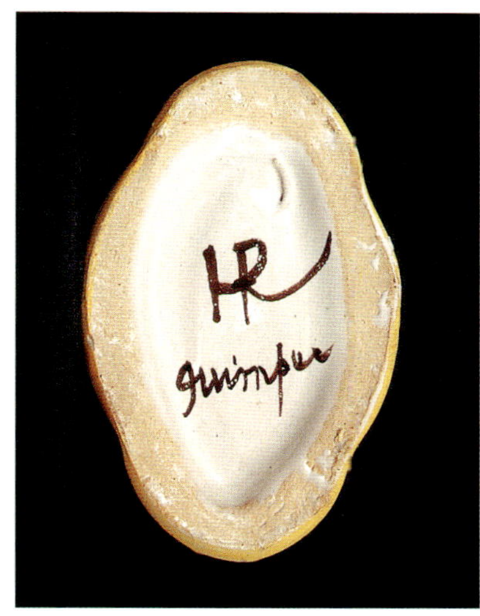

Pierre Henriot, great-grandson of Jules Henriot, explained the history of the original Henriot faïencerie signature HR.

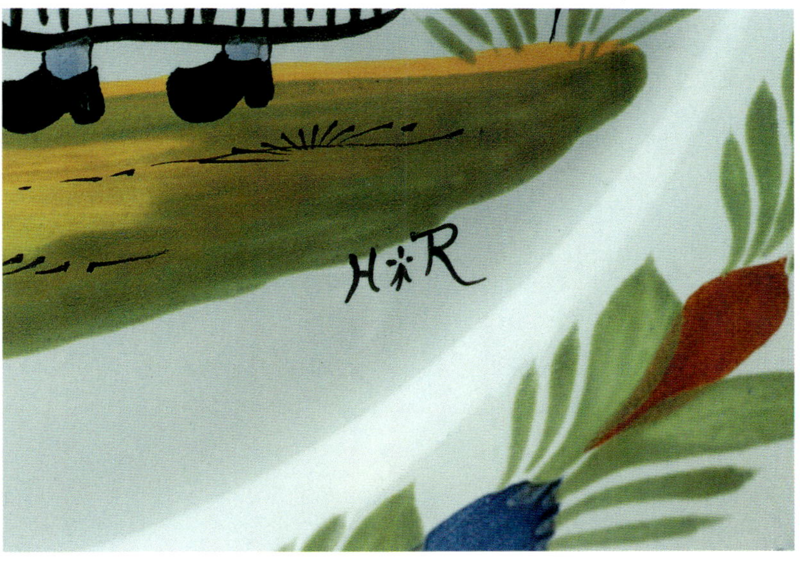

FAB registered a signature, designed to meet the 1922 court's ruling about separating the letters H and R. An ermine-tail device is used in this new mark developed by the Henriots. *Courtesy of Faïencerie d'Art Breton.*

The Henriot family recently has revived the HR mark. Following the 1922 court decision's instructions, the letters indeed are separated, this time with an ermine tail, the symbol of Brittany. *FAB* made a group of plates with this mark and applied to have the mark registered. Its use was challenged by the *Société Nouvelle des Faïenceries de Quimper*, which purchased the former *Les Faïenceries de Quimper* establishment in 1984. The local court in Quimper ruled the new mark met the guidelines of the 1922 decision; an appeal was registered with the regional court in Rennes.

When asked about the future of the faïenceries in Quimper, Pierre-Jules Henriot confidently believes Quimper will always be the home of fine faïence production. It is in their blood, he said. (*Conversations and correspondence with Pierre-Jules Henriot, January-March 2001.*)

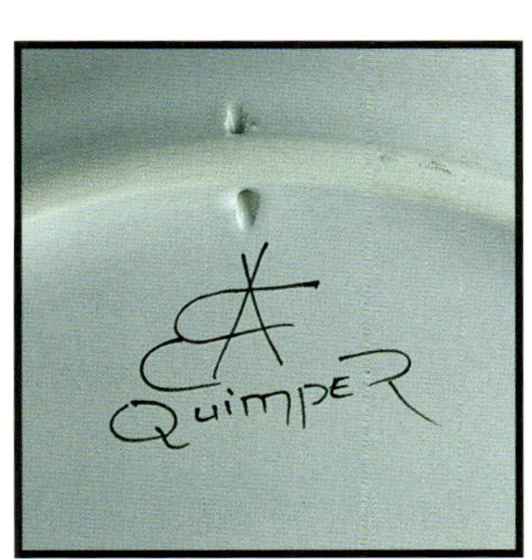

The familiar *FAB* signature remains on the back of plates with the ermine-tail-enhanced HR signature. *Courtesy of Faïenceries d'Art Breton.*

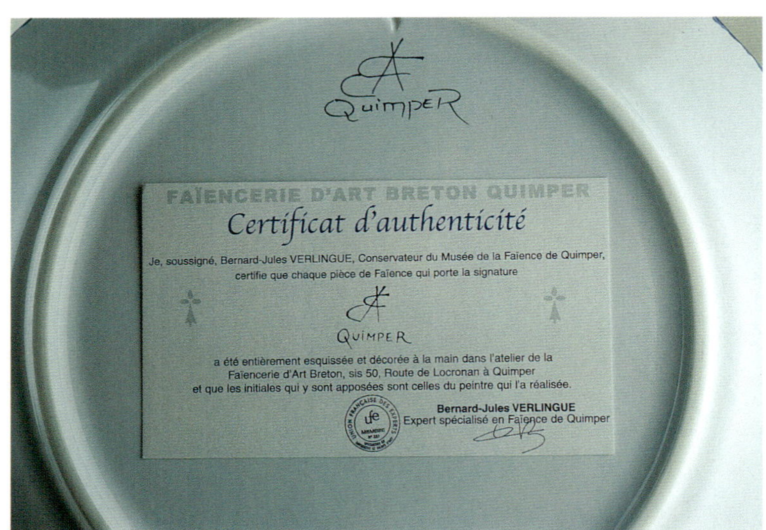

The *Faïencerie d'Art Breton* guarantees each item to be authentic, as documented by Bernard-Jules Verlingue, an *expert specialisé en Faïence de Quimper* (expert specializing in Quimper faïence). *Courtesy of Faïenceries d'Art Breton.*

The Generations Carry on the Quimper Tradition

Alphonse Breton was born in Landivisiau in 1902, and purchased a store in 1938 named *La Civette.* It was on *Rue de Parc,* overlooking the Odet River in the heart of Quimper. Among other things, Alphonse Breton sold Quimper poterie, and he became friendly with Joseph Henriot, co-director of the Henriot's *Faïencerie d'Art Breton.* Breton also came to know Quimper artists Renaud, Quillivic, Sévellec, Micheau-Vernez, and Leonardi.

In 1950, Alphonse Breton purchased the *Relais St. Corentin,* on the *Place de la Cathédral.* The *Relais* had been a hotel on the tourist route and was known to have dishes signed with a segmented fish, the logo honoring St. Corentin for whom the hotel was named. Prior to being the *Relais St. Corentin,* the establishment was called the *Hôtel Lion d'Or.* The building is more than 400 years old. On this site, Alphonse Breton created another store, *Art de Cornouaille,* where he featured Breton art, and particularly the work of artists from the local faïenceries.

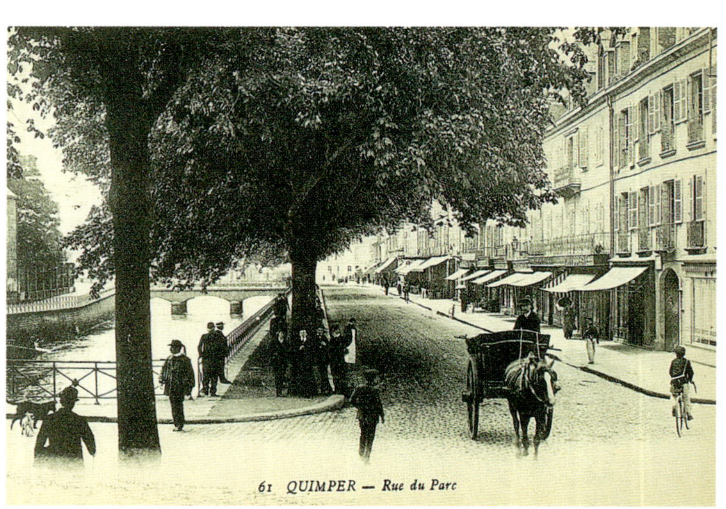

Quimper's *Rue de Parc* is seen in this turn-of-the-century postcard. Alphonse Breton's first *magasin* (shop) stands at the far end of the picture. *Authors' Collection.*

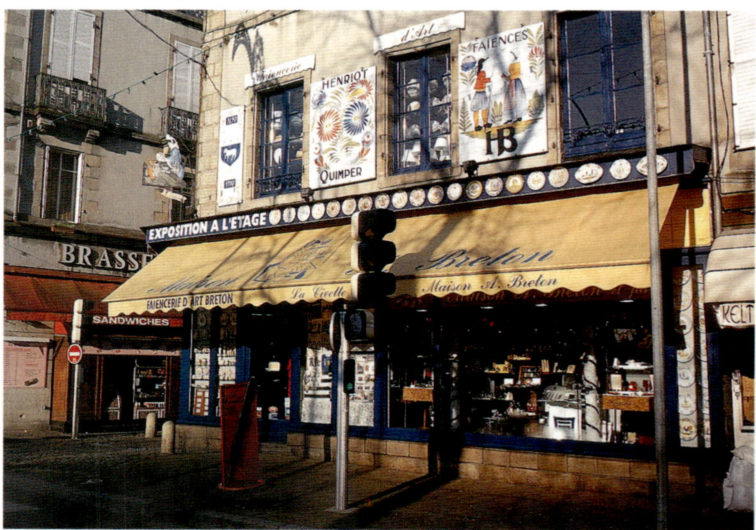

The first *magasin* owned by Alphonse Breton is *La Civette* on *Rue de Parc,* across from the Odet River in the center of Quimper. The Breton family expanded the shop from its original *petit* size.

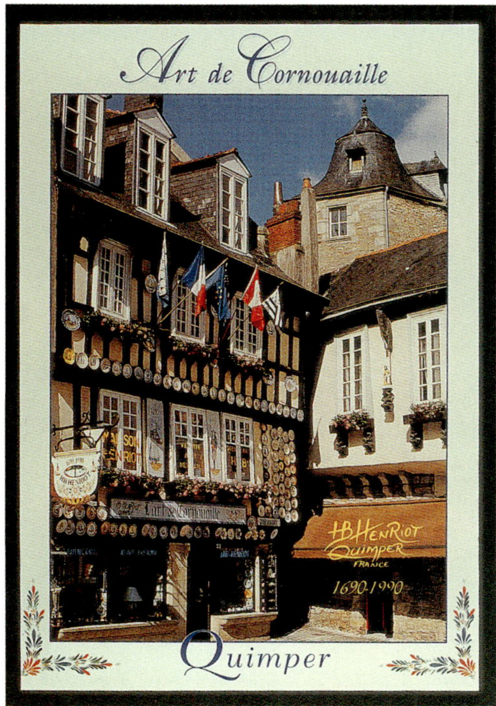

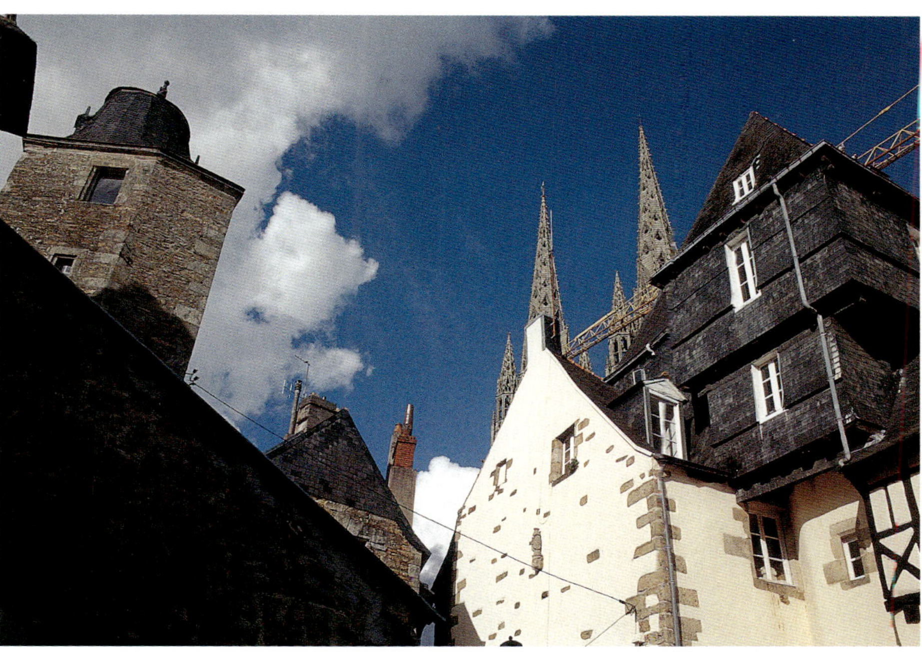

A second *magasin* purchased by Alphonse Breton is on the Cathedral Square and became the *Art de Cornouaille*. The building previously provided tourist lodgings and was called the *Relais de St. Corentin. Courtesy of Pierre Breton, Art de Cornouaille, Quimper.*

Art de Cornouaille was the *Hôtel Lion d'Or*, prior to being the *Relais de St. Corentin*. A photograph from the inner courtyard shows the early construction.

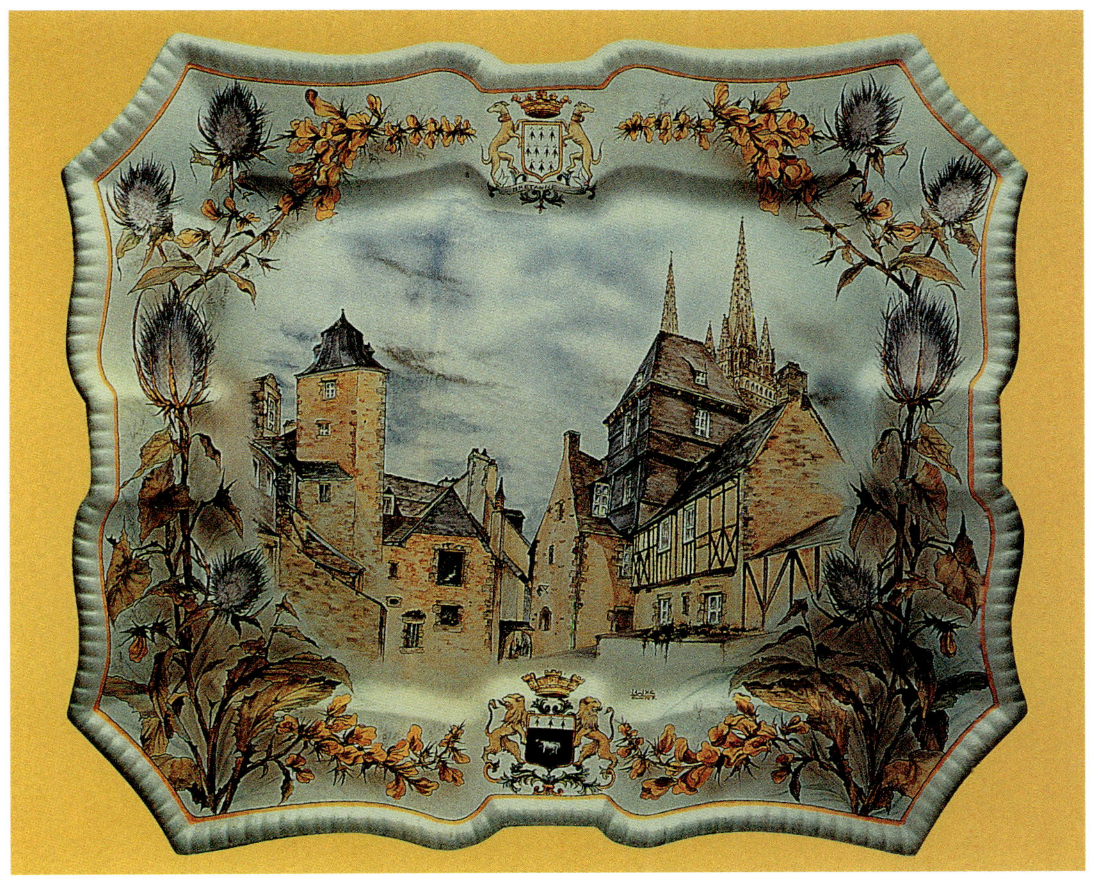

This scene from the inner courtyard of the present *Art de Cornouaille* was rendered on faïence by the noted artist Philippe Lalys. Lalys was previously the Artistic Director for the *Société Nouvelle des Faïenceries de Quimper,* but now is an independent artist in Quimper. *Courtesy of Pierre Breton, Art de Cornouaille, Quimper.*

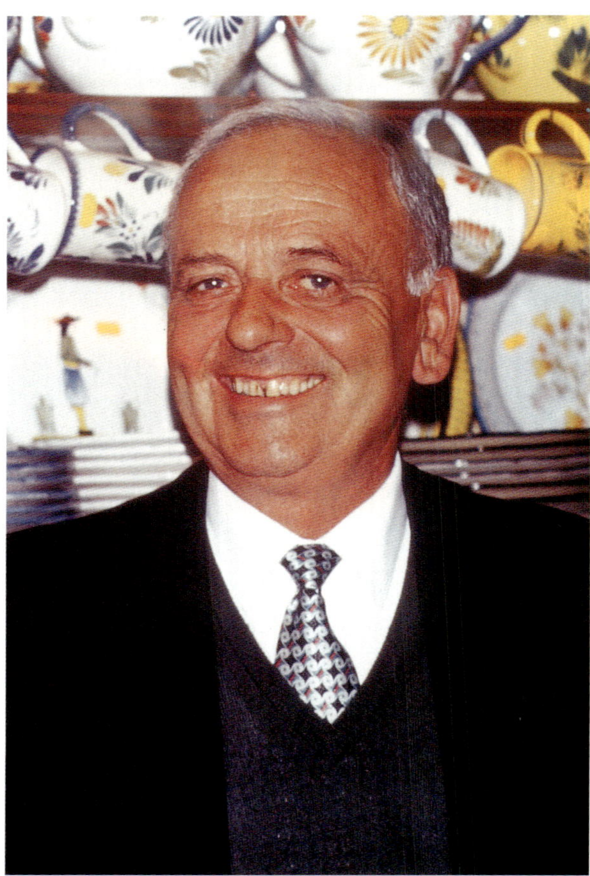

Jean-Claude Breton took the reins of *La Civette* on *Rue de Parc* and continued to sell Quimper, quality writing instruments, and tourist items.

In 1965, Pierre Breton took over the management of *Art de Cornouaille* on the Cathedral Square. He continued his father's tradition of presenting works by Quimper artists, as well as selling Quimper faïence and tourist items.

Enter Pierre and Jean-Claude Breton, Alphonse's two sons. In 1962, Jean-Claude Breton took over the management of the store overlooking the Odet, *La Civette*, which had expanded from its original, rather small size. In 1965, Pierre took over the direction of the store on the Cathedral Square, *Art de Cornouaille*. All Quimper collectors know of the Breton brothers. Pierre and Jean-Claude built their respective businesses and continued the family tradition of successfully marketing Quimper faïence. Alphonse Breton passed away in 1982.

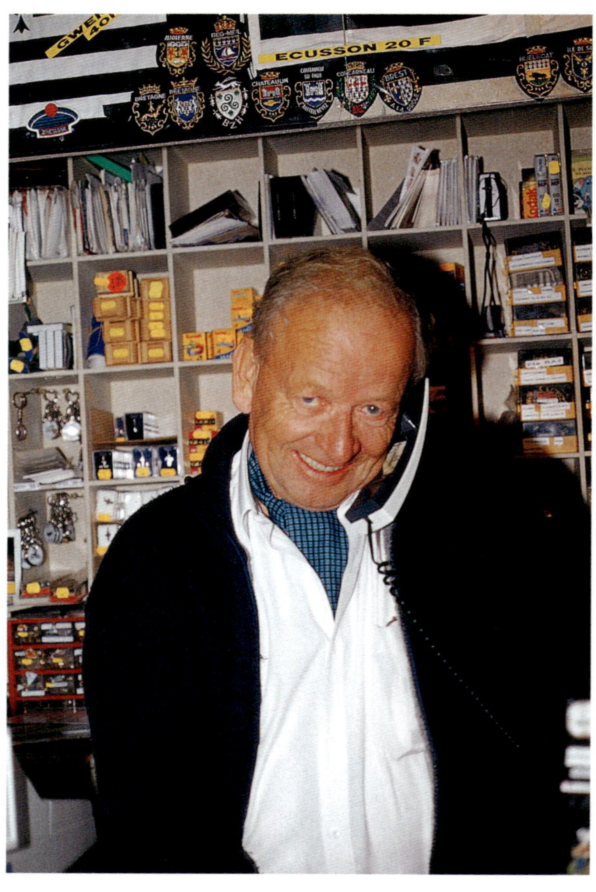

A group of the Families Breton and Henriot met in Jean-Claude's shop in January 2001. From left to right: Pierre Breton, Philippe Henriot, Jean-Claude Breton's daughter, Gwénola, Jean-Claude Breton, and Pierre Henriot.

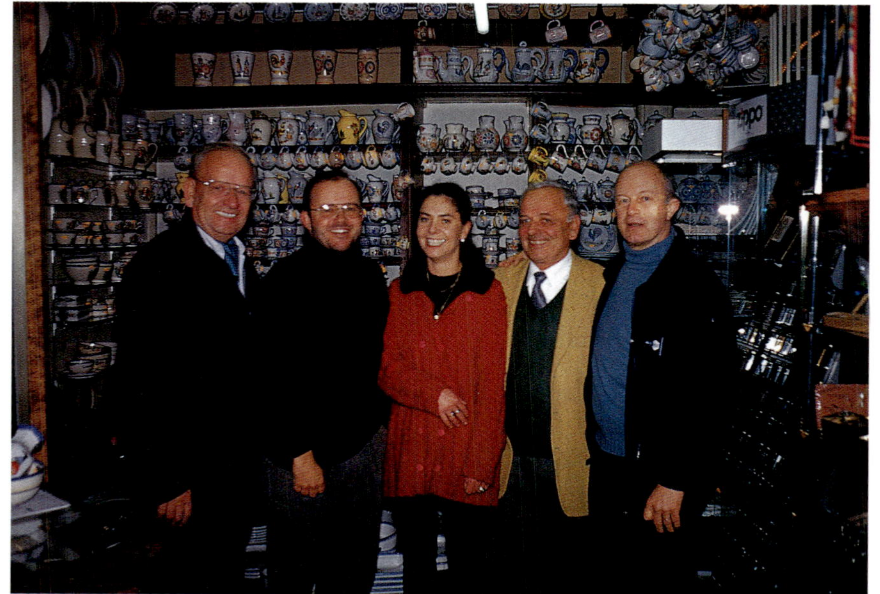

Enter the third generation. Jean-Claude's daughter, Gwénola, has become an active manager at *La Civette*, and Pierre's son, Michael, has become an active manager for *Art de Cornouaille*. Both families are proud of their longstanding connection with the faïenceries in Quimper, and the fact that Alphonse Breton designed some of the faïencerie décors, which can be identified by the addition of his signature, A. Breton to the factory mark. *(Les Amis du Musée de la Faïence Bulletin, August 1998; Mali, Old Quimper Review, October 1999; conversations and correspondence with Gwénola and Michael Breton, January 2001.)*

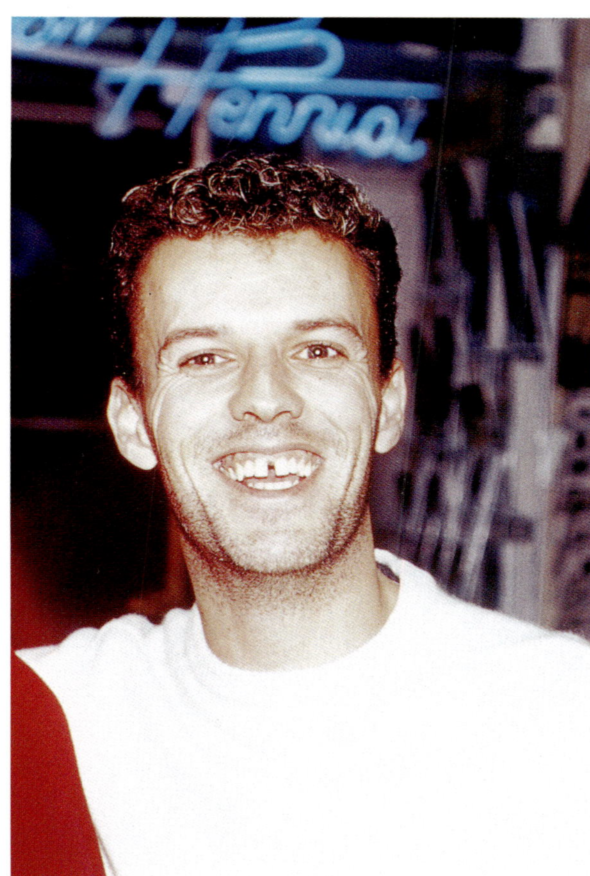

Missing from the group picture was Pierre Breton's son, Michael, who was in the midst of directing renovations at the *Art de Cornouaille.*

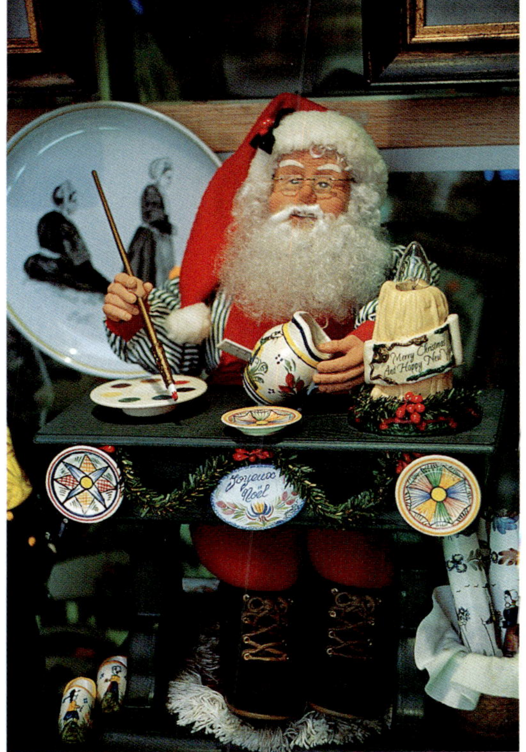

Michael Breton collects miniature Quimper items, and displays some in the *Art de Cornouaille* window during the Christmas season. *Courtesy of Michael Breton, Art de Cornouaille, Quimper.*

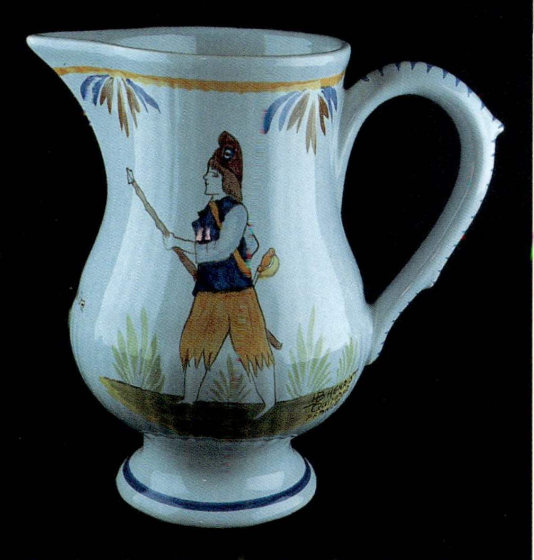

The Breton Family verified that Alphonse Breton created some designs for the Quimper faïenceries. This pitcher is one of his designs. *Courtesy of Charlie Walker.*

Jean-Claude Breton pointed out his father's mark on the bottom of the pitcher, A. Breton. *Courtesy of Charlie Walker.*

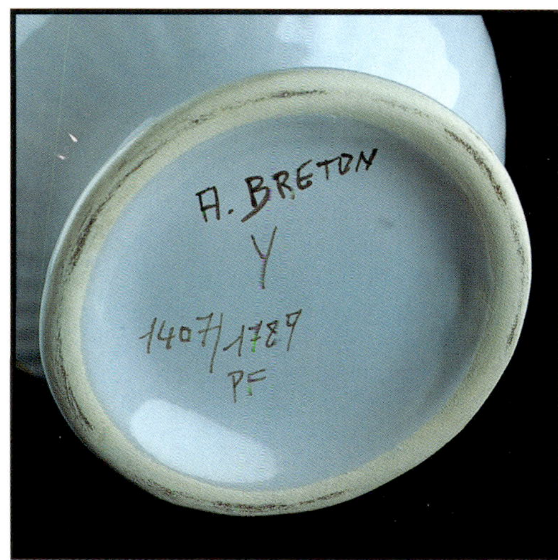

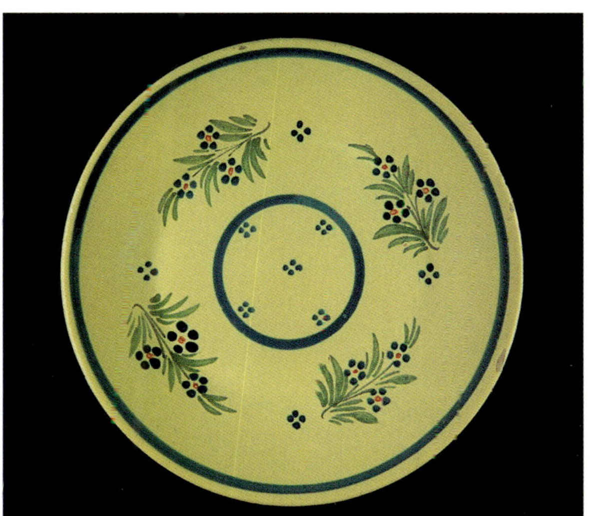

Several years ago, Pierre Breton had shown us an item designed by his father in the *soleil* décor. *Authors' Collection.*

On the reverse side was the name Breton in addition to the HB faïencerie artist's mark of dash and dot (- .) and the word Quimper. The Morse Code-like mark represents HB artist Monsieur Chapalain. (*Taburet*, p. 216.)

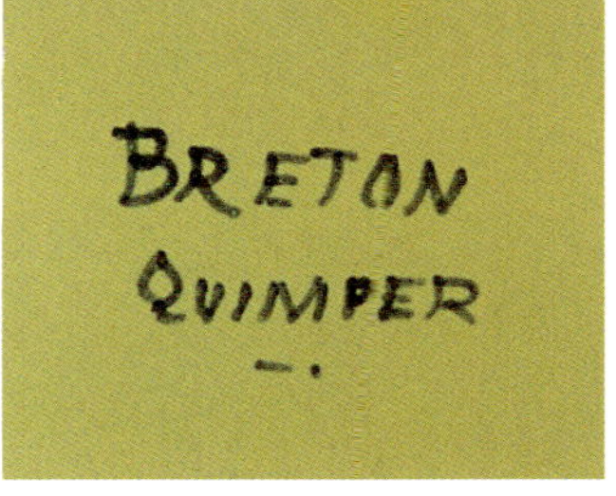

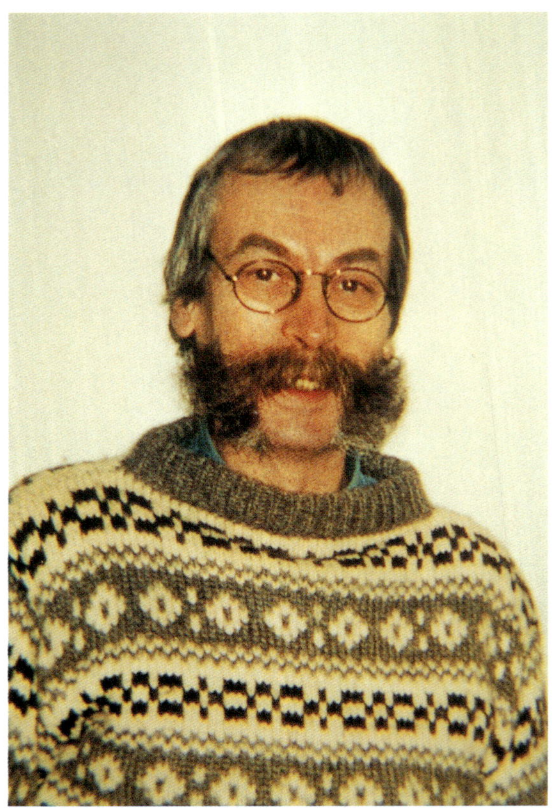

Bernard Verlingue is the director of the *Musée de la Faïence* in Quimper, and is a registered with the French Union of Experts (UFE), specializing in the *faïence de Quimper*. Bernard Verlingue is the grandson of Jules Verlingue, the purchaser of the *HB/Grande Maison* factory in 1917.

Verlingue

Most Quimper devotees quickly will recognize the name of Bernard Verlingue. He is a grandson of Jules Verlingue and curator of *Le Musée de la Faïence*, an emphatic must-see stop in Quimper. Bernard describes the origins of the privately-owned museum as a continuation of the Verlingue family faïence tradition begun in Boulogne-sur-Mer.

Bernard Verlingue's grandfather, Jules Verlingue, founded *La Faïencerie de la Madeleine* in Boulogne in 1903. In 1913, a fire destroyed part of the Boulogne factory, causing economic hardship and it became necessary for Jules Verlingue to sell the factory to banker Henri Delcourt. Verlingue remained on as the faïencerie director, a situation not to his liking. Therefore when his friend Guy de la Hubaudière decided to sell *La Grande Maison* in 1914, Bernard's grandfather began negotiations to purchase it. Because of World War I and the death of Guy de la Hubaudière in 1916, the sale wasn't finalized until 1917.

The name Verlingue quickly became a prominent fixture in Quimper faïence, and many creative innovations in faïence came about during Jules Verlingue's leadership. In 1932, according to Bernard Verlingue, his grandfather lost the majority shares in the business and was obliged to leave the *HB/Grande Maison* factory. Jules Verlingue became an insurance agent. When Bernard's grandfather died in 1946, Bernard's father, Jean-Yves Verlingue, took charge of the family and became the head of the insurance agency at the age of 18. By 1956, Jean-Yves bought back the majority shares of the faïencerie, and the *HB/Grand Maison* returned to the Verlingue family.

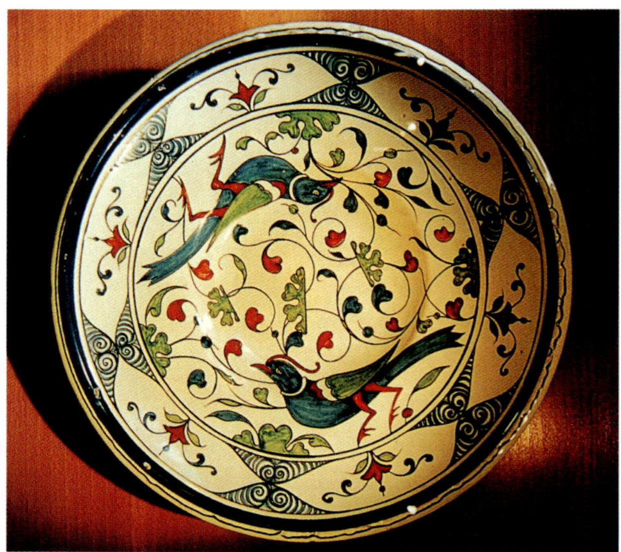

A Turkish-inspired plate is from the first quarter of the 20th century. After Jules Verlingue purchased the *HB/Grande Maison*, he collected various styles of poterie from throughout the world and incorporated design elements in the HB product. *Courtesy of Musée de la Faïence, Quimper.*

Jules Verlingue is reported to have originated the *chardon*, or thistle, décor shown on this plate, soon after his arrival at the *HB/Grande Maison* in 1917. *Courtesy of Musée de la Faïence, Quimper.*

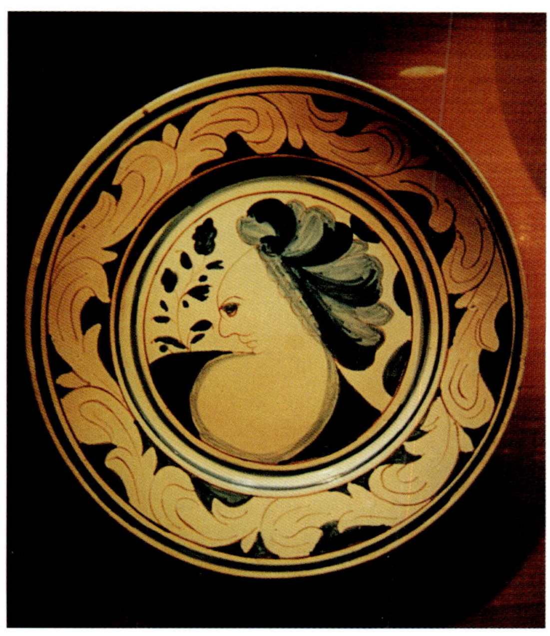

Another HB Quimper dish is in the *Hispano-Mauresque* style. It was produced in the first quarter of the 20th century, after Jules Verlingue came to Quimper. *Courtesy of Musée de la Faïence, Quimper.*

Twelve years later in 1968, the *HB/Grande Maison* firm absorbed the Henriot factory, which was ailing financially. The two businesses were consolidated within the same building, yet maintained separate clients, décors, and artists. This new firm became known as *Les Faïenceries de Quimper*, and a board with representatives from each of the original factories oversaw the business activities. This was the firm that was sold in 1984. *(Mali, French Faïence, p. 49.)*

Verlingue recalls the decline of the faïence business in France and in Quimper during the 1980s as he experienced it. Factory owners felt frustration, watching payrolls and production costs rise while working hours and product orders fell. This was compounded by French legal restrictions banning staff adjustments to accommodate market fluctuations. While this was occurring, labor costs, which previously were 60 percent of the final product, rose to 80 percent. Meanwhile, other countries were flooding the faïence market with merchandise made at lower costs with cheaper labor. In July 1983, despite worker protests and despair in the Quimper collecting community, production ceased at *Les Faïenceries de Quimper*.

Pierre Breton, whose family has been selling faïence in Quimper since the 1930s, reported a rush to buy Quimper both in 1968, when Henriot nearly dissolved, and again in 1983, when investors and collectors thought they might be purchasing the last of the line.

The approval of the Janssens' plan to purchase and revive the oldest ongoing faïence firm in Quimper also served to continue the Verlingue and Henriot presence. The *Société Nouvelle des Faïenceries de Quimper* hired Pierre Henriot as the Managing Director and Bernard Verlingue as the Technical Director, positions they held until 1987.

Bernard Verlingue recounted how his family owned the models and *aquarelles*, or watercolor models, and an extensive collection of faïence. After the sale of the factory, a gentleman's agreement was struck, dividing the *aquarelles* between the *Société* and the Verlingues. The faïence collection was to be retained by the family, but housed by the *Société* in the faïencerie's first and second floor museum. In 1989, the collection was boxed up and moved out of the faïencerie by the Verlingues, and the idea was born for the *Musée de la Faïence, Jules Verlingue,* to house the years of faïence history so lovingly accumulated by the Porquier, Henriot, and Verlingue/de La Hubaudiére establishments. *(Conversations and correspondence with Bernard Verlingue, January-April 2001.)*

Musée de la Faïence, Jules Verlingue

One museum in Quimper personifies all three characteristics of the history, the art, and the spirit of Quimper. It took three years for the dream of this new museum to become a reality, but it was well worth the wait. The *Musée de la Faïence* is on the site of an early Porquier factory, bordering the Odet. It's not far from the church, *Notre Dame de Locmaria* and is behind the present-day *Société Nouvelle des Faïenceries de Quimper,* or HB/Henriot, as their products are signed.

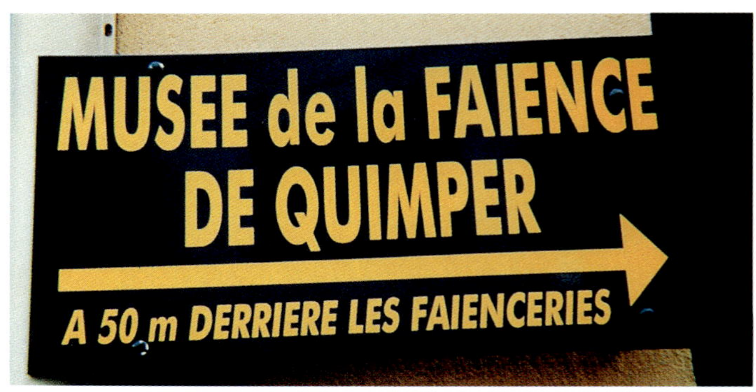

The *Musée de la Faïence* overlooks the Odet River at *14 Rue Jean-Baptiste Bousquet,* the site of an early Porquier factory.

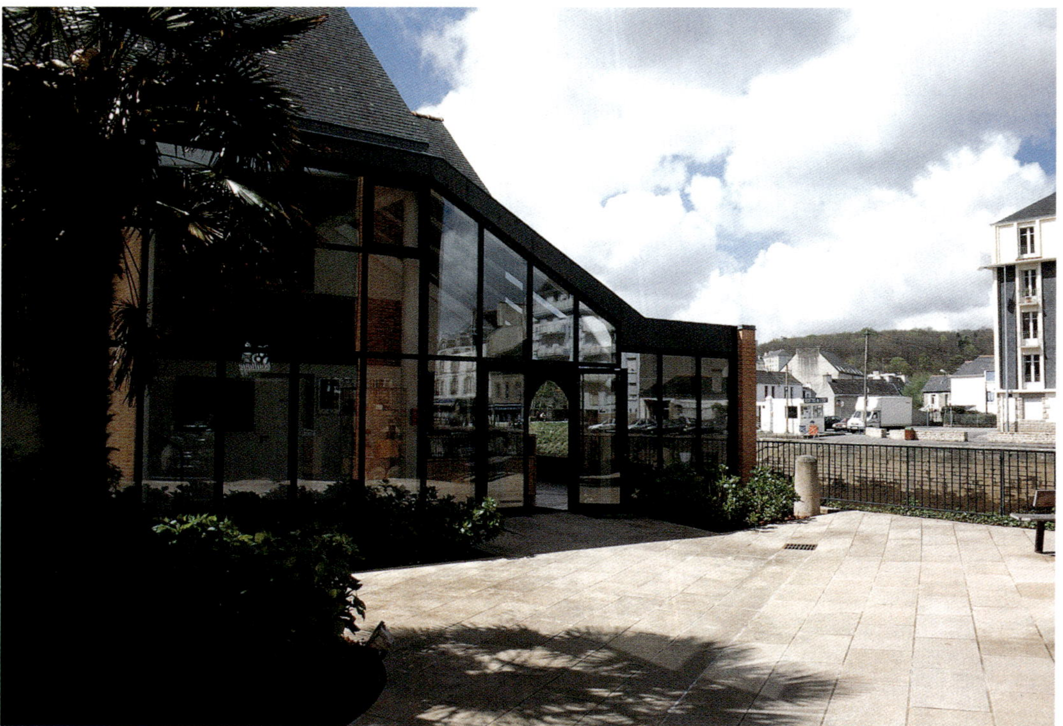

The museum building was designed to blend with the surroundings and to present the faïence collection in its best light.

Opening June 17, 1991, the *Musée de la Faïence* is designed and lit to create an entirely appropriate setting for the collection housed there. Bernard Verlingue describes it as a potter putting his life on display, and he believes the layout and presentation are an accurate depiction of the history and reality of the *faïences de Quimper.* The museum is an enriching voyage through eight rooms, chronicling the history of faïence. Visitors are guided through the various influences on Quimper artistry and special production periods.

The tour begins with replicas of the two saints connected with Quimper faïence, *Notre Dame de Locmaria* and St. Anthony of Padua, the potters' saint. A *triskele* of the natural elements, earth, water, and fire, is featured. These elements were prevalent in the Locmaria section of Quimper, making it a natural site to make pottery. In fact, Gallo-Roman remains of poterie-making have been found in this location. That, coupled with the quality clay or *argile* from the Toulven Cove a few kilometers southeast of Quimper, made the Locmaria area an ideal location for poteries to settle.

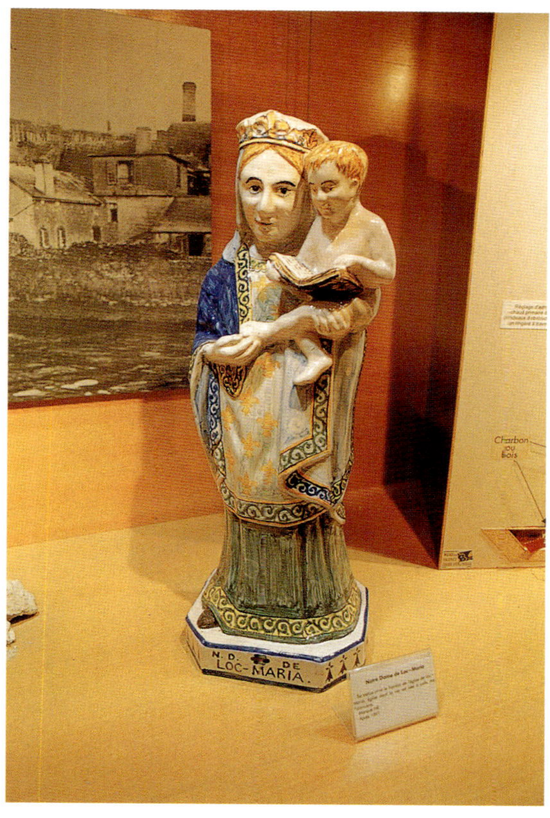

In the first display area, *Notre Dame de Locmaria* welcomes visitors to the home of Quimper faïence history. *Courtesy of Musée de la Faïence, Quimper.*

The second presentation is homage to Breton potters, as depicted by the artist Yvonne Jean-Haffen, and a display of the ingredients and technical instruments needed to bring the clay to life as Quimper faïence. Bernard Verlingue explained the five steps illustrated by Jean-Haffen in her remarkable, award-winning sculpture. The steps are: The clay is shaped; the object is fired for the first time; then it is decorated by the painter; it is returned to the kiln again; and then the object is fired for a second time. Voilà! The Quimper faïence process in ceramic by Yvonne Jean-Haffen.

Saint Anthony of Padua, the potters' saint, joins *Notre Dame de Locmaria* in greeting visitors. We are reminded that water, earth, and fire, all required for making poterie, were prevalent in Locmaria. *Courtesy of Musée de la Faïence, Quimper.*

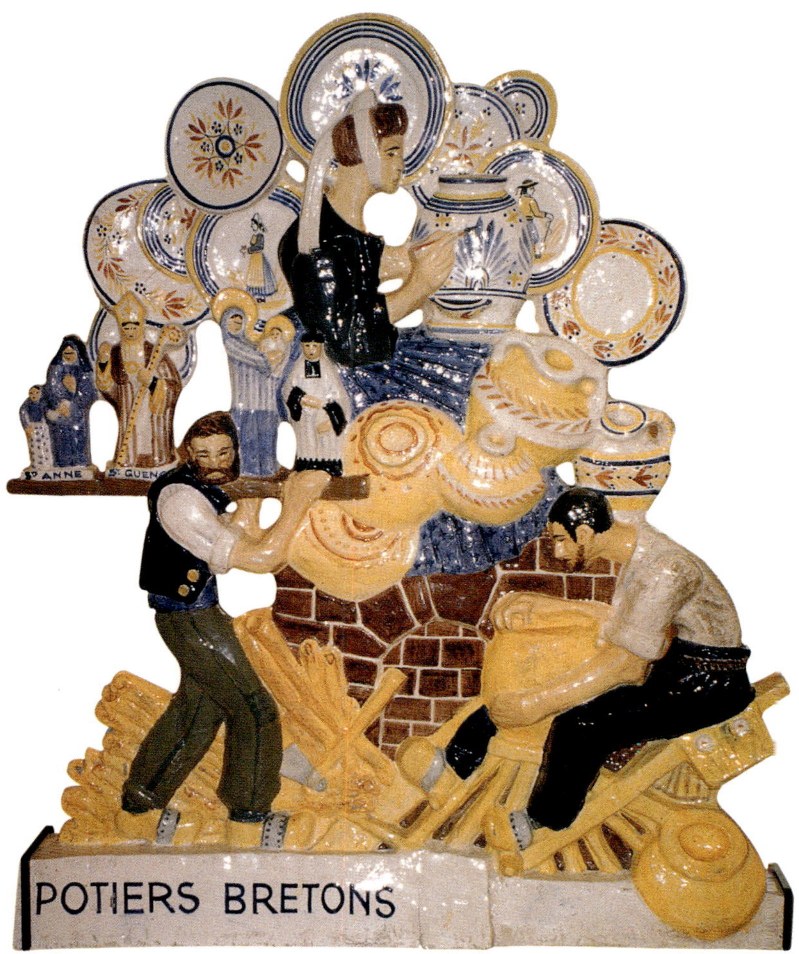

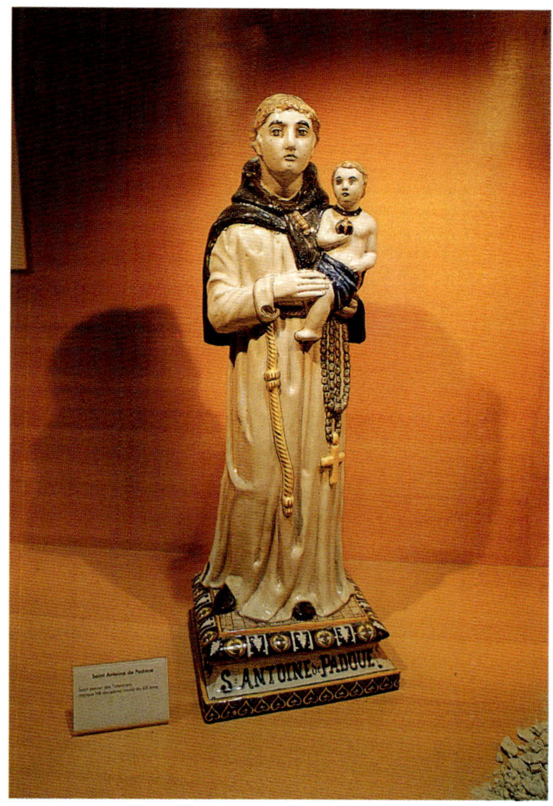

In the second display area, the remarkable work by Yvonne Jean-Haffen dominates the presentation of the artists' tools and techniques. Nearly six feet high, Jean-Haffen's *Potiers Bretons* shows the steps in making Quimper poterie. This remarkable work won a gold medal for the Henriot faïencerie at the 1937 Universal Exhibition held in Paris. *Courtesy of Musée de la Faïence, Quimper.*

The third display area shows the evolution of the Quimper style. An 18th century Quimper earthenware two-handled container, *sans* one handle, is on view. It is decorated with slip, or *aux engobes*. *Courtesy of Musée de la Faïence, Quimper.*

The third room presents early examples of Quimper, terra cotta decorated with various slips, and the Nevers and Rouen styles' first impact on the product of Quimper. The *petit Breton* appears about 1860 and is shown in various poses. Intricate early Quimper pieces are displayed, as well as unusual theme items.

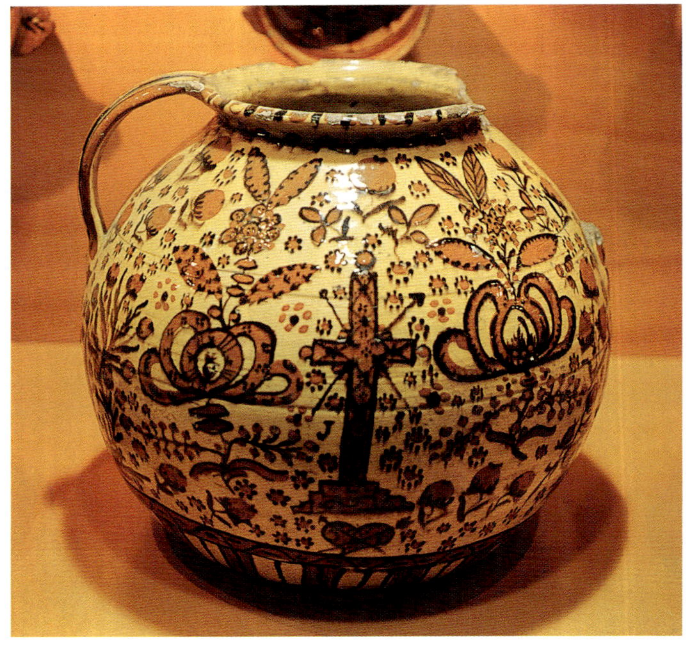

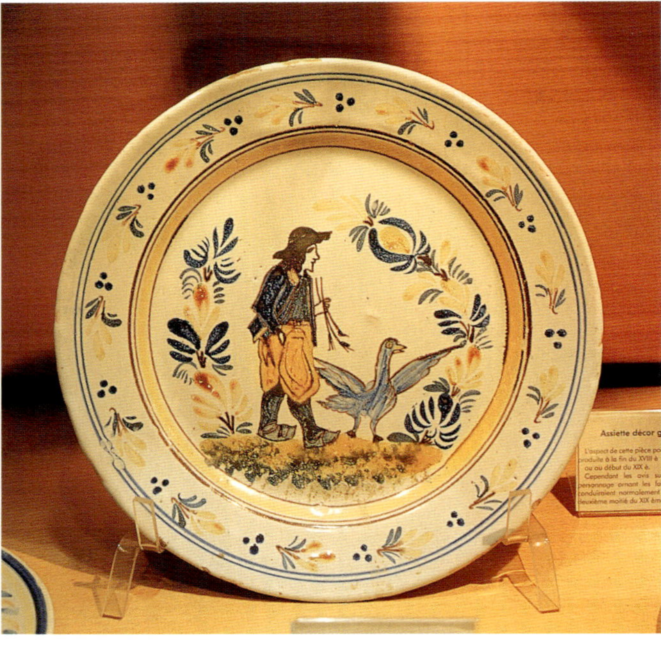

A novel rendition of the *petit Breton* is called a tender of geese (*d'oie*) from St. Thoix. The same design, but called St. Thois, is found on a Porquier-Beau plate with a *rinceaux* border. *(See Château de Quintin Exposition Catalogue, p. 100.) Courtesy of Musée de la Faïence, Quimper.*

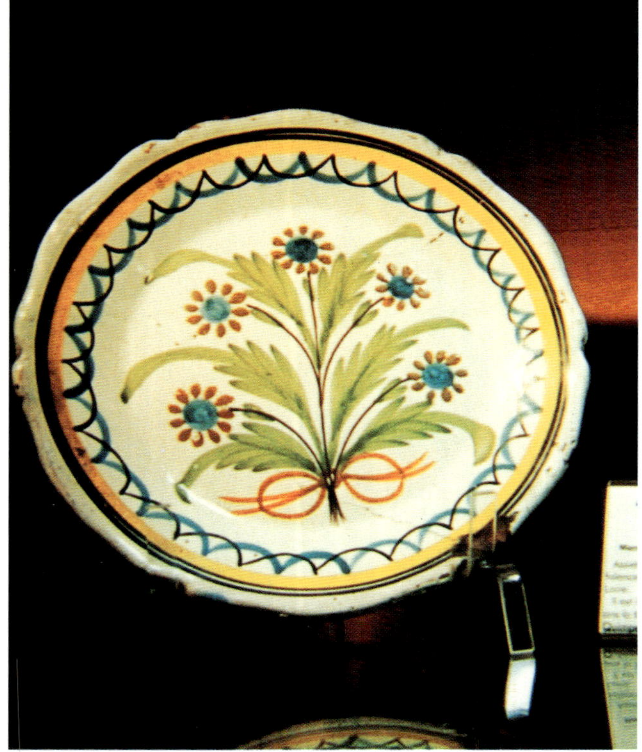

A late 18th century, 8.25" plate is Quimper, but the manufacturer is undetermined. The décor demonstrates the impact of the Nevers potters' *à la touche*, or freehand brush-stroke technique, on Quimper work. The floral bouquet, featuring blue, yellow, green, and manganese coloration, shows the technique brought to Quimper by the Nevers potter Pierre Bellevaux in the 1770s. *Courtesy of Musée de la Faïence, Quimper.*

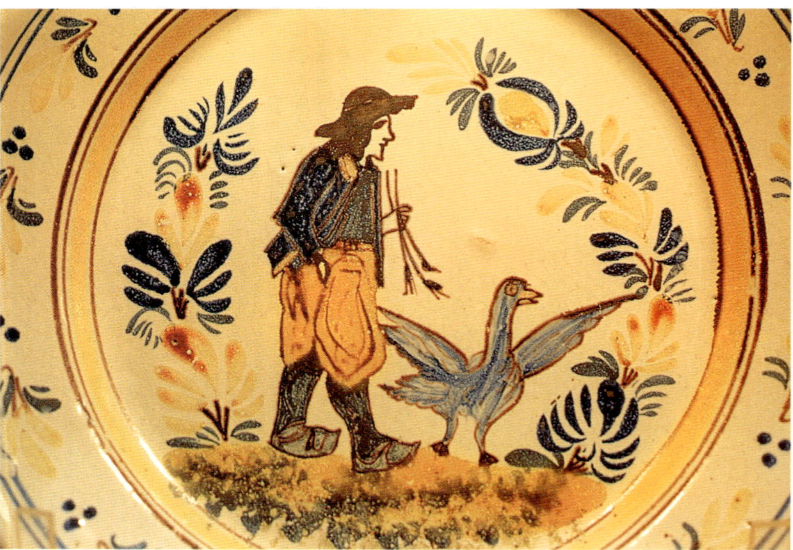

A closer look reveals delicate *à la touche* designs on the border and center of this Quimper plate from the mid-1800s. *Courtesy of Musée de la Faïence, Quimper.*

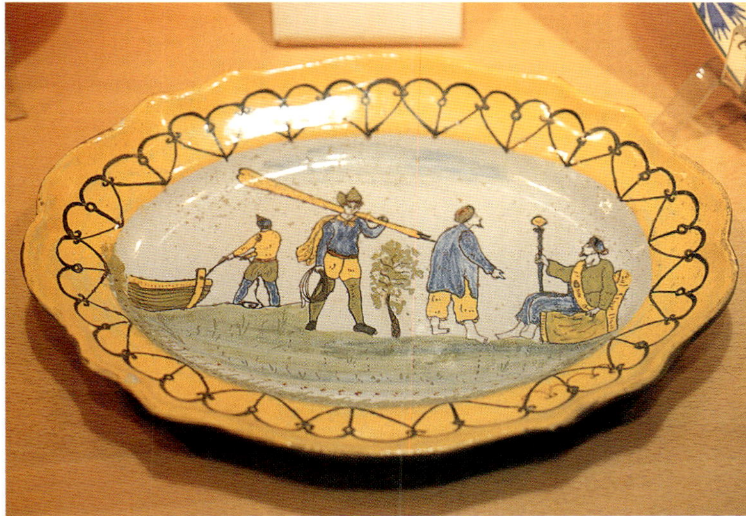

An oval plate from the 18th century has a border in the style of Marseilles. The center is a commemoration of the arrival of René Madec in India. Madec was born in a house on *Place Terre-au-Duc* in Quimper in 1736, and became an important military leader and diplomat. In India, he was given the title of *Nabab*, indicating a position of importance and influence. *Courtesy of Musée de la Faïence, Quimper.*

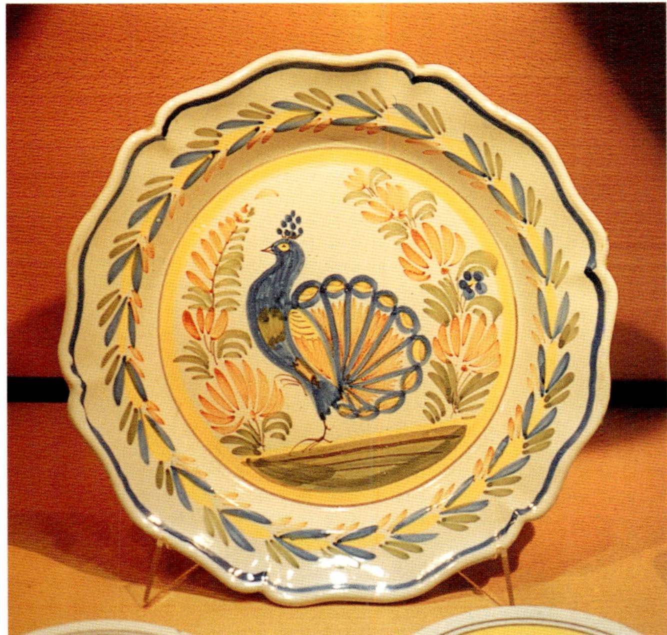

Another colorful plate represents the style of Delft, or the East India Company's influence on Quimper faïence. The rendition of the peacock, or *paon*, is stylish and bold. The plate dates from the first half of the 19th century and is unsigned Quimper. *Courtesy of Musée de la Faïence, Quimper.*

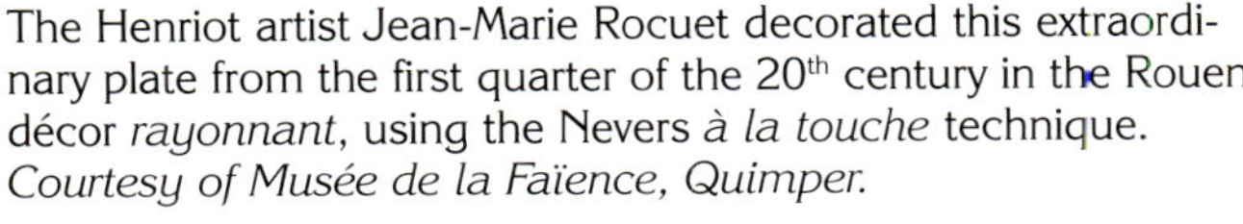

The Henriot artist Jean-Marie Rocuet decorated this extraordinary plate from the first quarter of the 20th century in the Rouen décor *rayonnant*, using the Nevers *à la touche* technique. *Courtesy of Musée de la Faïence, Quimper.*

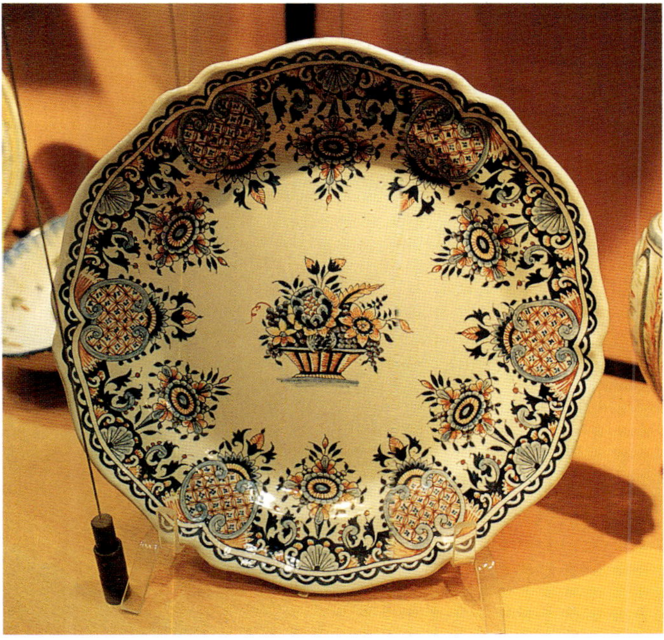

The Rouen potters' influence is seen on this Quimper plate from the late 19th century. Note the lambrequins and the lattice-work, also called *quadrillés*, in the medallions around the rim in the style of the Rouen Guillibaud factory. The central motif, a *panier fleuri* (basket of flowers), is another Rouen element. *Courtesy of Musée de la Faïence, Quimper.*

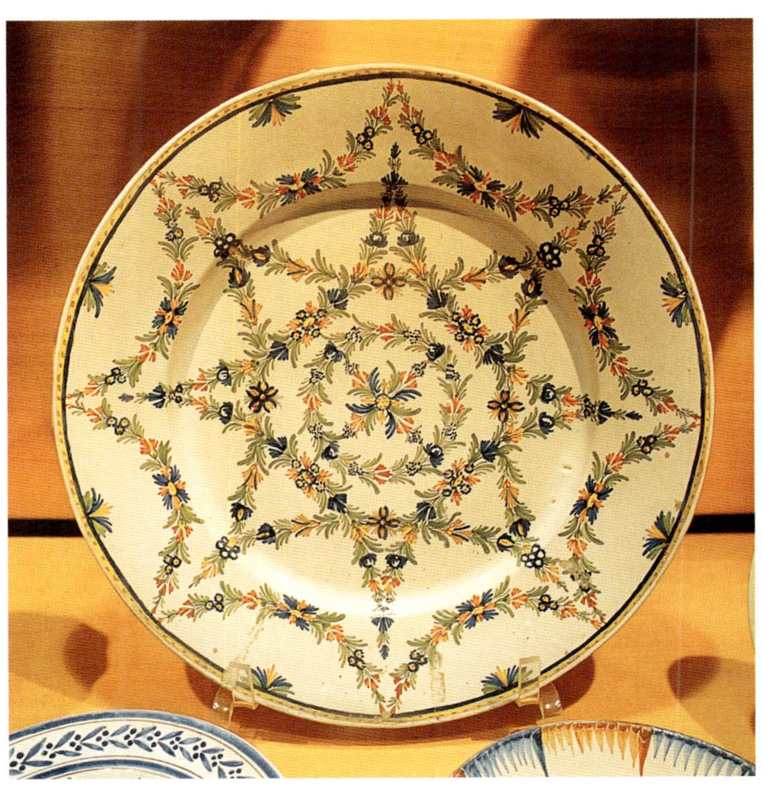

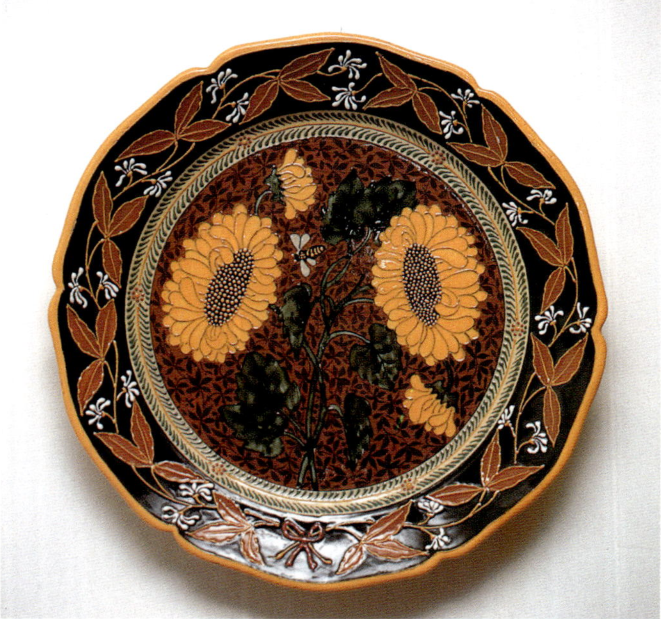

This gorgeous HB Quimper 17" diameter charger of sunflowers in various colored glazes is reminiscent of Longwy products. It dates from 1920 to 1925 and is a combination of styles and techniques, including *broderie,* which emulates the embroidery on Breton costumes. *Courtesy of Musée de la Faïence, Quimper.*

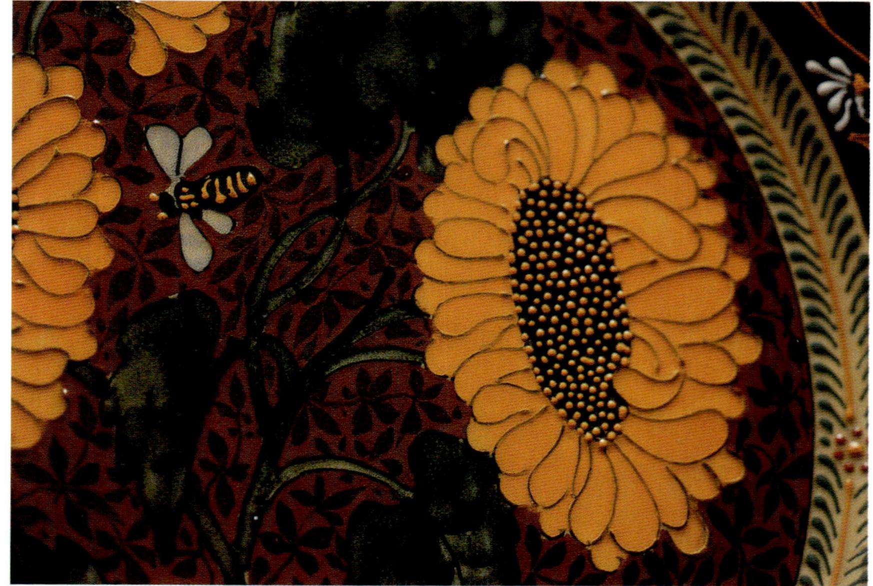

A closer look at the *tournesols* (sunflowers) reveals an insect among the flowers. Cloisonné is employed on this lovely example created and painted by Charles Trautman. (For additional examples see *Verlingue and Mannoni, p. 78.*) *Courtesy of Musée de la Faïence, Quimper.*

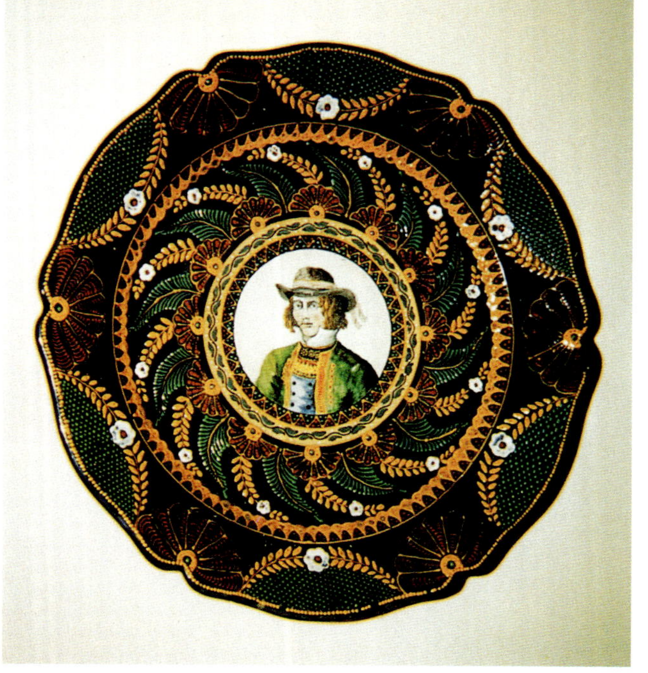

The technique of applying additional glaze with a special tool in a variety of patterns also is known as *à la poire* or *tubé.* The *broderie* décor is clearly observed on this nearly 19" diameter charger from the 1920s. It is signed HB Quimper and has a central medallion showing a Breton surrounded by various *broderie* designs. *Courtesy of Musée de la Faïence, Quimper.*

The fourth room presents a further, more intense look at the Nevers, Rouen, Marseilles, Delft, Turkish, Persian, and Hispanic-Moorish styles applied to Quimper. Bernard Verlingue's grandfather enjoyed collecting faïence from other countries and used the designs on HB products.

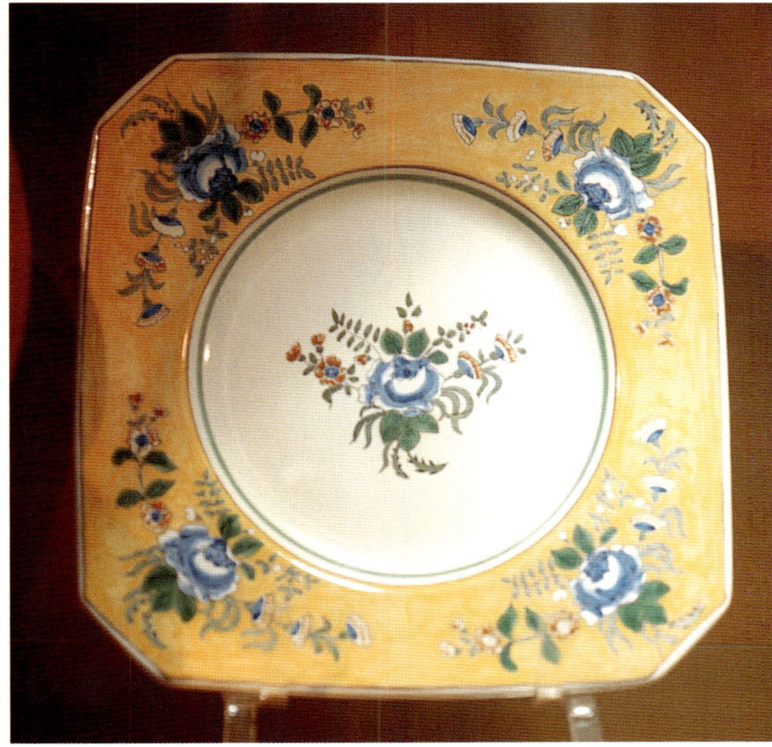

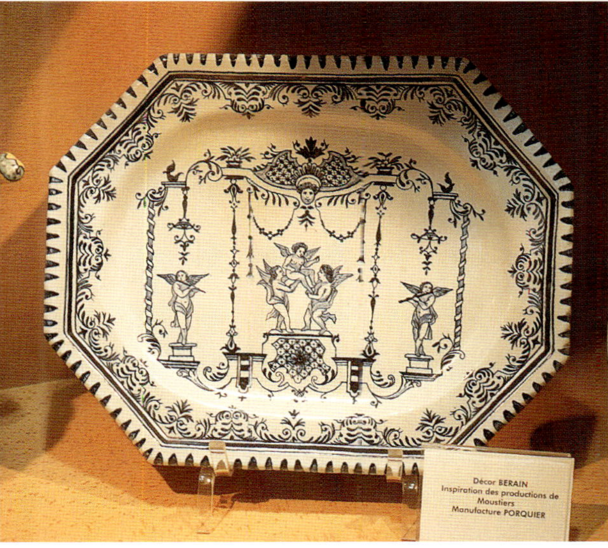

The décor on this Porquier faïencerie oval platter is called *Bérain*, another Moustiers design. Note the garlands and angels executed in dark *camaïeu bleu* on white faïence. *Courtesy of Musée de la Faïence, Quimper.*

In the fourth room, additional influences on Quimper production are displayed. An example of the Marseilles décor graces this faïence square plate with cut corners by HB. The color is a delicate yellow and the floral embellishments are rendered in blues with touches of rose and green. *Courtesy of Musée de la Faïence, Quimper.*

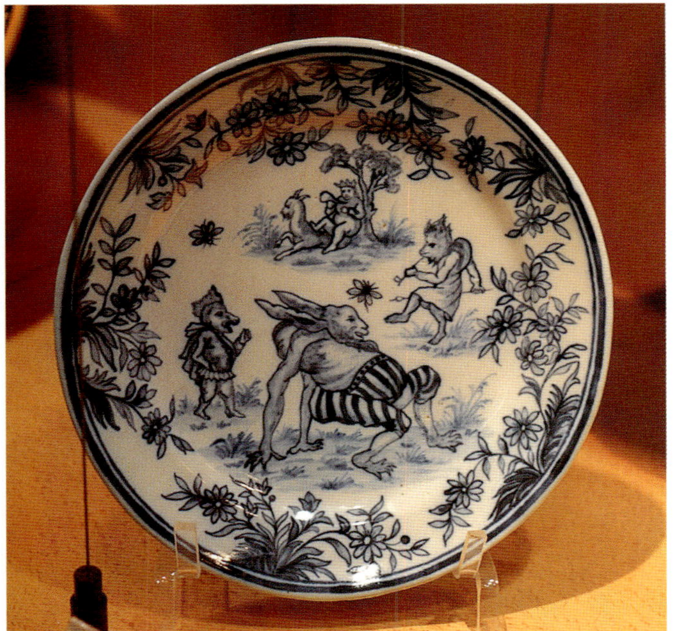

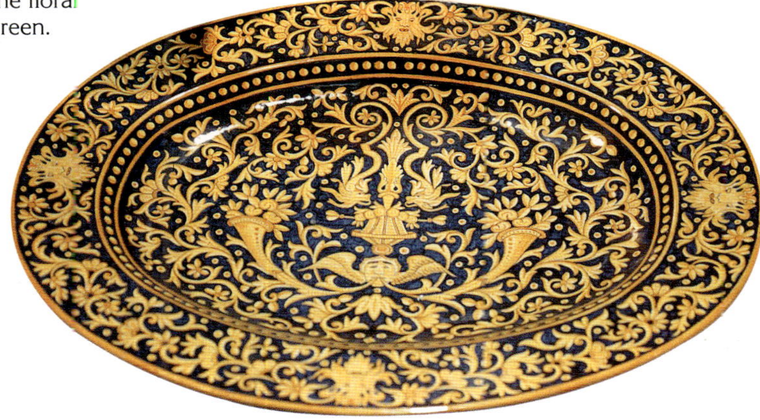

The Italian influence on Nevers potters was felt in Quimper. This 23.5" long platter is signed HB Quimper and P for the artist Poulain. Poulain came to Quimper with Jules Verlingue from the Boulogne-sur-Mer faïencerie. Poulain specialized in more formal décors such as this *Italo-Nivernais* example. *Courtesy of Musée de la Faïence, Quimper.*

Camaïeu bleu, or monochromatic blue, is the palette for this Moustiers-inspired décor plate with Italian *Commedia dell'arte* characters. The example was manufactured by the Porquier-Beau faïencerie in the last quarter of the 19th century. *Courtesy of Musée de la Faïence, Quimper.*

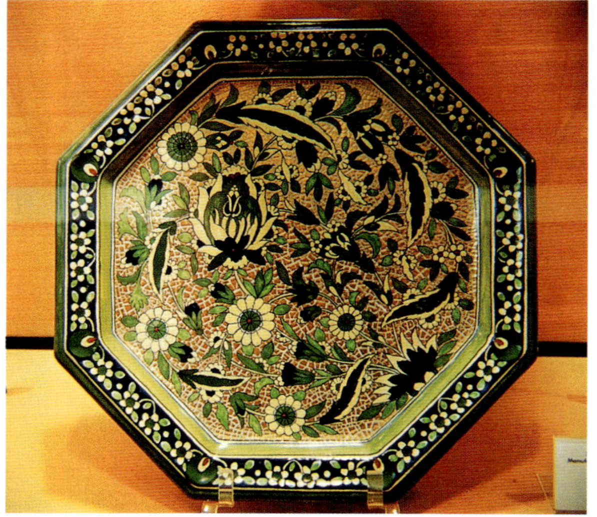

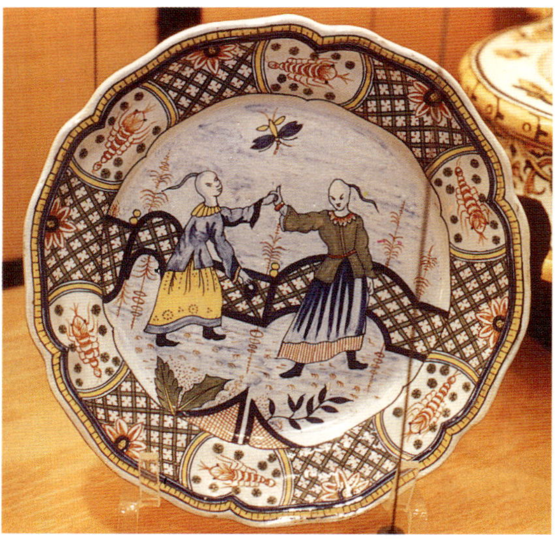

The Persian influence is seen on this Porquier-Beau faïencerie octagonal platter, from the last quarter of the 19th century. *Courtesy of Musée de la Faïence, Quimper.*

A 9.75" diameter scalloped plate in the Rouen *chinois* style features a border of *quadrillages* interspersed with medallions featuring prawns. The interior of this Porquier-Beau design features two Chinese greeting each other as an insect hovers. (For a similar example, see *Château de Quintin Exposition Catalogue, p. 29.*) *Courtesy of Musée de la Faïence, Quimper.*

A Rouen décor of Chinese influence presents a startling, vibrant, and somewhat menacing example from the last quarter of the 19th century. Note the Rouen red chain motif around the edge of this Porquier-Beau example of a dragon on the wing. (For another example, see *Trois Siècles de Faïences, p. 65.*) *Courtesy of Musée de la Faïence, Quimper.*

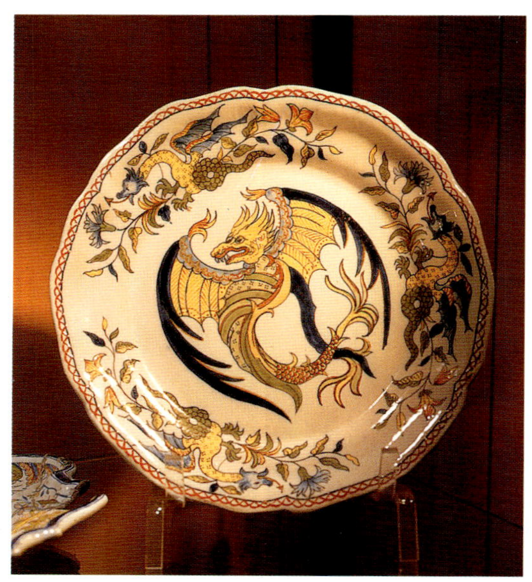

The fifth room is devoted to the magical works of Alfred Beau, and features botanical motifs, *légendes Bretonnes*, *scènes Bretonnes*, and more. Beau's contributions to the development of Quimper faïence cannot be underestimated. His skills as a photographer, his design and painting talents, and his commitment to art served the *faïence de Quimper* well. Beau's impact on the Quimper faïenceries continues today. He gave admirers of Quimper faïence lasting works of art, and he has been the impetus for other faïence artists to create important works.

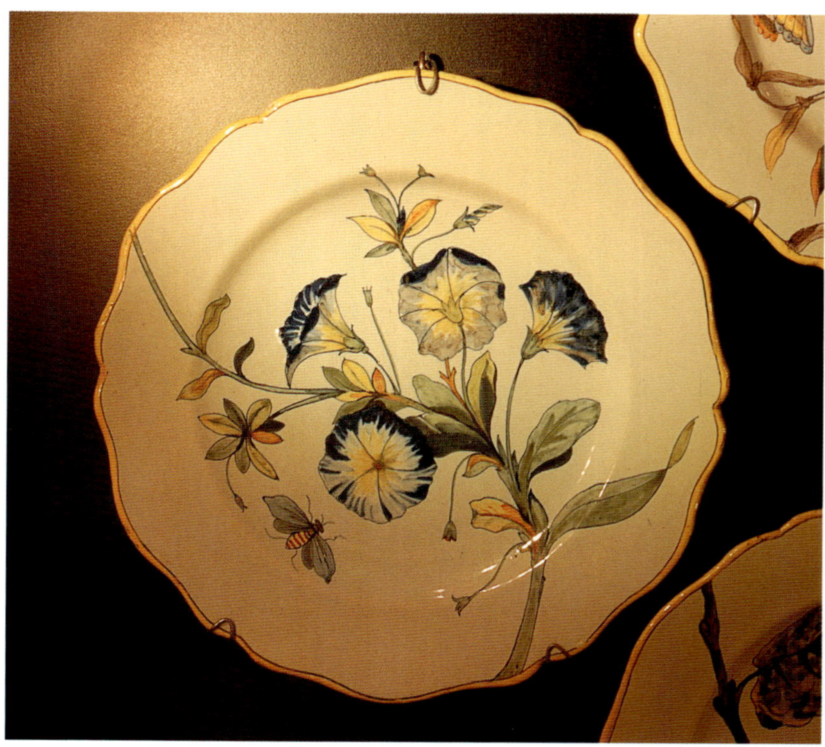

Alfred Beau's works have the fifth display room to themselves. Beau's creations decorated with his *botanique* designs have increased in popularity since their inception. Botanical plates usually measure between 9" and 10" diameter and are bordered in yellow. Some have colorful flowers like these morning glories … *Courtesy of Musée de la Faïence, Quimper.*

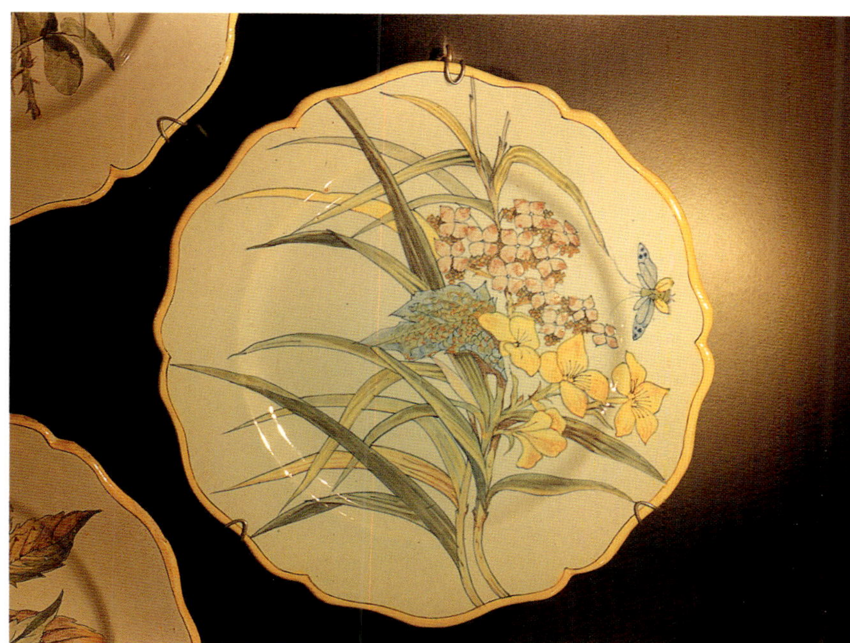

… And some of Beau's botanical plates have insects in addition to the flowers. *Courtesy of Musée de la Faïence, Quimper.*

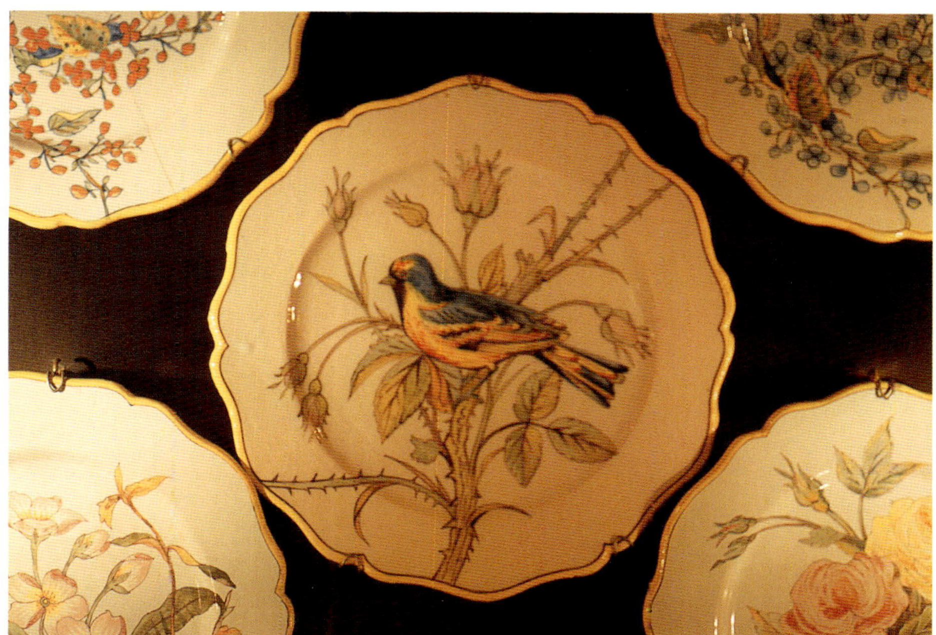

Other Beau *décor botanique* plates have birds perched on branches … *Courtesy of Musée de la Faïence, Quimper.*

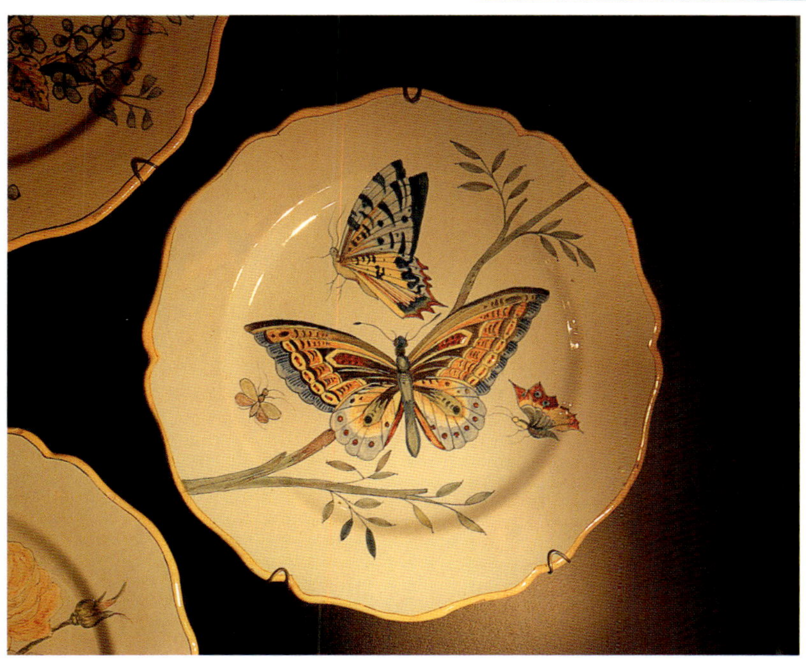

… Still others have beautiful butterflies. Beau's designs are reminiscent of English porcelain motifs. *Courtesy of Musée de la Faïence, Quimper.*

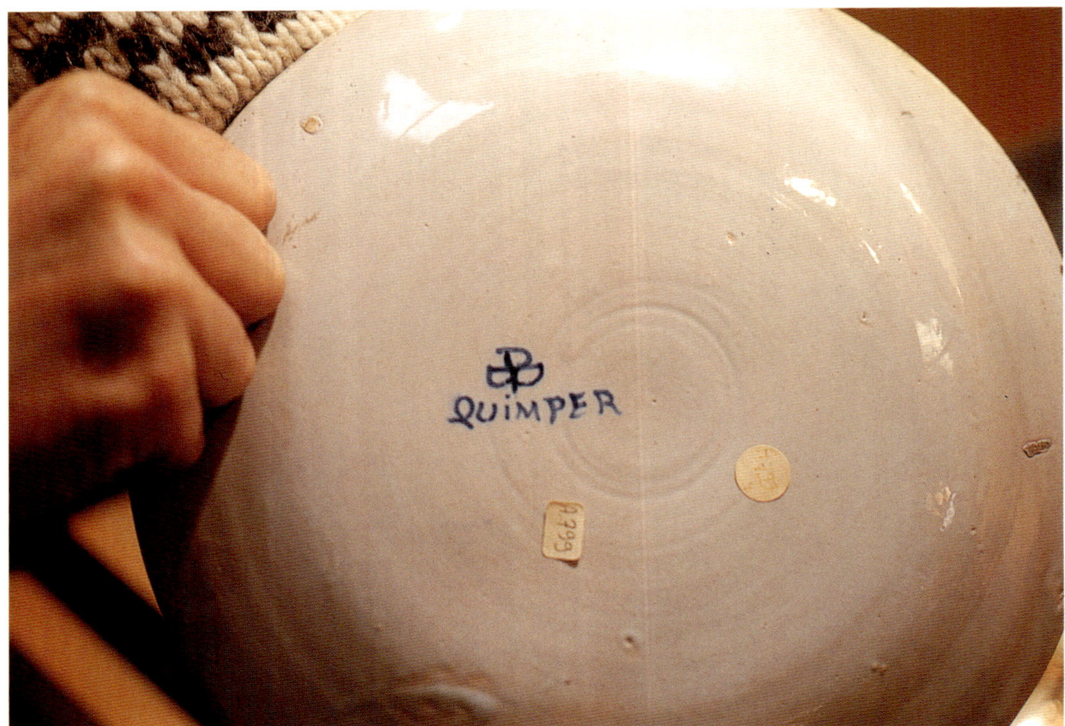

Many Porquier-Beau items are signed with only PB, but there are examples where items are signed with PB (for the Porquier-Beau faïencerie) and the word Quimper, as shown here. This signature on a Porquier-Beau plate, as demonstrated by Bernard Verlingue, is from the last quarter of the 19th century and should not to be confused with the re-issued works signed PB Quimper from the Henriot faïencerie. *Courtesy of Musée de la Faïence, Quimper.*

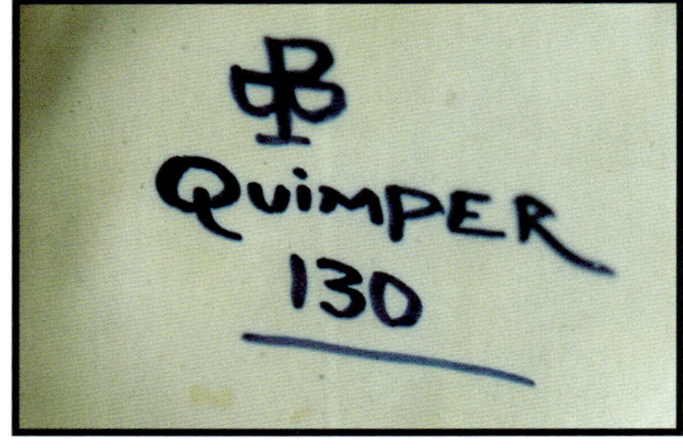

The newer items, made by the Henriot faïencerie beginning in 1919, have a PB Quimper signature but also contain an artist's number, as seen on this example. *Authors' Collection.*

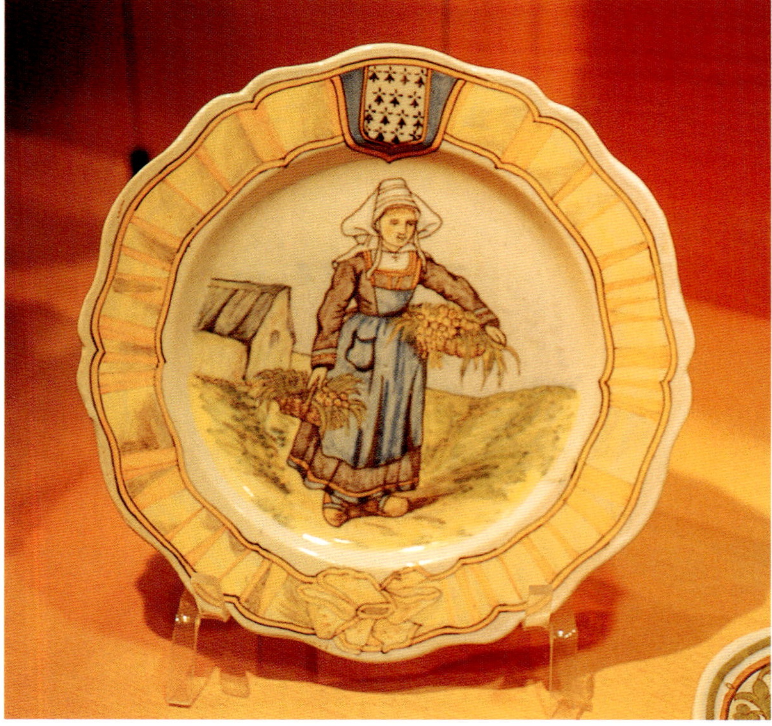

Alfred Beau also is known for his *scènes Bretonnes*, where *la vie quotidiene*, or daily life is documented. When these scenes are rendered in Beau's exquisite detail, the everyday episodes become classic expressions. A Bretonne produce seller is surrounded with a pleated yellow ribbon border, called *au ruban jaune plissé*. The armorial of Brittany is at the top of the border décor of the 9.25" diameter plate. *Courtesy of Musée de la Faïence, Quimper.*

Left:
Another Alfred Beau scene appears on a Porquier-Beau shaped dish, tied with a ceramic bow. A mother and child are playing outdoors in a sweet rendition of childhood in 19th century Brittany. This scene seems to fit the shape of the dish quite well. In some instances, elements of larger scenes were selected for use on smaller pieces. *Courtesy of Musée de la Faïence, Quimper.*

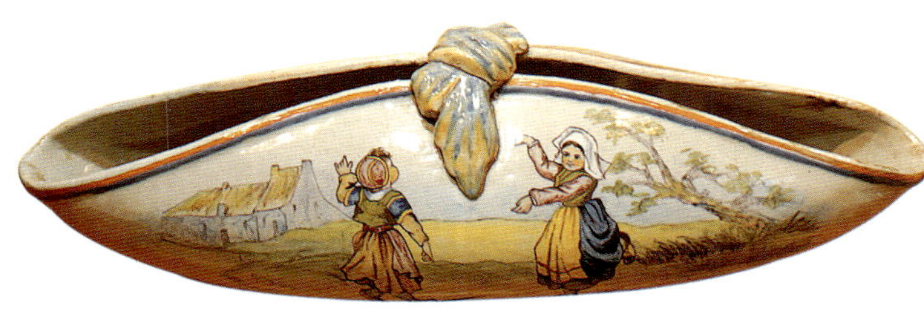

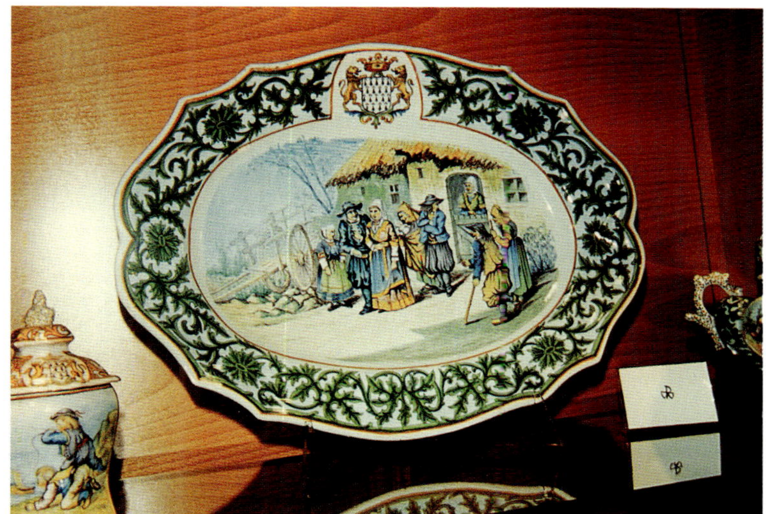

A large oval Porquier-Beau platter from the last quarter of the 19th century is rimmed with green scrolling foliage on blue background, and tells an entire story. Alfred Beau's artistry sets the scene of a family departing from a Breton thatched cottage. Nearby are *mendiants*, or beggars hoping to receive charity. *Courtesy of Musée de la Faïence, Quimper.*

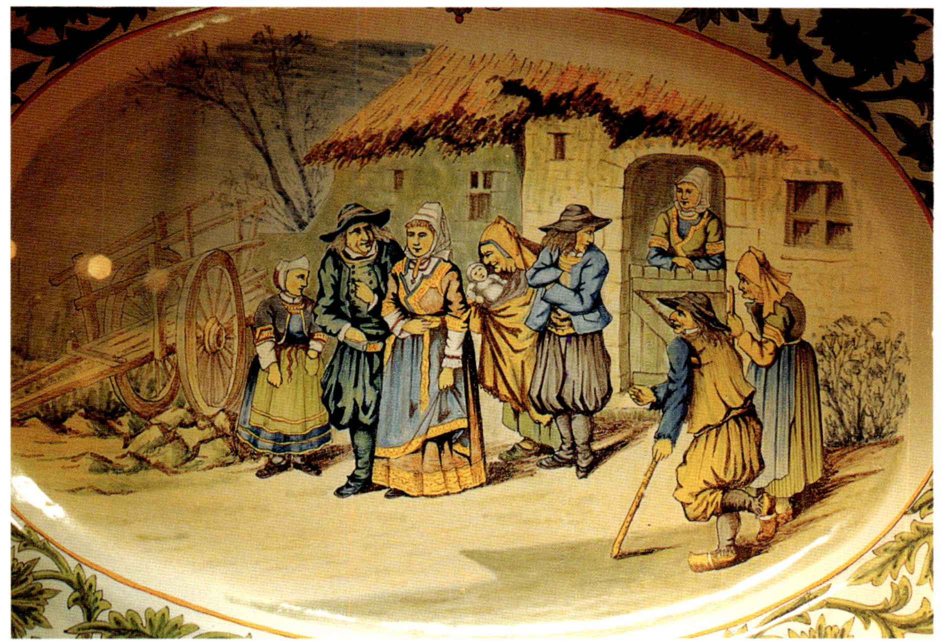

A closer look shows the detail and human interest achieved by Beau. The two Bretons and the young Bretonne are giving the *mendiants* a glance. The others seem intent on their journey, perhaps to a christening of the baby in the arms of *grandmère*. *Courtesy of Musée de la Faïence, Quimper.*

The sixth room features the artists who followed in Beau's footsteps, such as *Ar Seiz Breur* members James Bouillé, René-Yves Creston, Jorg Robin, Robert Micheau-Vernez, and Jules-Charles LeBozec. René Quillivic of *HB/Grande Maison* and Mathurin Méheut of Henriot also are featured, as are several other artists working prior to 1931. Grand and wonderful art is displayed from this host of important artists. The city of Quimper is known as a place of art and history, and its reputation is shown well in these displays.

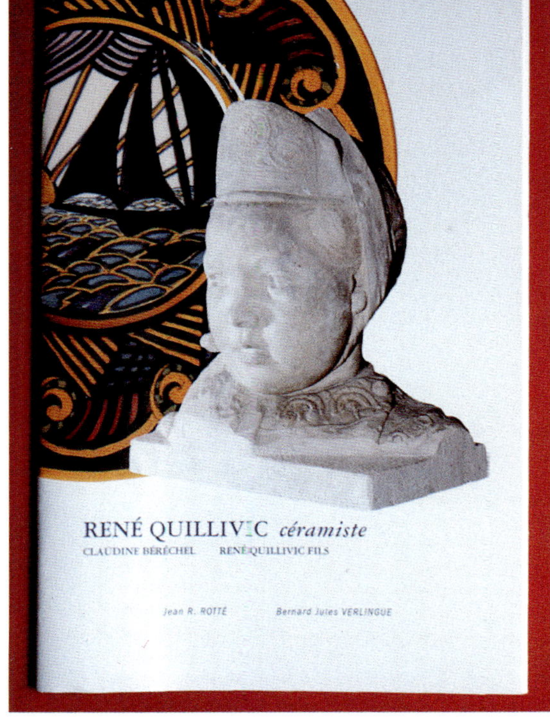

Another display room features major HB and Henriot artists, including Bouillé, Micheau-Vernez, and Robin among others. One of this group is HB artist René Quillivic. A retrospective was held for Quillivic in the museum's special exhibition room in 1997. In addition to his sculpting prowess, Quillivic developed a nautical décor called *Armorique Rustic. Courtesy of Musée de la Faïence, Quimper.*

Bold colors and simple lines tell the story of a strong and powerful ocean. The border décor on this 21" long *Armorique Rustique* platter contains white ram's horns alternating with blue squares containing lattice-work, all on a yellow background. The edge is a raised pearl effect, with alternating colors of violet and mauve, reflecting the colors of the sails. Signed: Armorique Rustique Quillivic with the monogram, or *chiffre*, of PF for Paul Fouillen. This means it was produced by Fouillen when he was *chef d'atelier* for HB in the 1920s. (*Rotté & Verlingue, p. 21.*) Courtesy of *Musée de la Faïence, Quimper.*

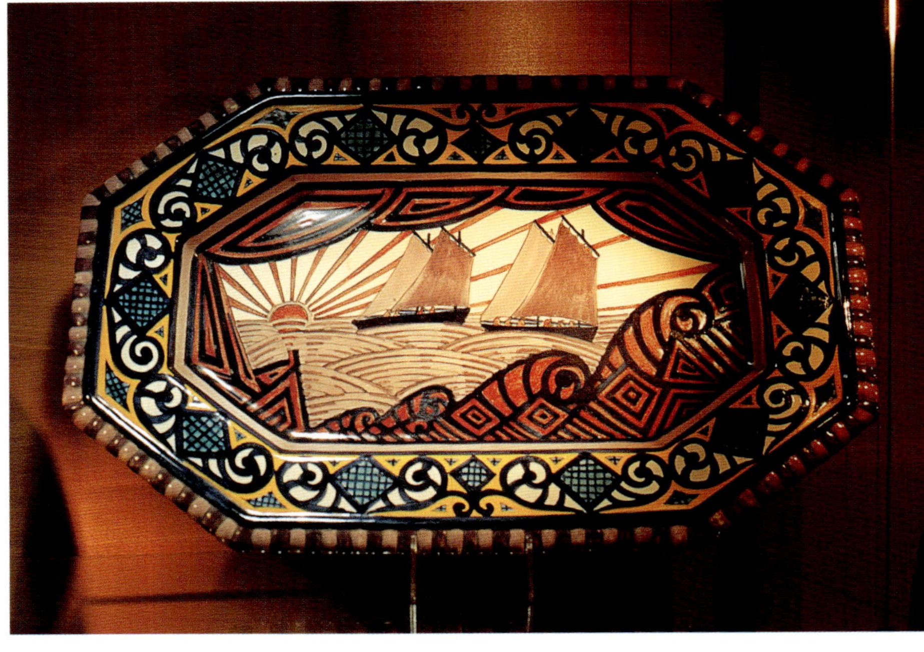

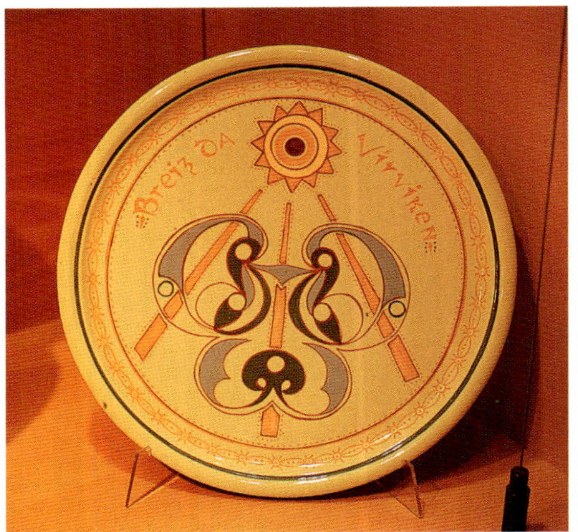

James Bouillé initiated the *Keltia* design based on Celtic symbols, many of which were gleaned from the Book of Kells. He was among a group of Bretons intent on raising awareness of their Celtic-Breton heritage through works of art. This plate by Bouillé is 12" diameter and carries the slogan *Brittany Forever*, in Breton. Celtic motifs complete the presentation. *Courtesy of Musée de la Faïence, Quimper.*

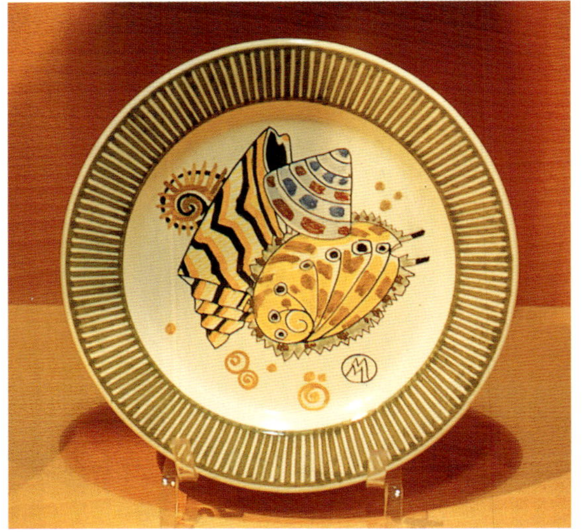

Another Méheut marine design graces this 9.5" diameter plate. His fanciful colors somehow reflect the actual world of underwater life forms. *Courtesy of Musée de la Faïence, Quimper.*

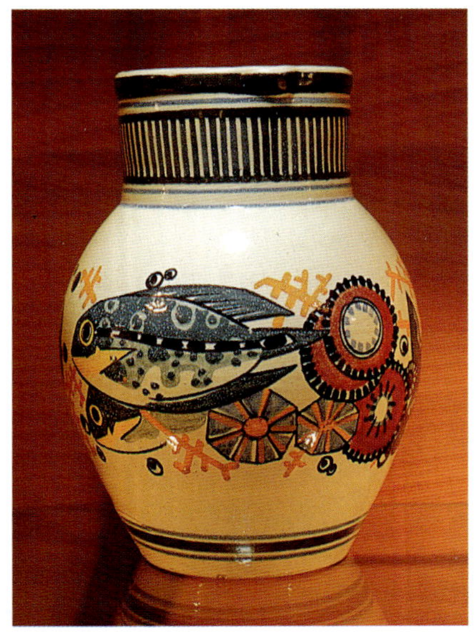

Left:
Mathurin Méheut developed many marine motifs in keeping with his love for the northern coast of Brittany and the sea creatures he observed there. A 9.25" tall Henriot pitcher sports stylized sea life by Méheut. *Courtesy of Musée de la Faïence, Quimper.*

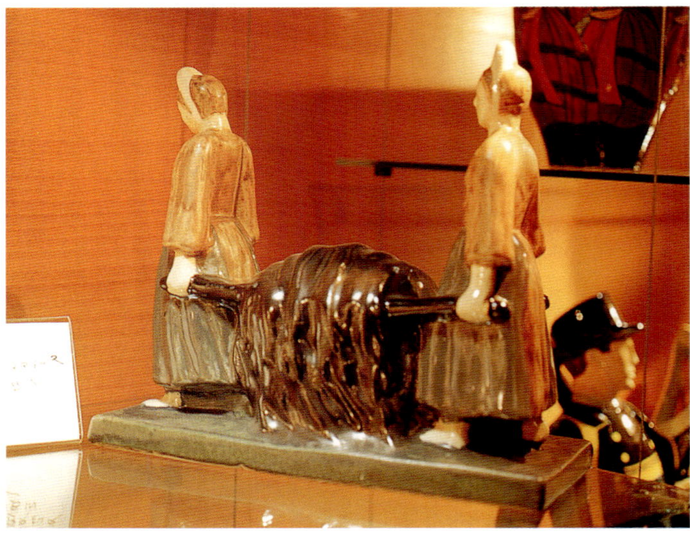

Jorg Robin designed this rendition of seaweed carriers, *Les Porteuses de Goëmons.* Robin was an *Ar Seiz Breur* member, intent on awakening an appreciation of things Breton through his art. When he sold the rights to a design of his work to the HB faïencerie, his name appeared on it as an anagram, Brion. *Courtesy of Musée de la Faïence, Quimper.*

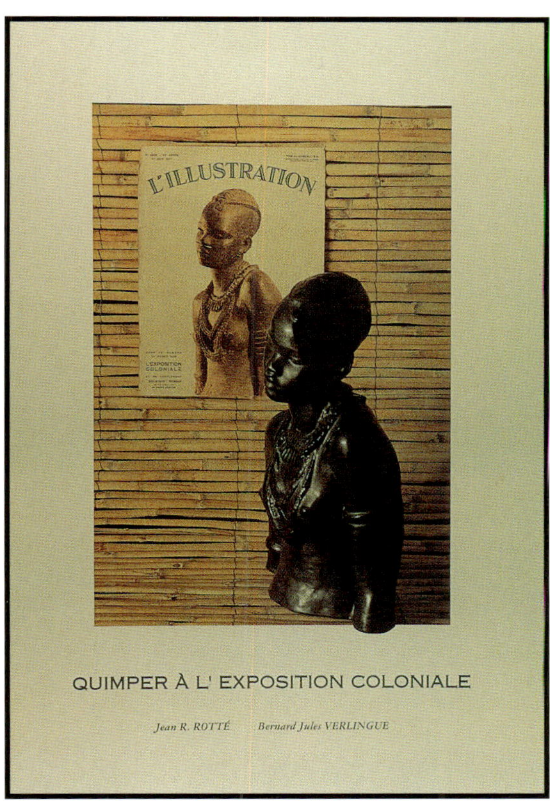

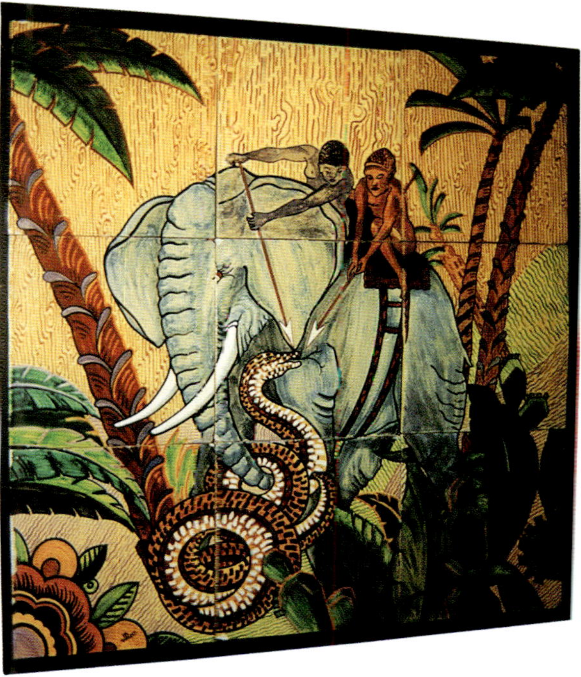

Renaud also designed this nine-tile painting measuring 23.5" square. It's entitled *Scène de Chasse en Afrique*, showing an elephant, two boys brandishing spears, and a threatening serpent. *Courtesy of Musée de la Faïence, Quimper.*

The Colonial period also has a special display in the sixth room. An exhibition was held in 1996 on Quimper and the Colonial Experience. A *Musée de la Faïence* publication features HB artist Anna Quinquand's 17.25" tall figure called *Femme du Fouta-Djalon*. It is juxtaposed with the French art magazine *Illustration*, where it appeared on the cover. *Courtesy of Musée de la Faïence, Quimper.*

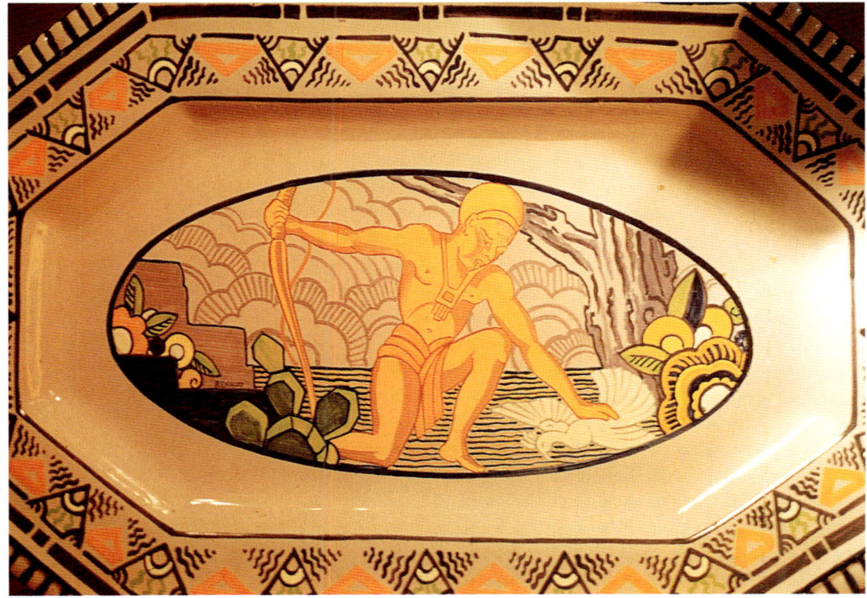

An 17.25" oval platter carries an African theme by HB artist Georges Renaud and was exhibited at the 1931 Colonial Exhibition in Paris. Entitled *Scène de chasse en exotique*, it shows an African archer with his prey. *Courtesy of Musée de la Faïence, Quimper.*

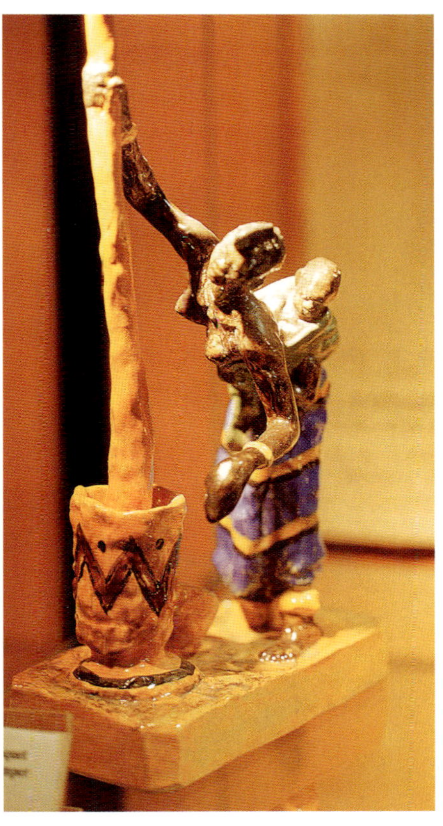

Another artwork for the Colonial Exposition by Gaston Broquet is entitled *Le Pilon*, representing an African mother with a baby on her back, using a large mortar and pestle. The statuette stands 8" tall and is signed HenRiot Quimper, #145. Broquet was a prolific sculptor associated with the Henriot firm. (Additional Broquet examples are in the *Colonial Exhibition Catalogue*, pp. 21-22.) *Courtesy of Musée de la Faïence, Quimper.*

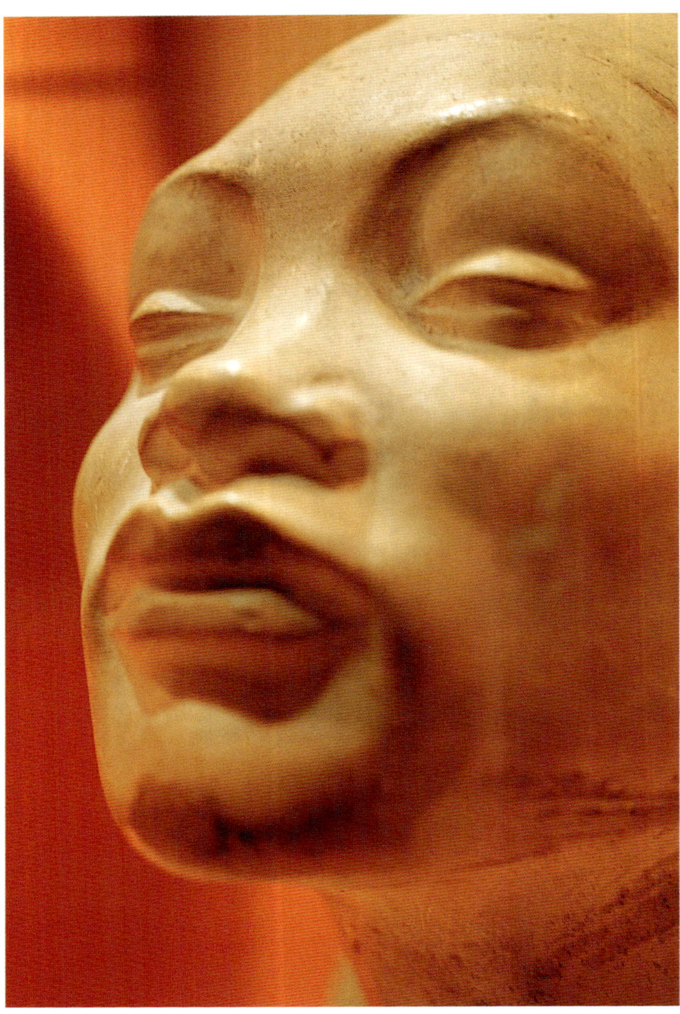

A proud visage greets visitors to the Colonial display. This is the plaster model made by the artist, Emile-Adolphe Monier of *Femme Mangbetou*. The statue was created for the 1931 Colonial Exhibition and was rendered in two sizes by the Henriot faïencerie. This original plaster model is 20" high. *Courtesy of Musée de la Faïence, Quimper.*

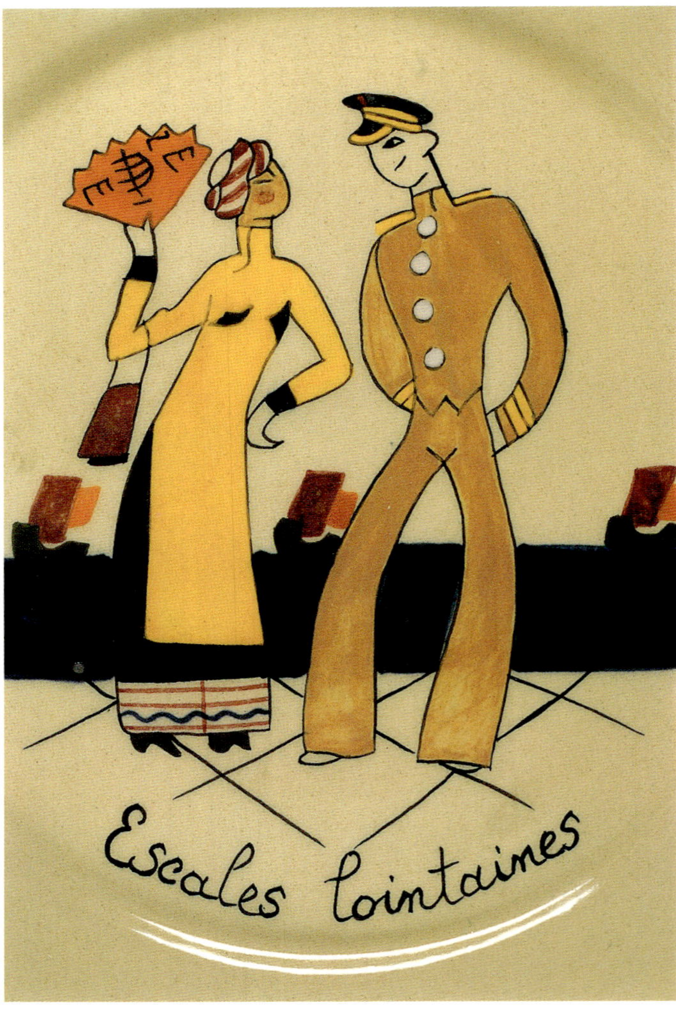

An interesting *aquarelle* for a plate in a series called *Escales Lointaines* (distant stopovers) by Georges Brisson is in the publication *Quimper à l'Exposition Coloniale, p.15.* We found a plate in this HB cake service set series and donated it to the *Musée* in gratitude for the warm reception we received on our quest for information about Quimper poterie in 2001. *Courtesy of Musée de la Faïence, Quimper.*

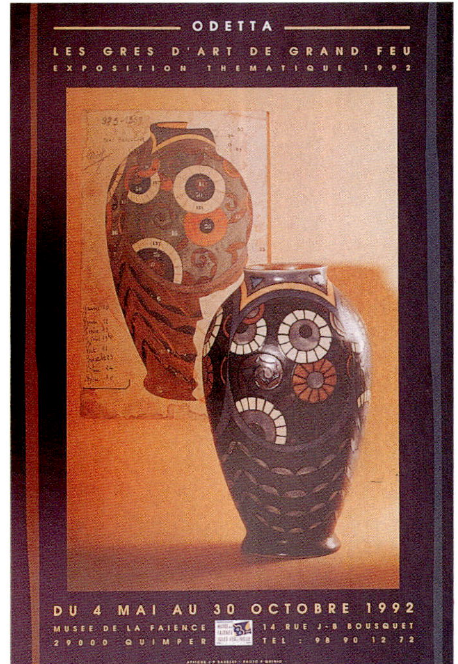

The seventh room contains a display of Odetta, and presents works by Louis Garin, George Brisson, and Alphonse Chanteau, among others. Odetta (pronounced o-day-TA) is a special art pottery developed at the HB faïencerie in the early 1920s. Most likely named for the Odet River in Quimper, Odetta is heavier than the usual Quimper faïence, and consists of a mixture of clay, sand, and ground pottery chips. It is fired at much higher temperatures, for longer periods of time than faïence, and is decorated with a different type of enamel. Collectors highly regard Odetta produced through the 1930s. *(Verlingue, Odetta, pp. 6-12.)*

The seventh display room at the museum features Odetta and an eclectic group of works by Quimper artists. Odetta (pronounced o-dey-TA) is an HB faïencerie art pottery initiated in the 1920s by Jules Verlingue. An exhibition devoted to Odetta was held in the museum from May through October 1992. *Courtesy of Musée de la Faïence, Quimper.*

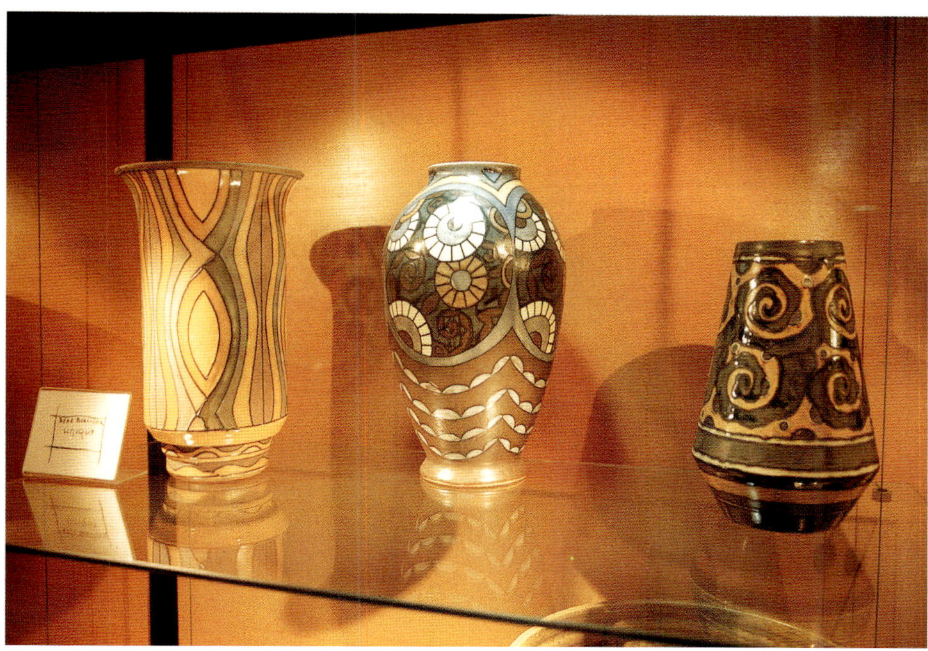

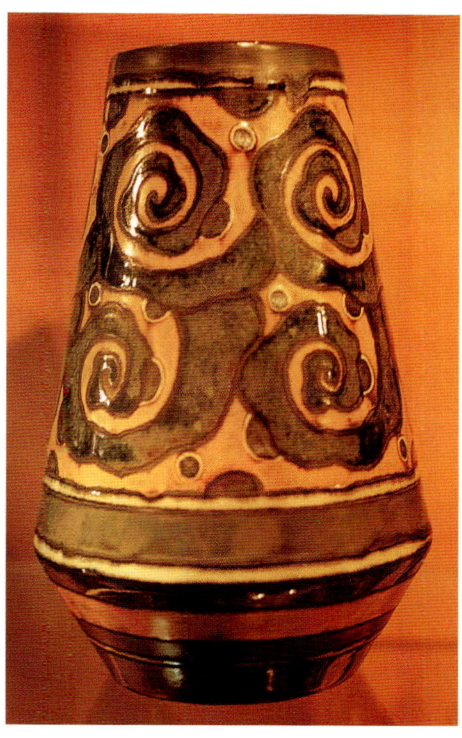

A trio of Odetta vases by HB artist René Beauclair sits proudly in the museum's showcase. The vase in the middle is the one featured on the poster celebrating the Odetta Exhibition in 1992. *Courtesy of Musée de la Faïence, Quimper.*

The vase to the right in the Beauclair trio is Odetta #282-1340, as listed in the *Odetta Catalogue* published in 1999 by the *Musée de la Faïence*. It stands nearly 9" high and is glorious in its own right.

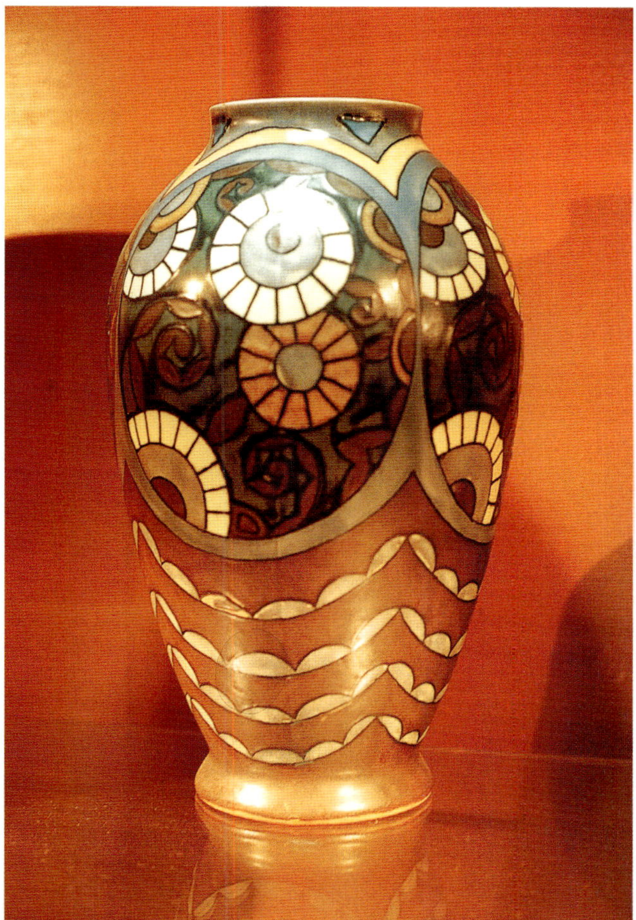

This beautiful Odetta example by Beauclair deserved a premier position in the exhibition. It is 11.75" tall and signed HB Quimper Odetta #973-1369. *Courtesy of Musée de la Faïence, Quimper.*

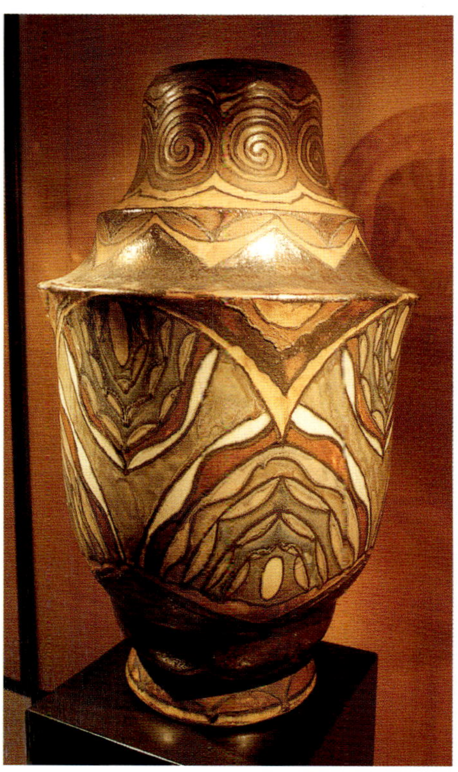

Right:
Another Beauclair Odetta beauty is 22" high and signed HB Quimper Odetta #673-1352. *Courtesy of Musée de la Faïence, Quimper.*

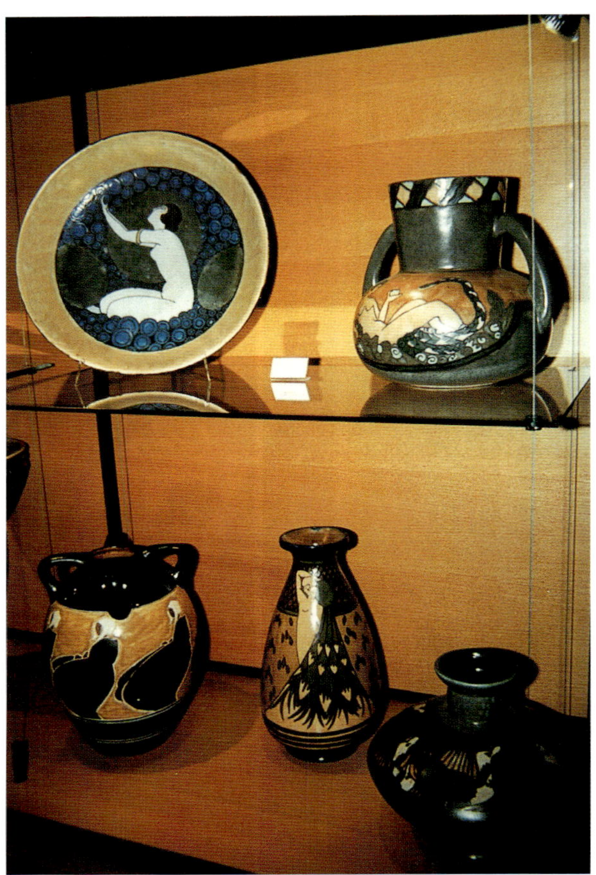

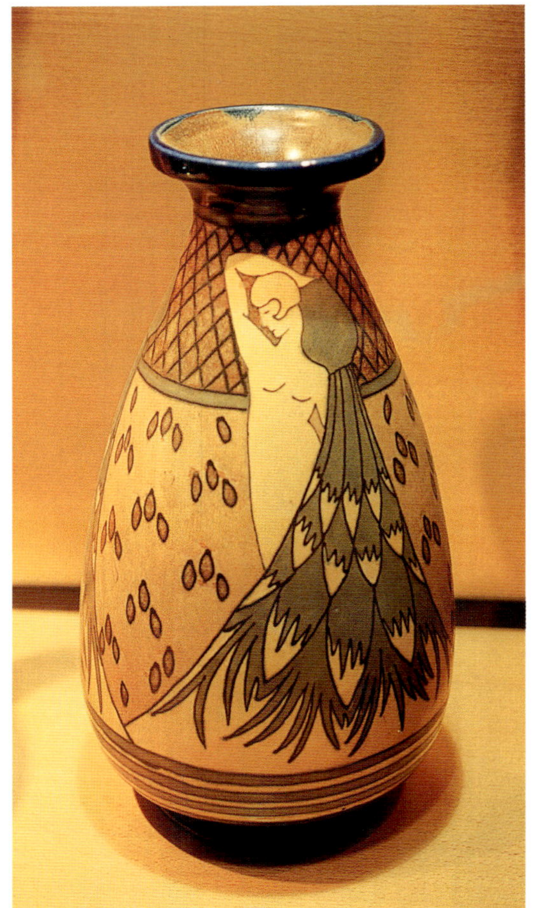

A potpourri of Odetta graces these showcase shelves in the museum. On the top shelf, left, is the Nicholas Pesce vase, *Eve with an Apple*. Louis Garin's vase, *Femmes au Vent*, or Women in the Wind, which stands 11" tall, is on the bottom shelf, left. *Courtesy of Musée de la Faïence, Quimper.*

The Odetta vase in the center, bottom shelf, is exquisite. It is similar in execution to Art Nouveau designs and entitled *Femme versant une cruche d'eau, or woman with a jug of water*. The vase is signed HB Quimper #340-1066 and is 13.5" tall. *Courtesy of Musée de la Faïence, Quimper.*

The room also contains renditions of animals in faïence by Marius Giot, Louise Bar, and Jacques Lehman, and the works of Emile-Just Bachelet, Berthe Savigny, Jim-Emile Sévellec, Paul Fouillen, and Giovanni Leonardi complete the eclectic presentation. Extraordinary works of art fill this room in another winning display.

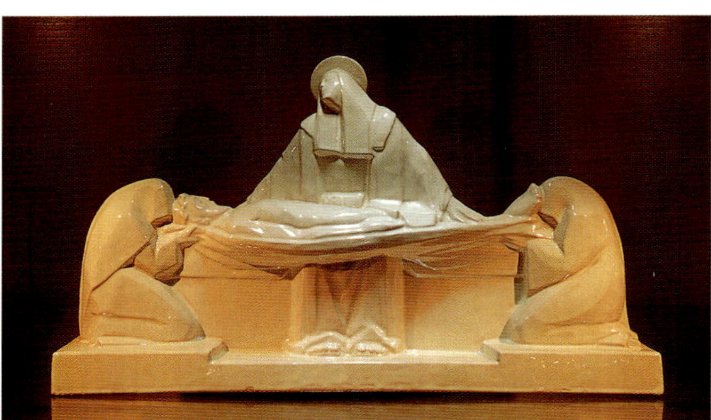

In addition to Odetta, other artists are featured in the seventh display room. One is Emile-Just Bachelet. Bachelet designed this touching religious scenario, entitled *Pieta*, in *email blanc* for the Henriot faïenceries. His initials EJB appear on the base. *Courtesy of Musée de la Faïence, Quimper.*

Jacques Lehman was the full name of the artist who signed his work NAM. His renditions of animals, particularly cats, are highly sought by collectors. This example in *grès* is 13.5" long. *Courtesy of Musée de la Faïence, Quimper.*

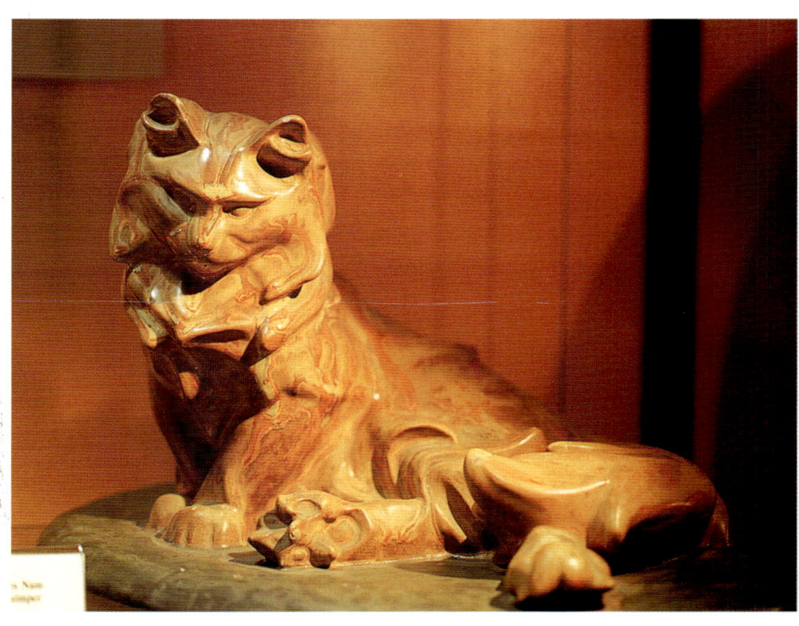

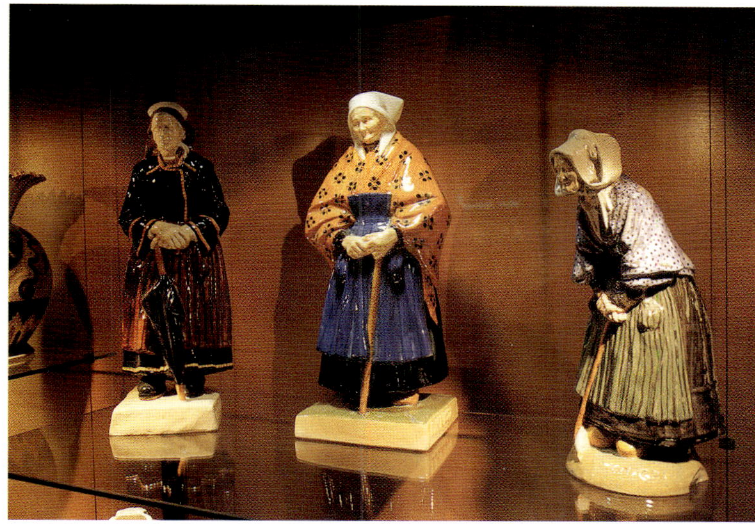

L.H. Nicot is known for his statues of Bretons, and this trio shows his talent. *Courtesy of Musée de la Faïence, Quimper.*

Les Deux Fumeuses by René Quillivic, c.1930, was made in a limited edition of 40 examples in *faïence polychrome*, but other examples exist in *grès*. The work stands 17.25" tall. Two women of *Pays Bigouden* are captured in a moment of relaxation as they smoke their pipes. *Courtesy of the Musée de la Faïence, Quimper.*

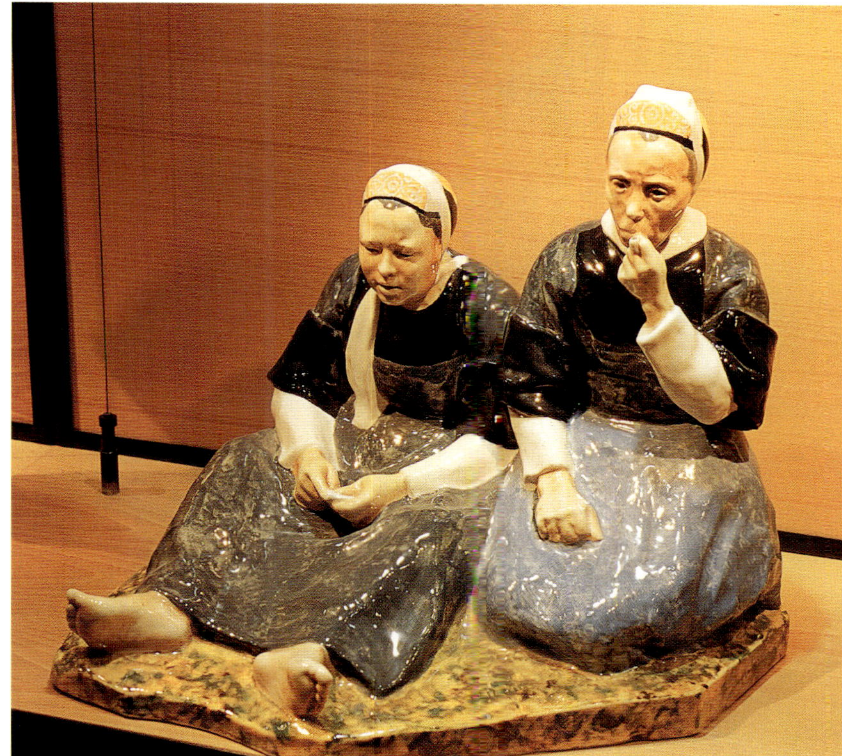

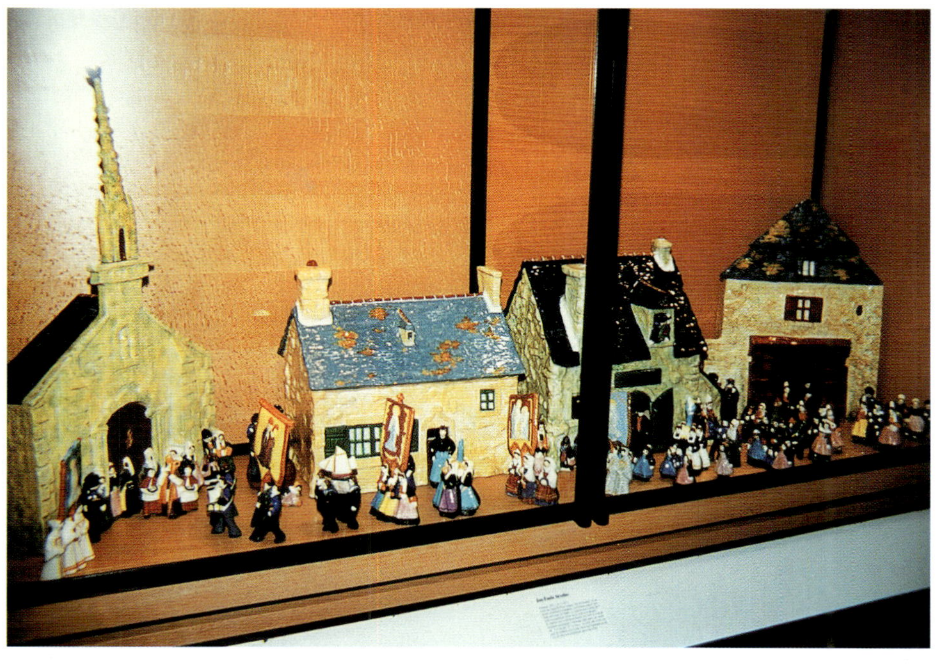

Jim-Emile Sévellec designed an entire village, including buildings and people. Characters from his village scene are more easily found than the church, hotel, café, or houses. Everyone seems to enjoy Sévellec's rendition of a Breton town celebrating a religious ceremony. *Courtesy of Musée de la Faïence, Quimper.*

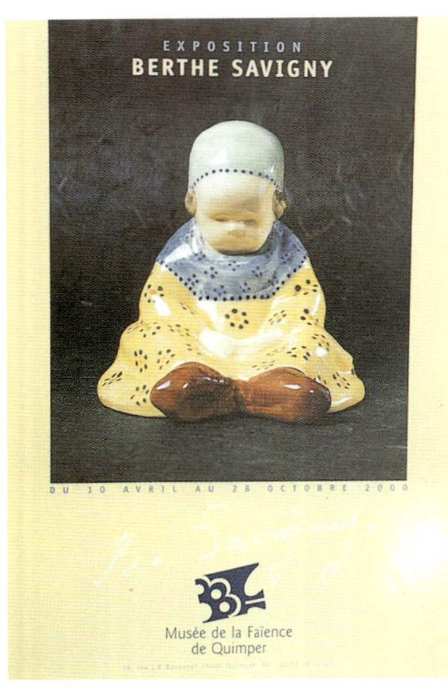

The eighth room is reserved for annual displays, with an eye to both the past and future of Quimper. The 2000 exhibit featured the works of HB artist Berthe Savigny. What a delight to see the array of *bébés*, as well as sketches and watercolors executed by Savigny. A poignant piece included in the display was her potter's wheel. The number of examples and the variety of her work impressed us and we look forward to seeing other featured artists in the future.

The eighth display room offers seasonal exhibits featuring artists or specific styles. In 2000, Berthe Savigny was the featured artist at the *Musée de la Faïence. Courtesy of Musée de la Faïence, Quimper.*

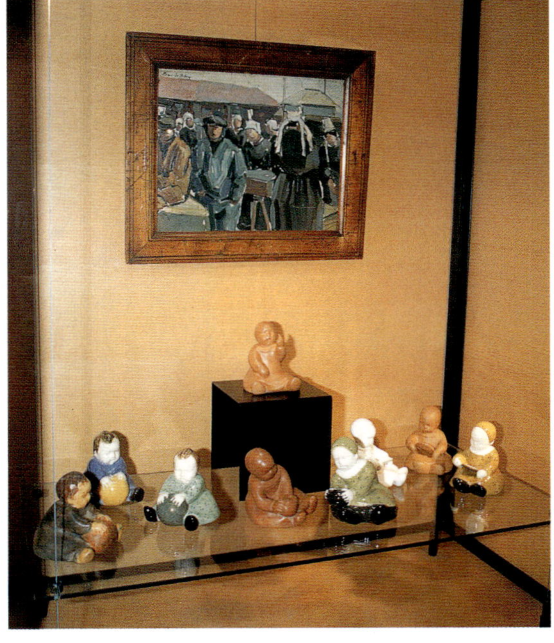

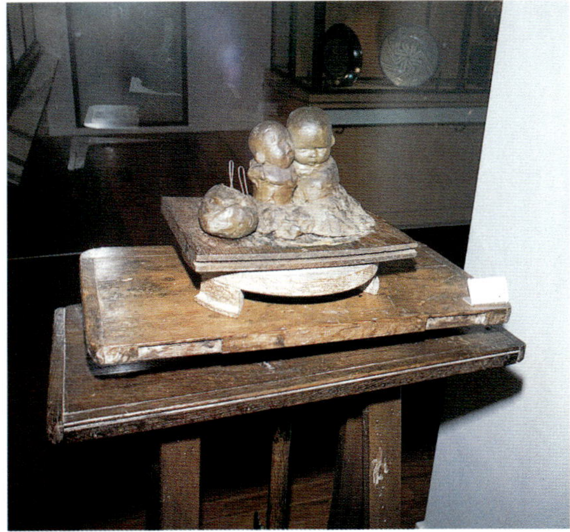

Savigny's potters wheel from her days at the HB faïencerie was a poignant display. *Courtesy of Musée de la Faïence, Quimper.*

Savigny's multiple talents as an artist in ceramic and paint were highlighted. As always, the Savigny *bébés* were present. *Courtesy of Musée de la Faïence, Quimper.*

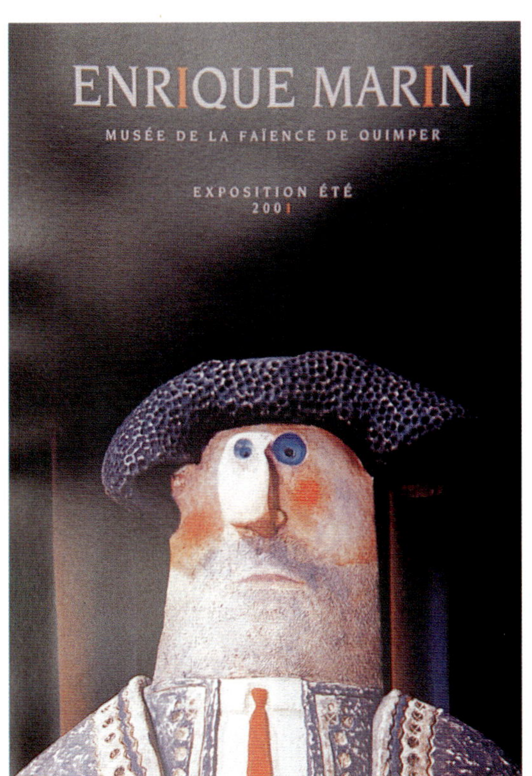

In 2001, the exhibit featured the works of Enrique Marin, a surrealist artist formerly with the *Keraluc* faïencerie. Marin, born in Spain, loves Brittany, and has a home in Pont Aven. He creates objects reflective of the beauty and cultural heritage of *Bretagne.*

Verlingue is an expert as decreed by the *Union Française des Experts*, specializing in Quimper faïence. He has co-authored several books on the subject, and has an amazing recall of the history of the *faïence de Quimper.* He strongly believes in supporting the development of artists who will continue the tradition of extraordinary works from the *faïenceries de Quimper.* Historically, a major event in France has brought about a major work in faïence, and Bernard Verlingue wants to preserve this practice for generations to come. It is a natural continuation of his family's faïence history. *(Conversations and correspondence with Bernard Verlingue, January-April 2001.)*

The featured artist for 2001 was Enrique Marin. An artist from Spain and formerly with the *Keraluc* faïenceries, Marin has a home in his adopted *Bretagne,* at Pont Aven. *Courtesy of Musée de la Faïence, Quimper.*

We spent many wonderful days exploring areas around the city of Quimper on our quest for the poterie that haunts us. North, south, east and west bring vistas and opportunities to gain a deeper understanding of the Breton spirit and culture. And more Quimper.

Locronan

One of those *it's a small world* coincidences that led us to explore Locronan. We had just returned from a three-week trip to Brittany several years ago, when an attractive couple arrived at the gallery as we reopened for business. They were looking for antique desks for their two sons, Alexandre and Raphael, and their French accent was delightful to hear. They were Jean-Baptiste and Caroline Monnier. We had just visited the La Baule area, which turned out to be Caroline's birthplace, and Jean-Baptiste told us of his great-grandfather, Charles Daniélou of Locronan, who had been the mayor of Locronan and a National House Representative for the region of *Finistère*. His wife, Madeleine Daniélou, was the first woman in France to achieve the degree of *aggrégation grammaire*, the most difficult literature degree. She founded a series of schools, *École Sainte-Marie*, well-respected private establishments for girls, which continue today.

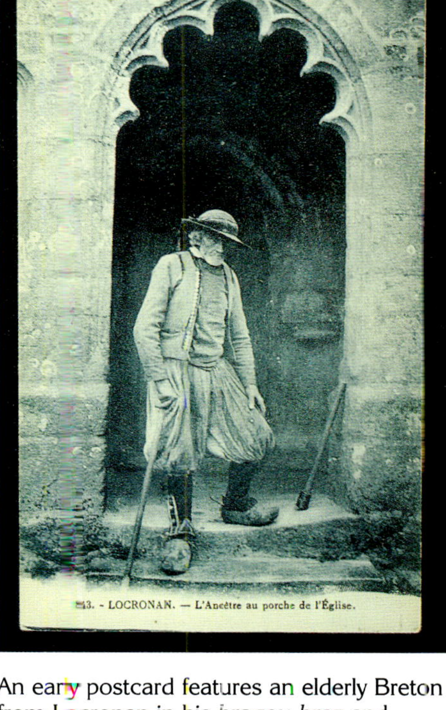

An early postcard features an elderly Breton from Locronan in his *bragou-braz* and *sabots* standing in the doorway of the church named after the town's founder, St. Ronan. *Authors' Collection.*

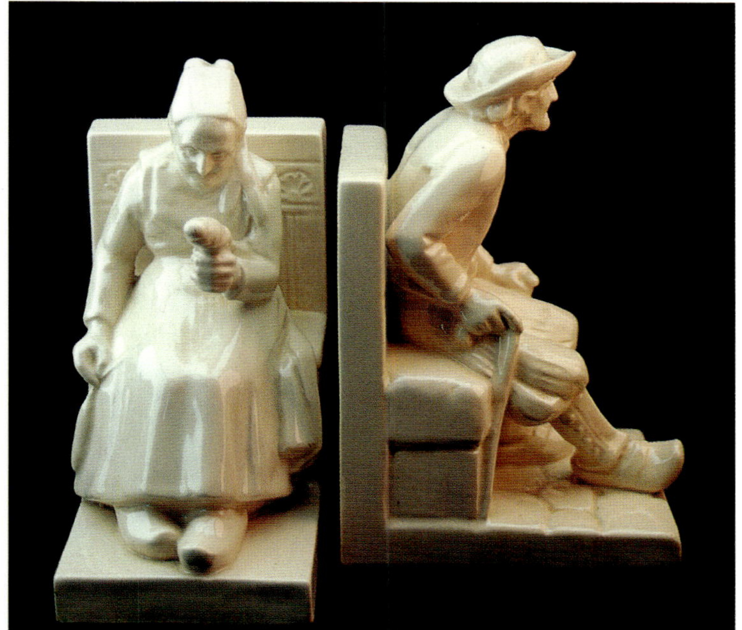

A pair of bookends by HB artist Bouvier, in *email blanc* (white glaze), stand 9" tall and feature elderly Bretons from Locronan. *Private Collection.*

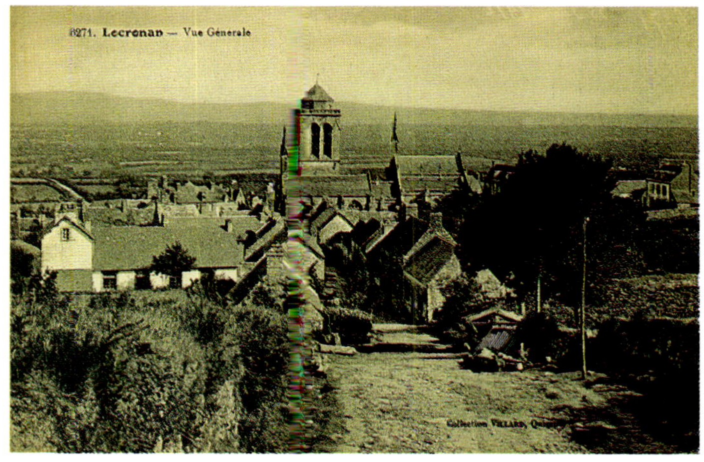

A general view of Locronan, c. 1900, is seen from part way up St. Ronan's Way, a section of the daily climb the saint made as an act of contrition. *Authors' Collection.*

147

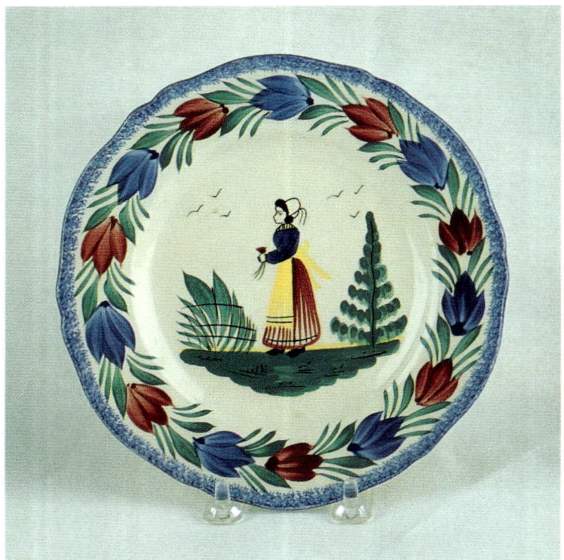

We found the grave of Charles Daniélou for Jean-Baptiste and Caroline Monnier. Daniélou was mayor of Locronan and a deputy representing *Finistère* in Paris.

Jean Baptiste's mother sent us a Quimper plate for our kindness in visiting Locronan. To us, the gift represents Breton hospitality. *Authors' Collection.*

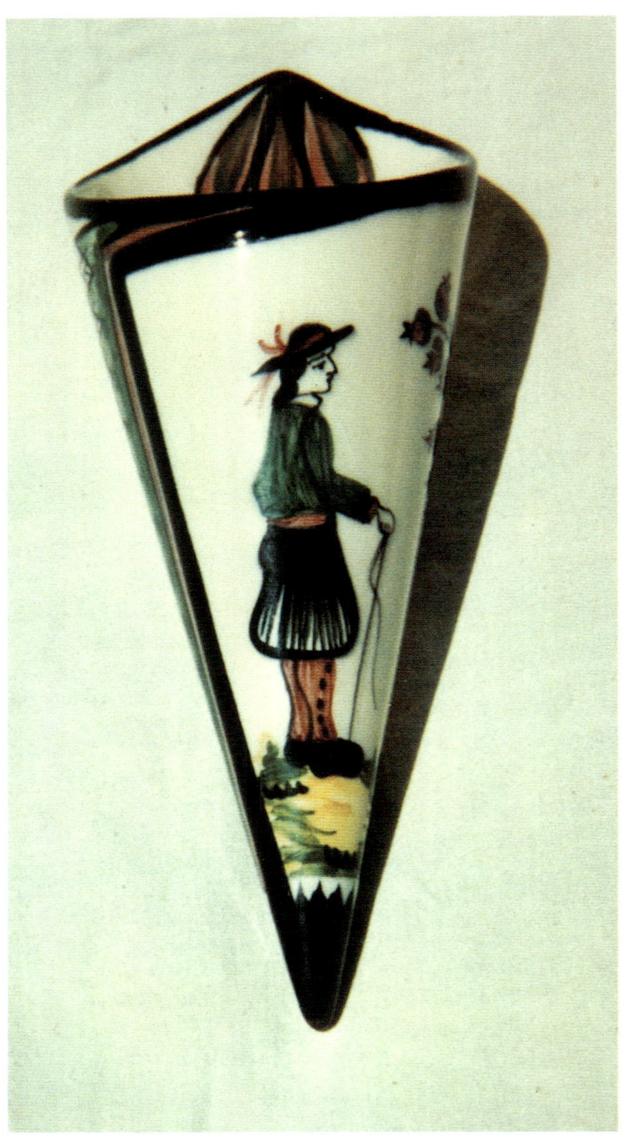

Another souvenir of Locronan is this 7.75" conical-shaped wallpocket from the Henriot faïencerie, mid-20th century vintage. *Private Collection.*

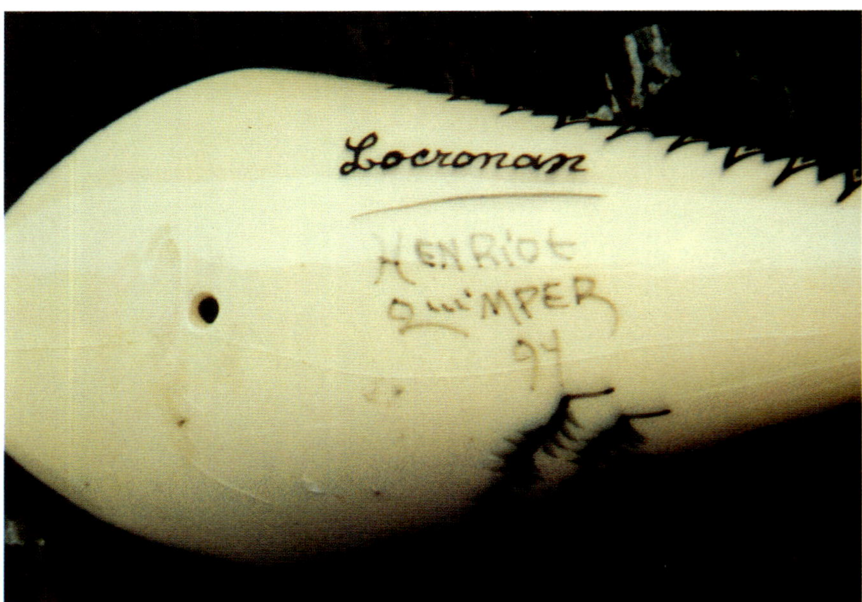

The names of towns on Quimper pieces usually mean they are souvenir items. This doesn't include Porquier-Beau pieces, whose town names represent the print or drawing from which the scenes were taken. *Private Collection.*

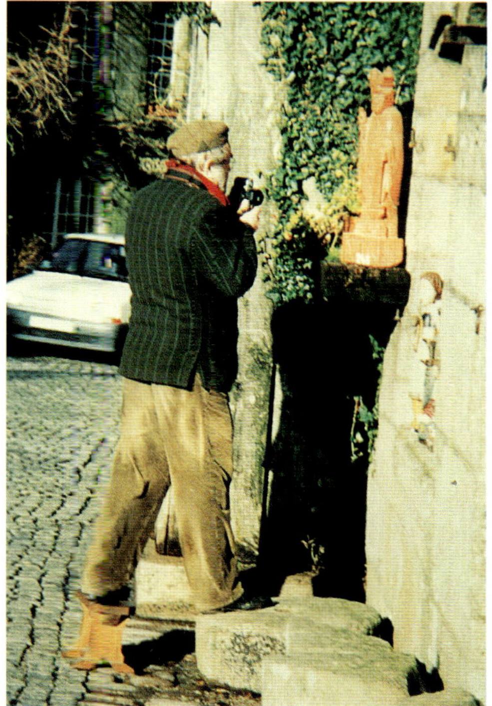

Locronan is now an artists' colony and a tourist haven. An artist photographs his work for publicity purposes on the sill of a house built in the 1500s.

While we were trying to cover as much of Brittany as we could on our quest for Quimper, this couple with a fabulous background in Brittany found our gallery in Chester County, Pennsylvania. Ah, the power of serendipity.

We made it a special point to visit Locronan on our next quest for Quimper in Brittany, as a result of learning about Charles Daniélou. Locronan is about 12 kilometers northwest of Quimper. We found his *manoir*, on a hill overlooking the town. It's now a museum called *Skritelleoueg*, devoted to conserving and restoring early posters of the politics and culture of Brittany. We also found his grave in the neatly kept cemetery, right behind the church named for St. Ronan, a 6th century Irish missionary. We took many photographs for Jean-Baptiste's family. In return his mother, who lived near Paris, generously sent us a book on *Bretagne* and a Quimper plate which we display in our home. Today, the Monnier family also includes a daughter, Victoire. Jean-Baptiste's sister, Emmanuelle Boysson, has written a book on the Daniélou family history.

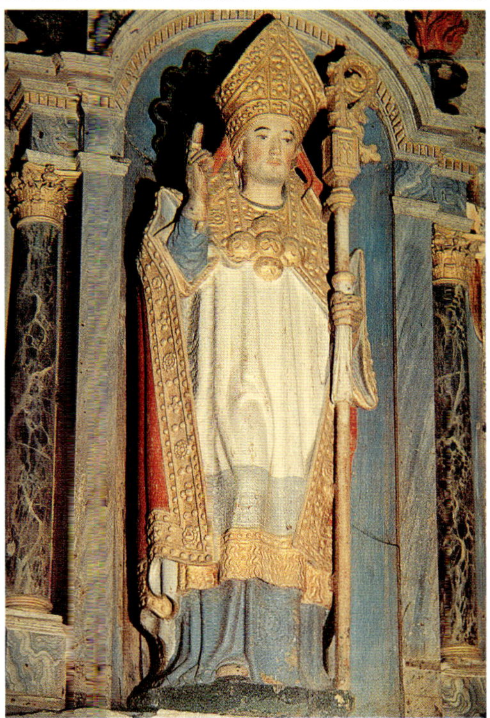

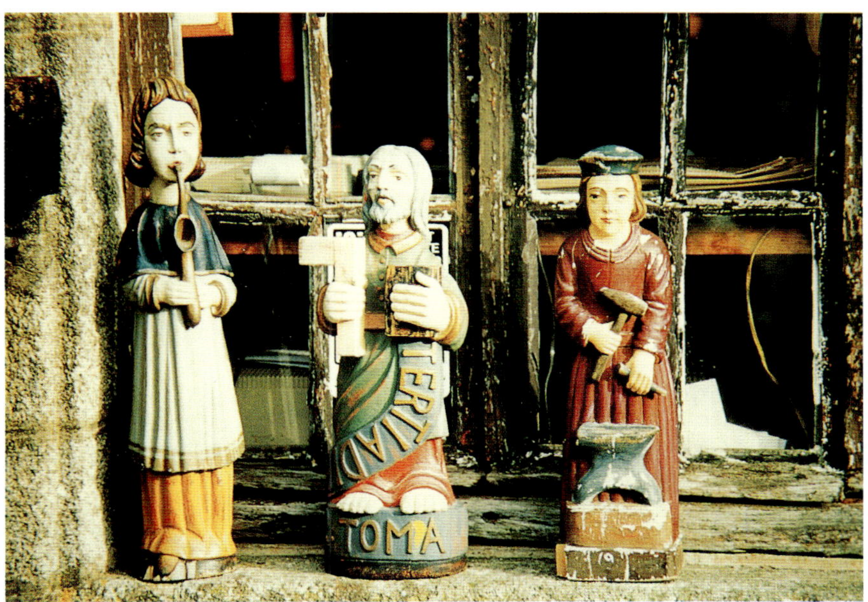

The works of art seen here on a Locronan windowsill seem very much at home in either the 16th century or today.

This statue of St. Ronan resides in the church bearing his name on the main square in Locronan. *Private Collection*

Locronan has been called a living museum. It has a large cobblestone square and is surrounded by impressive Renaissance-era granite houses. The homes originally were built for textile and sailcloth merchants, who made the town rich for a time. The houses are decorated with sculpted doorways, stone moldings, cornices and dormer windows. Now, tourists flock here. Visitors dine in the former homes of the town fathers, and shop for art where families once lived and attended St. Ronan, the 16th century church.

Many Breton town names grew out of religious references. For instance *Loc*, as in Locronan, means holy place or hermitage of Ronan. *Ple* or *plo* means parish, so the town name of Ploërmel translates as Armel's parish. *Lan*, or *lann*, means small monastery, therefore the town of Lannion is named for the monastery of St. Yon. *(LeCunff, p. 42)*

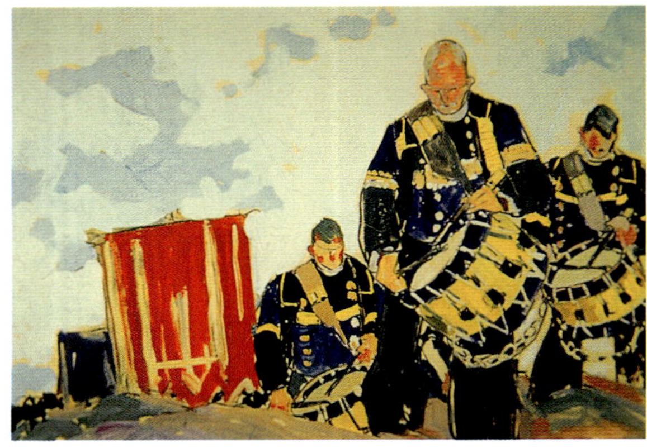

Quimper artist Mathurin Méheut created this scene of a *Grande Troménie*, or religious pilgrimage, held in Locronan every sixth year in July. The procession travels over seven miles around the mountain of Locronan, stopping at 12 stations where participating parishes display saints and reliquaries. *Private Collection.*

In addition to being a center for artisans and a well-preserved slice of history, Locronan is known for its religious pilgrimages, *Troménies*, which occur each July. These walks emulate St. Ronan, who as an act of contrition climbed the steep hill just outside of Locronan each day, in his bare feet. The way now is marked for tourists. If you follow the path out of town – 948 feet up – the chapel atop the hill offers a panoramic view.

Douarnenez

Douarnenz is a modern fishing port in Brittany, about 20 kilometers northwest of Quimper. But it is also an ancient town, with ancient legends. King Mark, of the legendary myth about Tristan and Isolde, is thought to be from Douarnenez. The real-life 16th century bandit La Fontenelle made his lair on the Bay of Douarnenez's Isle of Tristan. From there he mercilessly plundered villages in the *Pays Bigouden,* south of Quimper.

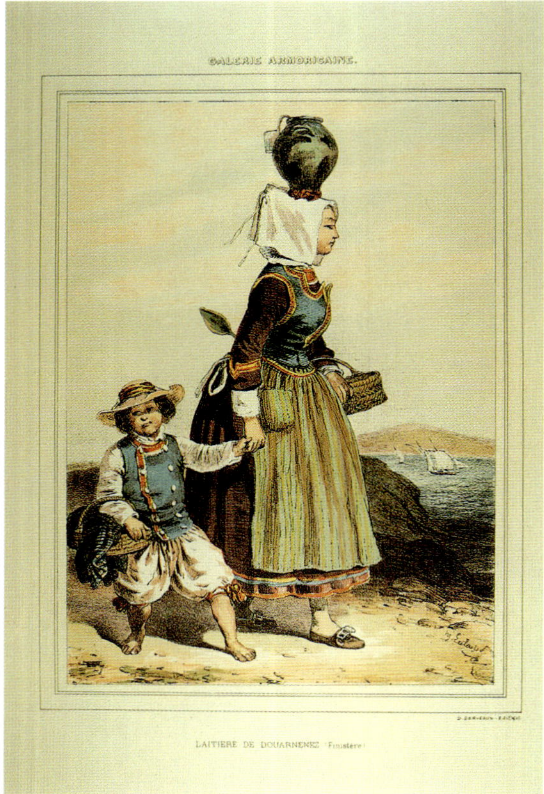

A *Galerie Armoricaine* print by F. H. Lalaisse shows a woman in an early *coiffe* from the Douarnenez area, carrying a milk container on her head. *Authors' Collection.*

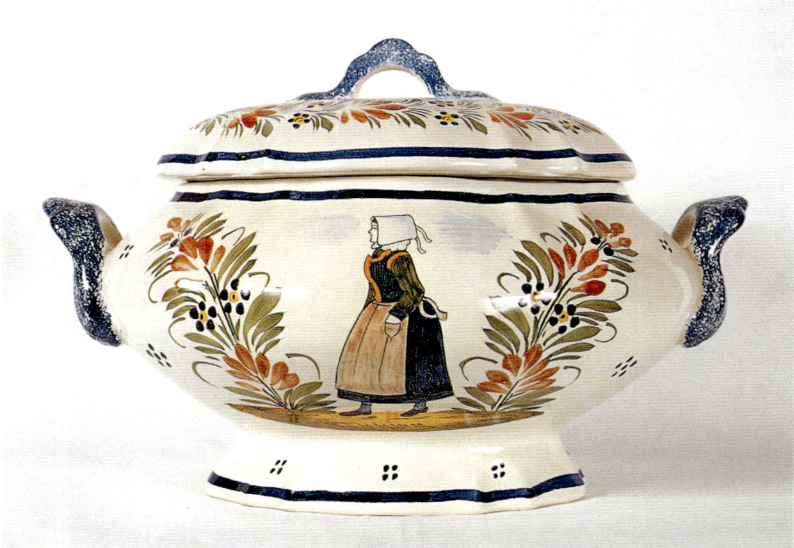

A Bretonne wears the same *coiffe* on this Henriot 10.25" long soup tureen, or *soupière,* from the second quarter of the 20th century. Also note the apron and vest worn in both scenes. *Courtesy of Barbara Cleaver Kroll.*

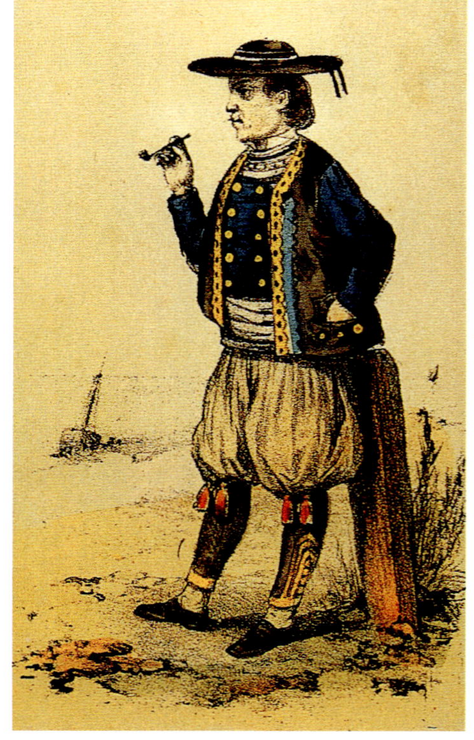

The gentleman on this postcard wears the costume of Douarnenez. Look closely at his attire and compare it with the couple on the following plate. *Authors' Collection.*

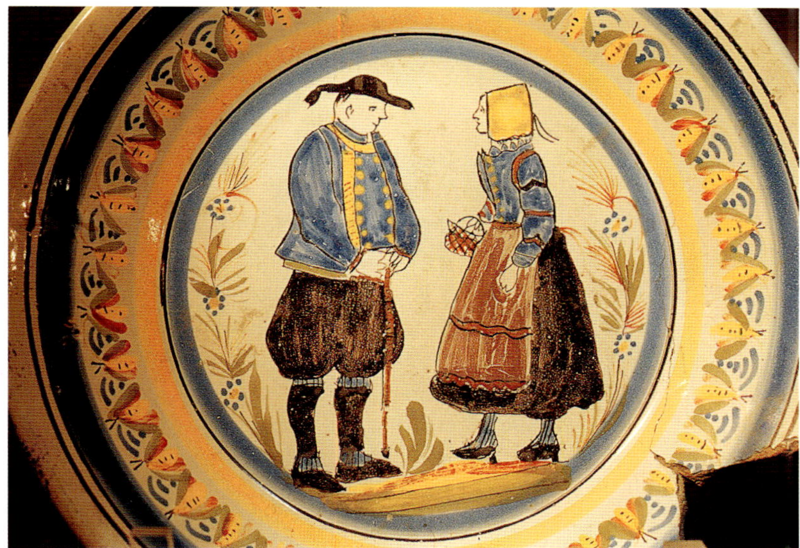

The same *coiffe* and a similar apron and vest of Douarnenez are worn by the Bretonne on this 19th century Quimper plate from the *Musée de la Faïence.* And the Breton with her obviously is in the attire of Douarnenez. *Courtesy of Musée de la Faïence, Quimper.*

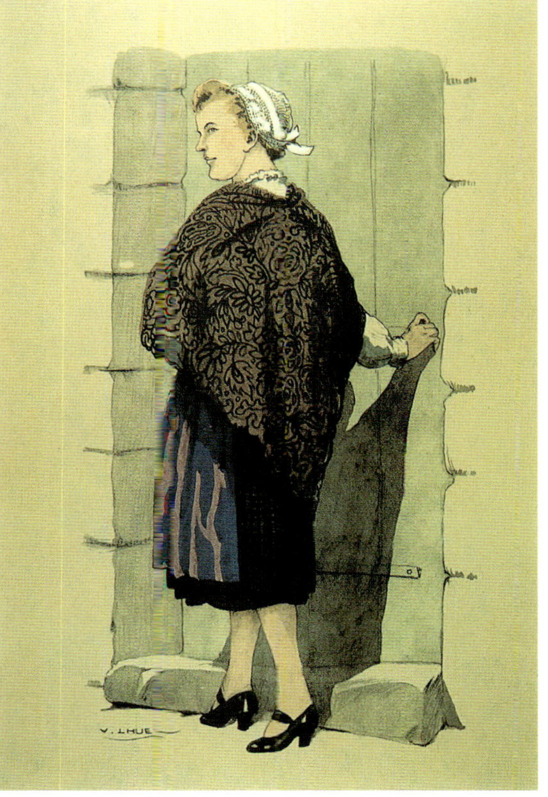

A print from the mid-20th century shows the change in the costume for the women of Douarnenez. *Private Collection.*

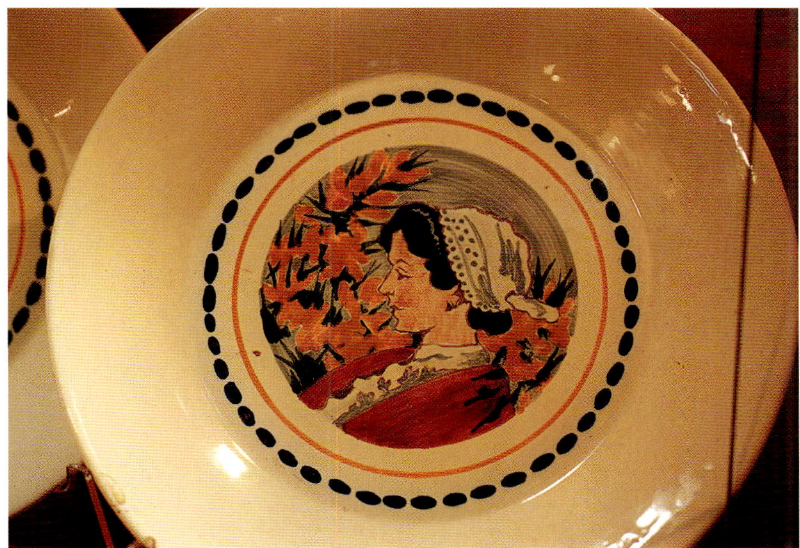

The updated *coiffe* of Douarnenez appears on this plate by the HB artist Alphonse Chanteau in his series on the *coiffes* of Brittany. *Courtesy of Musée de la Faïence, Quimper.*

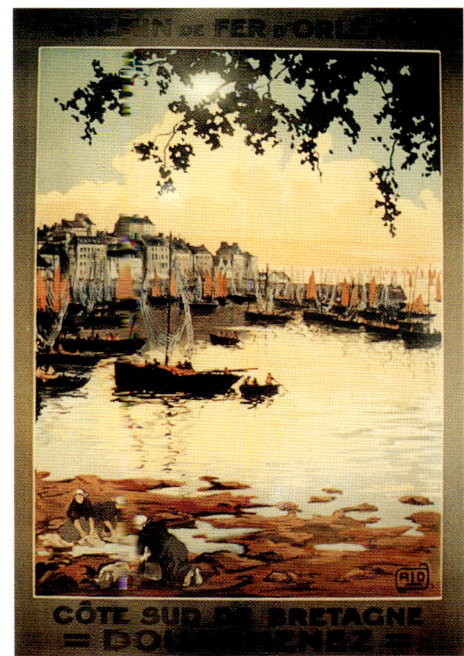

An early poster shows a peaceful Bay of Douarnenez. Women are washing clothes on the rocks of the calm waters in the quiet harbor. *Private Collection.*

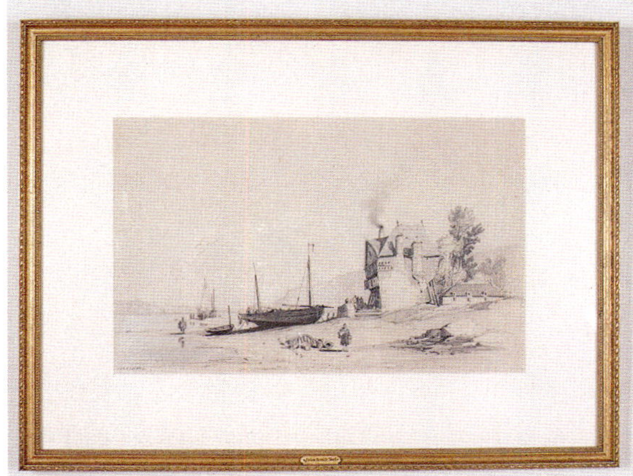

Jules Achille Noël (1810-1881) created a scene called *An Inlet Near Douarnenez.* Rendered in colored chalks on paper, the work is c. 1850. *Private Collection.*

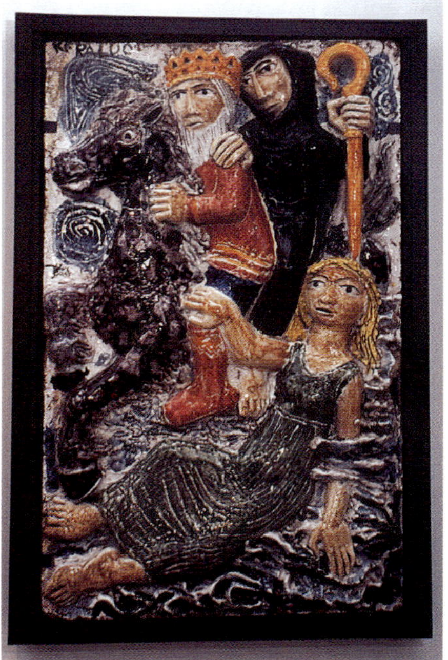

The city of Ys, or Is, Brittany's mythical Atlantis, is an island that supposedly sunk in the Douarnenez Bay. To some, the legend of Ys represents the triumph of Christianity over paganism. The legend concerns King Gradlon and his daughter Dahut, also spelled Dahud and Dahouet. She was the link to the pagan past, and King Gradlon, who had been converted by St. Guénolé, represented the new force, Christianity. Dahut's demise, when her father cast her aside as he escaped the waters engulfing Ys, was seen as her just punishment for unlocking the sluice gates that protected the city.

Dahut became a mermaid, according to legend, and still lures sailors to their death. Another part of the legend says that Ys will rise again when Mass is said in its submerged church, and Dahut will be redeemed from her *sirène* role. Some scholars have found that the sea levels did rise sharply on the coast of Brittany in this area around the 6th century. Legend and reality blend easily in Brittany.

Pierre Toulhaut rendered this image in bas-relief faïence for the *Keraluc* faïencerie. It shows Gradlon, Dahut, and St. Guénolé at the fall of Ys. *Courtesy of Musée Départemental Breton, Quimper.*

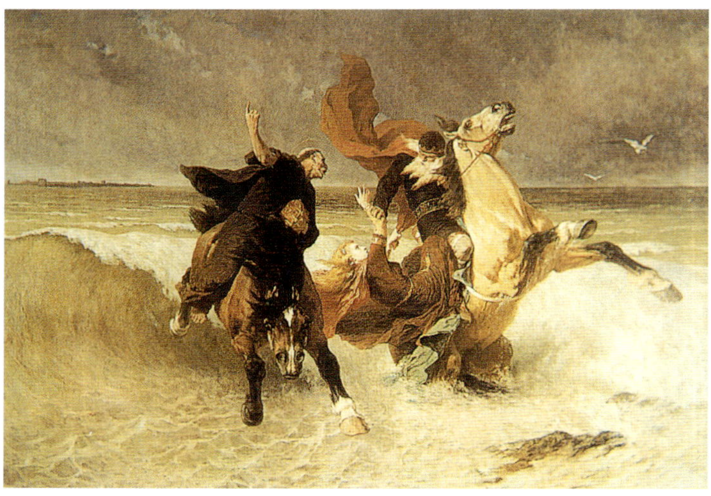

Legend tells that King Gradlon's bedeviled daughter Dahut was instrumental in unlocking the gates holding back the sea from the city of Ys. As Gradlon escaped with Dahut, St. Guénolé warned him to let go of her in order to save the city. Entitled *Fuite de Gradlon*, the painting is by Evariste Luminais, 1884. *Courtesy of the Musée des Beaux Arts, Quimper.*

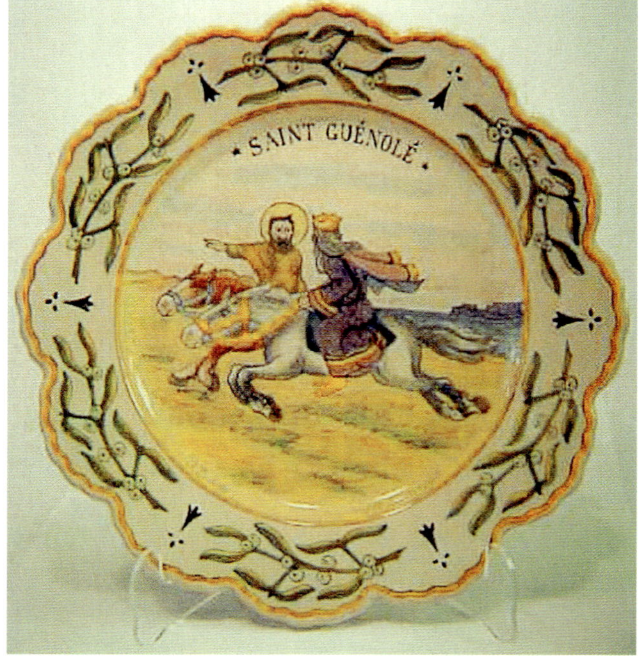

The legend of Gradlon, St. Guénolé, and the escape from Ys is told on an 10" Henriot plate in the saint series by Jacques Pohier. The good saint is warning Gradlon to save himself, as the waters engulf the city. Re-issues of the original series are in circulation, but are signed Henriot Quimper and do not carry Pohier's signature. *Courtesy of Lucy Williams.*

Today, Douarnenez is an important port, ranking just below Concarneau in size. There is a fish *criée* every morning and lobsters boats, deep-sea vessels, and sardine fleets all make Douarnenez their home. And Douarnenez is home to the Thierry & Lannon auction that offers remarkable examples of Quimper poterie several times a year. Bernard Verlingue serves as their expert-in-residence for appraising Quimper.

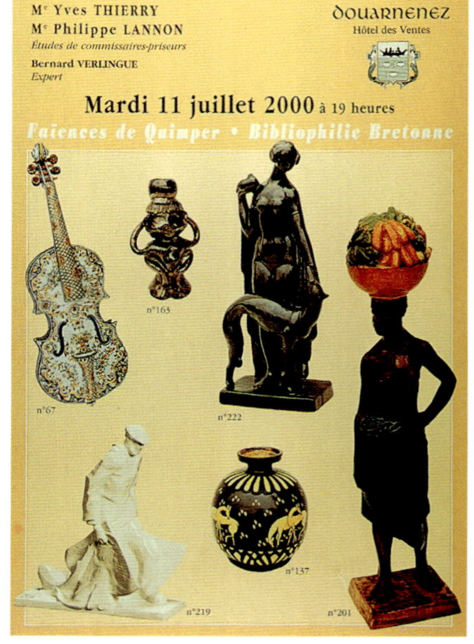

Another reason to visit Douarnenez is the quality Quimper auctions held by Thierry & Lannon several times a year. *Courtesy of Thierry & Lannon, Douarnenez and Brest.*

Pointe du Raz

This impressive point about 25 kilometers west of Douarnenez overlooks the Atlantic Ocean. *Pointe du Raz* is called one of the most dramatic headlands in Brittany and one of the western most points in *Finistère* and in France. (*Pointe de Corsen*, northwest of Brest is the most western point.) It was a clear, cold, windy day when we stood on the point and watched the afternoon sun descending in the west, and we wondered what lay across the horizon.

A statue, *Notre Dame des Naufrages* (Our Lady of the Shipwrecked), stands on the point reminding us of the treacherous waters not only here, but along most of the Breton coast. It also reminds us of the many mariners who never returned to their homes in Brittany. The wind and waves have taken a toll on the rocks. Numerous sightseers also have taken their toll on the land around the point, so reclamation projects to protect the area have been instituted.

Off-shore stands a lighthouse and beyond that is the *Île de Sein*, encircled by a reef. These waters are considered the most dangerous in the world. Legends say Druids rowed their dead to their burial grounds on the island from the *Baie de Trespássés*, or Dead Man's Bay, located to the right of *Pointe du Raz*. It was so named for the number of mariners who washed ashore.

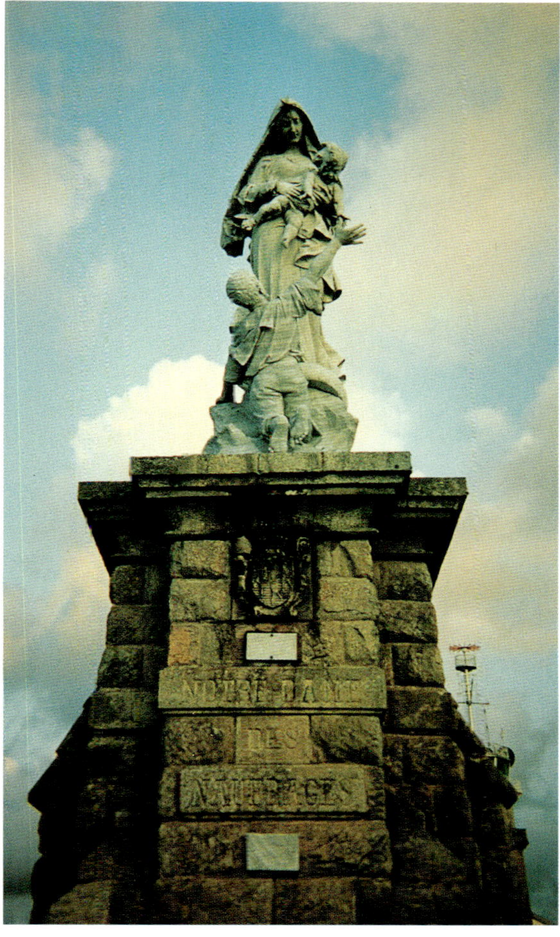

Notre-Dame-des-Naufragés, Our Lady of the Shipwrecked, stands on *Pointe du Raz* watching for the sailors lost at sea.

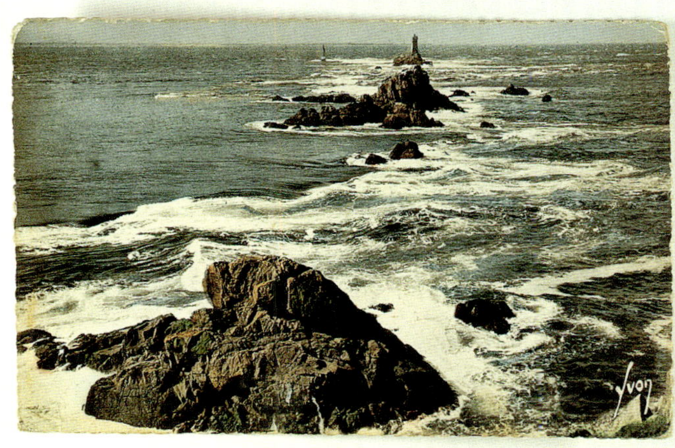

A vintage postcard shows the view from *Pointe du Raz*. It's an impressive rock formation jutting into the Atlantic Ocean, where treacherous waters have tested the mettle of Breton *marins* for centuries. *Authors' Collection.*

Pointe de Penhir

Another headland on the western coast of Brittany, this time on the Crozon peninsula, is *Pointe de Penhir*. Henriot artist Jim-Emile Sévellec was born on the peninsula in the port town of Camaret. HB artist Chanteau was from Crozon; Yvonne Jean-Haffen captured the peninsula town of Morgat on canvas.

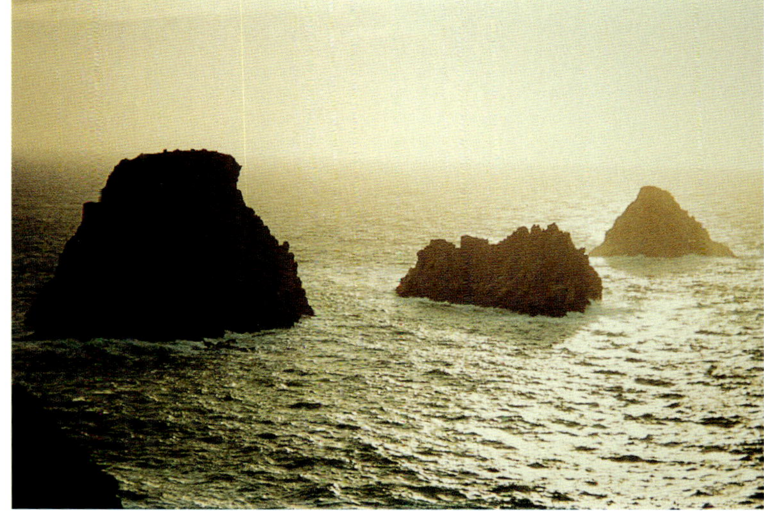

Directly off the *Pointe de Penhir* are the famous *Tas de Pois*. Meaning *heap of peas*, it's the name given to a row of isolated rocks offshore.

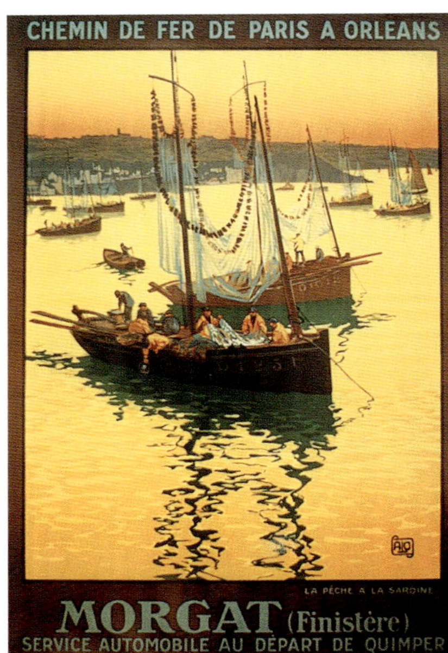

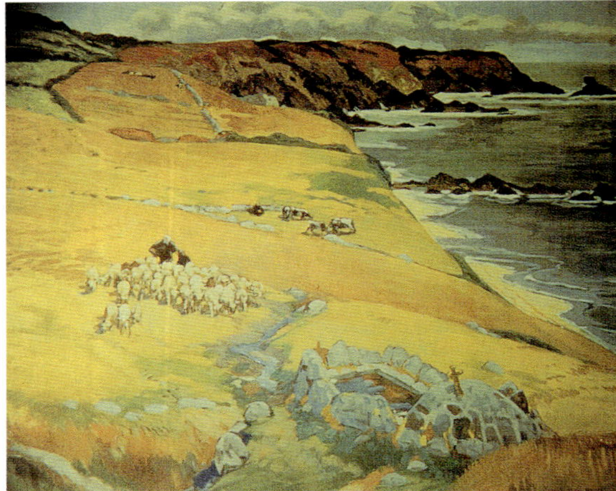

The *Tas de Pois* is shown in this painting of the same name by Henriot Quimper artist Yvonne Jean-Haffen. *Courtesy of Musée des Jacobins, Morlaix.*

The port town of Morgat, as seen in this vintage poster, is on the Crozen peninsula. *Private Collection.*

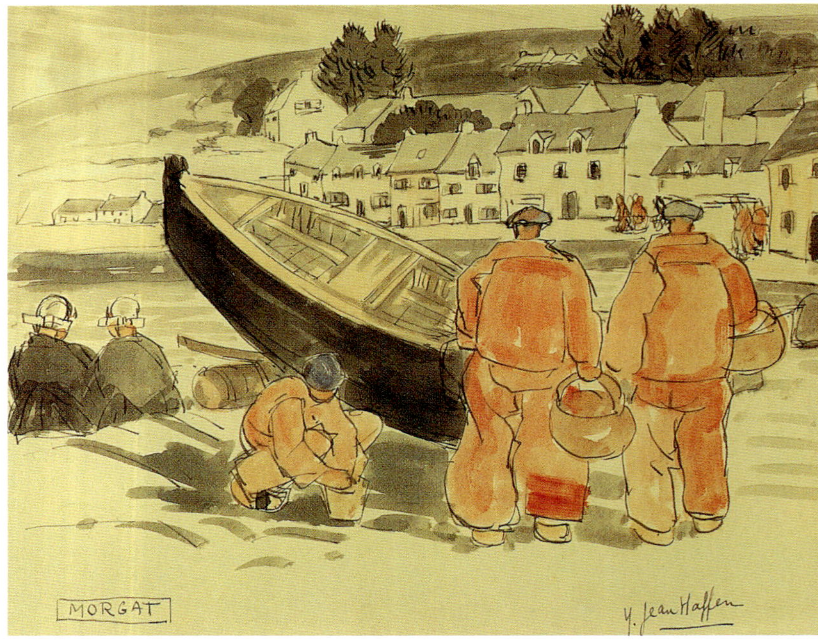

Morgat is depicted by Quimper artist Jean-Haffen, whose talent seems boundless. *Courtesy of Musée des Jacobins, Morlaix.*

Quimper artist Alphonse Chanteau designed a plate service featuring *coiffes* of Brittany for the HB faïencerie in the 1920s. This plate features the *coiffe* of Crozon, a town on the Crozon peninsula, about 9 kilometers from *Pointe de Penhir*. The *coiffe* is modeled by the artist's mother. *Courtesy of Musée de la Faïence, Quimper.*

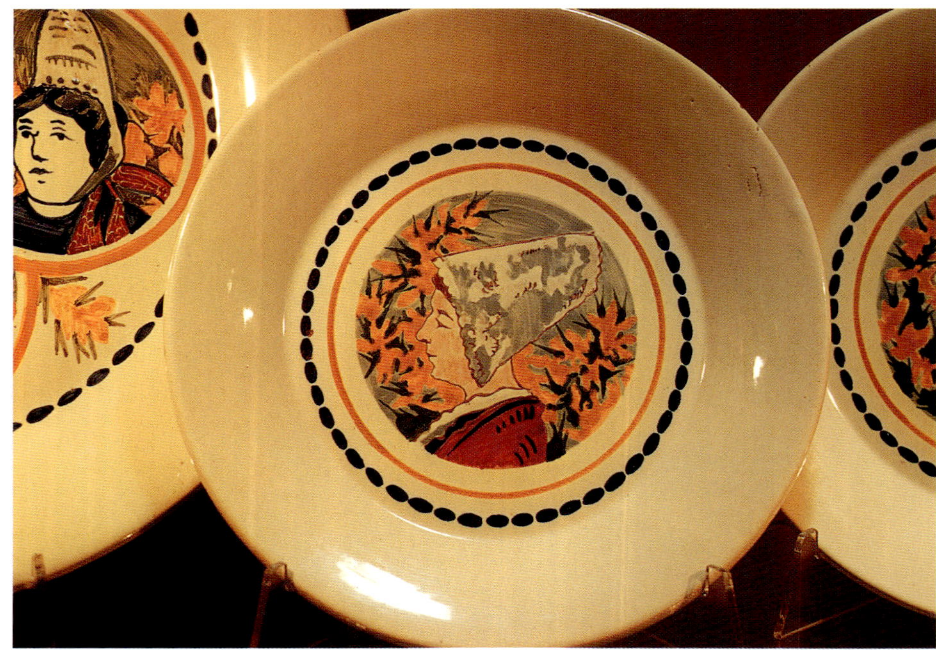

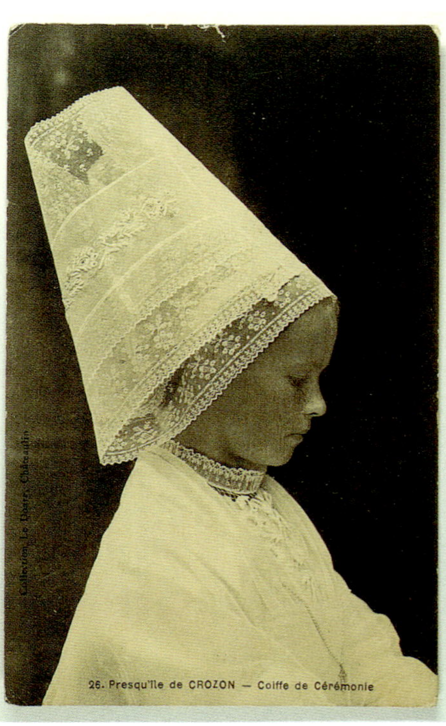

An early postcard shows the *coiffe* of Crozon worn for special holidays and festivals. The style hasn't changed much since the Middle Ages. *Authors' Collection.*

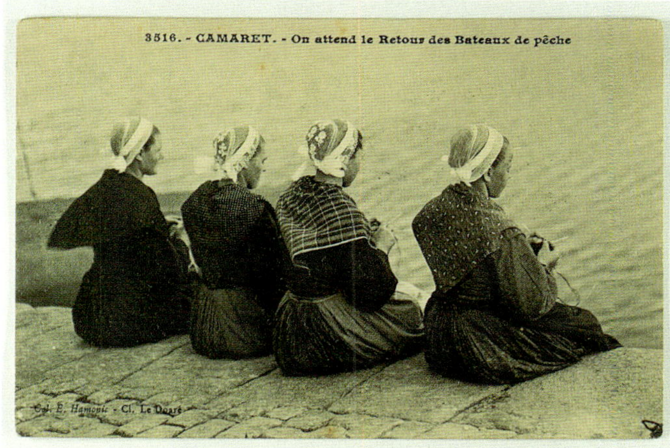

In the port town of Camaret, where Henriot artist Jim-Emile Sevellec was born, four young women await the return of the fishing boats. On this early 20th century postcard, note the *coiffes* of the region worn for everyday purposes. *Authors' Collection.*

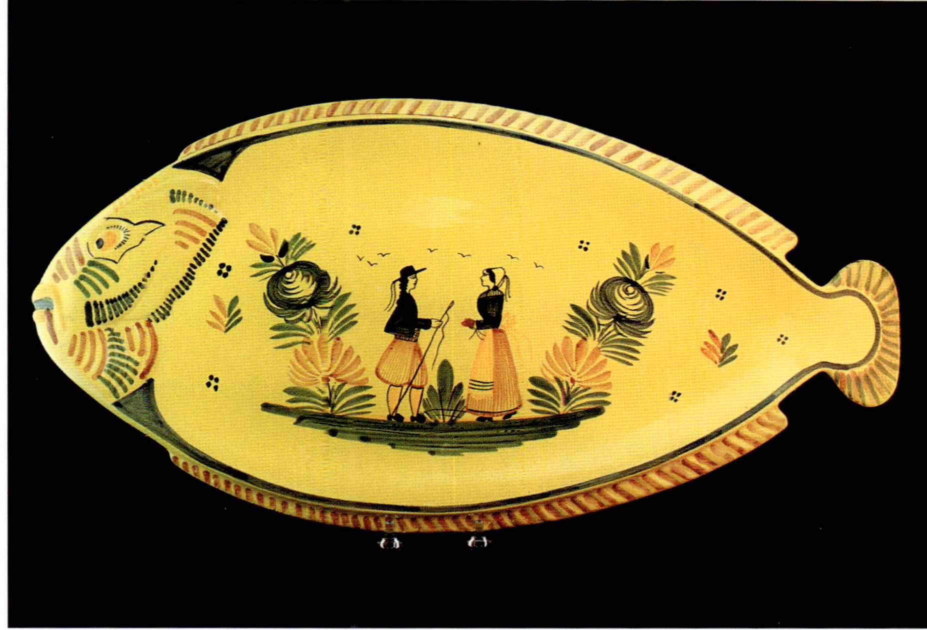

Renditions of fish forms are a favorite Quimper poterie theme. This large platter is used to serve fish. It measures 22" long, is from the HB faïencerie, third quarter of the 20th century, and is in the sunny *soleil* pattern. *Courtesy of Janice M. Longer.*

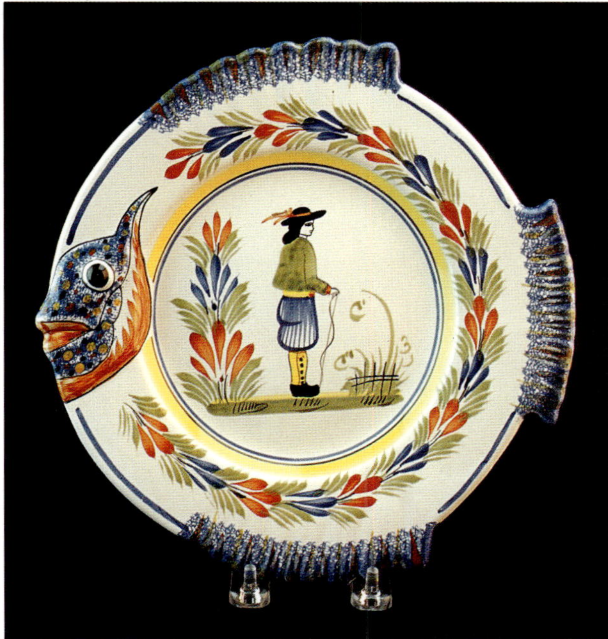

Another attractive fish-shaped dish in bright, cheery colors is post-1984, as the combined HB/Henriot signature indicates. *Courtesy of Janice M. Longer.*

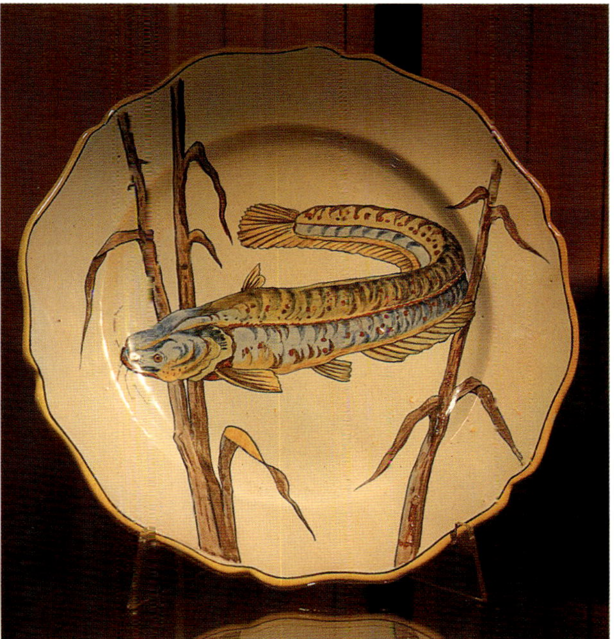

Alfred Beau's botanical series designs for Porquier-Beau also featured fish motifs. This fellow swims across a 9.75" surface, is c. 1900, and signed PB. *Courtesy of Musée de la Faïence, Quimper.*

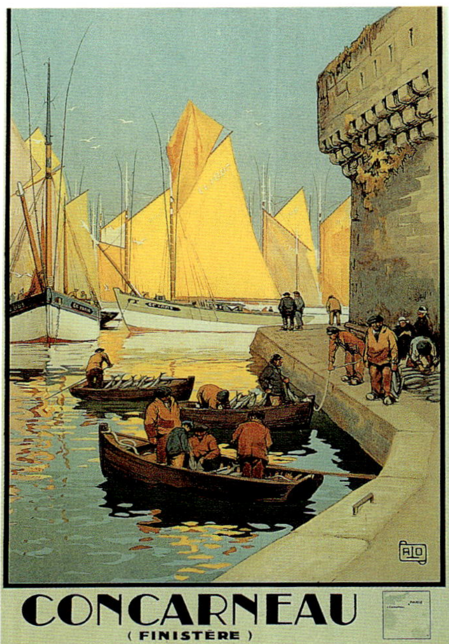

The old town section of Concarneau is on an island surrounded by ramparts begun in the 14th century.

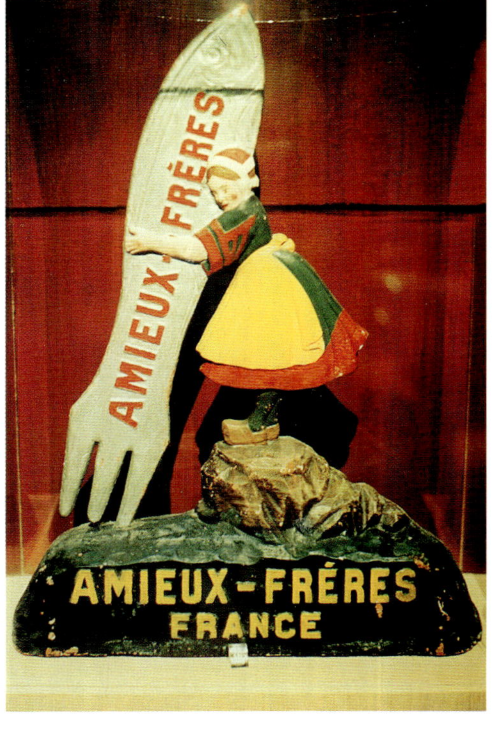

An early poster presents the harbor and serene setting of Concarneau. *Private Collection.*

Concarneau

Traveling southeast from Quimper about 20 kilometers, visiting the Breton port town of Concarneau is like taking a step back in time. We discovered this on a rainy Saturday afternoon. One hundred years ago, the walled town boasted a flourishing sardine trade; Théophile Deyrolle founded his school of painting there. Today, there is a daily fish *criée* and a resort area, but the town remains much the same as it was. Concarneau is on an island, accessible by small bridges and a gate, and is surrounded by ramparts, which were begun in the 14th century and completed in the 17th century. Narrow alleyways serve as streets on this island, which is less than a mile across.

Musée de la Pêche was enchanting and brought to mind how sardines fueled the town's economy. Times were hard when the sardine supply dwindled in the 1880s. The situation improved until the early 1900s, when the sardine catch fell off again. The *Fêtes des Filets Bleus,* or Festival of the Blue Nets, was established in 1905 as a way to raise funds to help beleaguered fishermen. (At that time the nets used to catch the sardines were blue, from being preserved in a solution of copper salts.) The festival is still held today, with music, folk dancing, and parades, all in regional costumes. (For a full description of the sardine industry in Concarneau see *Mali, Old Quimper Review, October 1997.*)

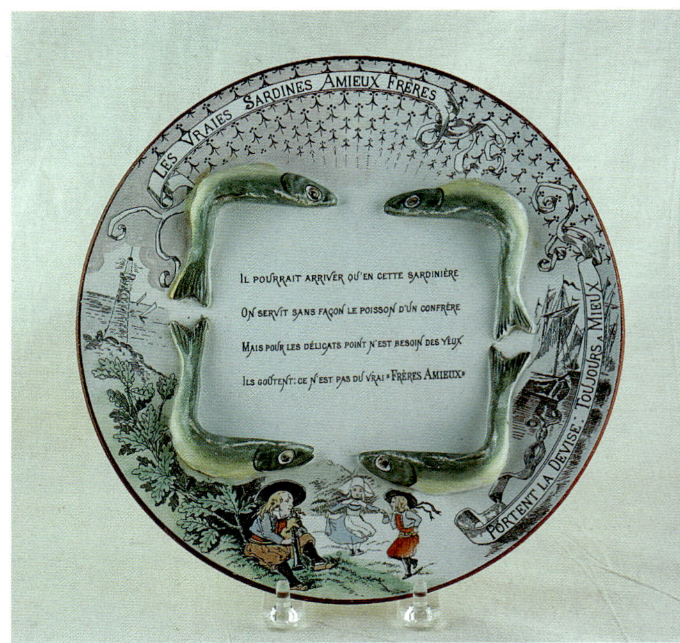

A 9.75" faïence plate to serve sardines advertises *Amieux Frères*. Design elements include the ermine-tail design of Brittany, a ship, lighthouse, and children looking more Victorian than Breton. The plate was manufactured in eastern France, perhaps Sarreguemines. *Private Collection.*

This advertising sign represents *Amieux Frères*, a well-known sardine distributor in France. The industry thrived as long as the sardines were plentiful. *Private Collection.*

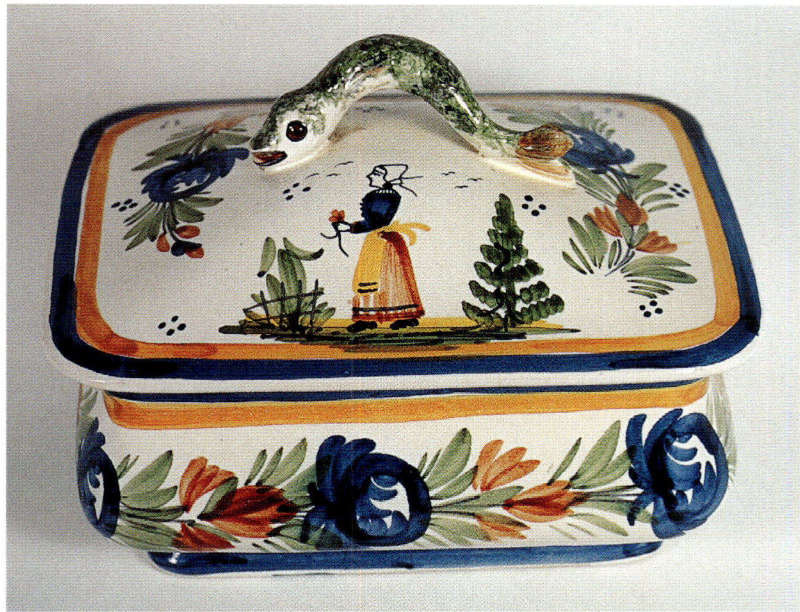

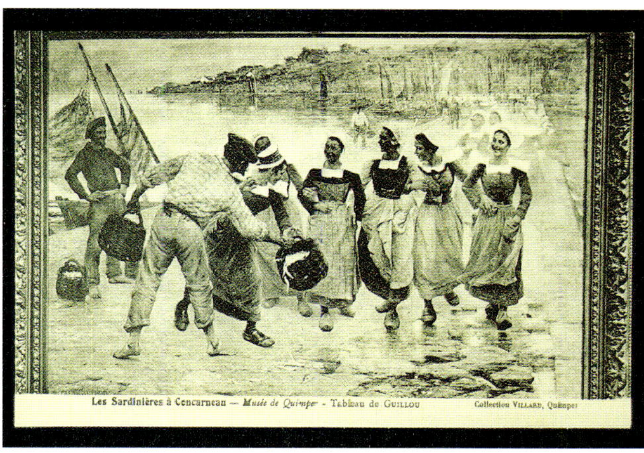

An early postcard depicts life at the Concarneau harbor. The scene is a painting entitled *Les Sardinières à Concarneau*, by Guillou. *Authors' Collection.*

An HB Quimper box to hold sardines is topped with a wiggly sardine. The *petit Bretonne* on the front carries a posy with *arbustes*, or shrubs, on either side of her. Bold *à la touche* flowers surround the base of the box, which measures 6.5" long and is from the second quarter of the 20th century. *Private Collection.*

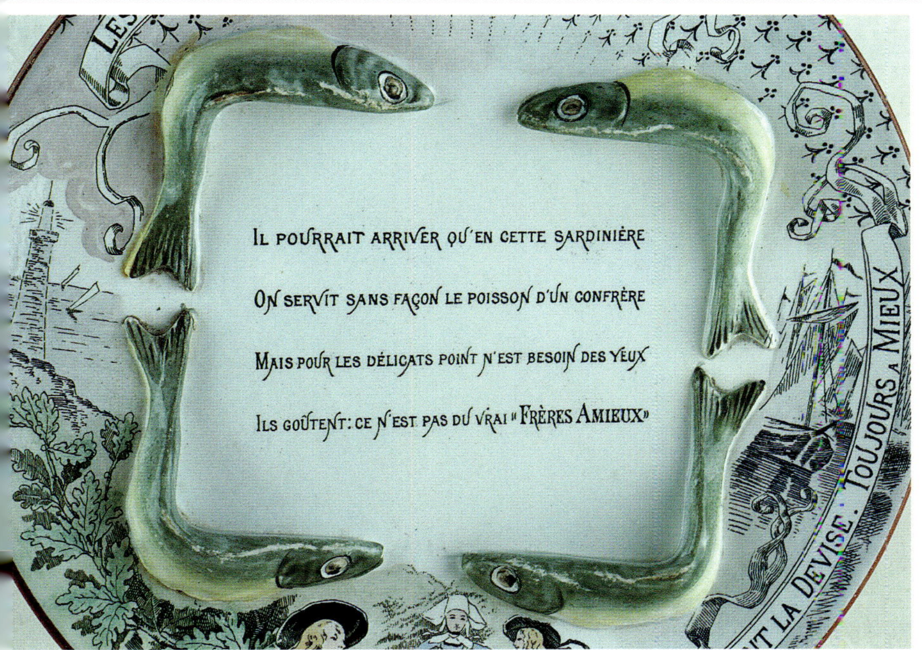

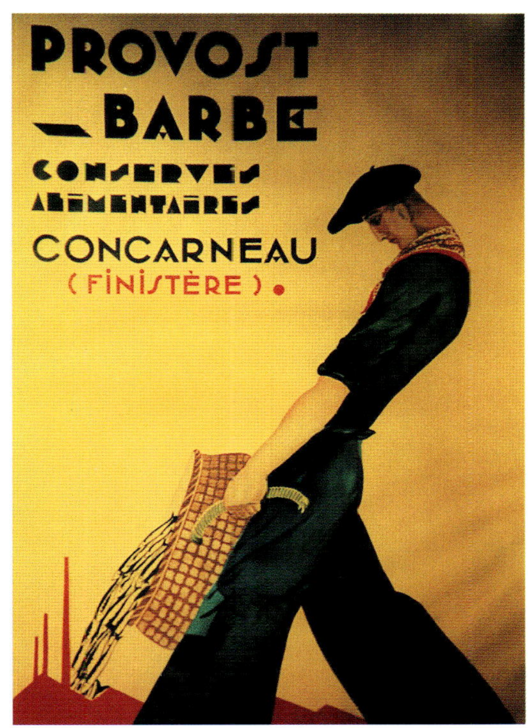

A colorful vintage poster advertises Concarneau and its sardine trade. *Private Collection.*

A close-up look at the center of the plate shows writing not common to Quimper work. It also reveals wonderfully rendered sardines. The HB faïencerie made a similar plate, but the difference in the decoration may be observed in *Mali, p. 44. Private Collection.*

While these young women from Concarneau, on an early 20th century postcard, wait for the fishing boats to return, they spend their time making lace and crocheting. These women were called *commises,* and bid on the catch as the boats returned. *(Mali, Old Quimper Review, October 1997.) Authors' Collection.*

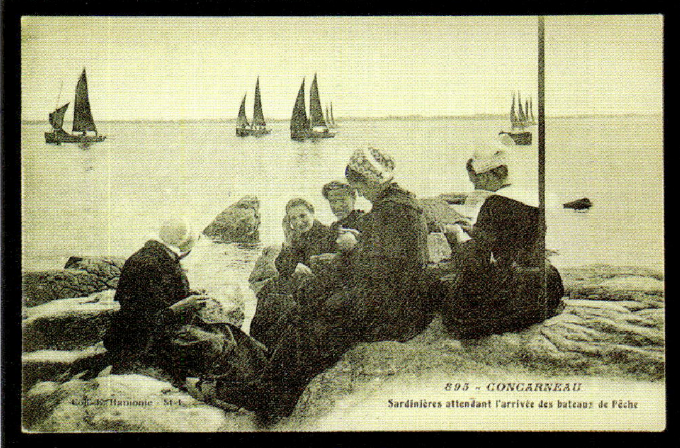

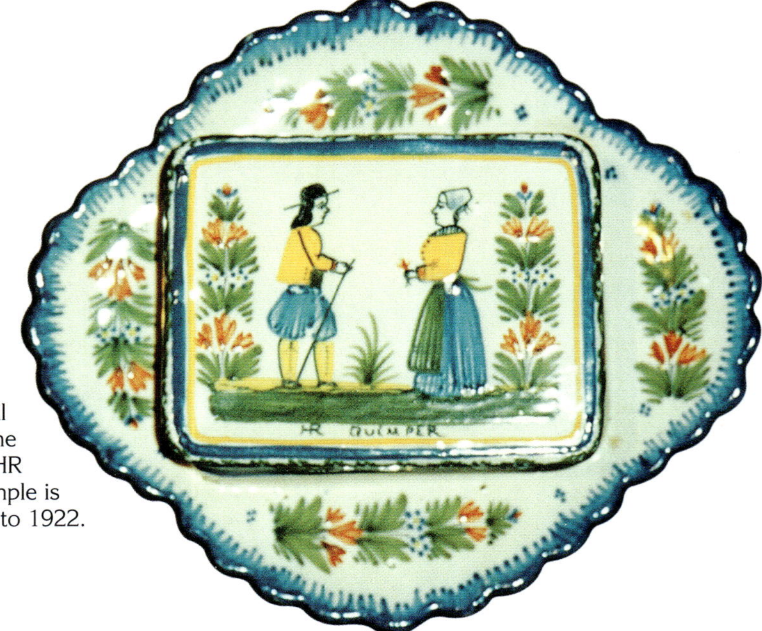

Another box for sardines, but this time it has an attached underplate. Note the delicate scalloped edge painted with blue and the attention to detail in the floral décor, including the blue four-dot design. Signed HR Quimper, this 9.25" long example is from the Henriot factory prior to 1922. *Private Collection.*

Pont-Aven

Our first look at Pont-Aven was startlingly beautiful! Coming down into town on a side road, we could see the water ahead. The Aven rushed by, as if flooding, and the sky was clearing above the hill on the other side of the narrow river. Rain clouds moved northeast, clearing the way for a brilliant blue sky where white cloud castles climbed each other's backs...an exquisitely memorable experience.

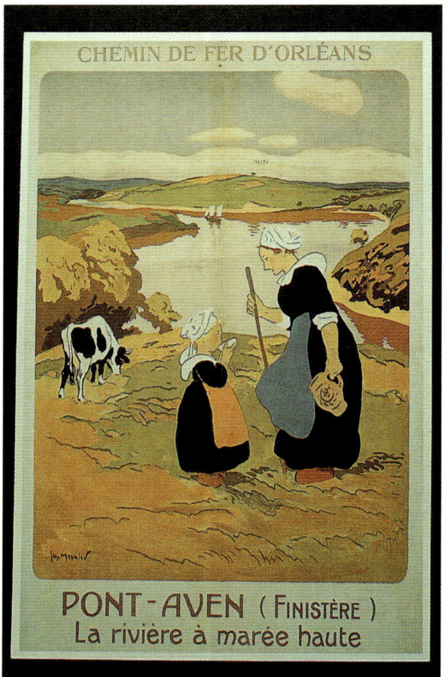

Pont-Aven is a delight to the eyes and soul, as seen on this idyllic poster from the early 20th century. *Private Collection.*

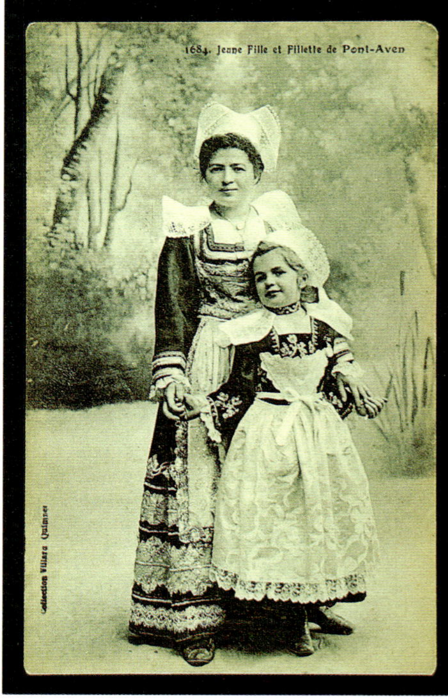

A young girl and a child from Pont-Aven pose for the photographer in a turn-of-the-20th century postcard. *Authors' Collection.*

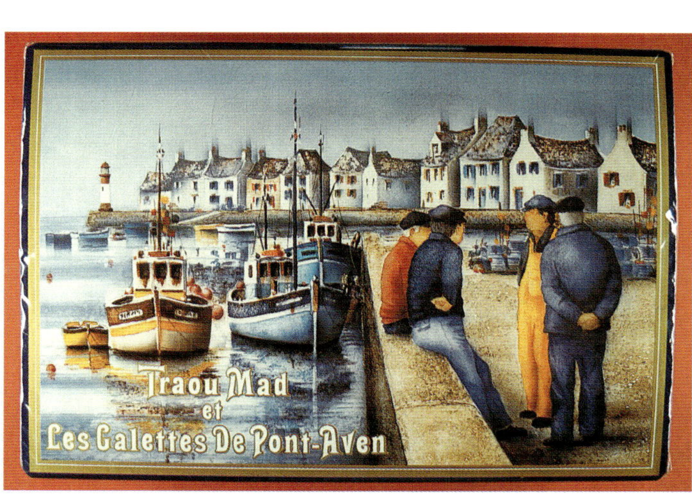

Les Galettes de Pont-Aven from *Traou Mad* are exceptionally tasty, as well as beautifully packaged.

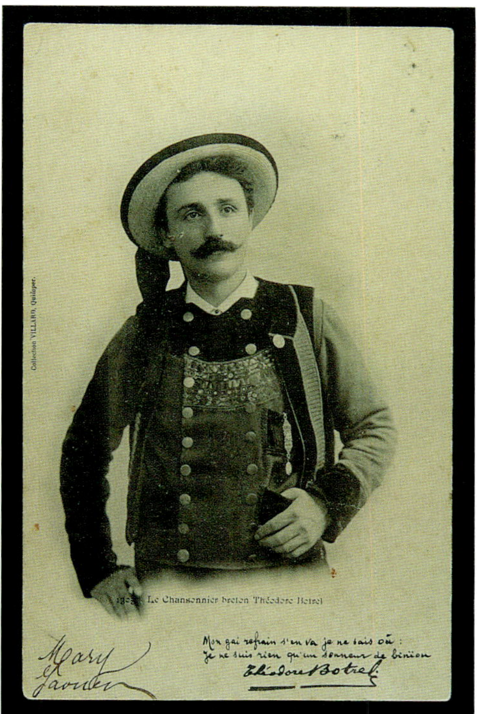

Théodore Botrel made Pont-Aven his home and settled into a life promoting all things Breton, as seen on a vintage postcard. *Authors' Collection.*

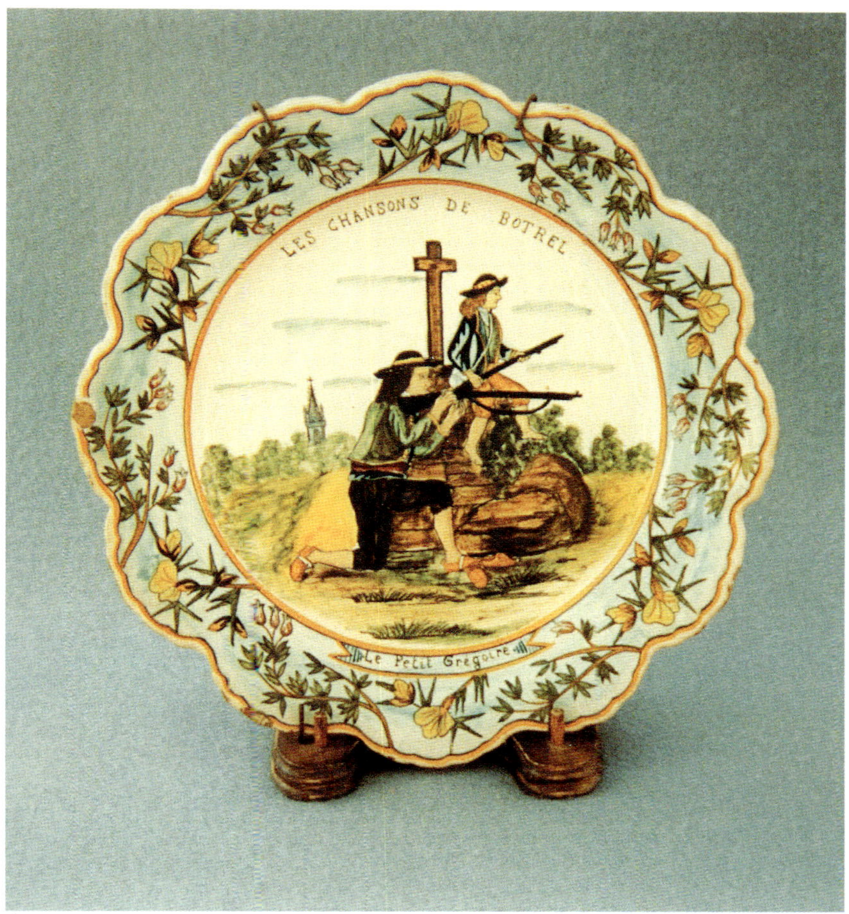

Botrel was renowned for his poems and songs, many of which glorified Breton themes. One series of plates created by the Henriot faïencerie, was called *Les Chansons de Botrel.* Illustrated here is the *chanson,* or song, entitled *Le Petit Gregoire.* The 10" plate has a *dentillé* border filled with *l'ajonc* and *bruyère,* Breton gorse and heather, and the center contains a well-painted scene. Signed HenRiot Quimper, #20, the plate is from the 1920s or early 1930s. Two similar plates from the Botrel estate sale realized $450 each at a French auction in 1981. *Private Collection.*

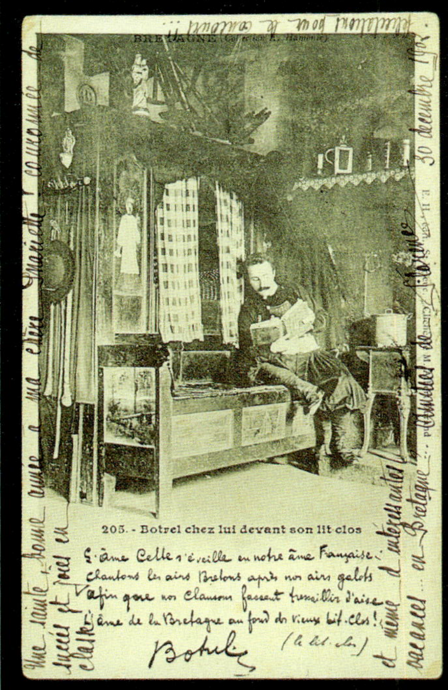

Botrel is pictured on this early 1900s postcard at home in front of his *lit clos,* a Breton enclosed bed. *Authors' Collection.*

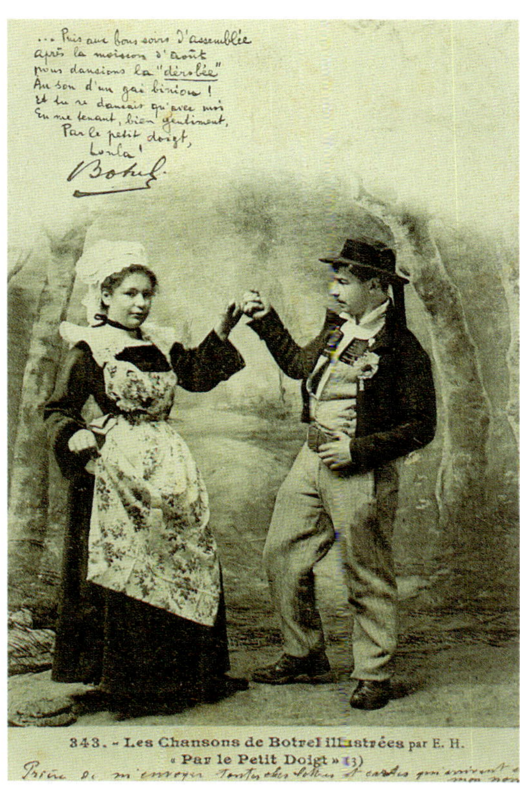

Another Botrel *chanson* is illustrated on a postcard from the early 20th century. This one is entitled *Par le Petit Doigt. Authors' Collection.*

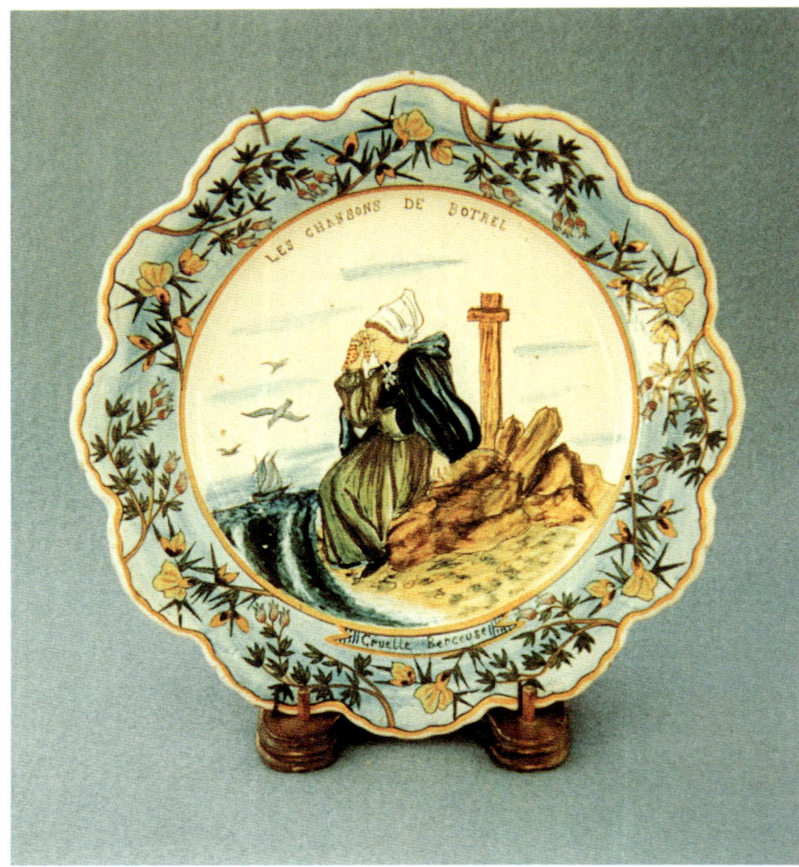

Cruel Lullaby, or *Cruelle Bercuese*, is the title of the Botrel *chanson* depicted on another Henriot faïencerie plate in the series. In addition to finely executed painting, note the *dentillé* rim and border décor. Signed HenRiot Quimper, #20, the plate is 10" in diameter, and dates in the second quarter of the 20th century. Two *Chanson de Botrel* plates, marked HR Quimper, sold through an American auction in 1997 for $1,300 each. *Private Collection.*

The Botrel *chanson* enacted on this early postcard is *Le Meunière de Pont-Aven*, or The Miller of Pont-Aven. *Authors' Collection.*

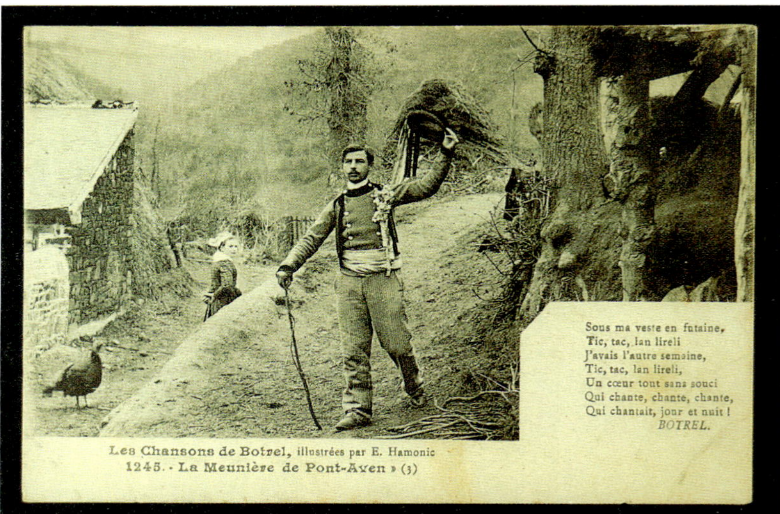

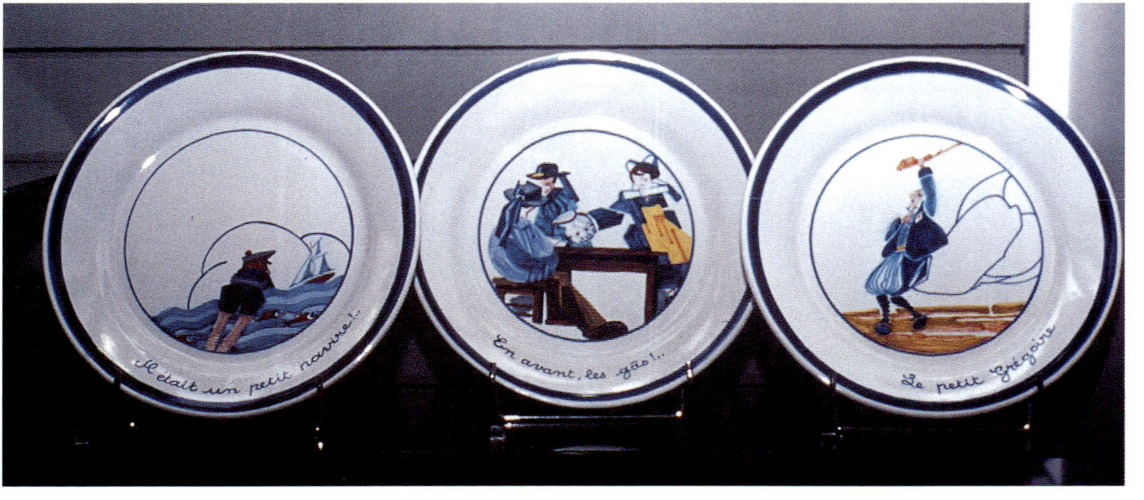

HB artist Marc'harit Houel designed a series of plates commemorating Botrel's chansons. Shown here are three in the series. *Courtesy of Musée Départemental Breton, Quimper.*

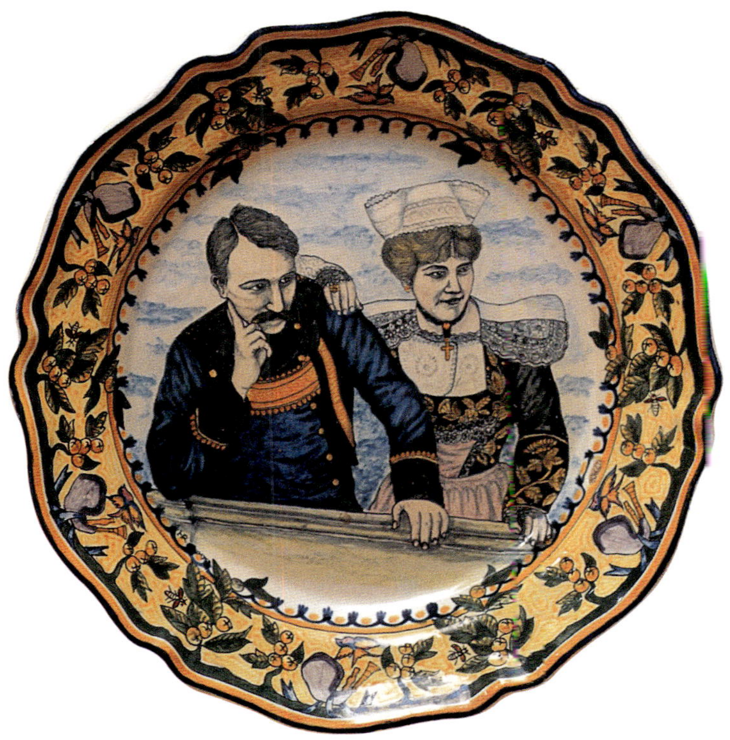

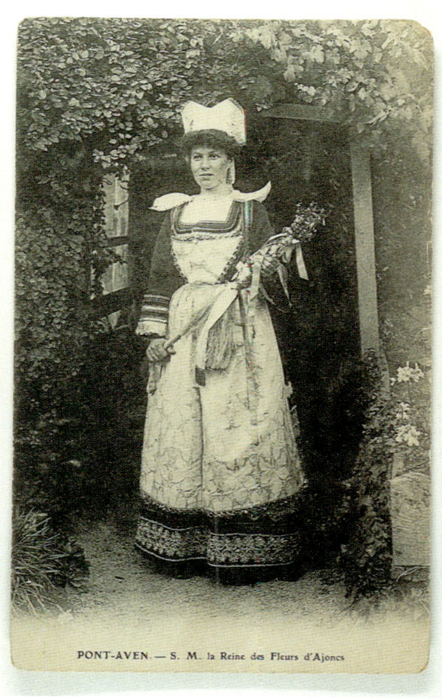

The Henriot faïencerie immortalized Théodore Botrel and his wife, Hélène, on a 9.75" diameter plate signed HR Quimper. The border is a unique combination of mistletoe and *binious*. The couple, whose Breton names were *Dorig* and *Léna*, is captured on faïence in a pensive and personal rendition. (*Mali, Old Quimper Review, March 1997*; also see *Taburet, p. 122* for an inscribed postcard from Botrel to his friend Jules Henriot.) *Courtesy of Musée de la Faïence, Quimper.*

The Queen of the Gorse Festival is depicted on this early 20th century postcard. Botrel initiated the *Pardon des Ajoncs d'Or* in August 1905. It later was renamed the *Fête des Fleurs d'Ajoncs*, and continues to be held in Pont-Aven in August. *Authors' Collection.*

It was our first trip to Quimper, and we took the southern route from Rennes through Vannes and Lorient. We decided to make a side trip to Pont-Aven, which is about 40 kilometers west of Lorient. We had no idea how lovely this town was, or the images we would see and capture on film. What a reception! No wonder artists have flocked to this spot for more than a century, initially congregating around Paul Gauguin. We parked and walked along the harbor, following the Aven into the heart of town in search of the butter cookies, *Les Galletes de Pont-Aven*, a delicate confection claimed by some to be nearly as famous as the artists of the Pont-Aven School.

I love Brittany. It is here I find the wilderness, the primitive. When my wooden shoes resonate on the granite ground I hear a haunting sound, muted and strong, that I search for in my painting.
Paul Gauguin, Letter to Schuffenecker; 1888. (LePaul; p. 24.)

Pont-Aven was known as fourteen mills (*moulins*) and fifteen houses. The *Moulin Rosemadec* remains today, as a restaurant and hotel for tourists. The quickly moving waters of the Aven rush by.

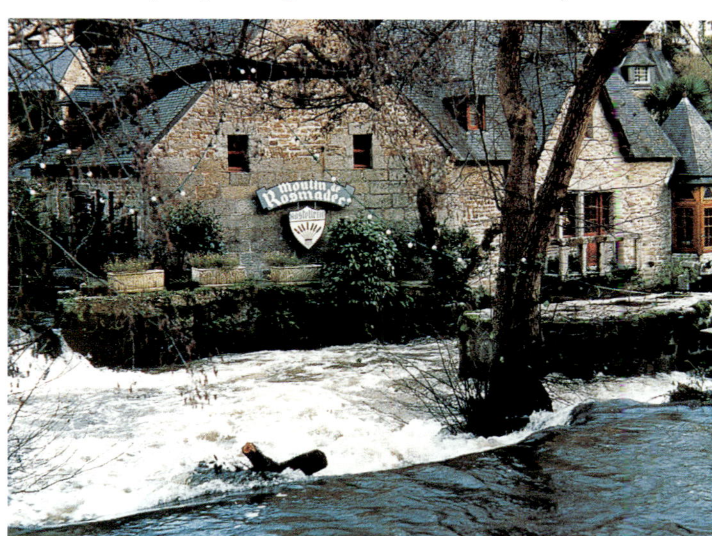

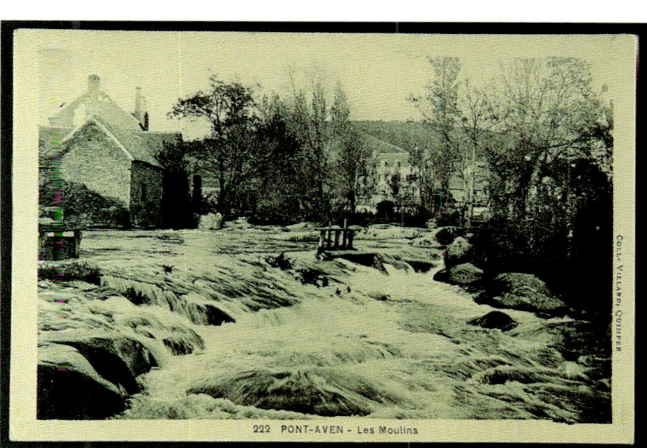

An early postcard shows the Aven tumbling by the mills in the center of town. *Authors' Collection.*

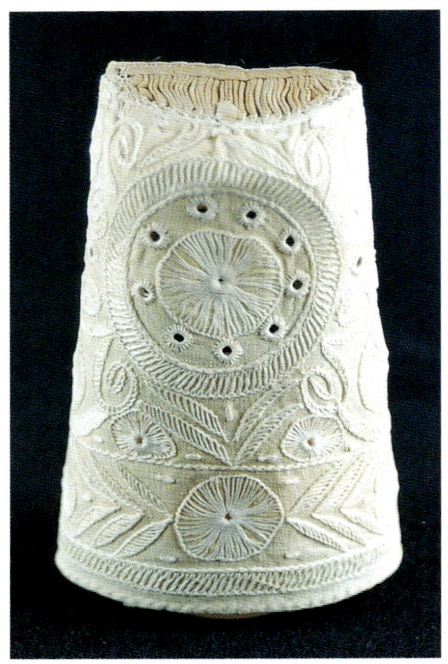

Our favorite purchase in Pont-Aven is this pre-1900, 5" tall *coiffe* from the *Pays Bigouden.* In the 20th century, the *coiffes* from the area grew in height to more than 12". *Authors' Collection.*

After purchasing many boxes of the butter cookies, we found two small shops in the heart of town selling old Quimper. Over the years we have purchased several pieces from these shops, but the dearest treasure is a 5-inch tall *coiffe* of *Pays Bigouden,* dating back to before 1900. In those days the *coiffes* were small, but as the 1900s progressed, the *coiffes* grew in size. *Coiffes* of recent vintage generally stand 12-to-14 inches tall.

To us, Pont-Aven is a sheer delight. We never fail to be enthralled by the history, the scenery, and the people. Because we usually visit in the off-season, we have been fortunate to see this beautiful town in its quiet mode, reflecting a simpler time of artists, romantic woods, and madly rushing waters. Pont-Aven, as Brittany, taught us to slow down, look around, and enjoy our journey.

An important stop in Pont-Aven is the Théodore Botrel statue and his home on the harbor. Botrel was born in 1868, and became the *célèbre bard Breton.* This poet and songwriter adopted Brittany and spent a great portion of his life in Pont-Aven. Botrel initiated Pont-Aven's *Pardon des Ajoncs d'Or* in August 1905. Also called *Fête des Fleurs d'Ajoncs,* this annual festival keeps alive the Breton customs that Botrel loved, and is a model for festivals emulated by other towns in Brittany.

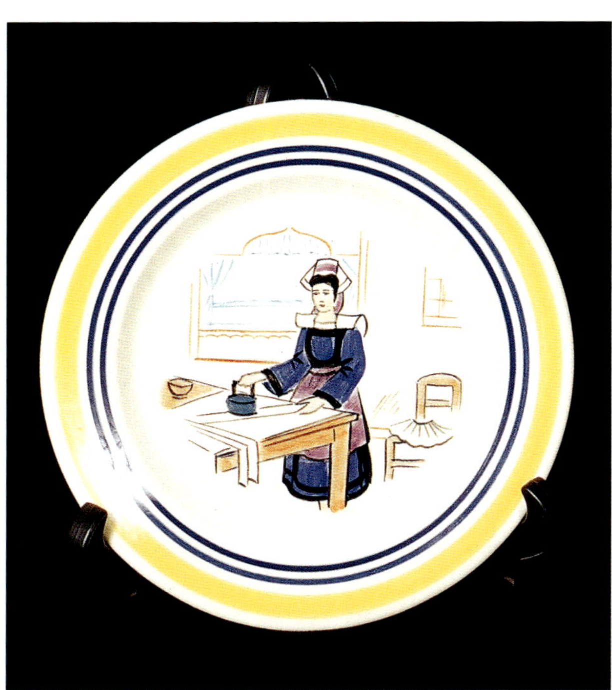

Another great find in Pont-Aven was series of plates showing various Breton professions. The first plate shows *la repassuese de coiffes,* the *coiffe* ironer. *Courtesy of Susan S. Temple.*

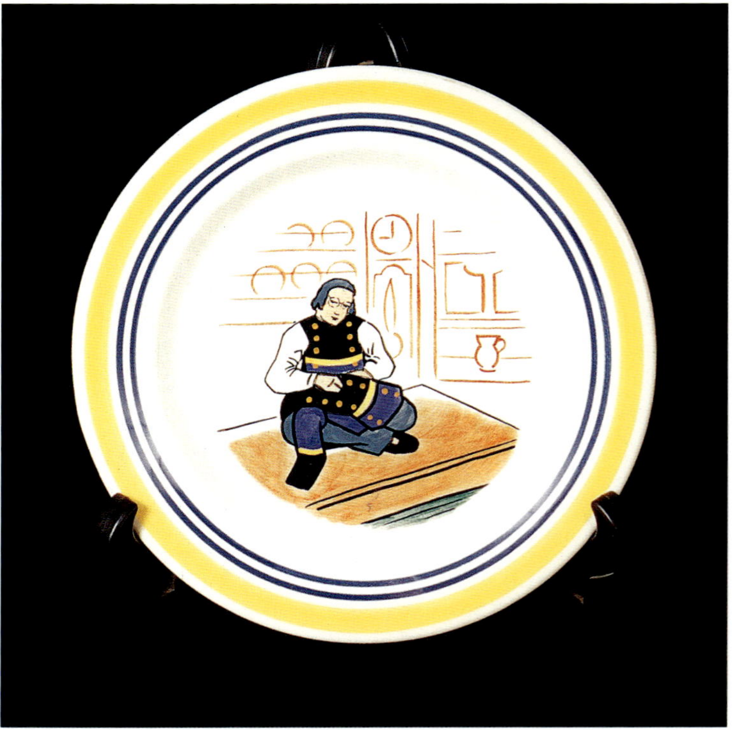

A second plate features *le tailleur,* the tailor, an honored profession in Brittany. The tailor was called upon to ready the wedding finery, not an easy task when elaborate embroidery was needed. *Courtesy of Susan S. Temple.*

Each plate is marked with the name of the profession and the signature Henriot Quimper Françe #11, and is second quarter of the 20th century. *Courtesy of Susan S. Temple.*

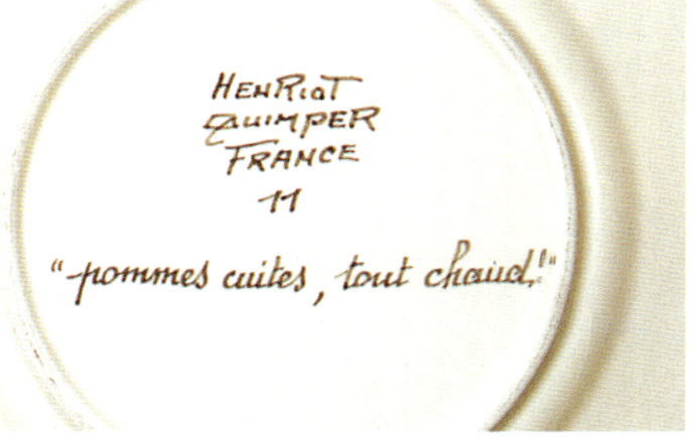

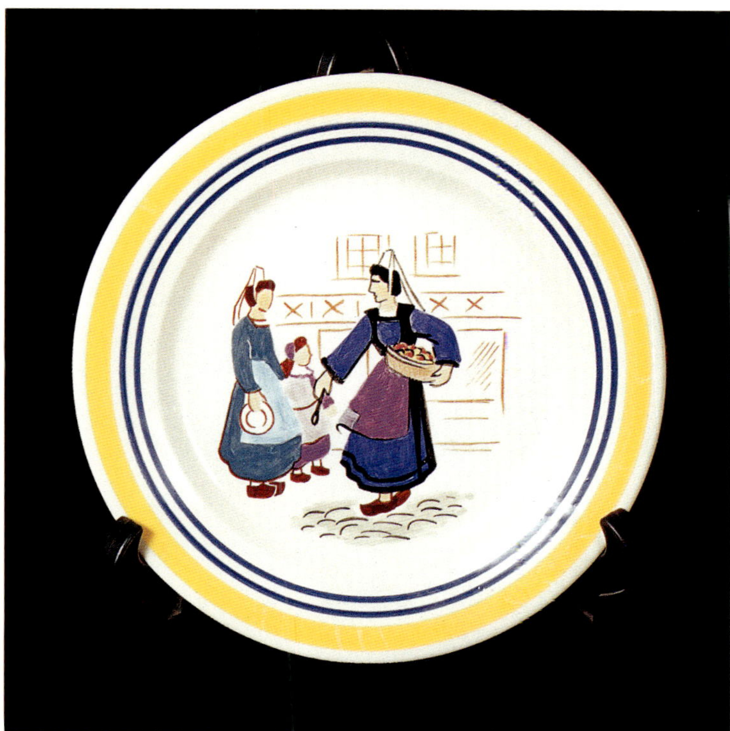

The third plate is entitled *pommes cuit tout chaud* – or cooked potatoes, all hot. Perhaps it's a glimpse into the profession of selling fast food *à la Bretonne, n'est-ce pas? Courtesy of Susan S. Temple*

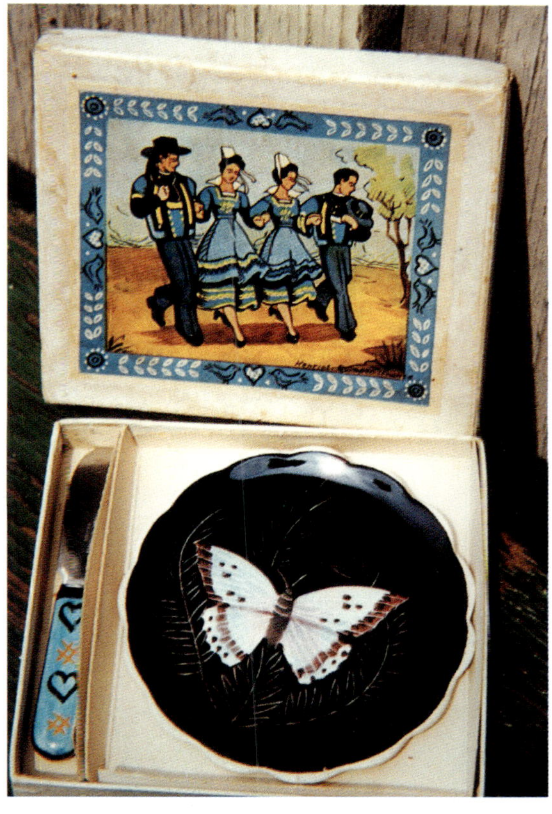

Another treasure we found in Pont-Aven, was this *papillion* (butterfly) design set of a 4.5" serving dish (for jam or cheese) with accompanying 4.5" knife, all in the original box. Signed Henriot Quimper, the set is from the mid-20th century. *Private Collection.*

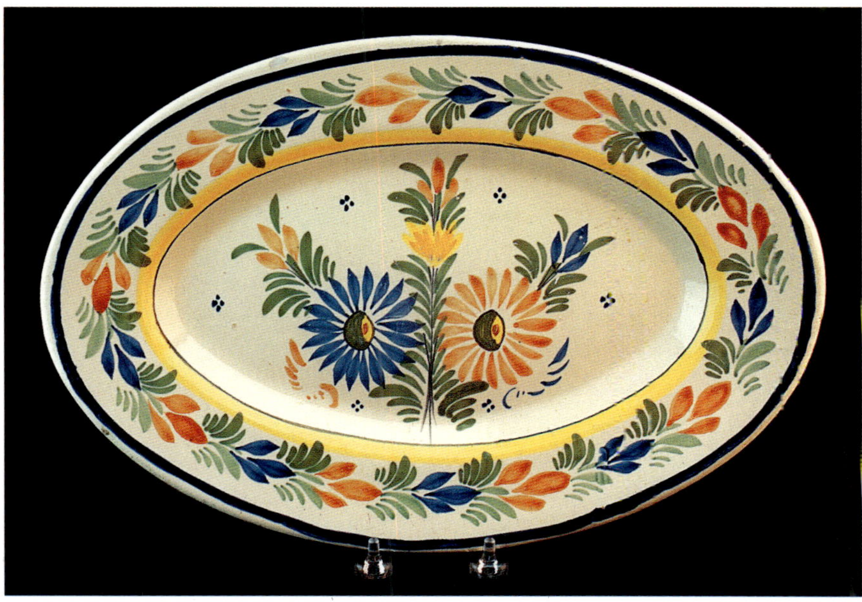

A large Henriot oval platter filled with wonderful *à la touche* flowers was waiting for us in a shop in Pont-Aven. The platter is 15" long and signed Henriot Quimper #93, and is second quarter of the 20th century. *Courtesy of J. Cameron and Kathleen Yorkston.*

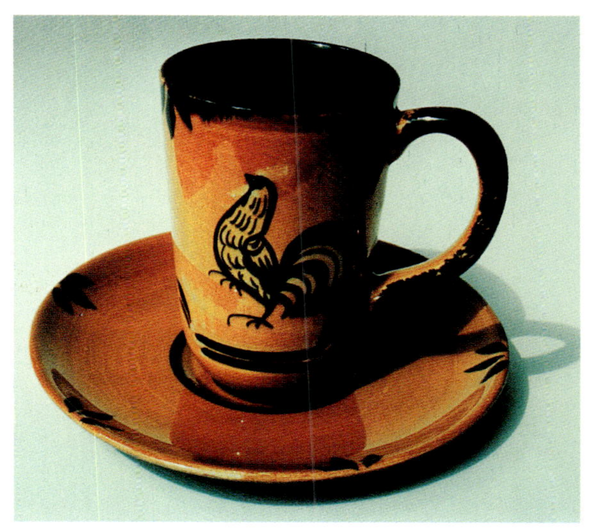

The rooster motif is always popular in France and with American collectors as well. This fellow looks particularly charming on the mid-20th century cup and saucer, signed Henriot Quimper, France. *Collection of Jen and Jeff Nowland.*

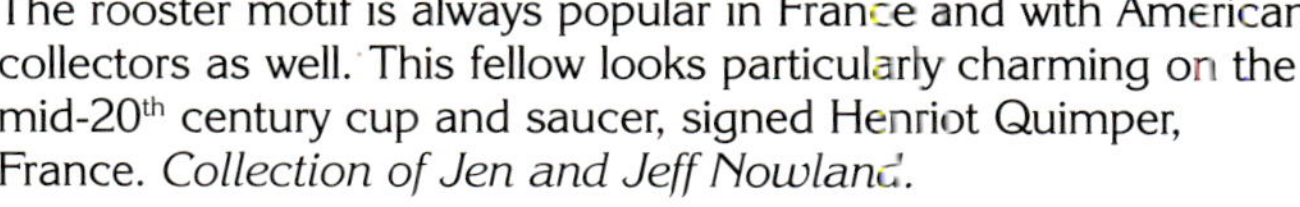

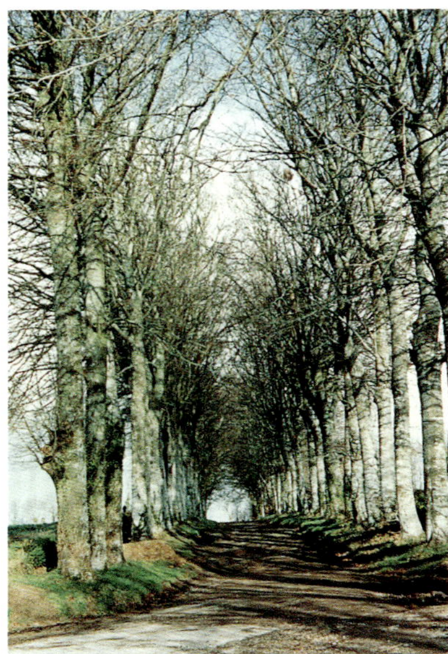

A trip to the *Chapelle de Trémalo* took us on a climb through the *Bois d'Amour* and up a tree-lined path.

The most joyous of our Pont-Aven discoveries actually came on the outskirts of town. Each time we visit, we walk the colorful side streets, follow the promenade Xavier-Grail, we frequent a *pâtisserie* in the heart of town, and of course, shop for antiques. But the fondest memories of Pont-Aven involve our climbs up through the hilly woods called *Bois d'Amour*, up past views made famous by painters a century ago, up and on to the *Chapelle de Trémalo*.

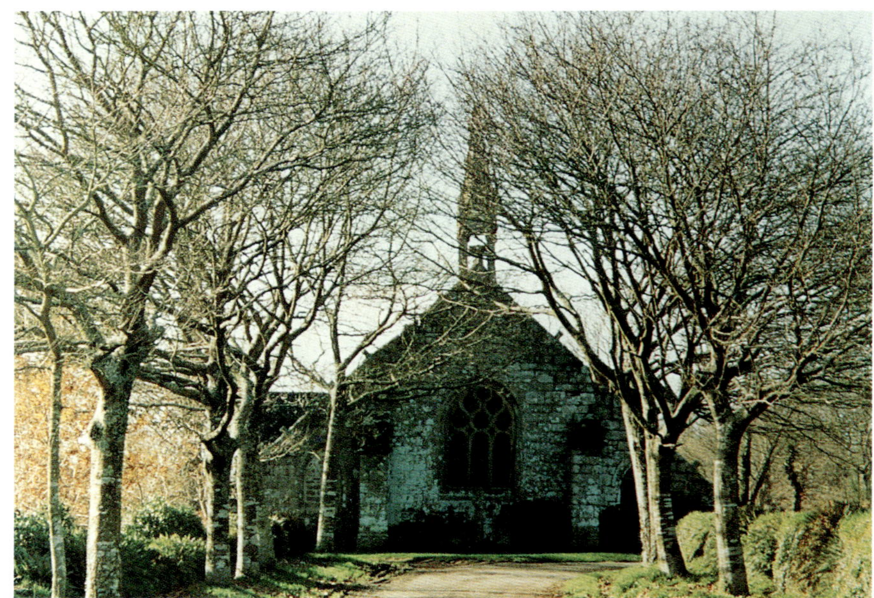

Trémalo waited for us at the end of a country lane.

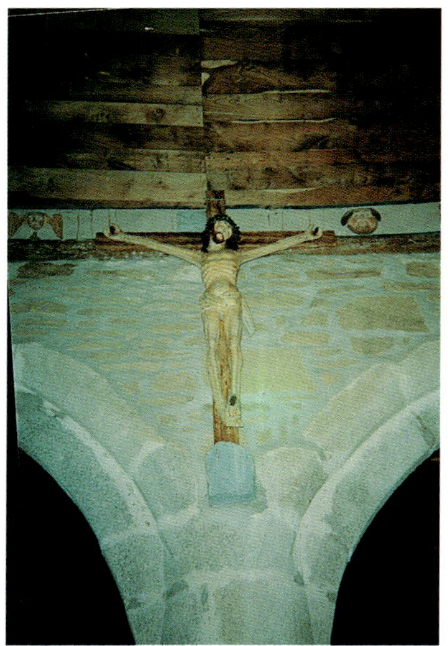

The interior was silent and spare, and home to the model for Gauguin's painting, *Christ Jaune* (Yellow Christ.)

Trémalo is the home to the model for Gauguin's painting entitled *Yellow Christ*. On our first visit, the chapel was dark and filled with silence. Our eyes slowly adjusted, allowing us to see the intricate, yet simple beauty of the interior. It is an early 16th century country chapel that has been lovingly tended over the centuries. Our last visit to the *Chapelle de Trémalo* is especially memorable. In a misty rain, we hiked through the *Bois d'Amour*, up the long country lane to the chapel. Inside we gazed again at the painted wooden inspiration for *Christ Jaune*, and the grinning gargoyle-style peasant faces carved along the upper beams smiling down on us. A few townspeople were meeting in the chapel, and we hoped we had not intruded.

It was on the walk back down into Pont-Aven that we saw the rainbow in the clearing January afternoon sky of Brittany, over the open field and into the line of trees, and the scene grabbed our hearts. Two townspeople, linked arm-in-arm, were walking ahead of us after their chapel meeting. We became acutely aware of stepping slightly into their lives, aware that both they and we have been younger, and aware of others who have gone before us. We also became aware of our own role in the parade of the present and future visitors who will appear momentarily in Breton lives, briefly visiting the reverie of Pont-Aven.

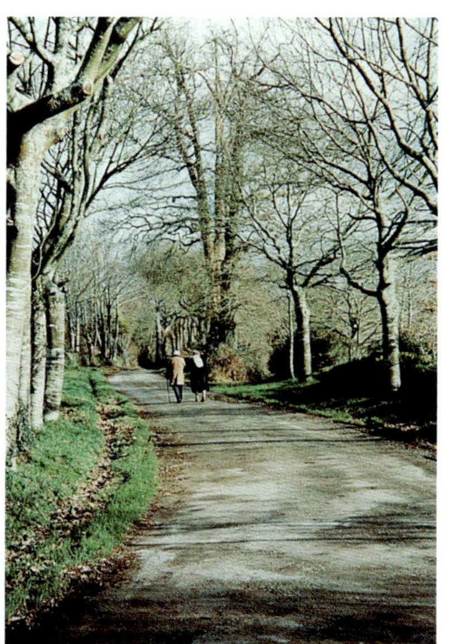

On our way back to Pont-Aven from Trémalo we followed a couple from the church meeting, hoping we had not imposed on their privacy.

Carnac

We made a detour on our first trip to Brittany, about 55 kilometers from Quimper. We took the southern route from Rennes toward Quimper, and veered off the main road toward Carnac, a megalithic site we'd heard about. We were not disappointed. While other alignments and megalithic constructs abound throughout Brittany and throughout the world, the massive alignments at Carnac have no equal in size, complexity, or age. It is one of the most impressive pre-history alignments in the world, with more than 3000 menhirs and dolmens. It was a grand introduction to the pre-history of Brittany.

Legends and religious myths about the alignments date back several hundred years. While colorful, no one takes the stories seriously about *korigans,* or goblins, who erected these monuments; soldiers frozen in stone as they pursued a saint; or dancers who turned to stone. Even the supposition that Carnac was a site for Druid rituals has been discarded, once historians showed that a Celt-like civilization's presence in Brittany coincided with the Iron Age — much later than the alignments' estimated age. A favorite theory claims an astronomical purpose; another speaks reverently of religious purposes. Despite generations of speculation, no one really knows why theses stones were set in place. One writer concludes: *It is the stones that ask the questions, and we who are required to supply the answers. (Giot, The Carnac Alignments, p. 32.)*

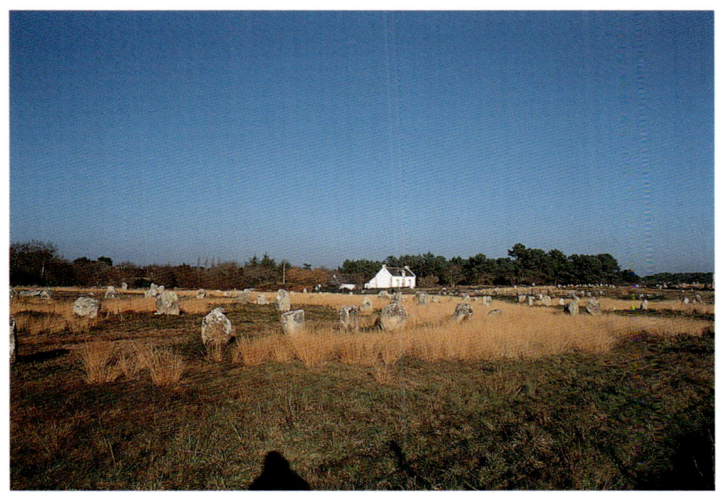

Fields of menhirs surround Carnac and are taken for granted by the local inhabitants. It's the tourists who are astounded. Fences have been erected to protect the countryside from overeager sightseers.

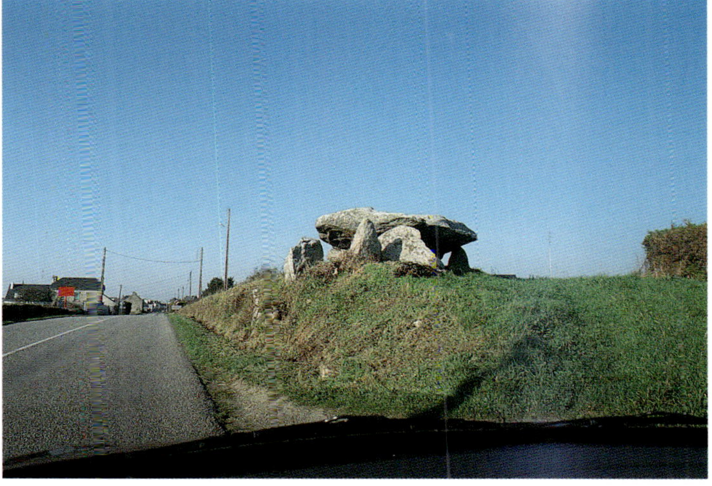

Carnac held many surprises for us, including a dolmen on the edge of a busy road, about 2 kilometers from a major intersection. Dolmens differ from menhirs; dolmens have a table-like configuration and are thought to have been graves. Menhirs are single standing stones.

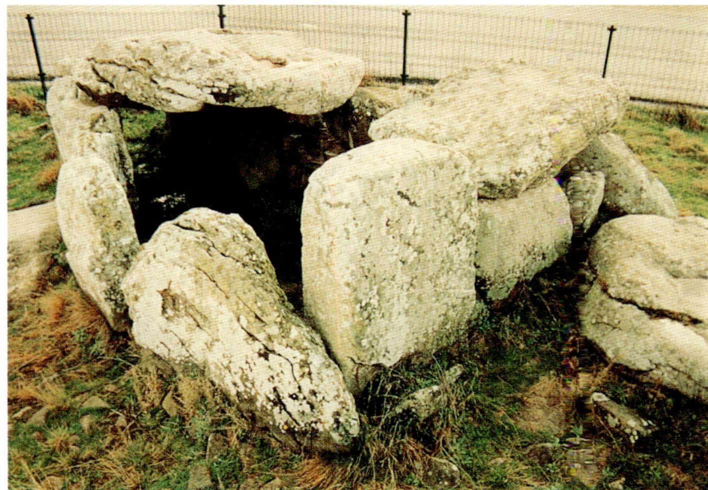

A closer look at another dolmen shows the reclusive nature of the structure. Some people thought early people lived in the dolmens.

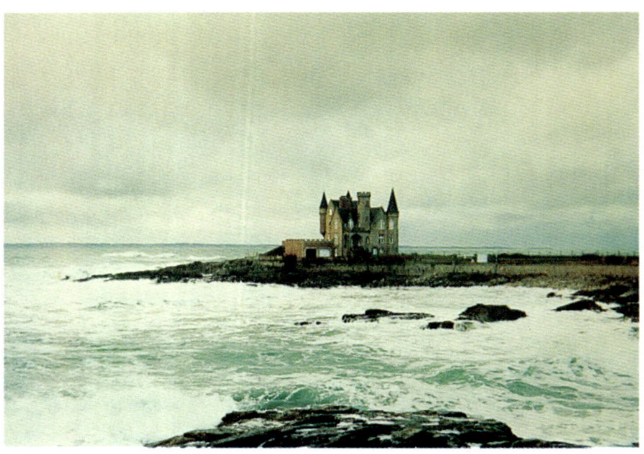

The eastern coast of the Penthièvre peninsula is calm in climate and weather. An inviting *crêperie* is located on its isthmus.

Presqu'île de Quiberon

Within a few kilometers of Carnac is a causeway of tidal sediment – in some spots barely 25 feet wide – which forms the isthmus connecting the Quiberon peninsula to the mainland. Fortress Penthièvre, built in the 1740s and rebuilt in the 19th century, guards the northern end or neck of the peninsula; at the far end is the town of Quiberon, a popular resort, fishing port and harbor. Port Maria is the departure point for boat service to *Belle Isle* and Houat and Hoëdic islands. Quiberon, like many other Breton ports, formerly had an active sardine fleet.

There are several small towns on the peninsula. We had no way of knowing that a winter storm in the United States would lead us to become guests in one of these homes several years later.

The wind and rain whipped us on the *Côte Sauvage*, as we tried to watch a fish *criée*. The hundred-year-old *Château de Turpault* looked forlorn against the stormy sky.

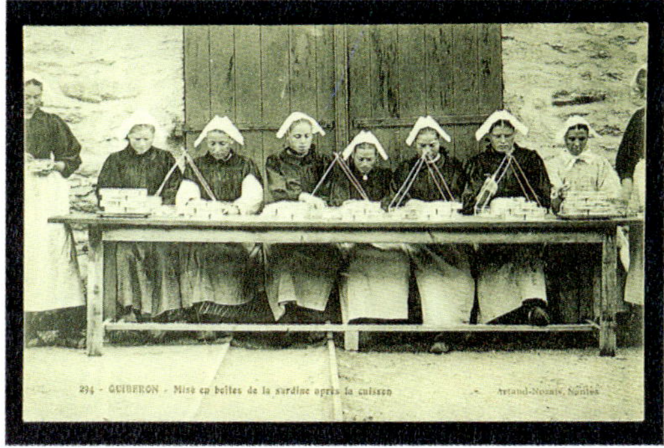

Quiberon also had a thriving sardine business. These young women (*friteuses*), on a turn-of-the-20th century postcard, are packing the cooked sardines in tins. *Authors' Collection.*

Yves and Claude

It was on a return trip from Brittany one January when we had the good fortune to meet a Breton couple returning to their home in the United States. They were traveling from their home on the Quiberon peninsula, which is about 90 kilometers southeast of Quimper. Our plane was routed to North Carolina for the night, because the Philadelphia airport was closed due to heavy snow. It wasn't until we got into Philadelphia the next evening that we met Yves and Claude. They were charming and we talked in the airport shuttle on our way home about their collection of Quimper poterie. They lived only about 20 minutes from us! They kindly invited us to visit them on our next trip to Brittany. Bretons are very cordial.

Even in January we found Quimper for sale on Penthièvre. A teapot and matching cup and saucer in the décor *ivoire corbeille* from the Henriot factory, from the 1950s, caught our eye. They made the trip home with us. *Private Collection.*

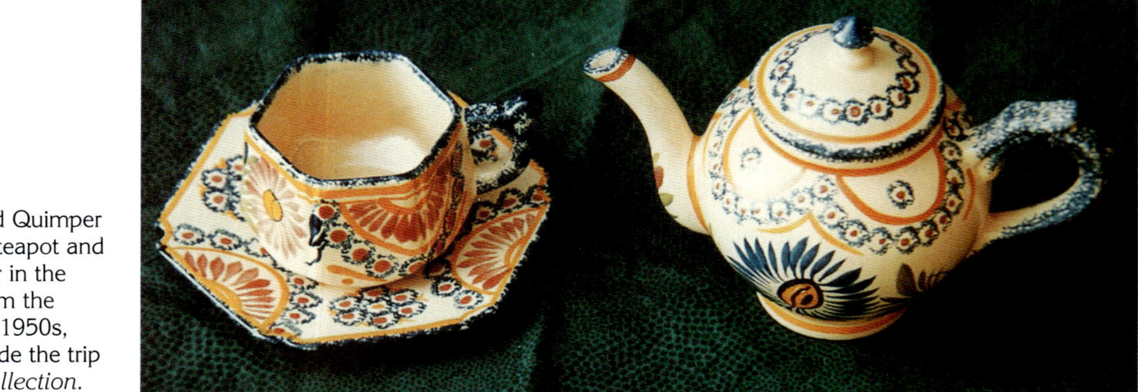

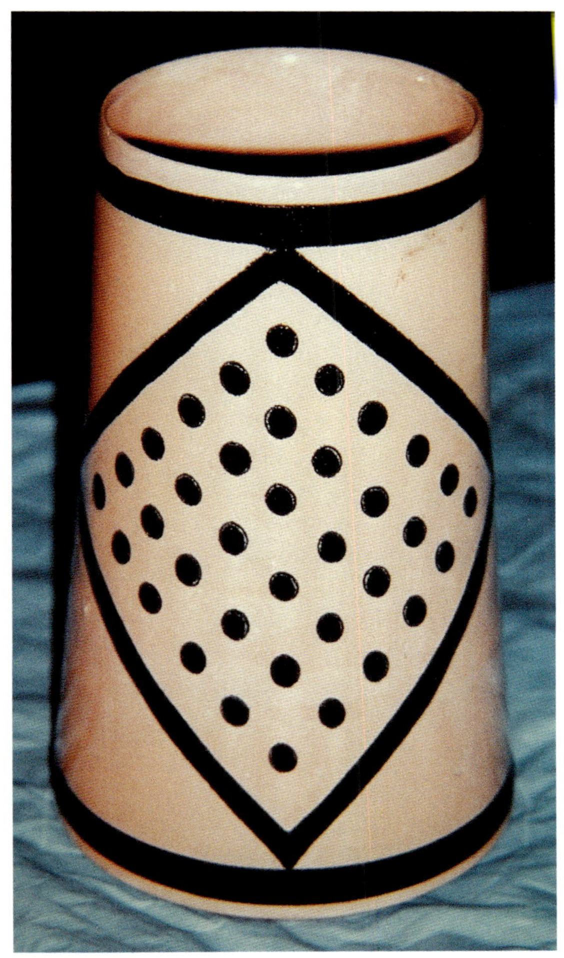

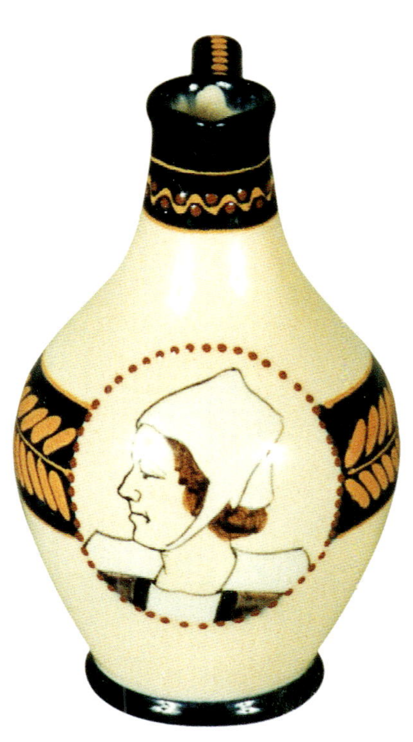

Left:
Another Quimper purchase was a 9.25" tall vase by the Henriot faïencerie. Pink with black polka dots is not a décor we were used to seeing! *Private Collection.*

Right:
HB is the maker of this 7.25" tall pitcher in the décor *broderie*, from the mid-20th century. Note the Bretonne in the medallion is surrounded by raised dots of colored glaze, a simple but clear look at the *à la poire* technique. *Private Collection.*

We thought about their offer and wrote to them about the possibility of photographing some of their Quimper. With typical Breton hospitality, we were invited to their United States home, as well as their home in Brittany. We visited them in both places and found them even more charming the more we talked. We discovered that Claude's family lived on *Presqu'île* for many generations. The home she and Yves purchased was close to her great-grandmother's home, which she often visited as a child. Yves and Claude have the best of both worlds!

In the Footsteps of Pierre-Jakez Hélias

The *Pays Bigouden*, the area around Pont-l'Abbe and Plogastel-Saint-Germain, west and south of Quimper, is considered the bastion of the old values, where *coiffes* sometimes still are worn and Breton is spoken by many. This is Pierre–Jakez Hélias country, so gloriously written of in his classic, *The Horse of Pride*.

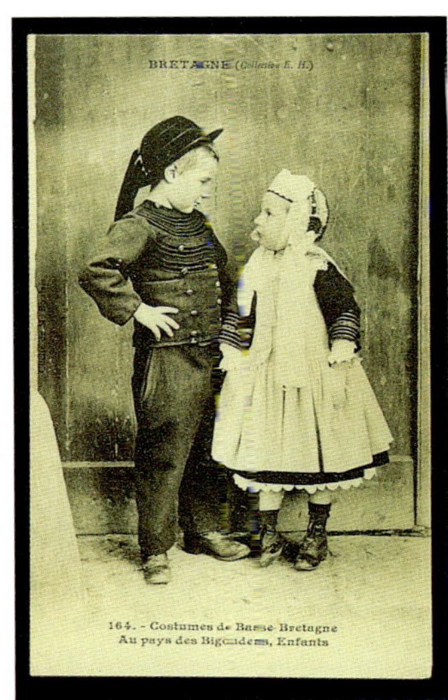

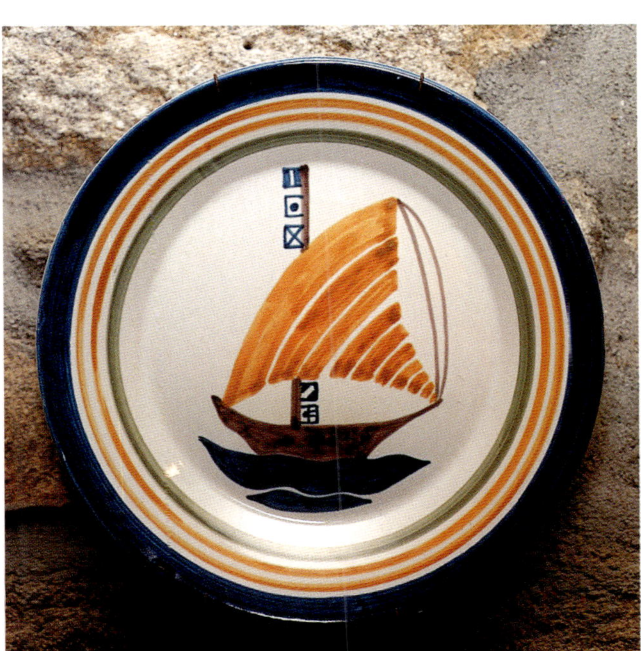

An HB faïencerie plate with a sailboat, manufactured in the first quarter of the 20th century, hangs on the interior stone wall of the c. 1700 home of our hosts. It looks wonderful! *Private Collection.*

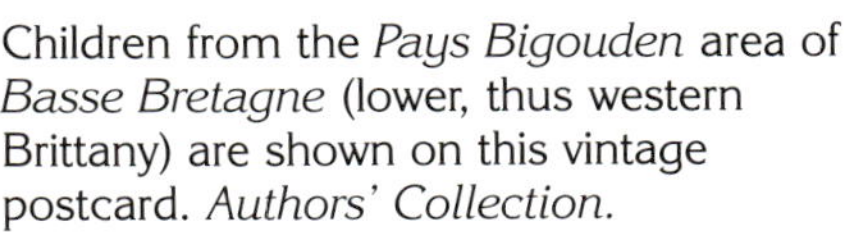

Children from the *Pays Bigouden* area of *Basse Bretagne* (lower, thus western Brittany) are shown on this vintage postcard. *Authors' Collection.*

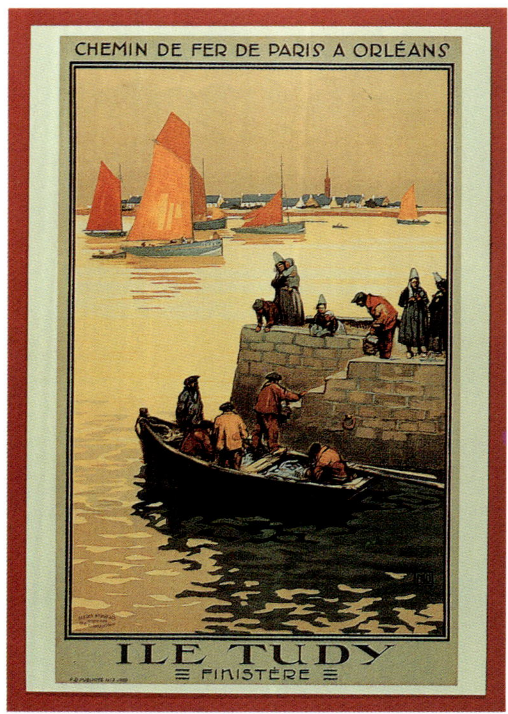

An early poster captures the good life on the coast of the *Pays Bigouden*, south of Quimper. *Private Collection.*

Before exploring this region we followed the advice given us by two sisters from Texas, Patsy McDonald and LaLita Taylor, to read Hélias' book. He does a wonderful job recounting golden childhood memories of a boy growing up in *Pays Bigouden* in the early 20th century, sometimes glorifying a hard way of life and sometimes exposing the harsh conditions of the era. The poverty he describes seems natural for the time. In retrospect, Brittany was behind the times compared with other parts of France. This came to be seen as a blessing by later generations, who cherish their heritage.

Hélias' goal was to promote respect for the culture which nurtured him, for families who cared for each other, grew their own food, worked their own land; for villages which supported each other through difficult times, passing on values which had sustained them for centuries.

But then change happened as change is bound to, and the pastoral scenes described by Hélias were no longer the way of life in *Pays Bigouden* or elsewhere in Brittany. The wars in Europe introduced Breton *conscrits* from many separate villages to a bigger, more sophisticated life, and the railroad brought people and ideas deep into Brittany. The use of French rather than Breton, the demise of the farms, the growth of manufacturing, gawking *Kodakeurs* (camera-toting tourists on paid vacations from their technical jobs in the cities), and the desire for an easier life and modern conveniences all pushed the old values into the *lit clos*, which was soon discarded for a modern bed.

We visited several places, from Pont-l'Abbe to Loctudy, from *Pointe de Penmarc'h*, to Penhors and on to Plozévet searching for some of Helias' roots, and for Quimper poterie. We traveled the roads and memories he conjured for us and felt glad to have such a worthy guide.

Manoir de Kérazan

One extraordinary destination in *Pays Bigouden* is the *Manoir de Kérazan*, between Pont-l'Abbe and Loctudy. We requested access to the *Manoir's* museum during off-season by writing to the Administrator, Monsieur Christophe Calbiac, months in advance. He responded quickly and kindly greeted us when we arrived on a gray January morning. The *Manoir* is a *château* located in a spacious park, and is furnished with original belongings from the Jacob Astor family. It contains a fine art collection, including a remarkable collection of Quimper by Alfred Beau.

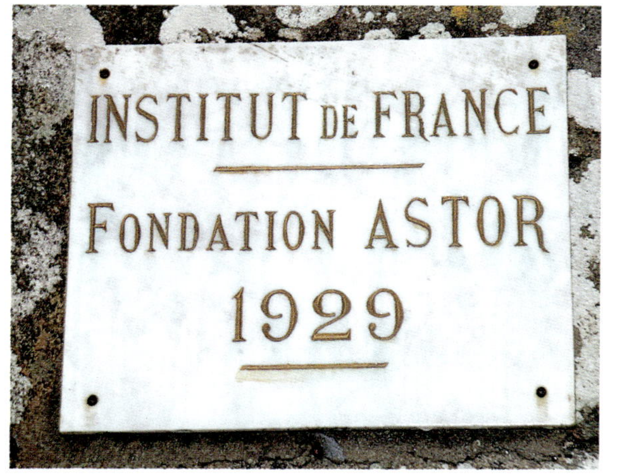

The *Manoir de Kérazan* was bequeathed to the *Institut de France* on Joseph Astor's death.

The *Manoir* is situated in a park, a grand setting for buildings that date from the 17th century onward.

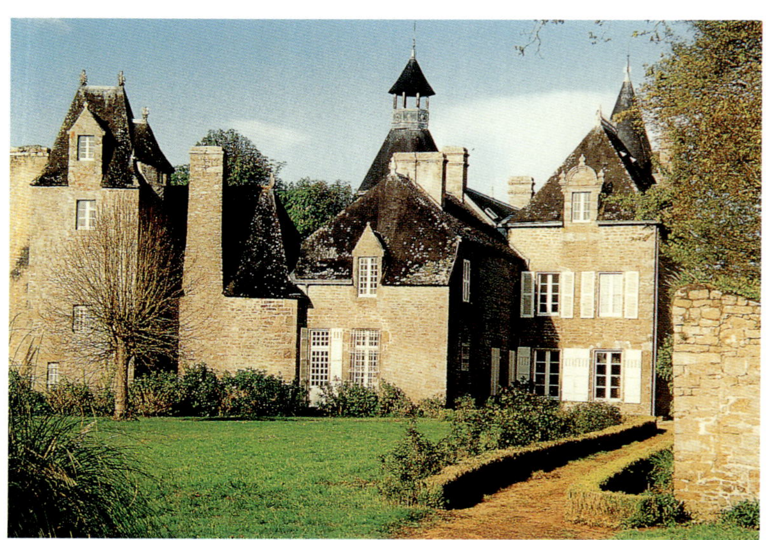

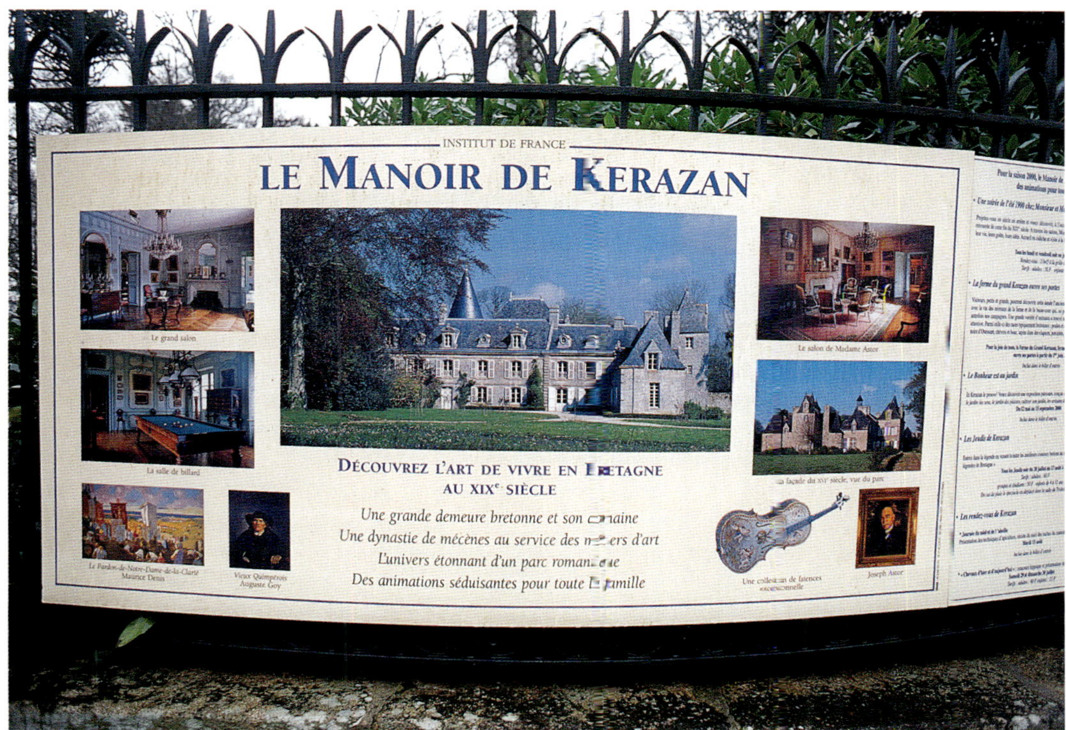

The *Manoir de Kérazan* houses a beautiful collection of furniture, paintings, and ceramic works of well-known Quimper artist Alfred Beau.

Unlike most museums where furnishings have been collected and strategically placed, the *Manoir* is much as it was when the Astors lived there, and Beau and Deyrolle visited. It was the country home of Joseph Astor while he served as mayor of Quimper and in other elected offices. (Under Astor's guidance the *Musée des Beaux Arts* was developed in Quimper, and Alfred Beau served as its first *conservateur*.) The attention to minute details, such as writing instruments poised to compose, create the feeling of the Astors' continued presence. In 1928, Joseph Astor's son bequeathed the property and contents to the *Institut de France,* which maintains it as a museum.

The *Manoir* features many original artworks, representing art schools from the 16th through the 20th centuries, showing Brittany and her way of life in an earlier time. Two large paintings on wooden panels in the dining room were painted for the Astor family by the famous artist, Théophile Deyrolle, founder of the Concarneau school. The Astors were close friends with Alfred Beau. Beau encouraged his friend, Deyrolle, to decorate the dining room for the Astors with hunting scenes. There is also a painting on faïence by Deyrolle, an unusual medium for him, and most certainly a result of Beau's influence.

The Beau collection once was kept in the dining room but now is maintained in the Blue Hall, formerly the Astor family chapel. It was a great moment to see so many exceptional works in one small room. But as Monsieur Calbiac explained, the *Institut de France* and *Fondation Astor's* mission is to create a special exhibition for the Beau collection and present it in an active way. The works eventually will be housed in two rooms on the second floor of the *manoir*, and the *Institut* plans to initiate a Friends of Art group to assist with this project.

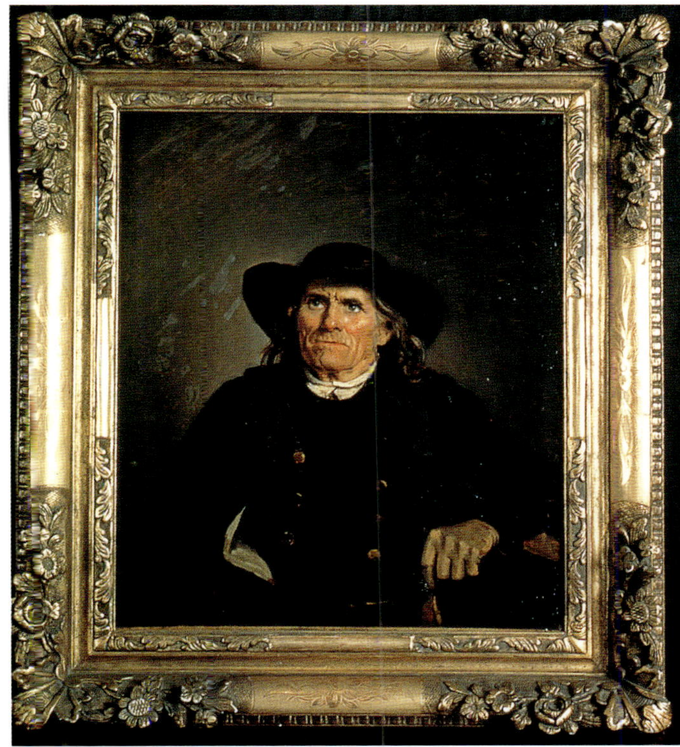

Le Vieux Quimperó's or *Le Celte* by Auguste Goy, 1849, is one of the paintings collected by the Astors portraying life in 18th and 19th century Brittany. Its two titles are *The Old One from Quimper* or *The Celt. Courtesy of Manoir de Kérazan, Institut de France, Fondation Astor. Photograph by Georges Fessy.*

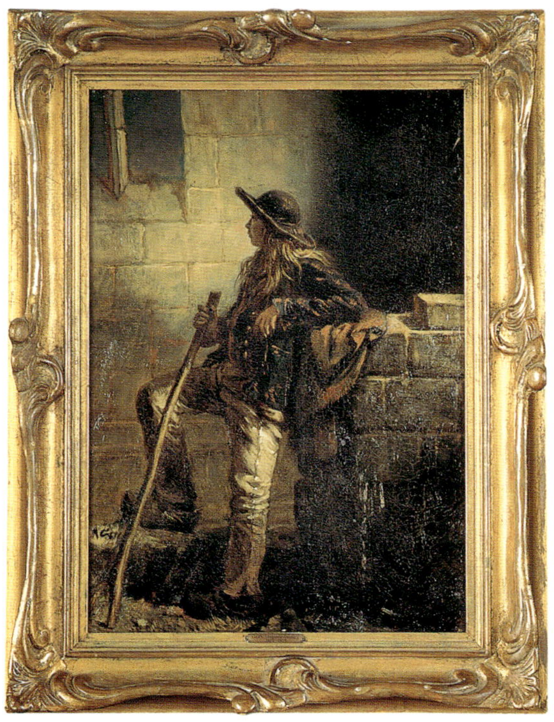

Another Auguste Goy painting entitled *Jeune Paysan auprès d'une ruine d'eglise,* or *Young Peasant Near a Church Ruin,* gives a glimpse into earlier times *en Bretagne. Courtesy of Manoir de Kérazan, Institut de France, Fondation Astor. Photograph by Georges Fessy.*

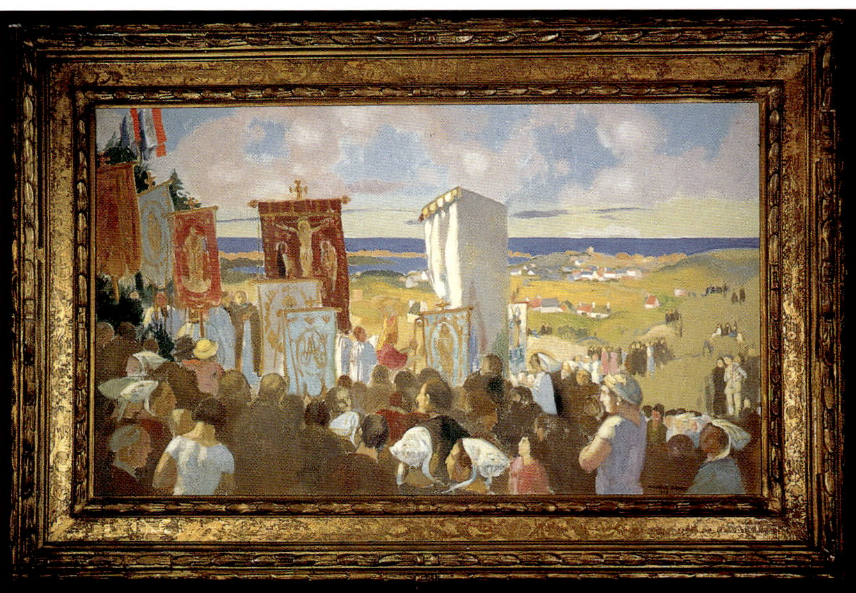

Maurice Denis painted *Le Pardon de Notre-Dame-de-la-Clarté* in 1926. It shows the religious gathering in Brittany known as a *pardon. Courtesy of Manoir de Kérazan, Institut de France, Fondation Astor. Photograph by Georges Fessy.*

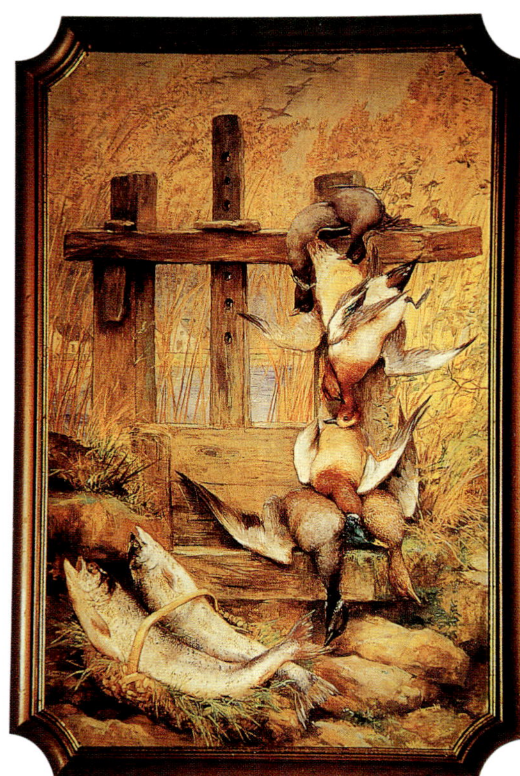

Alfred Beau's friend and famous artist Théophile Deyrolle painted this after-the-hunt scene on a wooden panel for the Astor family. It hangs in the dining room with a companion painting. *Courtesy of Manoir de Kérazan, Institut de France, Fondation Astor.*

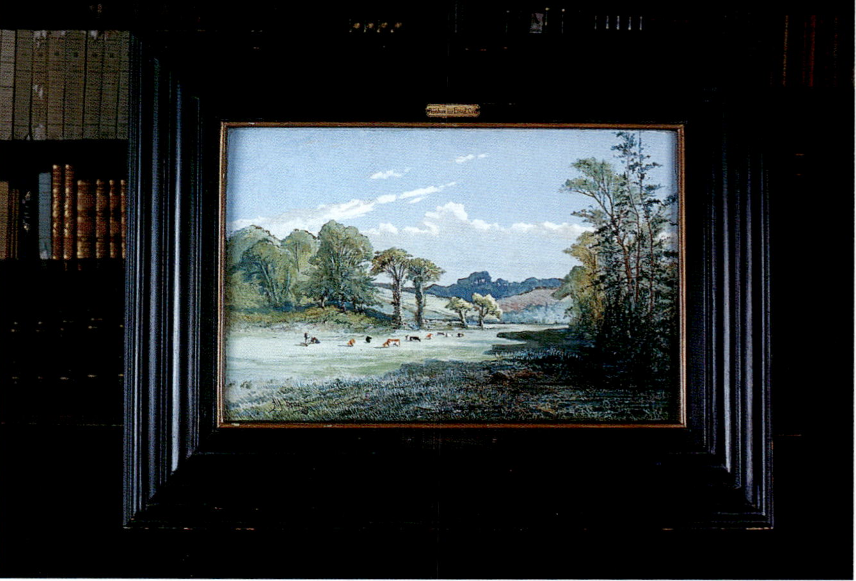

The Astor family's collection of works by Alfred Beau is displayed in a room that previously served as the family chapel. This painting on faïence signed Alf. Beau resembles a painting on board or canvas, and is entitled *Marais de Pluguffen.* It depicts an idyllic countryside with grazing horses, dates 1878-1879 and was displayed at the *Salon de Paris* in 1879. *Courtesy of Manoir de Kérazan, Institut de France, Fondation Astor. Photograph by Steven LeGrand.*

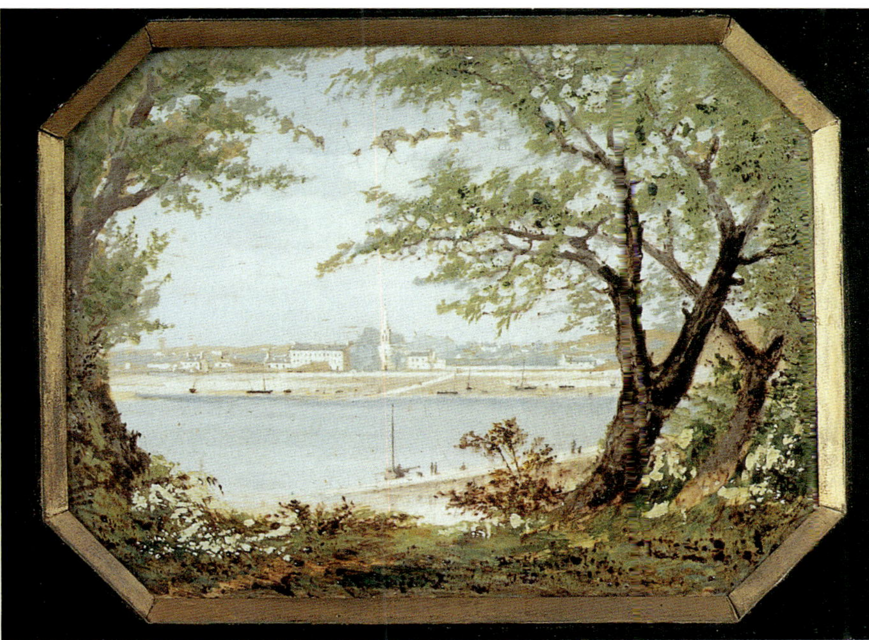

Another painting on faïence by Beau is entitled *Vue de Bérodet*, and is signed Alf. Beau, in addition to PB for Porquier-Beau. The painting technique is called *email cru*, or painting on a raw or unfired glaze surface. The artist from Lorient, Michel Bouquet, reportedly pioneered this technique. It's surmised Beau learned about it from Bouquet, when Bouquet had a studio in the Morlaix/Roscoff area. *Courtesy of Manoir de Kérazan, Institut de France, Fondation Astor. Photograph by Georges Fessy.*

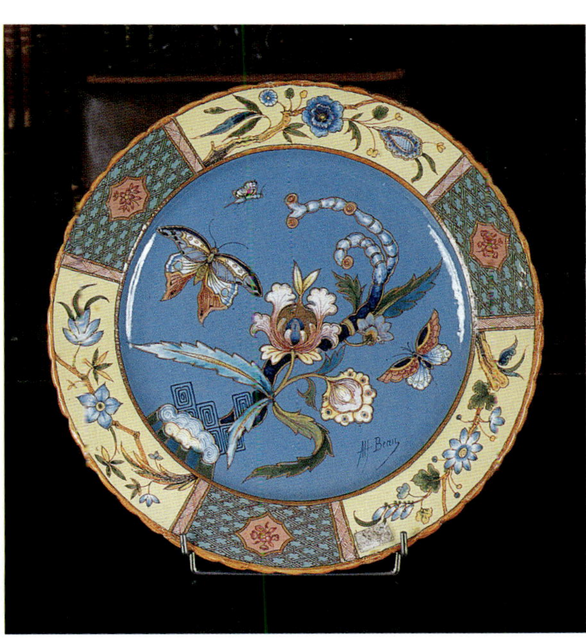

A gorgeous plate rendered in the *décor Japonisant* vibrates with color and activity. Butterflies and stylized flowers on a brilliant blue background are surrounded by an intricate border of flowers and a *croisillon*-like motif. Signed Alf. Beau, PB, it dates from the last quarter of the 19th century. *Courtesy of Manoir de Kérazan, Institut de France, Fondation Astor. Photograph by Georges Fessy.*

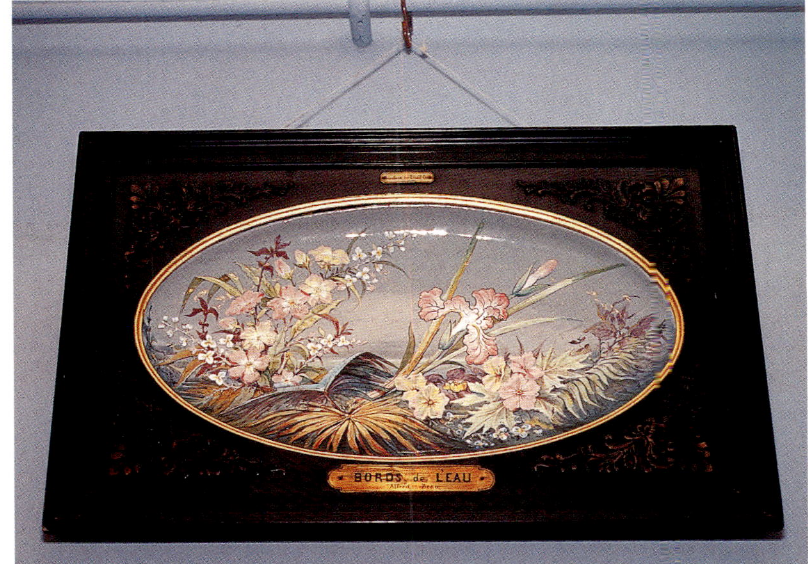

An oval painting on faïence by Beau is entitled *Bords de l'Eau* and is dated 1885-1886. This painting is framed in wood, as are the other paintings on faïence, and was exhibited at an exposition in 1886 at Nantes. *Courtesy of Manoir de Kéazan, Institut de France, Fondation Astor.*

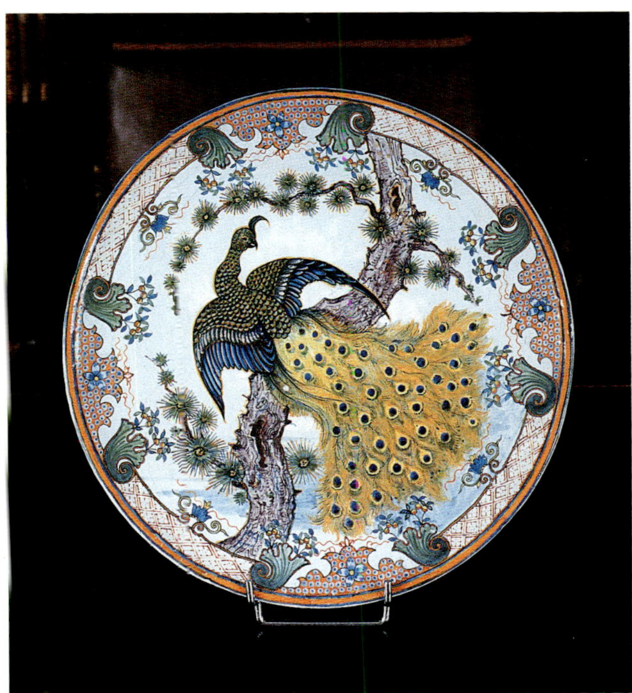

Another stellar plate from Alfred Beau in the *décor Japonisant* features a peacock sitting on a tree limb. His gold tail feathers, highlighted with blue, are draped gracefully across the plate. This example is unsigned but attributed to Beau, either when he was with the *HB/Grande Maison* or the Porquier firm. If HB, then it would be around 1872. If Porquier-Beau, it would be last quarter of the 19th century. *Courtesy of Manoir de Kérazan, Institut de France. Photograph by Steven LeGrand.*

This Alfred Beau oval platter in the *décor botanique* is signed HB and Alf. Beau, and dates from 1872. As an artist, Beau sought the right to sign his work. When the *HB/Grande Maison* forbade this practice, he sought employment at the Porquier faïencerie with the condition he could sign his work. Beau's relationship with the Porquier firm led to an association called Porquier-Beau. *Courtesy of Manoir de Kérazan, Institut de France, Fondation Astor. Photograph by Steven LeGrand.*

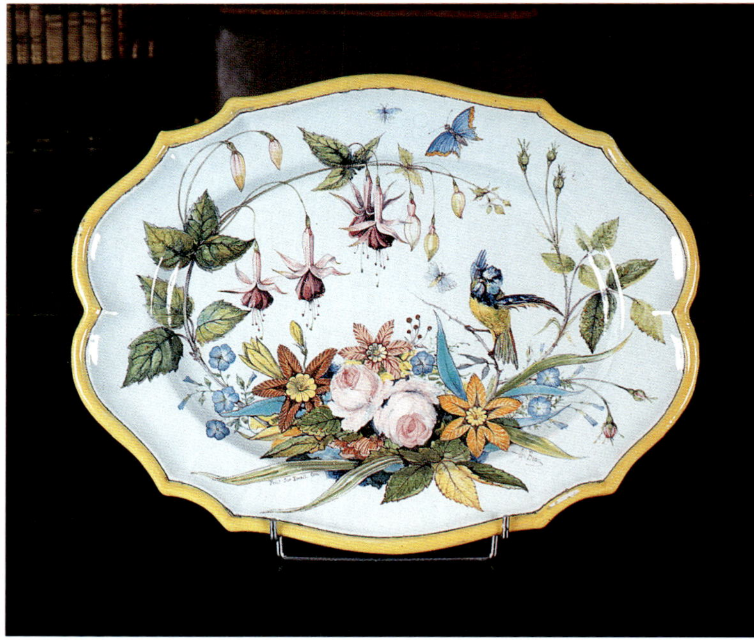

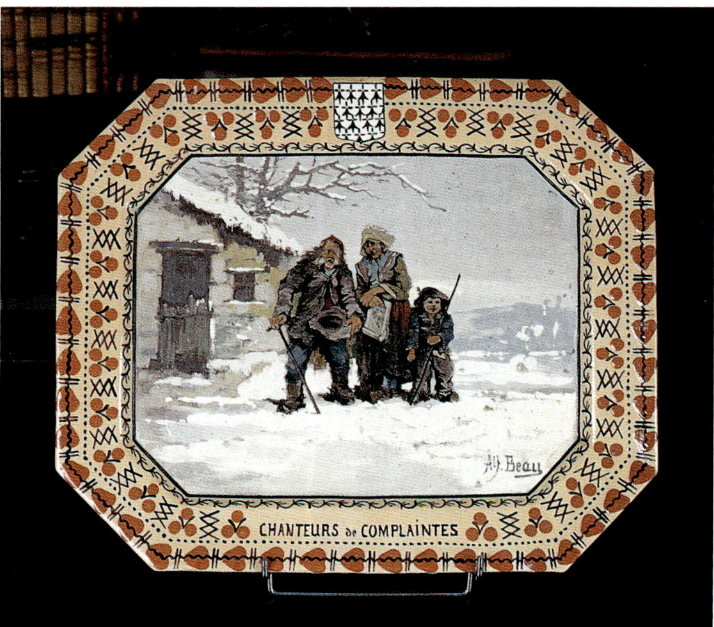

An important platter by Beau entitled *Chanteurs de Complaintes* is credited for the design of his later *Mendiants de Noël* scene. *(See Château de Quintin Exposition Catalogue, p. 79.)* The platter is signed Alf. Beau, PB and dates in the last quarter of the 19th century. *Courtesy of Manoir de Kérazan, Institut de France, Fondation Astor. Photograph by Steven LeGrand.*

A *banêtte,* or two-handled tray, by Beau and signed PB, is called *Le Masque.* It features a central décor of *angelots* with masks surrounded by lambrequins in the Rouen style. *Courtesy of Manoir de Kérazan, Institut de France, Fondation Astor. Photograph by Steven LeGrand.*

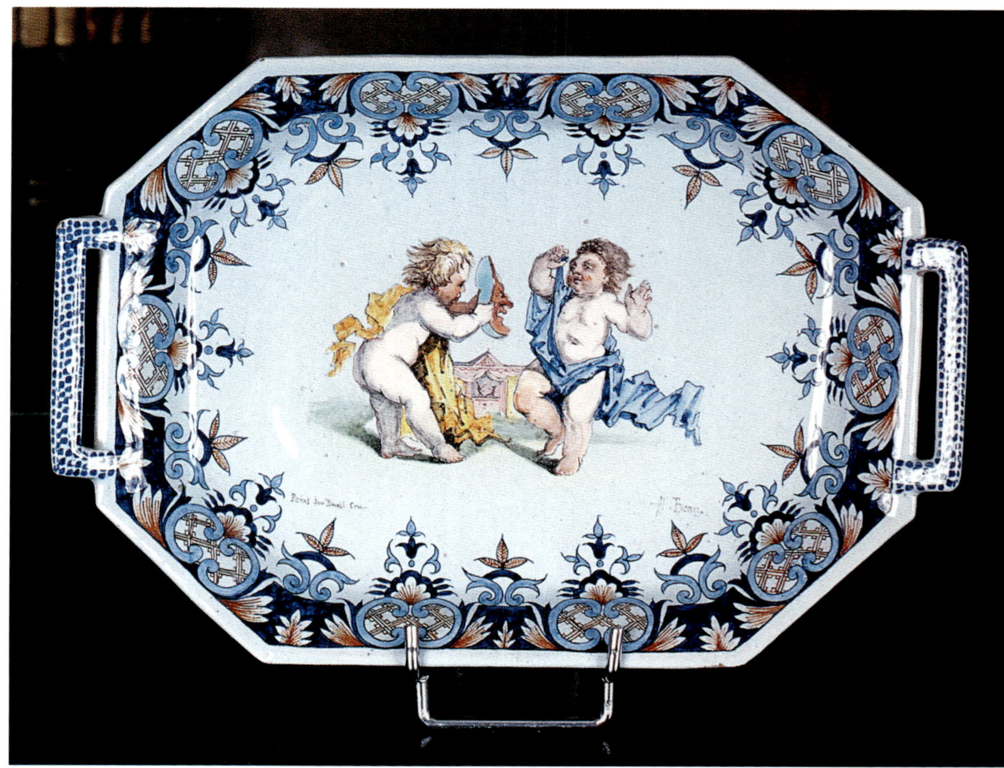

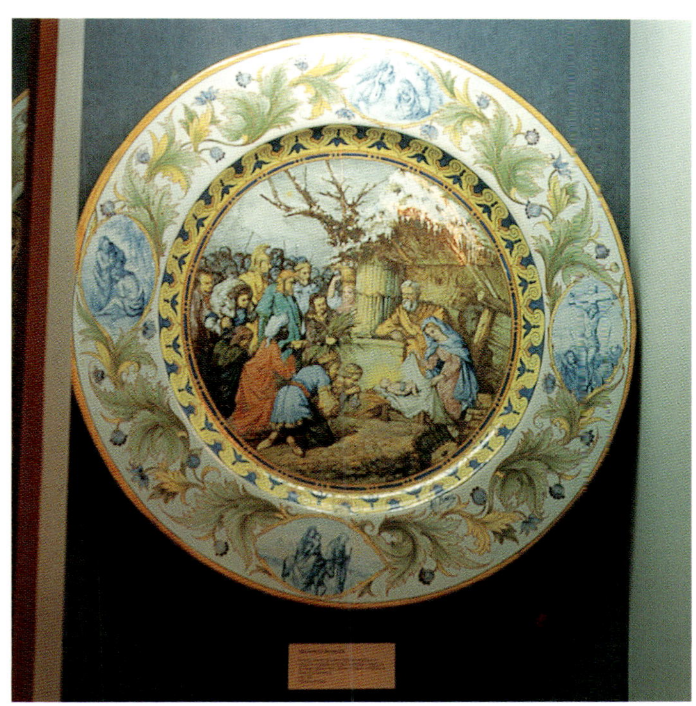

In a happier Christmas mode, a *grand plat décoratif* of the *Adoration of the Magi* by Alfred Beau is extraordinary in composition, color, and execution. *Courtesy of Manoir de Kérazan, Institut de France, Fondation Astor.*

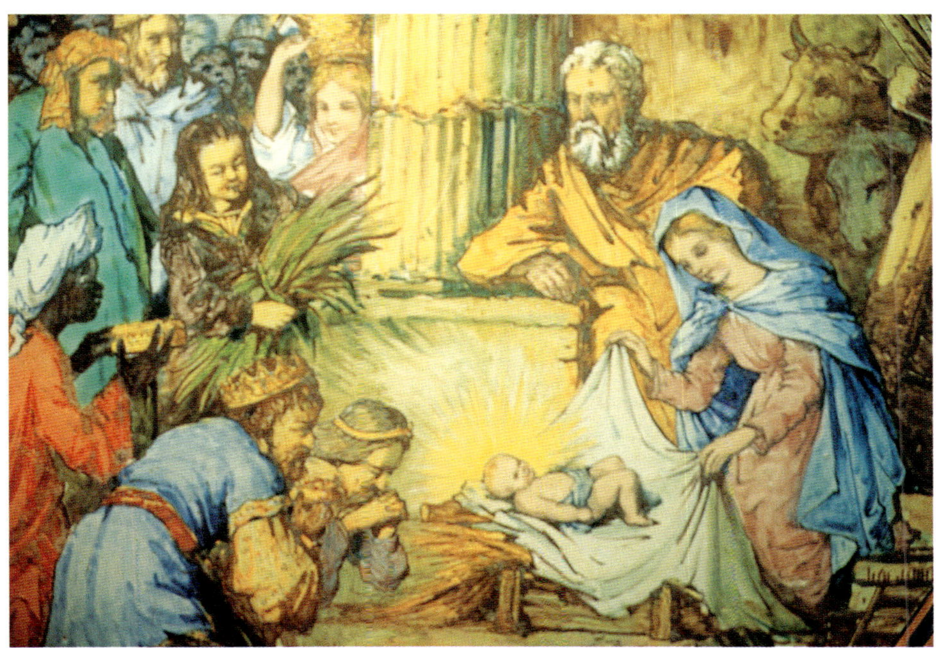

A closer look at the central figures shows the detail of this exquisite work by Beau for the Porquier-Beau firm. *Courtesy of Manoir de Kérazan, Institut de France, Fondation Astor.*

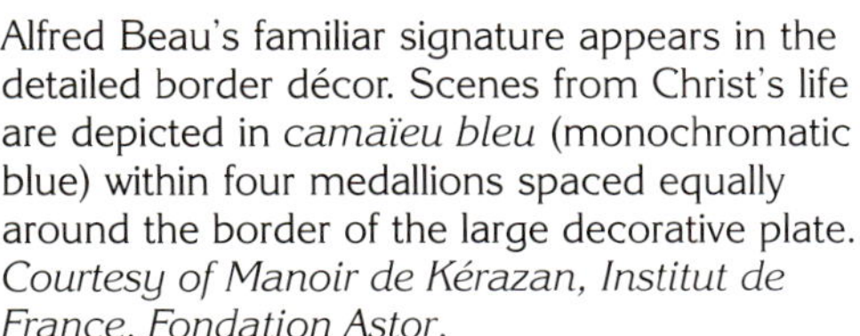

Alfred Beau's familiar signature appears in the detailed border décor. Scenes from Christ's life are depicted in *camaïeu bleu* (monochromatic blue) within four medallions spaced equally around the border of the large decorative plate. *Courtesy of Manoir de Kérazan, Institut de France, Fondation Astor.*

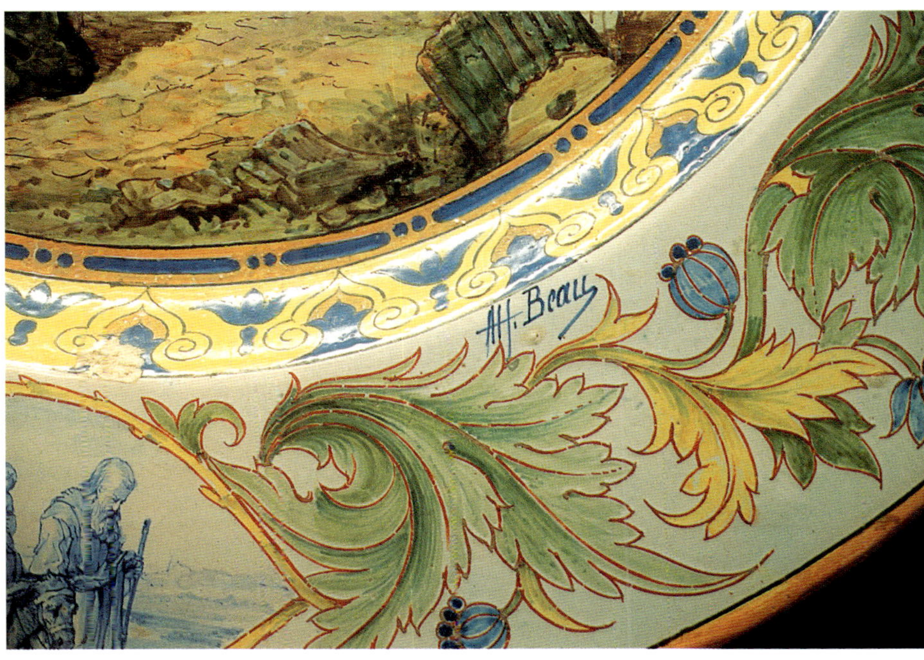

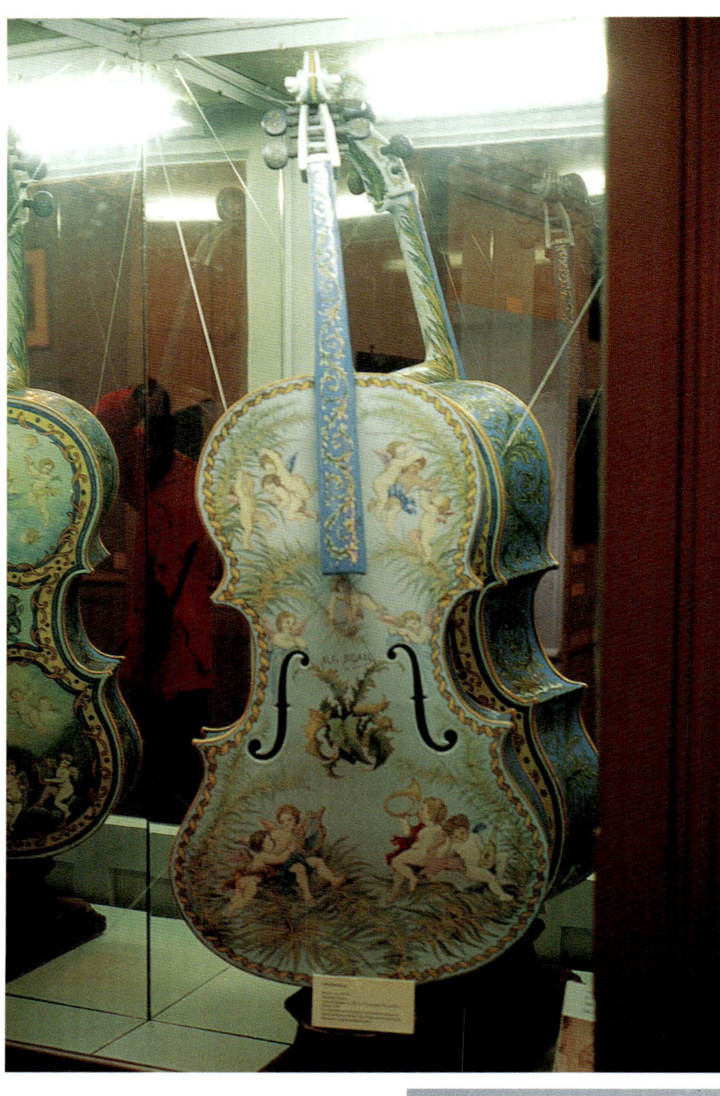

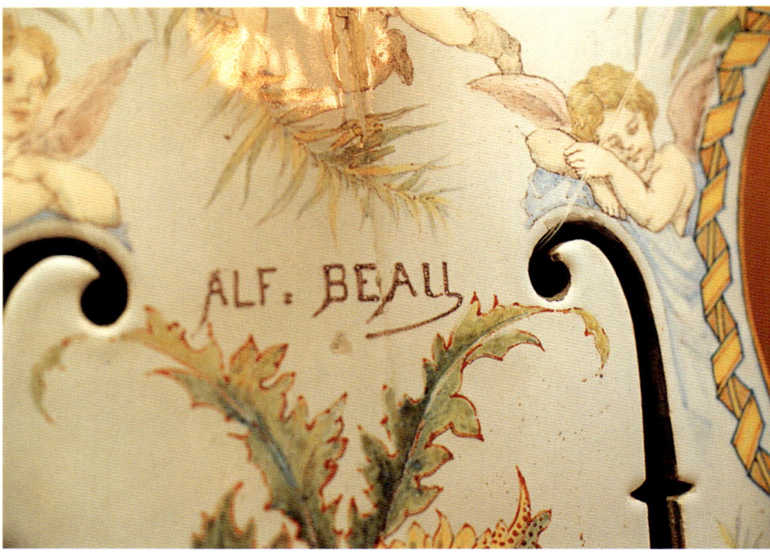

Again the familiar signature of Alfred Beau appears on the front of the instrument. *Courtesy of Manoir de Kérazan, Institut de France, Fondation Astor.*

The star of the Beau collection at *Manoir de Kéazan* is the life-sized viola in faïence. It is a masterpiece and required fifteen firings in the kilns of the Porquier-Beau faïencerie. *Courtesy of Manoir de Kérazan, Institut de France, Fondation Astor.*

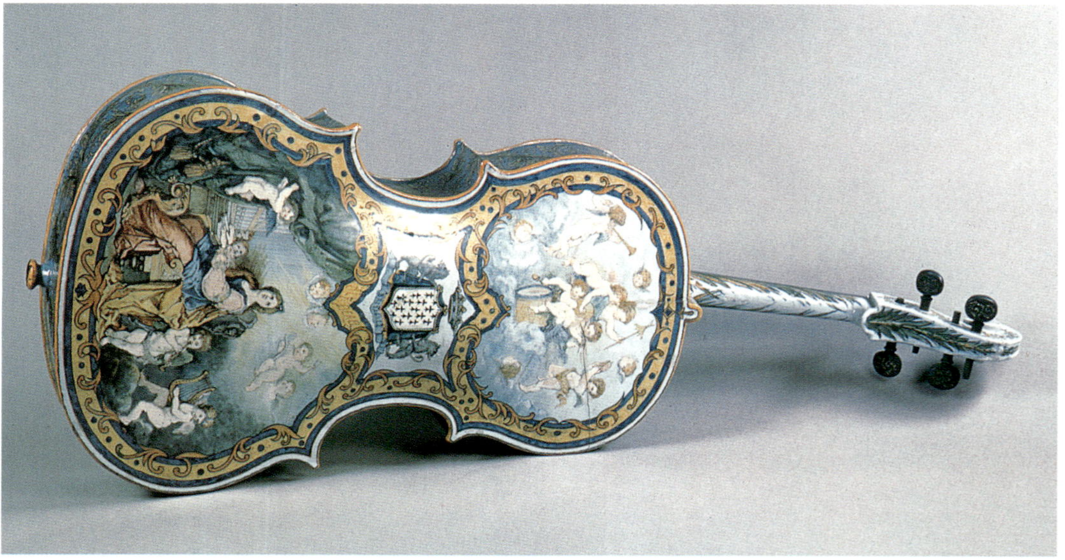

The reverse side of the faïence viola is a symphony in design and color also. *Courtesy of Manoir de Kérazan, Institut de France, Fondation Astor. Picture by J.Y. Husuet.*

From *Manoir de Kérazan* we headed back into Pont-l'Abbe, to see the Bigoudens Memorial by the Quimper artist and sculptor François-Victor Bazin, which stands opposite the quay in a grassy park. Then it was on to *Pointe de Penmarc'h* and the Eckmühl Lighthouse, which stands more than 200 feet high, yet seems encroached upon by the buildings and roadways; and then we stopped at the nearby church, *Notre Dame de la Joie*, about which Hélias also wrote.

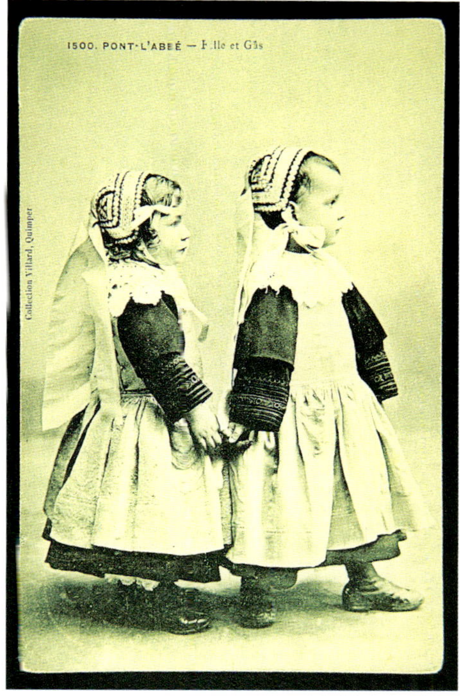

Two children from Pont-l'Abbé are dressed in their finest turn-of-the-20th century outfits. Look closely. The child on the left is a young girl and the one on the left is a young boy. In *Horse of Pride*, Hélias relates the experience of evolving from dresses to long pants about the age of six. *Authors' Collection.*

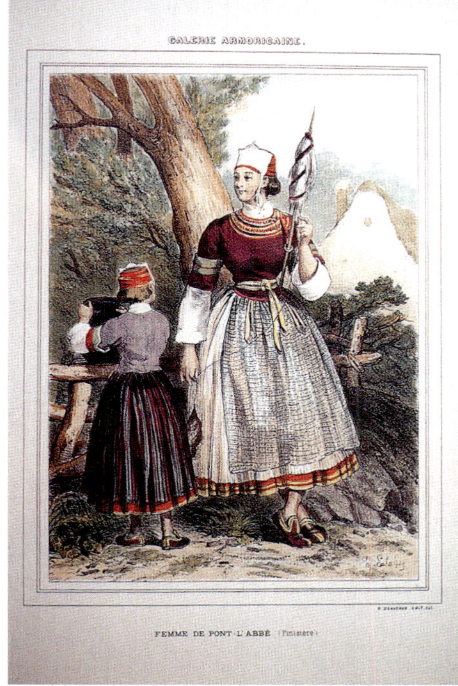

A *Galerie Armoricaine* print features the women's costume of Pont-l'Abbé in the mid-19th century. *Authors' Collection.*

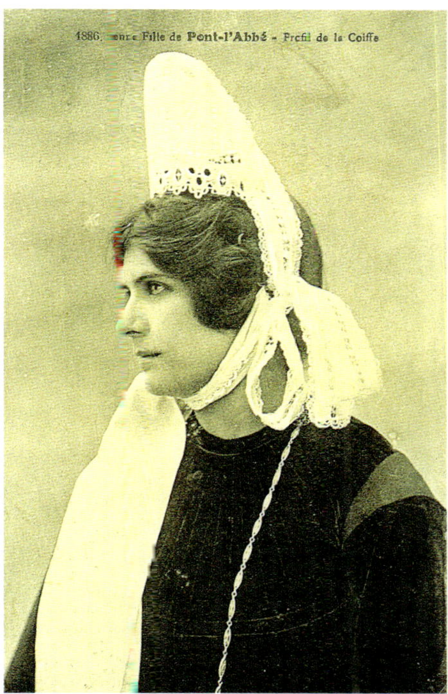

A young woman wears the Pont-l'Abbé *coiffe*, which was growing in height, as shown on this postcard from the 1920s. *Authors' Collection.*

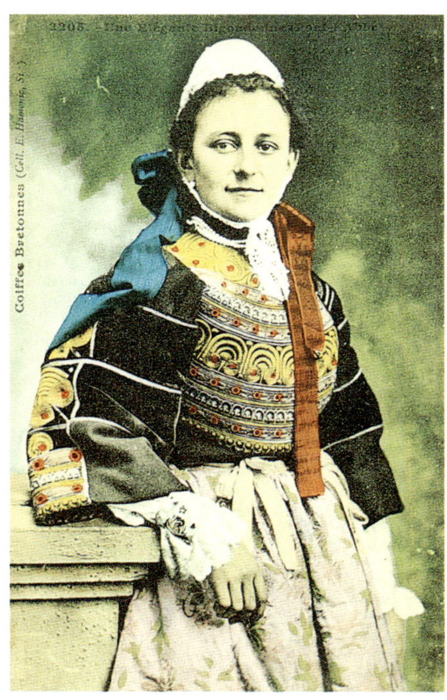

The costume on this woman from Pont-l'Abbé shows elaborate embroidery coming into fashion. This postcard dates from the beginning of the 20th century. *Authors' Collection.*

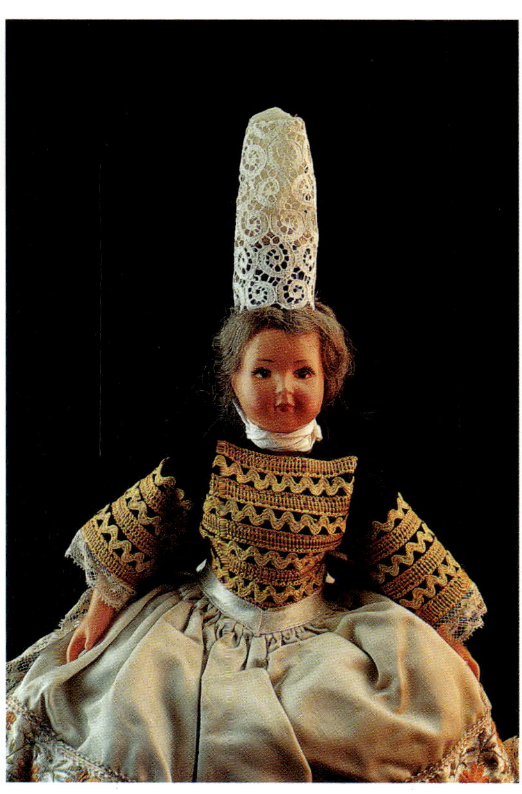

A doll sports the sugarloaf-size *coiffe* now worn by women of Pont-l'Abbé. *Authors' Collection.*

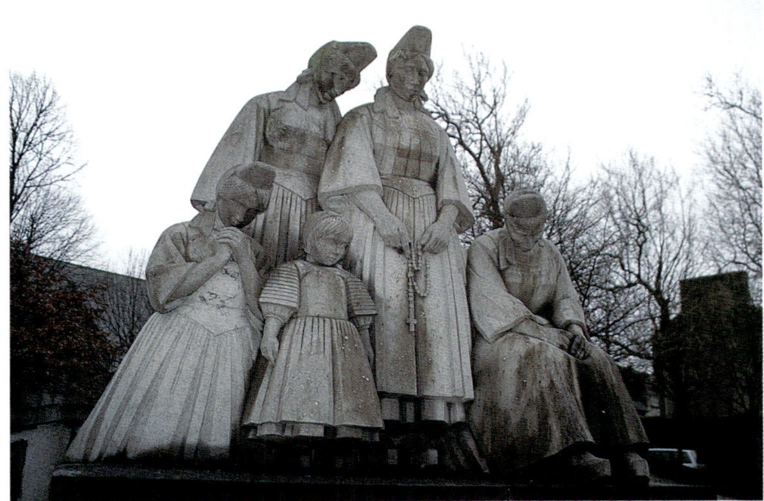

The memorial to Pont-l'Abbé's fallen of World War I is stark against a winter sky. *Monument aux Bigoudens* was designed by the HB artist François-Victor Bazin in 1929.

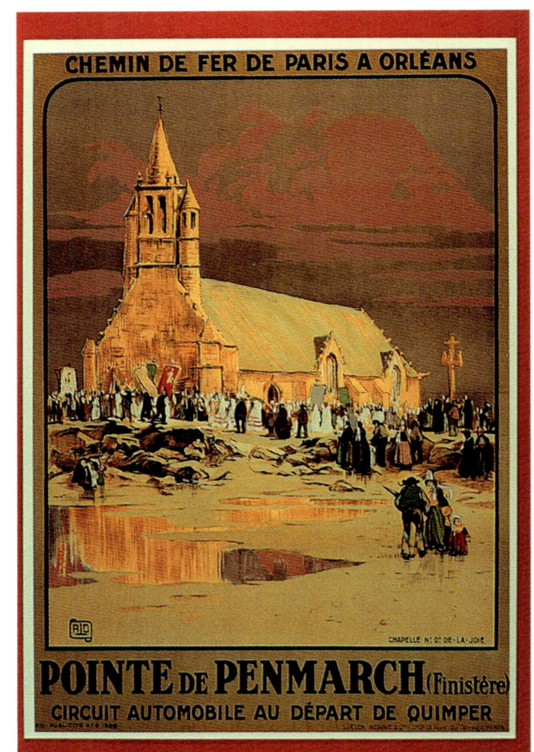

Right:
The church *Notre Dame de la Joie*, seen here on an early poster, was on our Hélias–inspired tour of the Penmarc'h peninsula. *Private Collection.*

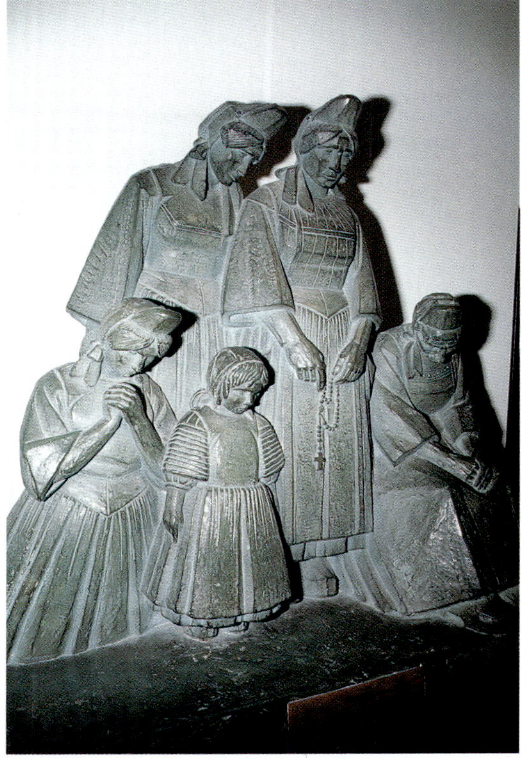

The original bronze statue of the group of mourners from Pont-l'Abbé stands in the *Musée de la Faïence* in Quimper. *Courtesy of Musée de la Faïence, Quimper.*

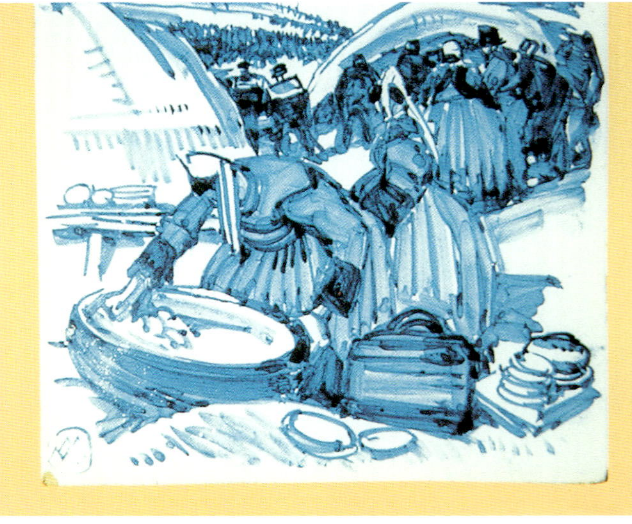

Mathurin Méheut designed this 8" by 8" *camaïeu bleu* tile for Henriot, depicting a scene after a *Pardon* at *Notre Dame de la Joie. Courtesy of Thierry & Lannon, Douarnenez & Brest.*

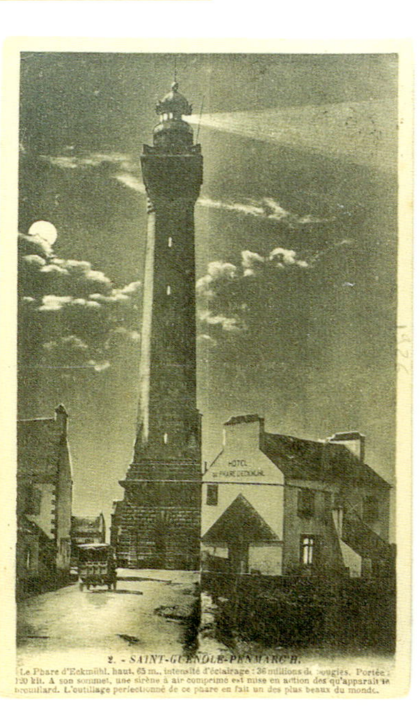

A postcard from the 1920s shows the famous Eckmühl lighthouse towering over the buildings in Penmarc'h. *Authors' Collection.*

Pointe de la Torche

We have a Quimper restaurateur to thank for leading us to our favorite sight along the western coast of Brittany. This was several years before we were introduced to Hélias. We had been telling Laurant, the owner of a mildly Americanized eatery in Quimper, about our excitement upon seeing *Pointe du Raz*. He suggested we go south of Quimper to a place called *Pointe de la Torche*. When we approached the site, we were not impressed. It looked very similar to the beach in Delaware about two hours from our home. The sand dunes' height and protective fencing were unremarkably similar. But when we crested the dune we were dumbstruck by the sight.

It was a beautiful, sunny January day with little wind. The roar of the surf was deafening, and the waves crashed all about the point where a tall, slender rock stood against the wind. A lone brave soul sat far out near the breakers' spray, dwarfed by the adjacent rocks. Hélias talks about *La Torche* in a gale, when rolling breakers knew no bounds, but this calm day was enough to convince us that we were seeing the most impressive sight on the Breton coast. This view of *La Torche* helped us first envision our logo, *the triskele*, as the never-ending waves breaking on the shores of Brittany.

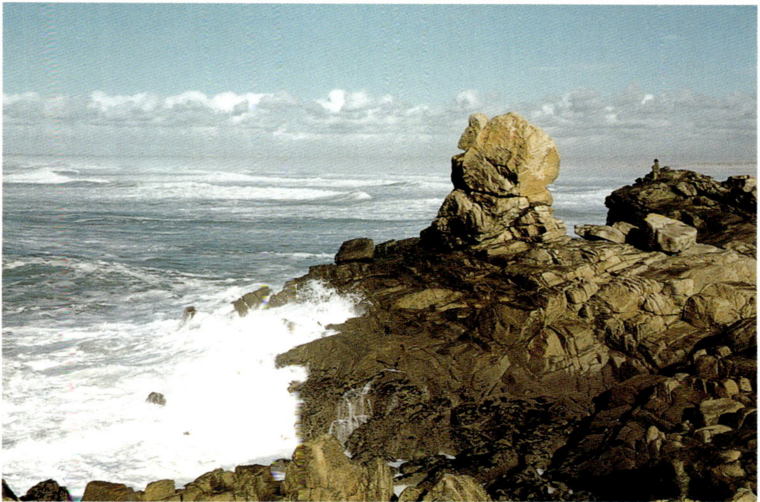

We never cease to be impressed by the power of the ocean and wind on the coast of Brittany. *Pointe de la Torche* still overwhelms us.

Penhors and Plozévet

The next visit on our Helias-inspired tour was Plozévet, stopping first at the chapel at Penhors. As a boy, Hélias attended the *Pardon of Notre Dame de Penhors*, held the first Sunday in September. *Pardons* are religious festivals held in one church, but attended by many parishes. *Pardons* usually commemorate a special saint's day or event. Secular festivities are held in conjunction with the religious rites and more than once were frowned upon by the local priests.

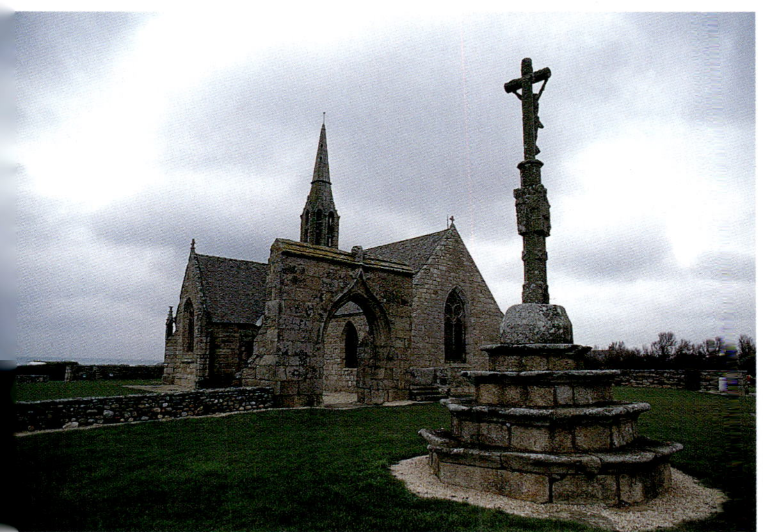

Next on our Hélias list was Penhors and the church on the beachfront, *Notre Dame de Penhors*.

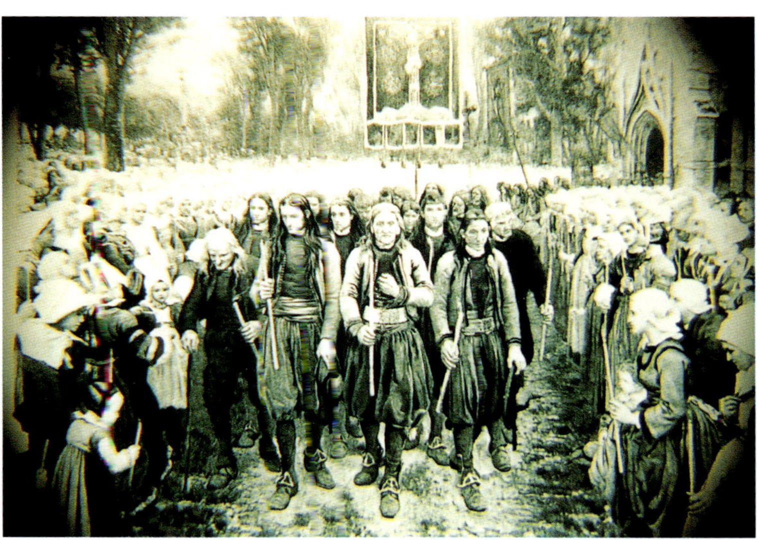

Hélias attended a *pardon* as a boy at *Notre Dame de Penhors*. *Pardons* are Breton religious events, usually followed by a festival of food and entertainment. This print by Jules Breton is entitled *A Grand Pardon in Brittany. Authors' Collection.*

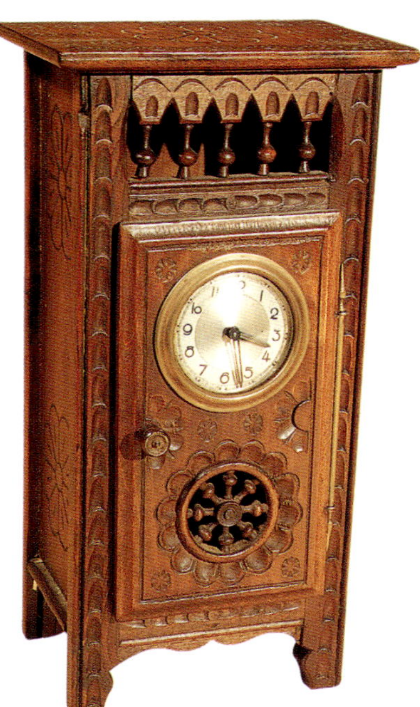

It was from the beach in front of Notre Dame de Penhors that Hélias claimed he could see all the way to *Pointe de Penmarc'h*, and all the sights in between. Since it was another overcast day for us, we took his word for the view, but we knew it was there. We have been enchanted for years by the surging ocean at *Pointe de la Torche*. It was enlightening, and evoked a sense of kinship when we read in *Horse of Pride* that Hélias could hear the wind sing through the *La Torche* rock from far inland as a child in his *lit clos* at night. *(Hélias, Horse of Pride, pp. 124 and 173.)*

Plozévet was on our must-see list. The children's toy furniture from the town is highly collectible, especially in forms such as this tall case clock. *Authors' Collection.*

There are two Quillivic statues in Plozévet. One stands in the churchyard as a memorial to Plozévet's fallen of World War I. The old man has his hand over his heart, next to the *Croix de Guerre*. He lost four sons and two sons-in-law in the war. This statue has been rendered in a faïence edition.

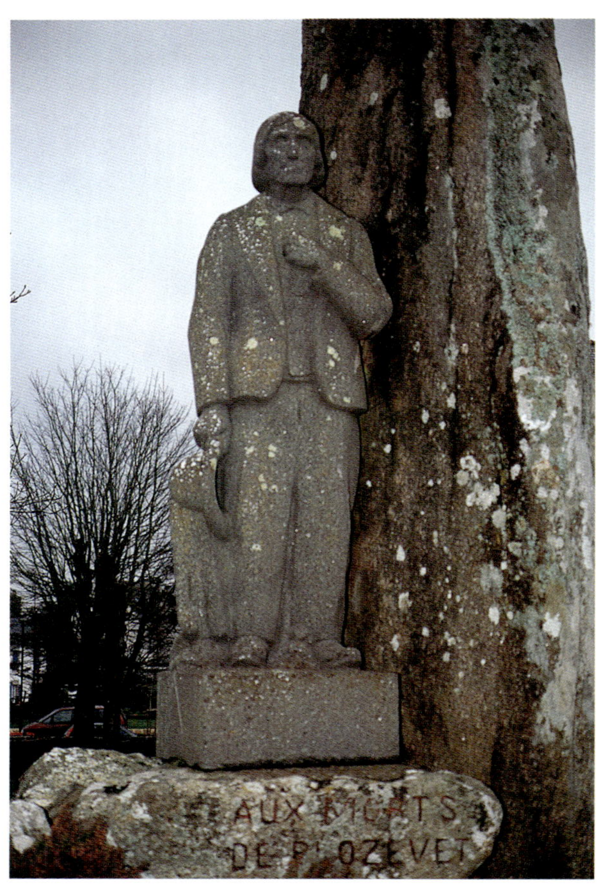

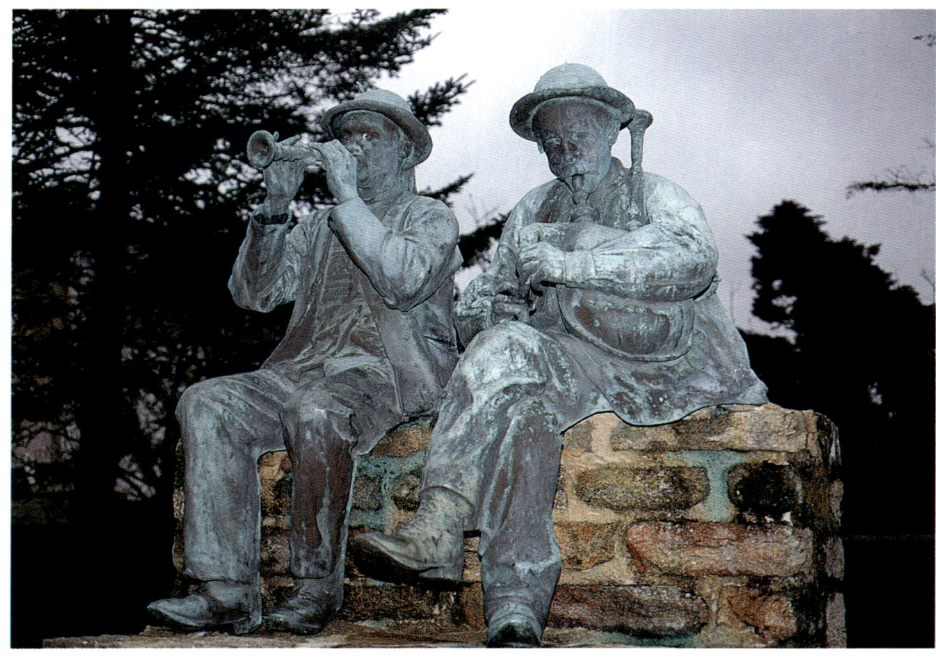

But it was this rendition of the Breton musical duo of *biniou* and *bombarde* that we came to see. Hélias attended the statue's unveiling in 1937. Many who attended did not realize they were bidding farewell to an era. The instruments would fall out of favor, until Celtic-Breton revivalists brought back the tradition of the *sonneurs*.

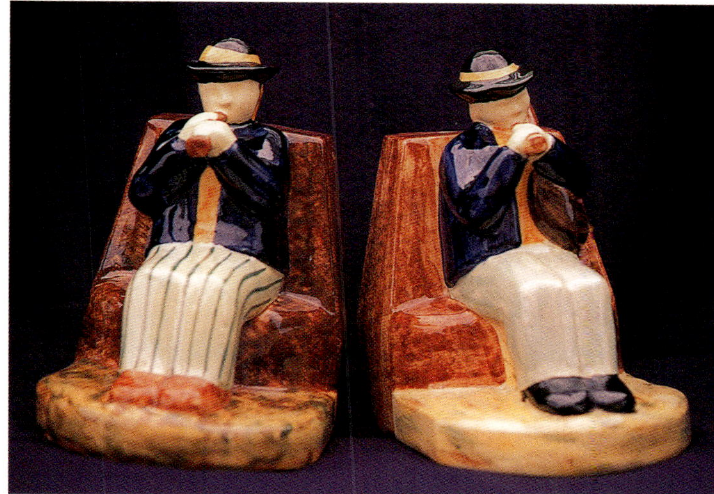

Sonneurs play their instruments in ceramic bookends designed by Jorg Robin. These are signed HB Quimper, Brion, showing that the mold was sold to the HB faïencerie by Robin. *Authors' Collection.*

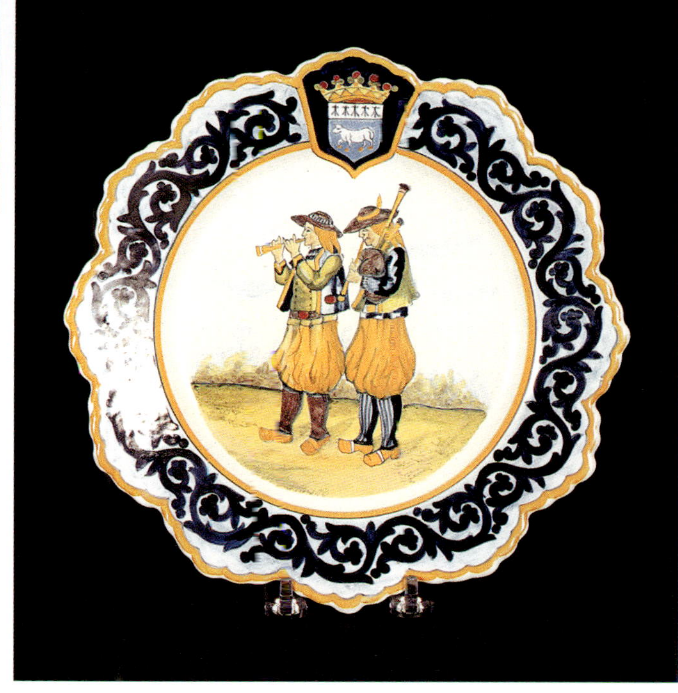

Sonneurs continue to play their Breton tunes or faïence. Signed Henriot Quimper #165, this 10" diameter plate features the duo encircled by a *décor riche* scrolling foliage border, with the armorial of the city of Quimper at the top. *Courtesy of Patricia Zimmerman.*

Plozévet was the home of Hélias' father, who moved southwest to his wife's home in Plouldreuzic where Hélias grew-up. Our goal in Plozévet was to see the famous sculpture, *Les Sonneurs,* by Quimper artist René Quillivic, which Hélias wrote about in such poignant terms. We found the statue across from the 12th century church and adjacent to the tourist bureau. Hélias recalls the day in August 1937 when the statue was unveiled, because, despite a crowd of 1,500 to honor the musicians who contributed to the customs held dear by many, the future was already upon them. The *biniou* and *bombarde* were being replaced by the accordion and clarinet. *(Hélias, p. 315.)*

A Word to Hélias

In the beginning we raced across the countryside on our *Quest for Quimper.* We didn't understand your words about earlier travelers, who were wise enough to learn from their journey, unlike the masses on the move today. We were like so many *Kodakeurs* bustling about on a quest for a piece of Brittany to take home. Perhaps your spirit will be patient with some of us who came to acquire the past, but who did slow down to look more intently at the country, the people, and the customs of this land. We gradually absorbed enough of her offerings to discover some of the mysteries and truths inherent in her hills, villages, forests, shores, cities, megaliths, songs, sun, wind, rain, colors, mountaintops, *triskeles,* churches and parish closes, laughter, and faïence.

Pierre Toulhoat designed this bas-relief faïence plaque featuring Breton musicians while he was with the *Keraluc* faïencerie. *Courtesy of Musée Départemental Breton, Quimper.*

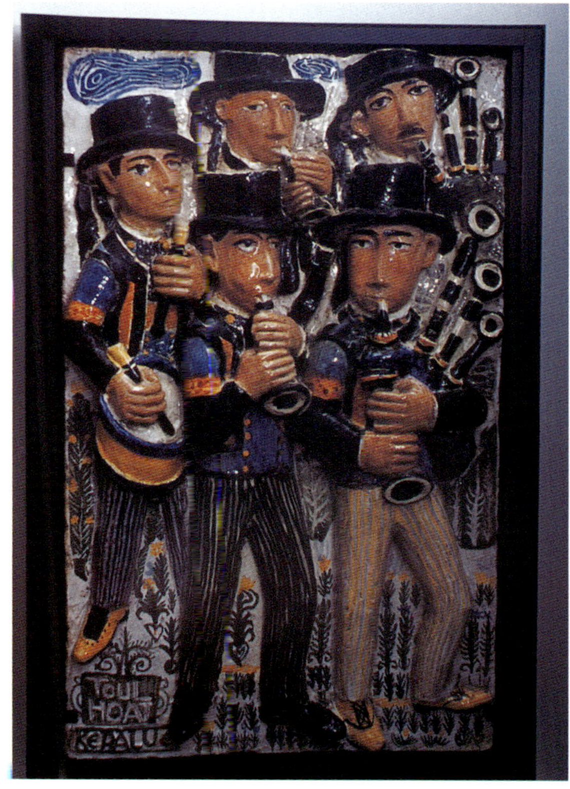

Internet auctions are a mixed blessing for lovers of Quimper poterie and for the dealers who have for so many years journeyed to France, searching for excellent examples to bring back for their buyer-collectors. When we first found Quimper selling on the Internet in 1997, our searches would reveal about 20 items for sale each day. Now it's not unusual to find sites listing more than 300 Quimper items for sale. More recently, personal Web sites developed by Quimper merchants offer additional avenues to explore.

One positive benefit of this phenomenon has been that we've now seen more examples of Quimper poterie on Internet auctions and Web sites than we saw in more than a dozen years of searching in the United States and France, (except of course for the glorious and incomparable Quimper in the Breton museums and certain private collections.)

In the beginning, mid-to-low range Quimper brought active bidding, and selling prices were appropriate for U.S. market demands at the time. Then, there was a shift in selling habits. New sellers, with aggressive marketing ideas, began to offer from 10-to-40 Quimper items at one time. Some were located in France, even in Quimper itself, while others were located in England, Belgium, and Switzerland. Even with this influx, the prices initially held.

Meanwhile, several customers who used to haunt our gallery waiting for our latest Quimper finds now were buying internationally via the Internet. This was understandable, because of the quantity and range of examples offered. Add that to the excitement of auction buying and the prospect of purchasing from abroad, close to where the poterie originally was manufactured. It seems natural that many buyers have hopped on board the Internet express.

Buying Quimper on the Internet

Pat Zimmerman is something of a typical example of people discovering their own interest in Quimper, and how it evolves into a specialty and passion. Pat discovered Quimper poterie about 14 years ago at a Montgomery, Pennsylvania, antiques show, and was drawn to the Breton figures with bright, happy colors. Even though the pieces were wonderful, she thought the prices were too high and didn't buy anything. About a year later she found another Quimper dealer at a show in Lititz, Pennsylvania, and purchased a pair of the traditional *petit Breton* plates with *gros filets* of yellow and blue, many American's first introduction to Quimper poterie.

Pat continued attending antiques shows trying to find more Quimper, but rarely found someone specializing in the Breton poterie. In frustration she bought some new Quimper, but it only increased her thirst for older examples. Eventually she found an older Quimper *cachepot* (flower pot), a set of four *petit dejeuners* (breakfast cups and saucers), and a teapot. Then, about five years ago, she found us in Avondale, Pennsylvania, and acquired several choice pieces. And she began to do what collectors do as they explore their passion. She refined her selections and began to narrow her purchases to a specific area. Pat now collects mainly HR signed pieces from the Henriot faïencerie.

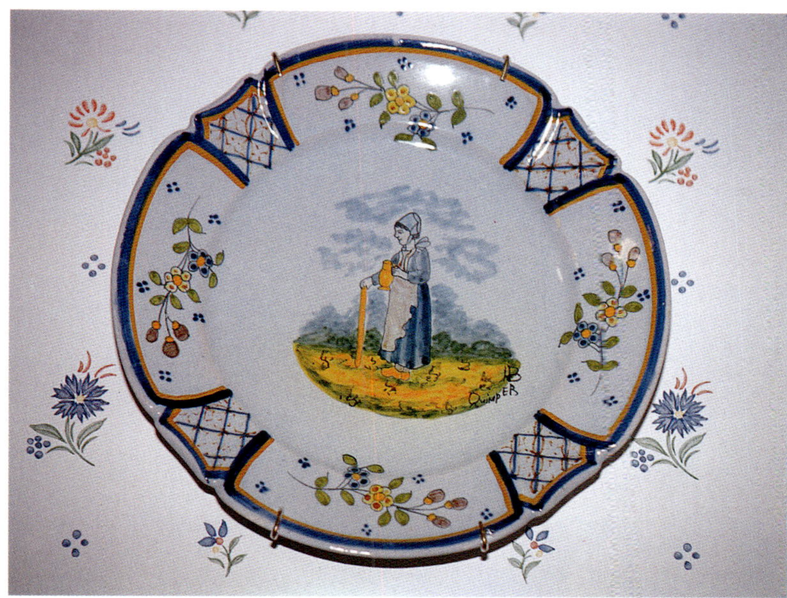

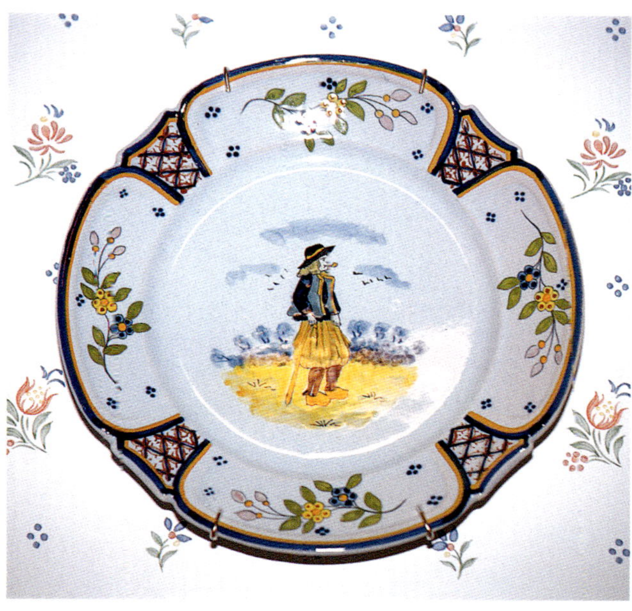

Pat Zimmerman has successfully purchased many Quimper items through Internet auctions. This HB 9.25" plate with *croisillon* and flower border with a blue four-dot design was purchased over the Internet. The sweet Bretonne carries an umbrella and a jug as she strolls in the countryside. Signed on the front and back HB Quimper, this example dates from the second quarter of the 20th century. *Courtesy of Patricia Zimmerman.*

The Bretonne's mate also came via the Internet. He has blonde hair, carries a walking cane and smokes a pipe as he strolls along in the country. Signed HB Quimper on front and back, this plate dates from the second quarter of the 20th century. Both plates hang in Pat's kitchen, which she covered with wallpaper containing Quimper motifs. *Courtesy of Patricia Zimmerman.*

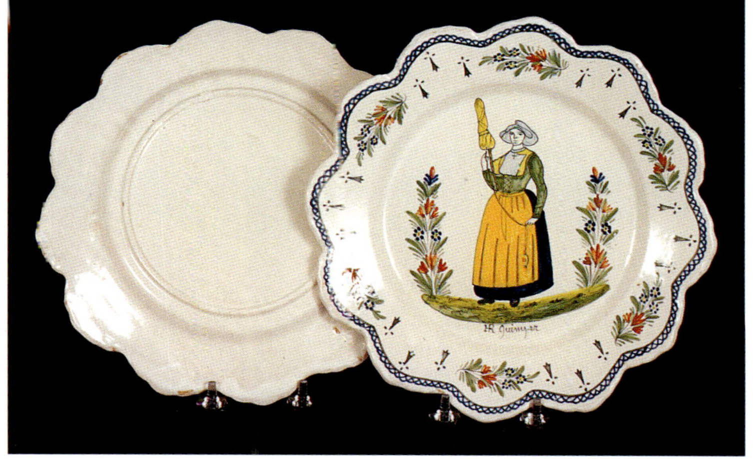

Pat began to narrow her focus to Quimper signed HR. This Henriot faïencerie plate has a *dentillé* rim. There is a dark-blue chain décor around the edge and the border contains alternating floral garlands and black ermine-tails. The Bretonne *filuse* holds a distaff used for spinning, and she wears the *Croix de Ste. Jeanette.* Signed HR Quimper on the front only, the plate measures 10" diameter. *Courtesy of Patricia Zimmerman.*

In September 1999, Pat discovered Internet auctions, which soon became her primary source of Quimper. Her initial reaction was like that of a kid in a candy store, she recalls, when she saw so many pieces at one time. She bought as much as she could. Then she looked beyond auctions, to individual sellers. Among these Web sites, she found an even larger world for those who cannot live without Quimper. Pat has decorated her home literally from top to bottom with wonderful examples of Quimper poterie, and she still searches for more. That's what it is like for those of us who are hit by the thunderbolt. We understand. *(Conversations and correspondence with Pat Zimmerman, October 2000-April 2001.)*

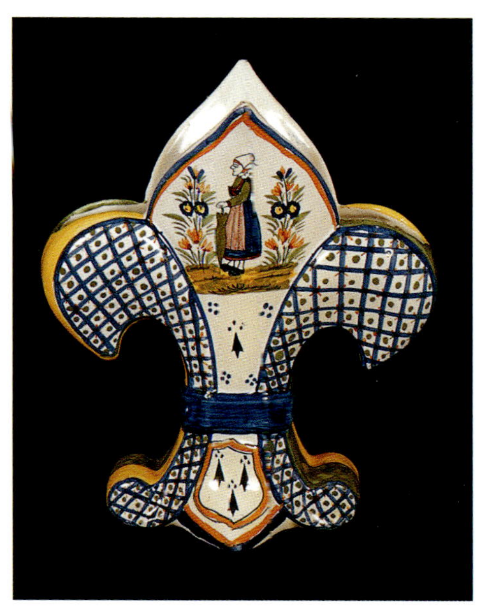

This 7.5" tall fleur-*de-lys* vase is signed Henriot Quimper France; it couldn't be passed by. It is from the second quarter of the 20th century and features a Bretonne holding her green umbrella. She is flanked by *à la touche* floral sprays. The remainder of the vase contains some wonderful design elements. *Croisillon*, black ermine-tails, and the blue four-dot configuration all add to the impact of this lovely piece. *Courtesy of Patricia Zimmerman.*

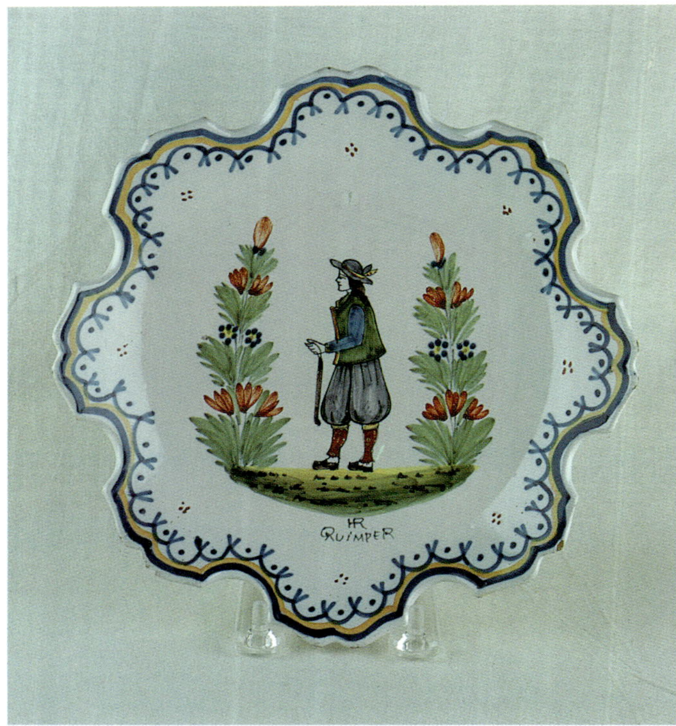

The Henriot faïencerie made this wonderful 8.5" diameter *coupe*, with *polylobé,* or deeply-scalloped edge. The colors are still bright after a century. There is a blue scallop-and-dot border, and a blue four-dot design spaced evenly around the rim. The Breton in *bragou-braz* is flanked by floral sprays. Signed HR Quimper. *Courtesy of Patricia Zimmerman.*

Buddy Styer's grandfather started him on his own quest for Quimper. He gave him this Henriot Quimper pitcher with a uniquely shaped body. Buddy began collecting Quimper pitchers first, then rapidly expanded his purchases to additional types of Quimper items. *Courtesy of A.W. Styer.*

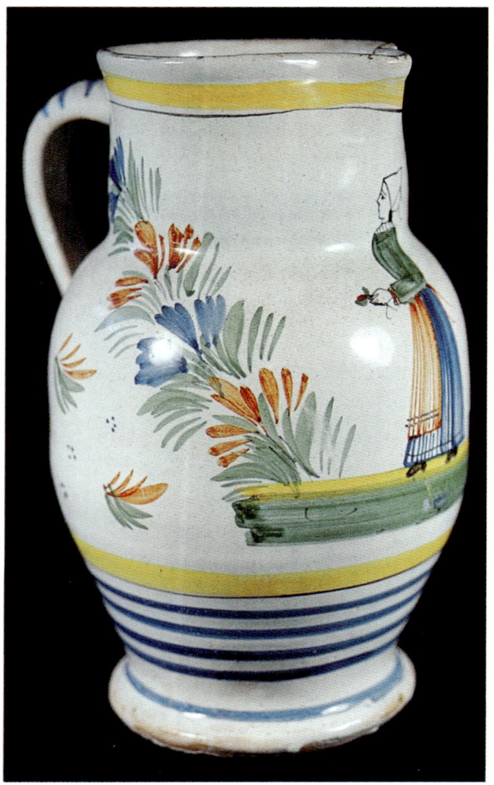

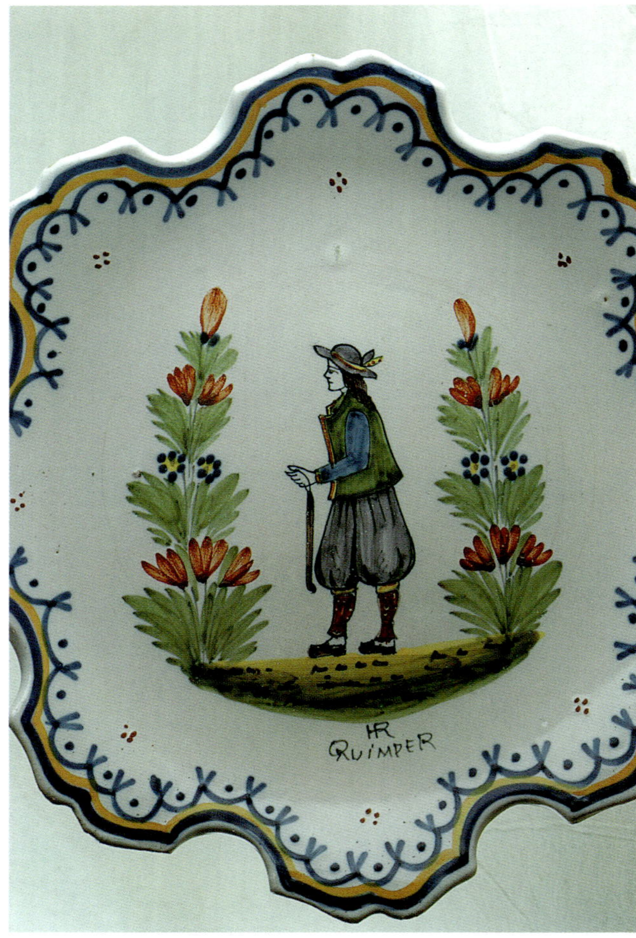

A glaze drip, consistent with early production, appears just above the Breton's head. This only makes the piece more endearing. The *coupe* dates from the first decade of the 20th century. *Courtesy of Patricia Zimmerman.*

At the same time, the Internet auctions afforded us the opportunity to sell Quimper to people across the United States and in England, to people who otherwise would not find our antiques gallery in Avondale, Pennsylvania. And some of those people, upon finding us on the Internet, began to visit us, and became gallery customers.

Grandfather's Gift Starts a Collection

A.W. Styer's story is typical of many who become collectors after a chance encounter with their soon-to-be addiction. Known as Buddy to his friends, this avid collector once planned to become a dentist while growing up in southeastern Pennsylvania, but discovered his real love was helping with his grandfather's auctioneering business. After graduating from college, he went to work full-time for his grandfather, learning on the job the photography skills required for the auction sales catalogues. He opened his own photography studio more than 23 years ago and has served the public since.

Buddy's interest in Quimper poterie was awakened when his grandfather gave him a Quimper pitcher, which still holds a place in his heart, as well as a prominent place in the kitchen of his lovingly restored Victorian home. The pitcher's unusual form fascinated him. Since then, he has sought out and bought about 90 more Quimper pitchers. But not one has the same shape or the sentiment as the gift from his grandfather.

At first Buddy searched local markets, including the ones at Adamstown, Pennsylvania, but the real breakthrough came for him when Quimper began appearing on Internet auctions in the late 1990s. For Buddy – and for many other people – it was the first time much so Quimper was available in one place, and the variety and quantity were amazing. He purchased numerous pieces from the United States, England, Switzerland, and France. He also found Quimper dealers through the Internet who were within reasonable driving distance of his home, including us at Antiques & Images, and as a result many more items were added to his collection.

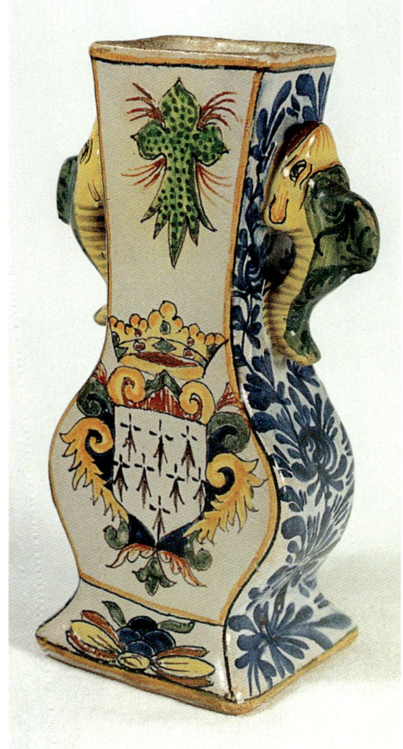

The reverse side is also charming. The armorial of Brittany, topped with a crown, predominates with a spotted-green ermine-tail above. The sides have a *décor riche* treatment. *Courtesy of A.W. Styer.*

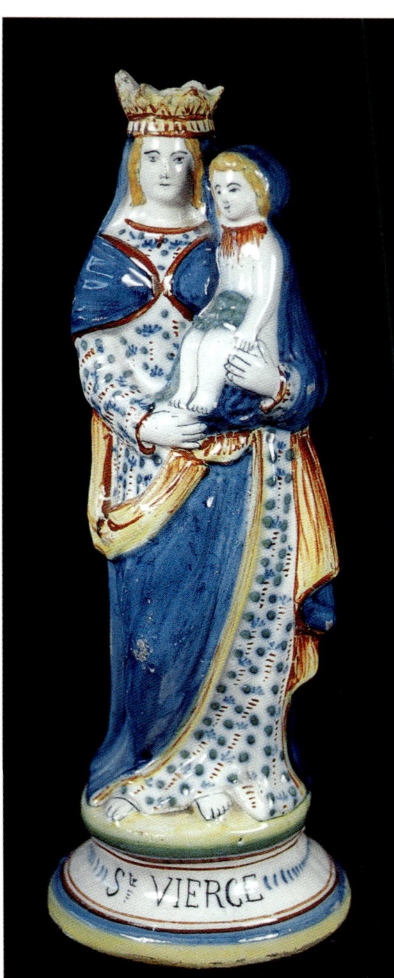

A treasured purchase through an Internet auction is this 10.5" tall *Ste. Vierge* from the Henriot faïencerie. Signed HR Quimper, the statue dates from the first quarter of the 20th century. *Courtesy of A.W. Styer.*

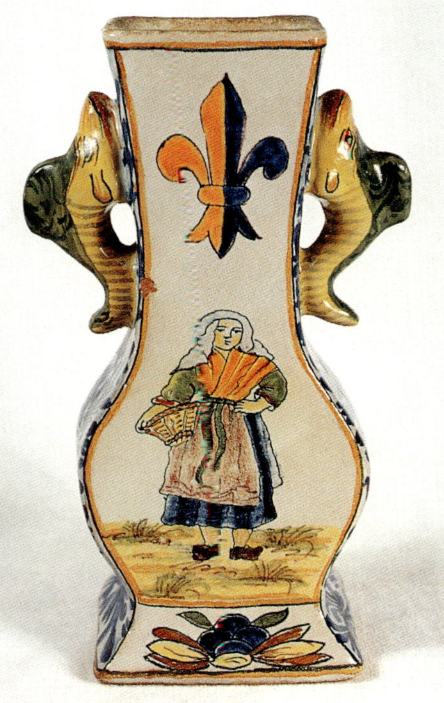

Buddy also found this Malicorne faïencerie vase on the Internet. It stands 5.5" tall, features a Bretonne, a two-toned *fleur-de-lys*, and sports whimsical fish handles. It is signed PBx and dates from the last quarter of 19th century. *Courtesy of A.W. Styer.*

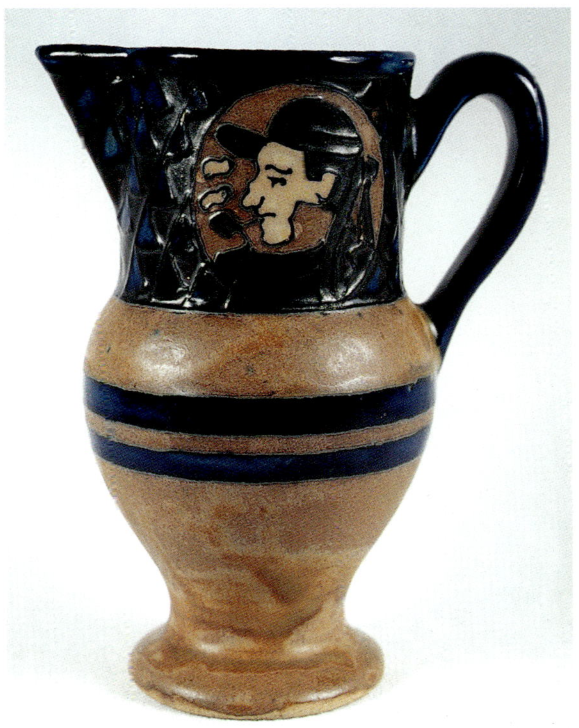

This Odetta pitcher was purchased in Avondale, Pennsylvania, after Buddy found our gallery via the Internet. The 6" tall pitcher is signed HB Quimper Odetta #369-1084, and is found in the Odetta catalogue under #1084. *Courtesy of A.W. Styer.*

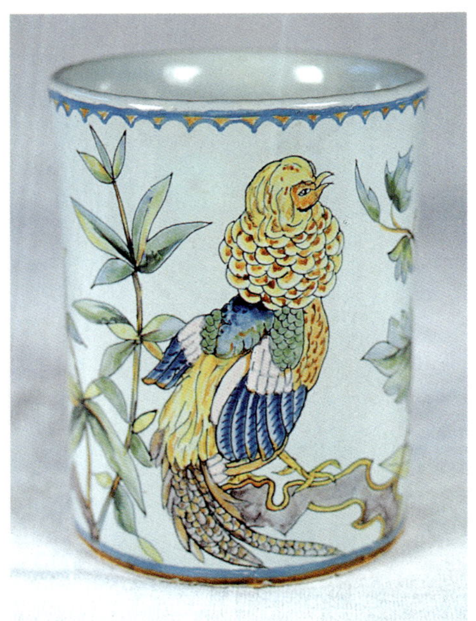

A cider mug in a gorgeous botanical motif was found by chance. Is this Porquier-Beau? It had the pale grayish blue background and a stellar bird sitting on a branch, surrounded by foliage. *Courtesy of A.W. Styer.*

One story Buddy loves to tell is about a very special prize acquisition. While his 10-year-old daughter, Claire, is his frequent partner on treasure hunts, it was 11-year-old Charlotte who accompanied him on this particular weekend morning. They stopped by a yard sale near their home, where a table held about a dozen ceramic mugs with advertising motifs. Among the items was a tall grayish-blue mug with a bird and floral branch motif. The price was written on the bottom in blue magic marker, blending with what appeared to be a maker's signature. As he wiped a bit of the marker price aside, an intersecting PB appeared.

He let out an *Oh no* under his breath, which drew his daughter's attention. Briefly explaining to her that all was fine, and with trembling hands, he asked the seller for a better price, which he got. They went home with a fantastic Porquier Beau cider mug for under ten dollars! This is the kind of experience that keeps Quimper poterie collectors devoted to their search. *(Conversations and correspondence with A.W. Styer, October 2000-April 2001.)*

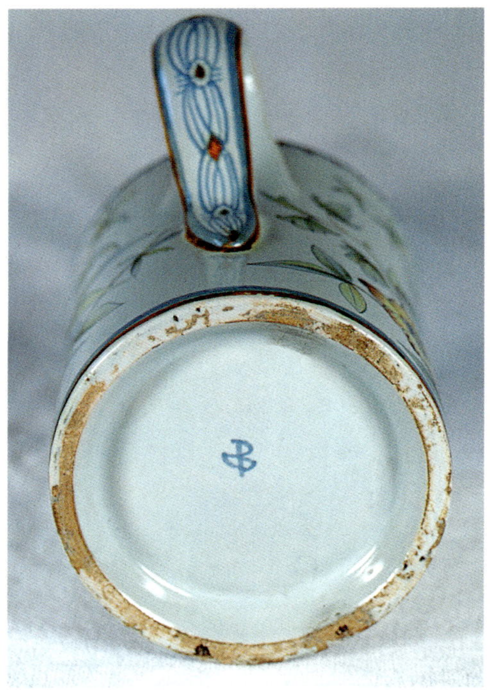

When Buddy removed the blue magic marker price, he found the Porquier-Beau signature of PB. Finding the mug at a roadside sale was exhilarating! *Courtesy of A.W. Styer.*

❧ Issues on Internet Auctions

Over the late 1990s, more and more Quimper appeared on Internet auctions and Web sites, as already active sellers increased their offerings and greater numbers of people worldwide began to participate in the Internet auctions. With this increased availability of Quimper selections, especially in the low-to-mid price range, the market became over-saturated and many prices for these items dropped sharply. Certain examples once considered rare to American customers now were easily obtained, even if it meant the buyer had to pay shipping and insurance, and sometimes wait weeks for delivery. Then hard-to-find higher dollar Quimper began appearing, and the buyers' attention turned to them. At the same time many lower-to-mid priced gems had no bids at all. Was Quimper becoming too easy to find?

There are other issues in this revolution of buying and selling. One factor that Quimper collectors must become aware of is the proliferation of misinformation about Quimper poterie, whether deliberate or unintentional. This has resulted in confusion for many buyers, who trust sellers and assume the sellers always know the facts. It bothers us when sellers describe items with little care for accuracy, such as the age, artist, maker attribution, and even condition. As buyers, we have experienced all of these manifestations. At times we found ourselves in the position of playing the *Kwimper Kops* in policing the Internet, as Millie Mali kidded us.

Another tactic is *shill bidding*, which crops up in online auctions. Shill bidding occurs when the merchandise owner and/or friends stimulate interest in a specific item by bidding on it. We have encountered several sellers who have used this ploy, whether it is for Quimper, folk art, books, paintings, toys, or quilts, to name only a few possibilities. This behavior occurs at live auctions too, where consignors cover their merchandise costs by bidding on the item to achieve the price they want. Reputable auctioneers will not tolerate this, but it still can occur through friends, relatives, and business partners of the consignors. Because of the anonymity offered by the Internet, this behavior is less easily observed and can be a haven for those who wish to use this selling technique. In fact in 2001, one Internet auction purchased and implemented anti-shill bidding software to ferret out those stooping to this practice. *(Industry Standard, p. 55-57.)*

We suppose whenever there is money to be made, some people will find ways to misuse the situation to their advantage. We suggest these tips about purchasing Quimper on the Internet auctions:

• Know your seller. Does he/she have an established record and respond forthrightly to your questions?

• Learn the marks of the various Quimper faïenceries and request to see the entire mark on the screen.

• Beware of intentionally blurred images that may camouflage size or defects not mentioned in descriptions.

• Read the descriptions thoroughly. The true condition, age, or maker may be hidden in the last sentence.

• Question references to anonymous experts or books used to authenticate item descriptions.

• Remember, geographic location does not make the seller an expert, nor do verbose descriptions.

• Resist the urge to win it all! Internet auctions are still auctions; set your limit and stick to it.

We are hopeful that both buyers new to Quimper and more experienced buyers will become more adept at selecting from Internet auctions offerings, and will be pleased with their purchases. All collectors grow, change, and refine their tastes, and it is the same with collecting Quimper. The addition of Internet auctions has given all of us another avenue to educate ourselves about what makes this faïence so unique.

❀ Quimper Club International

The Quimper Club International is a product of the Internet and the hearts and minds of two Californians, Lucy Williams and Katie Wiggins. These two collectors wanted a central resource for information, research, and communication about their favorite faïence. In early 1999, Lucy and Katie began placing a notice about forming a club or an Internet Web site devoted to Quimper poterie. Feedback generated by that posting, coupled with advice from Millicent Mali and Gary Fritzhand, quickly brought about the Quimper Club International. The Club published its first newsletter in July 1999. The first annual meeting was held in September 1999 in Santa Monica, California. The second annual meeting followed in September 2000 in Washington, D.C., and the third one was planned for Quimper itself, in October 2001.

Club president Lucy Williams believes that while members join for the Quimper Club International's yearly meetings and newsletters, the relationships members have developed over the Internet, through the mail, over the phone, and even in person, become the real attraction. There is an immediate bond when you find others who share your dedication and fascination with this wonderful faïence. But perhaps more significant are the friendships that naturally evolve into a feeling of family, enduring side-by-side with the love of Quimper poterie. *(Correspondence and conversations with Lucy Williams, September 2000-April 2001.)*

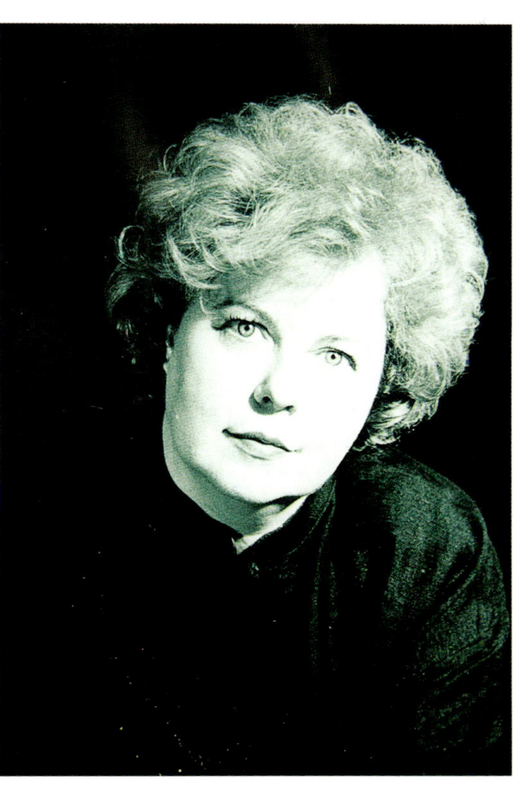

Lucy Williams is the co-founder of the Quimper Club International and served as Club president for three years. The QClub's goals are to increase knowledge and promote research about Quimper faïence. *Courtesy of Lucy Williams.*

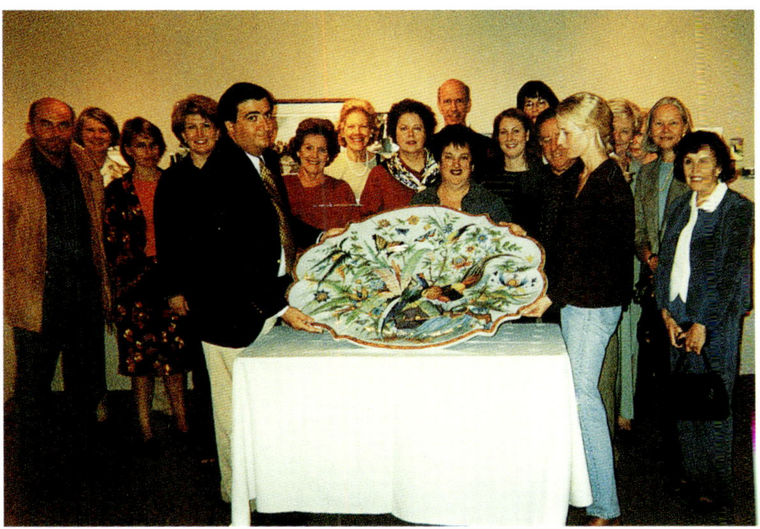

The Quimper Club International held its second annual meeting in Washington, D.C. One activity was a visit to the Woodrow Wilson House to view the famous platter by Alfred Beau. It was given to President Wilson when he attended the Paris Peace Talks after the First World War. *Courtesy of Lucy Williams.*

Over the past dozen years, we have kept a detailed file of the Quimper poterie we have owned, some of it only briefly, and we catalogued examples we have observed in the marketplace and in private collections. The examples we are sharing with you do not by any means represent a complete and thorough list of all possibilities, but a sample of the numerous forms and styles of Quimper. We want to thank the many collectors and customers, as well as the members of the Quimper Club International, for sharing a portion of their collections, which are included in this chapter.

Printed price guides once set the standard in Quimper pricing, prior to the rapid growth of the Internet. But these price guides often were outdated before they reached the collector. Now, up-to-date pricing information is only a mouse-click away, thanks to online auctions and personal Web sites. It must be remembered however, that this instant information· does not reflect trends in the market, but instead offers only a microscopic, point-in-time glimpse. Many of our examples will reflect the serendipitous nature of Internet prices.

All prices are based on our observations over a 12-year period, including our experience in buying and selling Quimper, reports of marketplace pricing, and results of French, American, and Internet auctions. Buyer premiums, which range from 10-to-15 percent, and shipping, handling, and insurance are not included. Amounts are rounded to the nearest dollar. In most cases, we list high and low prices for items, demonstrating either the staying power or fluctuations for certain forms and styles.

As always, condition, personal taste, availability, and geographic location are factors affecting prices for individual pieces. Keep in mind that French buyers may pay more for certain items than U.S. buyers, and vice-versa, depending on what is valued by each sector. In our opinion, beginning in 1999 the proliferation of Quimper on the Internet created a glut in the market. The effect has lowered prices for certain low-to-middle range items, and raised prices, perhaps temporarily, for other examples. Quimper is no longer difficult to find!

❧ A is for...

Advertising pieces (*les objets publicitaires*) have been made by the Quimper faïenceries since the 1870s.

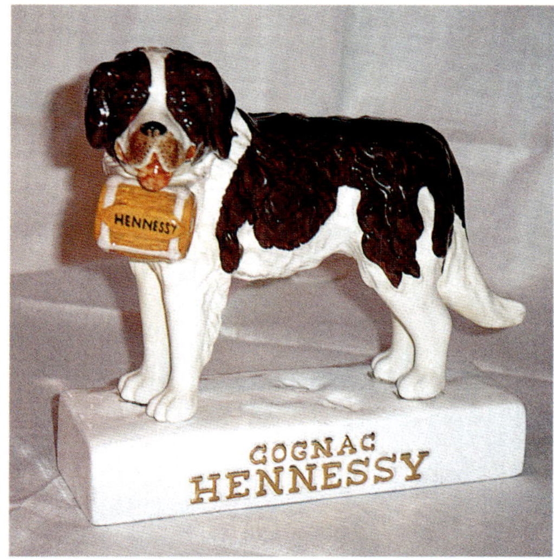

A St. Bernard dog from the HB firm advertises Hennessy Cognac. Signed HB Quimper, France, the piece stands 10.25” tall. One was offered through a French auction in 1999 for $350-$450. Price range: $450-$550. *Courtesy of Lucy Williams.*

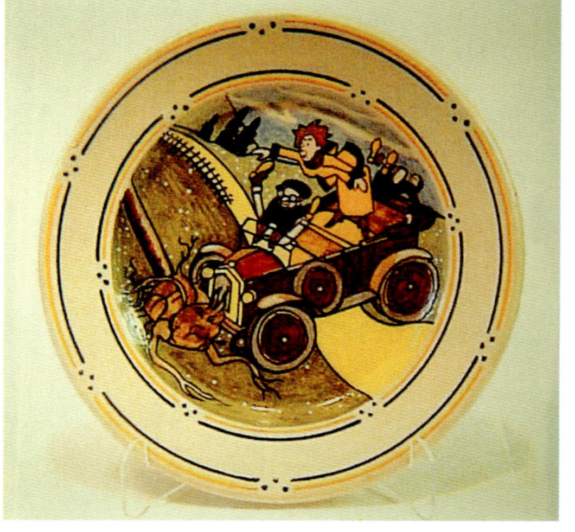

The Henriot faïencerie made this 9.5” diameter advertising plate for the Michelin Tire Co. in 1927. Signed Henriot Quimper, E. Guyard. Price range: $500-$750. *Courtesy of Lucy Williams.*

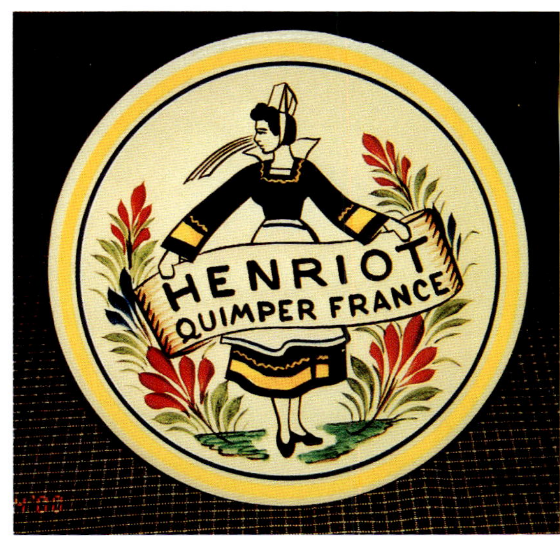

An Henriot 7.5" diameter faïence advertising sign has no signature on the back. This particular style is not seen often in the United States. One like it sold on an Internet auction in 2000 for $400. Signs like this were used in shops as product advertisement for the faïenceries. Date is mid-20th century. Price range: $250-$350. *Courtesy of Jay Luttrell.*

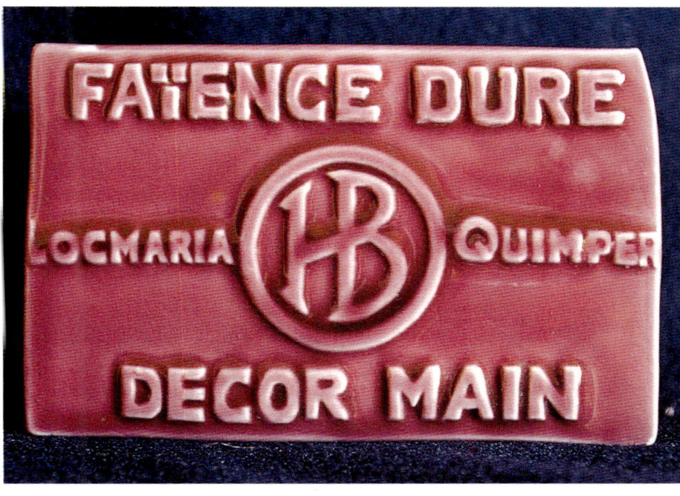

HB, Henriot, HB *Faïence Dure* and HB/Henriot advertising sign prices have fluctuated in the past decade. In the 1990s, they brought up to $300. After 2000, prices fell by 50 percent and more in many instances. This c. 1950 HB *Faïence Dure* sign sold for $150 in 1999. Price range: $125-$225. *Private Collection.*

Ajonc is Breton gorse and grows wild throughout Brittany. In the first decade or so of the 20th century, Perrig Rocuet designed the *l'ajonc* and *bruyère* décor accents for the Henriot faïencerie. *(Mali, Old Quimper Review, March 1991.)* The décor became very popular and appears often on Quimper pieces.

Ajonc and bruyère, Breton gorse and heather, are a popular combination on Quimper products. Here they grace the reverse side of a 10" tall vase in décor *broderie*. *Courtesy of Silvia and Gary Fritzhand.*

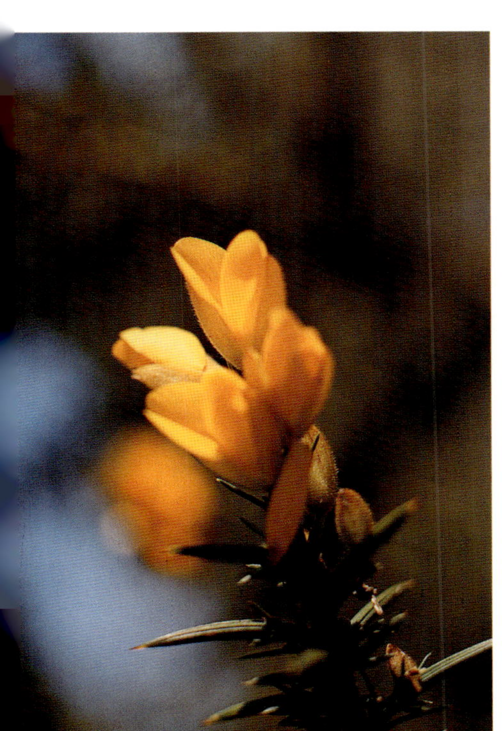

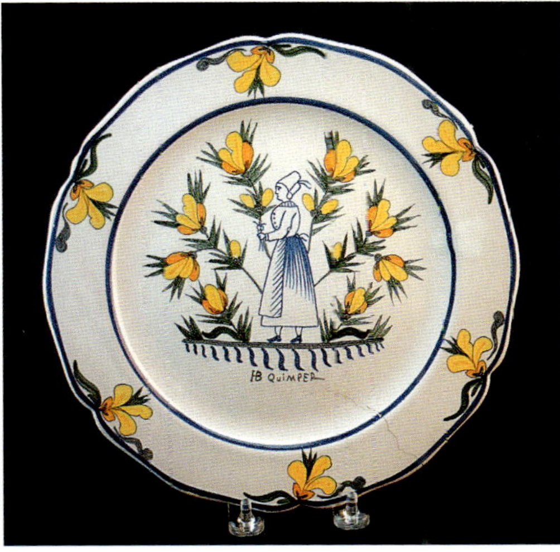

Ajonc is the primary accent décor on this *petite Bretonne* plate, which may have been an experimental model. Signed HB Quimper, it is 9.5" diameter. Price range: $275-$325. *Courtesy of Carter Yeatman.*

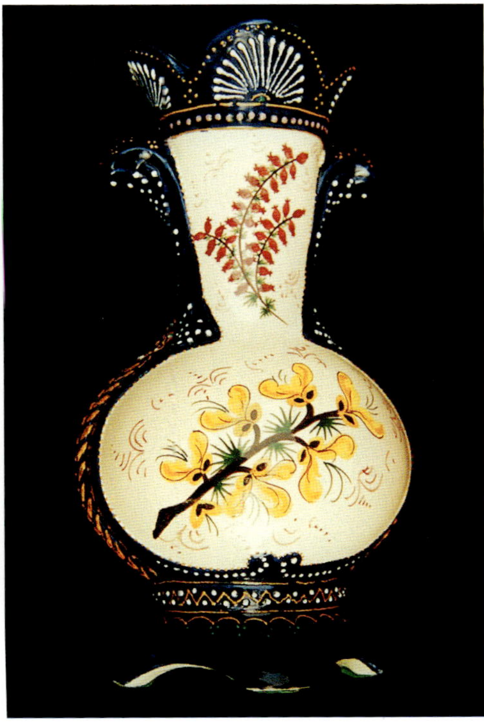

Left:
L'ajonc grows wild along Breton roadways and glows golden in the sun.

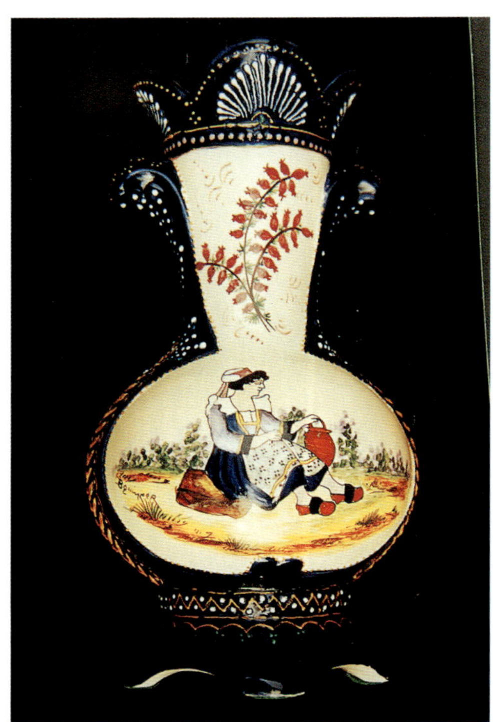

Signed HB Quimper, the front of the vase reveals a Bretonne sitting in the countryside on a rock. Above her is spray of *bruyère*. *Courtesy of Silvia and Gary Fritzhand*

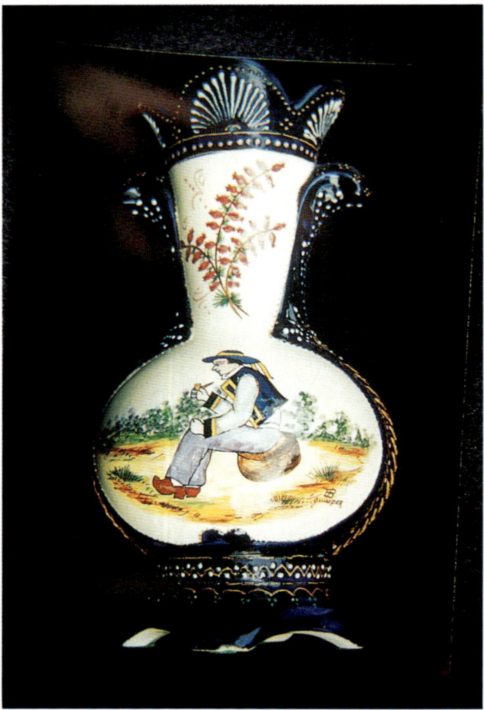

Her Breton mate also sits in the countryside, perched on a rock while smoking his pipe. Both vases are HB Quimper from the second quarter of the 20th century. A matched pair commands a higher price than if sold separately. Price range: $1,400-$1,800. *Courtesy of Silvia and Gary Fritzhand.*

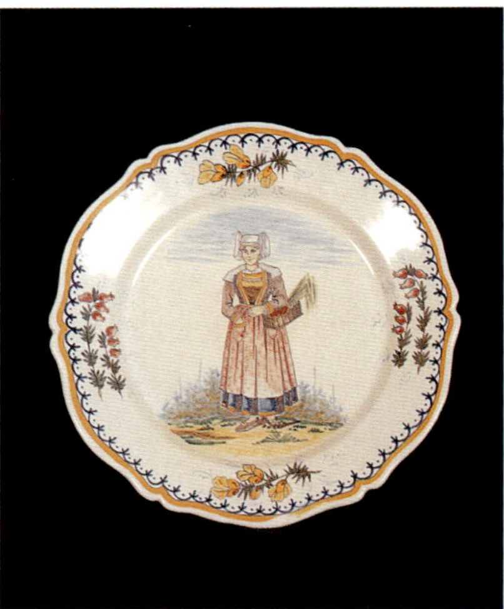

Ajonc and *bruyère* accents alternate on the rim of this Henriot 9.5" plate, which dates from the second quarter of the 20th century. Prices for this style have jumped around in the past several years. In 1999, the highest price for a similar style plate was about $400 and the lowest was $290 through an Internet auction. A similar pair from Henriot brought $700 through a French auction in 2000. Price range: $300-$325 per plate. *Courtesy of Patricia Zimmerman.*

Aquarelle is an original watercolor model used in faïencerie workshops as a guide when painting items and for catalogue advertisements.

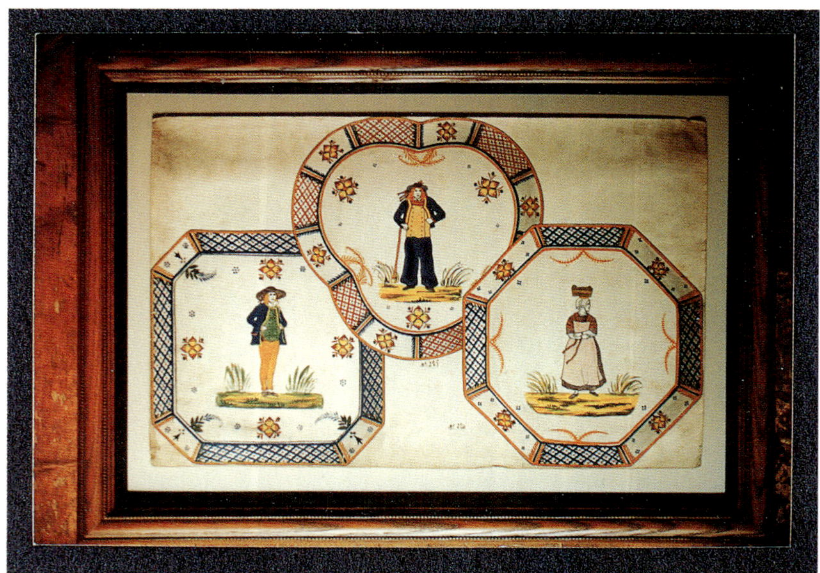

Croisillon, or lattice-work, and stylized blossoms surround the central subject on these Henriot faïencerie *aquarelle* designs called *croisillé*. (See *Mali, Old Quimper Review, October 2001* for definition of *croisillé*.) In American auctions in the 1990s, *aquarelles* consistently ran between $300 and $900. Some décors such as *croisillé* brought the higher prices. A similar framed example brought $600 in 1998. Price range: $300-$1,000, depending on the décor. *Private Collection.*

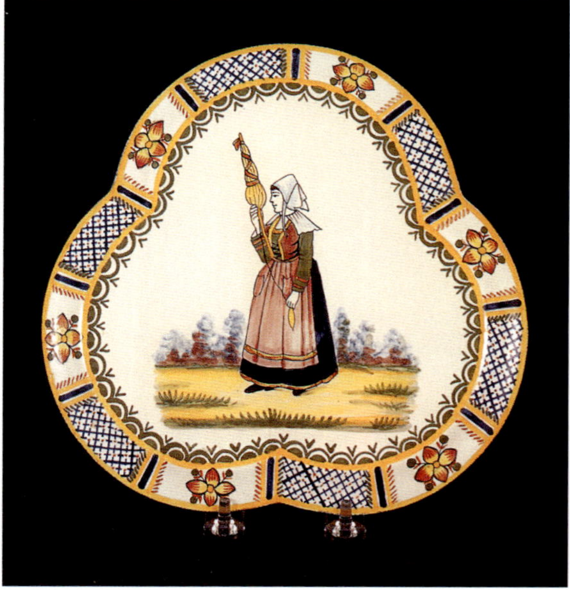

A 9.5"diameter *trefoil* tile with *croisillé* décor demonstrates the desirability of the design shown on the *aquarelle*. The labor-intensive nature of this particular rim décor led to a reduction in its output after World War II, and finally its discontinuation. Therefore, examples with the *croisillé* décor have risen in value. Price range: $425-$475. *Courtesy of Patricia Zimmerman.*

✾ B is for…

Banks (*tirelires*) include figural banks and the ever-popular pig bank.

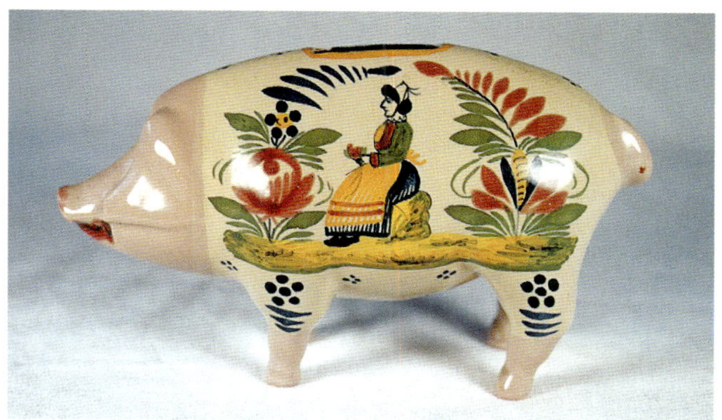

This pig bank, signed Henriot Quimper #72. is c. 1950, and measures 8" long by 4.5" tall. Prices for pig banks have fluctuated in the 1990s. A similar bank sold for $190 in 1993, but then, in 1994, it only brought $70 through the same American auction. However in 1998, a pig bank with a bit more detail brought $425 through the same venue. In 1999, Internet auction prices were more consistent; four similar pig banks sold between $202 and $228. Price range: $200-$250. *Courtesy of A.W. Styer.*

Baskets (*corbeilles*) come in a variety of styles, sizes, and designs, including very simple renditions of the *petit Breton* to more complicated forms.

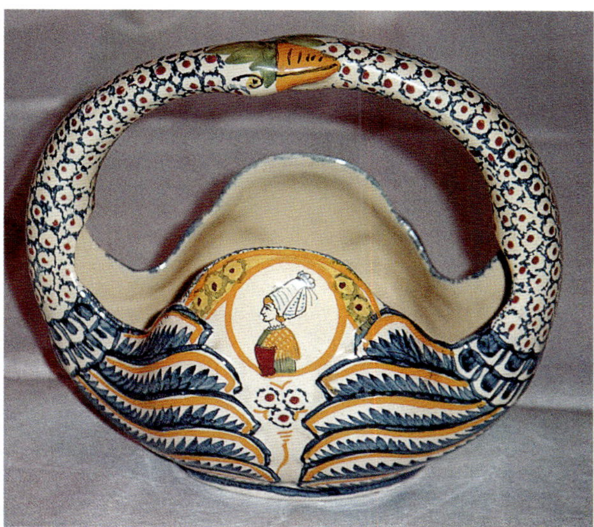

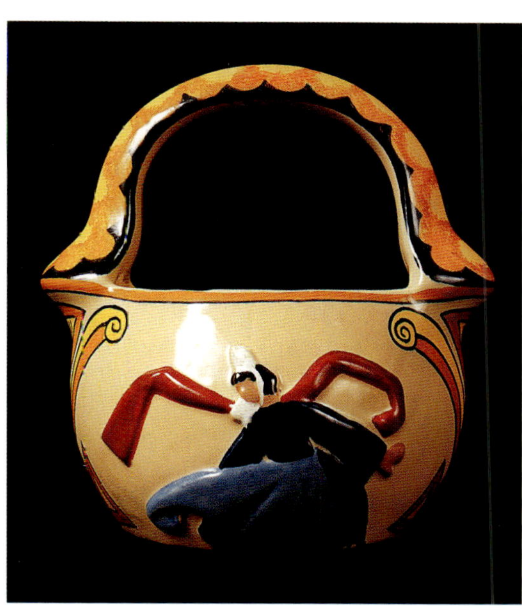

This Henriot faïencerie basket consists of two swans, whose necks and heads form the handle. Feather motifs decorate the sides. The basket, which also has been called a jardinière, measures 8.75" long by 7.25" tall, and dates from the second quarter of the 20th century. The décor on the swans is the sponged circle motif seen on *ivoire corbeille* items, and there is a medallion of a Bretonne on one side. Internet auction prices were between $400 and $650 in 1999 and 2000, depending on the quality of the décor. Price range: $475-$650. *Courtesy of Lucy Williams.*

Jim-Emile Sévellec designed this basket with bas-relief *Bigoudènes* swirling around the side. Signed Henriot Quimper J.E. Sévellec, and measuring 5" long by 4.25" high, this model dates from the 1930s. Price range: $425-$475. *Private Collection.*

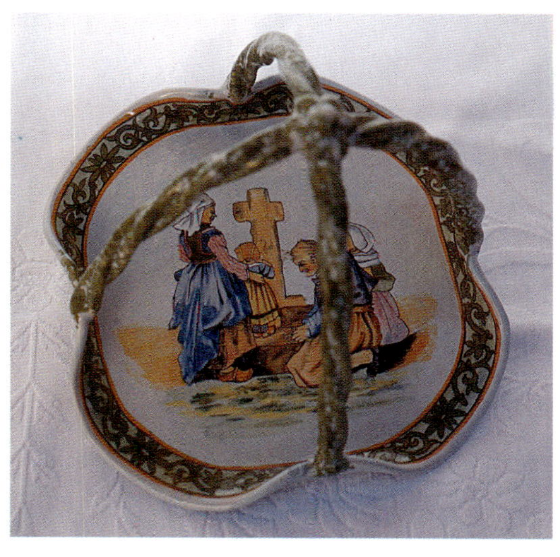

A basket (or dish) from Porquier-Beau features a *scène Bretonne* named *Les pérerins d'Hanvec*, where pilgrims worship at a wayside *calvaire*. The piece is edged in green scrolling foliage on a yellow ground and capped with a set of sponged-green *anses torsadées*, or twisted handles. It is signed PB. (See *Château de Quintin Exposition Catalogue, p. 106* for a similar example.) Price range at French auctions: $400-$500. *Courtesy of Pierre Breton, Art de Cornouaille, Quimper.*

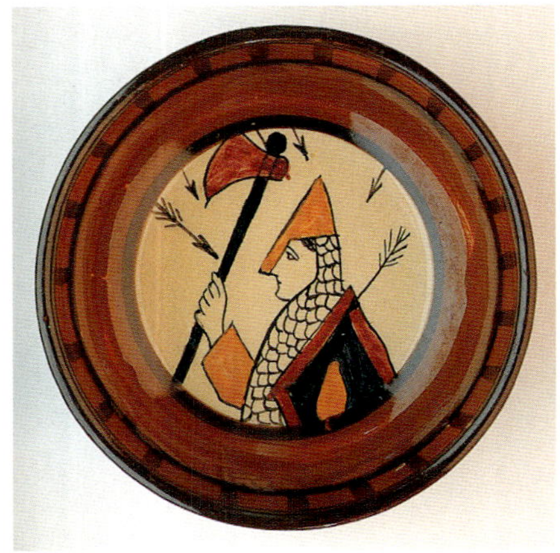

Bayeux Tapestry is about 230 feet long. It gives historians a visual record of events occurring in conjunction with William the Conqueror's invasion of the British Isles.

Bayeux Tapestry characters appear on Odetta examples. This 4" diameter dish has a Norman on the attack as the central theme. The dish appears in the Odetta Catalogue #1227, and is signed HB Quimper Odetta, #1227. Prices range: $55-$125. *Private Collection.*

Another Bayeux scene, this time on an 8" tall Odetta pitcher. Again a *cavalier Norman* readies for battle across the English Channel *(Manche).* This Odetta pitcher is from the 1920s-1930s, is signed HB Quimper #369-1221, and can be found in the *Odetta Catalogue* under #1221. Price range: $500-$600. *Private Collection.*

Bells *(clochettes)* have many forms such as *biniou* and figural. Some ordinary examples have unusual finials, such as bows, fleur-de-lys, *petit Bretons*, and even fish heads of the famous St. Pol bell.

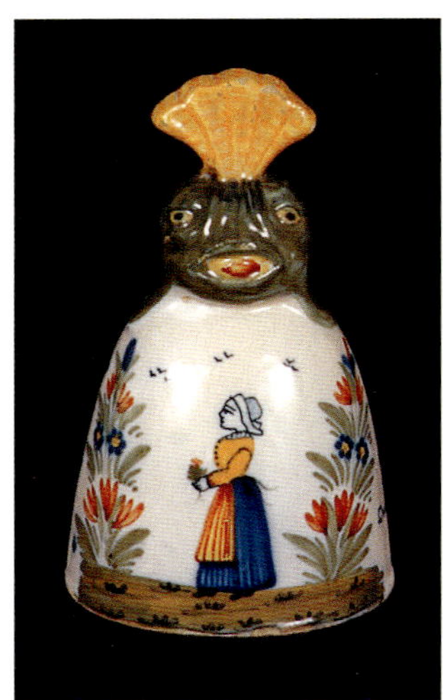

The St. Pol-de Léon bell with the fish-head handle by the Henriot firm is 4" tall and signed HR Quimper. There's a Breton on one side and a Bretonne on the other. Similar bells have realized between $125 and $275 through Internet and American auctions in the late 1990s and early 2000s. Price range: $175-$275. *Courtesy of Patricia Zimmerman.*

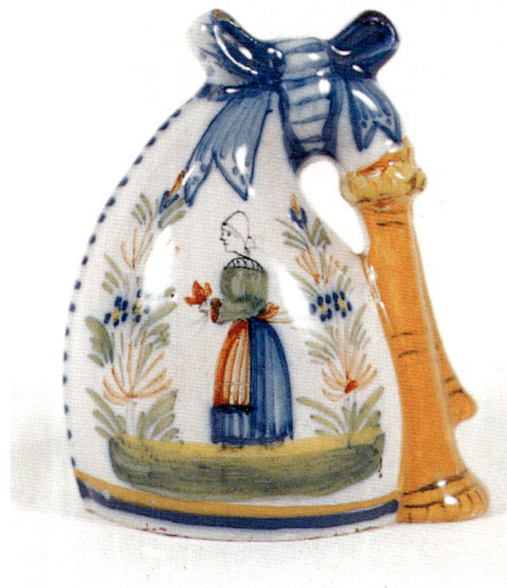

This bell is in the shape of a *biniou* (Breton bagpipe.) It's 3.5" tall and features a Bretonne flanked by floral sprays, with a bow at the top. The bell shows the early flowing coloration of Henriot at the beginning of the 20th century and is signed HR Quimper. American auction prices in the 1990s were $100 to $200. Internet prices in 2000 were $95 to $175. Price range: $125-$200. *Collection of Barbara Cleaver Kroll.*

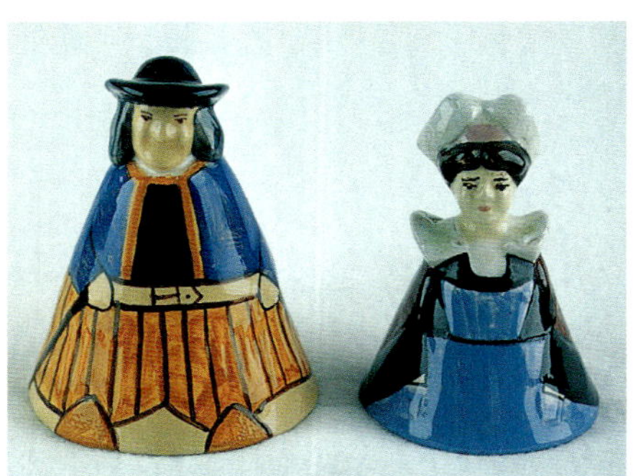

Another type is the figural bell. In this case, it's a pair of figural bells by the Henriot artist André Galland. She stands 3.5" tall and he 3.75" tall. The Bretons are depicted in modern movement colors and form. *Private Collection.*

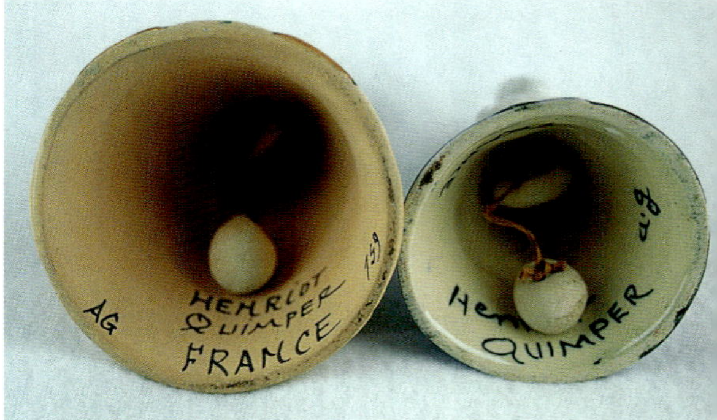

Signed Henriot Quimper and AG on one and Henriot Quimper ag on the other, these bells are an example of how painters sign marks differently. American and Internet sales in the late 1990s and early 2000s brought $350-$425 for the pair. Price range: $375-$475. *Private Collection.*

Bookends *(serre livres)* come in figural forms by such Quimper artists as Bouvier, Galland, Fouillen, Maillard, Savigny, and Sévellec, to name a few.

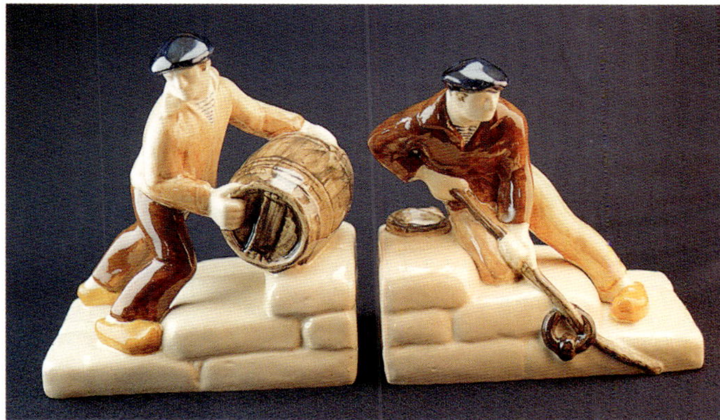

These bookends showing *marins* at work are by Bouvier. They stand 8.25" high at the tallest part, and are signed HB Quimper with Bouvier written on the *socle,* or base. A similar pair sold at a late 1980s American auction for $475. In 2000, a similar pair did not meet their reserve on an Internet auction. Price range: $525-$675. *Collection of Carter Yeatman.*

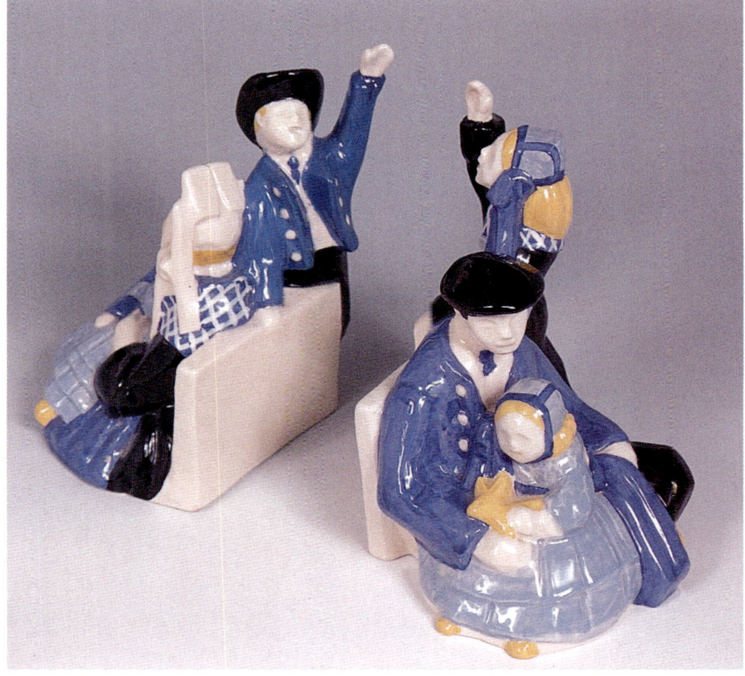

Bookends in a wonderful rendition of a Breton family, perhaps on a train ride, show children climbing and looking about as their parents hold them. The remarkable Henriot artist Yvonne Jean-Haffen designed these precious 8" tall bookends, c. 1930. In 1998, U.K. prices were below $300. *Courtesy of Gaynor Smith, Russethouse.*

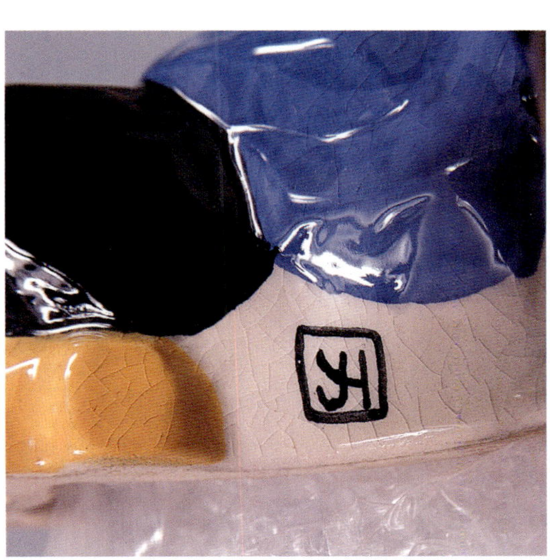

Jean-Haffen's *chiffre,* or monogram, is on the base of one of the *serre livres.* A single Jean-Haffen statue of similar size with monogram sold for $650 at a French auction in 2001. Price range in France: $700-$800. *Courtesy of Gay Smith, Russethouse.*

Bottles *(bouteilles)* come in a variety of forms. Sometimes they hold perfume, sometimes liqueur.

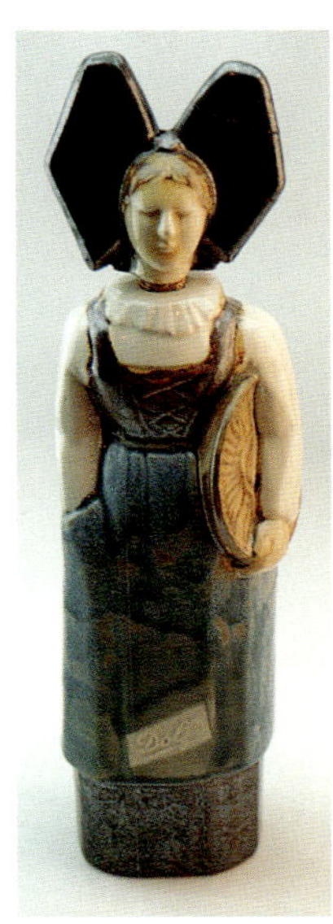

The HB faïencerie made this liqueur bottle in Odetta-like stoneware. The female stands 12" tall and is dressed in the costume of Alsace. She is a liqueur decanter marked Dolfi. *Courtesy of Janis Maxwell and Mike Feldman.*

The mate to the female bottle is this 11.5" tall male liqueur decanter or bottle marked Dolfi. A similar pair sold at a late 1980s auction for $160. Because of the advertising component, the bottles have increased in value. American price range: $275-$375 for the pair. *Courtesy of Janis Maxwell and Mike Feldman.*

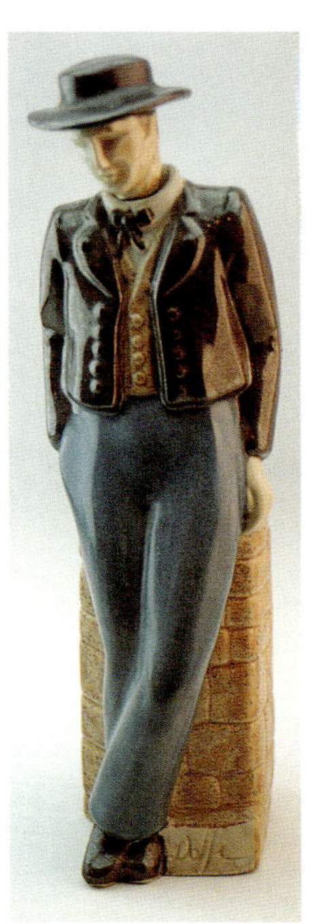

Bottle holder (*panier porte-bouteilles*) is an interesting and unusual form. Many are seen with *scènes Bretonnes* and *décor riche* borders.

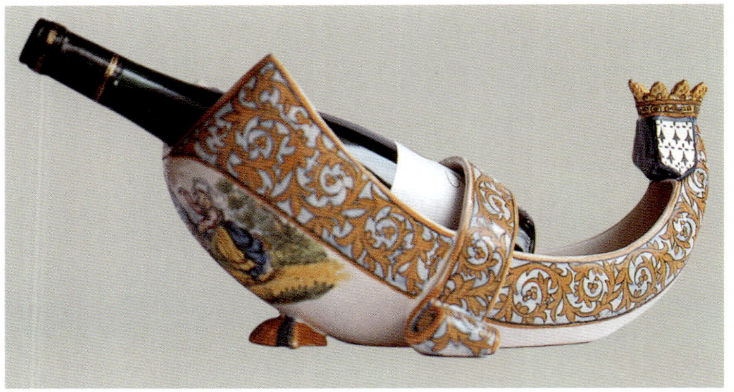

This Porquier-Beau *panier porte-bouteilles* is ready for a bottle of wine, perhaps Vouvray! An example sold at a 2000 French auction for $1,000, while another French auction sold one the same year for $2,571. But then in 2001, a French auction realized only $900 for an example with damage. The especially well-rendered model shown here is in the range of $2,700. *Courtesy of Pierre Breton, Art de Cornouaille, Quimper.*

Bowls (*bols, coupes, jattes*) are more abundant due to their utilitarian nature, but do come in a surprising number of forms and styles.

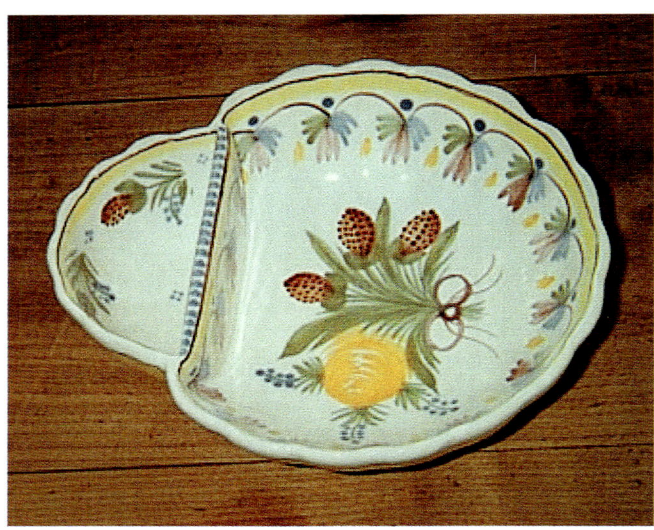

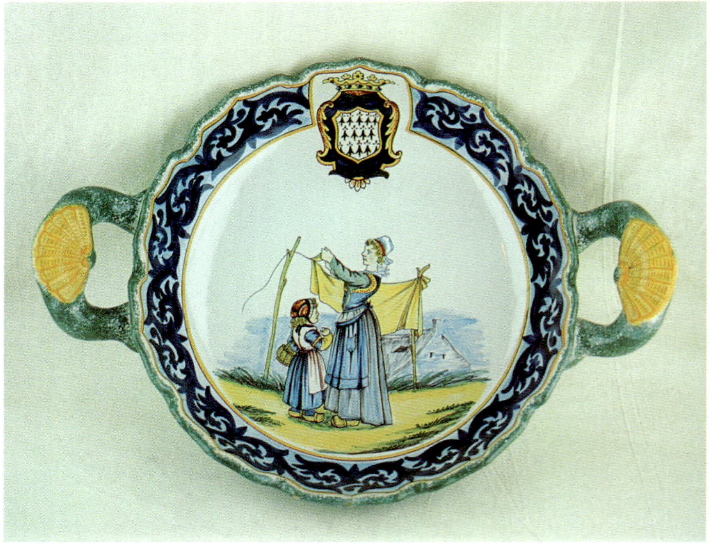

This berry bowl features a section for your choice of berries and a section for cream or sugar for dipping. Signed HB Quimper, this example is 9" long and dates from the third quarter of the 20th century. Price range: $275-$350. *Private Collection.*

This interestingly shaped round bowl with two handles is called a *melonnière*. The handles are sponged and contain a scallop-shell motif. An armorial of Brittany is at the top of border design. A *scène Bretonne* showing a mother and daughter hanging wash fills the center, and a blue *décor riche* border surrounds the scene. Other *melonnières* may be square with square-shaped handles. Depending on the décor and age, *melonnières* realized between $600 and $1,200 through Internet and American auctions in the late 1990s and early 2000s. This 10" diameter example is signed Henriot Quimper #159 and is mid-20th century. Price range: $850-$1,000. *Private Collection.*

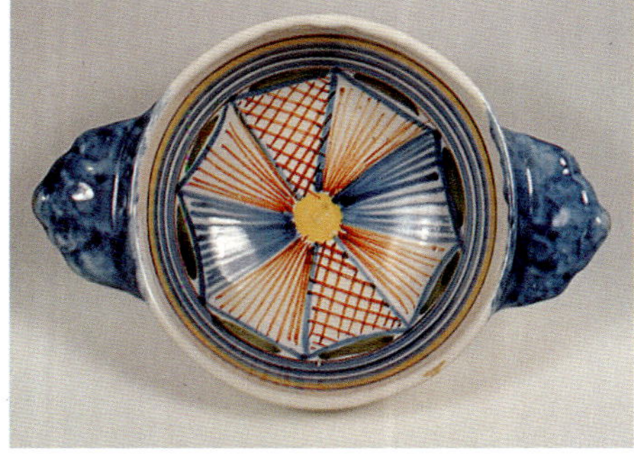

Small bowls with ears (*bols à oreille*) are porringers. Some are only 3" diameter, while others are 9" and larger. This example with geometric décor measures 4.5" diameter, dates from the second quarter of the 20th century, and is signed Henriot Quimper. Prices for porringers are determined by the décor and age. A simple *petit Breton* model of this size and age ranges between $45-$60. A pair of HR porringers brought $95 through an American auction in 2001. The desirable décor makes this example more expensive. Price range: $65-$85. *Private Collection.*

Vegetable bowls sometimes are covered and sometimes not. Signed Henriot Quimper France, this example is from the second quarter of the 20th century. The bowl is 5.5" diameter and the 7.5" diameter lid has sponged blue button-style finial. Sponged horseshoe handles complete an interesting work. Price range: $300-$425. *Courtesy of J. Cameron and Kathleen Yorkston.*

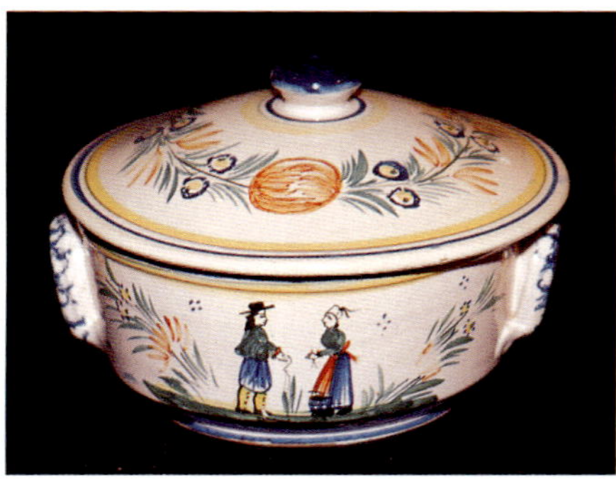

Boxes with lids *(boîtes avec ses couvercles)* come in many styles.

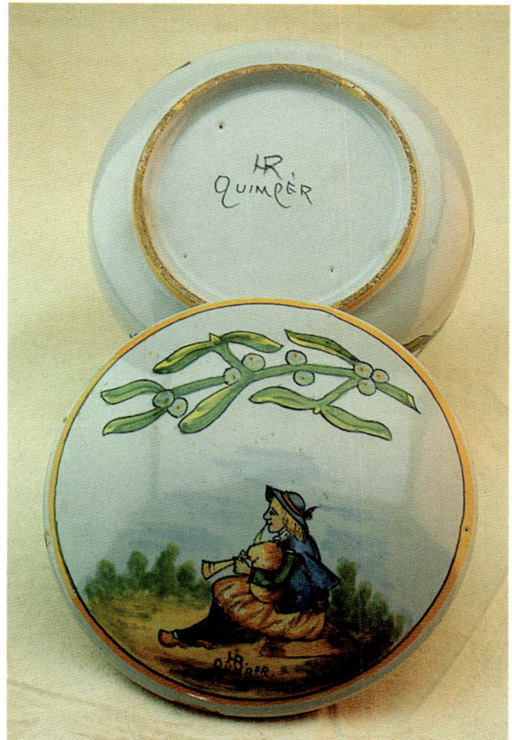

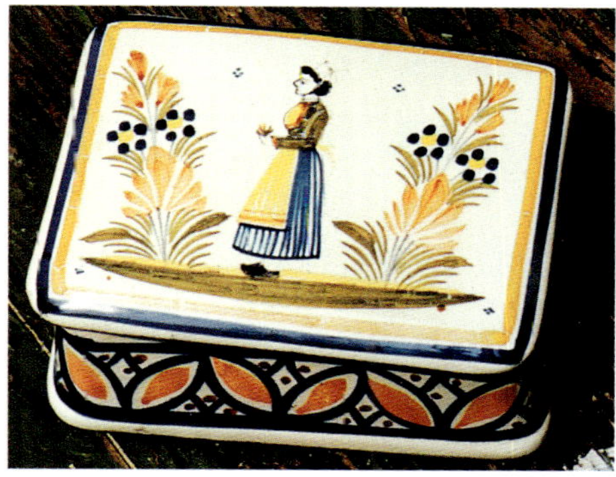

Sardine boxes are rectangular boxes with lids especially designed to hold the popular treat from the coast of Brittany. Of course not all rectangular boxes are for sardines, but this model is. Signed Henriot Quimper France, it measures 4.5" long and dates from the mid-20th century. Prices have held steady in American auctions and Internet sales. This model brought $200 in late 1990s. Price range: $200-$250. *Private Collection.*

Left:
This 4' diameter box, signed HR Quimper, may have been used as a *bonbonnière*, or candy dish. The rendition of the *biniou* player is very painterly. *Décor riche* examples brought from $150 to $475 through Internet and American sales in the early 2000s, but the excellent painting, mistletoe décor, and age earn this early 20th century item four stars! Price range: $450-$525. *Courtesy of Nancy Wyman.*

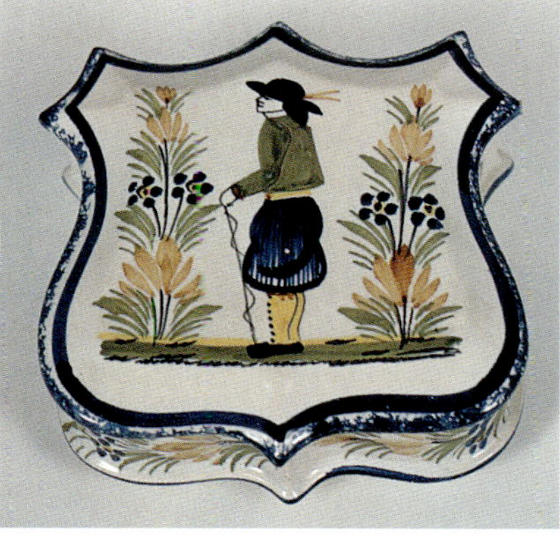

Shield-shaped boxes have been very popular on Internet auctions and at American sales. One *décor riche* example brought $450 in 2000 on an Internet auction. This shield-shaped box, signed Henriot Quimper, measures 4.5" at its longest point. It features a Breton between two floral sprays, but the shape is the biggest draw. Price range: $350-$425. Private Collection.

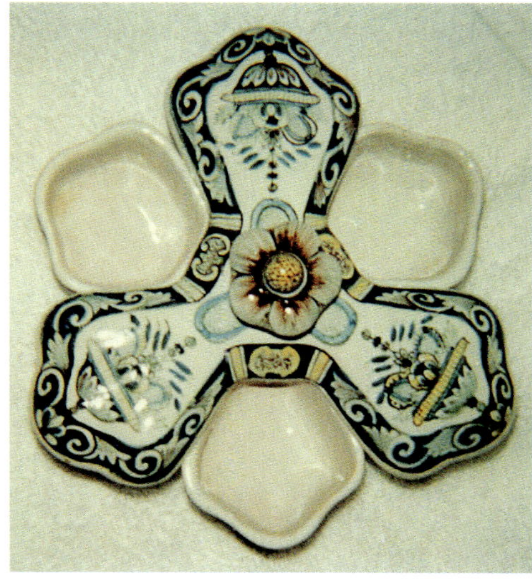

Spice box *(boîte à epice)* is the definition of this unique piece with a pivoting top. A 19th century HB example brought $650 in an American auction in 1996, and another was estimated to bring $850 at a 1990s French auction. This 19th century model is signed with the first mark HB, and has a unique flower finial and Rouen décor. *Courtesy of Janey Levine.*

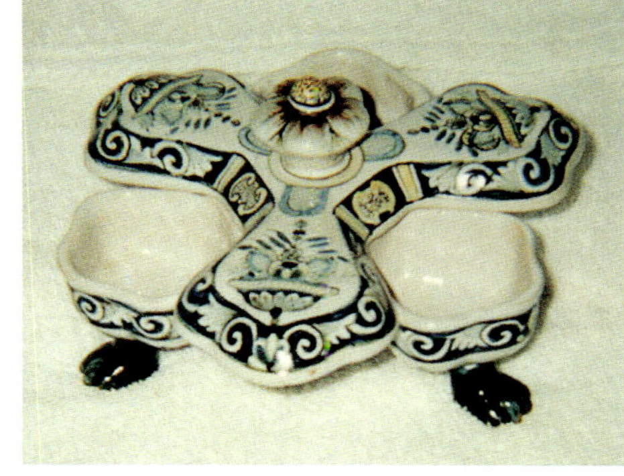

The spice box measures 8" diameter, stands on three little sponged animal-type feet. It has all the whistles and bells. Price range: $900-$1,100. *Courtesy of Janey Levine.*

Butter pat or doll dish, that is the question.

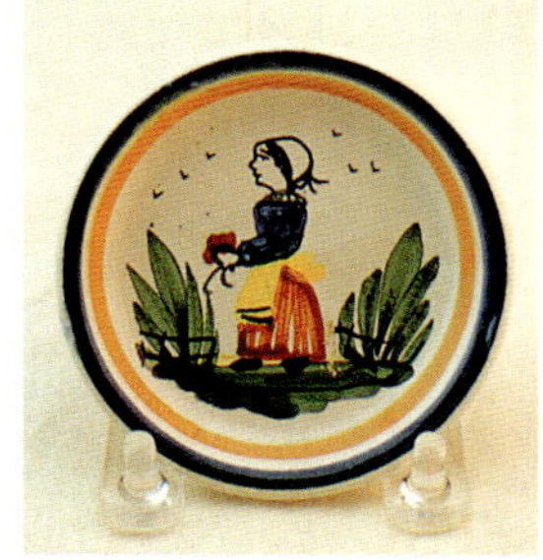

Butter pats often are mistaken for doll plates. This model is a 2.75" diameter butter pat from the 1940s-1950s and is signed Henriot Quimper France. More decorative models or shaped forms would bring higher prices. Price range: $25-$35. *Private Collection.*

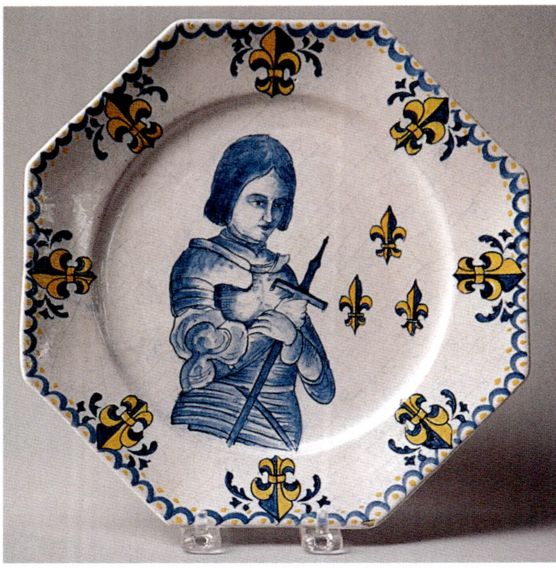

A CA octagonal plate, form #448, features *Jeanne d'Arc*. The plate is 9.75" diameter, is marked CA, and its colors are limited to blues and yellow. Missing are the red accents around the rim so common in CA border décors. Price range: $400-$475. *Private Collection.*

✂ C is for...

CA is the name of a previously unidentified French faïencerie in Paris. After twenty years of research, Millicent Mali named the elusive CA factory as belonging to the Chaumeil family.

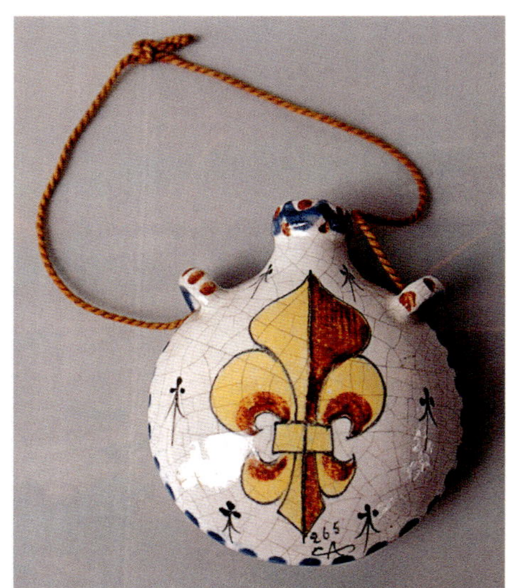

Another CA example is a round snuff flask, form #265, with typical two-toned CA *fleur-de-lys* décor. Measuring 3" diameter, this example still had the cord attached to the little loops near the top. The signature CA and the number 265 are just below the *fleur-de-lys* design. Price range: $250-$300. *Private Collection.*

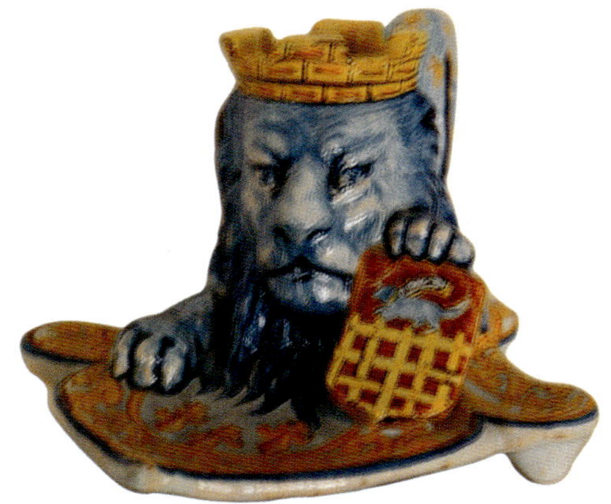

A unique *bougeoir* from the Porquier-Beau faïencerie is a real winner! It has a lion's head with a crown as the candle socket. The lion holds a shield in his paws, and scrolling gold foliage decorates the tray of the chamber stick. It is signed with the first PB mark and is 7" at its widest point. This model is listed in an 1887 Porquier-Beau price list as costing 8F. *(Bondhus, p. 101.)* A lion statue holding a shield rendered by HB in the 1880s brought more than $3,000 at a French auction in 2000. Price range: $1,400-$1,600. *Private Collection.*

Candlesticks *(flambeaux)* are taller than chamber sticks *(bougeoirs)*, but they are all in the same family.

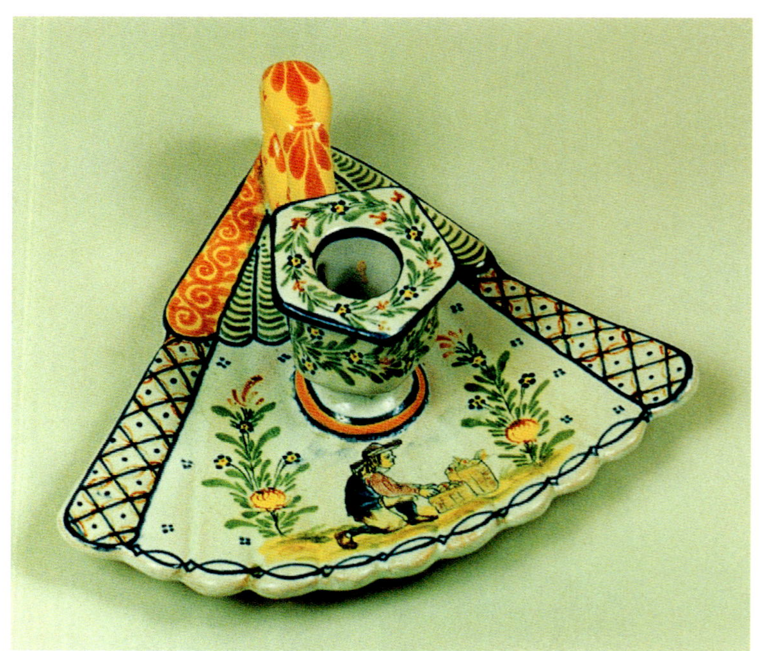

Bougeoirs have a loop for steadying with one finger. This example is an Henriot faïencerie fan-shaped chamber stick called *éventail*. The *croisillon* décor is complemented by a scattered blue four-dot design, a boldly colored handle, and *petites guirlandes* around the candle socket. Signed Henriot Quimper France, it measures 7.25" across the widest part. An unusual scene of a Breton digging in his garden further enhances the value of this piece. Price range: $400-$475. *Private Collection.*

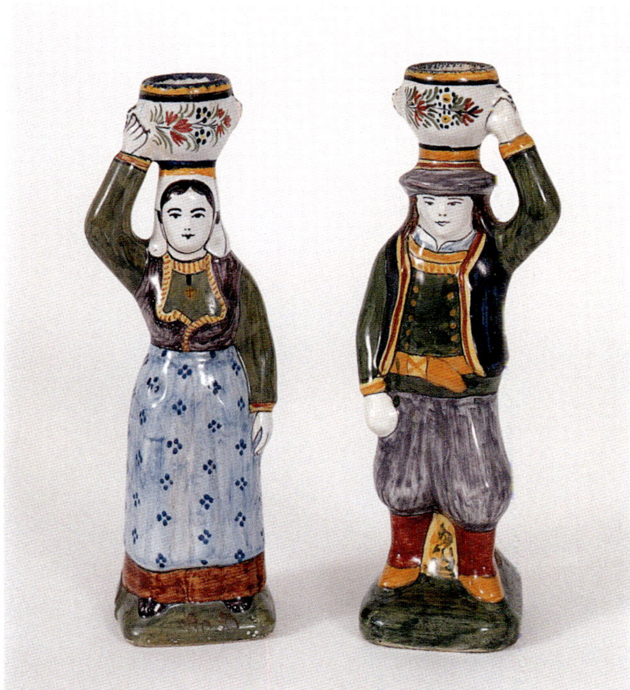

Figural candlesticks are popular, popular, popular. The Henriot pair seen here has climbed in price, even for brand-new examples. Perhaps they personify the elusive 19th century Bretons sought by visitors to Brittany. This pair from the second quarter of the 20th century brought $1,000 in 1996 at an American auction, and they continue to bring $700-$1,000 each time they appeared on the Internet in 2000. Price range: $950-$1,200. *Courtesy of S.D. State Agricultural Heritage Museum Photographic Collection.*

Christmas (*Noël*) items have retained their standing over the past 12 years, especially the nativity figures.

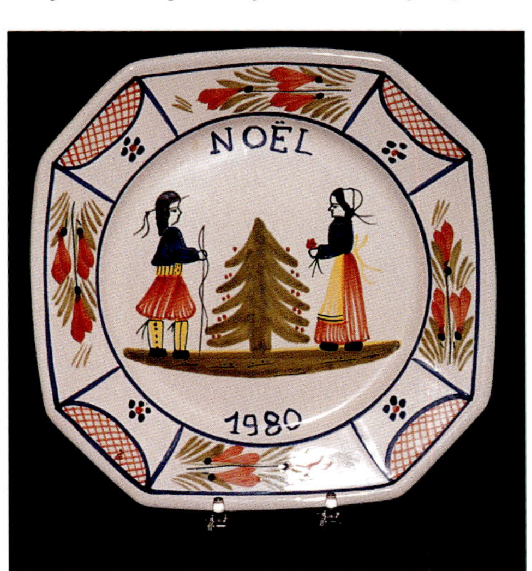

Plates and ornaments still command dollars around the holidays, despite their relative newness. A similar *Noël* plate dated 1980 brought $60 in a 2000 Internet auction. Price range: $60-$80. *Courtesy of Charlie and Donna Walker.*

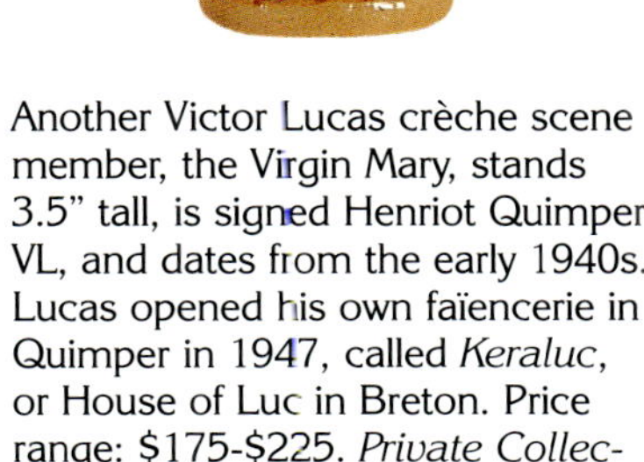

Nativity or crèche scene figures by Victor Lucas, while at Henriot, brought strong prices through an American auction in the late 1990s. Advertised as a starter set, the four figures, St. Joseph, the Virgin Mary, baby Jesus in a manger, and a donkey sold for $1,350. This Christ child in the manger is 3.5" long, signed Henriot Quimper VL (for Victor Lucas), and dates from the early 1940s. Price range: $175-$225. *Private Collection.*

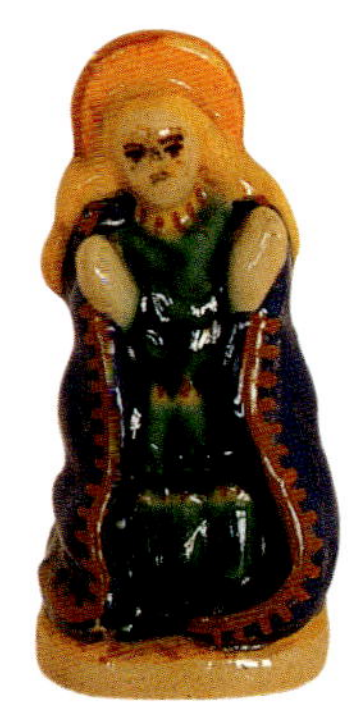

Another Victor Lucas crèche scene member, the Virgin Mary, stands 3.5" tall, is signed Henriot Quimper VL, and dates from the early 1940s. Lucas opened his own faïencerie in Quimper in 1947, called *Keraluc*, or House of Luc in Breton. Price range: $175-$225. *Private Collection.*

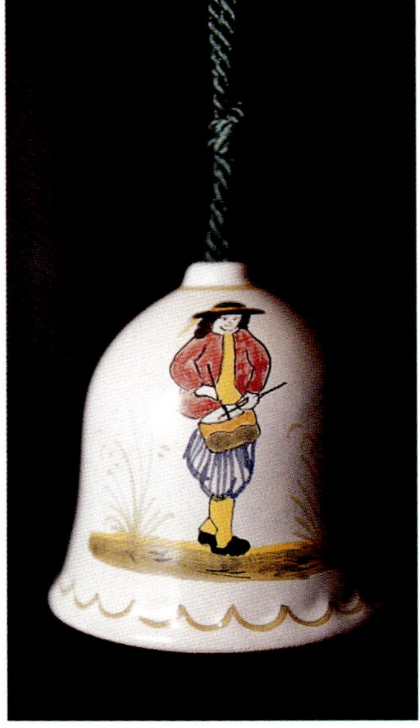

At the same time, relatively new ornaments for the Christmas tree like this one from HB/Henriot brought $50 on an Internet auction in 2000, versus $33 in a 1994 American sale. In 2001, one was offered for less than $20, but it was after the Christmas season. Price range: $40-$60. *Private Collection.*

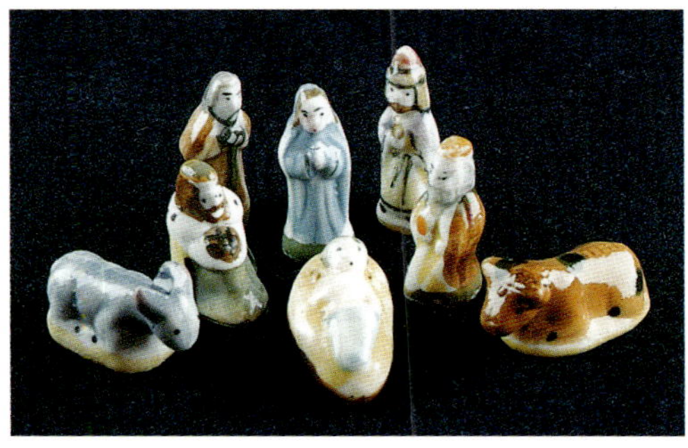

Feves are small ceramic people connected with the Nativity story, and are not Quimper faïence. These figures measure 1.5" and smaller. Many times they are given away by French merchants or placed in Christmas cakes during the *Noël* holiday in France. Price range: $1.25-$1.50 each. *Authors' Collection.*

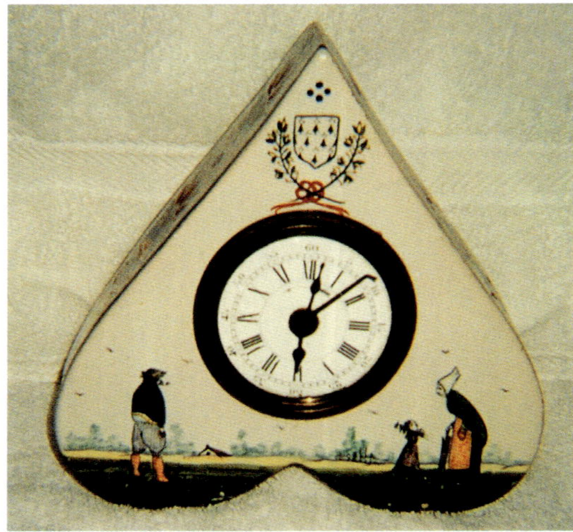

A *pendule* is a table or mantle clock. In a 1980s American sale, a 9.5" tall *décor riche pendule*, signed Henriot Quimper France, realized $2,900. A 1999 Internet auction brought $1,675 for an early 6.75" tall clock in the shape of a heart, marked *HB Déposée,* similar to this example. Price range: $1,700-$1,900. *Courtesy of Janey Levine.*

Clock (*pendule*) is an uncommon form that brings high dollars.

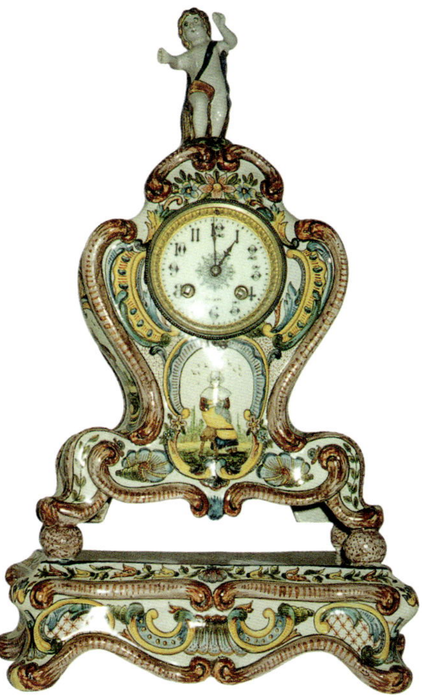

The extraordinary clock presented here is turn-of-the-20th century HB production and stands a full 21" tall, including the *angelot* on top. *Courtesy of Janey Levine.*

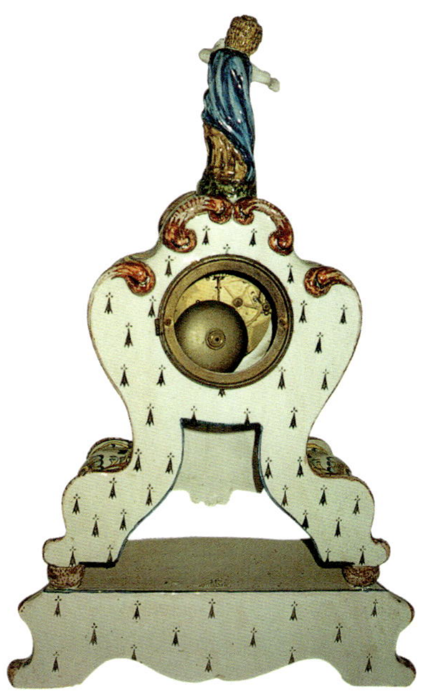

Even from the reverse side, the clock is stellar. The scattered ermine-tail design is a perfect complement to the rococo elements on the front and sides. A master-piece! Price range: $6,000-$8,000. *Courtesy of Janey Levine.*

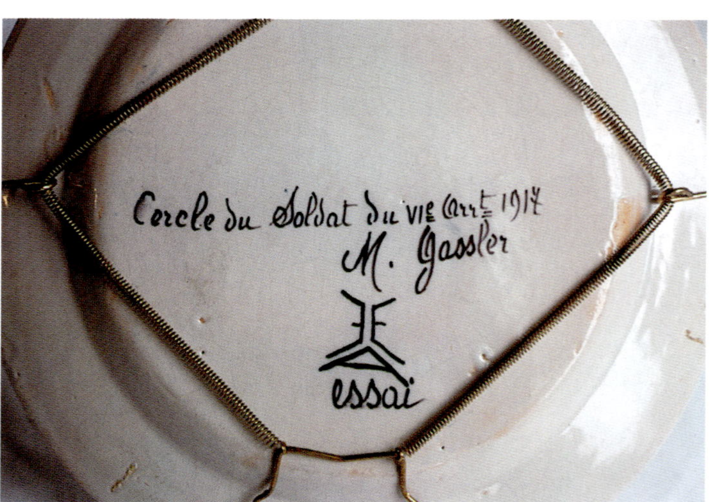

Several motifs of this commemorative plate series were made by the Henriot faïencerie. This example shows a generous gift of armaments, soldiers, and money being given to France by Uncle Sam. Note the white stars on a blue ground and the red-and-white stripe border treatment. It reads: *A gift from Uncle Sam. Courtesy of Pierre Breton, Art de Cornouaille, Quimper.*

Commemorative (*commémoratif*) items include war memorabilia.

The back of the commemorative plate says: Circle of Soldiers of the *6th Arrondissement* (an administrative section in Paris), 1917. It is signed M. Gassler. This example is from a series of plates commis-sioned by a group called *Cercle du Soldat* as a method to raise funds for veterans of World War I. *(Mali, Old Quimper Review March 1991.)* A French auction in 2001 sold similar plates for around $700 each. Signed HR Quimper. Price range: $775-$850. *Courtesy of Pierre Breton, Art de Cornouaille, Quimper.*

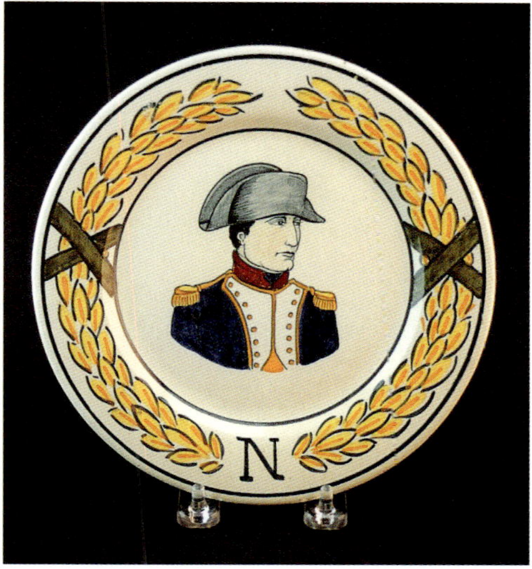

Another commemorative plate, this one from the third quarter of the 20th century, features Napoleon. It is 7.75" diameter, has the initial N for Napoleon, and is signed Henriot Quimper France, #133. A set of five plates, some with damage, sold on an Internet auction in 2000 for $100, a good buy! Price range: $125-$145 each. *Courtesy of Carter Yeatman.*

Coupe or *presentoir* is a cross between a dish and a bowl.

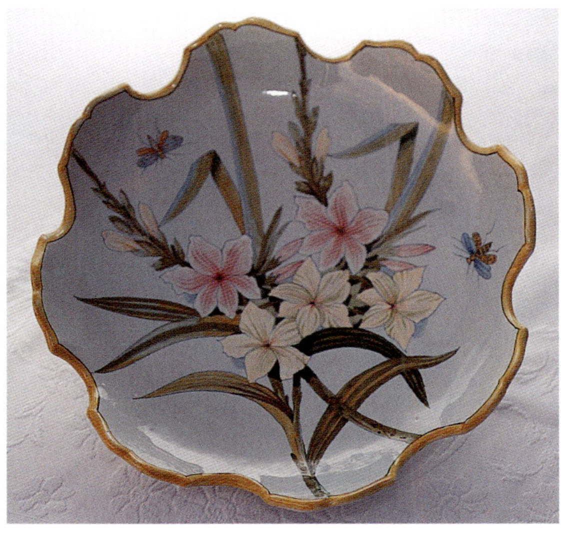

This prime example of a *coupe* is Porquier-Beau *décor botanique.* It is *polylobé,* or deeply scalloped, and edged with a band of yellow. The yellow and pink flowers attracted two colorful insects on this 8.5" diameter *coupe* signed PB. A French auction in 2000 sold two *polylobé coupes botanique.* The prices differed greatly. One PB model with similar décor realized $860. The other, with a branch of strawberries, brought $2,790. American auction prices in the 1990s ranged from $840 to $1,450 for similar PB botanical *coupes.* Price range: $1,200-$3,000, depending on the rarity of the décor. *Courtesy of Pierre Breton, Art de Cornouaille, Quimper.*

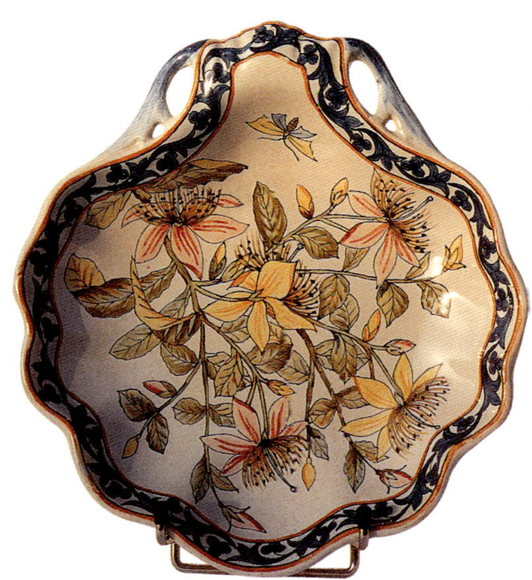

A Porquier-Beau botanical design graces another *coupe,* this time in a fancier mold, *forme de coquille* or scallop shell form. Notice the interior border has blue scrolling foliage, but the gently scalloped rim is edged in golden yellow. The botanical is St. John's Wort and insects are hovering in expectation. This 8.5" tall form is less frequently seen and therefore commands more. Price range: $1,400-$3,200, depending on the rarity of the décor. *Courtesy of Pierre Breton, Art de Cornouaille, Quimper.*

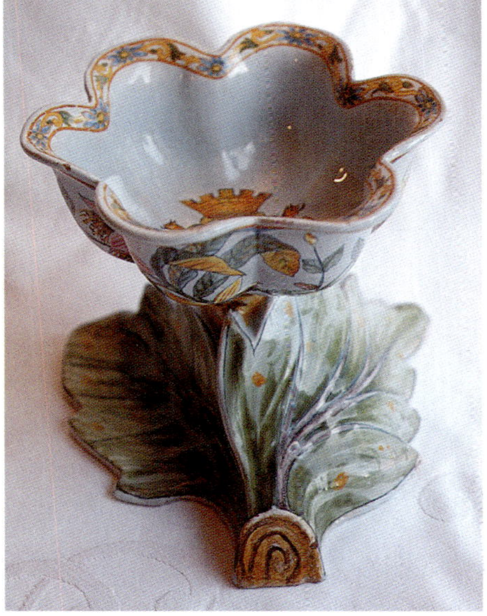

A rare *coupe* in the form of a *chou-fleur,* or cauliflower, is a remarkable work of art. Three leaves form the foot of the *coupe,* the bowl section is deeply scalloped (*polylobé*) with floral decor, and the interior is decorated with an armorial. (Other examples are seen in *Trois Siècles de Faïences, p. 143,* and *Bondhus, p. 37.*) This 6.5" tall piece by the Porquier-Beau faïencerie is signed PB, and is seen more often in French auctions than American sales. Price range: $2,000-$3,500. *Courtesy of Pierre Breton, Art de Cornouaille, Quimper.*

Cruet sets *(hulliers et vinaigriers)* are readily available and can be reasonably priced.

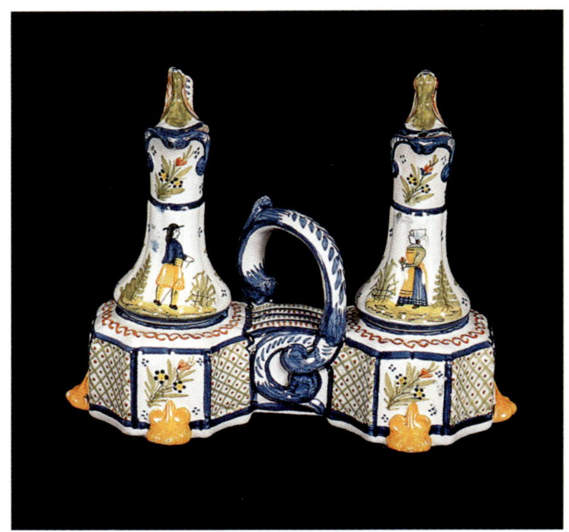

This HB cruet set has the oil and vinegar bottles with stoppers, and a 9.75" long carrier with handles. The overall height is 7.5". The décor features *croisillon, fleur-de-lys* feet in deep yellow, red chain link, and blue four-dot accents. The carrier's handle has a rococo flair. The Breton and Bretonne are sitting pretty on this prime example, signed HB Quimper. Price range: $450-$550. *Courtesy of Patricia Zimmerman.*

Cups and saucers *(tasses et soucoupes)* are available in great quantities and décors, since a set of six, eight, or twelve usually accompanied tea or coffee pots. Some forms are *demi-tasse, petit déjeuner,* trefoil, and unusual shapes.

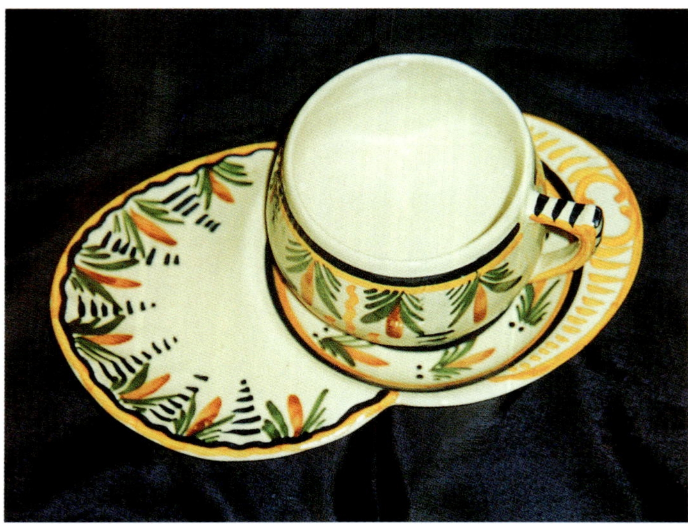

This example is a *petit déjeuner,* or breakfast set. It dates from the mid-20th century and measures 11" long, leaving plenty of room for a croissant next to the large cup of morning coffee. Price range: $145-$200. *Private Collection.*

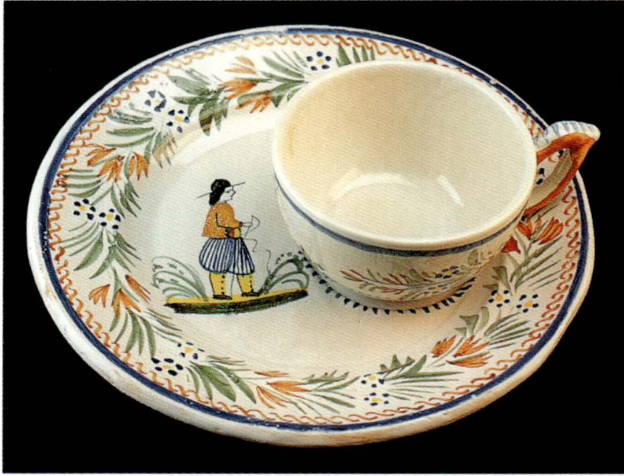

This set is for luncheon. It is signed Henriot Quimper France, #74. It dates from the 1920s-1930s and measures 8" diameter. Some call this décor *demi-fantasie.* Confusion with this term arises from an earlier time when *demi-fantasie* was used to describe a variety of décors. This luncheon or teatime set is bordered by a red chain accent, and the *petits Bretons* are very much at home on this charming rendition. Price range: $250-$275. *Courtesy of J. Cameron and Kathleen Yorkston.*

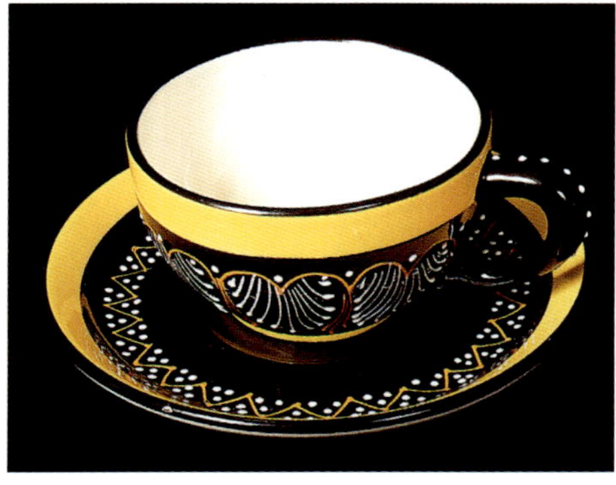

This large cup and saucer is in the modern rendition of *broderie,* and manufactured by HB. It contains the F, or form number and D, or décor number, elements added in the 1960s. Price range: $35-$45. *Courtesy of John Temple.*

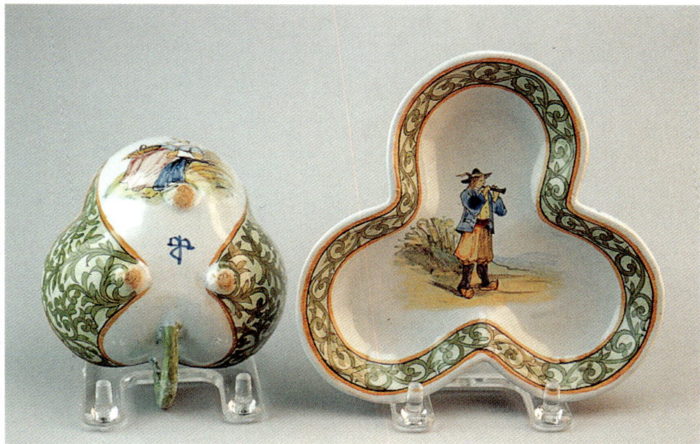

A lovely Porquier-Beau trefoil-shaped *soucoupe et tasse* set is signed PB. The 5.25" diameter saucer features a Breton *bombarde* player surrounded by dark green on light green scrolling foliage border. The shaped cup has the same border décor around another scene of a Bretonne sitting in the country-side. (A similar set is seen in the *Château de Quintin Exhibition Catalogue, p. 69*.) Price range: $275-$375. *Courtesy of Carter Yeatman.*

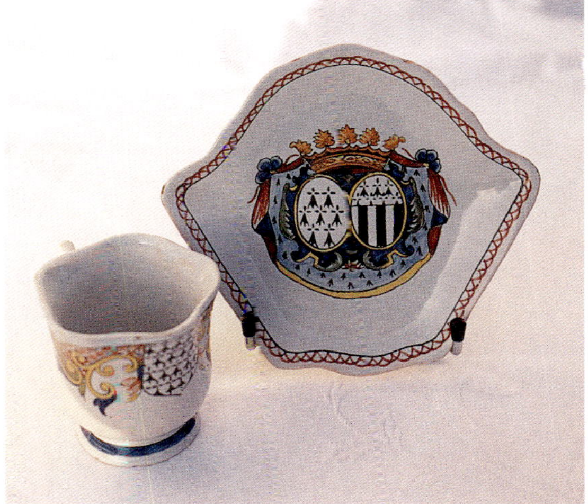

Another type of Porquier-Beau cup and saucer is this *soucoupe et tasse* for tea or chocolate. Armorials of various cities, departments, or families are featured on shield-shaped plates and cups. A dual emblem represents Brittany and Rennes on this set, rimmed in a red chain décor and signed PB. Price range: $275-$375. *Courtesy of Pierre Breton, Art de Cornouaille, Quimper.*

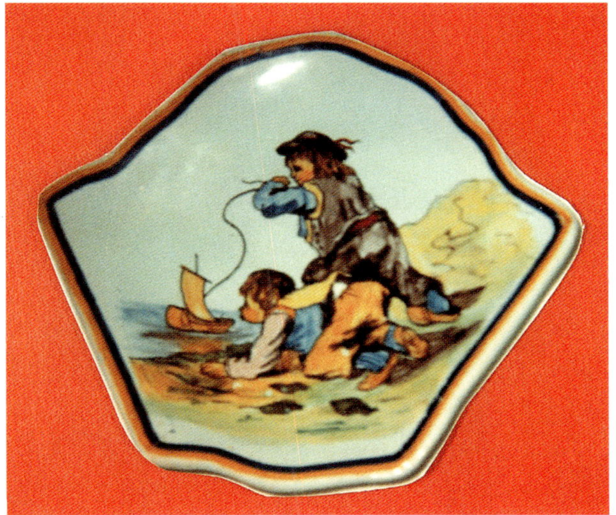

A *soucoupe* in a shield-shape with a *scène Bretonne* by Porquier-Beau stands alone as a work of art. Two young boys playing with a boat along the water's edge are outlined in dark-blue and gold. The *soucoupe* measures 5.5", is signed PB, and dates from the last quarter of the 19th century. Internet auction prices in 2000 ranged from $300 to $381. Price range: $375-$425. *Courtesy of Janey Levine.*

❧ D is for…

Dish (plat) is a generic term for many styles of utilitarian tableware. Some forms are stellar.

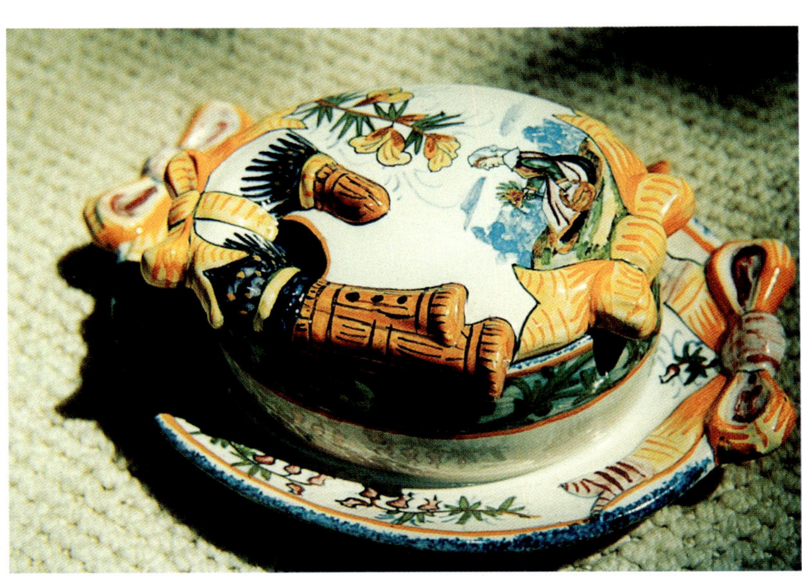

The *biniou*-shaped dish is popular in small sizes as holders for spoons, tea bags, nuts, and condi-ments, and in larger sizes for butter or cheese. A 10.75" long Henriot *décor riche* covered cheese dish in the *biniou* shape brought $510 on an Internet auction in 1999. In 2001, an Internet sale realized only $300 for a similar model. The *biniou*-shaped cheese dish shown here is signed Henriot Quimper, measures 9" long, and is a lovely example of the form. Price range: $625-$700. *Collection of Silvia and Gary Fritzhand.*

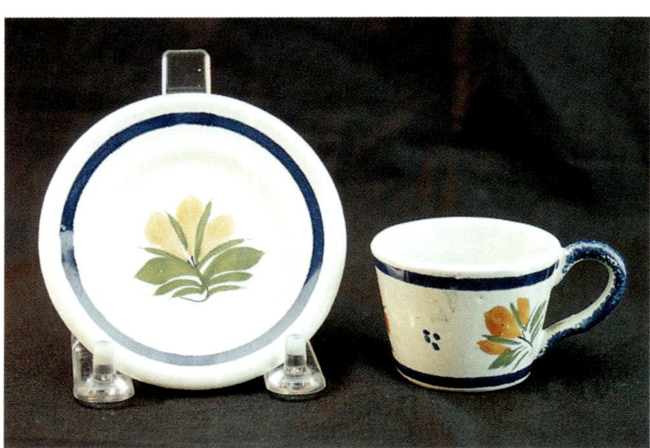

Doll dishes as children's toys are a favorite. This little cup and saucer set is signed Henriot Quimper; the saucer measures 3.25" diameter. Doll dishes are highly collectible, but sometimes difficult to differentiate from miniatures made for adults or other tableware, such as butter pats and condiment servers. Price range: $55-$75. *Collection of Reilly Nowland.*

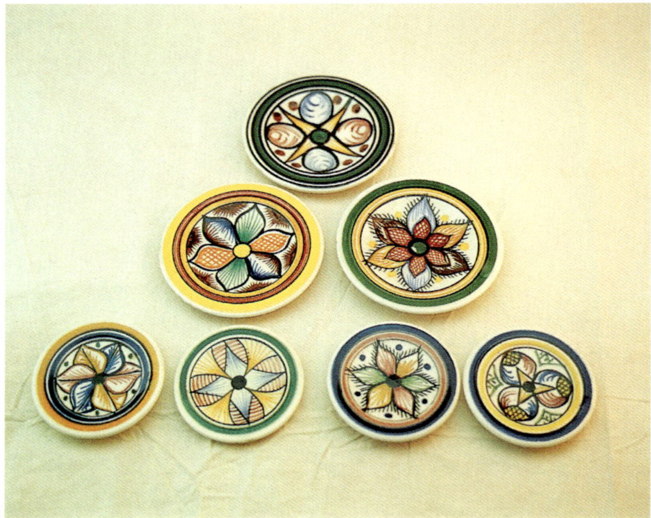

An assortment of doll plates shows the variation in size and décor. Sometimes these are confused for butter pats. Smaller is better is the rule for doll plates, which bring higher prices. The three plates on the bottom row are doll plates measuring 2.75" diameter. The three 4" diameter plates above are not doll plates, but rather are used for individual jam or honey servings. All the examples are Henriot. Price range: $40-$80 for doll plates. Price range: $35-$50 for condiment servers. *Private Collection.*

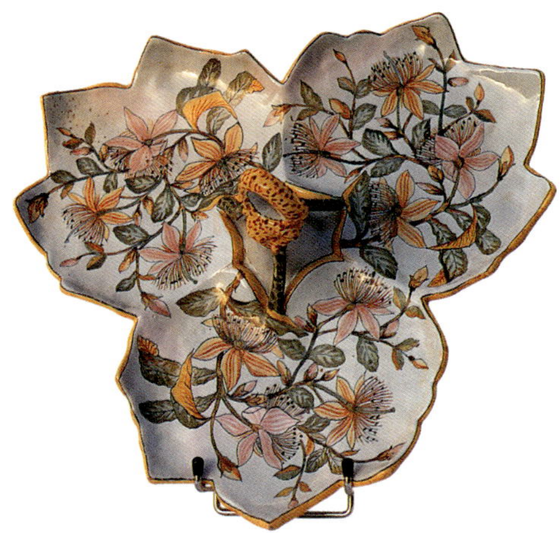

Sectioned dishes are used for serving hors d'oeuvres or vegetables. This Porquier-Beau tri-lobed example is stunning. The deeply scalloped or *polylobé* sections are rimmed with a yellow border. Each section is filled with the floral St. John's Wort, and the shaped handle is green and yellow with dark green and brown spots. Signed PB, this dish dates from the last quarter of the 19th century, and is a rare model. Price range: $2,800-$3,600. *Collection of Pierre Breton, Art de Cornouaille, Quimper.*

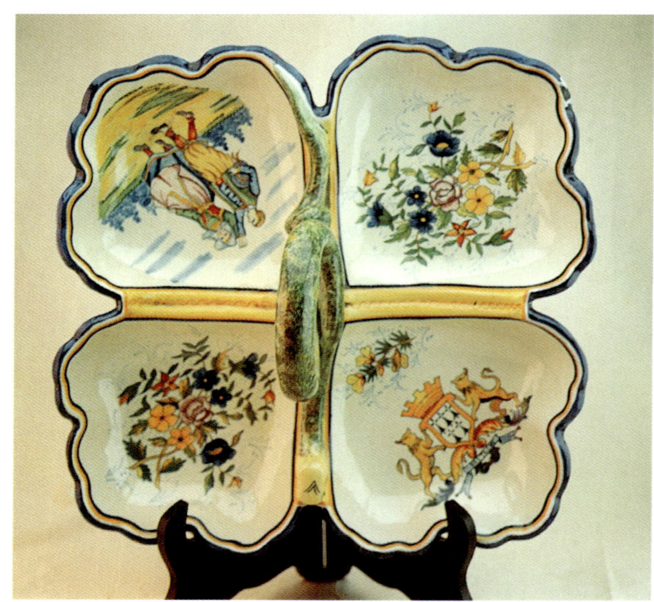

A four-part serving dish from the first quarter of the 20th century is signed HR Quimper. The four sections have scalloped edges, but not the deep scallops of *polylobé.* Each section is bordered with a blue and a black line. Within one compartment a couple dances a *gavotte*, and in another the armorial of Brittany is topped with a crown. The remaining two sections have delicately rendered floral bouquets, and a charming snake handle tops the serving dish. Price range: $550-$675. *Private Collection.*

Duck *(canard)* forms come in many styles, such as pipe holders, egg cups, vases, inkwells, and serving dishes.

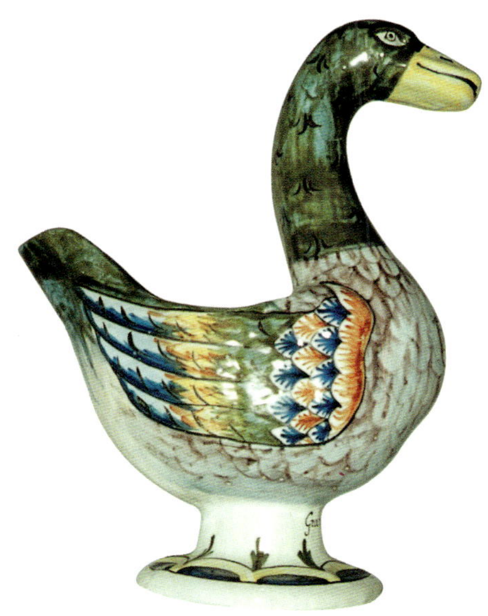

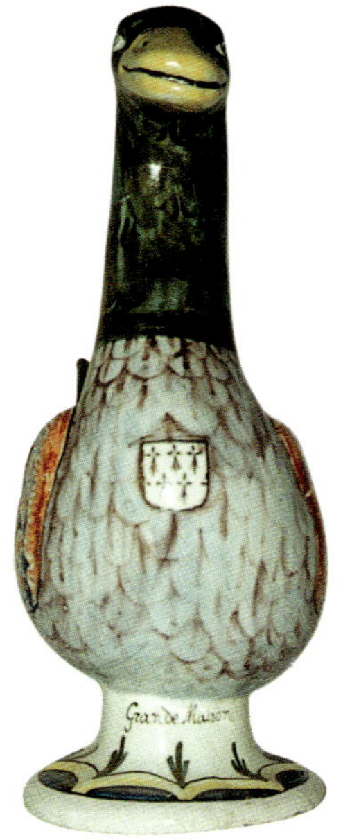

A look at the duck's breast shows the armorial of *Bretagne*. At the base, written in script, is *Grande Maison*. This is an uncommon and desirable form, which brought $800 on an Internet auction in the 1990s. Roullet catalogued this form in a 1990s French auction as being a rare *porte-bouquet en forme de canard*. An American auction realized $825 in 2000 for this example. Price range: $1,100-$1,200. *Courtesy of Janey Levine.*

This early duck vase is signed only HB on the bottom, dating it from the late 19th century. Standing 12" tall, it is a remarkable piece in form and color. *Courtesy of Janey Levine.*

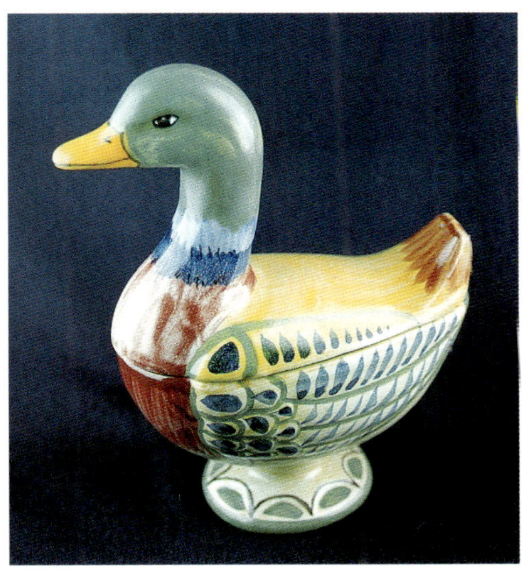

This modern duck form comes apart to be used as a container. Signed HB/Henriot, this colorful fellow stands 7.5" tall and dates post-1984. Price range: $150-$225. *Courtesy of Jen and Jeff Nowland.*

❡ E is for…

Eggs *(oeufs)* are plentiful in France and a number of ways to serve them on Quimper faïence have been devised.

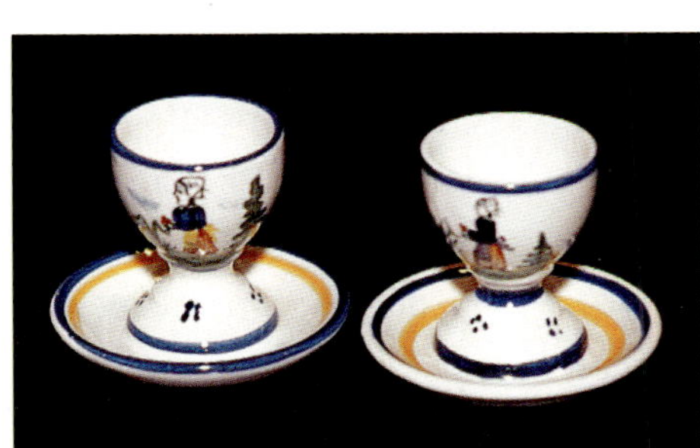

Individual eggcups *(coquetiers)* have an attached foot and stand 3.75" tall. These are signed HB Quimper and date from the 1930s. Price range: $150-$175 for the pair. *Courtesy of J. Cameron and Kathleen Yorkston.*

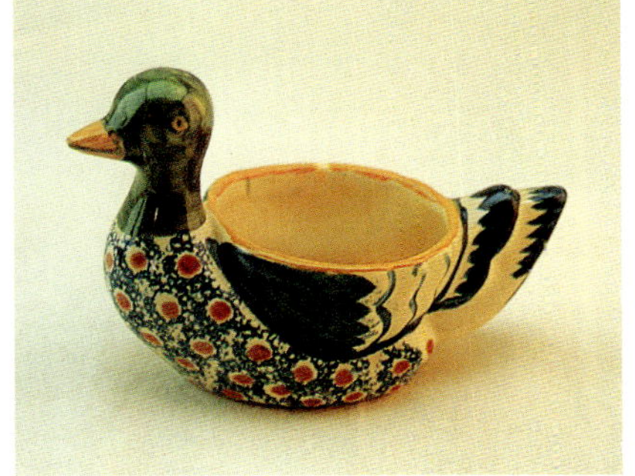

Another version of an eggcup is the figural-type. In this instance the form is a duck, which is 4" long and signed Henriot Quimper #86. This fellow dates from the 1920s-1930s. Single forms like this have brought healthy prices on the Internet in 1999-2000. Price range: $125-$150. *Courtesy of Nancy Wyman.*

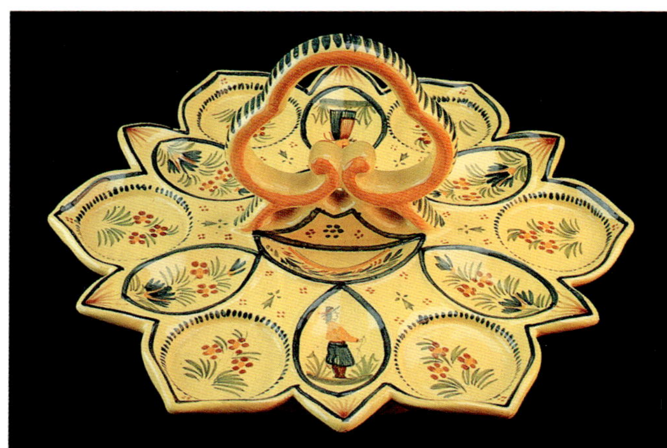

A plate to serve eggs *(porte-oeufs)* in the *soleil* décor looks like a bright, sunny flower. It measures 10.75" diameter and is signed Henriot Quimper France, #71. Dating from the 1920s-1930s, this beautiful plate would have had six eggcups for the round indentations, which alternate with the oval-shaped receptacles. With or without the eggcups, this design makes quite a statement. Price range: $275-$325. *Courtesy of Janice M. Longer.*

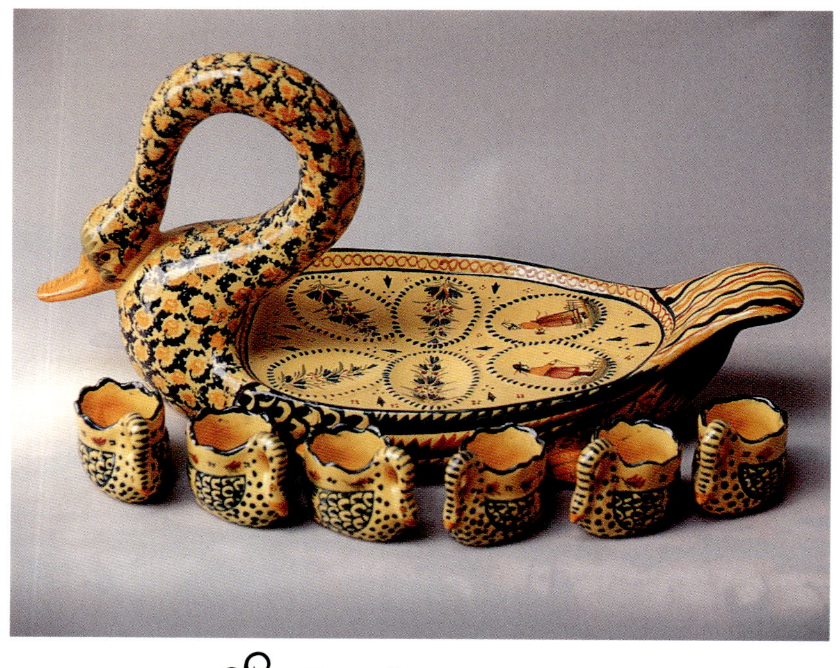

The most extraordinary *porte-oeufs* are shaped like swans. This example is in the sunny *soleil* décor and measures 16" long and 7.75" tall. Six 3" tall matching swan eggcups complete the set. There are oval receptacles for them on the swan's back; two are decorated with a male and female Breton, and the remaining four contain floral garlands. Black ermine-tails, a scattered red four-dot design, and a red chain design complete the interior décor. Remarkable painting, including sponged circles and *à la touche* feathers complete the picture. It is unusual to find a complete set with all six swans. Signed Henriot Quimper, this set dates from 1920-1930s. American auctions in the late 1980s through the 1990s realized $1,600-$2,100 for HR models. Price range: $1,400-$2,000 for stellar examples. *Courtesy of the M. Donilon Collection.*

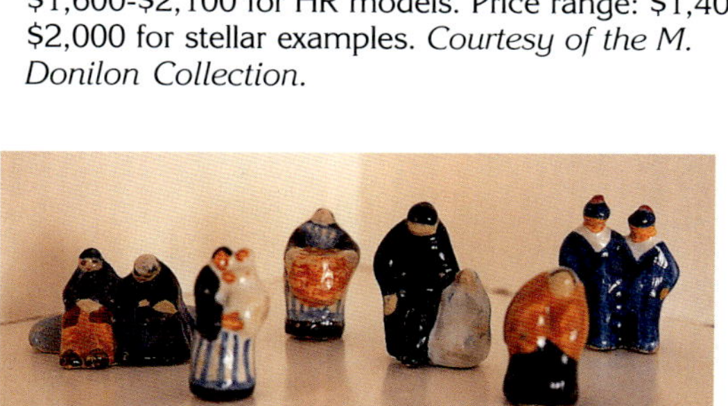

These examples from Méheut's *Mon Village* stand only 1.25" tall at maximum, and are signed Quimper France. Collectors are challenged to find all the pieces to the set. Price range: $500-$575 for a group of six. *Private Collection.*

✤ F is for...

Figurines, statues *(statues, statuettes)* are very popular with many Quimper collectors. Méheut's *Mon Village* and Sévellec's *Village Breton* contain numerous small figurines, as well as some buildings.

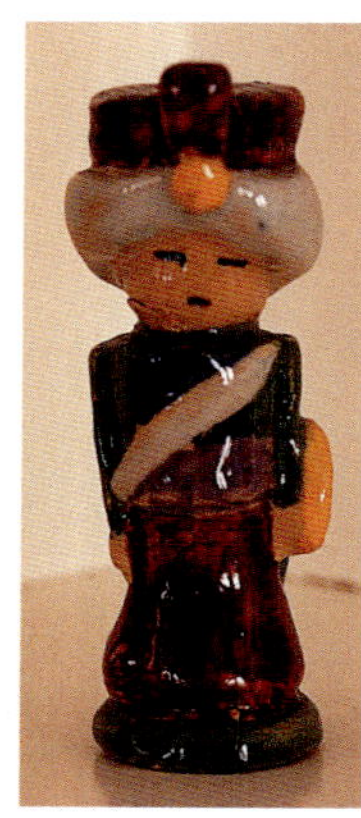

The next four figures are by the Henriot artist Geo-Fourrier.

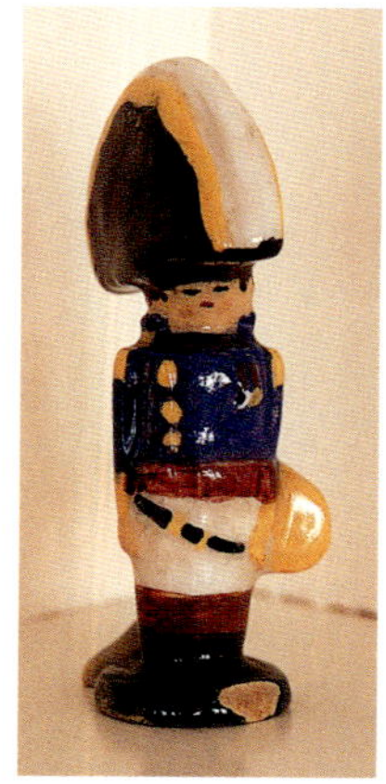

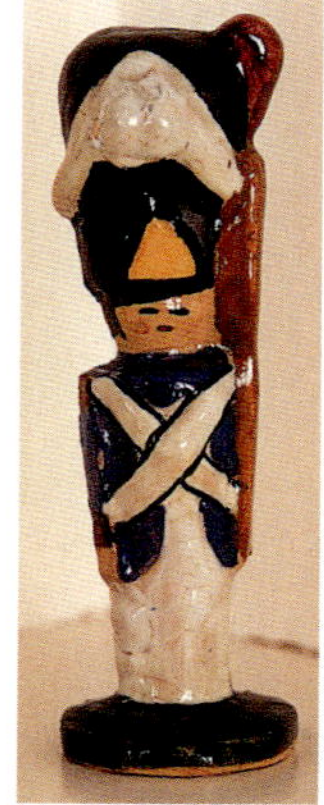

Each soldier stands about 3.25" or less ...

... and has the Geo-Fourrier monogram and the word France.

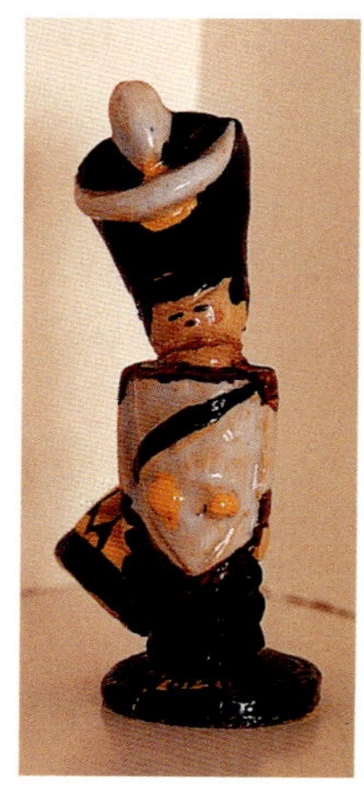

Right:
For another look at Geo-Fourrier soldiers, see *Mes Plus Beaux Quimper*, p. 70. There they are referred to as figures from the coronation of Napoleon. Price range: $175-$225 per figure. *Private Collection.*

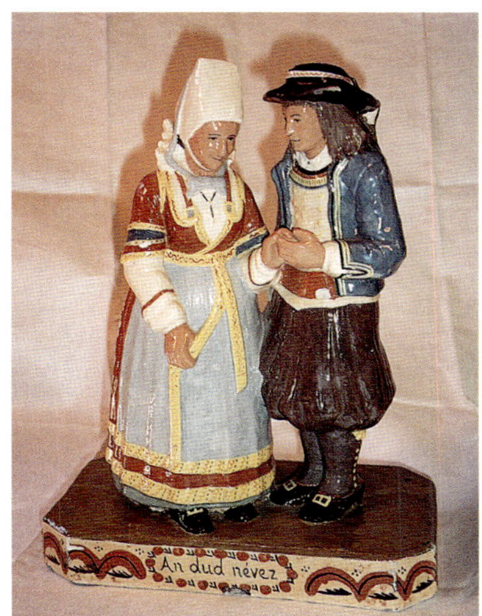

Single figurines come in all sizes, shapes, and décor. This unsigned example is entitled *An dud névez*, or Newlyweds. (Their likeness can be seen on the cover of Joseph Henriot's *Mémoires d'un faïencier quimpérois* and in *Trois Siècles de Faïences, p. 219*.) The couple, in *terre cuite vernissée,* stands 16.5" tall and date from the last quarter of the 19th century. The statue did not meet its reserve on an 2001 Internet auction. Price range: $1,000-$1,400. *Courtesy of Lucy Williams.*

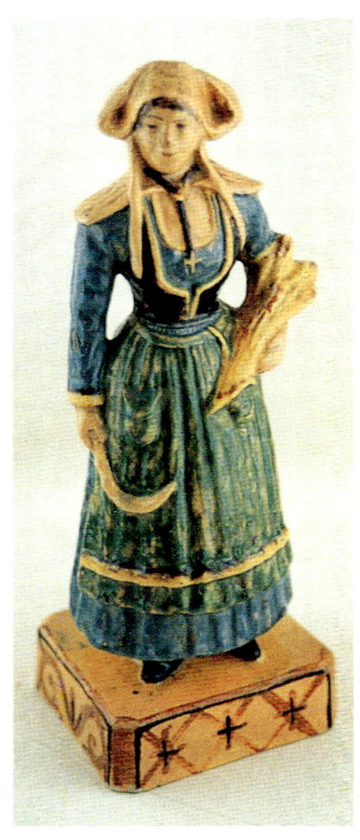

A 9" tall figurine of a female in *terre cuite vernissée* holding a scythe in her right hand and a sheaf of wheat in her left arm is signed HR, and dates in the 1890s. The base of the figurine has very simple décor. Statues of this type are not easily found. One similar model of later vintage sold through an American auction in the 1990s for $235. Price range: $450-$550. *Private Collection.*

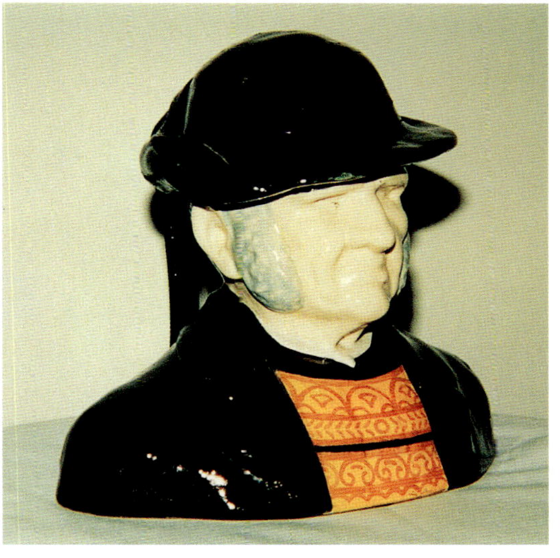

A bust of a Breton by the Henriot faïencerie stands 6.75" tall and personifies the character of Brittany in its stoic demeanor. The piece is signed Henriot Quimper and Roger.Le.Gall; it dates from the second quarter of the 20th century. Price range: $350-$500. *Courtesy of Christine T. Lindstrom.*

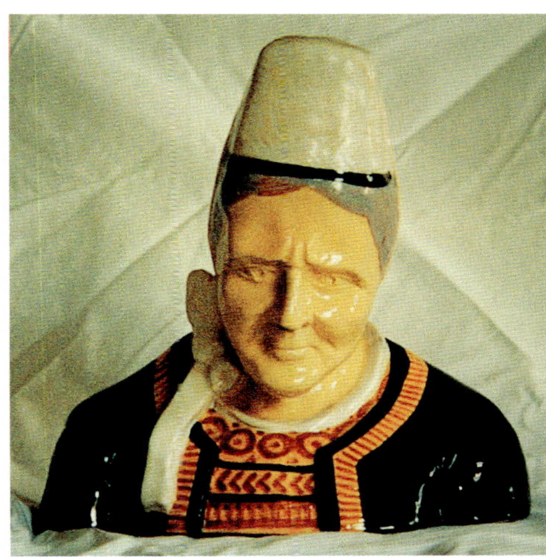

A near mate to the Breton is this Bretonne bust by LeBozec. This also is signed Henriot Quimper, but it stands 8.25" tall. The painter has misspelled the artist's name as Le Brozec. Models were developed by the artists, but the painting usually was done in workshops by squads of painters under the direction of a *chef d'atelier*. Price range: $400-$550. *Courtesy of Claire and Jon Scarborough.*

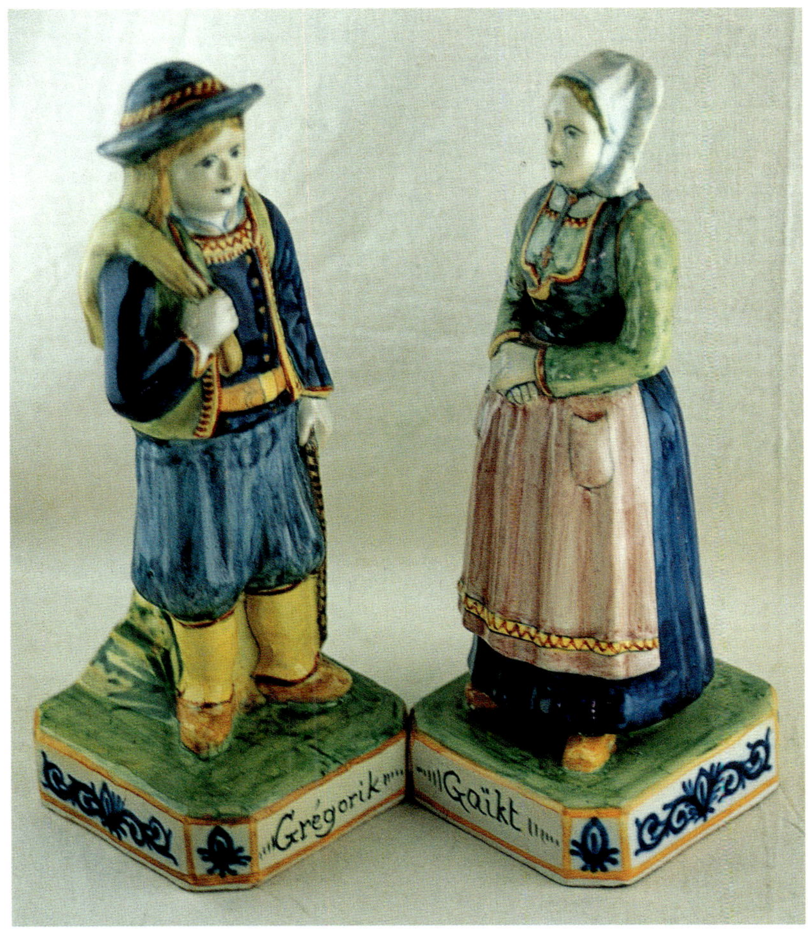

Left:
Two 8" tall figurines signed HR Quimper are a few years newer than the previous HR example. Called *Grégoire* and *Gaïkt*, the charming pair has lovely flowing colors, which were achieved by a process introduced in first quarter of the 20th century at the Henriot faïencerie. Touches of *décor riche* are on each base, and the pair dates prior to 1922. Collectors of figurines are a passionate group and the 1990s brought prices more than $400 apiece for such examples at American sales. Internet sales have produced $900 for a 5.5" tall similar pair. Price range: $1,200-$1,600 for this pair. *Private Collection.*

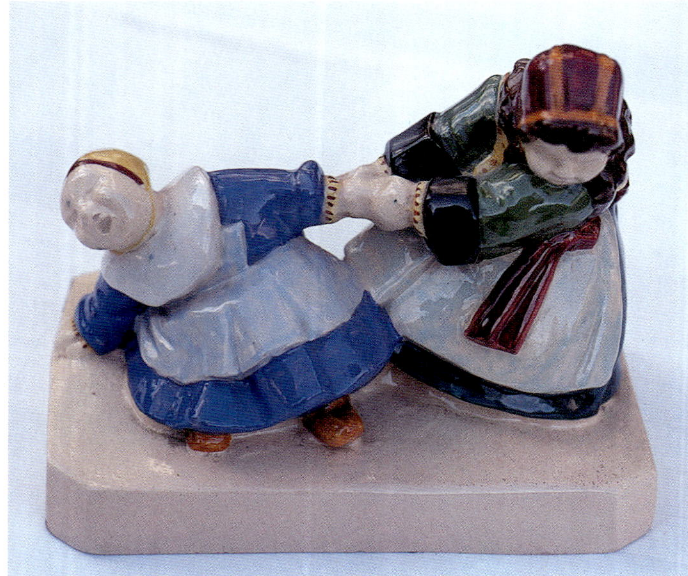

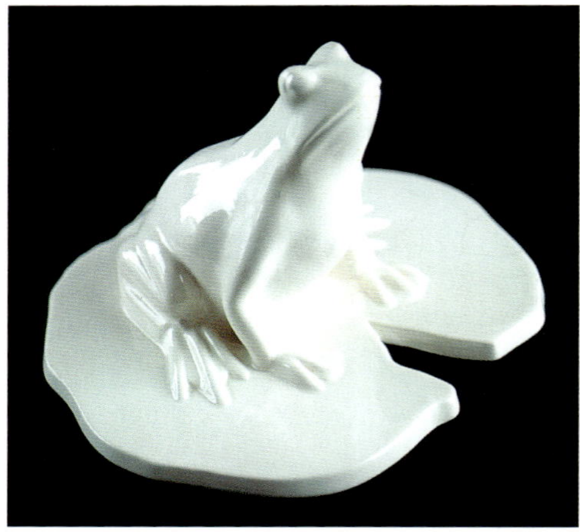

A frog *(grenouille)*, just a wart shy of 4" tall, stands on a 7" wide lily pad in *email blanc*, a winsome scene. Signed HB/Henriot, this model is post-1984 when the *Société Nouvelle des Faïenceries de Quimper* took over the factory. Price range: $175-$200. *Courtesy of Charlie and Donna Walker.*

Sisters is the name lovingly given by the owner of this charming statuette by the Henriot artist Jim-Emile Sévellec. Standing 6.5" high, it shows the struggle that sometimes can erupt between siblings. U.K. prices in the 1990s were in the $200 range, but in 2000 a French auction realized over $900 for this example. Price range: $550-$650. *Courtesy of Gaynor Smith, Russethouse.*

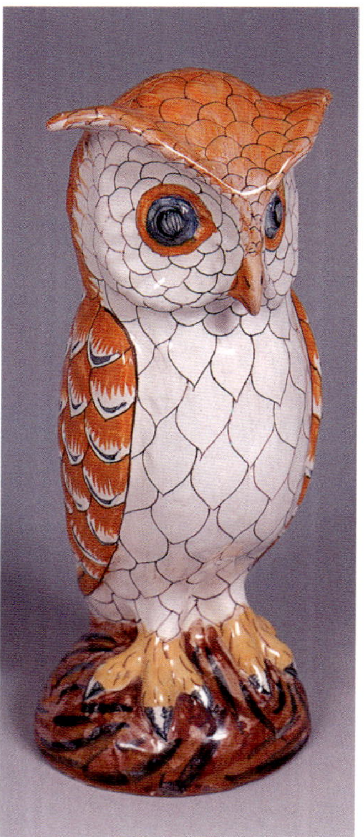

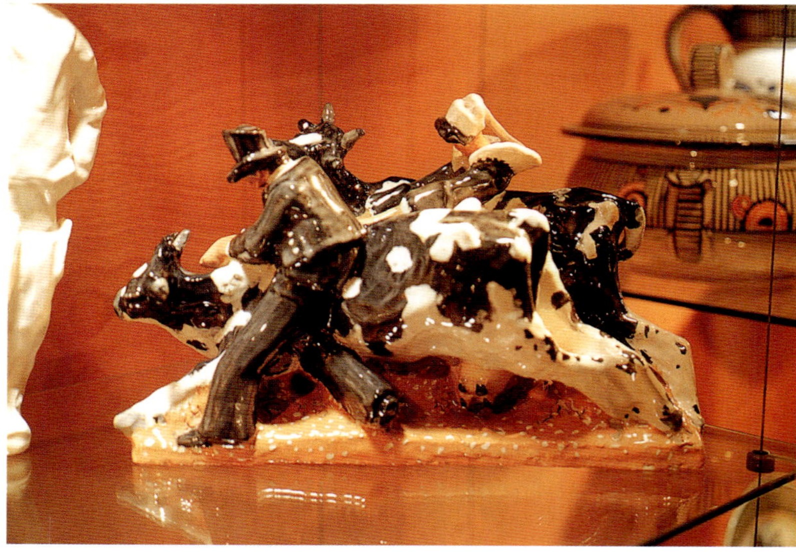

An Henriot owl *(chouette)* stands 10" tall, with a wise countenance. He has seen so much, but have we? Signed Henriot Quimper, he dates from mid-20th century. Other examples of c. 1930 owls shown sitting on limbs brought over $600 in the 1990s. One similar to this one sold through a 2000 French auction for $571. Price range: $500-$600 for this model. *Courtesy of Gaynor Smith, Russethouse.*

Mathurin Méheut designed this statue in the 1920s for the Henriot faïencerie. It's named *Le Depart pour la Foire* and shows Bretons trying to get their cows *(vaches)* to market. This version has sold well previously, but in 2000 it did not meet its reserve of $3,000 at a French auction. Price range: $1,200-$2,000. *Courtesy of Musée de la Faïence, Quimper.*

Right:
The Card Players, or *Jouers de Cartes*, is a statue by the Henriot artist Micheau-Vernez and features a *Bigouden,* from the area south and west of Quimper, matching wits with a *Glazik,* from the area of Quimper, including Locronan, Plogonnec, Le Juch and Quéménéven. It measures 8.75" tall and 12.25" long. In 2000, a French auction realized $1,072 for this model. Price range: $850-$1,075. *Courtesy of Musée Départemental Breton.*

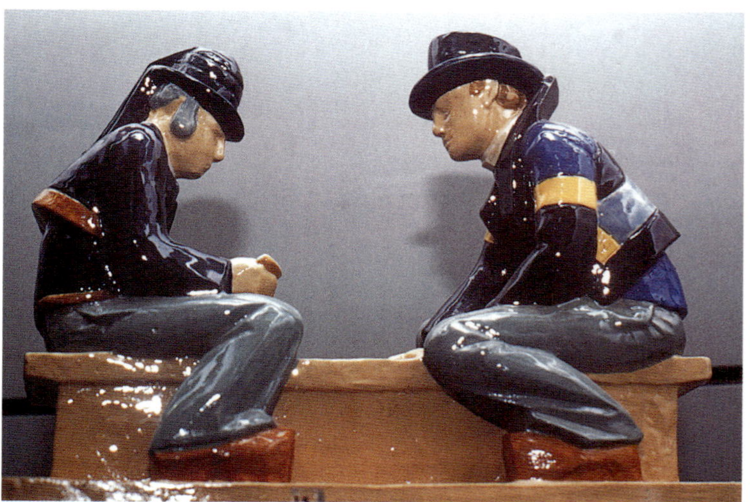

Fouillen is a famous name in Quimper for contributions to the growth of design in Quimper poterie. Paul Fouillen originally worked for the HB faïencerie, beginning in the early 1920s. He quickly rose to *chef d'atelier*, workshop leader. The *petit Breton* changed with Fouillen's touch; more angular lines and bolder colors were used to portray his versions. Fouillen opened his own workshop in Quimper in the late 1920s, located on *Place Styvel*, near the *HB/Grande Maison* and Henriot factories. After World War II, Fouillen purchased his own electric kiln and continued to experiment with form and décor. After his death in 1958, his son Maurice continued the business, signing his work with MFouillen.

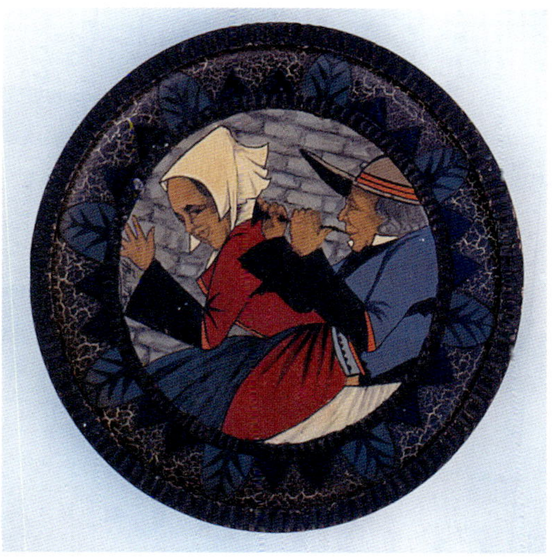

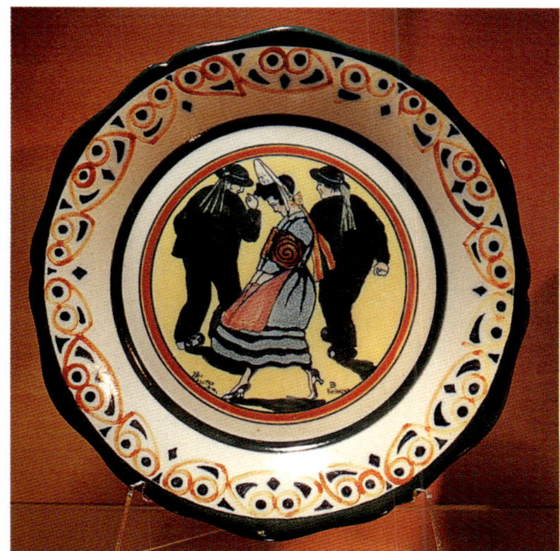

A faïence plate by Paul Fouillen made while at HB in the 1920s features stylized Bretons in the center and an interesting border décor around the rim. *Courtesy of Musée de la Faïence, Quimper.*

in Fouillen's own workshop run jointly with his brother-in-law, Hervé Patérour, wooden items were decorated with a pyrogravure technique. Price range: $375-$425. *Courtesy of Christine T. Lindstrom.*

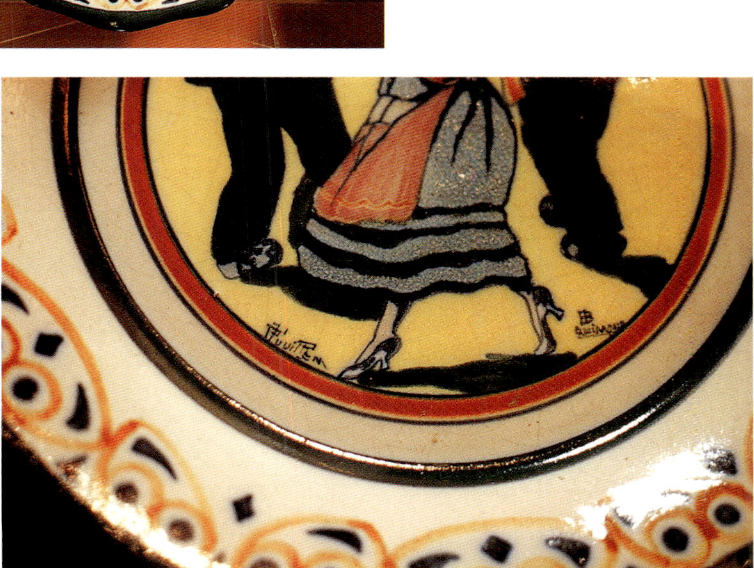

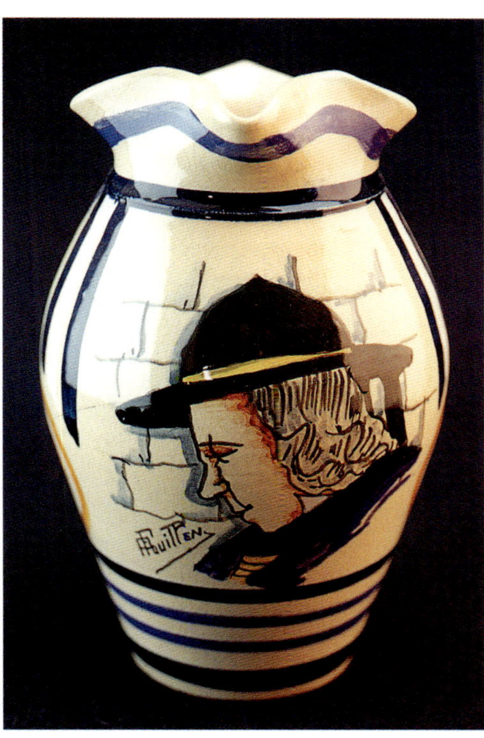

A closer look shows the signature, PFouillen and HB Quimper. *Courtesy of Musée de la Faïence, Quimper.*

Fouillen designs were made in ceramic as well, which he fired in the Henriot faïencerie kilns. An example of Fouillen's work after he left HB is seen on this 7.5" tall pitcher, signed Henriot Quimper. The décor replicates the designs Fouillen used on wooden items. Price range: $300-$375. *Courtesy of Carter Yeatman.*

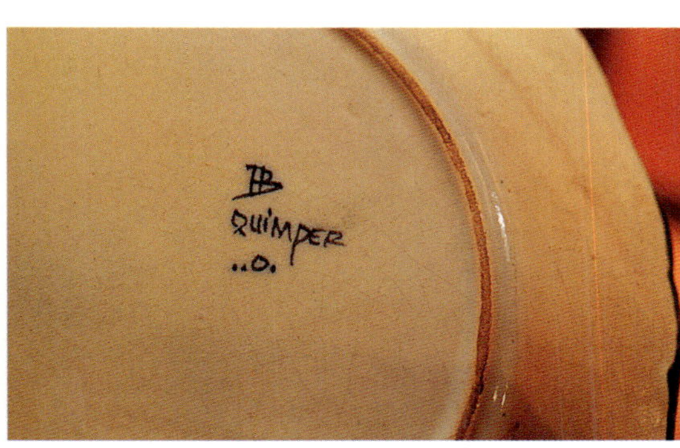

When the plate is turned over, the signature HB Quimper is accompanied by the Morse Code-like marks used by painters at HB in the 1920-1930s. This is not Paul Fouillen's signature. Rather it is the mark of the painter, as-yet-unidentified, who decorated the border of the plate. Price range: $550-$650. *Courtesy of Musée de la Faïence, Quimper.*

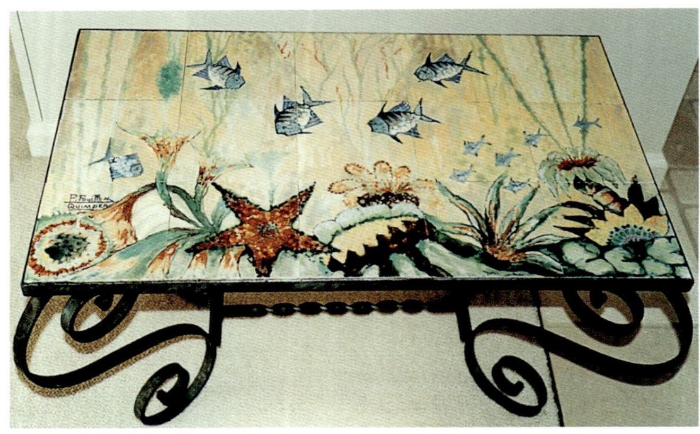

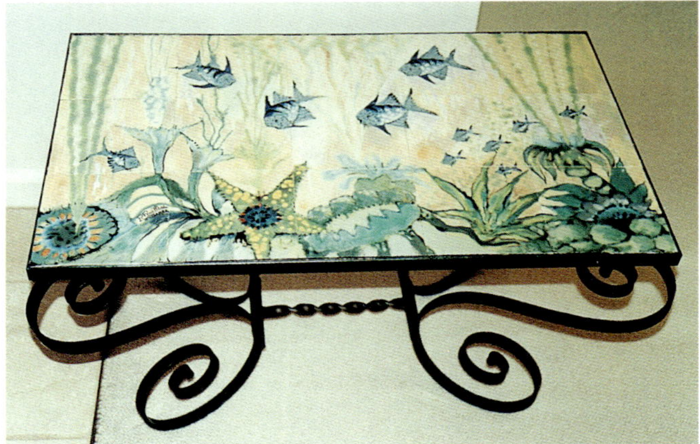

Another remarkable work by Paul Fouillen after he left HB is this tile table. It measures 30.5" long and 18.5" deep. There are fifteen 6" by 6" tiles, embraced by a wrought-iron frame. *Courtesy of Jo and David Wood.*

Look! The Paul Fouillen tile table has a mate. The pattern is the same, but the colors a bit different. *Courtesy of Jo and David Wood.*

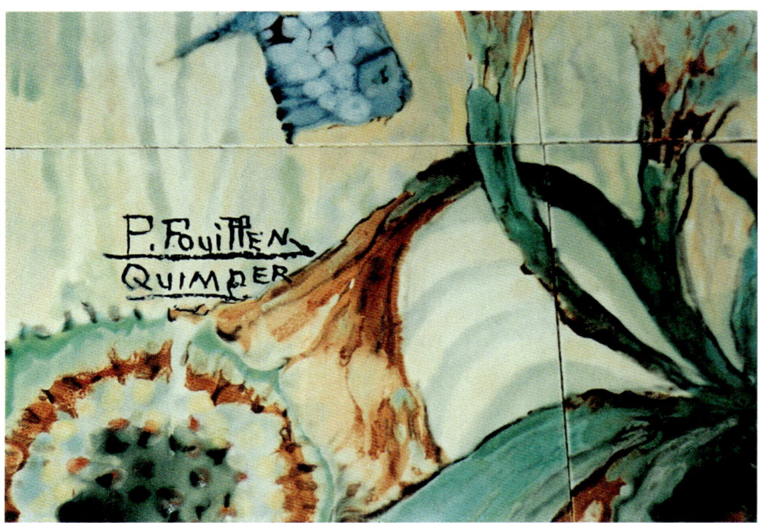

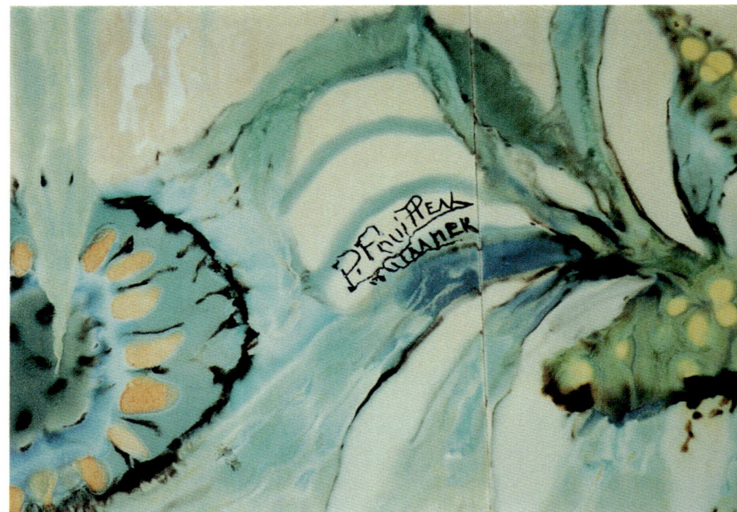

The signature is certainly Paul Fouillen. *Courtesy of Jo and David Wood.*

The signature on the second table is in the same location. This close-up view shows the variation in color from the first example. Appraised value for the pair: $12,000. *Courtesy of Jo and David Wood.*

Frames *(cadres)* for pictures and mirrors are rare and highly desired by collectors

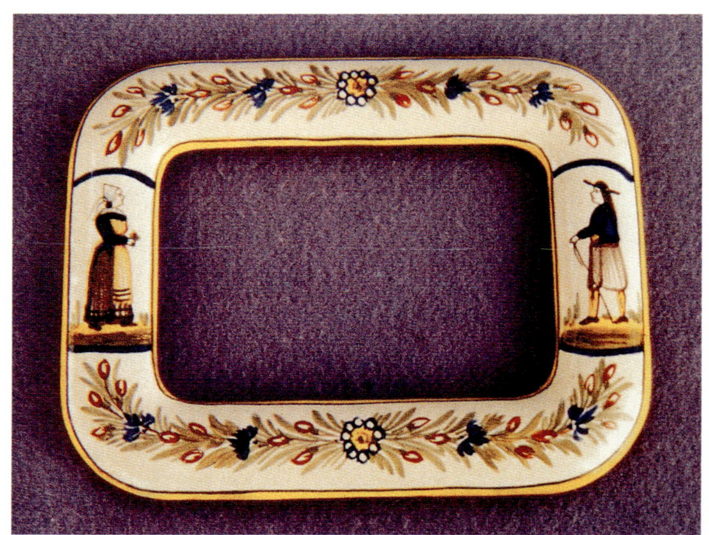

Picture frames come in a variety of shapes. This unsigned rectangular example measures 8" long by 6.5" wide. A similar model, attributed to the Porquier faïencerie, signed AP, sold through an American auction for $1,700 in 1998. Price range: $1,700-$1,900. *Private Collection.*

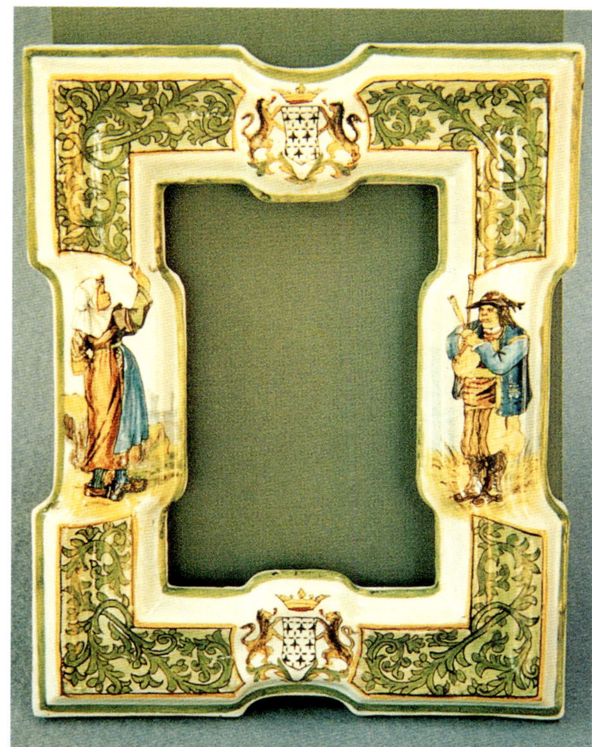

Frames for mirrors *(mirror)* are an exciting form. A 16" wide by 18" long PB Quimper beveled mirror with glass, in a dark-blue Rouen motif with two Bretons, sold in a 1980s American auction for $1,900, despite an age crack. In 2001, a Porquier-Beau beveled mirror frame, *sans* reflecting mirror, measuring 10.5" tall by 8.5" wide, with the arms of St. Malo and Brittany at top and bottom, two Bretons, and light-blue scrolling foliage on a yellow ground, brought $3,400 at a French auction. In 2001, a similarly sized mirror realized $3,700 through an American auction. The model shown here is unsigned and 10.5" tall by 8.5" wide. It has dark-green scrolling foliage on light-green ground, the arms of Brittany at both top and bottom, and two Bretons on either side. Price range: $2,800-$3,700. *Private Collection.*

❦ G is for...

Garniture de cheminée, or mantle ornaments come in a variety of combinations.

A Porquier-Beau *garniture de cheminée* consists of a *pendulette en forme de borne,* a small clock in the shape of a milestone, and two matching vases. All three have *scènes Bretonnes,* the same border of bas-relief leaves along the base, and the arms of Brittany. The clock features a fisherman and a spinner, with a view of St. Corentin in the background. A couple from Quimper is on one vase and a grinder from Briec is on the other. All are signed PB and date in the last quarter of the 19th century. In 2001, two Henriot *garniture* sets with jardinières in lieu of clocks brought $3,560 and $4,950 respectively, in Internet and American auctions. This set is early and extraordinary. Price range: $8,000-$10,000. *Collection of Pierre Breton, Art de Cornouaille, Quimper.*

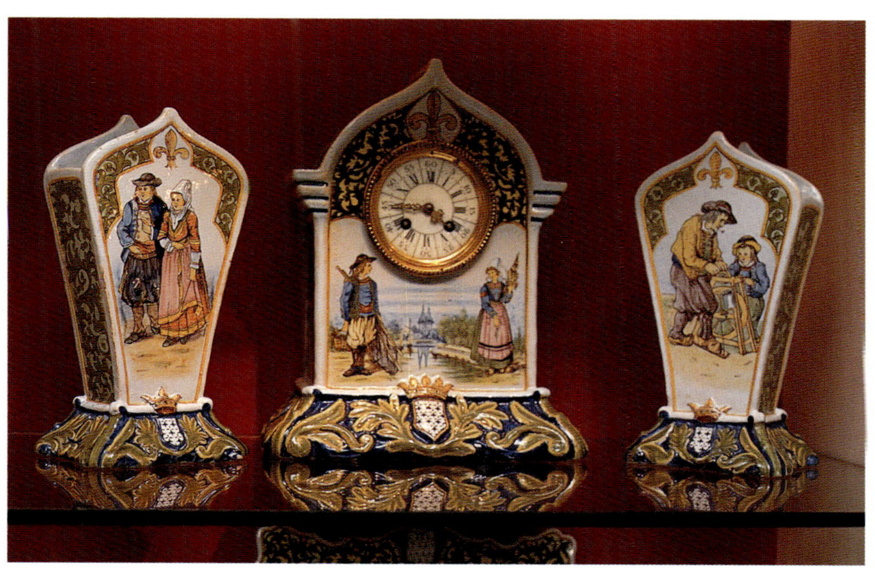

Glasses *(verres)* for drinking were made with the *petit Breton* décor by an American company, Libbey Glass.

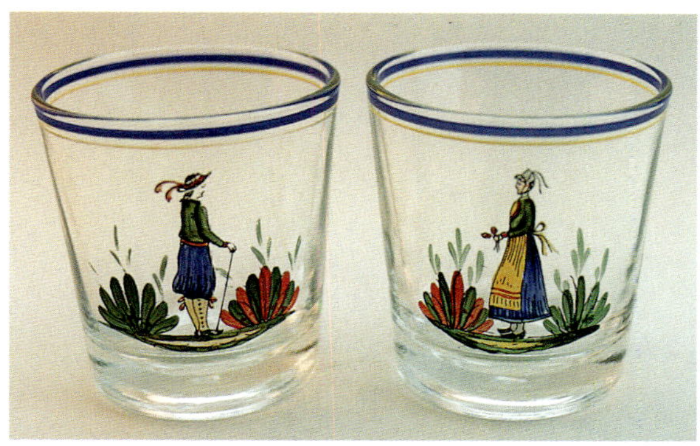

A set of eight 5.5" tall glasses sold in a 1980s auction for $165. In 1997, a set of four of the same size sold for $140. This pair of shorter 3.75" tall glasses is in mint condition. Price range: $55-$75 for the pair. *Private Collection.*

ℰ H is for...

Handkerchief (*mouchoir*) shaped items are interesting enough to have their own category.

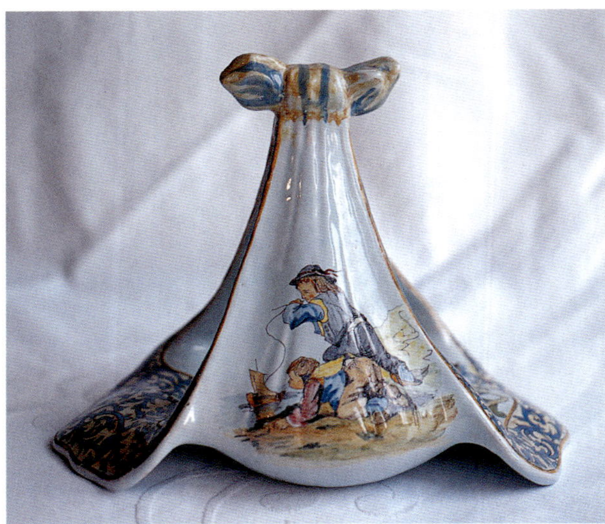

A Porquier-Beau form in the shape of a handkerchief is 8" tall, c.1900, and signed PB Quimper, *Environs de Quimper*. It features the scene of two young boys sailing a boat at water's edge, with a border of light-blue scrolling foliage on yellow ground. A second period Porquier-Beau 8" tall model from the Henriot faïencerie sold through an Internet auction in 2000 for $1,700, despite two hairline cracks. Price range: $1,750-$1,850. *Courtesy of Pierre Breton, Art de Cornouaille, Quimper.*

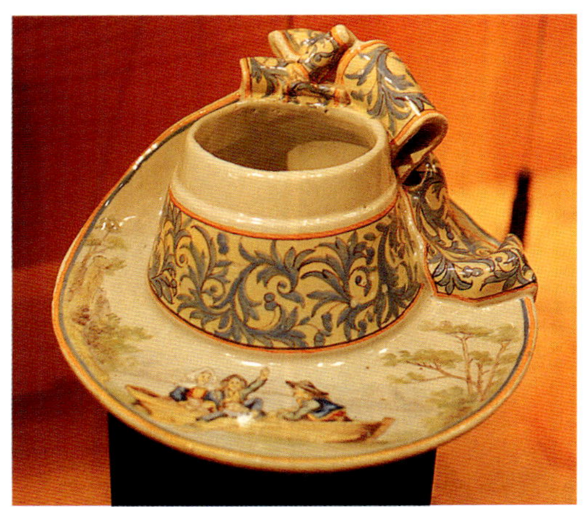

Hats (*chapeaux*) for Bretons come in ceramic as well as cloth.

This unique hat-shaped model in faïence is Porquier-Beau, last quarter of the 19th century, and very rare. A delicately painted scene shows young people in a boat along a tree-lined shoreline. The piece is capped by a hatband of ceramic ribbon in light-blue scrolling foliage on yellow ground. No price available. *Courtesy of Musée de la Faïence, Quimper.*

ℰ I is for...

Inkwells (*encriers*) come in single, double, and triple models, as well as a multiplicity of shapes and décors.

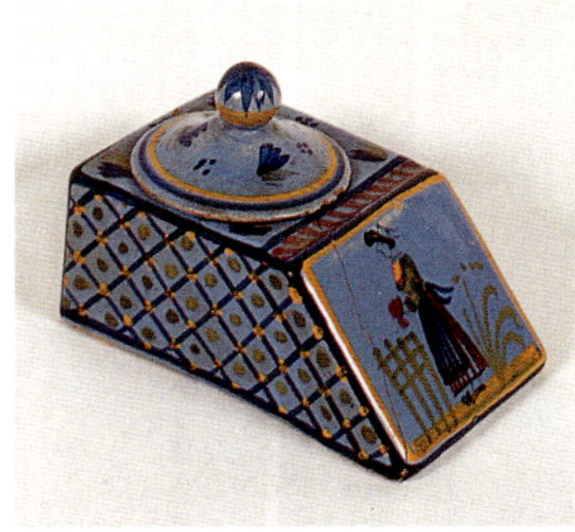

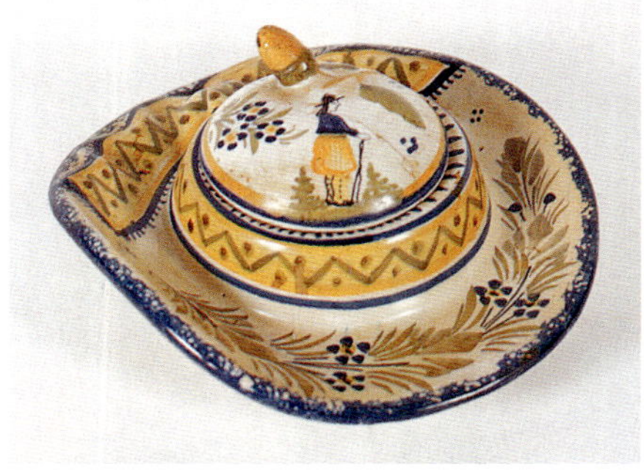

This single inkwell in blue features a Bretonne with a posy and *croisillon* décor on the sides. It measures 4" long and is not signed. It appears to be Henriot, post-World War II, when this color palette came into use. Internet auction prices for simple single inkwell models have dropped. In 1998, they were $250-$300. By 2001, the prices were in the $100 to $150 range. Price range: $100-$175. *Courtesy of Barbara Cleaver Kroll.*

A more complex design in a single inkwell is the hat form. This one has a yellow ribbon, with a zig-zag and dot design banding the crown, and a sprig of mistletoe. The rim of the hat is sponged with dark-blue, and a Breton amid *demi-fantasie* floral work completes the design. It measures 5.5" diameter, is signed Henriot Quimper, and dates from the second quarter of the 20th century. A 1999 Internet auction brought over $500 for a similar example. The same year this same model sold for $325, but in 1998 it brought only $195 through the same Internet auction. Price range: $225-$300. *Collection of Barbara Cleaver Kroll.*

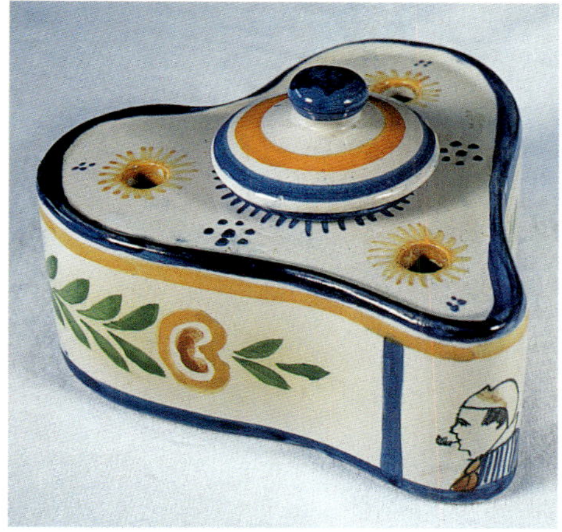

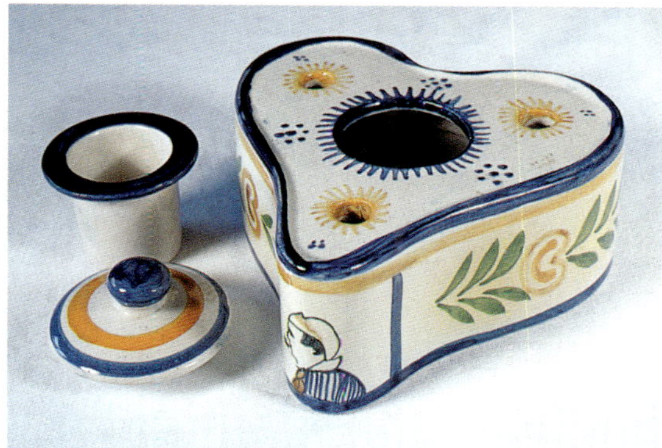

With all of the parts out, the soundness of the inkwell can be examined. This one is all together. Price range: $225-$300. *Courtesy of A.W. Styer.*

This heart-shaped inkwell with one pot is a sweetheart. It has a male from Normandy as the primary focus, with stylized apple décor accents. *Courtesy of A.W. Styer.*

The most interesting aspect of the inkwell is the signature, VB, which is found on many items with a Normandy design. We were told the initials represent the Verlingue and Bolloré, association. Jules Verlingue took on a partner, Louis Bolloré in 1922, and the firm was renamed *Société Jules Verlingue, Bolloré et Cie, Etablissement de la Grande Maison, HB. Courtesy of A.W. Styer.*

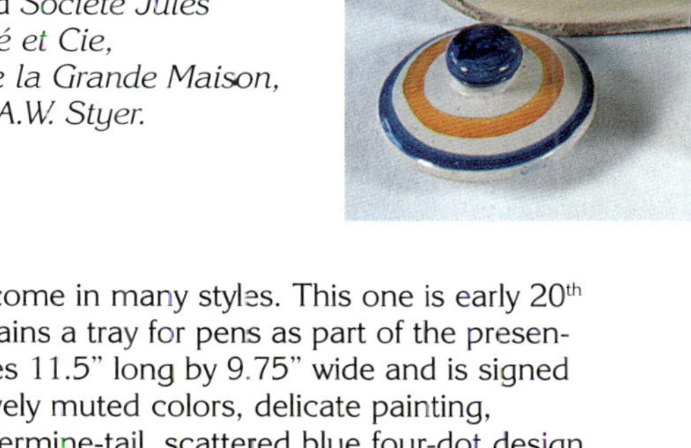

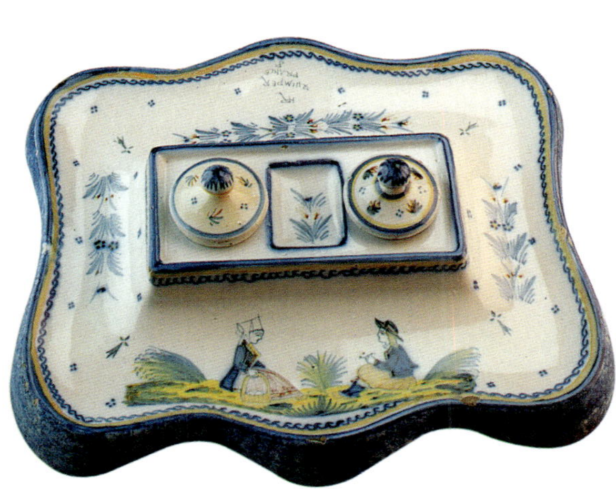

Double inkwells come in many styles. This one is early 20th century and contains a tray for pens as part of the presentation. It measures 11.5" long by 9.75" wide and is signed HR Quimper. Lovely muted colors, delicate painting, accents of black ermine-tail, scattered blue four-dot design, and a blue-chain border all make this example a winner. Price range: $1,250-$1,450. *Private Collection.*

This more formal rococo-style double inkwell is a stunning example. It measures 14" long by 5.25" deep and is signed Henriot Quimper. The Breton *sonneurs* are accompanied by sprays of *l'ajonc* and *bruyère*, the armorial of Brittany, and blue and gold embellishments to the swirling accents. This is an excellent rendition of a favorite with collectors. A late 1980s auction realized $1,700 for a similar model and an Internet auction brought $1,525 for another in 2000. Price range: $1,700-$2,225. *Courtesy of Silvia and Gary Fritzhand.*

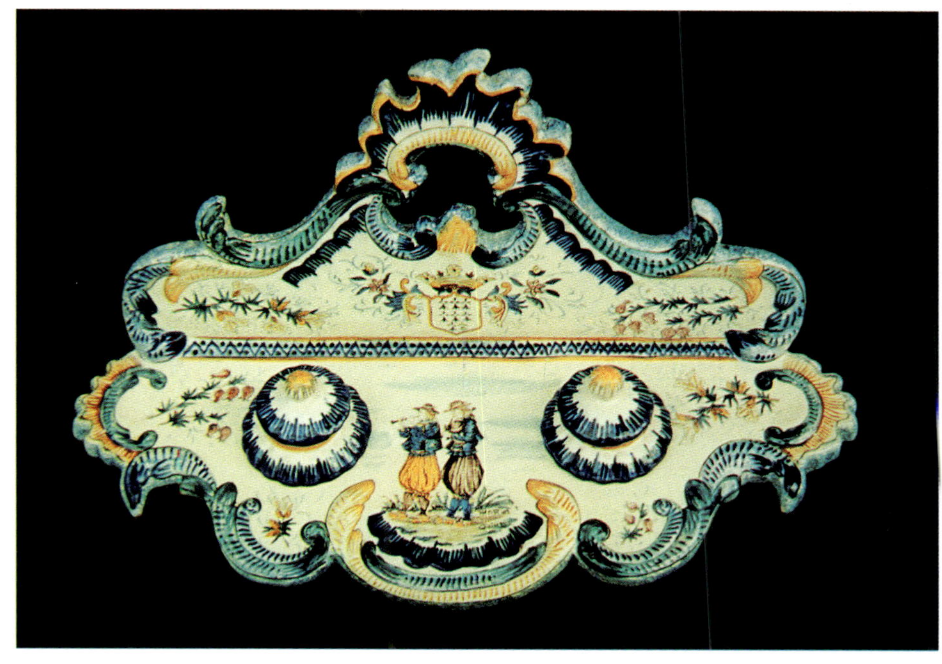

A Porquier-Beau example takes the cake. The shape is called commode, and the model has a drawer *(tiroir)*, two inkpots *(godets)*, and a pair of candleholders *(bougeoirs)*. The *scène Bretonne* is a couple from Quimper, with the armorial of Brittany over the scene. Scrolling light-blue foliage on a yellow ground completes the presentation. The commode inkwell measures 11.25" wide, 5.75" deep and is signed PB. A less-stellar, but similar model with the drawer missing brought only $500 at a French auction in 2001. Maybe someone had an extra drawer! In 2001, an Internet auction realized $2,381 for a model like this one. Price range: $2,500-$2,750. *Courtesy of Pierre Breton, Art de Cornouaille, Quimper.*

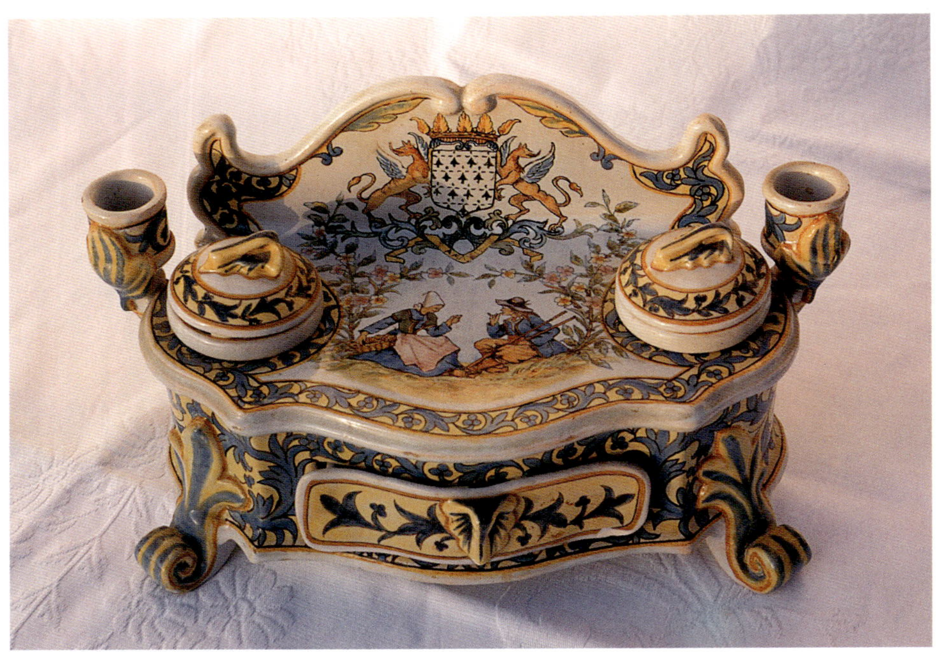

❀ J is for…

Jardinières or flower arrangement holders are highly popular and come in many forms and prices.

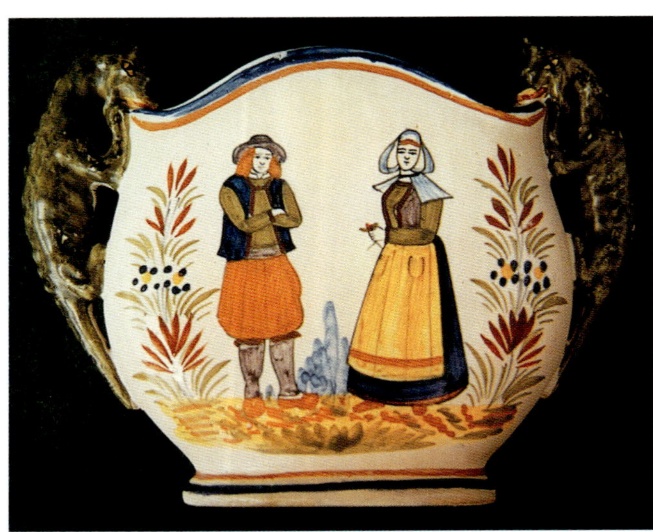

This moon-shaped jardinière with lizard handles is Henriot's version of an earlier model by Porquier-Beau. Standing 9.5" tall, this one is signed Henriot Quimper France, #82, and is from the 1920s-1930s. Price range: $550-$675. *Private Collection.*

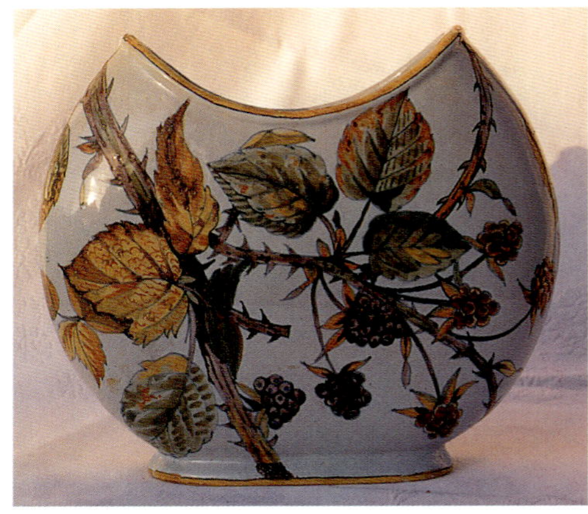

This Porquier-Beau jardinière is embellished with the botanical décor of blackberry branches. It doesn't have lizard handles as the previous Henriot example. Similar models from the last quarter of the 19th century have realized more than $2,000 at French auctions. Price range: $2,000-$3,000. *Courtesy of Pierre Breton, Art de Cornouaille, Quimper.*

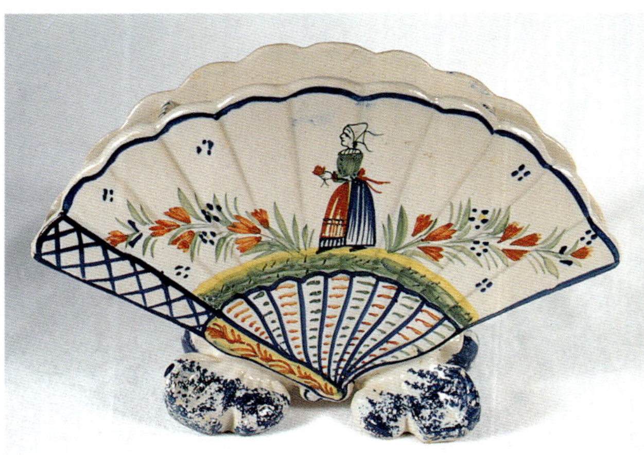

Another jardinière form is *éventail*, or fan-shaped. Although sometimes called a vase, it is more commonly known as a jardinière. This 4" tall and 6" wide example from the Henriot faïencerie is mid-20th century and has various décor elements which spice it up. The blue *croisillon* (lattice-work), red-and-blue scallop shell effect, sponged blue butterfly feet, and scattered blue four-dot accents make this piece interesting. Several Internet auction buyers paid more than $400 for similar models in the late 1990s. In 2001, a similar model was offered for $139 and did not sell. Price range: $425-$475. *Courtesy of A.W. Styer.*

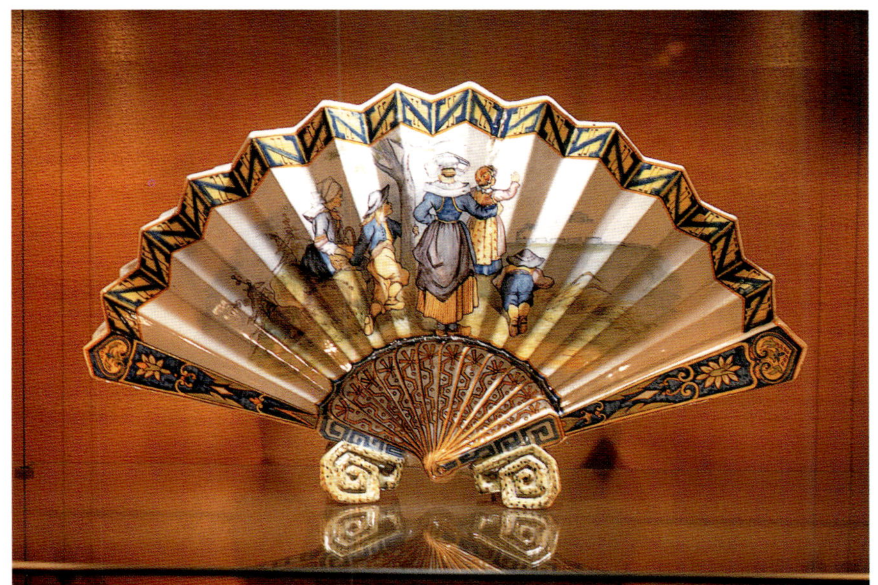

An earlier *éventail* example shows the sophistication of the potters and artists of the Porquier-Beau firm. The fan folds are sharper, and the *scène Bretonne* is beautifully painted. Called *Arrivée du train à Guengat*, it shows a family waving to a train probably bringing tourists to Brittany. The border details are just as delicately rendered. This model stands 6.25" tall and 8" wide, and is signed PB. Models like this have brought over $3,000 at French auctions. Price range: $3,000-$4,000. *Courtesy of Musée de la Faïence, Quimper.*

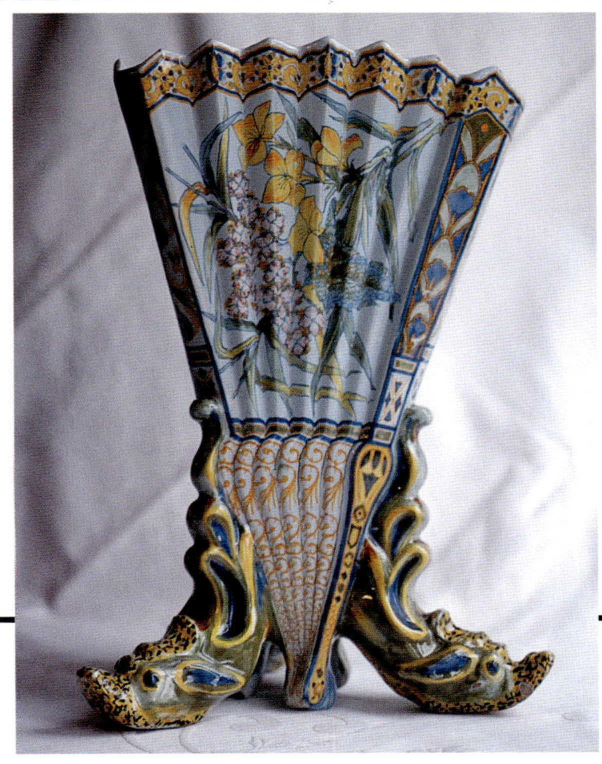

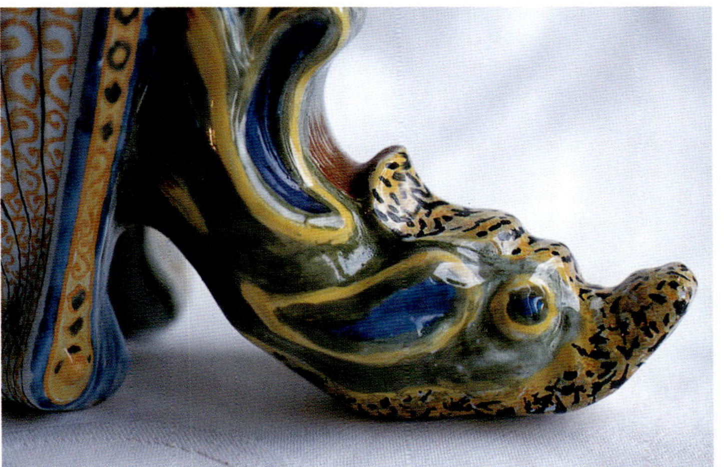

And then there are the feet! Sweet-faced dolphins executed with a fine touch hold the folded-*éventail* form. Price range: $2,500-$3,000. *Courtesy of Pierre Breton, Art de Cornouaille, Quimper.*

An 11.5" tall, folded fan-shaped vase or jardinière by Porquier-Beau is absolutely stunning. Botanical floral décor is painted on the form, as well as decorative multi-colored border designs. *Courtesy of Pierre Breton, Art de Cornouaille, Quimper.*

And just when you think you've seen the best, another one pops up to claim the top prize. This extremely rare jardinière is in the form of a butterfly *(papillon),* and is Porquier-Beau. At a French auction in 2000 it brought 62,000F, or a little more than $8,800. Price range: $9,000-$9,500. *Courtesy of Thierry & Lannon, Douarnenez & Brest.*

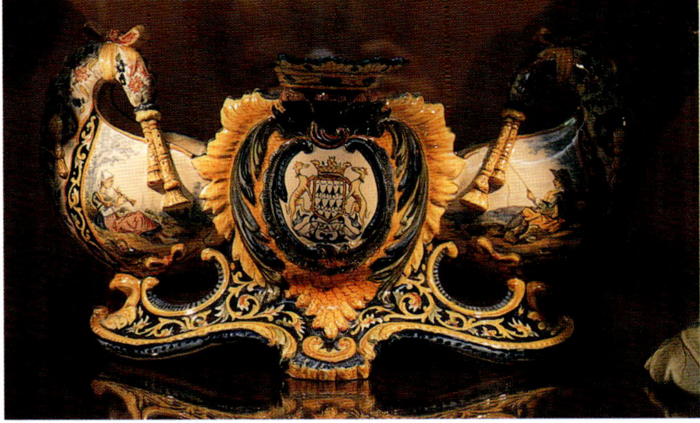

Now this is a jardinière! The form is a double *biniou* with a crest and crown molded in the center. It is lavishly decorated with rococo elements. The armorial of Brittany is in a center medallion, with a Bretonne playing a *bombarde* (the only time we've seen this), and a Breton fishing on either side. The jardinière measures 16.5" long and 9.75" high. The same form was offered in a late 1980s auction as Henriot Quimper #134 with an estimate of $2,500-$3,000. While it only achieved $1,650 then, it is well worth the original estimate and more. Price range: $2,500-$3,000. *Courtesy of Musée de la Faïence, Quimper.*

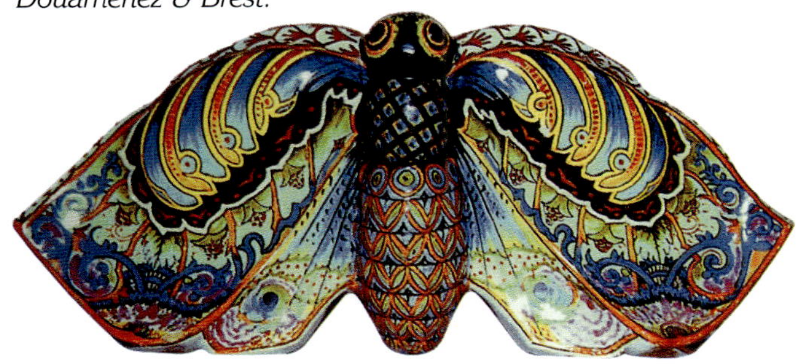

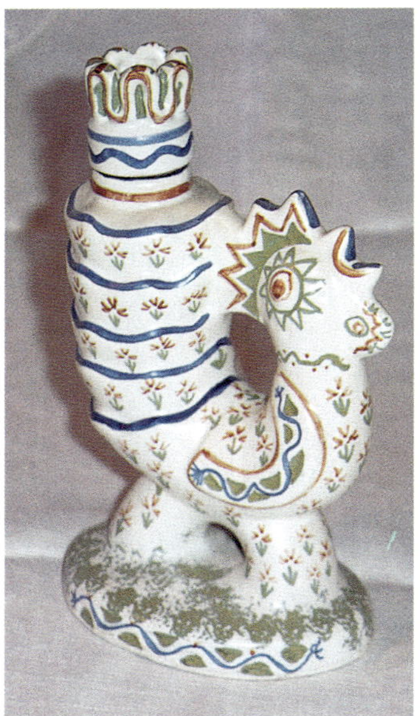

A 12.5" tall liqueur bottle in the shape of a rooster is a popular *Keraluc* motif. Price range: $175-$225. *Courtesy of Lucy Williams.*

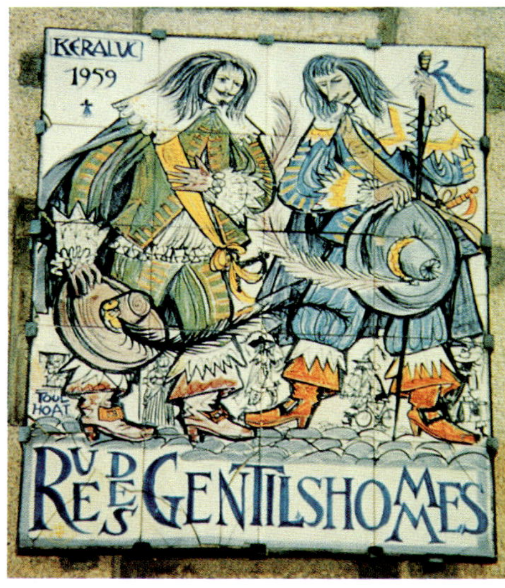

Keraluc in Breton means the house of Luc, an apt name for the faïencerie of Victor Lucas. The *Keraluc* faïencerie made this street sign for Quimper's *Rue des Gentilhommes*, dated 1959. Price not available.

❧ K is for...

Keraluc faïencerie in Quimper was started by Victor Lucas in 1947, after leaving both the Henriot and HB faïenceries for a mission to Paris after World War II. In 1985, the *Keraluc* faïencerie was purchased and the name changed to Stylform. In 1993, the faïencerie's molds, marks, and designs were purchased by the *Société Nouvelle des Faïences de Quimper*.

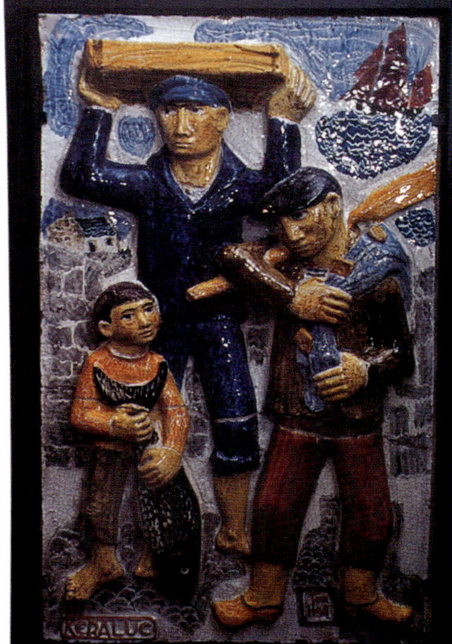

Left:
Pierre Toulhoat created this faïence plaque while at *Keraluc*. It shows Bretons working, and is part of a series Toulhoat designed depicting the life and legends of Brittany. Price not available. *Courtesy of Musée Départemental Breton.*

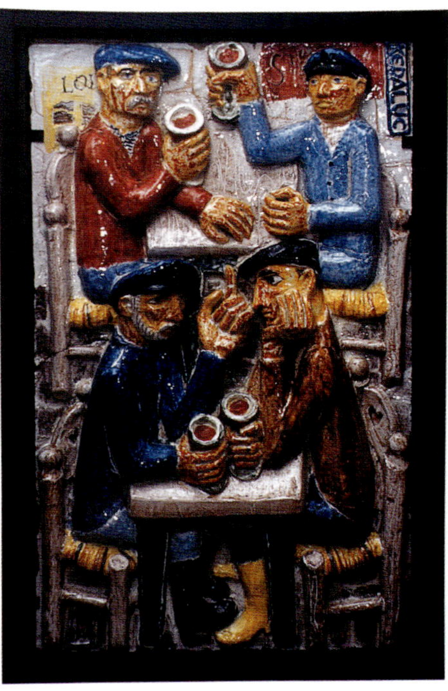

Right:
Another Toulhoat plaque shows Bretons relaxing at the end of the day in a café. Price not available. *Courtesy of Musée Départemental Breton.*

Knife rests (*porte-couteaux*) come in two basic forms, a ceramic cylinder or a figural shape.

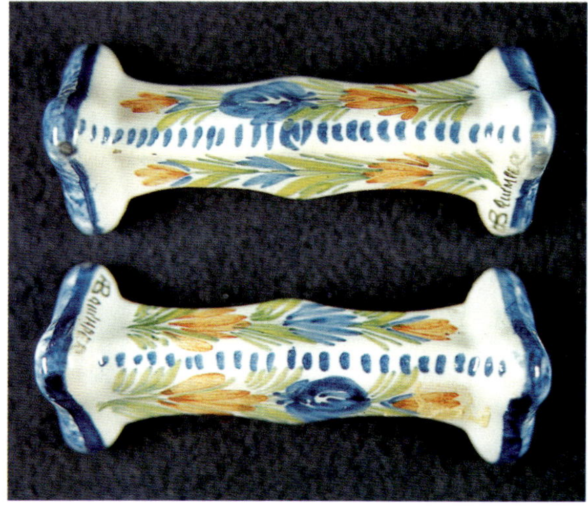

A cylinder-shaped pair of knife rests has a floral motif in blues and reds that covers their 3.5" length. These are from the second quarter of the 20th century, and signed HB Quimper. Knife rests are a favorite collector's item and prices on Internet auctions in the late 1990s were higher than in previous American sales. Things have settled down. Knife rest prices have fallen in 2001 Internet sales. Price range: $65-$85 for the pair. *Private Collection.*

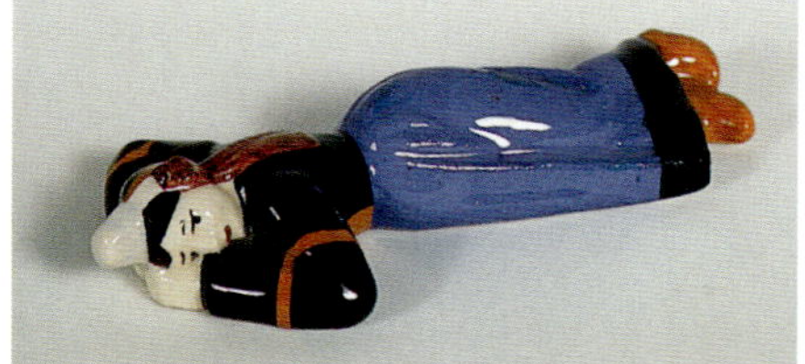

Figural knife rests are another story. This example by the Henriot artist Charles Maillard shows a reclining Bretonne with her head resting on her hands, and measures 4.5" long. Maillard is known for a series of knife rests with both male and female Bretons in similar poses. Signed C.M. Henriot Quimper. A collector paid $375 through a 1999 Internet auction for a reclining male in this series. Price range: $175-$275. *Private Collection.*

✜ L is for...

Lamps *(lampes)* are available in two forms. One is a made-to-be lamp. The other is a piece of Quimper, which has been converted into a lamp.

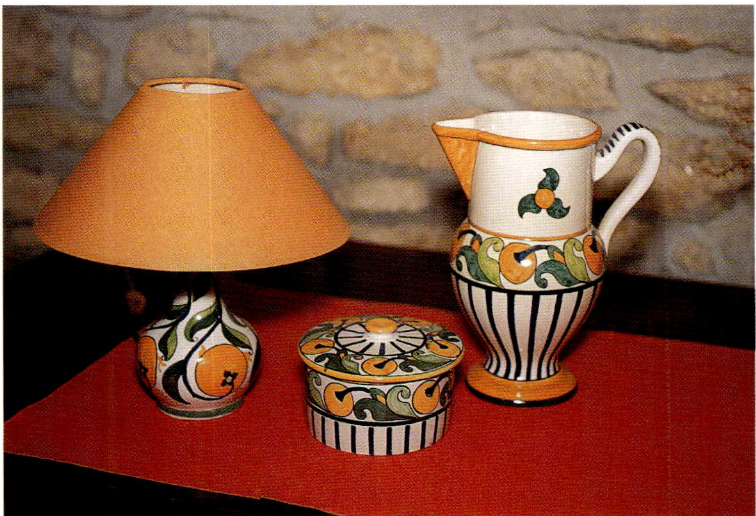

The 8" tall lamp shown here is a converted vase. The HB faïencerie made this décor #9 called *Genre Moderne* in the 1930s. The style works well with the bedroom furnishings in a Breton coastal home. The pitcher, powder box, and lamp make a great statement as a group. Price range: $100-$125 for the lamp, $150-$175 for the box, and $200-$300 for the pitcher. *Private Collection.*

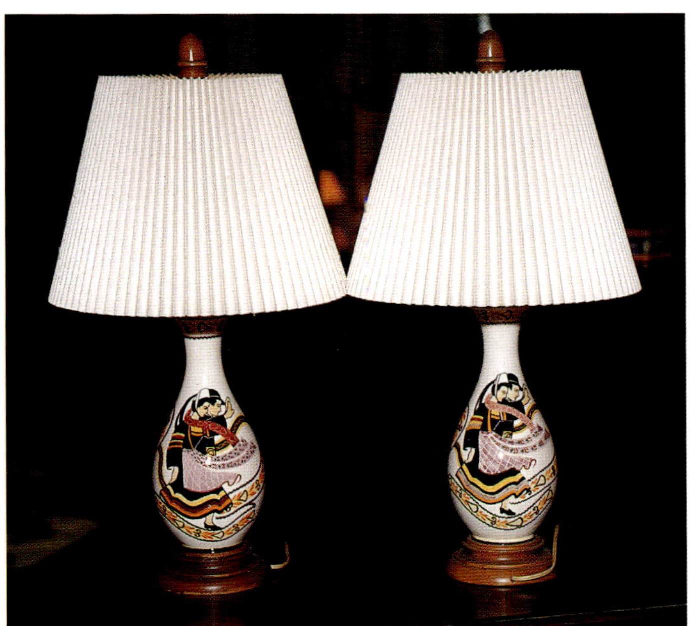

This pair of Quimper lamps in modern movement colors is from the third quarter of the 20th century and stands 27" high. Price range: $400-$500. *Private Collection.*

Lavebo (wall fountain) contains three parts, a bowl, a water dispenser or reservoir, and a lid to the reservoir.

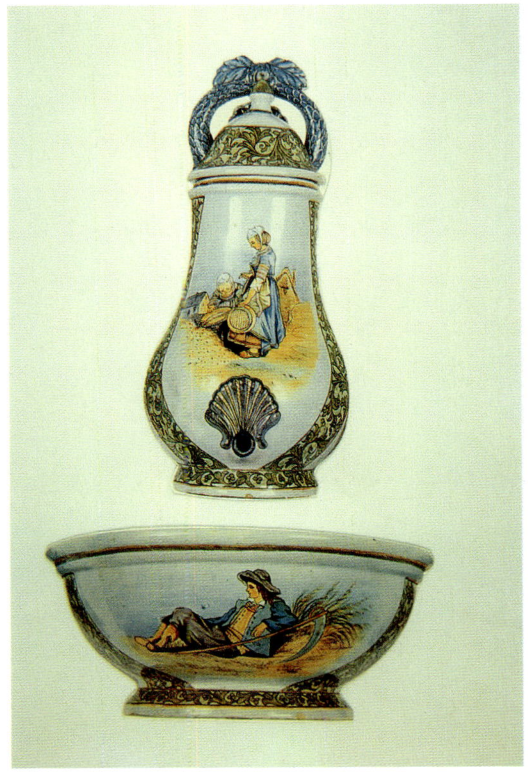

This Porquier-Beau *lavebo* was offered at a French auction in the 1990s. The *scène Bretonne* on the bowl is *Faucheur de Fouesnant* (the reaper of Fouesnant) and *les cribleueses de blé de Pont-l'Abbé*, the wheat sifters from Pont-l'Abbé, is on the reservoir. A PB reservoir with lid with the scene *Dévideuse de Penhars* (winder of Penhars) sold for $1,975 on an Internet auction in 2000. A complete model by PB from the last quarter of the 19th century commands more. Price range: $2,500-$3,500. *Courtesy of Oriot & Dupont, Morlaix.*

M is for...

Mayflower ship décor is found on several Quimper poterie items. It features a three-mast sailing ship ironically flying French flags, with the title *Mayflower* beneath the ship. The Henriot faïencerie is thought to have developed the design for an American department store.

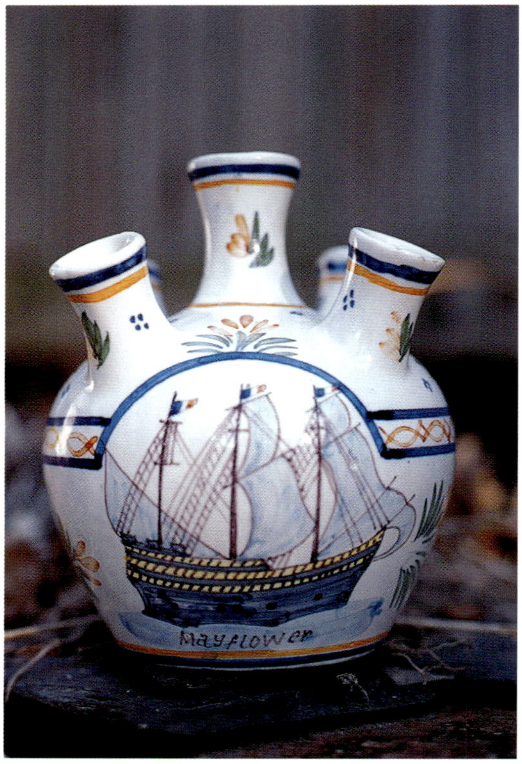

A *quintel* is a five-fingered vase for flowers. This 5.75" tall model signed Henriot Quimper France, #71, sports the Mayflower motif. This model dates from the 1930s. A similar model sold via the Internet in 2000 for $118, and another in 2001 for less than $120, real bargains. Then, another 2001 Internet sale brought $355 for a Mayflower *quintel.* Price range: $200-$250. *Courtesy of Carter Yeatman.*

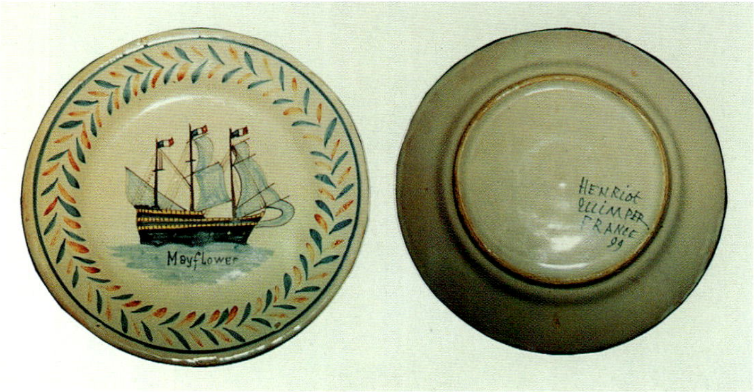

Most commonly seen Mayflower designs are on plates. This example measures 9.25" diameter and is signed Henriot Quimper France, #99, and is from the late 1920s. Prices for Mayflower plates fluctuated in the 1990s, with a high of $325 through an American auction and a low of $155 through an Internet auction. Price range: $250-$350. *Private Collection.*

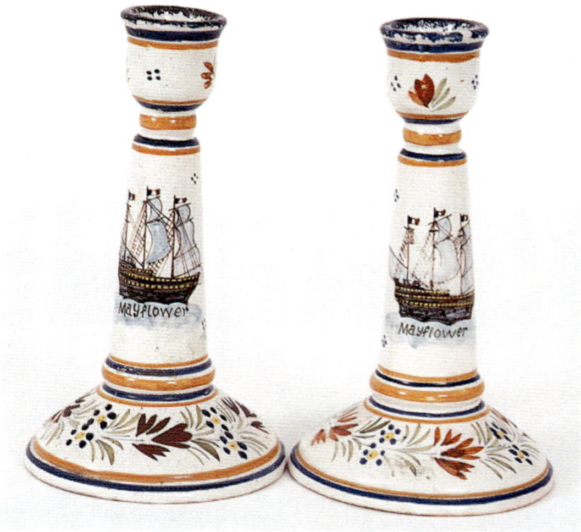

These remarkable candlesticks were part of a Quimper collection donated to South Dakota State University. They measure 8.5" tall and are an unusual form for the Mayflower motif. They have *à la touche* flowers and the blue four-dot design in addition to the ships, and they date from the 1930s. Price range: $475-$550. *Courtesy of the S. D. State Agricultural Heritage Museum Photographic Collection.*

Ménagère literally translated means a housewife, but it is the term used for a three-sectioned serving piece. It can be as simple as a small, covered center pot with two attached open compartments for salt and pepper, or as complex as a figural-shaped mustard pot with two compartments integral to the design.

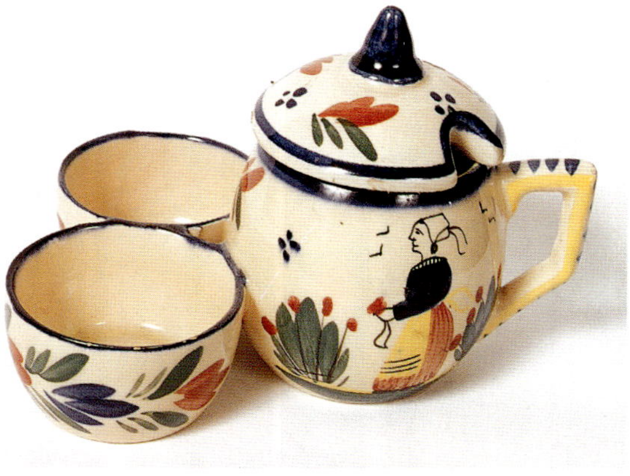

This *ménagère* form by HB is from the 1920-1930s. It is identified by the Morse Code-like signature of an exclamation mark (!) used by the painter Madame Kerbourc'h from the *Grande Maison. (Taburet, p. 216.)* It stands 5.5" tall and has a sweet Bretonne on the center mustard pot. Many times the lid is missing, but this example is complete. A similar, but later, HB model sold in 2000 for $60 and was called a *salonier* by the Internet seller. An Internet seller called another model by Henriot an eggcup with salt and pepper; it brought $245 in 2000. Price range: $175-$225. *Courtesy of Susan S. Temple.*

Menu *(porte-menu)* is a ceramic form that sits on the dining table and either has a slot in which to place the menu or is large enough to write the fare of the day on the surface.

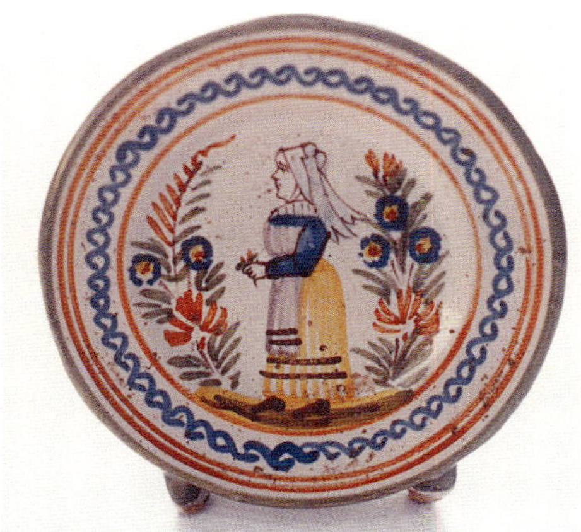

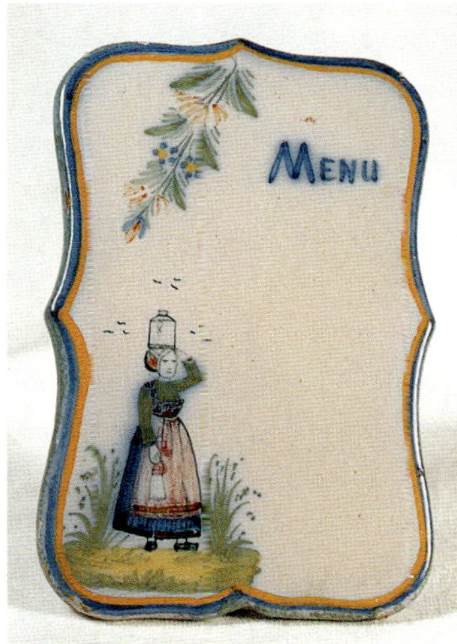

Left:
A 3" diameter version believed to be AP, similar to the menu or place card holder shown here, realized $300 in a late 1990s American auction. This example features a Bretonne with a complex *coiffe* surrounded by a blue-chain border, supported by a bracket foot. It is signed AP, a mark originally developed for the Adolph Porquier faïencerie. The AP mark was re-registered and used by Adolph's son, Aurther, in the late 1890s and the first few years of the 20th century. This menu most likely dates from that period. Price range: $325-$400. *Courtesy of Pierre Breton, Art de Cornouaille, Quimper.*

This Henriot faïencerie example of a *porte-menu* shows a Bretonne with a milk can atop her head. It did not reach its reserve the first time around on an Internet sale from France, but the menu now resides in the U.S. It has lovely flowing colors, is 5" tall, and is signed HR Quimper. Price range: $300-$400. *Courtesy of A.W. Styer.*

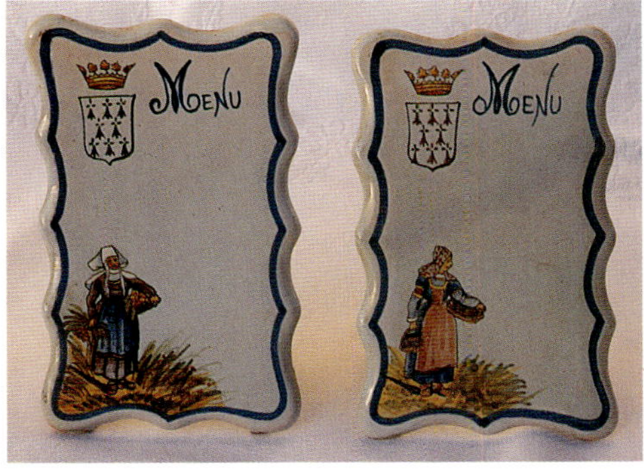

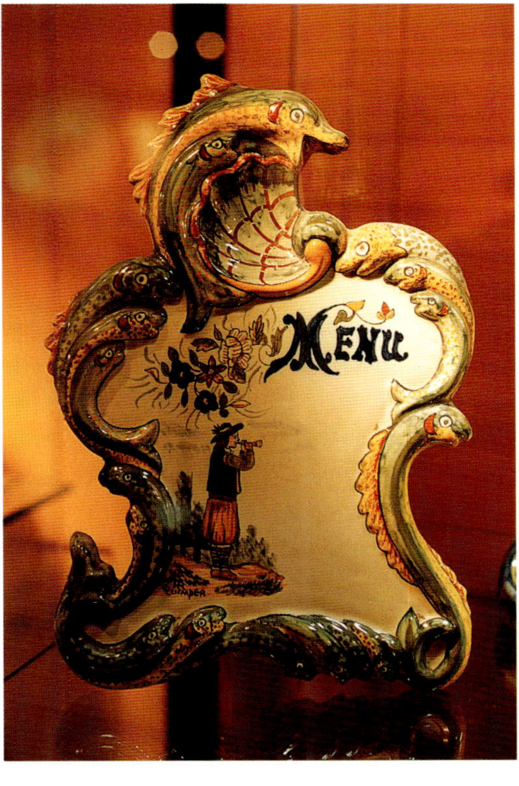

A pair of menus from the Porquier-Beau firm shows the more sophisticated artistry of Alfred Beau. Bretonnes carrying baskets in the countryside stand beneath the shield of Brittany topped by a crown. The scalloped edge is outlined with a dark-blue line. A similar menu with some damage to the bracket support sold for $220 in a mid-1990s American auction. In better condition these examples sell for much more. Price range: $350-$450 each. *Courtesy of Pierre Breton, Art de Cornouaille, Quimper.*

A rococo-style menu takes the prize. A dolphin swirls high above a shell on the top of the menu and other fish decorate the sides and the bottom edge of the piece. It's a gem. The Breton playing the *bombarde* seems overshadowed by the rest of the décor. Less detailed rococo-style menus from Henriot brought $425 in a late 1980s auction and more than $500 in a 1999 Internet sale. Price estimate: $800-$1,000. *Courtesy of Musée de la Faïence, Quimper.*

Miniatures are collectible items sometimes confused with dollware.

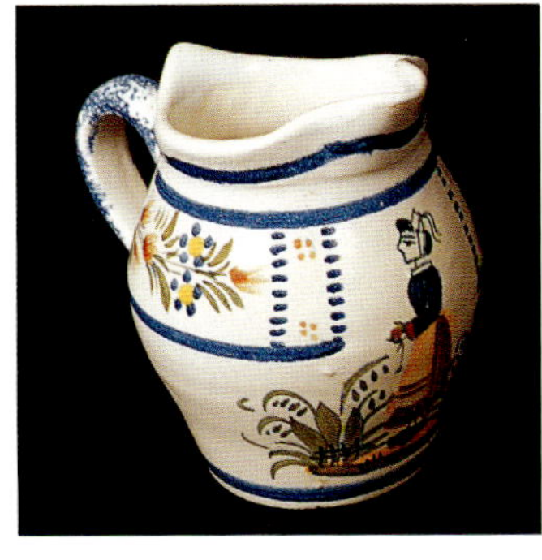

This miniature pitcher measures 2.5" tall and is signed Mt. St. Michel, Henriot Quimper #139. It was intended for the tourist trade and dates from the 1940s. On the other hand, a doll pitcher, 1.5" tall, signed Henriot Quimper France #432, realized $110 at a 2001 American auction. Price range: $125-$145 for the St. Michel souvenir miniature. *(See Mali, Old Quimper Review, March 1993, for a discussion of miniatures and dollware.)*

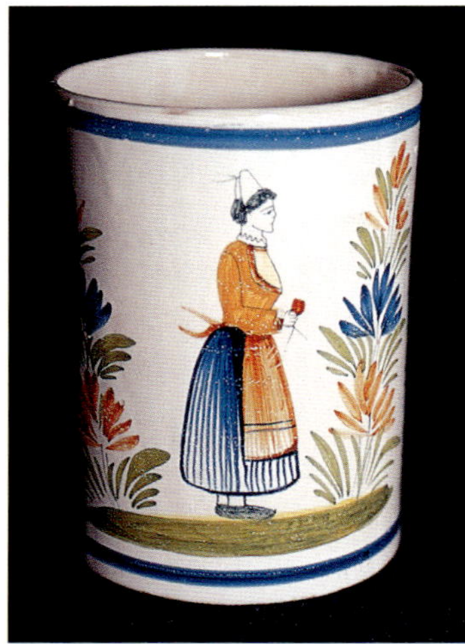

Now this is a mug! The Henriot faïencerie made this huge 6.75" tall by 4.25" wide mug, which holds nearly a liter of liquid. What beverage do you think was served in this piece, which dates from the first quarter of the 20th century? Price range: $275-$325. *Courtesy of Pam Moore.*

Mugs (*grande tasse* for coffee, *chope* for beer or cider) come in a variety of décors and sizes.

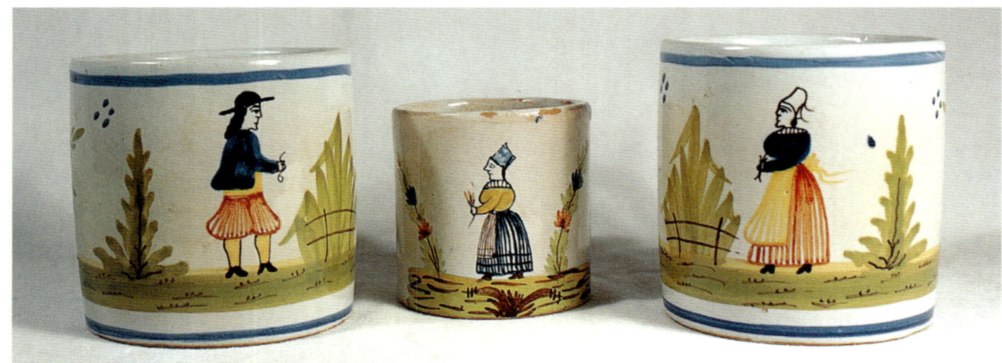

The two larger mugs measure 3.5" tall and 3.25" wide. They are signed HB Quimper and date from the first quarter of the 20th century. The smaller mug is unsigned Malicorne faïence, measures 3" tall, and dates from the end of the 19th century. Price range: $150-$175 for the HB pair; $55-$65 for the Malicorne product. *Collection of A.W. Styer.*

❧ N is for…

Noces or wedding, as in *Les Noces Bretonnes*, was the subject of many Quimper faïence décors, particularly platters showing the wedding procession or the celebration following the nuptials.

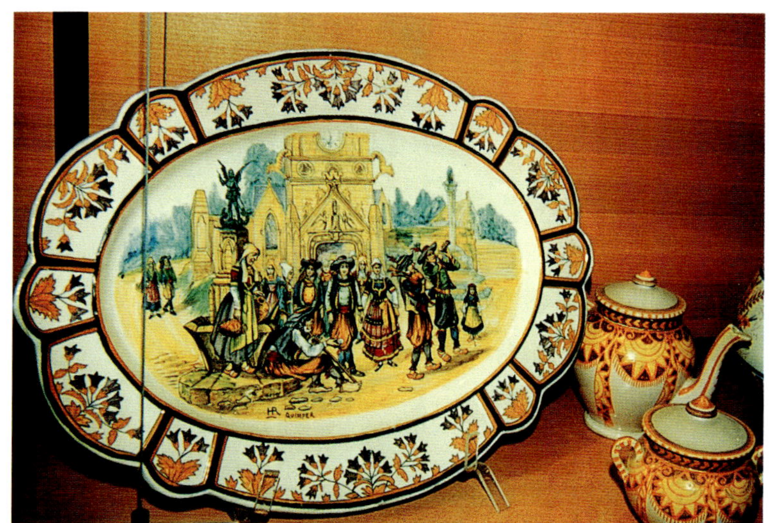

The *sortie* or exit from the church by a wedding party is captured on 13.5" platter by the Henriot faïencerie. Signed HR Quimper, it is c. 1900. The border treatment is highly unusual. Price not available. *Courtesy of Musée de la Faïence, Quimper.*

A close-up view shows the Breton musical duo called *sonneurs*, a *biniou* and a *bombarde* player, leading the way after the church services to the reception. *Courtesy of Musée de la Faïence, Quimper*

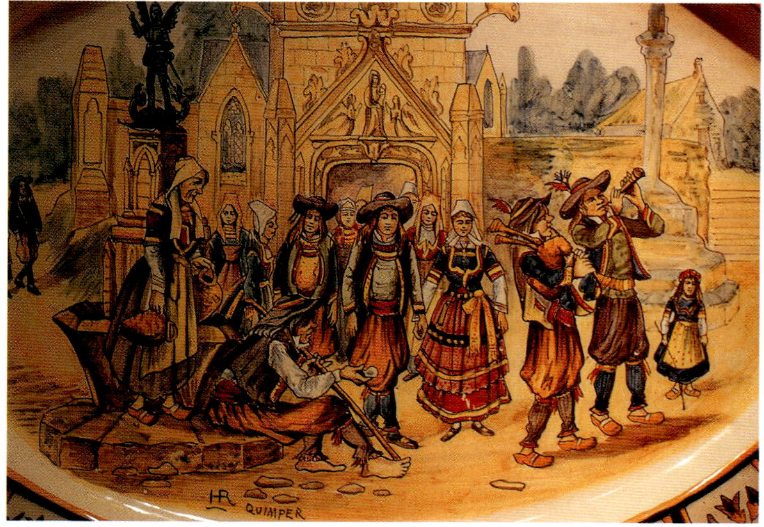

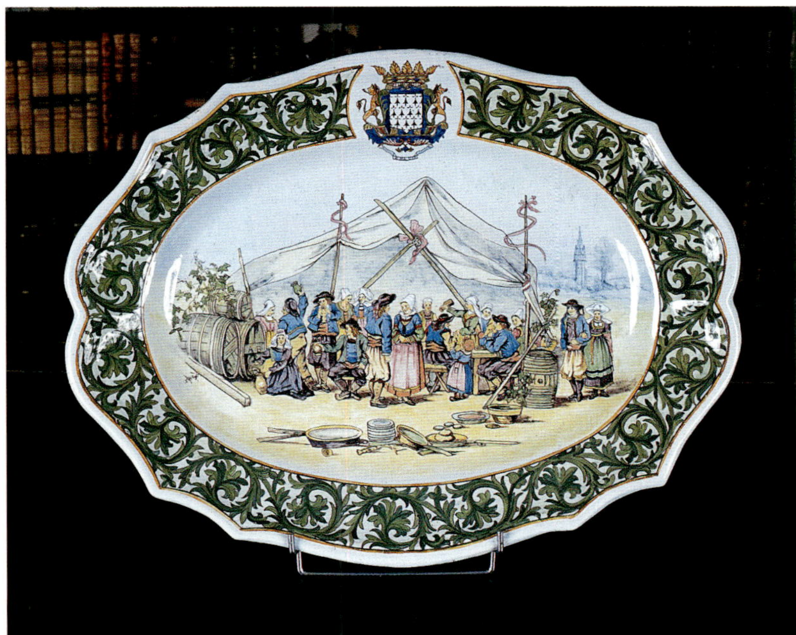

Repas de Noce sous la Tente depicts a wedding breakfast under a tent, by the Porquier-Beau faïencerie in the last quarter of the 19th century. The platter measures 21.25" long and is surrounded by dark-green on light-green scroll décor and the arms of Brittany. There are 17 people celebrating the nuptials. The scene is full of life and promise. A comparable platter sold through a 2000 French for 39,000F, or $5,570. Price range: $6,000-$7,000. *Courtesy of Manoir de Kérazan, Institut de France, Fondation Astor.*

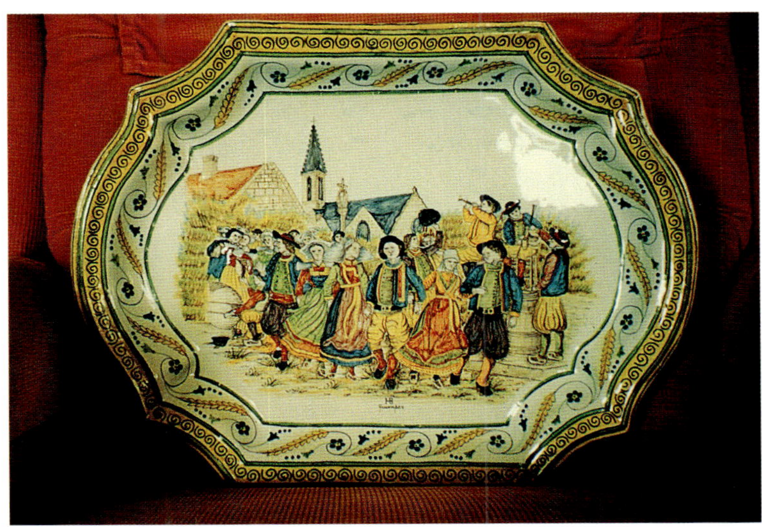

Another platter shows the party after the service. Dancers whirl around the seated *sonneurs* and details such as church spires and buildings are visible behind the merrymakers. It is signed HB Quimper on the front, HB on the back, and is 18" long. The unusual border is simple yet attractive, making this example from the first quarter of the 20th century very desirable. Price: $900-$1,200. *Private Collection.*

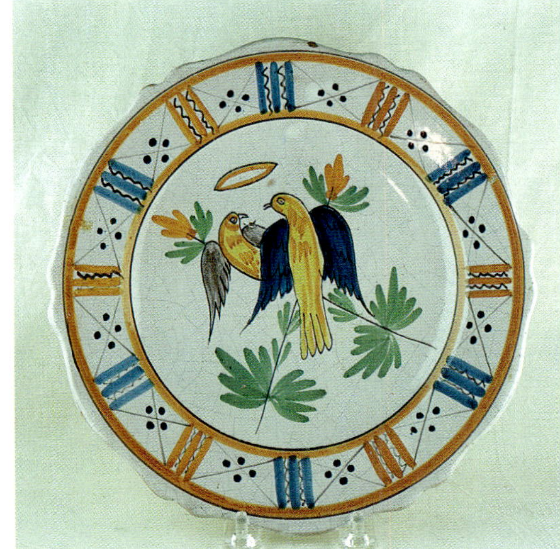

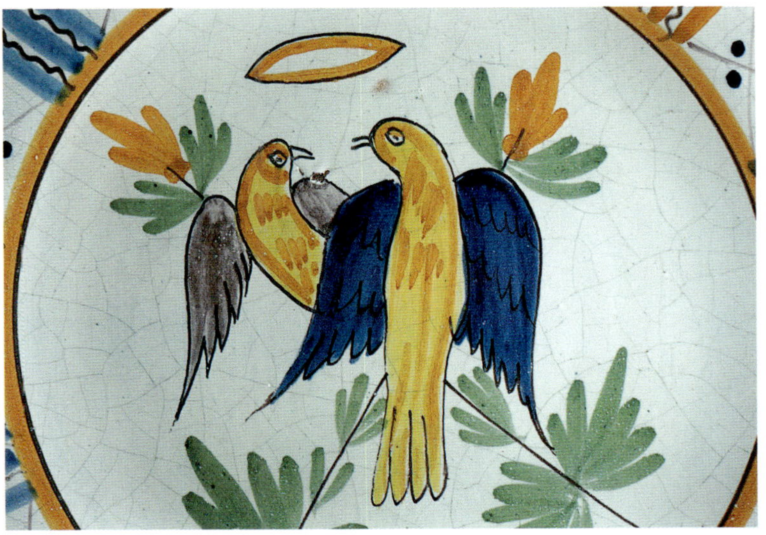

Two turtle doves *(colombes)* with a wedding ring above them signifying marriage, grace this 10" diameter plate from the last quarter of the 19th century. The rim is slightly scalloped and decorated with blue-and-gold stripes with black accents. *Courtesy of David and Linda Schaumann.*

A closer look at the central motif reveals age lines and a pit in the finish. These attributes, coupled with the pontil marks on the back, help identify this as an earlier piece. It is signed PBx, for the Malicorne factory of Pouplard. A similar plate is in the *Musée Départemental Breton* in Quimper. Price range: $325-$400. *Courtesy of David and Linda Schaumann.*

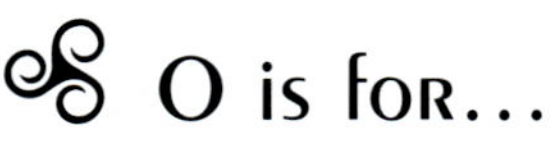

O is for...

Odetta (pronounced o-dey-TA) is a heavier *grès* ware art *poterie* made by the HB faïencerie beginning in the 1920s. Odetta's period of great accomplishment was between the World War I and World War II, although Odetta *grès* ware was made through the 1950s. Odetta is made with different ingredients, is fired at higher temperatures, and uses different glazes than faïence products. The following examples are all from the pre-World War II heyday of Odetta.

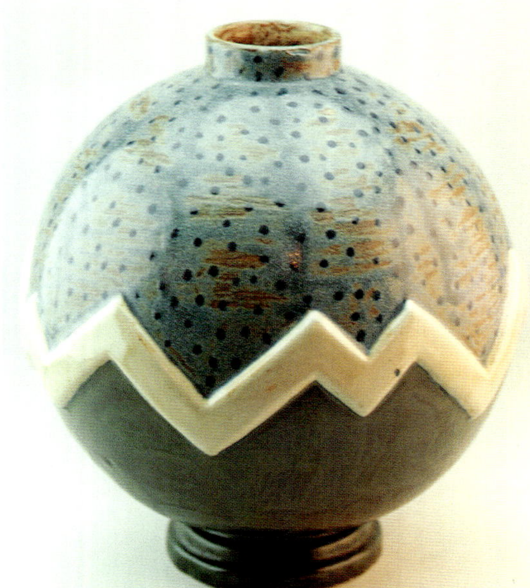

This first example of Odetta is found in the *Musée de la Faïence Odetta Catalogue* as #1447. The well-known Quimper artist Georges Renaud designed this globe-like vase, which stands 9.5" high, and has a 27" circumference. Signed HB Quimper Odetta #392-1447. Price range: $850-$975. *Courtesy of Janis Maxwell and Mike Feldman.*

Here's another gem from the Odetta art poterie production period at HB. This lovely 11.75" vase appears in the *Catalogue* as #1097. It is signed HB Quimper Odetta #450-1097. The three-digit number refers to the form and the four-digit number refers to the décor. A swirled motif in white is an excellent counterpoint to the browns and grays of the remaining décor. Price range: $900-$1,050. *Private Collection.*

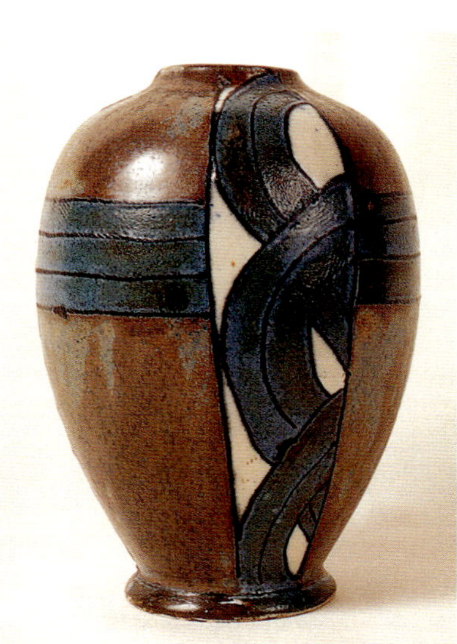

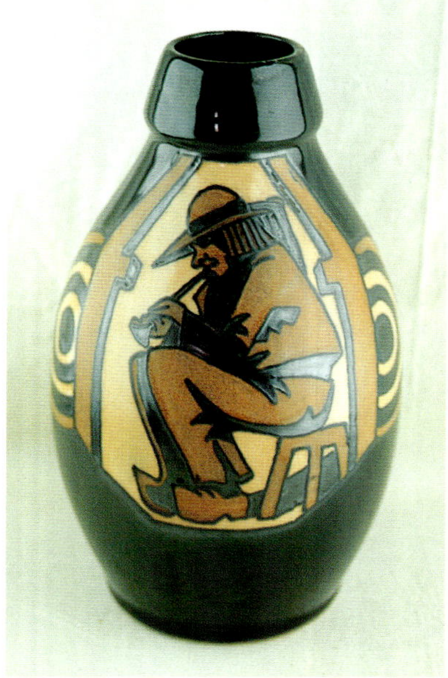

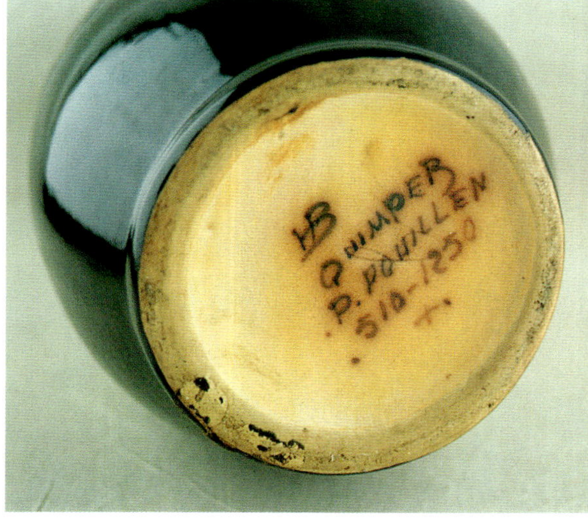

Paul Fouillen is the designer of this Odetta example, #1250. It stands 10" tall and features a *bombarde* player, in a typical Fouillen profile-pose, wearing oversized *sabots*. The vase is signed HB Quimper P. Fouillen #510-1250. *Private Collection.*

The Fouillen design vase also carries the 1920s-1930s Morse Code-like signature of (+.), an as-yet-unidentified HB artist. According to Verlingue, Odetta artists were not the regular house-artists. (See *Mali, Old Quimper Review, October 1999,* for a further discussion of Odetta anomalies.) Some Odetta examples do not contain the word Odetta, as seen in this example. There is an incised g visible. Price range: $900-$975. *Private Collection.*

The incised g can be seen more clearly on this Odetta model #1040. This signified the form was made in faïence too.

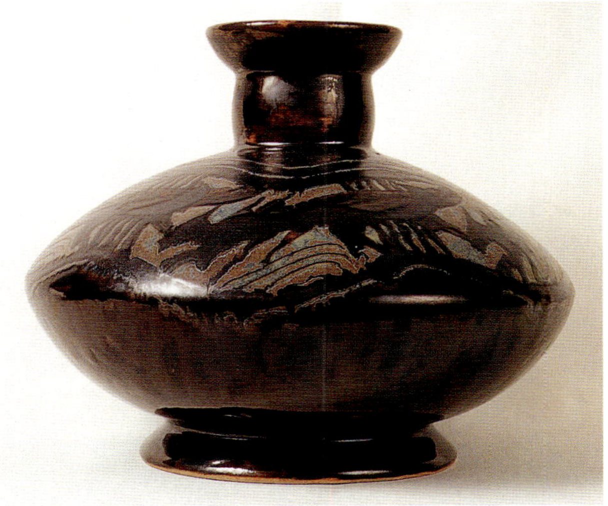

The Odetta item #1040 is a vase which stands about 8.25" tall with a 10.75" circumference. This model is rendered in mottled brown, black and tan. Price range: $650-$775. *Private Collection.*

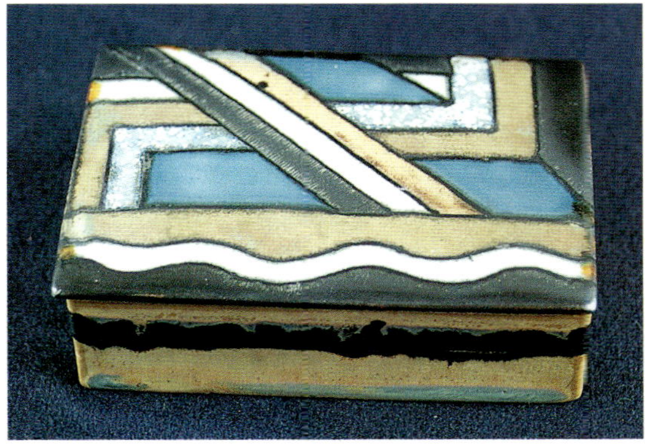

Another winner in the color category is this Odetta 4" long rectangular box, possibly for cigarettes. The blue, beige and white colors complement each other in the linear design. Odetta models are highly regarded by French collectors, who appreciate the difficulty of achieving the Art Deco motifs. A clay mixture different than that used for faïence, and very high firing temperatures helped create this art poterie. But this process resulted in production failures, sometimes as high as 50 percent. Price range: $375-$475. *Private Collection.*

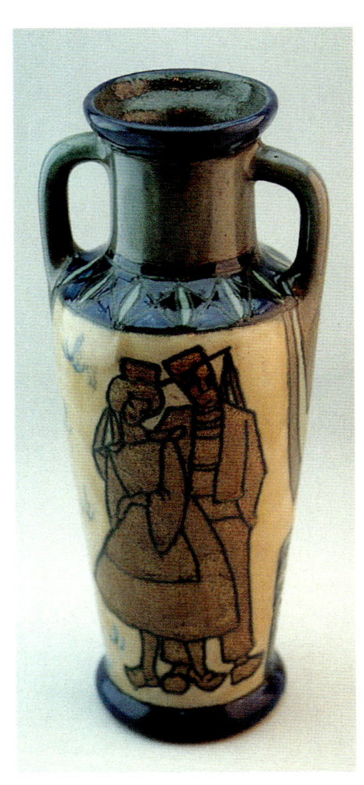

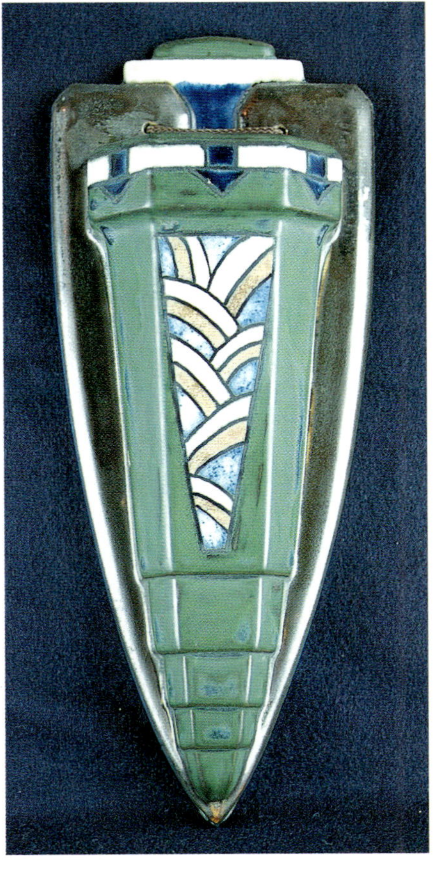

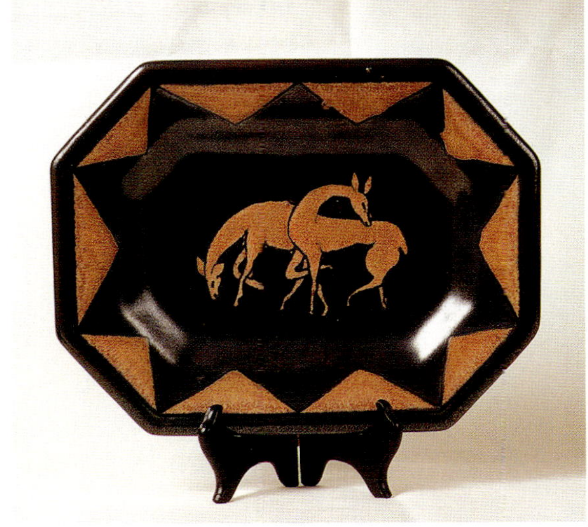

Odetta plates and platters are highly desirable. This example is executed entirely in cocoa and charcoal brown and features two stylized deer. It measures 10.25" long by 7.75" wide and is signed HB Quimper Odetta. It is #1168 in the *Odetta Catalogue.* A similar model sold through an American auction in the late 1980s for $475. Price range: $675-$800. *Private Collection.*

Odetta #1041 is a charming two-handled vase with a Breton couple as the focus on the front. Some researchers have thought this model was Fouillen, due to the angular pose of the couple. The vase stands 10" tall and is signed HB Quimper Odetta #1041. Price range: $550-$650. *Private Collection.*

An Odetta 11.25" long wallpocket in gorgeous colors, including cobalt blue touches, is marked HB Quimper Odetta #872. This example is unique and reminiscent of Renaud's work. Price range: $475-$650. *Private Collection.*

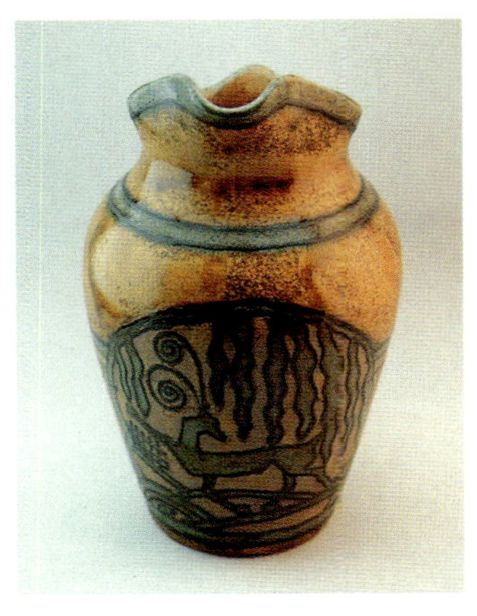

An Odetta pitcher in brown tones standing 9" tall features a scene with a stylized antelope in a medallion. It is signed HB Quimper Odetta #295-1141 and is attributed to Scherdel. Price range: $425-$575. *Courtesy of Janis Maxwell and Mike Feldman.*

Oyster set (*huîtres*) is a spectacular form.

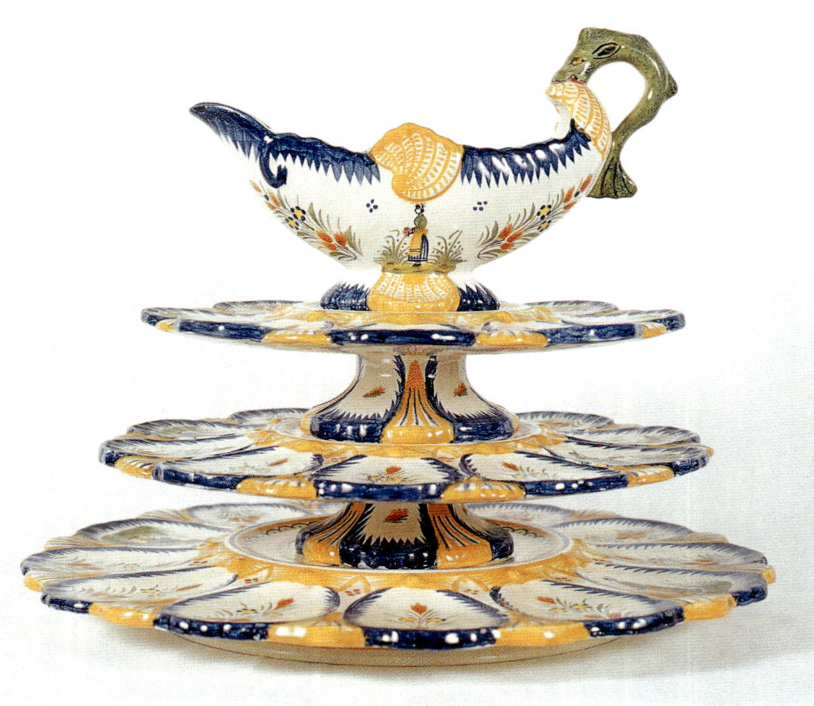

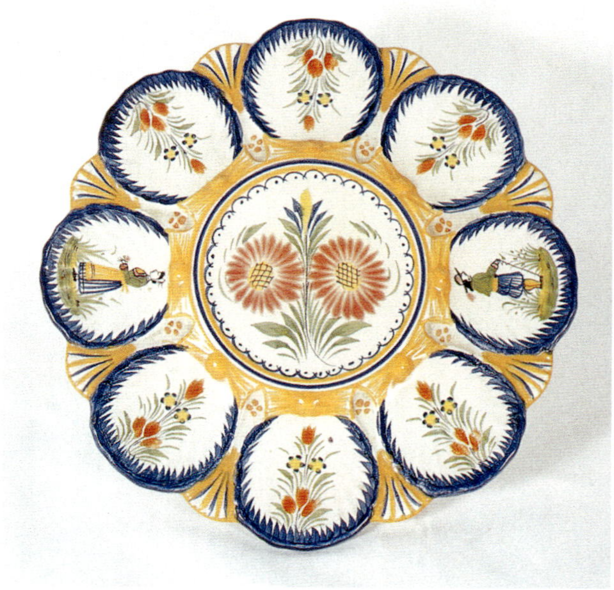

Many times oyster plates are sold separately, but this 12" tall ensemble, topped with a sauce serving boat, demonstrates what a full set can be. It is signed Henriot Quimper France #992, and dates from the 1930s. (See *Bondhus, p. 208.*) *Courtesy of Barbara Cleaver Kroll.*

The oyster plate on the lowest level measures 13.5" in diameter and features a Bretonne and a Breton in two of the oyster receptacles. The others contain *à la touche* florals. The other two oyster plates, each smaller in diameter, sit on top with pedestal bases supporting them. There are shell motifs on the pedestals. *Courtesy of Barbara Cleaver Kroll.*

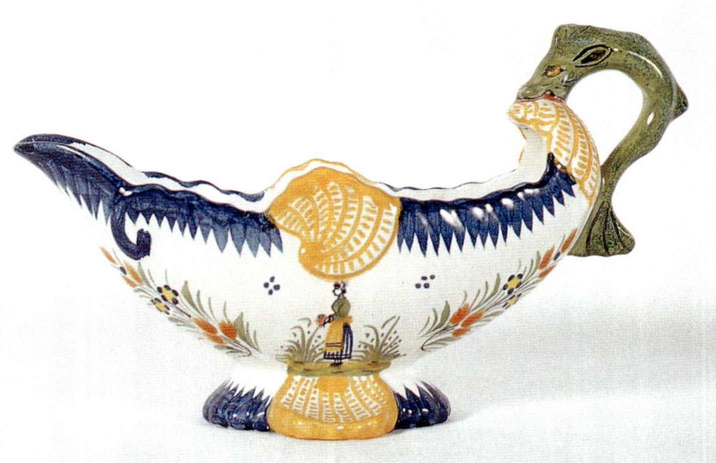

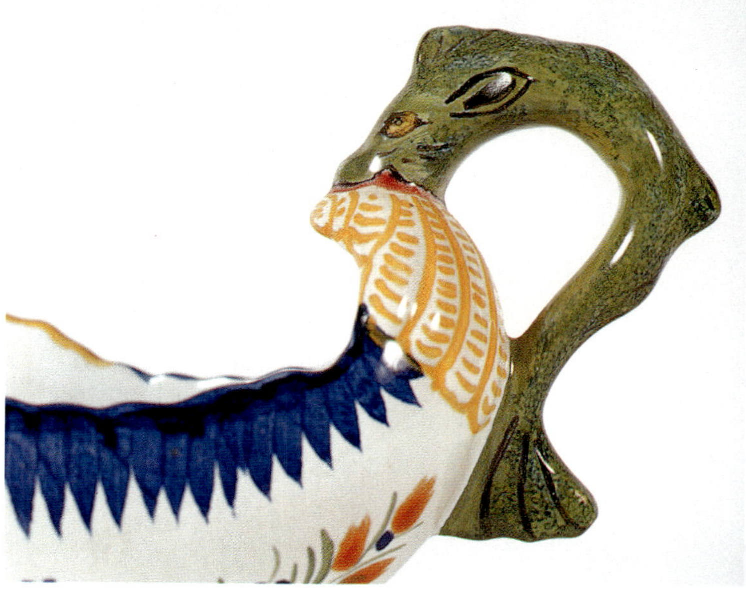

The 9" long sauce boat for the oyster ensemble is stellar by itself. A Bretonne is one side and her Breton mate on the other. The server's rim is edged in feathered blue and a scattered blue four-dot design springs-up among the *à la touche* floral sprays. Scallop shell motifs are at the base and the rim. *Courtesy of Barbara Cleaver Kroll.*

But look at the handle on the serving boat. It is a stylized fish latched onto a scallop shell. What a presentation! Finding a complete oyster set is unusual and therefore valuable. Some oyster plates achieved $500 to $1,000 each and more on Internet auctions in 2001. The price for this ensemble should not surprise anyone. Price range: $2,500-$3,500.

❦ P is for…

Pen tray or holder *(porte-plume)* is a category that could be included with inkwells, but demand dictates it stand alone.

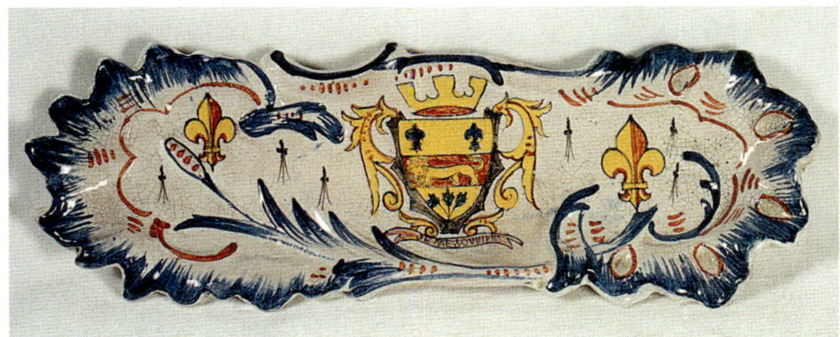

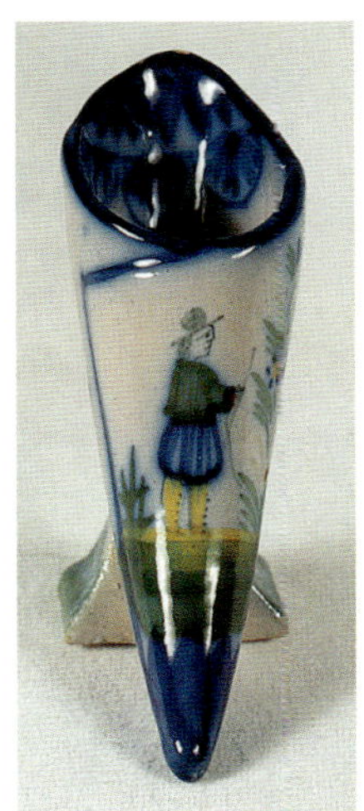

This pen tray is CA faïence and measures 10.5" long and 3.25" wide. It features the two-toned yellow and gold *fleurs-de-lys* and black ermine-tail design familiar on CA products. Rococo flourishes and an armorial complete the décor. This form is #531 in Mali's book, *CA, A French Faïence Breakthrough.* Price range: $375-$450. *Courtesy of A.W. Styer.*

Another version of *porte-plume* is this *cornet* (horn) on a bracket. Some sellers identify this as a pen-holder, others as a *porte-bouquet.* This example stands 3.5" tall, is signed HR Quimper #30, and features a Breton with a whip surrounded by *à la touche décor.* The flowing blue colors resulted from a glazing process introduced to the Henriot faïencerie after the beginning of the 20th century. Price range: $150-$225. *Courtesy of A.W. Styer.*

Pipes *(pipes)* for smoking by the Quimper faïenceries are not seen too frequently.

In the mid-1990s, a 19th century pipe with a ceramic bowl decorated with a Breton playing the *biniou*, and a wooden stem, sold for $525 through an American auction. More recently the same venue sold a similar 6" long unsigned model for $70. A unique example with a wooden stem and ceramic bowl in the shape of a Bretonne sold for $190 through an Internet auction in 2000. The pair of pipes shown here are 6" long and signed Henriot Quimper France. They feature a Breton on one and a Bretonne on the other. They are totally ceramic and the stems have blue striping design with gold-rimmed mouthpieces. Price range: $375-$450 for the pair. *Courtesy of Patricia Zimmerman.*

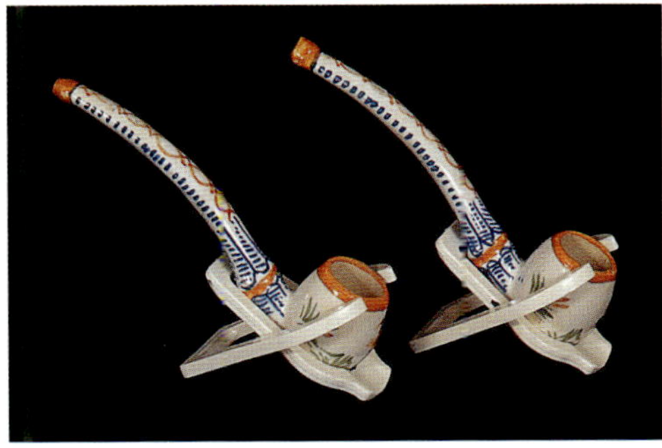

Pipe holder or rack *(porte-pipe)* comes in two distinct forms, the individual pipe holder or rest, and the pipe rack meant to be hung on the wall.

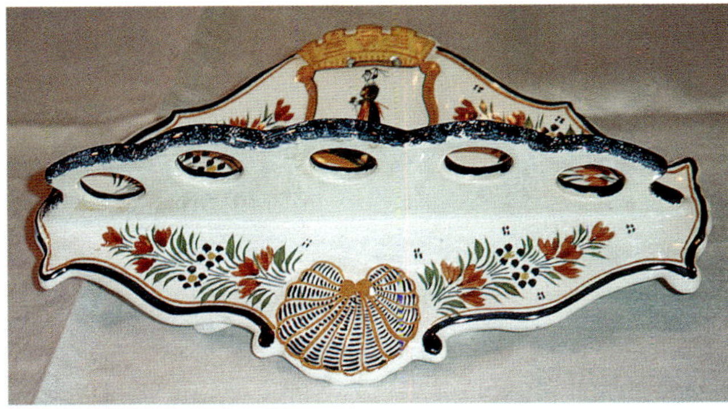

The pipe rack form seen here is grander and more expensive. It is the *biniou* form, 11" long with room for four pipes, and topped with a cartouche of ermine-tails topped by a crown. Similar ones signed Henriot Quimper did not meet sellers' expectations in an Internet auction in the late 1990s. Price range: $675-$775. *Courtesy of Musée de la Faïence, Quimper.*

This *porte-pipe* is the wall model, is signed Henriot Quimper France #505, and dates from the mid-20th century. It is 11" wide, 6.5" tall, and has a Bretonne and half-shell accents. There are five holes to hold the pipes. This model brought more than $500 from a 1980s American auction and less than $300 in a late-1990s American auction. Price range: $325-$425. *Courtesy of Lucy Williams.*

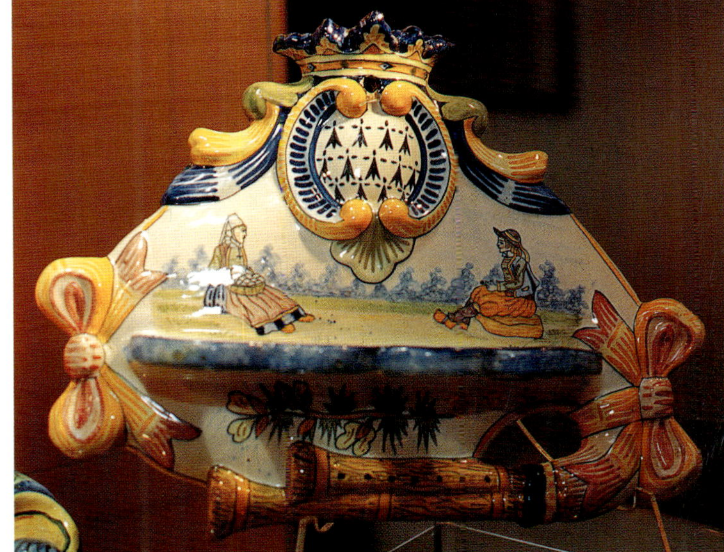

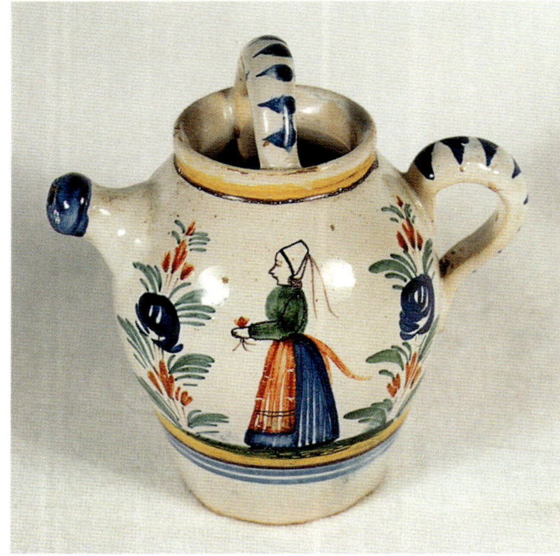

The model seen here is called a *biberon*, or baby feeding bottle, in faïence. Larger versions have been called cider pitchers. Biberons range in size from 4" to 6". This example is 4" tall, is signed HR Quimper, and dates from the first quarter of the 20th century. Prices on Internet auctions in the late 1990s ranged from $95 to $200 for similar models. Price range: $110-$175. *Courtesy of A.W. Styer.*

Pitchers (pichets) come in numerous sizes, shapes, and prices. The selection can be delightful or overwhelming, depending on one's perspective.

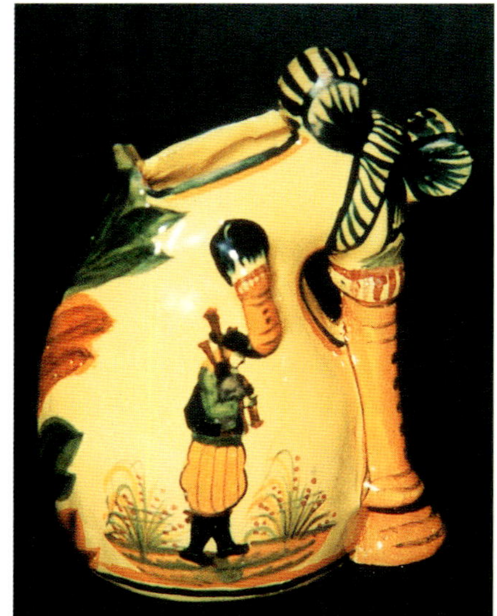

A *biniou* shaped pitcher features a *biniou* player… how appropriate! This fellow stands 6" tall and is the sunny *soleil* décor. A model of the same size sold through a late 1980s American auction for $185. In 1999, an American dealer offered a similar pair of *biniou* pitchers (5.75" tall), marked Henriot Quimper France, for $495. Price range: $225-$300 for one. *Private Collection.*

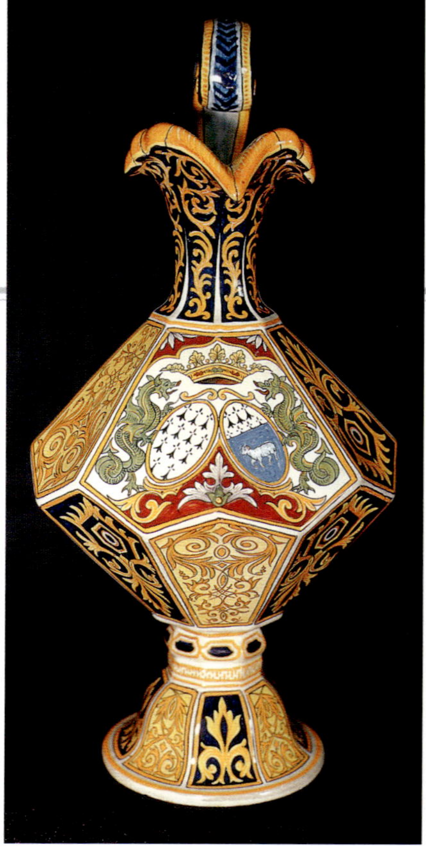

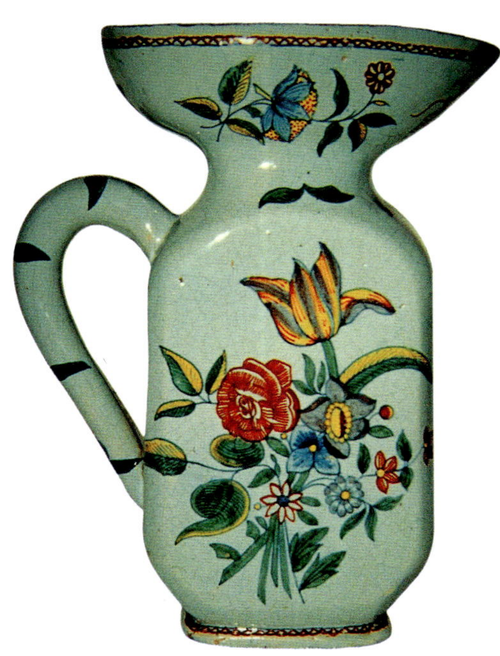

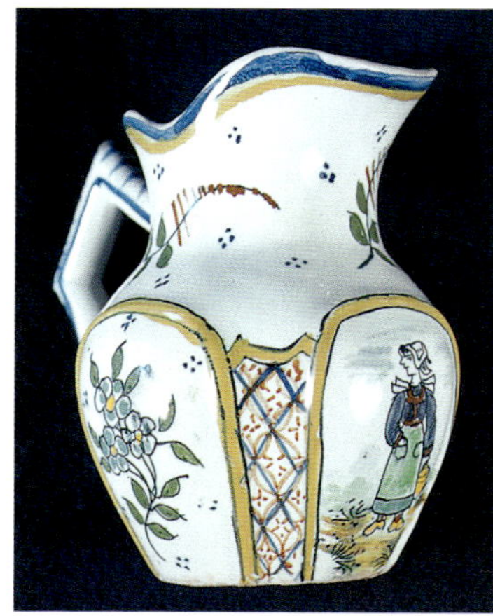

A cream pitcher *(crémier)* by HB is stunning in its décor. It stands 4.5" tall, has red *croisillon* accents, and the readily identifiable HB flower sprays, all capped by a scene of a Bretonne carrying a milk jug. *Courtesy of A.W. Styer.*

Cider pitcher is an interesting category. Many forms exist, but the Porquier-Beau examples are the most highly regarded. This PB model stands 10.75" tall and is covered with brilliantly colored flowers. A red-chain accent borders the base and the lip of the pitcher, and the décor is in the Rouen-style. A similar model sold through an American auction in the late 1990s for $1,450. Other Porquier-Beau examples with *scènes Bretonnes*, botanical designs, and *décor riche* accents combined on one example, have brought more than $2,500 in an Internet auction in 2000. Price range: $1,200-$1,400. *Courtesy of Janey Levine.*

Ewers are tall pitchers with narrowing at the neck. Some smaller versions, called *aiguieres,* are more cruet-like in size, although some American sellers also label taller models *aiguieres*. This ewer is fantastic. Its décor and shape set it apart from ordinary examples. *Private Collection.*

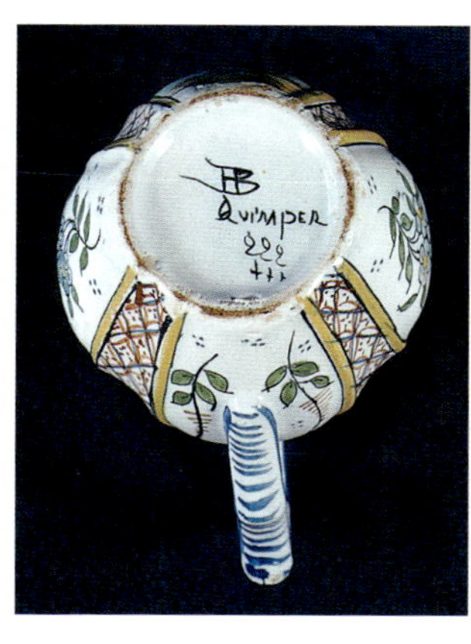

The signature clearly shows this HB creamer was made in the 1920s-1930s by the Morse Code-like signature of (+++) under the HB Quimper mark. The form is #222 and the piece has a lot going for it. Price: $125-$175. *Courtesy of A.W. Styer.*

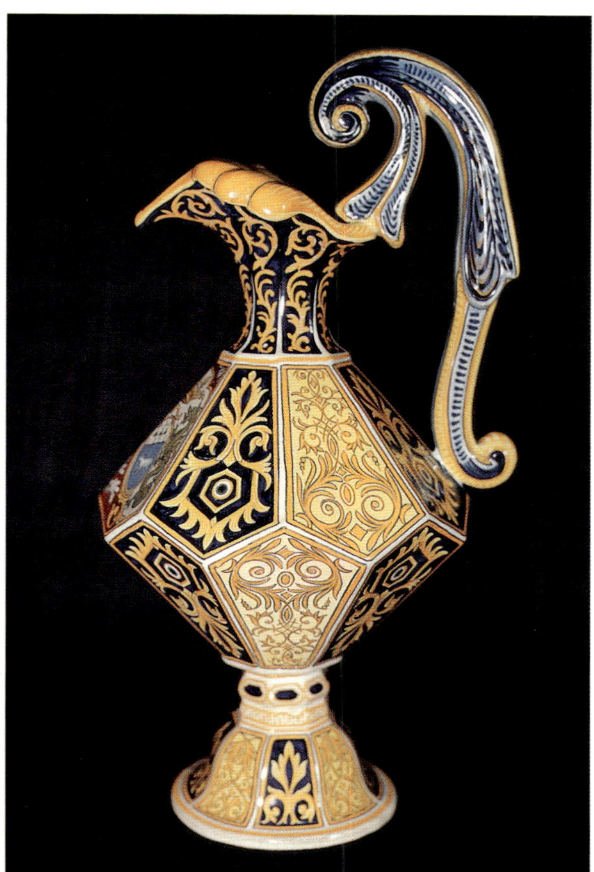

An *Italo-Nivernais* décor is used overall. The molded body is eight panels on the top section, over eight on the bottom section. The ewer stands on a pedestal base and the handle and pouring rim are additional extraordinary elements. The Henriot faïencerie re-issued this Porquier-Beau model, signed PB Quimper #130, c.1930. Price range: $2,500-$3,500. *Private Collection.*

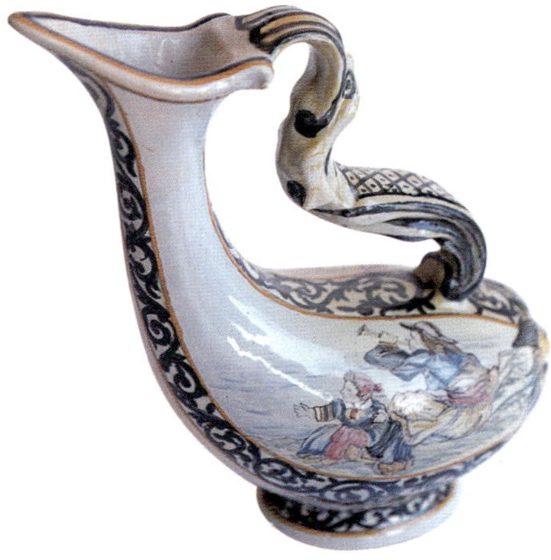

A second version of a ewer has been called fish-shaped. Actually this is a gently curved ewer, with a face on the end of the bowl. It's first period Porquier-Beau, from the last quarter of the 19th century, and measures 10" tall by 8" long. The piece is marked *Environs de Quimper* and PB. A similar ewer resides in the *Musée de la Faïence* in Quimper. *Courtesy of Pierre Breton, Art de Cornouaille, Quimper.*

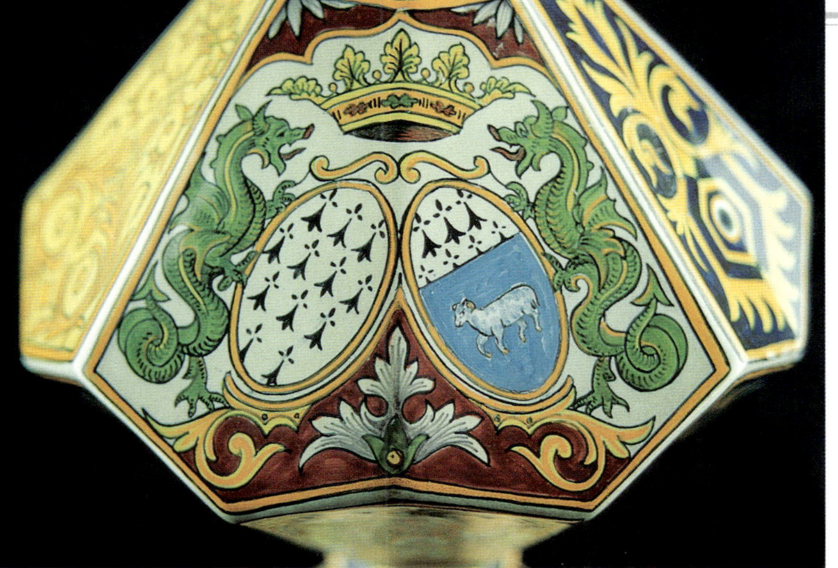

This model, shown at left, features the armorials of Brittany and Quimper in cartouches held by dragons surmounted by a crown. *Private Collection.*

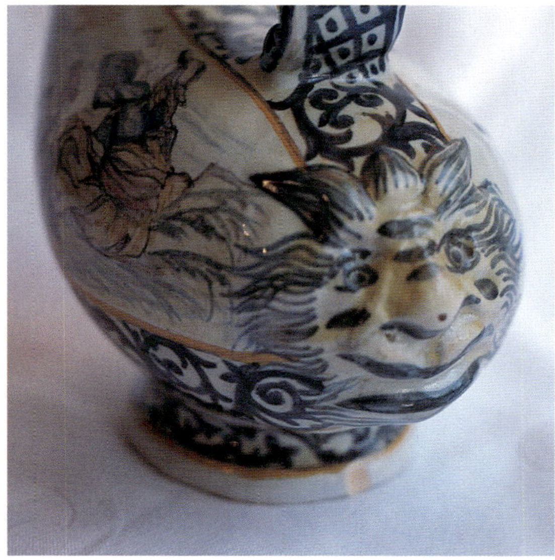

This ewer is featured in the *Château de Quintin Exposition Catalogue, p. 107*, and it is called a *cruchon anthropomorphe*, or small jug with anthropomorphic form. *Scènes Bretonnes* by Alfred Beau grace either side and are bordered by *décor riche* elements. An Internet auction in 2000 brought $4,500 for a similar model. Price range: $3,500-$4,500. *Courtesy of Pierre Breton, Art de Cornouaille, Quimper.*

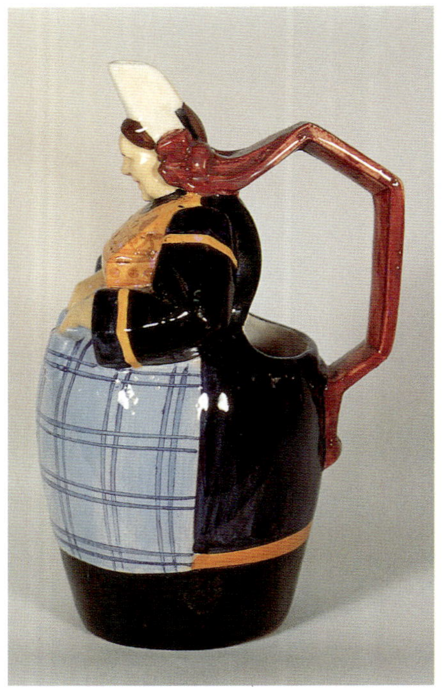

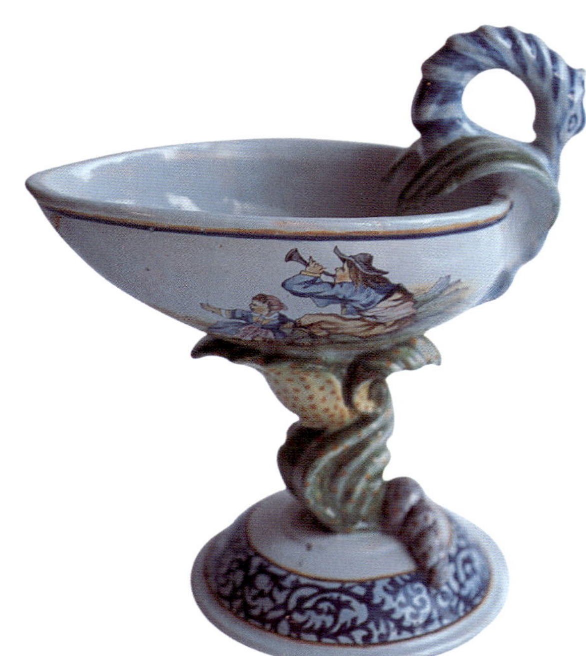

Grand hanap is the title given to this pouring vessel from the Porquier-Beau faïencerie. It stands nearly 10" tall to the top of its swan's neck handle. The *Jouer de bombarde de Pont-l'Abbé*, or Horn player from Pont-l'Abbé, highlights one side of the piece. Nevers-style garlands embellish the remaining surface. Note the elaborately decorated pedestal, including a shell and *décor riche* border. Signed PB, it dates from the last quarter of the 19th century. Price range: $3,000-$4,000. *Courtesy of Pierre Breton, Art de Cornouaille, Quimper.*

Figural pitchers come in a variety of styles. This one is by Henriot artist Charles Maillard, known for his rendition of portly *Bigoudènes* in either a rose or blue apron. A 10.5" tall version sold through a 1980s American auction for $900. In 2001, a similar model only brought $172. Our lady pitcher shown here is 8" tall, is signed Henriot Quimper #161, and dates from the 1930s. Price range: $350-$475. *Private Collection.*

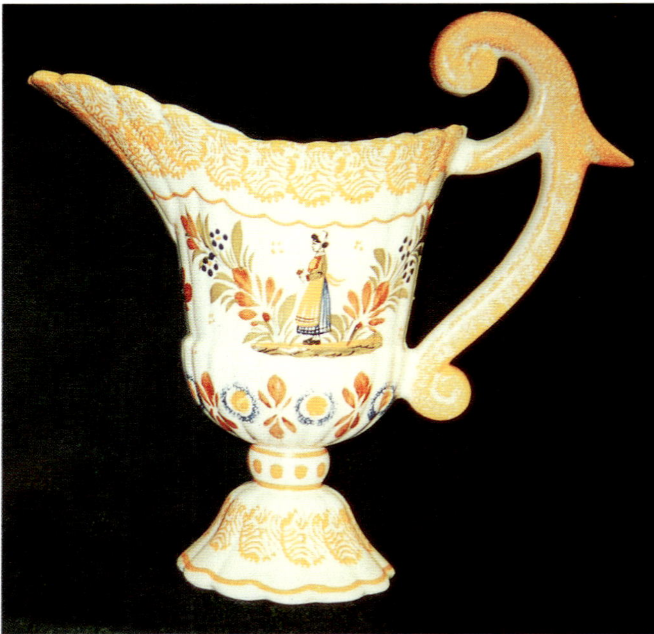

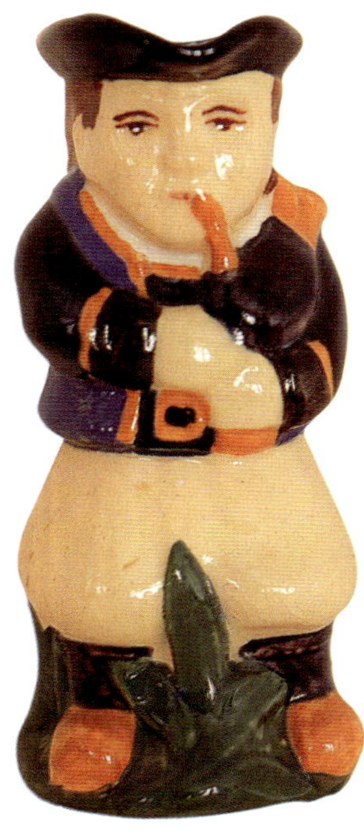

A Toby *(Jacquot/Jacqueline)* also is a figural pitcher. It sometimes is large enough to hold beer or cider. This example is a smaller version, standing 4.5" tall, and it is signed AG, for the Henriot artist André Galland. It is from the 1920s-1930s and is a sweet rendition by a well-known artist. A Toby of similar size and age by Henriot sold through a 1999 Internet auction for $320. Price range: $250-$350. *Private Collection.*

Helmet-shaped *(casque)* pitchers have been offered through Internet auctions and through personal Web sites. This model, signed Henriot Quimper France #90, stands 10.5" tall and 11.5" wide. The orange sponged handle and orange lace-like design around the top and bottom are unique. Price range: $325-$375. *Courtesy of Phil and Arlette Griner.*

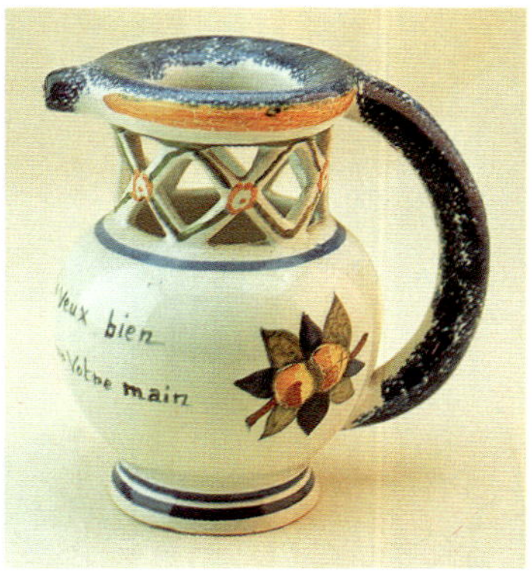

Puzzle pitcher *(pichet trompeur)* received a lot of attention in the mid-1990s. The saying, *Buvez je le veux bien, Mais sachez placer votre main,* warns the user to know where to place their hand to prevent the contents from spilling. Grapevines and leaves or an apple motif are the usual décor. The apple version here stands 4" tall and is signed Henriot Quimper #101. In a late 1980s American auction, this example brought $180, and in 1998, an American dealer offered a 6" tall model for $210. In 1999, an Internet sale garnered $235 for a 6" model in the *soleil* décor, but then in 2001, $145 was the best one example could garner. Price range: $175-$245. *Courtesy of Nancy Wyman.*

Plaque-de-porte or door push-plate is sometimes confused with *plaque-de-propriété,* which is a house number.

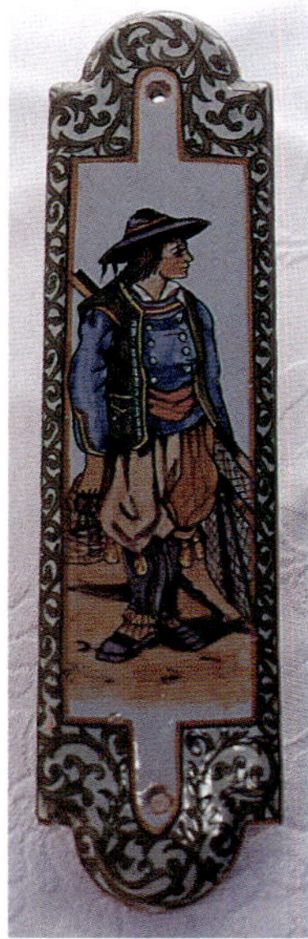

This *plaque-de-porte* is 10" long and features a portion of the *Pêcheur de Douarnenez* scene. Elements of the *aquarelles* or models were used to fit the piece, as seen in this case. Signed PB, this example dates from the last quarter of the 19th century. In 1999, an American seller offered an Henriot Quimper door push-plate for $125. A pair of HR-signed *plaques-de porte* sold through the Internet in 2001 for more than $800, but the same year a pair of Henriot plaques offered for $589 did not receive a bid. Price range: $400-$500. *Courtesy of Pierre Breton, Art de Cornouaille, Quimper.*

Plates *(assiettes, plats)* are the largest category, obviously because of their utilitarian and decorative uses.

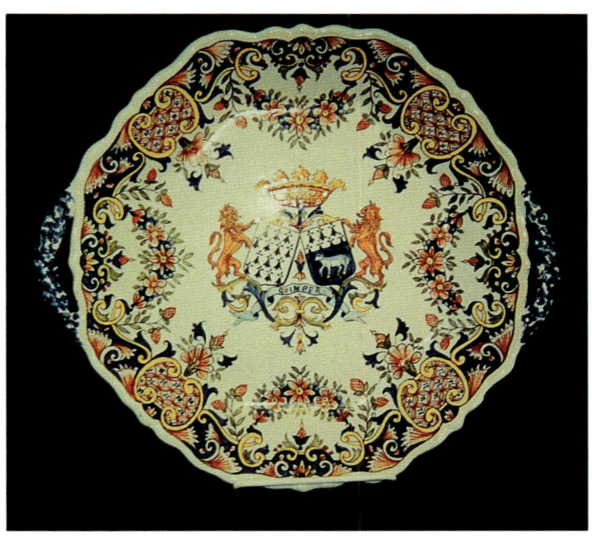

Armorial plates contain the shield of a city or family surrounded in some cases by intricate décor. This example is from the Porquier-Beau faïencerie, has two handles (and may be called a *banêtte*), is 10" diameter, and contains the armorial of the city of Quimper. (See *Château de Quintin Exposition Catalogue, p. 128.*) Similar plates without handles have brought $400 to $600 through French auctions in the 1990s. An American auction sold an armorial plate signed PB in 2000 for $700, and a French auction sold one with handles for $643. Price range: $800-$1,100. *Courtesy of Phil and Arlette Griner.*

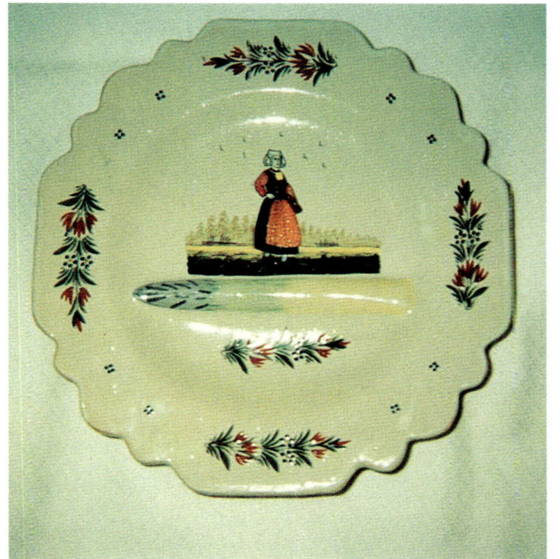

Asparagus *(asperge)* plates come in a variety of styles, from simple plates with an asparagus stalk as a divider to complex asparagus holders with attached underplates. This model is signed only HB, is a tad over 9" diameter, and has a lovely scalloped edge and naïve décor. The plate dates to the 1880s. In 1999, a similar model sold through an Internet auction for $602, while the same year a similar example brought $500 through an American auction. Price range: $550-$675. *Courtesy of Janey Levine.*

Bas-relief plates have been made by Quimper faïenceries for more than 100 years. This version is mid-20th century in modern movement colors and features *sonneurs,* the Breton musical duo of *biniou* and *bombarde.* The plate measures 10" diameter and is signed Henriot Quimper France. An American auction sold the same model for $75 in 1995. Price range: $75-$125. *Private Collection.*

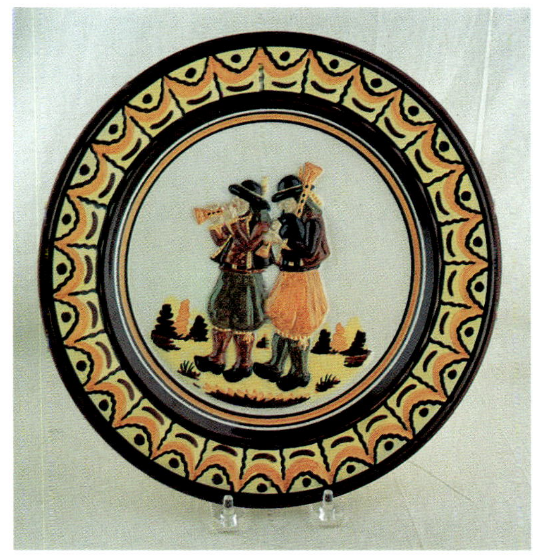

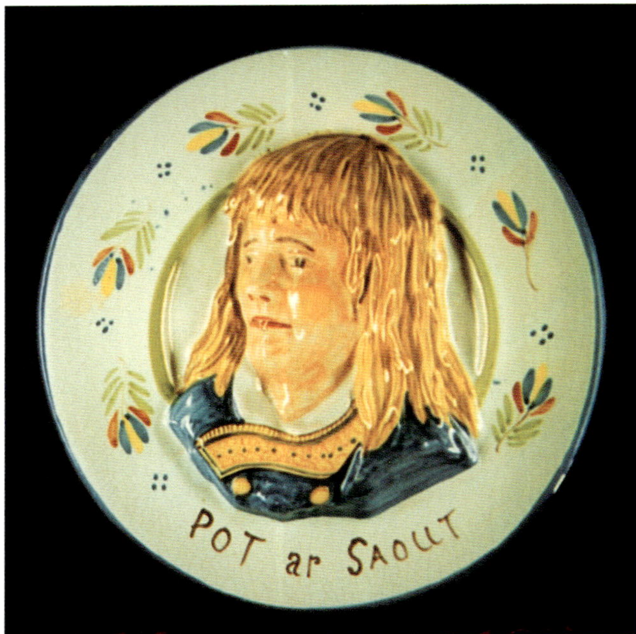

An unsigned 8" Porquier-Beau faïencerie 9.25" diameter bas-relief plate or plaque is entitled *Pot ar Soat* and is from the last quarter of the 19th century. *Private Collection.*

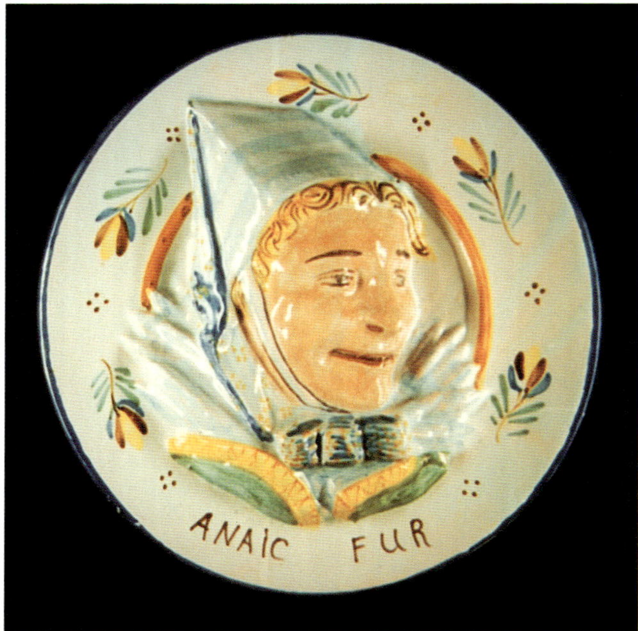

His mate, *Anaic Fur*, also is Porquier-Beau. Delicate *à la touche* floral sprays surround both bas-relief images, and he has a blue four-dot design, while she has a red four-dot design. Prices realized in the 1990s were more than $400 each. Price range: $800-$950 for the pair. *Private Collection.*

Another style of Porquier-Beau *terre vernissée* bas-relief plaque is rectangular with a reticulated or pierced edge containing ermine-tails, *fleur-de-lys*, and other decorative elements. The central character appears to be dressed in a Basque costume and stands next to a basket. The piece measures 11" tall by 8.5" wide and is signed PB on the back. A similar pair sold through an American auction in the late 1980s for $750 and $775 each, but a 2000 French auction only brought about $225 for the pair. The market has changed for this style. *Courtesy of Jo and David Wood.*

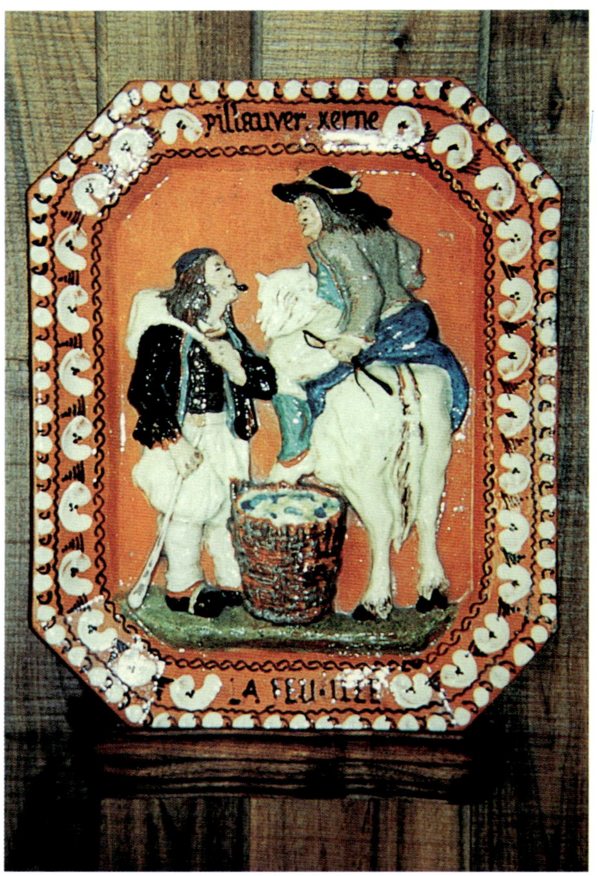

Bas-relief plaques come in a variety of sizes, shapes, and décors. Armorials of towns and profiles of famous figures are two types of plaques. This example is a Porquier-Beau rectangular plaque in *terre vernissée* named *La Feuillée* (leaf gatherer), and is signed PB in black on the back. It measures 18" high and 14" wide and shows two Bretons, one on a horse, and the other with a sack over his shoulder, and a basket is in the foreground. Similarly sized plaques sold through American auctions in the late 1980s and late 1990s for $1,700 and $1,200 respectively. This particular example was offered through an Internet auction in 1999 for $1,500. Price range: $1,500-$2,500. *Courtesy of Jo and David Wood.*

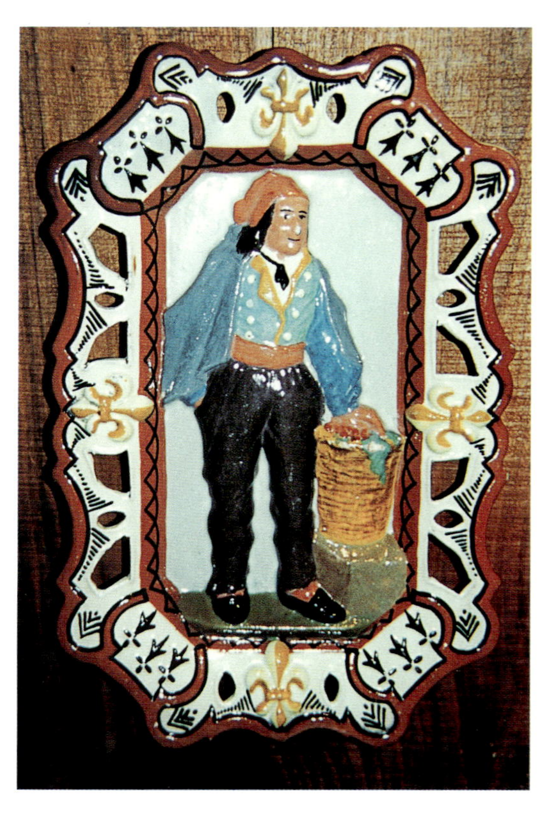

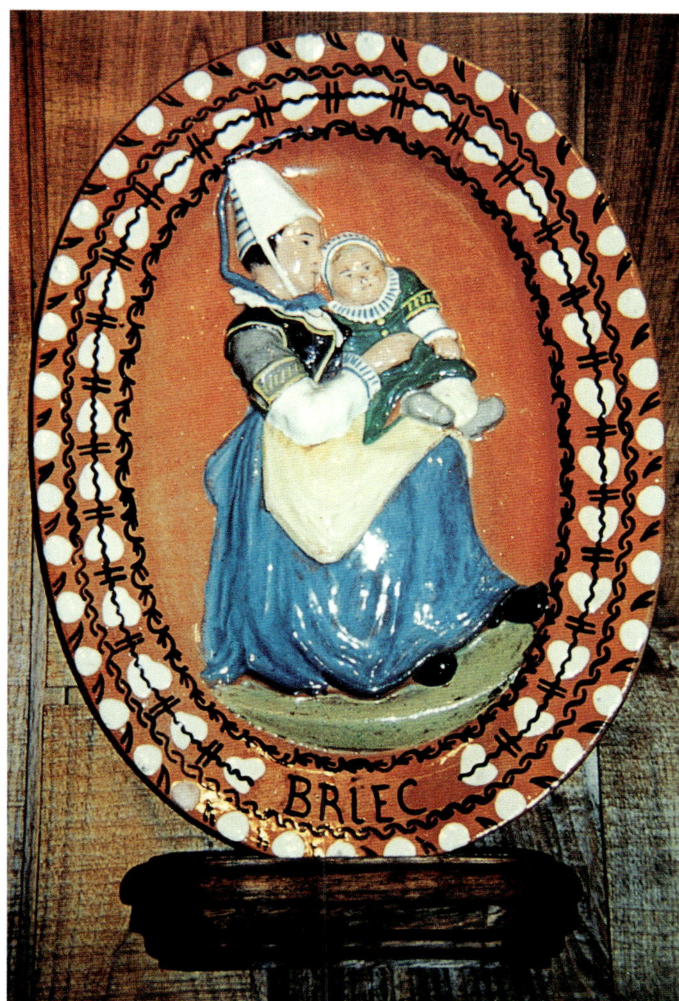

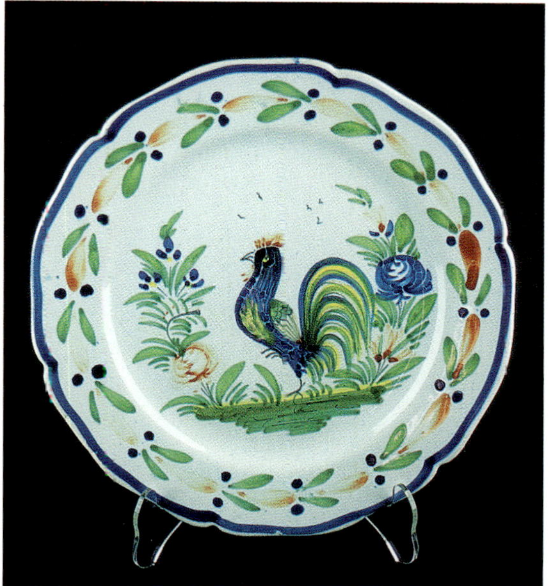

Bird motif plates come in many species. This 8.25" example shows a French national symbol the *coq*, or rooster, surrounded by colorful *à la touche* floral décor. It is signed HB Quimper. Price range: $110-$125. *Private Collection.*

A third type of *terre vernissée* plaque by the Porquier faïencerie is oval. This model features a mother holding a child and is entitled *Briec*, a town in Brittany. The border is simpler in design with white-and-black double strands surrounding the inner design. The plaque measures 15" tall and 11.75" wide and is signed PB on the back. A similar model only realized $300 in a 2000 French auction. Again the market has fluctuated in 2000-2001 for this style. *Courtesy of Jo and David Wood.*

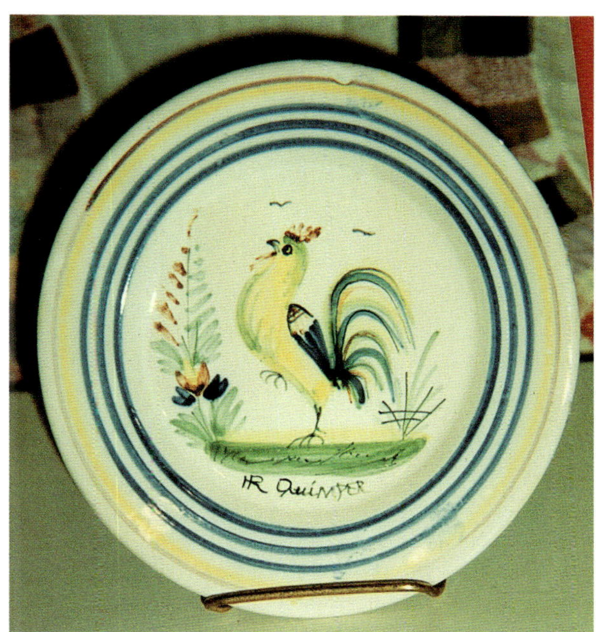

This *coq* was rendered by the Henriot faïencerie in the first quarter of the 20th century. This fellow is 8" diameter, signed HR Quimper, and encircled by *gros filets* of blue and yellow. Price range: $110-$125. *Private Collection.*

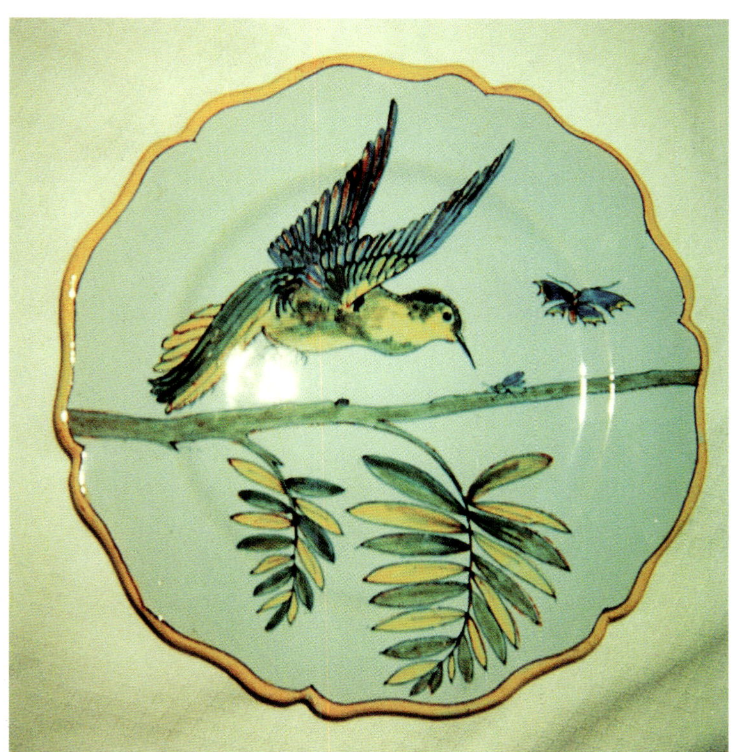

The Alfred Beau bird botanicals for the Porquier-Beau faïencerie in the last quarter of the 19th century rate highly with collectors. This example of Beau's artistry features a fluttering bird approaching a leafy branch with a butterfly nearby. Beau botanicals have brought between $1,500 and $4,000, depending on the subject, in both American and French auctions. This particular model sold for more than $2,400 at a French auction in 2000. Price range: $2,000-$2,500. *Courtesy of Janey Levine.*

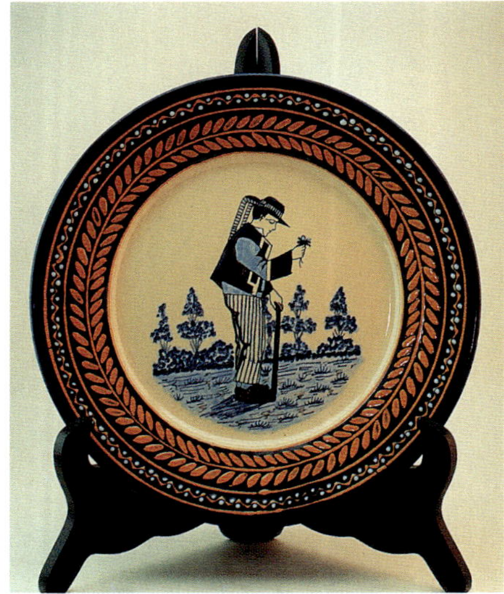

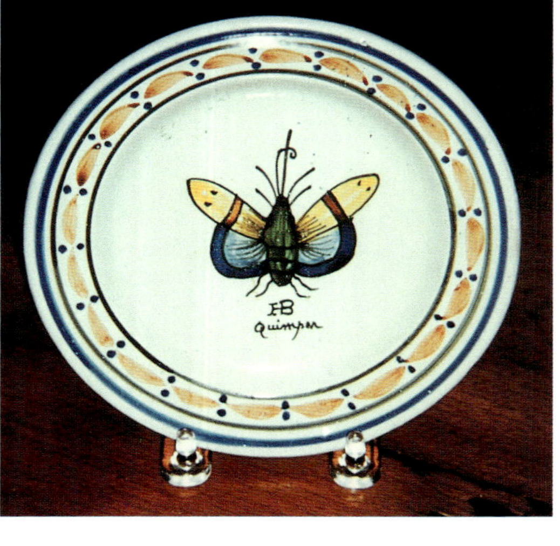

Butterfly *(papillon)* plates always have a following. This 5.5" diameter turn-of-the-20th century model is signed HB Quimper on the front. The simple border décor highlights the colorful fellow. An American auction sold this example for $220 in 1999. Price range: $225-$275. *Private Collection.*

Broderie is a design established by the *HB/Grande Maison.* A special tool is used to place additional enamel decoration, in a variety of designs. It is called *à la poire, tubé* or *perlé.* This example of *broderie* design is fairly straightforward. The male Breton holding a flower is rendered in *camaïeu bleu* and surrounded by a raised surface application in gold-colored enamel some call the wheat pattern. *Courtesy of Nancy Wyman.*

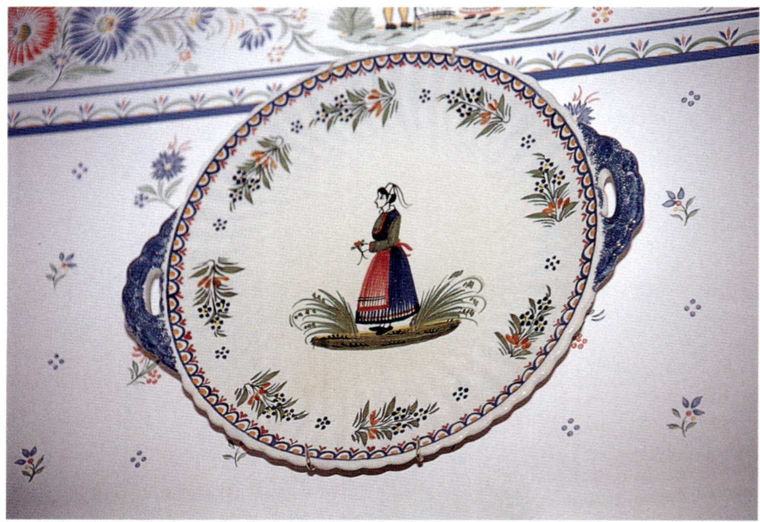

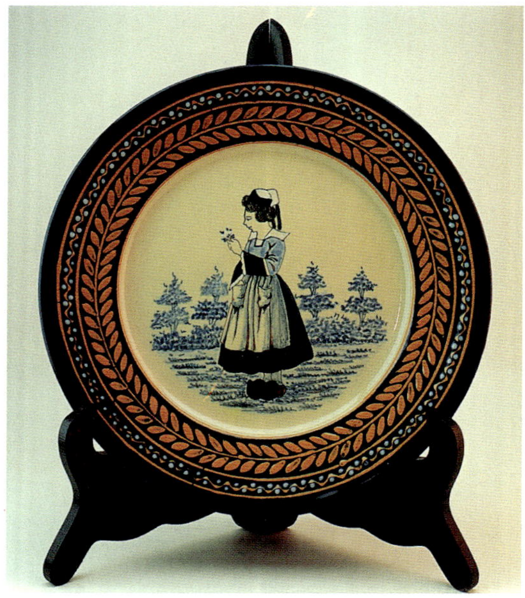

Cake *(gâteau)* plates come in several forms. One version is the two-handled example seen here, which measures 11.25" in diameter. It features a Bretonne with a posy and *à la touche* garlands around the plate's gently scalloped edge. American auctions in the 1990s realized between $140 and $350, depending on the complexity of the décor, for this type of cake plate. Price range: $275-$350. *Courtesy of Patricia Zimmerman.*

His mate, a Bretonne, also done in *camaïeu bleu,* seems to have received the gift. Both plates measure 10" diameter and are signed HB Quimper. They date from the second quarter of the 20th century. Price range: $375-$475 for the pair. *Courtesy of Nancy Wyman.*

The rococo form of this Henriot faïencerie cake plate is stunning. The example is 13" long and features a couple dancing a *gavotte* in the countryside, with sprays of *l'ajonc* and *bruyère* adding to the presentation. Internet and American auctions have realized between $600-$1,000, depending on the age and décor elements. Price range: $600-$800 for this second quarter of the 20th century model. *Private Collection.*

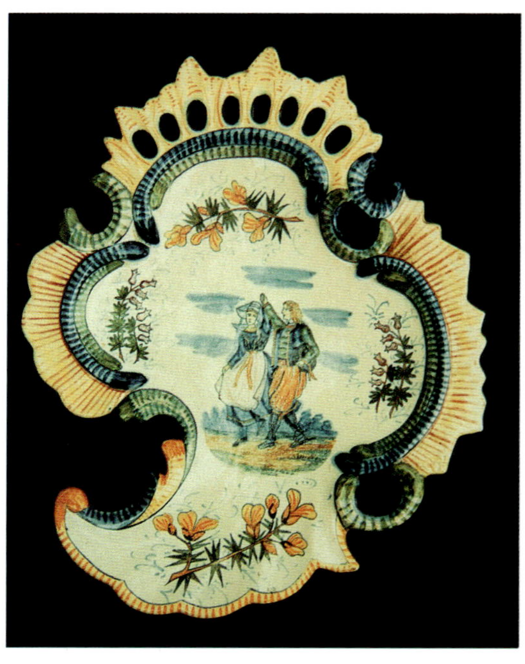

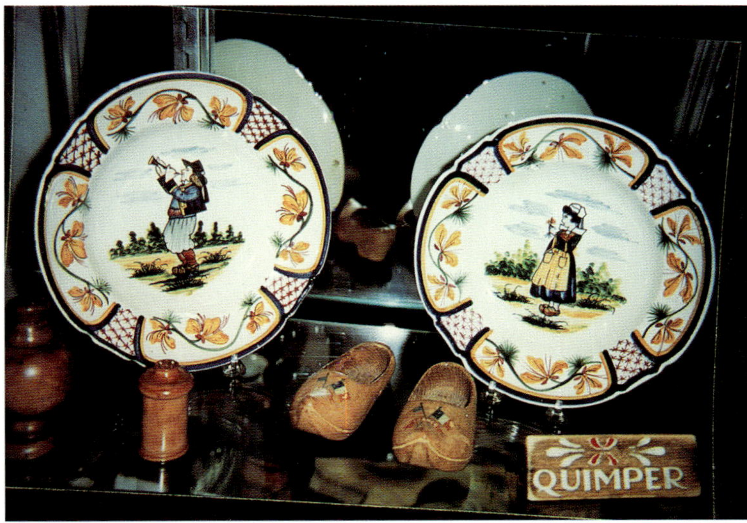

Calotte (soup plate) style is shown in this pair by the HB faïencerie. One features a Breton playing the *bombarde*, and the other a Bretonne with a posy. *Ajonc* sprays and *croisillon* accents make this version very desirable. The prices in the late 1990s through mid-2001 consistently ranged between $190 and $250 each in an American auction. But in 2001, an Internet auction sold four of these same calottes for $450. Price range: $175-$225 each. *Private Collection.*

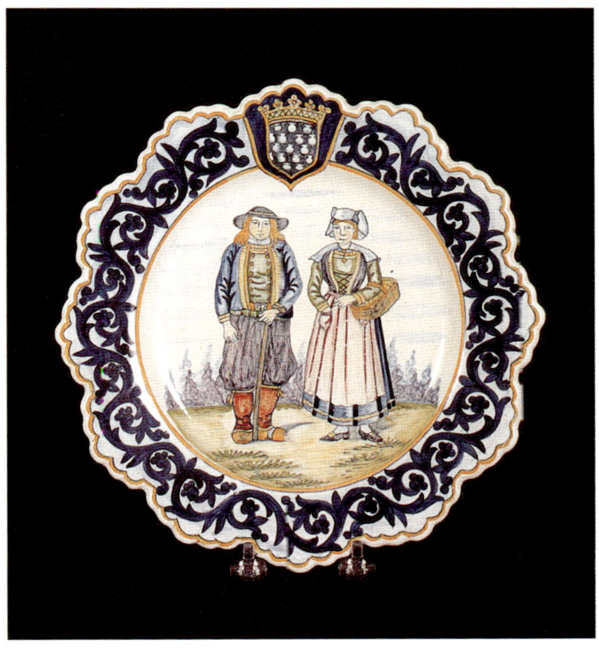

Décor riche is the name given to pieces carrying the border elements called scroll, scrolling foliage, *rinceaux, arabesque,* or *torsades,* depending on individual preference. The design has many variations and a keen eye can differentiate between several types. In this example with the *décor riche* border, a Breton couple poses happily in the countryside. The diameter is 10" and the plate is signed Henriot Quimper #144, and dates from the second quarter of the 20th century. Price range: $375-$425. *Courtesy of Pat Zimmerman.*

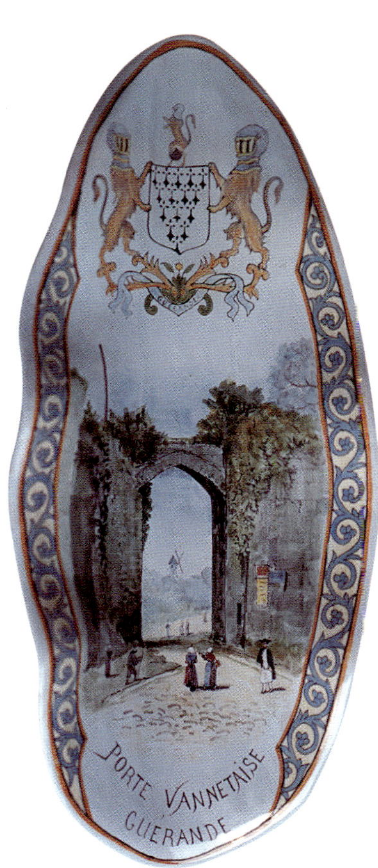

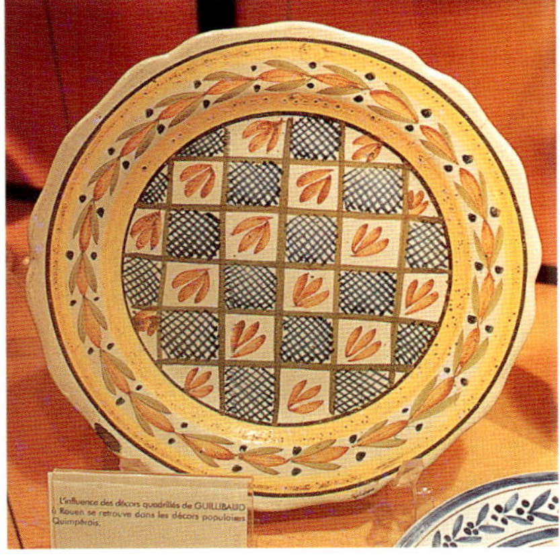

Croisillon is a lattice-work or cross-hatching technique thought to originate in the Guillibaud faïencerie in Rouen. It also is called *quadrillé*. This 19th century plate exhibits squares of blue *croisillon* alternating with squares of red three-stroke flowers. An *à la touche* garland encircles the slightly scalloped rim. Price not available. *Courtesy of Musée de la Faïence, Quimper.*

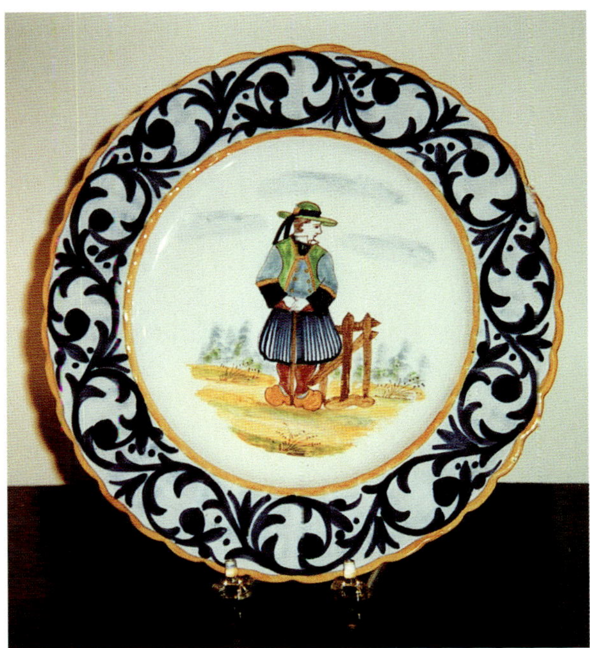

Crêpe plates do come in designs less grand than this 13" long example by Porquier-Beau. A scene on the interior is *Porte Vannetaies Guérande*, and the back is signed PB déposé PP. Price not available. *Courtesy of Pierre Breton, Art de Cornouaille.*

This HB *décor riche* plate also measures 10" diameter, but look closely at the scroll border. It differs from the Henriot version. The plate is a charming rendition of a Breton in large sabots, reminiscent of Fouillen, leaning against a fence with a walking stick in his hand. Prices have fluctuated through the 1990s. American and Internet auctions have brought from $100 to $475. Price range: $275-$375. *Private Collection.*

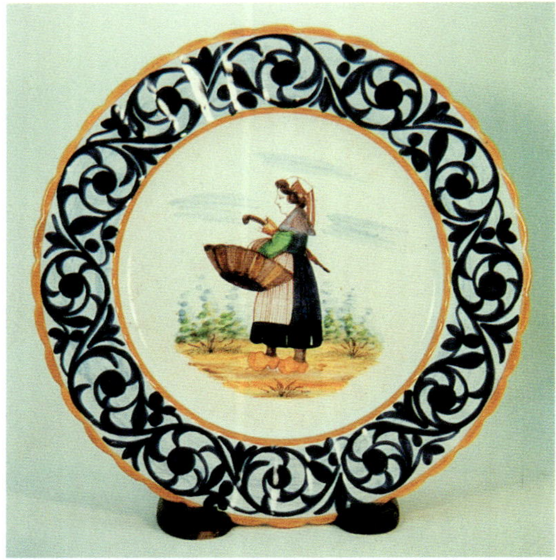

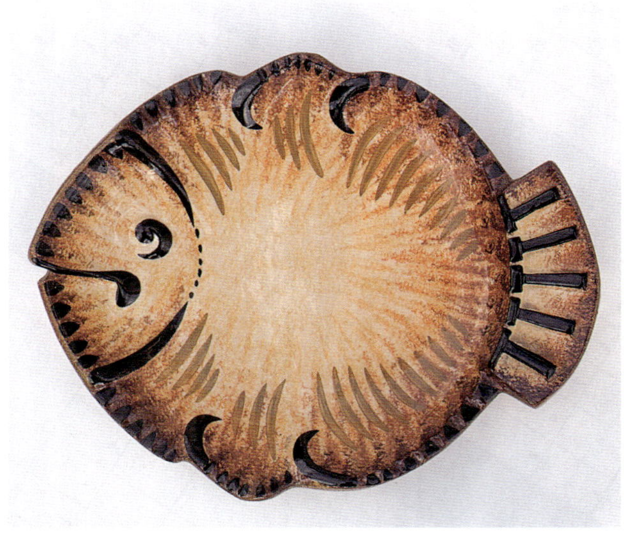

The Breton's mate strolls through the countryside with her *parapluie* under one arm and a market basket on the other. Look closely at the *décor riche* design on this plate. There are slight variations in execution, even though both plates were decorated by the same HB artist, and signed (—), the 1920s-1930s mark for Mme. LeMeur. The borders may have been executed by another painter, as happened with HB artworks by Paul Fouillen. *(MFouillen et al, p. 20.)* Price range: $275-$375. *Private Collection.*

Fish plates are a popular form in Quimper poterie. This example is signed P. Fouillen Quimper, and it measures 9.75" diameter from nose to tail. This Fouillen piece was part of a set of dishes and realized between $50 and $60 in the mid-1990s. Price range: $75-$125. *Courtesy of Gaynor Smith, Russethouse.*

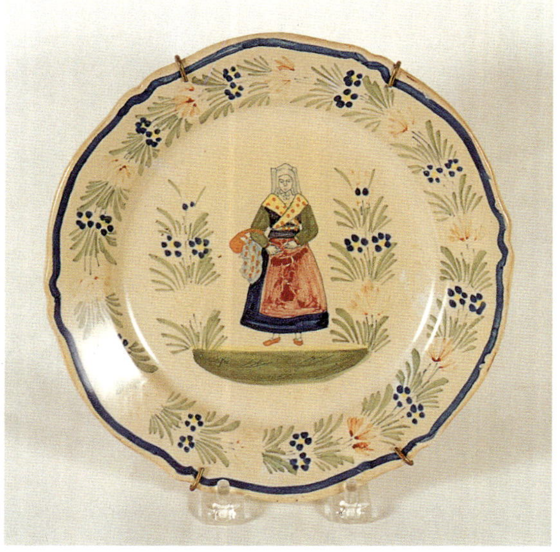

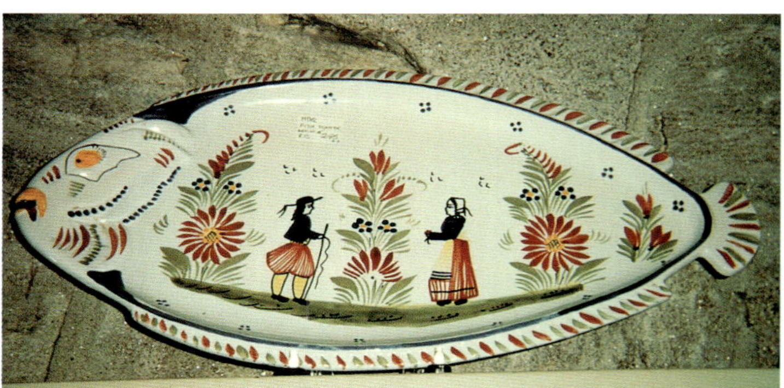

A grouchy fish adorns this 22" long HB model from the mid-1950s. The plate is decorated with a Breton couple and accented with floral sprays, a blue four-dot design, and red, blue, and green striping around the edge. In the late 1980s, a newer version of this model brought $160 through an American auction. In the mid-1990s, this model brought $245. Price range: $325-$375. *Private Collection.*

Demi-fantasie is the name associated with one décor even though the term can refer to several styles. In America, this is the pattern that *demi-fantasie* conjures in collectors' minds. A colorful Bretonne graces this 8" diameter plate by Henriot from the 1920s. The reds are dry, an indicator of age, but the lady is still lovely. Plates in this décor, size, and age realized between $150-$250 in the late 1990s through 2001 on Internet auctions, as well as American auctions. Price range: $175-$275. *Courtesy of Barbara Cleaver Kroll.*

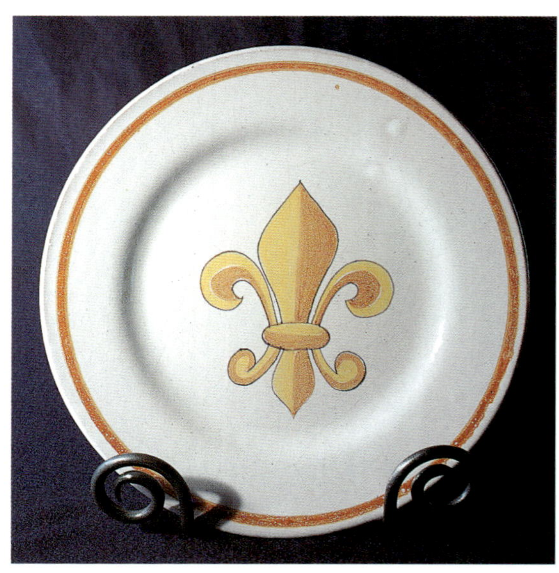

Fleur-de-lys plates usually come in two-toned colors. This example is 9.5" diameter and signed PBx, representing the Pouplard factory in Malicorne. *Fleur-de-lys* models sold between $100 and $300 on Internet auctions in 1998-1999. Size, maker, and condition were determining factors. Price range: $125-$225. *Courtesy of A.W. Styer.*

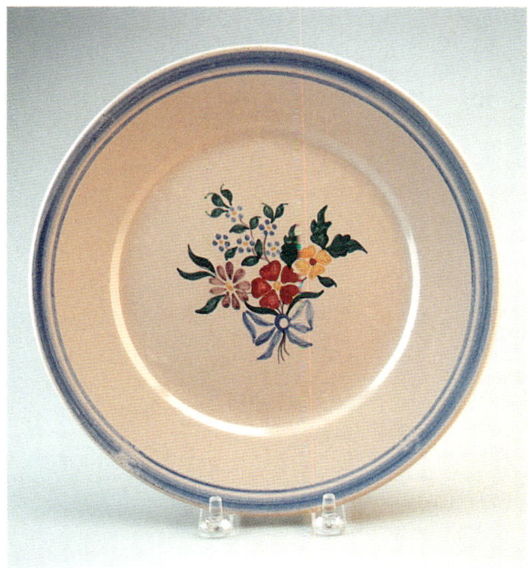

Floral plates come in many styles. A very simple bouquet sits in the center of a pink plate by the HB faïencerie. It is signed HB Quimper France, the artist's signature (..++), and #136. An Internet auction realized $35 for this example in the late 1990s. Price range: $50-$75. *Courtesy of Nancy Wyman.*

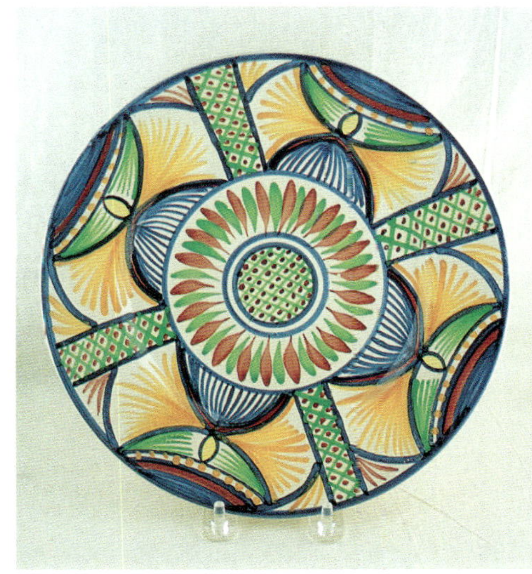

Geometric designs are always popular, especially on plates. This model is from the 1920s-1930s, as revealed by its HB Quimper artist's signature of (!), representing Mme. Kerbourc'h. The plate measures 9.5" in diameter and is stellar in composition and color. Prices in the late 1990s ranged from $150 to $250 on Internet auctions and American sales for similar models. Price range: $200-$225. *Private Collection.*

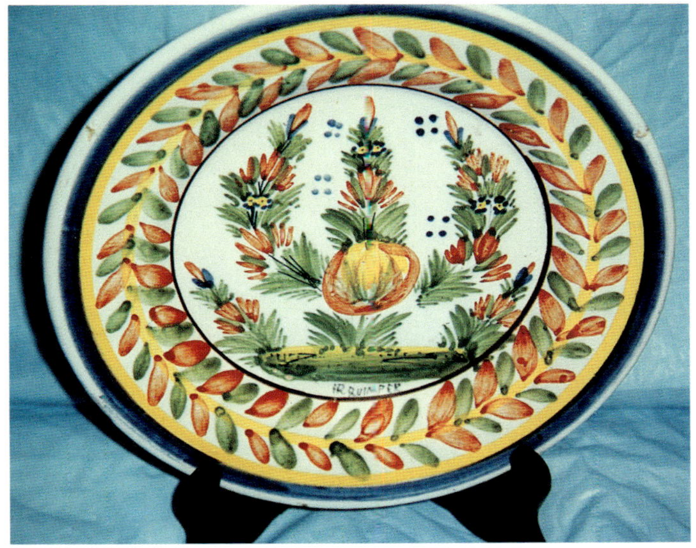

A 10" diameter plate signed HR Quimper is executed in the style called *exubérant*. The flowers sing with color and the border is a bold *à la touche* design. A 1998 sale realized $275 for this example. Price range: $325-$375. *Private Collection.*

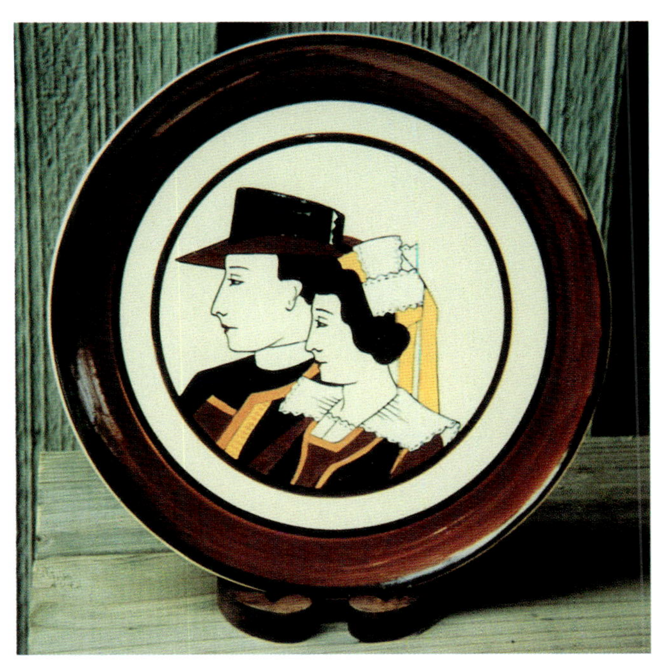

Modern Movement plates cover many décors. This example is fairly simple in design and color, with browns and deep yellows predominating. The HB Quimper charger measures 12.5" diameter and is from the mid-20th century. Prices have fallen for this décor in the late 1990s. Price range: $150-$200. *Private Collection.*

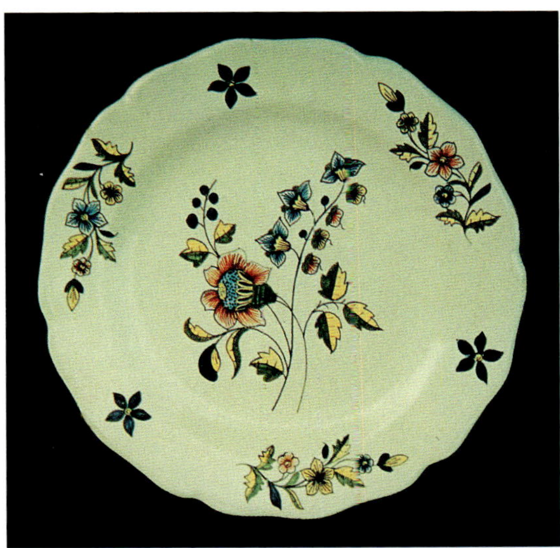

This 9.75" diameter floral plate is signed on the back with only HB. It is third quarter of the 19th century and a stellar rendition of an early motif. Price range: $550-$650. *Courtesy of Silvia and Gary Fritzhand.*

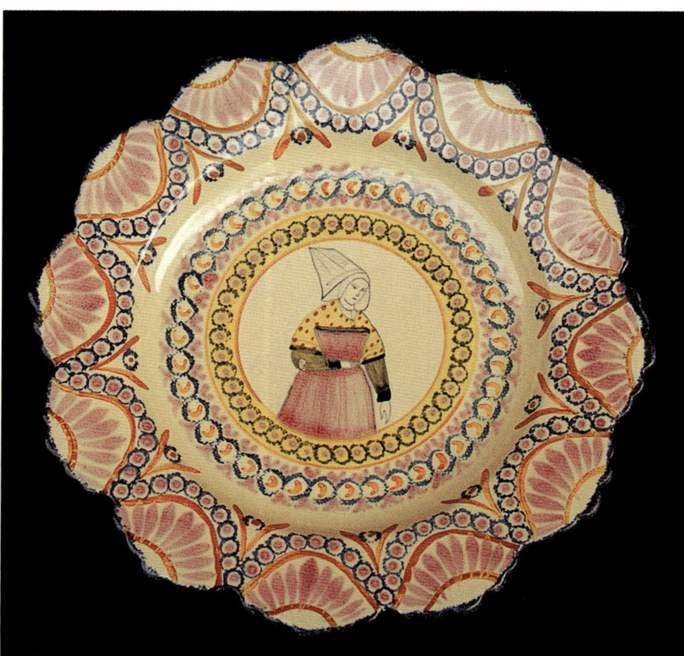

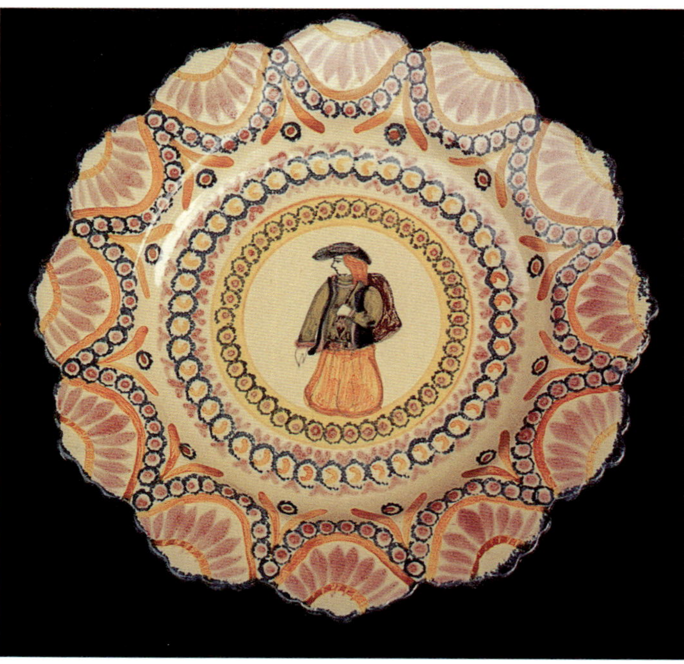

Ivoire corbeille is a décor featuring sponged circles filled with an alternating color, a *demi-fleur* motif on an ivory-colored ground. This example is scalloped with a blue-rimmed edge and features a colorful Bretonne. The plate is 10.25" diameter, and signed Henriot Quimper. *Courtesy of Silvia and Gary Fritzhand.*

The mate to the *ivoire corbeille* plate is just as attractive. It shows the Breton with a sack over his shoulder and a walking stick in his hand. Also signed Henriot Quimper, the pair date from the second quarter of the 20th century. Price range: $375-$450 for the pair. *Courtesy of Silvia and Gary Fritzhand*

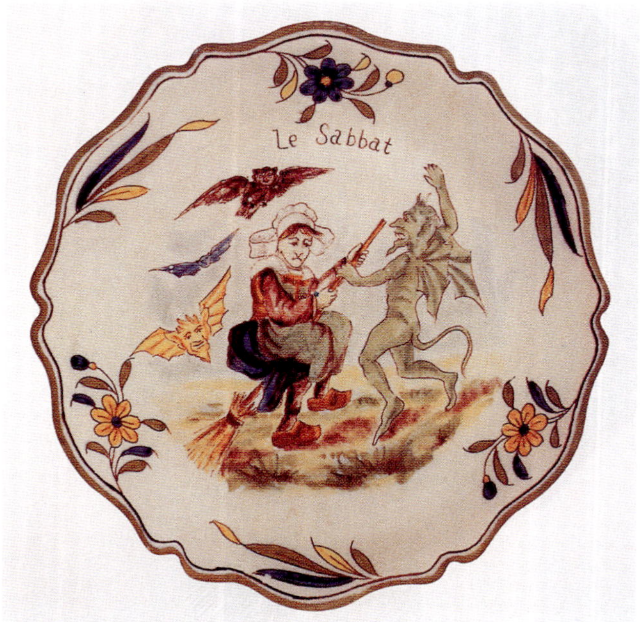

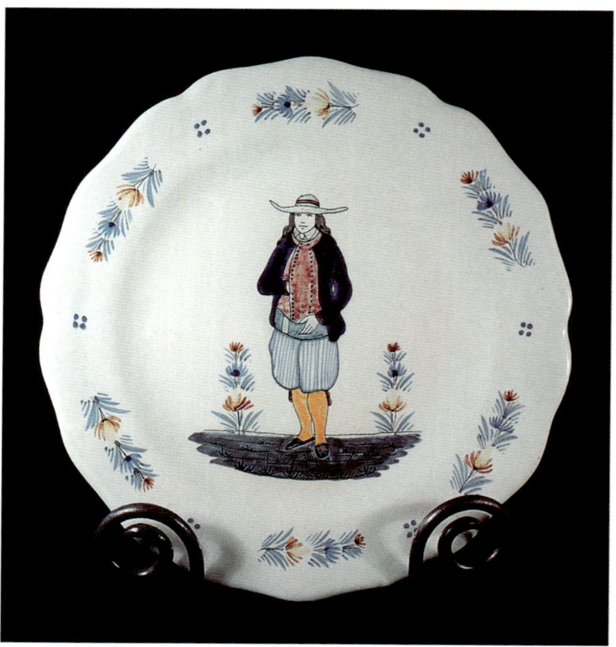

Légendes Bretonnes plates by Porquier-Beau brought $1,100-$2,400 at French auctions in 2000 and 2001. This unsigned model is 9.75" in diameter. Some experts have suggested it might be from the Pouplard faïencerie, due to the deep rim indentations. Other models' edges are less pronounced. *(Mali, Old Quimper Review, March 2001.)* *Légendes Bretonnes* plates brought between $740 and $2,400 in French auctions in 2000. Price range: $600-$800 for this version. *Private Collection.*

Naïve-yet-detailed is the description offered for this HB product, which has declined in price in the American market in the early 2000s. HB naïve-style plates range from 9.25" to 10" in diameter, and have ranged in price to $450. This same model received no bids on an Internet auction in 2000. A French auction in 2000 brought $300 for each piece in a set of four HB naïve-style plates, and an American auction in 2001 garnered between $180 and $325 for HB naïve plates. The chap on this 9.75" HB plate has colorful clothing and is surrounded with *à la touche* sprays and a blue four-dot border design. Price range: $200-$325. *Courtesy of A.W. Styer.*

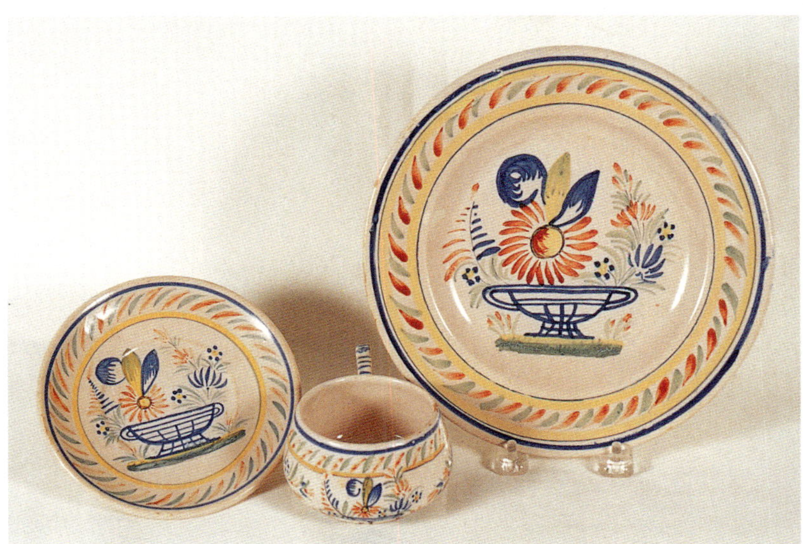

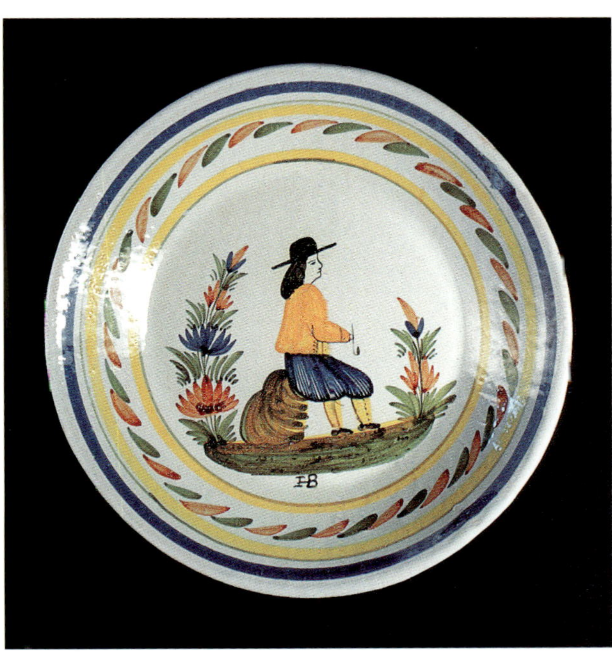

Panier fleuri (basket of flowers) motif is popular on plates and other items, as seen in this grouping. The central theme of a basket of flowers was adopted from the Rouen faïenceries. This version of the motif by Henriot is from the second quarter of the 20th century. Prices for this design have not been overwhelming. Price range: $135-$155 for the plate; $55-$75 for the cup and saucer. *Courtesy of A.W. Styer.*

This HB faïencerie rendition of the *petit Breton* shows him relaxing on a rock, holding a pipe. The 8" diameter plate is signed only HB on the front. Early plates like this still are highly regarded by American collectors. Price range: $150-$200. *Private Collection.*

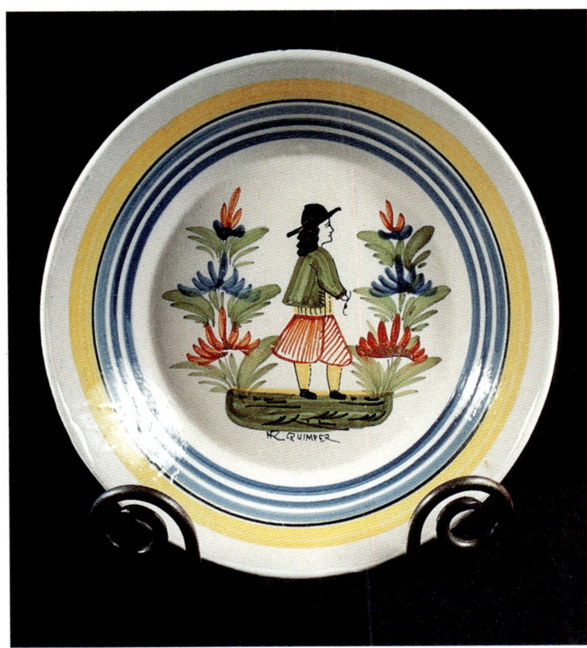

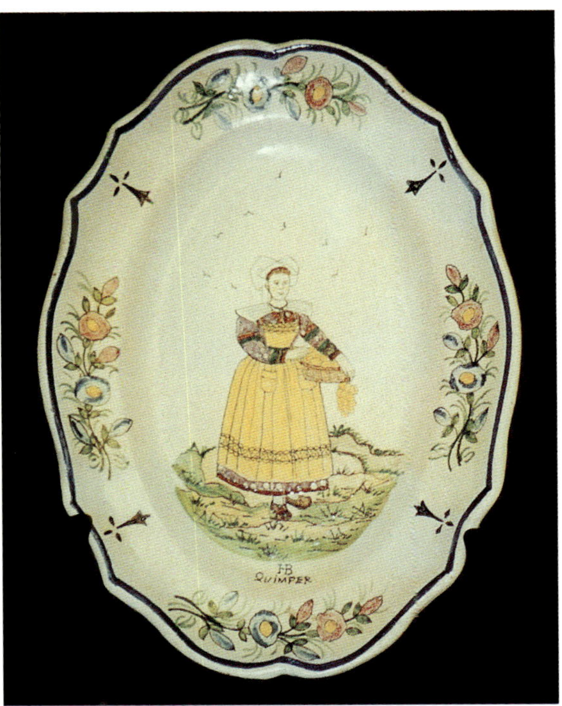

Petit Breton décor is the most widely-recognized design of all Quimper products. This early rendition is by the Henriot faïencerie in the first quarter of the 20th century. The plate measures 8" in diameter and is signed HR Quimper. It shows the *petit Breton* holding a pipe with floral sprays on either side of him. Prices have held for these earlier models. Price range: $150-$200. *Private Collection.*

A *petite Bretonne* graces this lovely *HB/Grande Maison* rendition from the first quarter of the 20th century. Ermine-tail accents and delicately rendered floral sprays make the border delightful. But the Bretonne is stunning. She is painted with great detail, and birds are seen flying in the sky behind her. This 11" long piece, signed HB Quimper, was purchased in France, but the American price range is higher than the French price! Price range: $325-$375. *Collection of Phil and Arlette Griner.*

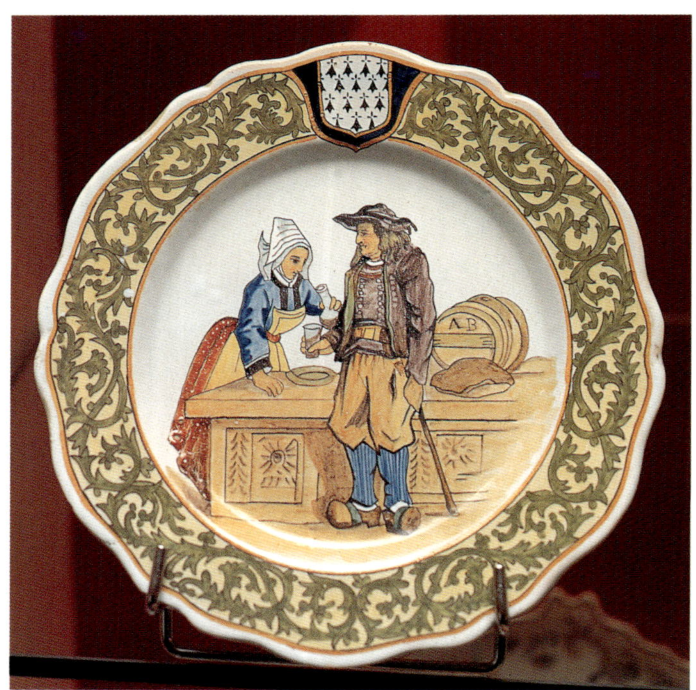

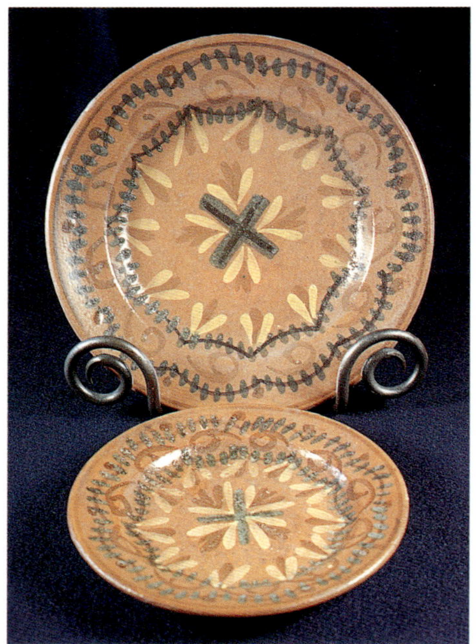

Redware plates? They certainly look like it, but they're signed in script on the back, Henriot Quimper France. The larger plate measures 8" in diameter and the other 6" diameter. These are unusual, but we have seen other examples. Price range: $125-$175 for the pair. *Courtesy of A.W. Styer.*

Scène Bretonne in this instance is a plate entitled *Scène d'auberge à Pleyben*. A border of green scroll with the armorial of Brittany surrounds the central scene. A Bretonne is serving a Breton a drink at an inn. A keg in the background has the initials AB; some believe these are for Alfred Beau. The plate measures 9.25" in diameter and is signed PB for Porquier-Beau. One just like it sold in 2000 at a French auction for $1,144. Price range: $1,200-$1,400. *Private Collection*.

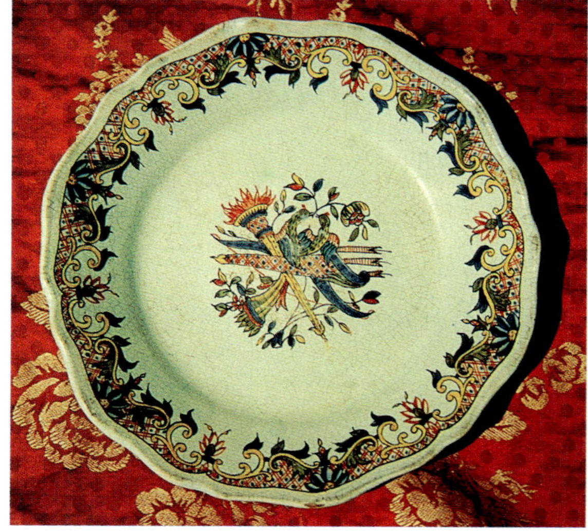

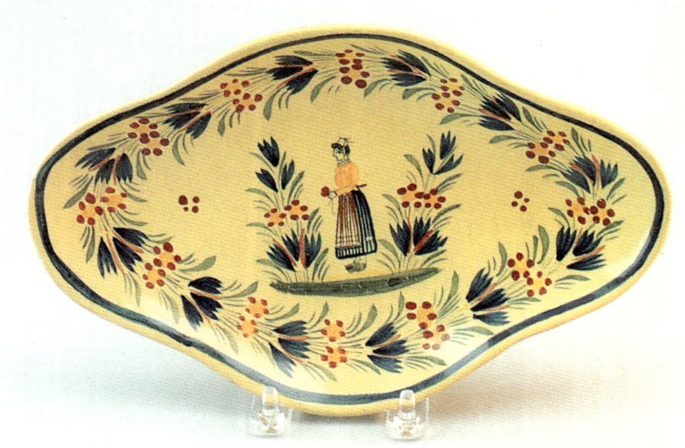

Ravier is a term for plates about 6" to 10" long generally used for serving hors d'oeuvres. This example in the *soleil* décor is 9" long and has a lovely Bretonne with a red posy in the center of a gently scalloped plate. Price range: $125-$195. *Collection of Ralph and Becky DeStefano.*

Rouen décor came early to Quimper faïenceries, when Pierre Bousquet's granddaughter married Rouen-area potter Pierre Clement Caussy in 1749. The quiver-and-arrow motif was one of the Rouen designs on Quimper poterie. This example shows the quiver-and-arrow central design with lambrequins and Guillibaud lattice-work in red filled with blue accents. A Porquier-Beau example can be seen in *Château de Quintin Catalogue, p.* 23, where the motif is called a symbol of chivalrous love. *Courtesy of Sylvain Acher, The French Rendez-vous.*

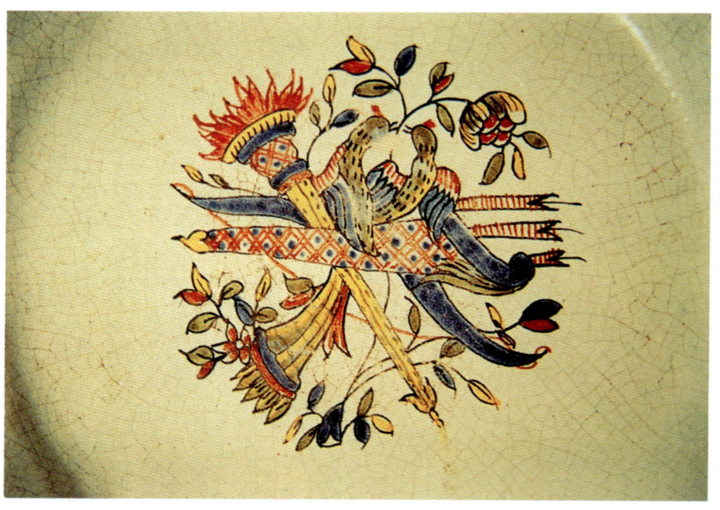

A close-up view of the center of the 19th century unsigned 10" diameter plate shows the quiver and arrows, a torch, and the two love birds. American and Internet auctions did not bring bids in 1998 and 2000. Price range: $300-$400. *Courtesy of Sylvain Acher, The French Rendez-vous.*

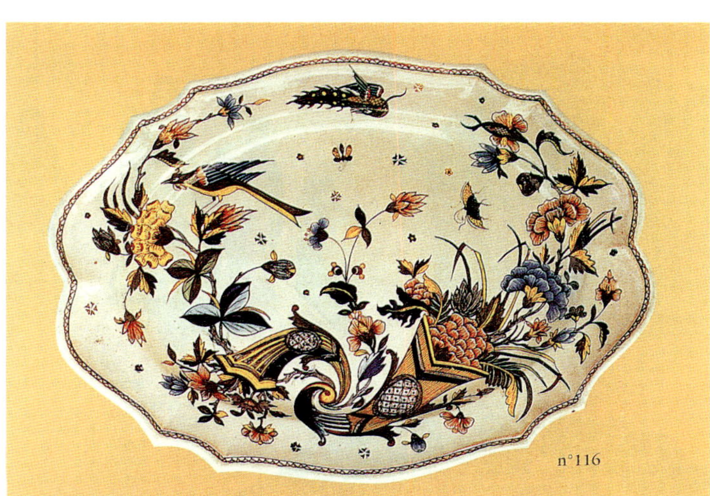

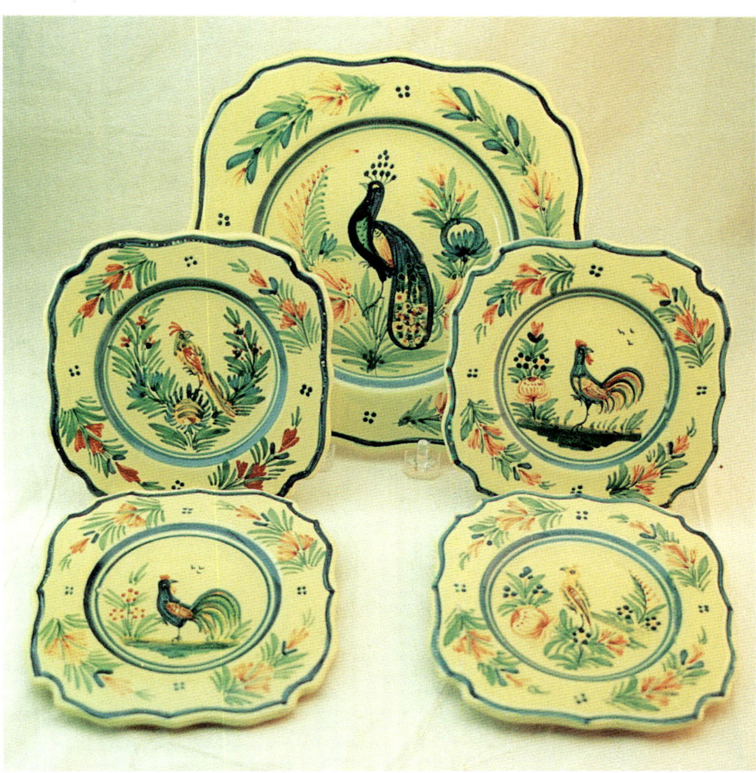

Rouen motif fills this *grand plat oval festonné,* or large scalloped platter, which measures 19.25" long. The inner décor is a double cornucopia with insects, a bird, and flowers filling the platter, surrounded by *chainette Rouen.* It is signed with the first mark HB for the de la Hubaudière faïencerie. This example brought over $2,700 in a French auction in 2000. Price range: $2,000-$3,000. *Courtesy of Thierry & Lannon, Douarnenez and Brest.*

Soleil or sunny yellow décor is a favorite with many collectors. The shade of yellow does differ on many examples according to faïencerie and production era. This group of plates from the HB faïencerie features exotic birds, including a peacock, although the sturdy French rooster is present. The large plate is 8" in diameter and the smaller ones are 5.5" in diameter; they are second quarter of the 20th century, and most likely a dessert set. The signature is HB Quimper, *Ovington's,* a New York City department store. Price range: $350-$450 for the group. *Collection of Nancy Wyman.*

Porte-Lettres (letter holder) is a handy desk top item.

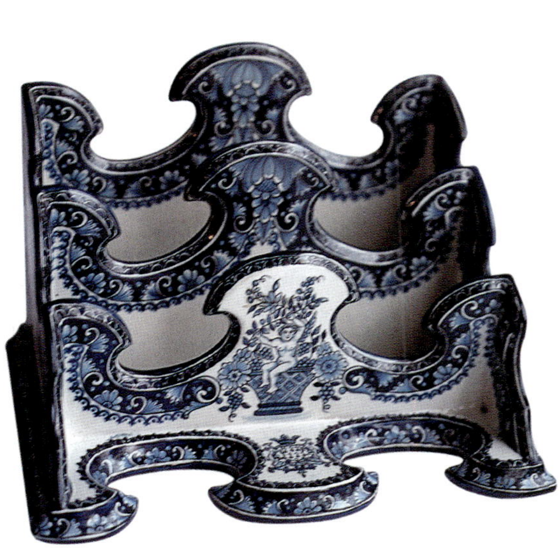

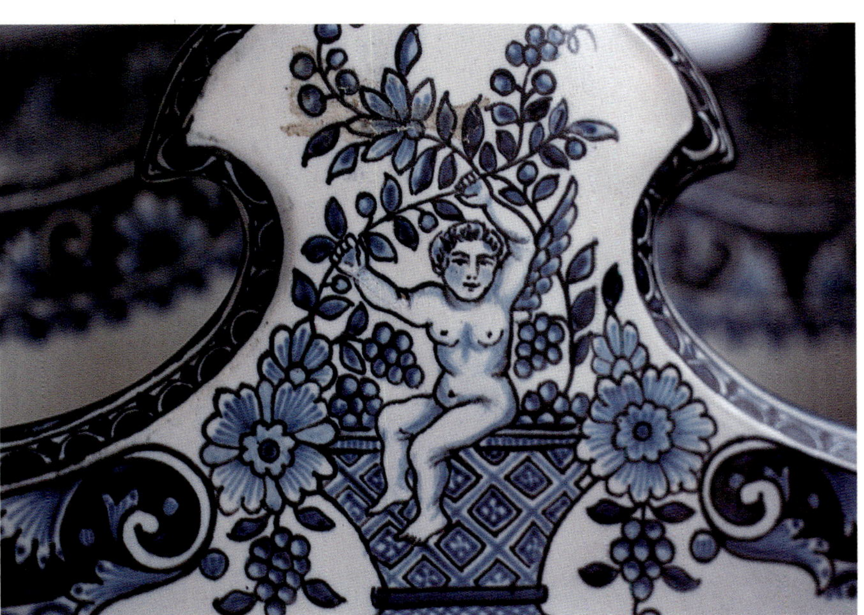

A *porte-lettres* by the Henriot faïencerie is in *camaïeu bleu,* a monochromatic blue décor. It is signed Henriot Quimper #130, and dates from the second quarter of the 20th century. *Courtesy of Pierre Breton, Art de Cornouaille, Quimper.*

The *porte-lettres* features a Nevers-style *anglot* sitting on a *panier fleuri.* This piece is unusual and desirable. A later model called *classeur de courier* by Henriot brought $566 on a 2001 Internet auction. Price range: $750-$950. *Courtesy of Pierre Breton, Art de Cornouaille, Quimper.*

Pots *(pots)* come in varying sizes, shapes, and purposes.

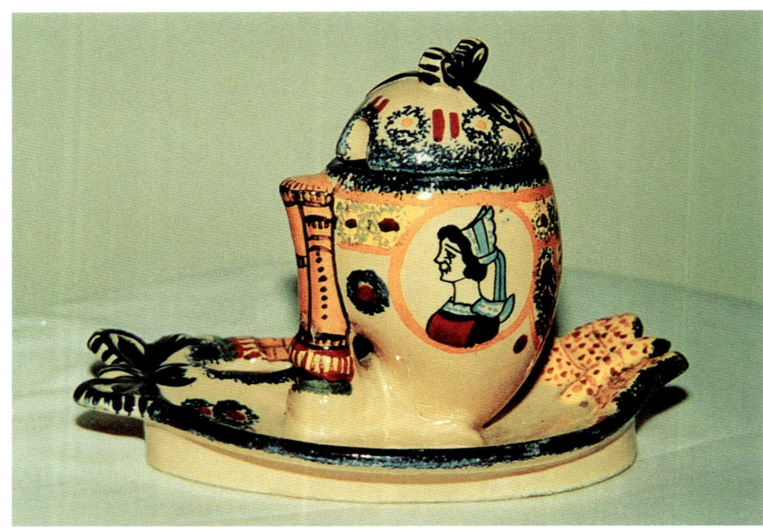

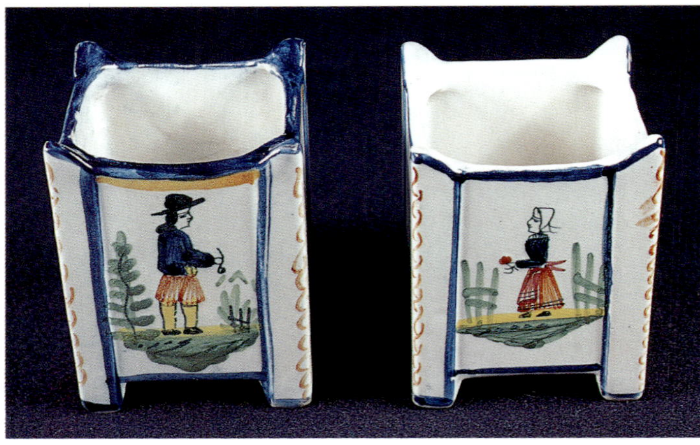

This pot is for jam or mustard. It is in décor *ivoire corbeille* and the pot itself is *biniou*-shaped. (Note the pipes on the pot's side.) A cartouche or medallion features a Bretonne and the attached undertray has a blue bow and pipes also. Signed Henriot Quimper #104, it is c.1930. Similar examples have realized $300 or more on Internet auctions in the late 1990s. Price range: $325-$375. *Courtesy of Christine T. Lindstrom.*

Cache-pot (flower pot or planter) is a *cache-all* phrase, oops, catch-all phrase to cover a number of variously shaped pots. This pair of HB faïencerie planters seems to match, except for the lack of blue edging around the rim on the Bretonne example. They stand 4" tall and date from the 1920s-1930s. *Courtesy of A.W. Styer.*

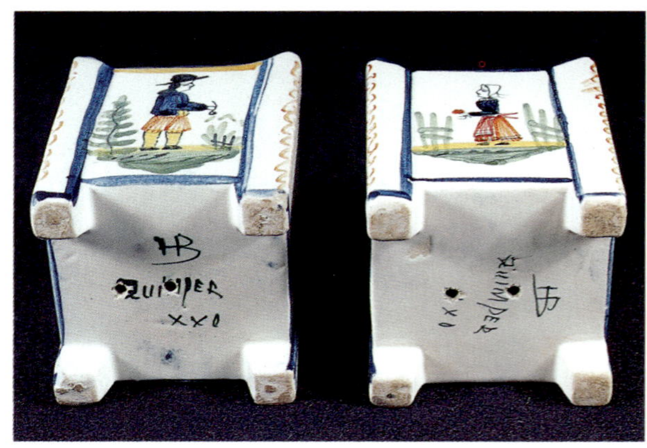

A close look at the bottom of the *cache-pots* reveals the HB Quimper signature, with the artist's mark (++o). It also reveals that this pair was drilled post-manufacture to allow water to drain. Price range: $175-$225 for the pair. *Courtesy of A.W. Styer.*

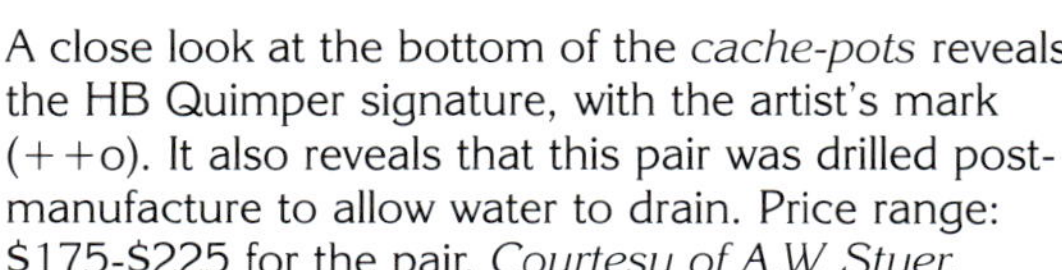

❧ Q is for...

It's all Quimper!

❧ R is for...

Religious items are prevalent in Brittany due to the strong influence of the church.

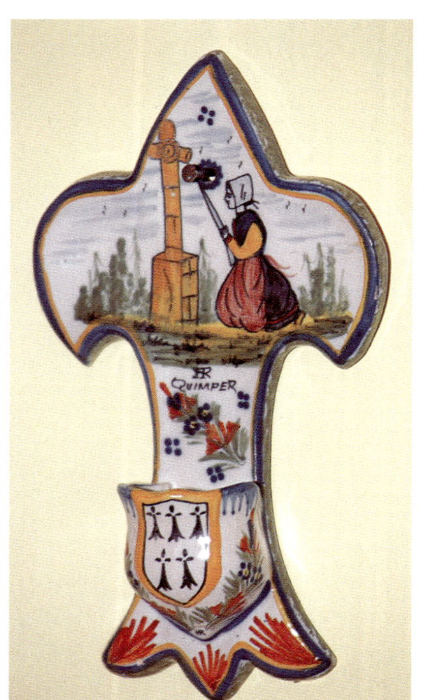

A *bénitier* or holy water font is an example of religious articles made by the Quimper faïenceries. This model is *fleur-de-lys*-shaped and shows a young Bretonne with a votive taper kneeling before a wayside cross. Marked HR Quimper and standing 8" tall, this is a sweet rendition by the Henriot faïencerie. Internet sales in the late 1990s brought between $200 and $500, depending on the décor and shape. A similar *bénitier* sold through an American auction in the early 1990s for $250, and through a French auction in the late 1990s for $260. Price range: $325-$425. *Courtesy of Patricia Zimmerman.*

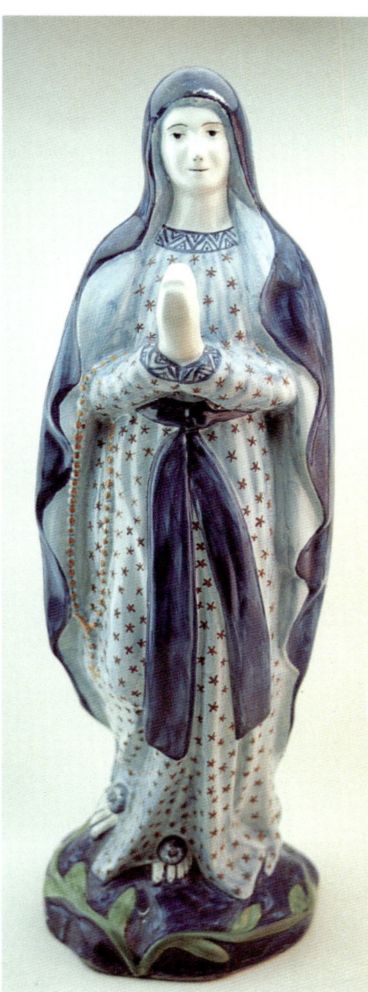

Saint figurines are the most prominent religious category. This statue stands 17.5" tall, is signed Henriot Quimper France, and dates from the 1950s. It's a glorious rendition found at a local antique market in the United States. It carries no designation as to saint name and an exact example is not found in *Cahn, Vierges et Saints de Faïence de Quimper*. A *Vierge Immaculée* attributed to Henriot is found in *Verlingue & Lécossois, p. 36*. It is in a similar stance and design. We finally found this example in *Bondhus, p. 236*. Price range: $800-$1,000. *Courtesy of Elizabeth C. Ross.*

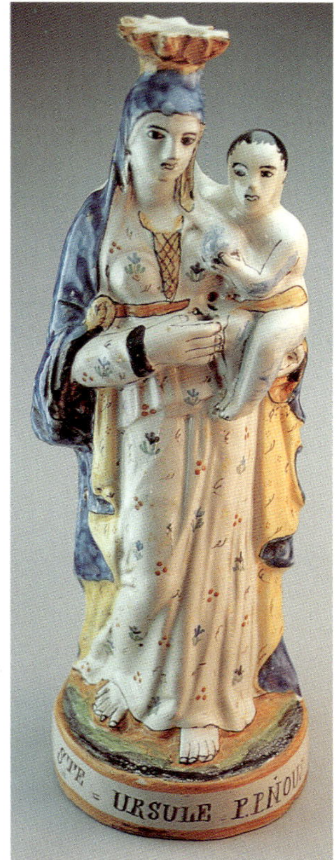

This saint statue is entitled *Ste.=Ursule= P. P. Nous* and stands 15.5" tall. *P. P. Nous* on the round base means, *pray for us*; on some statues only P. P. N. appears. The crown contains a narrow diameter hole for a candle. In *Cahn, p. 36*, variously sized receptacles are seen in this style, called *accouchée*. A candle is placed in the crown and lit during childbirth to bring blessings on the mother and baby. The robe is covered with red three-dot design and blue *à la touche* flowers. The only mark is a #9. Price range: $800-$1,000. *Courtesy of Carter Yeatman.*

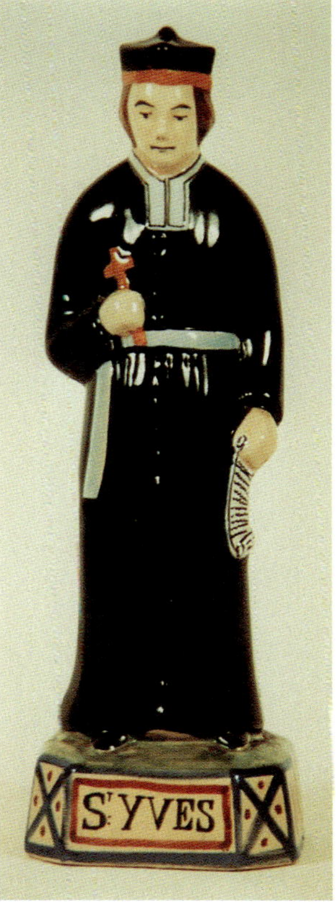

Saint Yves, the lawyer who became a saint by helping the poor, is pictured here in a 9.5" statue from the HB faïencerie. He stands on a rectangular base with cut-corners that are decorated with an X and red dots. This model dates mid-20th century. St. Yves is the patron saint of lawyers and was canonized in 1347. *(Bondhus, p. 86.)* Superior examples of St. Yves statues brought between $325 and $825 in the 1990s in the U.S. A French auction realized only $286 for an HR model of St. Yves in 2000. Price range: $350-$650. *Private Collection.*

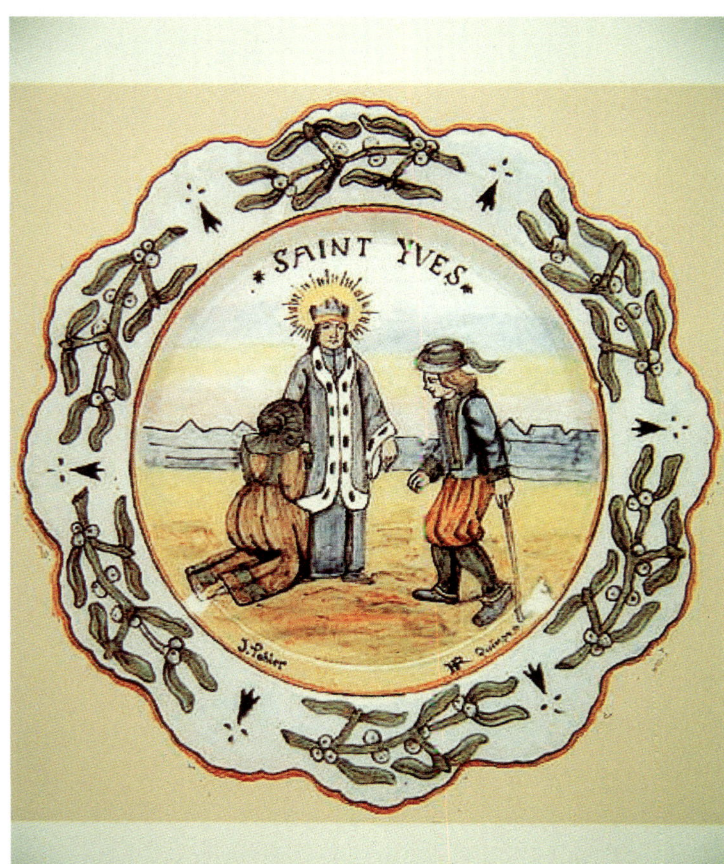

Collectors seek saint plates by Jacques Pohier. The series was made in the first decade or so of the 20th century. Mali states there are 12 in the original series. *(Mali, Old Quimper Review, March 1991.)* We have seen later versions signed Henriot. The example seen here is of St. Yves, the lawyer-saint. The plate measures 10" in diameter and is signed HR Quimper and J. Pohier. These plates have brought between $350 and $800 in Internet and American sales. A French auction realized nearly $2,000 for a 12" diameter example with a saying included in a cartouche and a rim filled with *l'ajonc, bruyère* and the armorial of Brittany. Price range: $675-$875. *Courtesy of Lucy Williams.* (For additional examples see Chapters *Rennes and Environs,* and *Environs de Quimper.*)

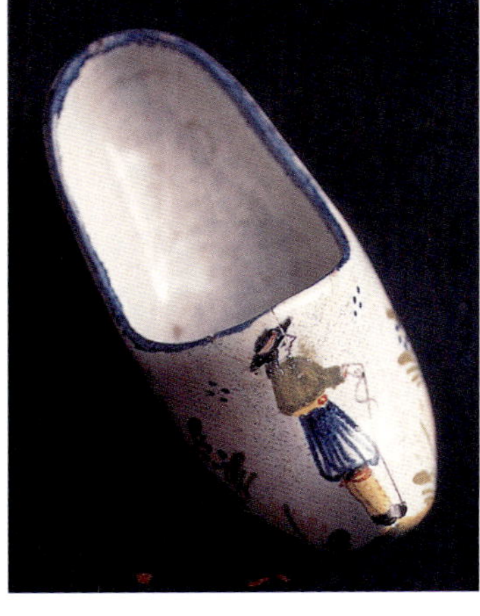

This 4.5" long *sabot* is faïence and marked only France. Looks like Quimper and most likely is Henriot. Price range: $35-$55. *Private Collection.*

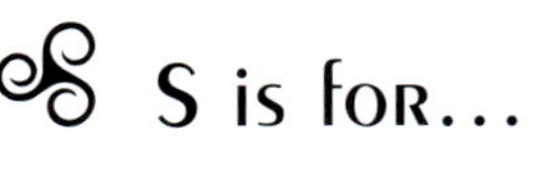

S is for…

Sabots are wooden shoes worn in Brittany.

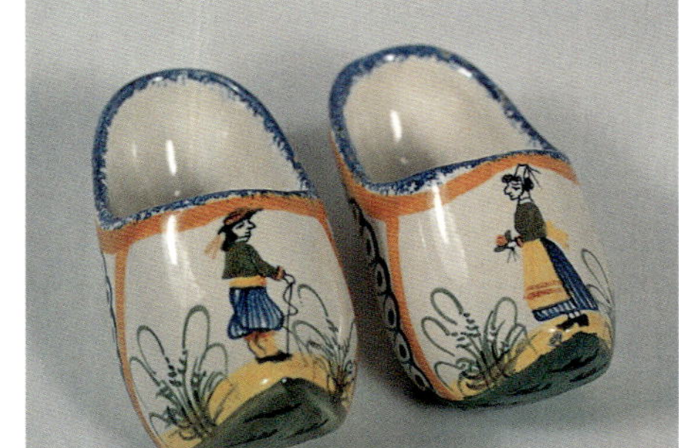

A pair of 4" long *sabots*, c. 1930, are marked Henriot Quimper #95. Prices have fallen for this type of item due to the selection now available on Internet auctions. In the 1990s, a matching pair like this would bring $65 to $85, or more. In 2001, many such examples received no bids or sold for less than $40. Price range: $40-$65. *Private Collection.*

Salt *(sel)* containers range from very simple to grand.

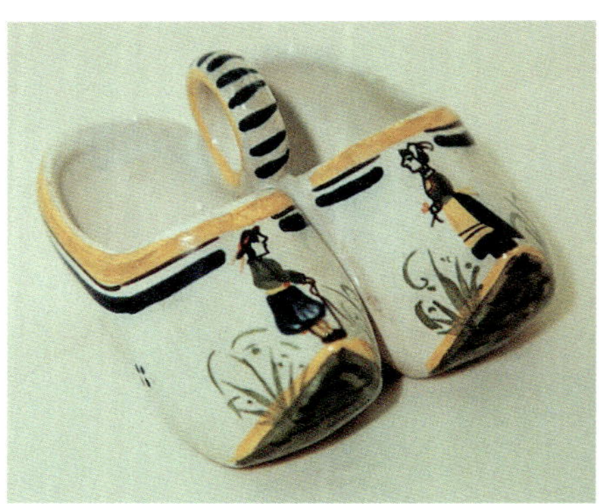

A linked pair of *sabots* double salts is signed Henriot Quimper, and dates from the mid-20th century. Double salts sabots with unusual décor have brought more than $400 through American auctions in the past decade. This example is frequently seen and ranges much lower. Price range: $65-$75. *Private Collection.*

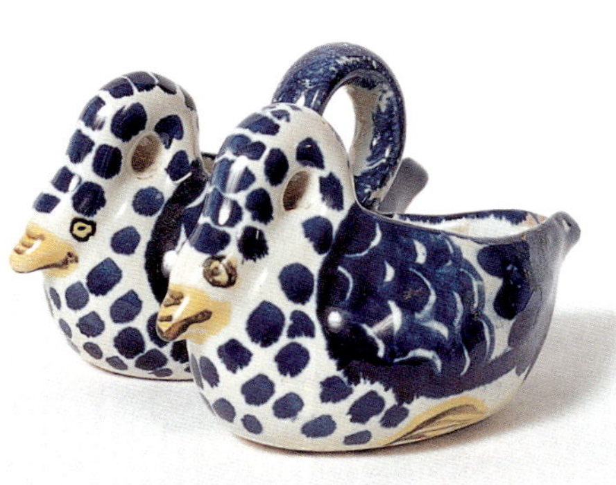

Swan double salts are another matter. Their unique shape has attracted collectors, and this 4" long version by Henriot brought more than $200 in 1999 from an Internet sale and more than $200 in an American auction in the mid-1990s. Prices have settled down and the pair brought $75-$125 in 2001. Price range: $75-$125. *Courtesy of Susan T. Temple.*

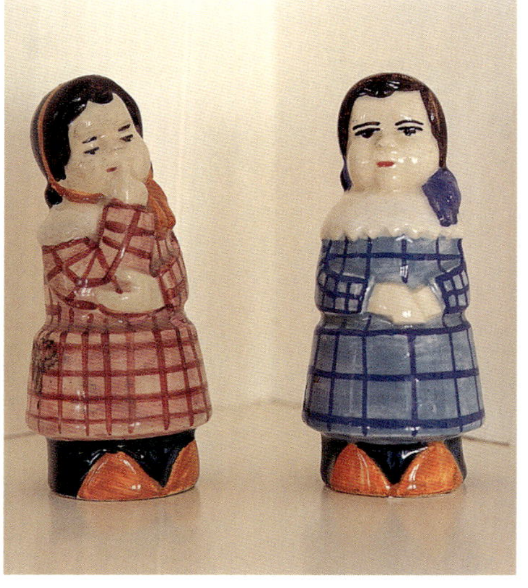

Salt and pepper shakers in figural forms are rarer than the *sabot* or swan versions. This adorable pair stands 3.5" tall and is by the Henriot artist André Galland. They are signed with the artist's initials AG and Quimper. Similar pairs sold through an American auction in the 1990s for between $180-$300. An Internet auction in 1999 sold a similar pair for $61. Nice buy! Price range: $175-$275. *Private Collection.*

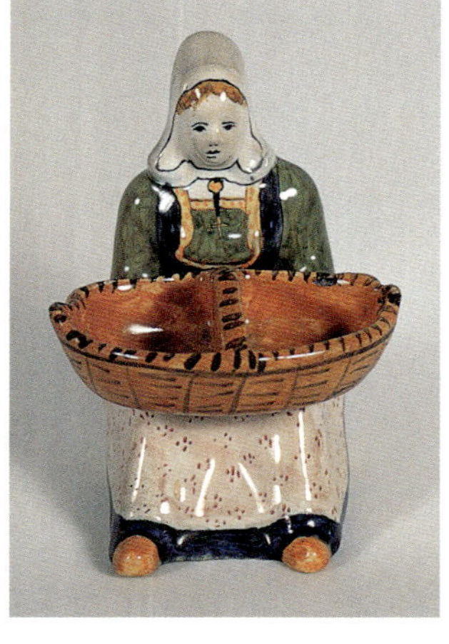

A Bretonne sits with a double basket on her lap to hold salt. She measures 5" tall and has a 4" base, and is signed Henriot Quimper France #131. The figural double salt dates from the 1930s and is an attractive model for collectors. This same model brought $400 in 2000 through an American auction and a more recent model brought $246 through a 1999 Internet auction. Price range: $350-$425. *Private Collection.*

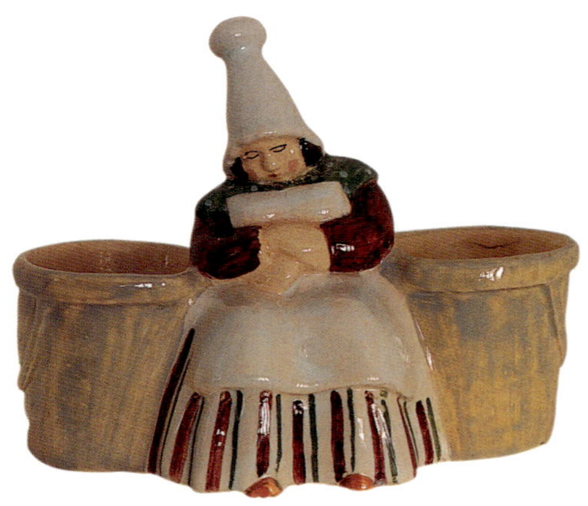

Another woman, this time from Normandy, sits with a basket at each side. She appears to be napping. André Galland designed this 5" tall double salt signed *Normandie* and AG, which is from the 1920s-1930s. Galland's work has a devoted following. (This example can be seen in *Mali, Old Quimper Review, October 1993*, along with other examples and information on salt production in Brittany.) Price range: $200-$295. *Private Collection.*

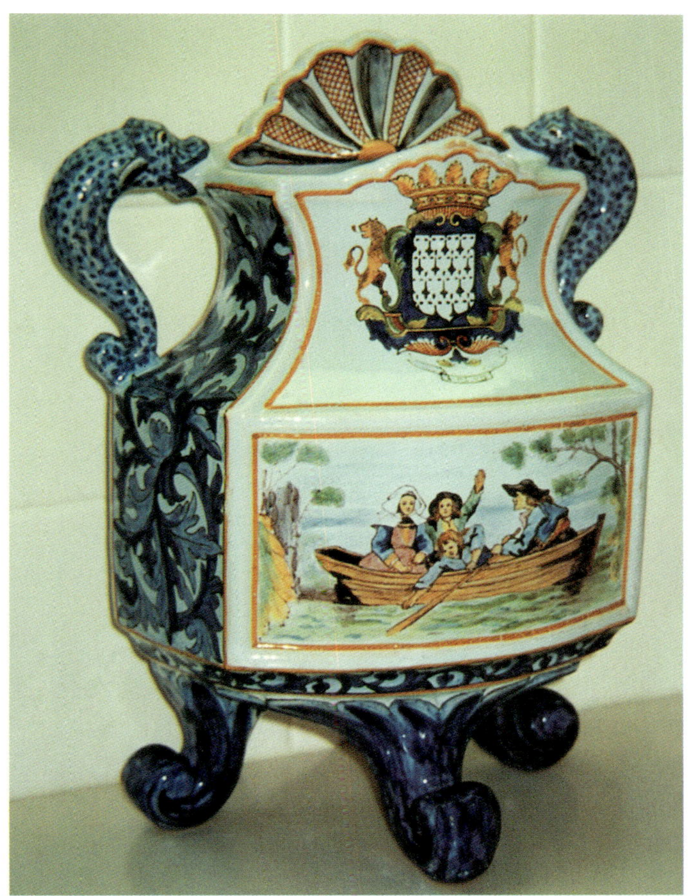

Although the rest of France was taxed heavily on salt, *Bretagne* had a much lower rate, a *petite gabelle*. Thus, a large salt container, or a *Main à sel*, came in handy. This 11.5" tall by 9.5" wide model by Porquier-Beau has handles in the shape of lizards and it stands on three scrolled feet. The lizards are done in light-blue with dark-blue spots, and the sides are two-toned blue scroll on a blue ground. The armorial of Brittany and a *scène Bretonne* of boaters fill the front of the piece, and a demi-shell with alternating red *croisillon* and blue accents tops it. A French auction realized about $1,350 for a similar model in 2001. The American market commands more. Price range: $2,100-$2,800. *Private Collection.*

Sets of faïence items are not easy to find.

Creamer and sugar sets are not always easy to find. This particular set is unusual, besides being very attractive. The paneled form, wishbone handles, and *à la touche* detail are wonderful, as are the renditions of the peasants on each piece. But the peasant dress was unfamiliar and the signature on the bottom of each confusing, until we did some research. *Courtesy of A.W. Styer.*

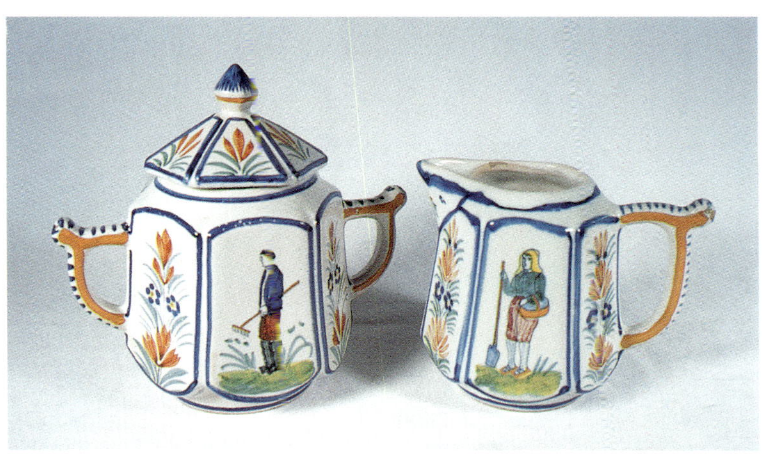

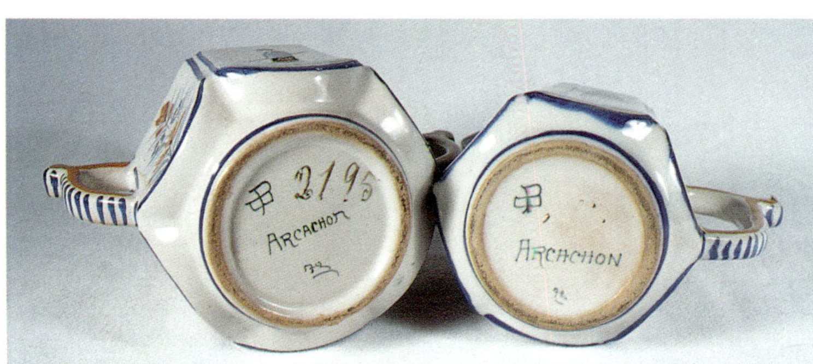

The bottom of the creamer and sugar told the tale. *Arachon* is a town and area on the Atlantic coast of southwestern France. A *Les Provinces Françaises* design by HB Quimper and the costumes on this sugar and creamer set matched. (See *Bondhus, p. 182.*) But a new mystery arose. The set is also signed PB for Porquier-Beau and #72, but the design appears to be Henriot. (See *Bondhus, p. 146.*) Could this be a clue to Porquier-Beau painters working for Henriot and signing their work PB? Was the *Arachon* design initiated before the series *Les Provinces Françaises*, which dates in the 1920s-1930s? Was this set possibly painted sometime between 1904 and 1914? Mali reasons that after Porquier-Beau painters were hired by the Henriot faïencerie in 1904, they may have continued to use the former signature, PB. *(Mali, conversations 2000-2001.)* The set is lovely and the mystery makes it more so. Price range: $225-$325. *Courtesy of A.W. Styer.*

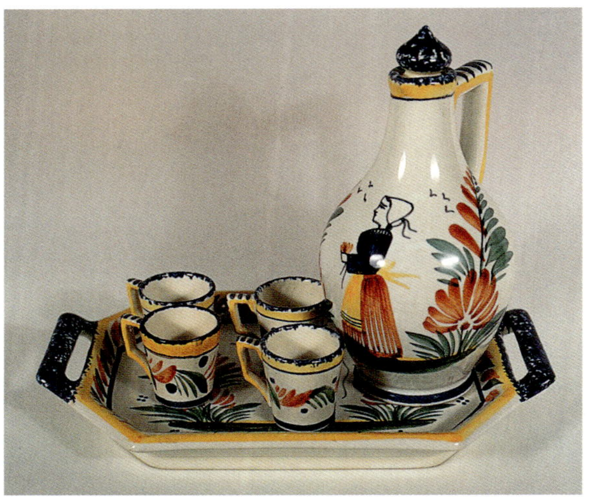

A liqueur set consists of a decanter, cups and matching tray. This example by HB is from the 1920s-1930s and is signed HB Quimper #58 and (…), the mark for the painter Mssr. Cojan. The decanter stands 7" tall including the stopper, the tray is 9" long, and each cup is 1.5" tall. A similar set in the *soleil* pattern with six cups sold through an American auction in the late 1990s for $375. Price range: $325-$375. *Private Collection.*

Slipper or fancy shoe is a favorite with collectors.

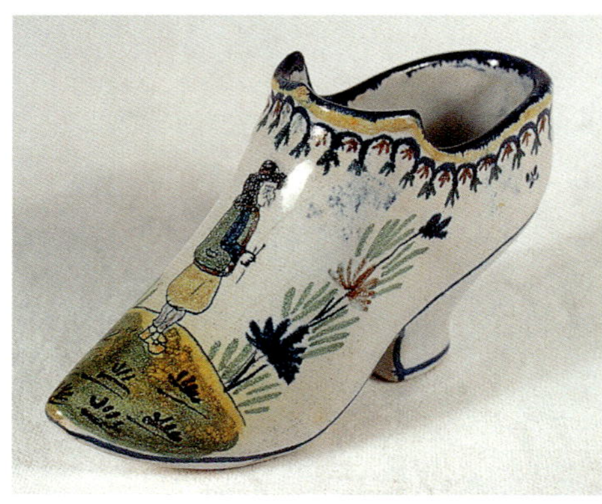

This 7" long slipper with a high heel is in the Louis XV-shape and decorated with a tassel border around the rim. Additional décor is a *petit Breton* in yellow *bragou-braz* flanked by floral sprays. This example is signed with the mark of the Leroy-Dubois factory and dates from 1899 to 1918. A similar slipper with no maker identified sold for less than $200 in an American auction in 1998. In 2000, American auctions sold a version attributed to the Porquier faïencerie for $160, while another marked only HB brought $100. In 2001, an Internet auction brought $110 for a 6.5" long AP model. Price range: $100-$165. *Courtesy of A.W. Styer.*

Smoking-related items are numerous.

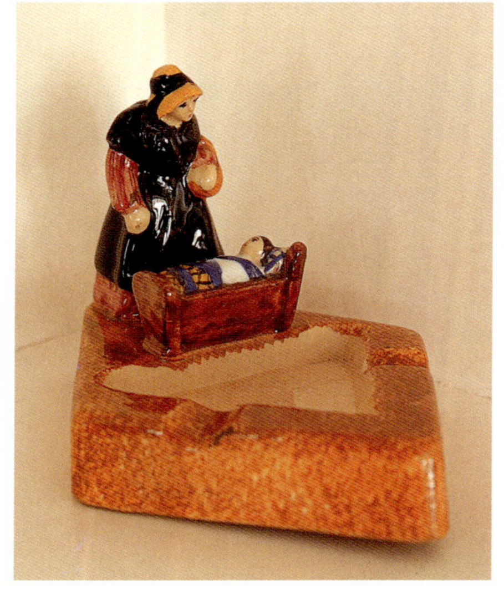

Ashtrays or *cendiers* come in a variety of sizes, shapes, and motifs. Some contain advertisement, others armorials, proverbs, or even figurines. This example incorporates figures. Henriot artist André Galland designed this 6" long ashtray, featuring a Bretonne looking down on a baby in a cradle. Galland is known for his figurines and also for the *berceau* (cradle) design. Signed Henriot Quimper France, the ashtray dates from the 1920s-1930s. A Sévellec figural ashtray of smaller size brought $160 at an American auction in 1999. Price range: $175-$225. *Private Collection.*

Another type of ashtray carries a proverb or motto. This example is stamped Henriot Quimper France and is 4.5" long with a sponged décor around the saying. Approximate translation: *Virgins are on strike against love.* Prices at American auctions have held between $25 and $55 over the past dozen years. Price range: $25-$55. *Courtesy of Charlie and Donna Walker.*

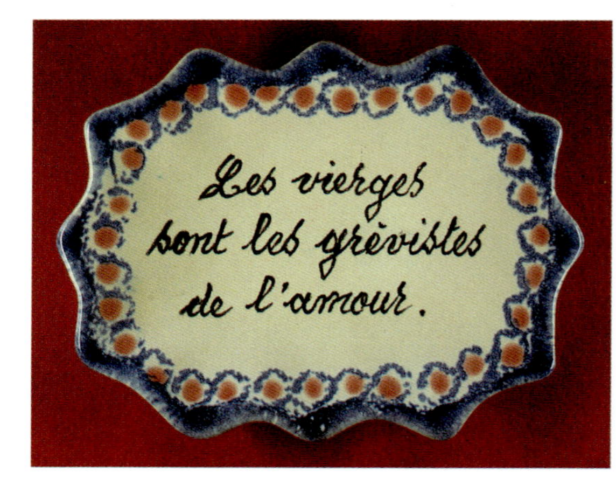

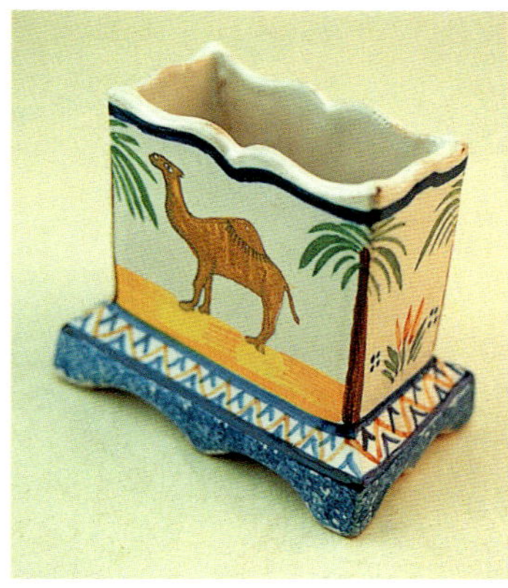

Smoking-related items include cigarette holders such as the popular camel motif. This version stands 3" tall and is signed Henriot Quimper. Because of the camel design, this model has sold for between $200 and $300 in American and Internet auctions in the late 1980s and 1990s. Price range: $225-$325. *Courtesy of Nancy Wyman.*

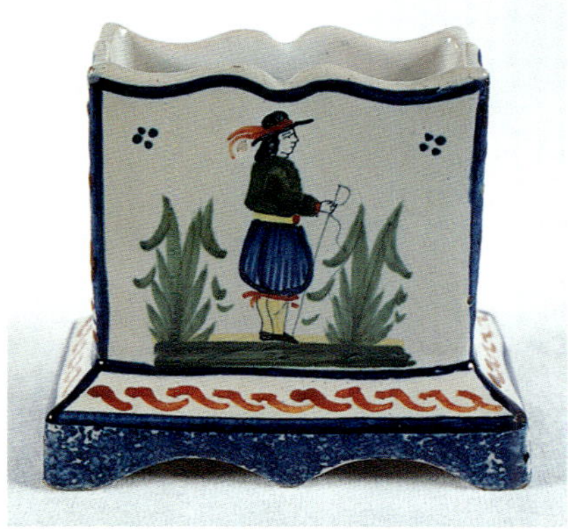

In contrast, the same mold, but with a *petit Breton* décor, signed Henriot Quimper France #75, realized under $200 in the 1990s. Price range: $175-$225. *Courtesy of A.W. Styer.*

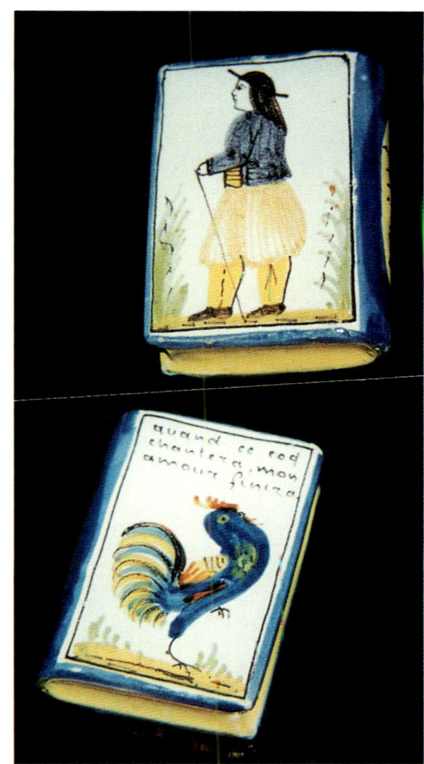

Snuffs *(secouettes)* come in plain and fancy forms. (For a look at auction prices for unusual snuffs, see Chapter *Morlaix*.) This version in the *biniou*-shape is one of the more frequently seen. The maker is undetermined in this 3" long model, but Pouplard is a good guess. A Malicorne *biniou* snuff sold through an American auction in 1997 for $220, and in 1998 for $210. Price range: $200-$245. *Private Collection.*

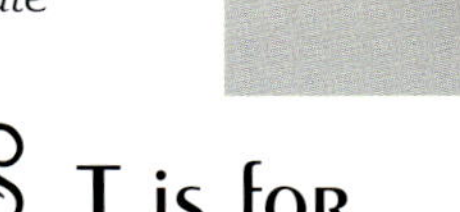

Another frequently seen snuff model is called book-shaped. Many versions have a rooster on one side and a Breton or Bretonne on the other, and many times the spine of the book has the word *souvenir* in a medallion. The saying above the rooster reads: *Quand ce coq chantera, mon amour finira*, or When this cock crows, my love will be ended. Age and décor help determine price. This HB Quimper version from the 1930s achieved between $150 and $200 at 1990s French auctions. In 2001, it brought $185 at an American auction. Price range: $225-$275. *Private Collection.*

ℰ T is for…

Tea (thé) and coffee (café) services come in a variety of Quimper décors.

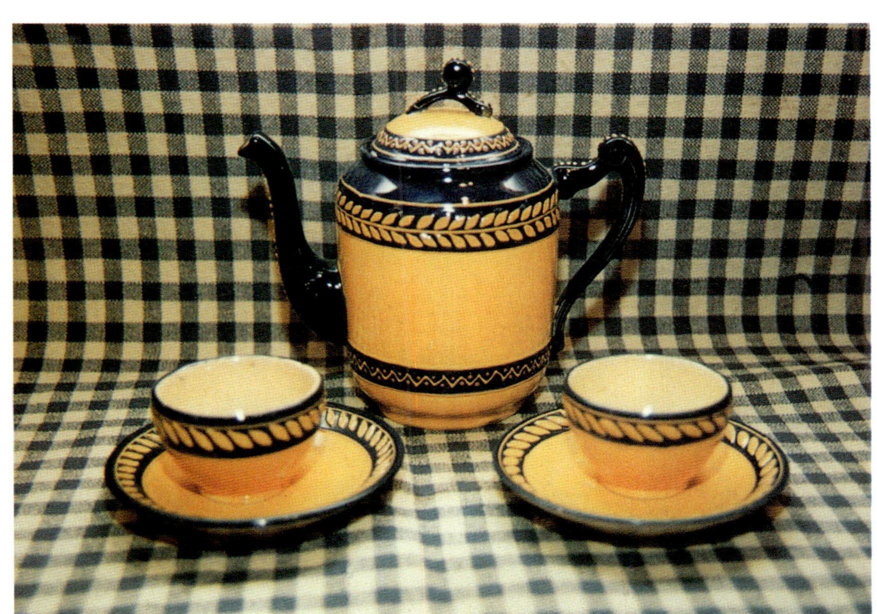

This teapot with matching cups and saucers is in the *broderie* design. The bold golden color is an early model, c.1930. The pot stands 7.5" tall and the cups are 2.5" tall. This trio makes a lovely display. Prices have held very well for *broderie* décor, especially of this vintage. Price range: $325-$425 for the set. *Private Collection.*

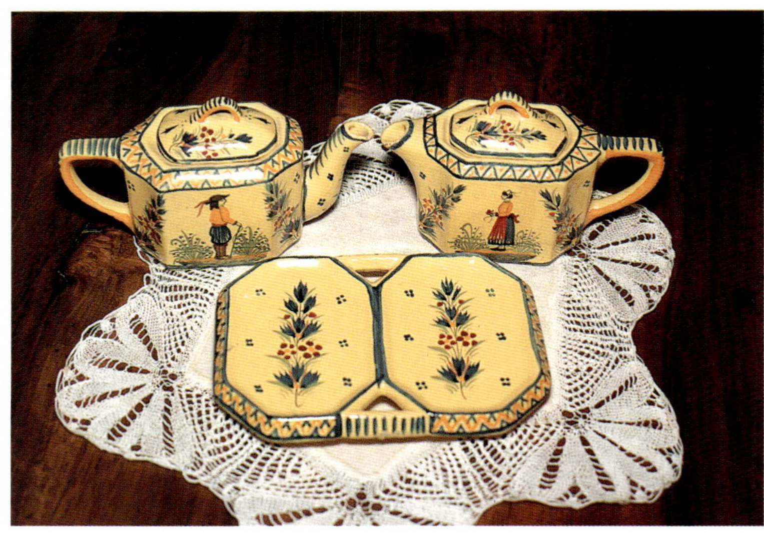

The Henriot faïencerie manufactured this sweet cozy set, as seen in its 1920s Catalogue. (*Bondhus, p. 146.*) It is even more charming in the *soleil* décor. Sets with the tray are hard to find. This one was handed down in a French family very carefully and now resides in Brittany. Sentimental value: $1,000,000. Price range: $425-$525. *Private Collection.*

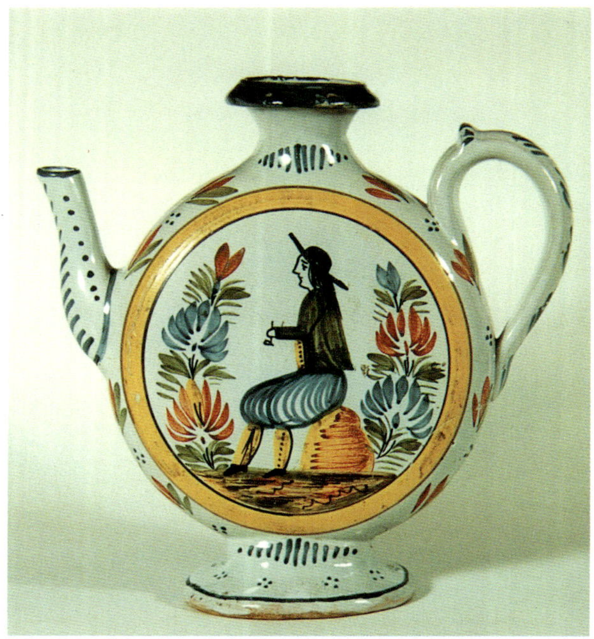

A canteen or circular teapot also is a rare find, especially one made before 1900. This model is signed only HB. A Breton enjoys his pipe as he sits on the ever-present rock of Brittany. *Private Collection.*

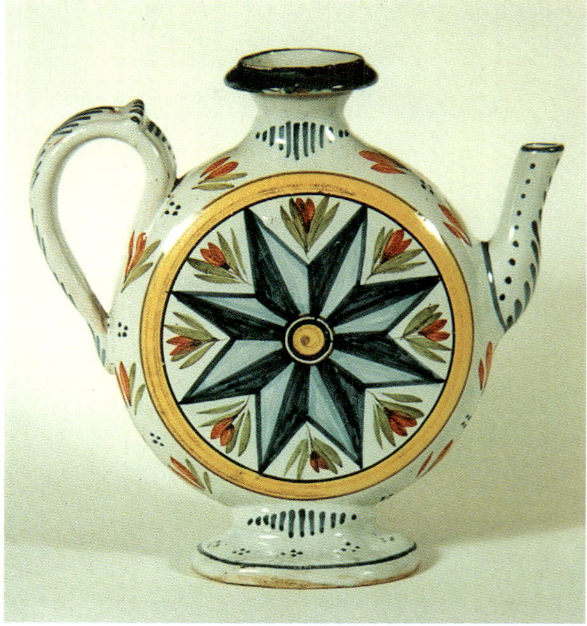

The other side of the teapot features a bold blue, two-toned geometric surrounded by *à la touche* sprigs and a blue four-dot design. A real charmer! Prices through 1990s American and Internet auctions for examples in this age and condition were between $400 and $900, while U.K. sellers advertised similar models at $1,300. Price range: $875-$1,075. *Private Collection.*

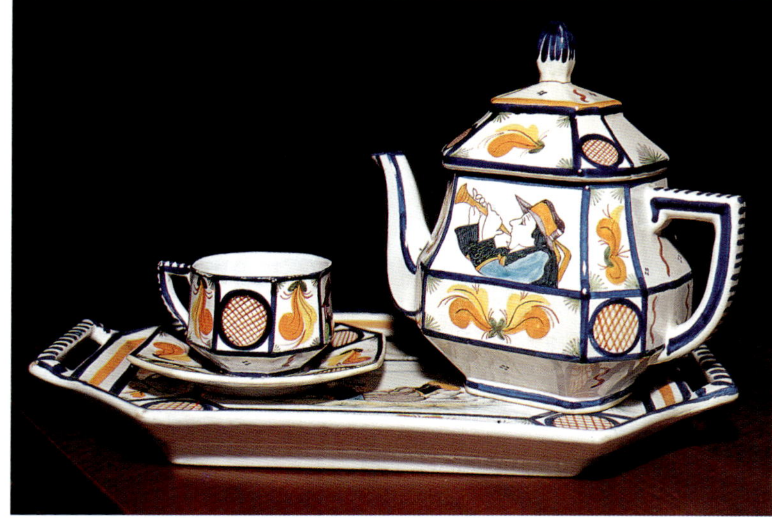

HB is the maker of this teapot, cup and saucer, and matching undertray. The style contains red *croisillon* accents in circles, which some call the tennis ball motif, with *l'ajonc* and *bruyère* accents. The jolly *bombarde* player is echoed on the cup and the tray. This design is from the 1920s-1930s and very popular with collectors. Price range: $675-$750 for the set. *Private Collection.*

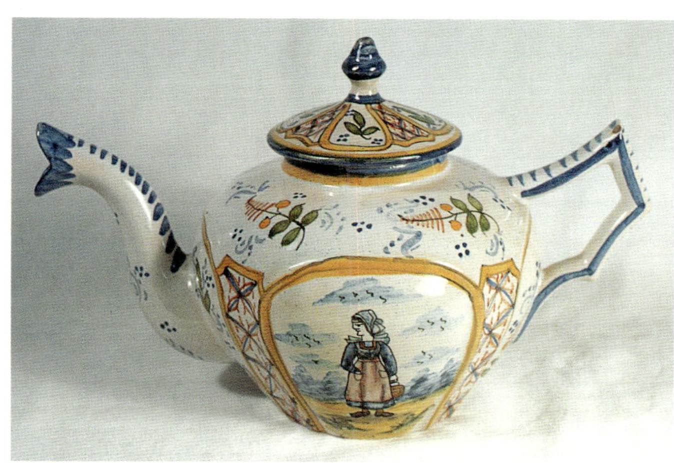

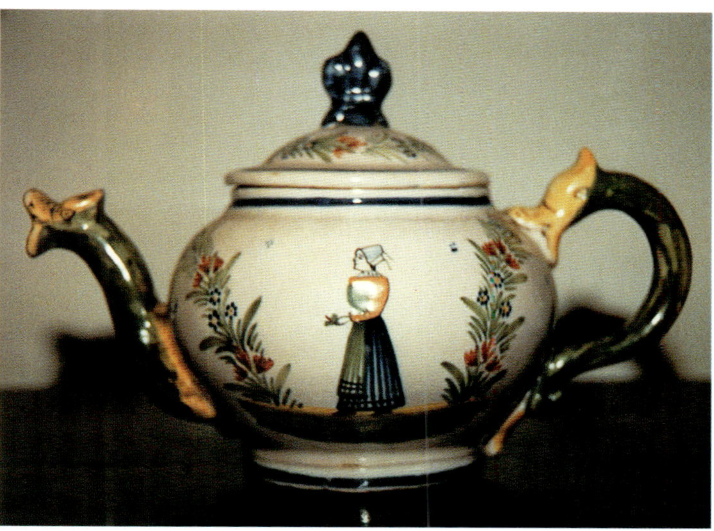

Another HB teapot from the 1920s-1930s has red and blue *croisillon* décor insets and HB floral accents. The design is called *demi-riche* by some collectors. Most noteworthy are the extended spout with flared opening and the wishbone handle. The Bretonne in a cartouche on the front completes the presentation. Prices have increased for this model since the early 1990s. Price range: $425-$525. *Collection of A.W. Styer.*

The Henriot faïencerie produced this dragon-handled teapot in the first decade or so of the 20th century. It's always a favorite style, and the fact it's signed HR Quimper makes it even more precious. Price range: $425-$475. *Private Collection.*

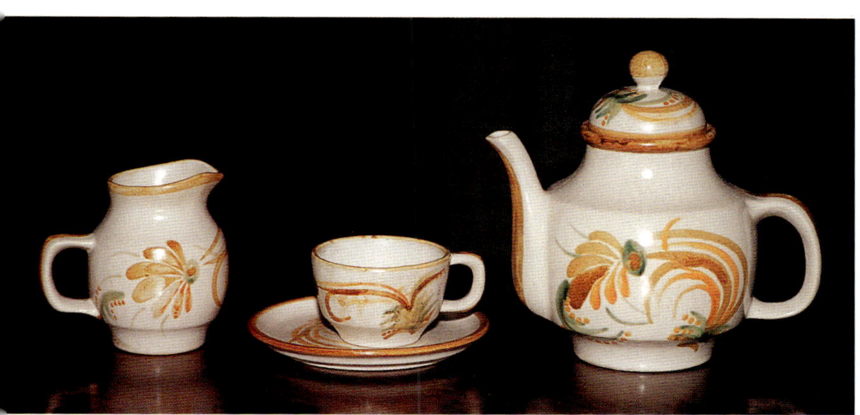

This tea set in *grès* ware was found in a shop in Quimper, high on a shelf behind other items. We were told it dated from the 1970s, when HB and Henriot shared the same facility while maintaining their own clients, marks, and inventory. *Authors' Collection.*

But the *grès* is stamped with the double signature HB and Henriot. We didn't know if this was an anomaly or whether the *marchand* was mistaken. The form is by Jean-Claude Taburet and the *Automne* décor by Tony Walch, c. 1977. (*Taburet, p. 205.*) Were some items signed with the double signature of HB/Henriot prior to purchase by the *Société Nouvelle*? Price range: $200-$225. *Authors' Collection.*

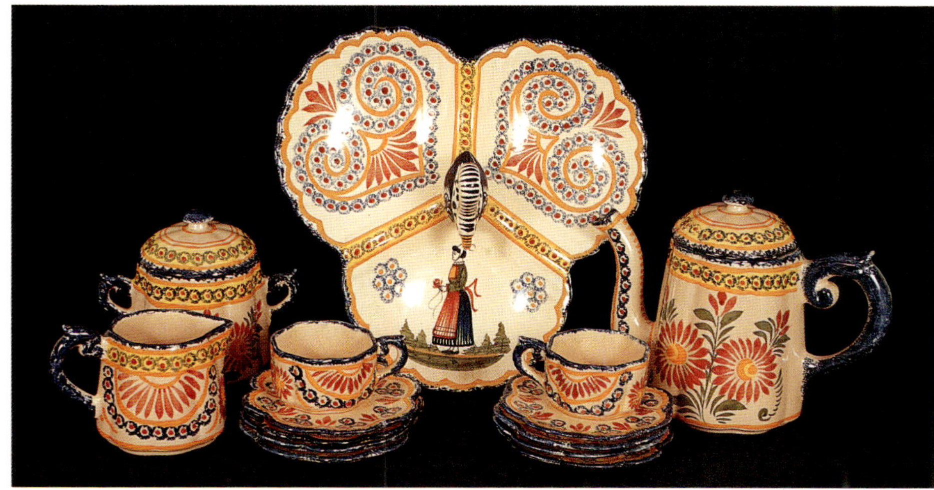

Ivoire corbeille is a décor sought by certain collectors. An *ivoire corbeille* trefoil server with a swan handle complements this lovely Henriot tea set with six cups and saucers, creamer, sugar, and 7.25" tall teapot. What a great serving set for afternoon tea or after dinner dessert. Internet sales in 2000 offered similar sets with success, reaching more than $550 for fewer pieces. The additional trefoil dish raises the price for this combination set. Price range: $775-$875. *Courtesy of Patricia Zimmerman.*

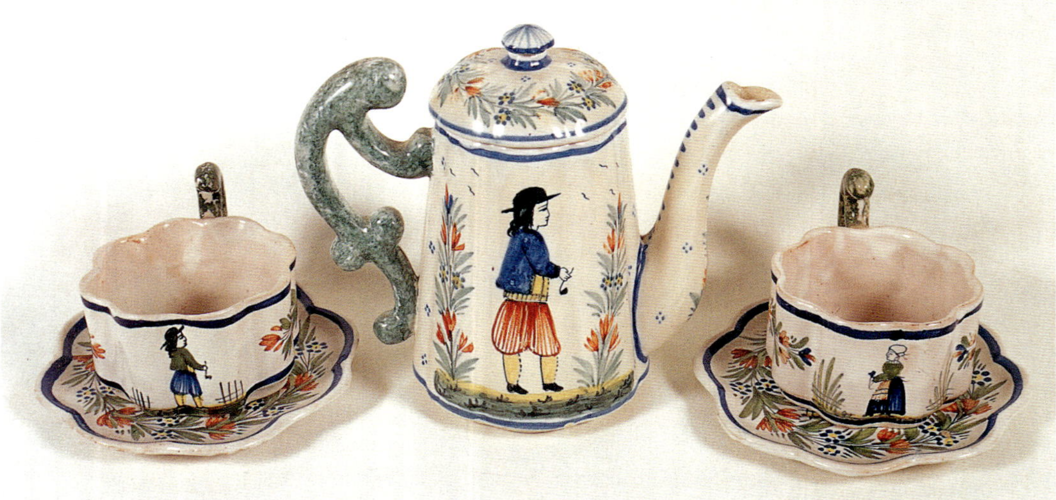

The mark on this sweet set is HR Quimper, dating it in the first quarter of the 20th century. The pot is only 5.75" tall to the tip of its finial, and the matching cups and saucers are 3" and 4.5" in diameter, respectively. The gently scalloped form of the set is highly desirable and the green-sponged shaped-handle on the teapot is another feature adding to its value. Price range: $525-$575 for the set. *Courtesy of Barbara Cleaver Kroll.*

Tiles or trivets (*dessous plats*) come in many décors.

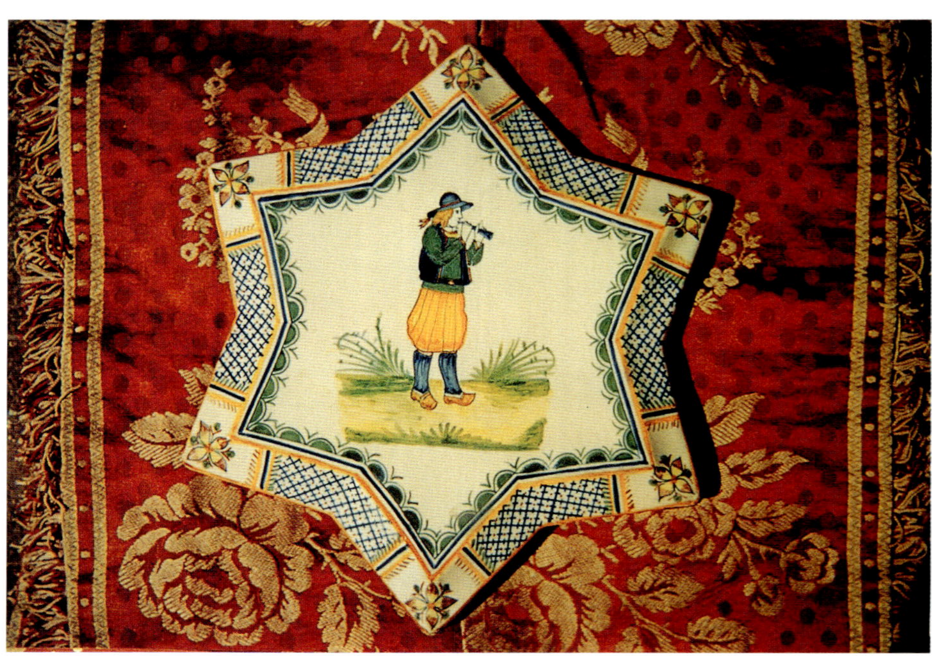

This hexagonal tile is stellar. It features the décor *croisillé* developed by Corentine Huitric. Formerly with the Porquier faïencerie, Huitric joined Henriot, bringing with her many Porquier design ideas. At Henriot, she developed a *croisillié* design based on the *quadrillé* décor from the Guillibaud faïencerie in Rouen. Henriot copyrighted the pattern, but by the 1950s the labor-intensive nature of the décor made it difficult to continue producing at a profit. (See *Mali, Old Quimper Review, March 1993.*) This 9.75" diameter example includes stylized blossoms in each point of the tile, in addition to the blue lattice-work detail. It is signed Henriot Quimper France #159 and dates in the 1930s. A similar example brought more than $400 in a 1990s Internet auction. Price range: $425-$525. *Courtesy of Sylvain Acher, The French Rendez-vous.*

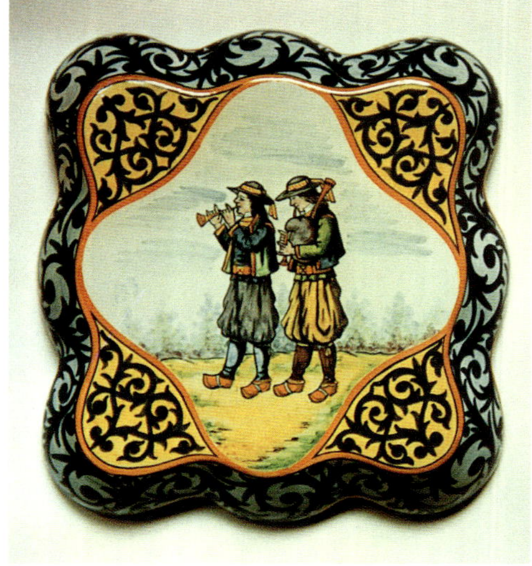

Another type of serving tile or trivet is this 10.5" square version by Henriot. It has *décor riche* scrolling elements in both blue-on-blue and blue-on-yellow. *Sonneurs* in the countryside are featured on the top surface, where cheeses or desserts were presented. An Internet auction realized $595 for a similar model in 2000, but in 1999 this same model failed to meet its reserve in the same venue. (Serendipity of the Internet, or any sale for that matter.) Price range: $525-$625. *Private Collection.*

Trays *(plateaux or banêttes)* are desirable collector items.

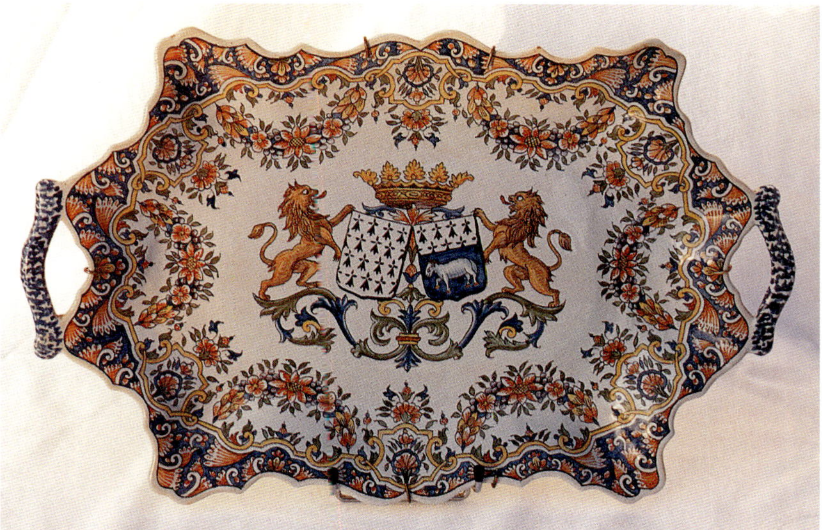

Either tray or *banêtte* applies to this over 20" long example in the Rouen motif, featuring the armorials of Brittany and the city of Quimper surmounted by a crown. What a beauty from the Porquier-Beau faïencerie! Price not available, but expensive! *Courtesy of Pierre Breton, Art de Cornouaille, Quimper.*

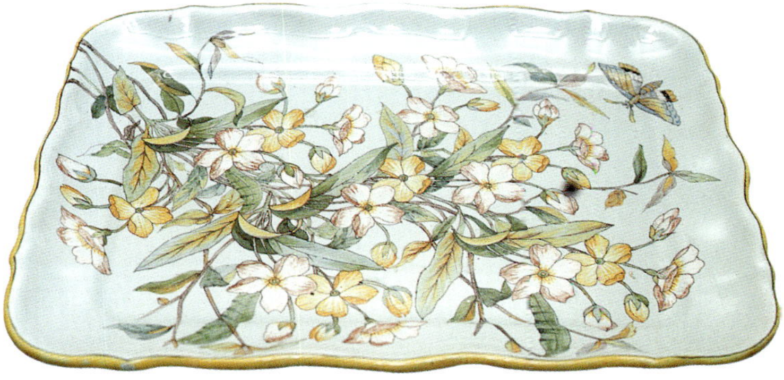

A 15" long tray in the botanical décor from Porquier-Beau faïencerie is another stunning example. *Plateaux* of this size and décor have brought up to $6,000 in French auctions in the early 2000s. Price range: $4,500-$6,500. *Courtesy of Musée Départemental Breton, Quimper.*

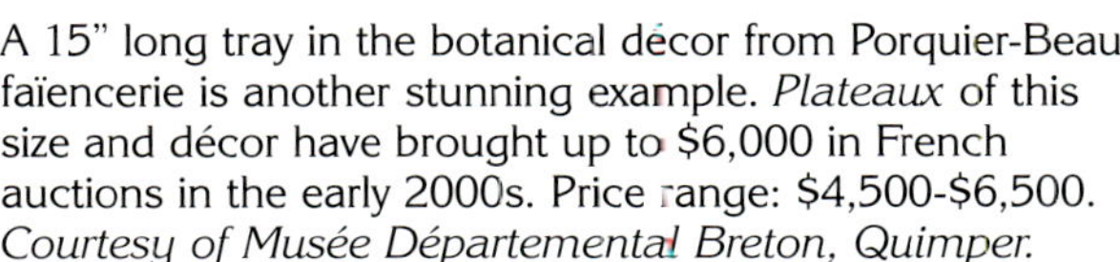

U is for...

Urns *(urnes)* are not seen as often as other examples.

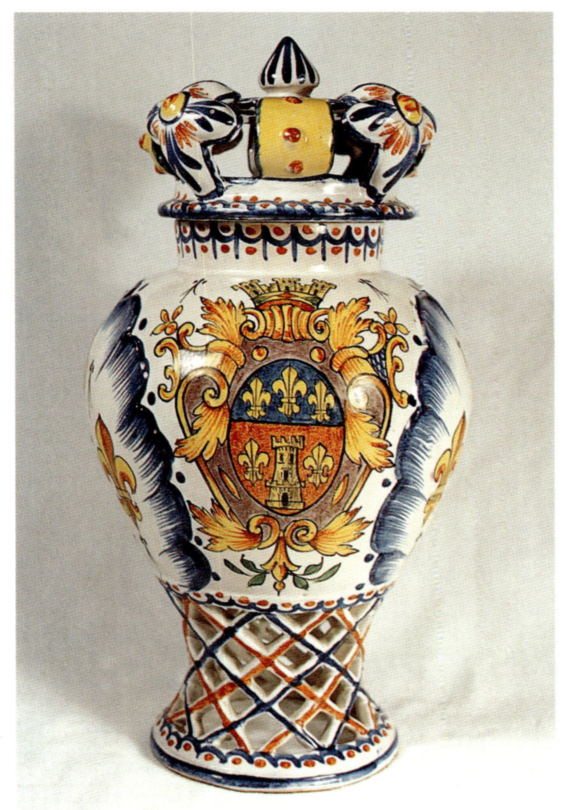

This urn is a gem, even though it's not Quimper. A close look spells CA faïence, and indeed it bears the CA signature and #497. The urn stands 12" tall and has a reticulated base, an armorial on the front, and a crown-like lid. Price range: $875-$1,150. *Courtesy of A.W. Styer.*

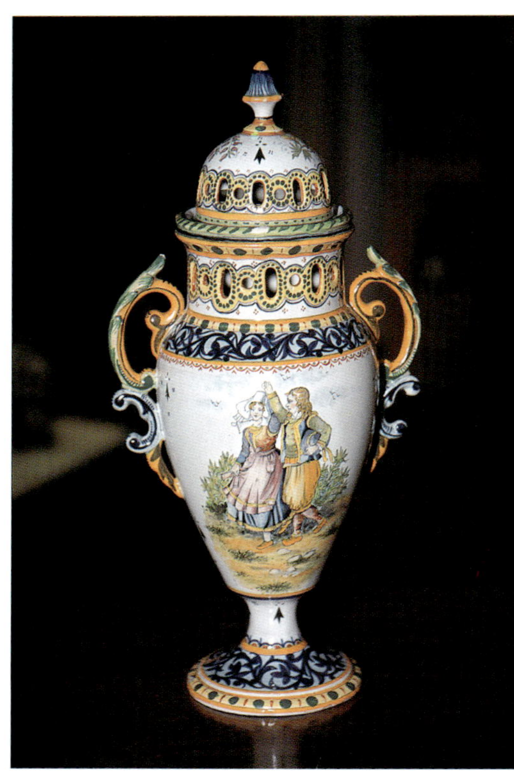

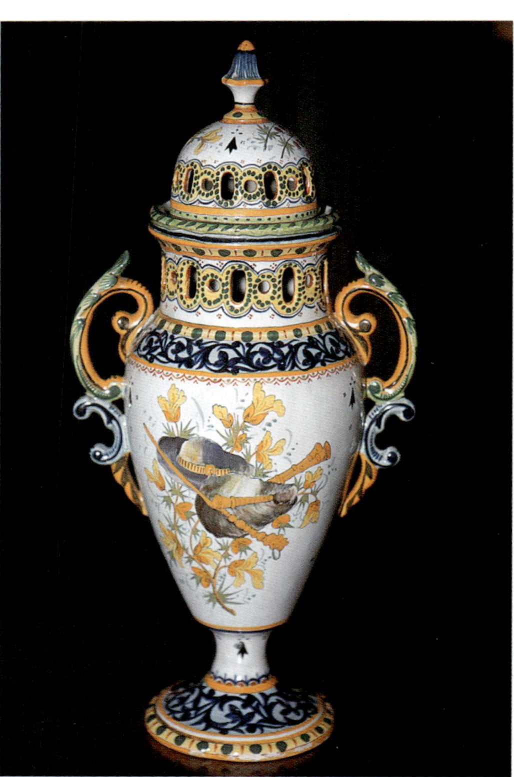

Left:
The HB faïencerie is the maker of this 14" tall urn with *décor riche* elements and reticulated neck and lid. Many times urns are *sans* lids, and incorrectly labeled vases. The front features Bretons dancing a *gavotte*. *Private Collection.*

Right:
The reverse side features a *biniou* and Breton hat, a complement to the dancers on the reverse. The graceful handles are another plus. Prices have increased for this type of urn. In 2000, a pair signed HB Quimper brought more than $4,400 through an Internet auction, despite repairs. Price range: $1,400-$1,800. *Private Collection.*

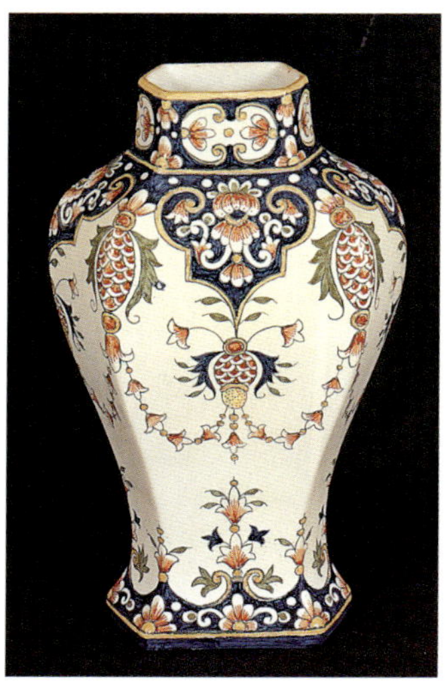

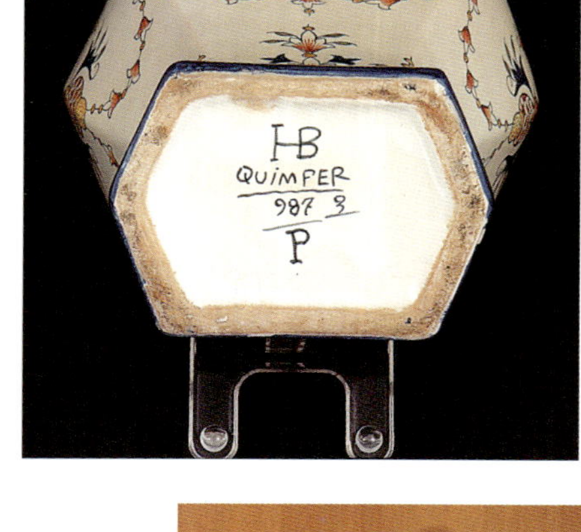

A look at the bottom shows it was made by the HB faïencerie and the artist Poulain, who signed his initial P, executed the décor. Poulain accompanied Jules Verlingue from the Boulogne faïencerie to Quimper, and is known for the intricate décor shown on this item. Price range: $525-$725. *Courtesy of Patricia Zimmerman.*

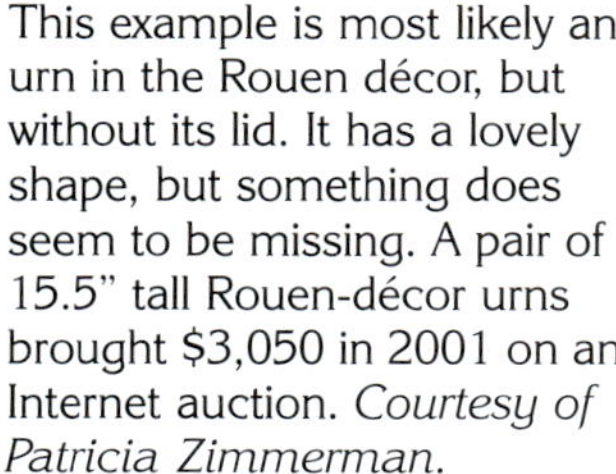

This example is most likely an urn in the Rouen décor, but without its lid. It has a lovely shape, but something does seem to be missing. A pair of 15.5" tall Rouen-décor urns brought $3,050 in 2001 on an Internet auction. *Courtesy of Patricia Zimmerman.*

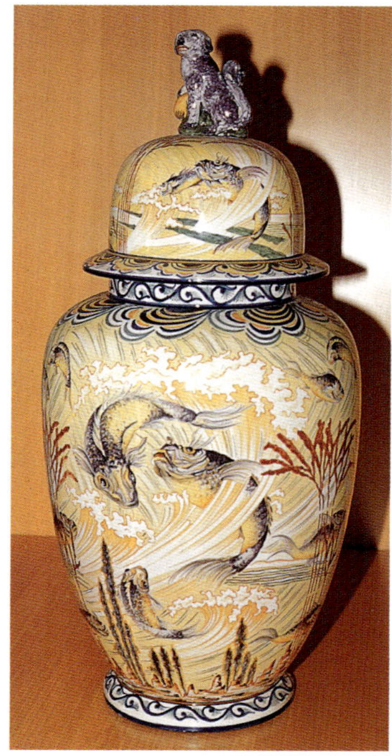

Now this is an urn! Painted by the artist Marguerite Soudane, the urn ripples with fish swimming gracefully in an underwater scene. *Courtesy of Musée de la Faïence, Quimper.*

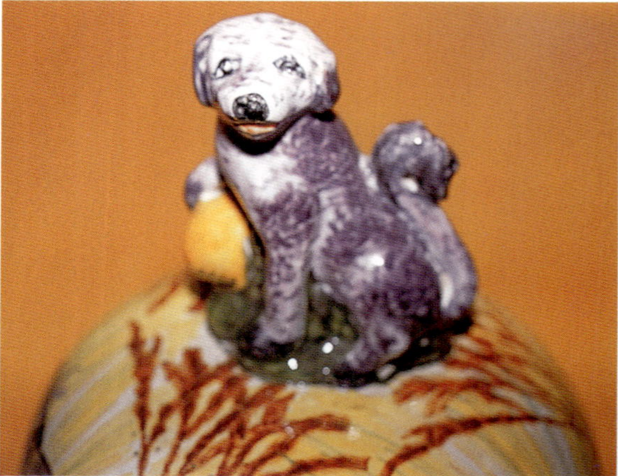

And the finial is the tops, literally. A sweet dog sits above the watery scene below. Soudane, like Poulain, followed Verlingue to Quimper from the Boulogne faïencerie. Her work for HB was displayed at the *Ti Breiz* exhibit in 1925, where *HB/Grande Maison* won a silver medal. Price not available. *Courtesy of Musée de la Faïence, Quimper.*

❦ V is for...

Vases *(vases)* come in all sizes, shapes, and décors.

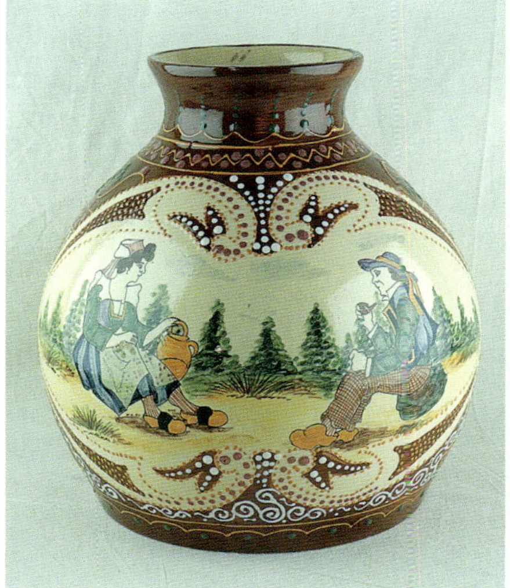

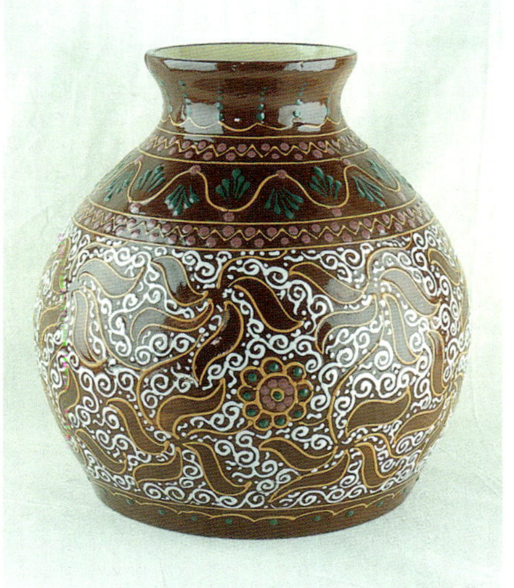

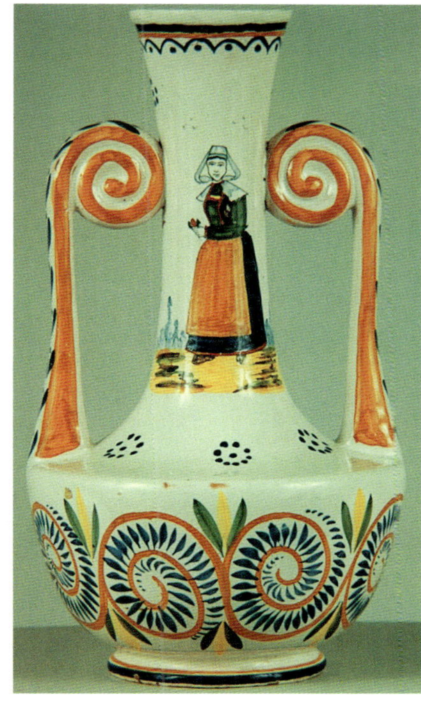

This vase in the *broderie* décor has a motif that seems very Fouillen-like. A couple sits facing each other in the Breton countryside, surrounded by extraordinary *à la poire* décor. The vase measures 8.25" tall, is signed HB Quimper P. H., and dates post-1942. *Private Collection.*

The reverse side is beautiful, too. *Petits fleurs*, swirls, and dots in the *broderie* technique shimmer. Similar examples have achieved more than $700 on Internet auctions in 2000-2001. Price range: $600-$700. *Private Collection.*

This vase is stunningly enveloped in Celtic swirls, which also carry through in the handle design. It stands about 16" tall, is signed Henriot Quimper, and dates from the 1930s. In the late 1990s, American and Internet sales brought $550-$800 for similar models. Price range: $650-$750. *Private Collection.*

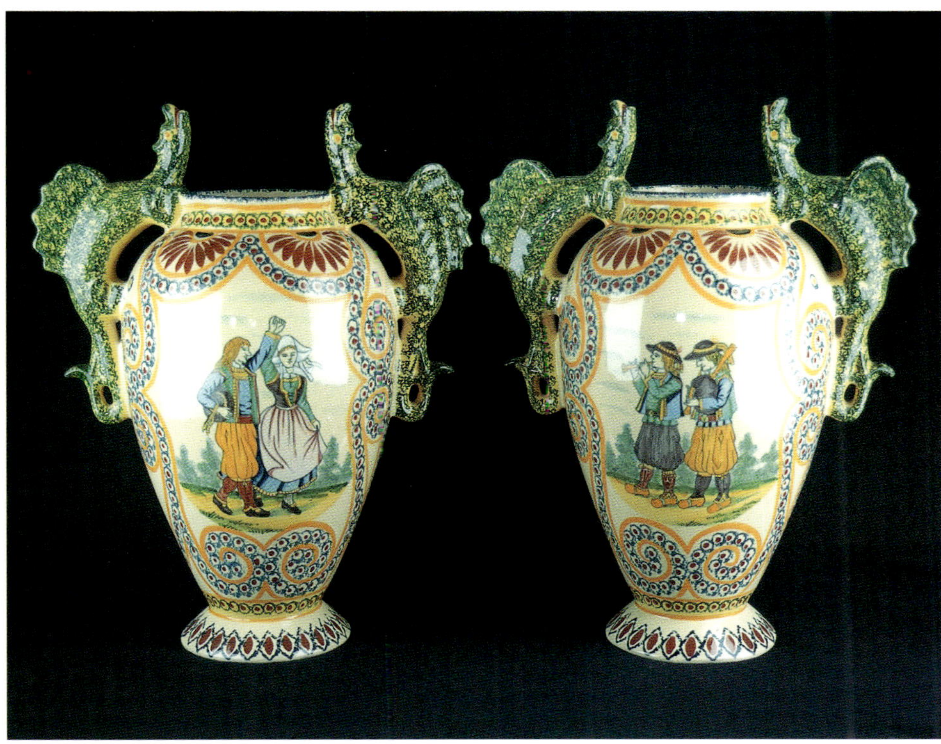

Are dragon motifs a result of the popularity of Chinese décor in the 19th century, or are the dragons integral to Breton folklore? The wings on these dragons are spread menacingly, as they climb the sides of a pair of Henriot 14.5" tall vases in the décor *ivoire corbeille*. The *gavotte* dancers and *sonneurs*, the Breton musical duo of *bombarde* and *biniou*, don't seem disturbed by the dragons' presence. *Courtesy of Lucy Williams.*

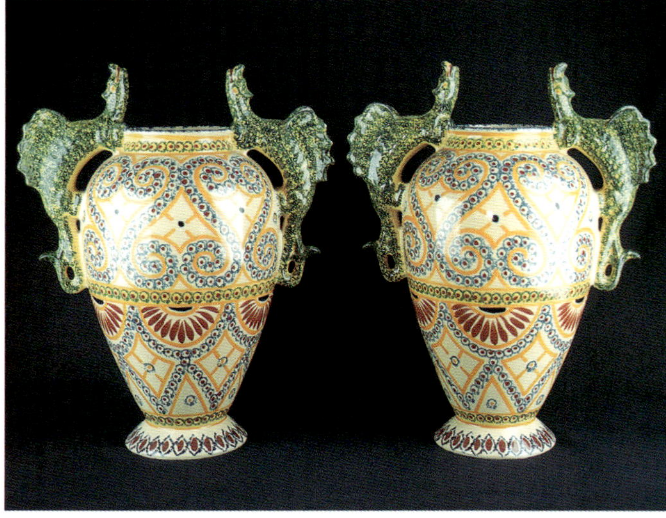

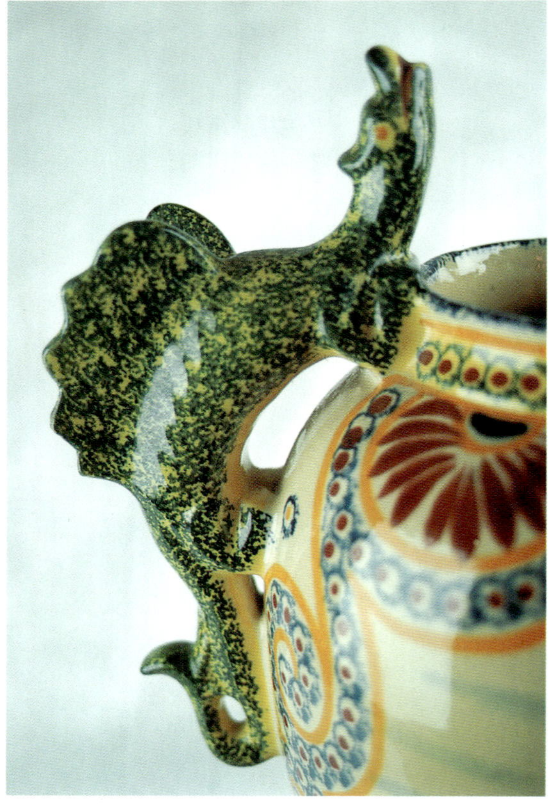

The reverse side shows Celtic designs covering the vases, along with the *demi-fleur* design, sponged circles and diamond shapes on the base. Dragon-handled vases are very popular with Quimper collectors, and these take the cake! *Courtesy of Lucy Williams.*

Dragons climb the sides of the vase. Charming! Price range: $2,200-$2,500 for the pair. *Courtesy of Lucy Williams.*

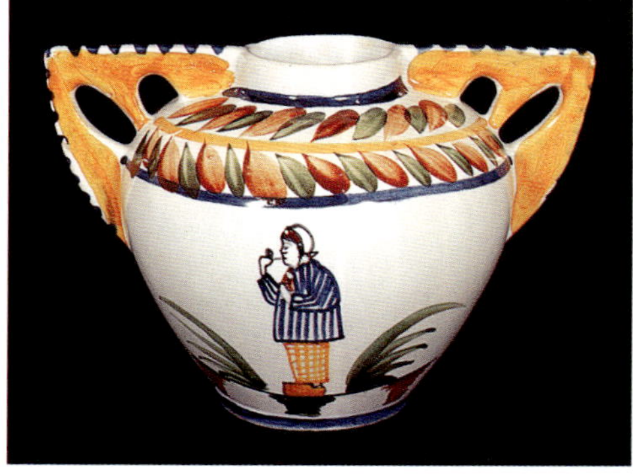

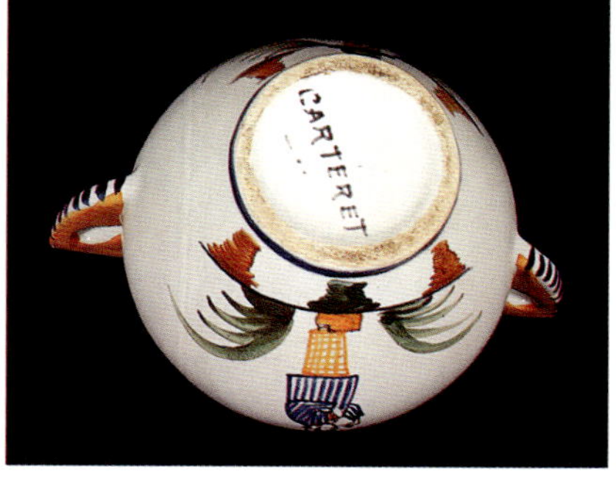

An unusual handle configuration causes this vase to measure 6" across while it's only 4.5" tall. A fellow from Normandy with a pipe is on the front and a lady in a Norman *coiffe* on the reverse. The piece appears to be Quimper. *Courtesy of Patricia Zimmerman.*

A look at the signature let us know it was made as a souvenir item from Carteret, a town on the coast of Normandy, and is from the 1920s-1930s. The HB painter's signature is (-..) and represents Mssr. Levenez. *(Taburet, p. 216.)* Price range: $225-$250. *Courtesy of Patricia Zimmerman.*

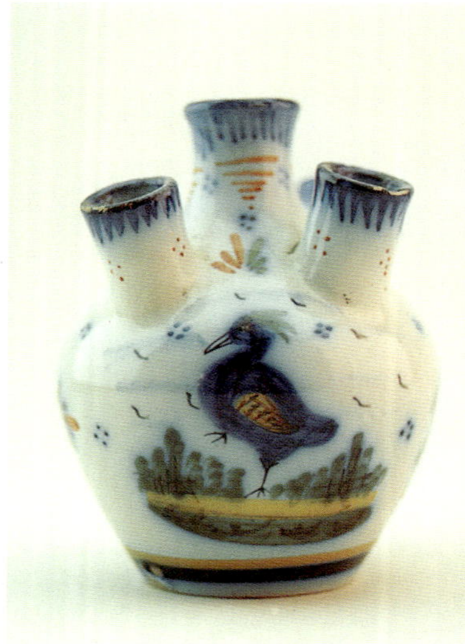

Left:
A *quintel* is a five-fingered vase for flowers sometimes called a *margoulette*. This sweet model is 4" tall, signed HR Quimper, and has a flowing glaze initiated after the turn of the 20th century at the Henriot factory. An additional glaze was added to create the watery appearance of the surface. Prices in the 1990s and early 2000s held steady in American and Internet auctions. Price range: $175-$225. *Courtesy of Elizabeth C. Ross.*

Right:
A more modern-looking version of a *quintel* is this 4.5" tall model by the Henriot artist Jim-Emile Sévellec. Done in modern movement colors of a cream background with black on gold-colored openings, it is a sharp contrast to the Henriot model shown previously. Sévellec's touch is apparent in the rendering of the figures. A Breton on the reverse is offering a flower to the Bretonne on the front. She refuses! Signed Henriot Quimper J.E. Sévellec. This model was offered through American auctions in the 1990s, realizing $100-$160. Sévellec is a favorite in France. Price range: $225-$275. *Private Collection.*

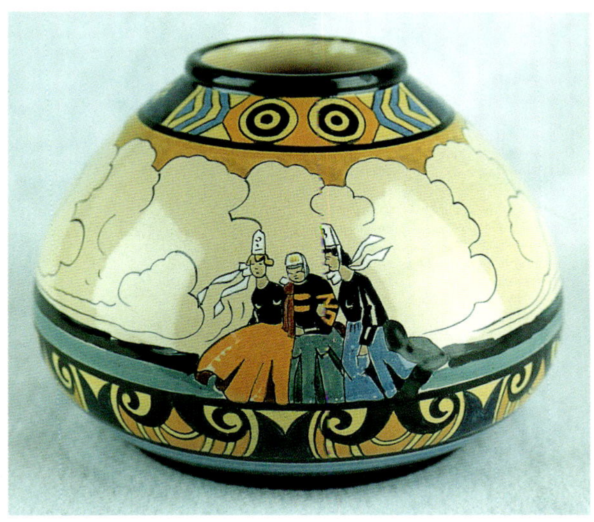

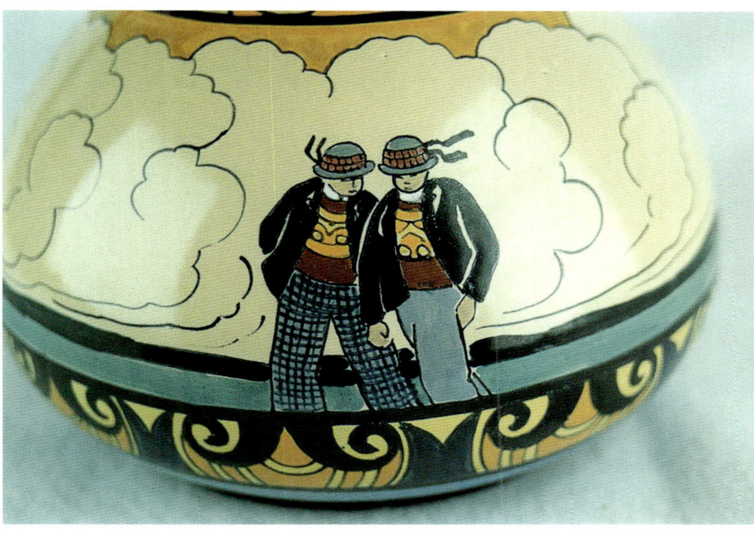

Sévellec strikes again, this time in a *vase boule* that is 5.5" tall and 8.5" diameter. It's decorated with a trio of *Bigoudènes* walking by the ocean, with the clouds billowing behind them. *Private Collection.*

On the other side of the Sévellec vase are two *Bigouders* also enjoying the seaside. The ever-present water of the coast of Brittany appears on Quimper faïence many times! In the late 1980s, this model brought $475. In 2001, it realized 4000F, or more than $572, at a French auction. Price range: $625-$675. *Private Collection.*

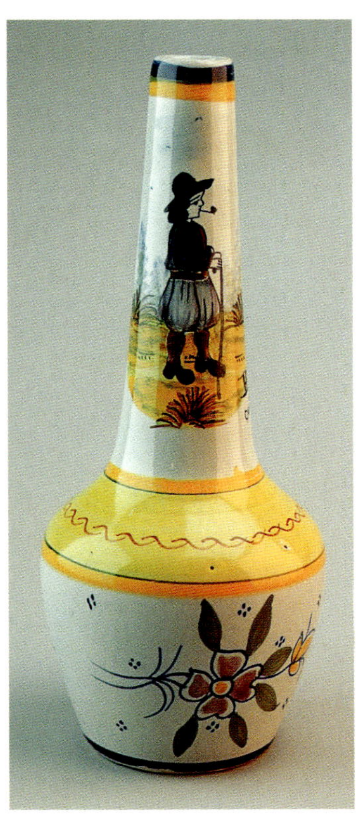

This style of vase is called a *soliflore* and it's meant to hold a single flower or bud. It stands 7.75" tall, is signed HB Quimper, and dates from the 1920s-1930s. Internet and American auction prices in the late 1990s for comparable *soliflores* were between $100 and $200. This example features a Breton with pipe and walking stick and the easily identifiable sweet HB floral sprays. Price range: $210-$245. *Courtesy of Patricia Paloni.*

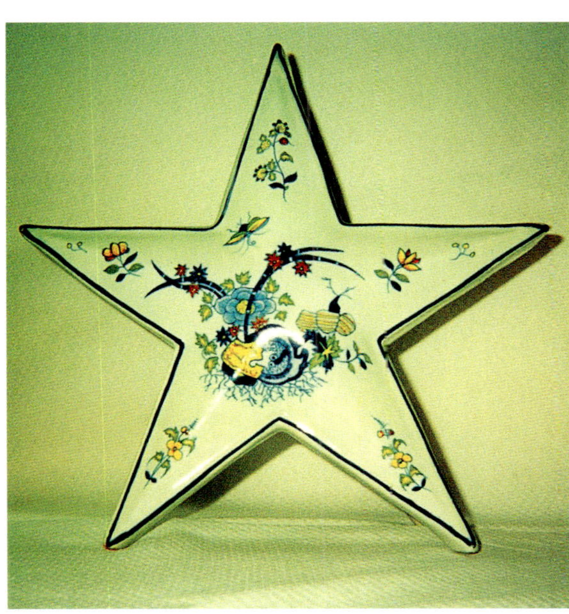

This rare star-shaped vase or jardinière from the *Grande Maison* stands over 12" tall and is signed only HB. On the front are lovely botanicals, including a butterfly, while the reverse contains whippets holding a double armorial surmounted by a crown. The star-shape is outlined with a single blue line on both sides. A similar vase with a scene of *boules* players in lieu of the botanicals sold through a late 1980s auction for $1,000. Price range: $1,500-$2,000. *Courtesy of Janey Levine.*

Left:
What is a spill vase? We're not sure, but that's the title given to this vase in the U.K. and it seems to have spilled over to the U.S. This interesting vase features a Breton and Bretonne flanking the armorial of Quimper, which is surmounted by a crown. The vase measures 6" tall and 7" wide and is signed HR Quimper, dating it in the first quarter of the 20th century. Prices for later models were $375 to $500 through late 1990s and early 2000s American and Internet auctions. Price range: $675-$875. *Private Collection.*

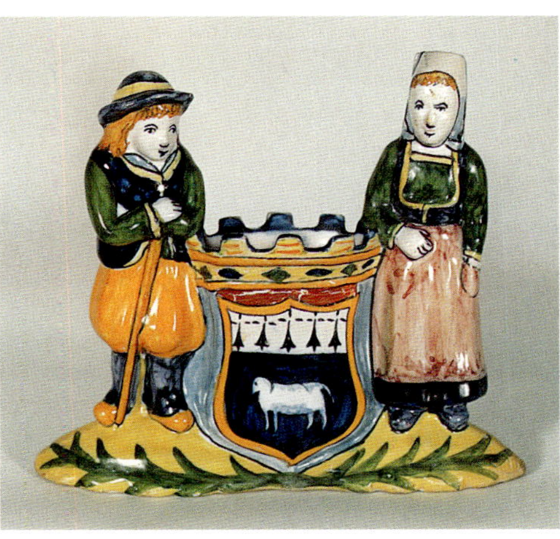

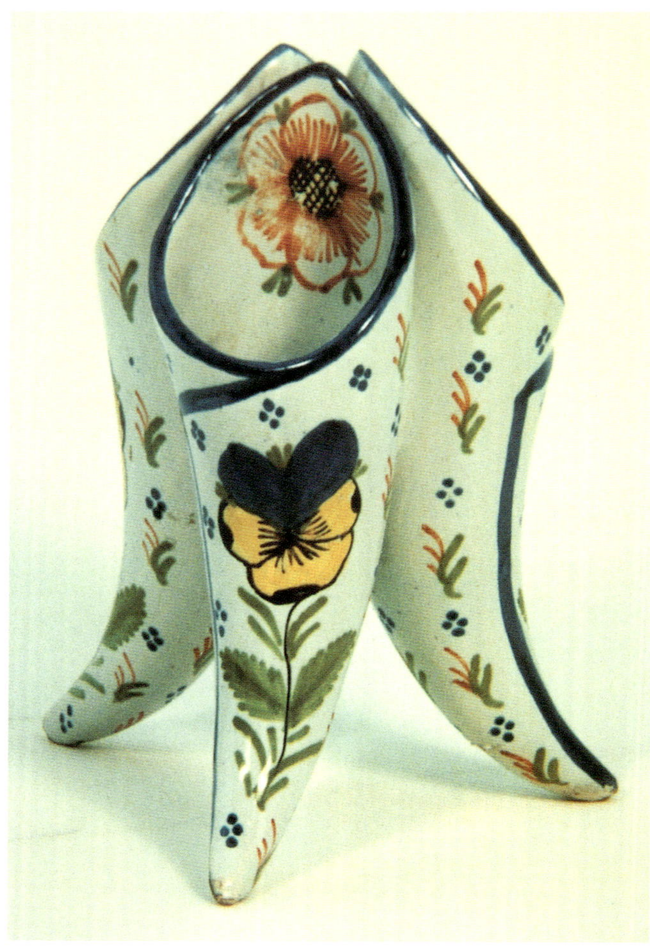

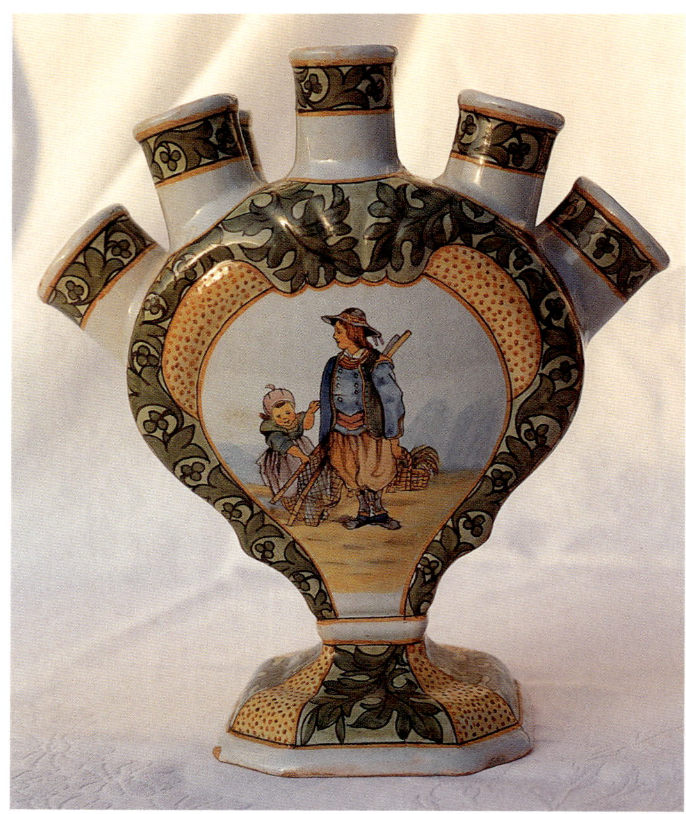

A Porquier-Beau *tulipière* stands 10" tall and contains eight holders for flowers. The *scène Bretonne* featured is Fishermen of Douarnenez. Dark-green on light-green scroll and orange dots on a yellow ground are border décors completing a spectacular presentation. Signed PB and *Environs de Douarnenez*, this example dates from the last quarter of the 19th century. An American auction realized $1,500 for a similar example in the late 1990s, but this version is worth more than that. Price range: $2,200-$2,400. *Courtesy of Pierre Breton, Art de Cornouaille, Quimper.*

A *tricornet,* or vase with three horns, is a unique configuration. This particular model features a favorite with collectors – pansies. Standing 5.5" tall, this 19th century model contains a colorful blue-and-yellow pansy surrounded by floral sprigs and the blue four-dot motif. It's unsigned but most likely Porquier production, (AP). Due to its age and décor, this model commands more than other *tricornets* seen on the Internet or American auctions. Price range: $400-$500. *Private Collection.*

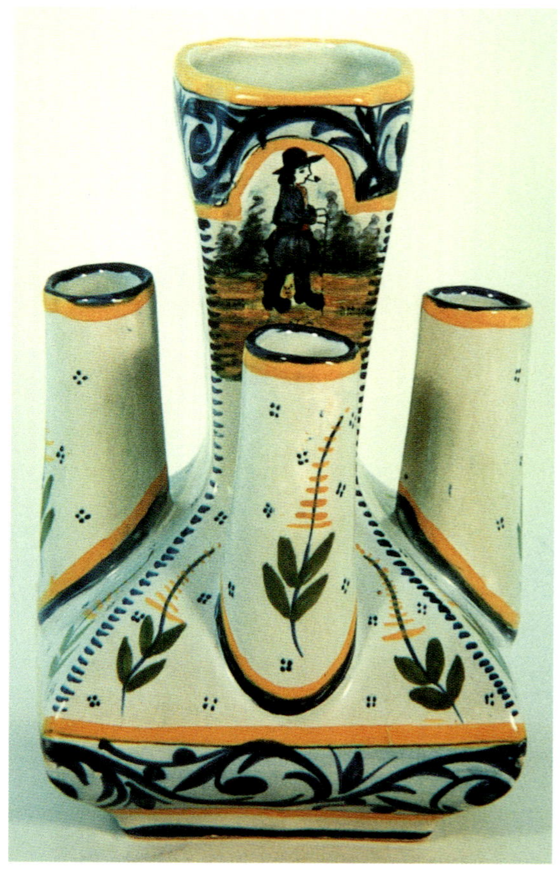

Tulipière or tulip vase is a form some confuse with the smaller *quintel* vase. A *tulipière* can have from three to eight holes for the flower stems. This version stands 7.75" tall and has one large center receptacle and four smaller ones around the base. It is HB Quimper from the 1920s-1930s. Décor elements are dark-blue on light-blue *décor riche* bordered with a dark-yellow band, in addition to stylized vines. A Breton with pipe and walking stick is in the central décor. Price range: $550-$675. *Courtesy of David and Linda Schaumann.*

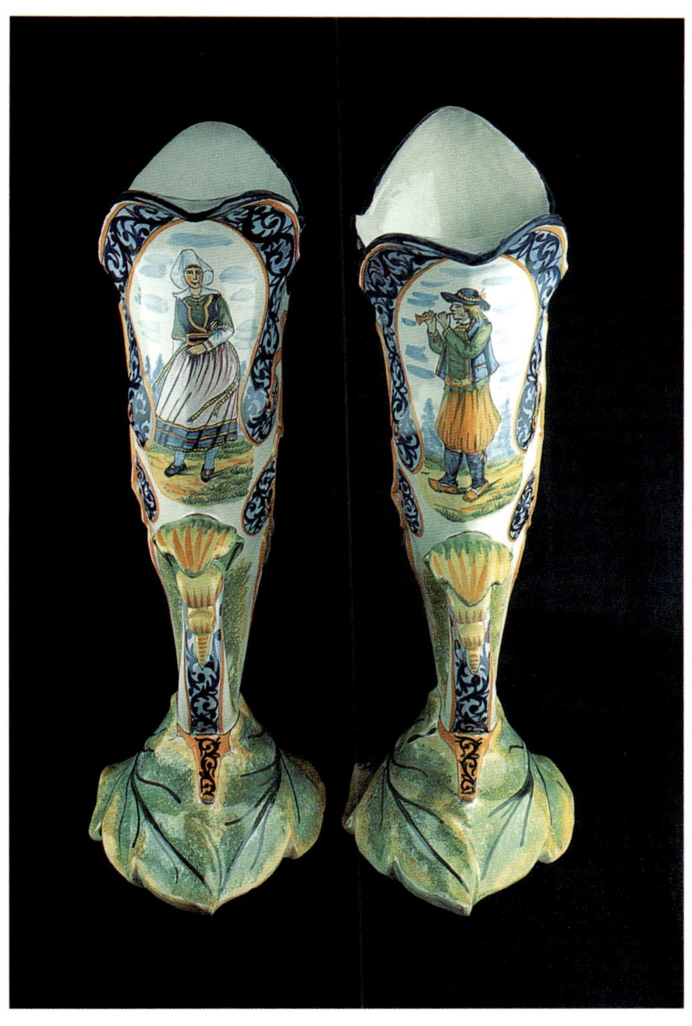

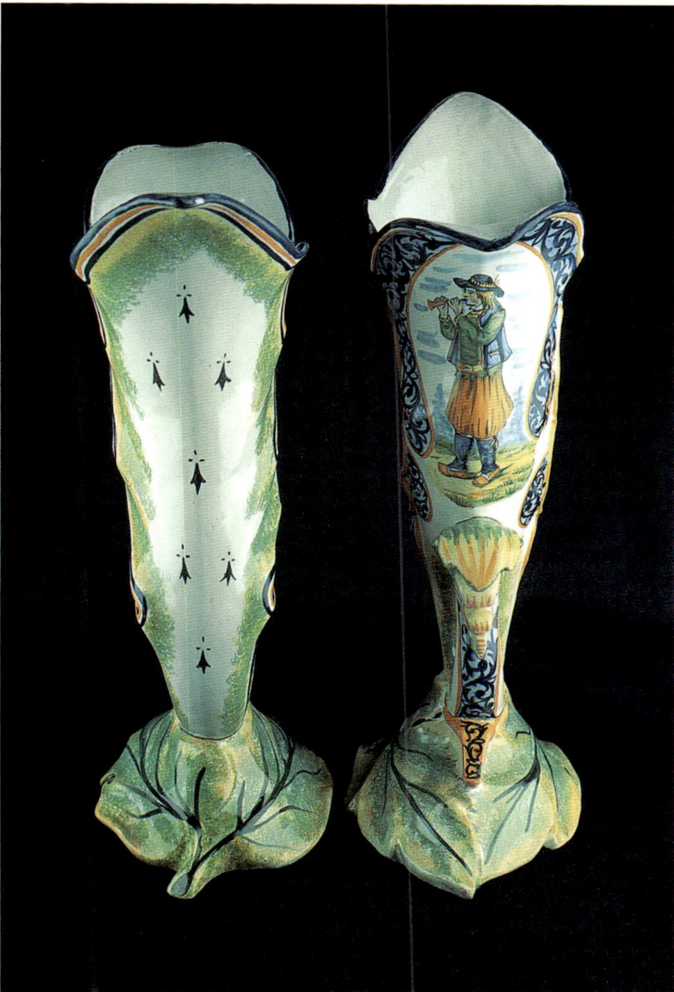

The reverse side of the pair also is stellar. Black ermine-tails are scattered over the white ground. *Private Collection.*

An unusual shape graces this pair of HenRiot faïencerie vases from the 1920s. A similar pair is in the *Musée de la Faïence* in Quimper, with an additional terra cotta figure added to the front of each on the petal-like shelf. This form is rare and finding a matching pair is wonderful. The bases are shaped like leaves and the rest of the vases look like flower petals unfolding. The Breton and Bretonne are encircled with *décor riche* scrolling foliage. *Private Collection.*

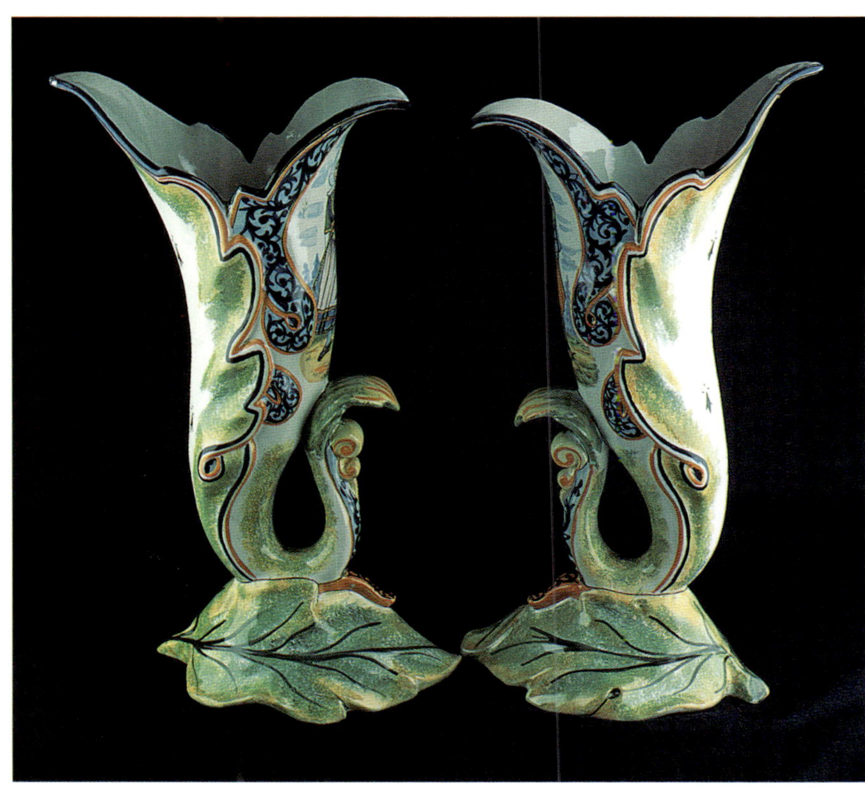

Even the vase profiles echo flowers unfolding. A grand form. Signed HenRiot Quimper #154, they are from the second quarter of the 20th century. Price range: $2,400-$2,800 for the pair. *Private Collection.*

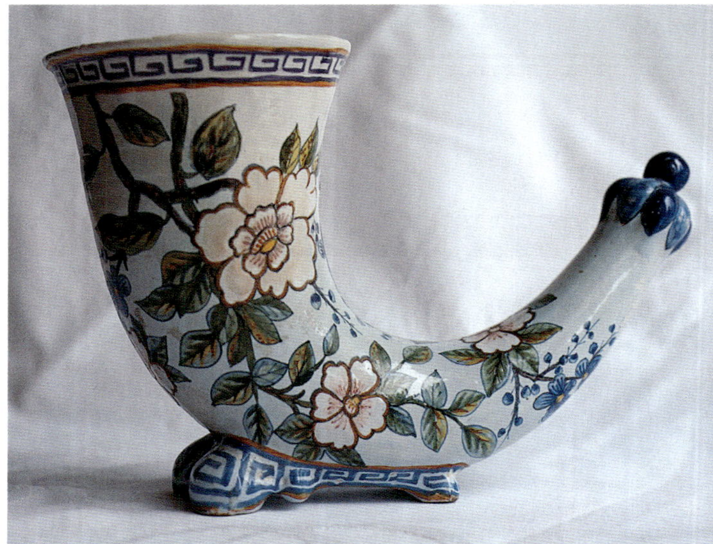

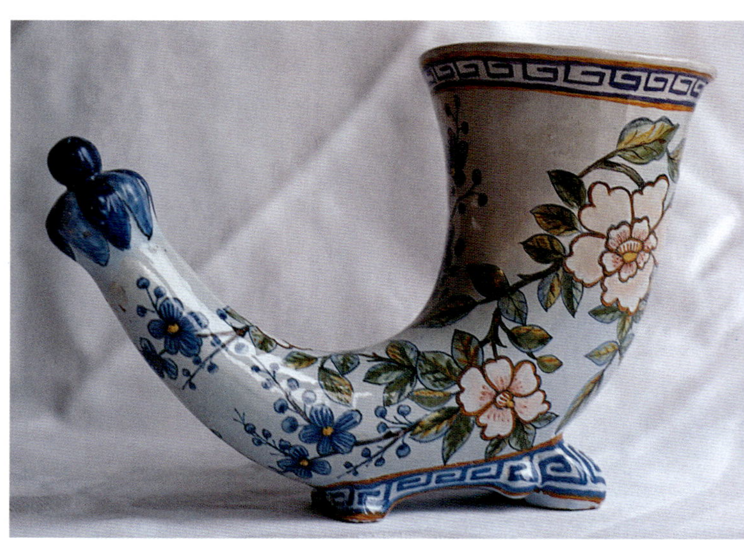

One unusually-shaped vase is this model called *oliphant* or elephant. It looks like a horn, or perhaps an elephant tusk. Examples labeled *oliphant* vases appear in French Quimper texts. (*Trois Siècles de Faïences, p. 110; Château de Quintin Exposition Catalogue, p. 50.*) Most interestingly though, the name *Corne de Rolland* appears in an 1887 Porquier-Beau price list under musical instruments, with a price of 60F. (*Bondhus, p. 102.*) In the medieval adventure narrative Song of Rolland (or Roland), the battle horn is called *Oliphant. Courtesy of Pierre Breton, Art de Cornouaille, Quimper.*

The other side of this version also contains pink and blue Porquier-Beau botanical flowers and a Greek key border around the rim and on the foot. In 2000, an Internet auction offered an *oliphant* vase with a *scène Bretonne* by Porquier-Beau, but the reserve was not met, even at $1,725. In 2001, an American auction sold a *scène Bretonne* Porquier-Beau *oliphant* vase for $1,550. This botanical version will command more. Price range: $1,750-$2,000. *Courtesy of Pierre Breton, Art de Cornouaille, Quimper.*

W is for...

Wallpockets (*porte-bouquets*) come in a variety of shapes, sizes, and uses.

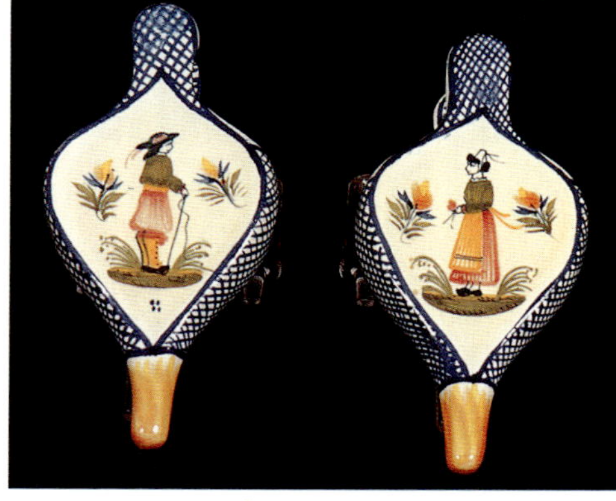

These 5.25" long, bellows-shaped wallpockets are intended to hold matches, and are signed Henriot Quimper France. One has a Bretonne, the other a Breton, and both have *croisillon* décor on the edges and golden points. A sweet set. One similar model brought $250 in an American auction in the late-1990s. Price range: $225-$275 for the pair. *Courtesy of Patricia Zimmerman.*

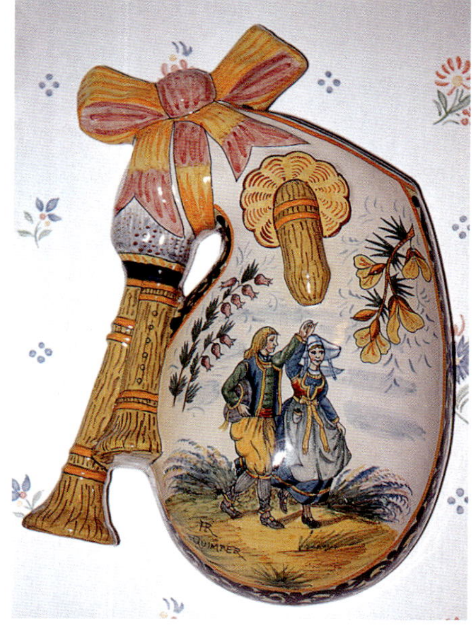

Biniou-shaped (bagpipe) wallpocket is a favorite and displays well. The artist Le Borgne is credited with adding this form to the Henriot line in the first decade or so of the 20th century. It became the specialty of the HR production and is found on cheese and butter dishes, vases, salts, and of course, wallpockets. (*Mali, Old Quimper Review, March 1993.*) This superb example measures 11" tall and 7.5" wide and is signed HR Quimper. A well-painted design shows a Breton couple dancing a *gavotte* with sprays of *l'ajonc* and *bruyère* above. A pink bow tops the pipes and *décor riche* borders the sides of the wallpocket. In 1999, this model sold through the Internet for about $375. A smaller and later version sold for about $295 the same year. In 2001, this same size and date model brought $475 through an American auction. Price range: $395-$495. *Courtesy of Patricia Zimmerman.*

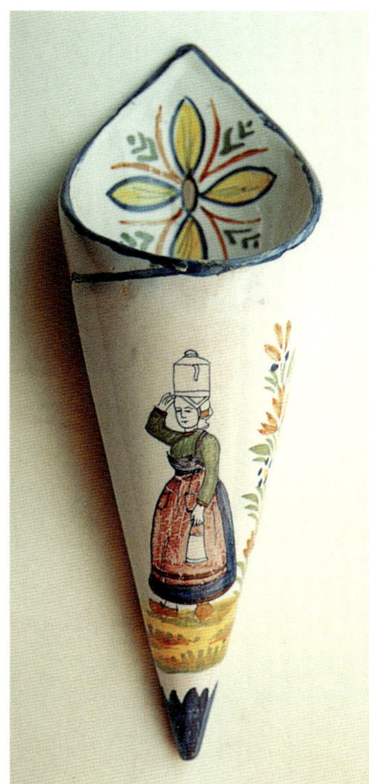

Cone-shaped or *cornet* is readily available form of wallpocket. This example is 10" long and signed Henriot Quimper France. The Bretonne carries a milk pail in her hand and balances a milk container on her head. Notice the red in her apron is dry looking, which helps to gauge this as an earlier Henriot piece, probably from the late 1920s. The hole for hanging the wallpocket is surrounded by a colorful flower, another enhancement to a balanced design. American sales prices for single wallpockets ranged from $75-$175 in late 1990s to early 2000s. Price range: $150-$200. *Courtesy of Elizabeth C. Ross.*

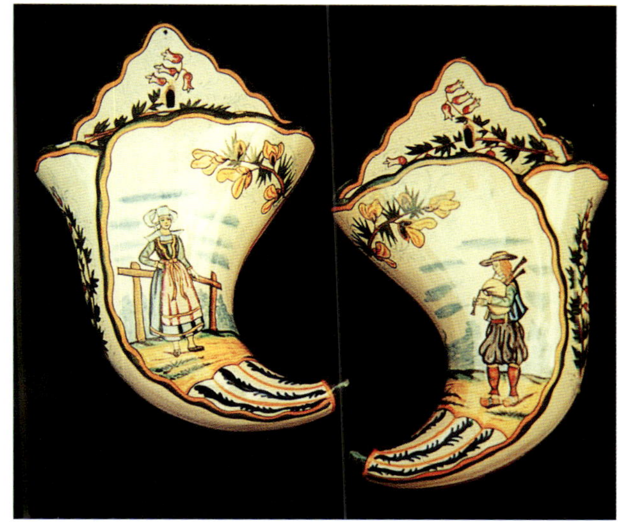

Cornucopia or gently curved wallpockets command higher prices. This pair exhibits all the finer qualities of the style. Copious sprays of *l'ajonc* and *bruyère* accent the scenes of a Breton playing the *biniou* on one and a Bretonne leaning against a fence railing on the other. He appears to be playing just for her. The wallpockets measure 10" tall and 7" wide, are signed HenRiot Quimper, and are c. 1930. In the late 1990s, a similar pair sold through an American auction for $750. Price range: $950-$1,250. *Courtesy of Silvia and Gary Fritzhand.*

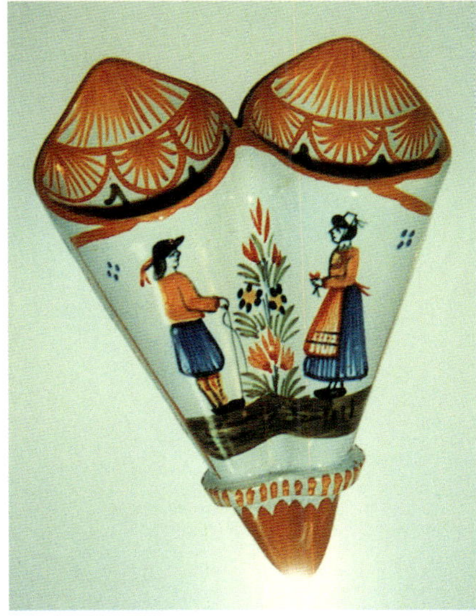

This model is a *double-cornet* and is in mustard, blues and greens. A Breton couple gaze at each other across an *à la touche* spray of flowers. The piece is signed Henriot Quimper France and dates from the 1930s. American and Internet auction prices in the 1990s were between $100 and $325, depending on the age and décor. Price range: $225-$250. *Private Collection.*

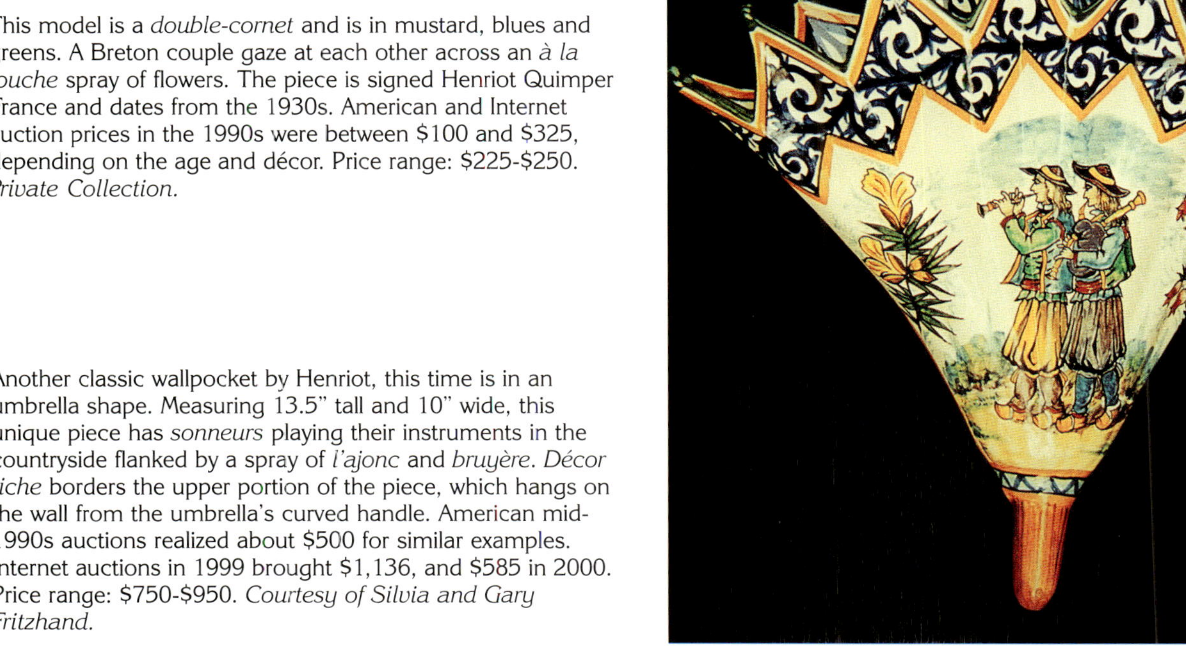

Another classic wallpocket by Henriot, this time is in an umbrella shape. Measuring 13.5" tall and 10" wide, this unique piece has *sonneurs* playing their instruments in the countryside flanked by a spray of *l'ajonc* and *bruyère*. *Décor riche* borders the upper portion of the piece, which hangs on the wall from the umbrella's curved handle. American mid-1990s auctions realized about $500 for similar examples. Internet auctions in 1999 brought $1,136, and $585 in 2000. Price range: $750-$950. *Courtesy of Silvia and Gary Fritzhand.*

Wooden *(en bois)* items from Quimper.

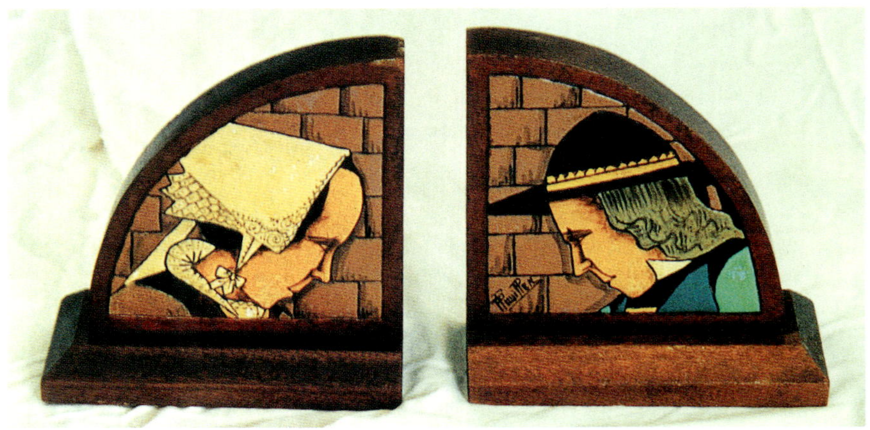

Wooden wares immediately bring to mind Paul Fouillen. These bookends in pyrogravure are from Fouillen's studio on *Place Styvel*. They each stand 6" tall and 5.5" wide and personify Fouillen's Art Deco approach to the *petit Breton*. Price range: $275-$325. *Courtesy of Claire and Jon Scarborough.*

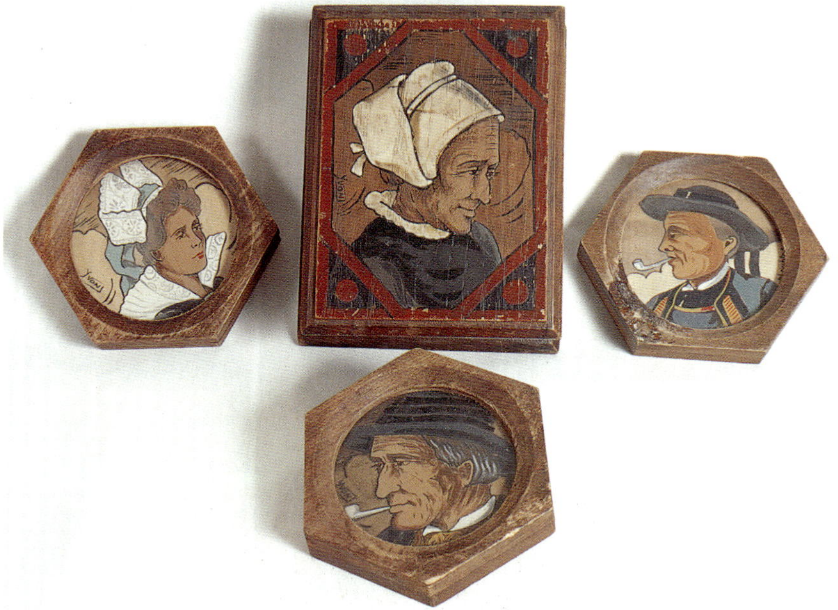

This potpourri of wooden objects is from another Breton artist who worked in wood. A close look helps confirm these are not Paul Fouillen, but they are nice. Price range: $100-$125 for the group. *Private Collection.*

❦ XYZ...

Another time!

Part IV Look-Alike Faïence

Quimper faïenceries copied other French and Italian faïencerie décors. Then French, other European, American, and even Japanese faïenceries copied Quimper designs. Following is a list of some of the look-alike faïence from both perspectives.

❧ Quimper Adopts other Faïencerie Décors

Marseilles is a potting center south of Moustiers in southeastern France. The Marseilles influence on Quimper production is seen in the mid-to-late-19th century Quimper décor with delicately rendered flowers and pastel palette.

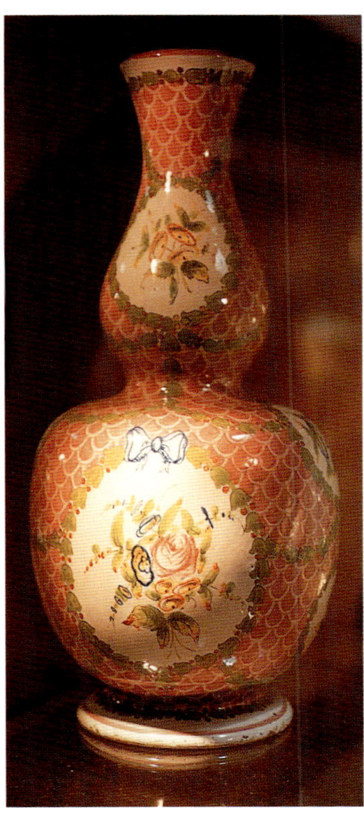

The décor on this Quimper vase is in the softer colors associated with Marseilles faïence. *Courtesy of Musée de la Faïence, Quimper.*

Moustiers is a potting center in the mountains of southeastern France. Because of its proximity to the Italian centers, it became a major force in the French faïence industry in the 18th century. One Moustiers faïencerie, Olerys-Laugier, produced items in the style of Callot's engravings of the *Commedia dell'arte.* The Olerys-Laugier faïencerie also used garlands and swags in the style of Berain. The Quimper faïenceries adopted these décors with success. (For other Moustiers styles, see *Mali, pp. 15-17; Château de Quintin Exposition Catalogue, pp. 42-43.*)

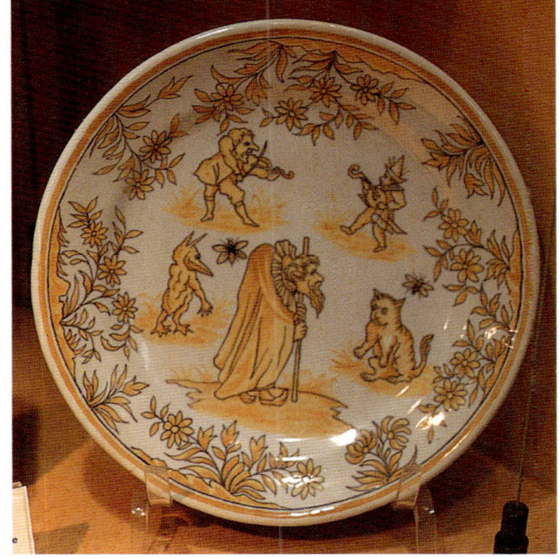

Olerys-Laugier produced items in the style of Callot's engravings of the *Commedia dell'arte,* seen here on a Porquier-Beau piece. *Courtesy of Musée de la Faïence, Quimper.*

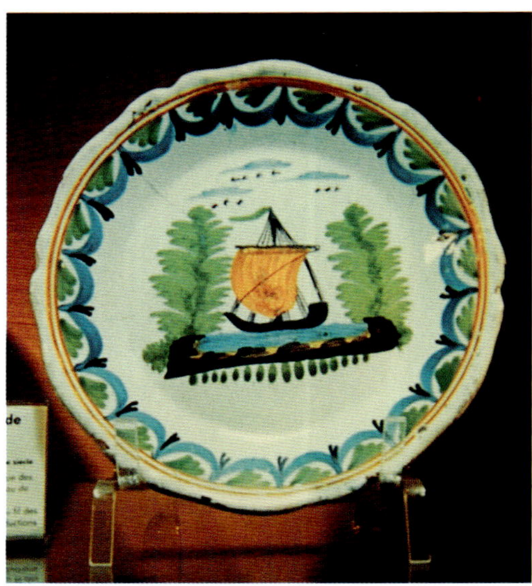

The Nevers-inspired decoration on this plate features a boat on the Loire River, which would pass by Nevers on the way to the sea. This 8.25" example is unsigned Quimper from the late 18th century. The *à la touche* technique remains in use on Quimper faïence today. *Courtesy of Musée de la Faïence, Quimper.*

Nevers is a potting center in central France. Styles brought from the Italian potting centers by migrating workers influenced the Nevers décor. Motifs included the *stile bello*, a central cartouche surrounded by other decorative elements, and *stile istoriati*, with mythological or historical scenes. (*See Mali, p. xv; Château de Quintin Catalogue, p. 37-41.*) Nevers is best known to Quimper followers as the home of Pierre Bellevaux, who brought Nevers designs and techniques (particularly *à la touche*) to the Bousquet faïencerie in 1731, when he married Pierre Bousquet's daughter. The Quimper faïenceries incorporated Nevers designs and techniques into their work.

Rouen décors, like Nevers décors, came to Quimper through marriage. In 1749, Bousquet's granddaughter married Pierre Clément Caussy, a potter from Rouen. Caussy brought with him Rouen techniques, *poncifs* (paper design stencils), the formula for Rouen red, and an historical journal about poterie-making. Within years Quimper poterie décor became more Rouenesque, replacing the earlier décors from Moustiers and Nevers. Rouen designs include the quiver-and-arrow motif, *au couchon aile* (flying pig), and *panier fleuri*, or basket of flowers. Borders from Rouen include lambrequins, *arabesques*, *chainette*, and *torsade*, as well as the *quadrillé* technique from the Guillibaud faïencerie in Rouen. (*Verlingue and Lecossois, p. 59.*)

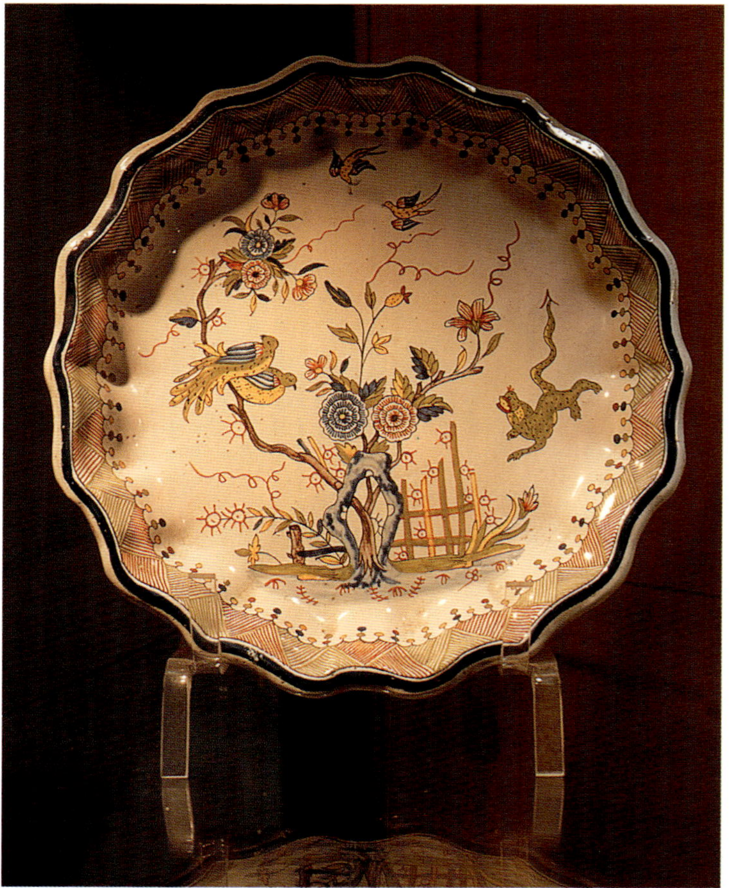

Rouen décor in the *chinois* manner fills this 19th century Quimper scalloped *calotte* with colorful images and border. *Courtesy of Musée de la Faïence, Quimper.*

American faïenceries that adapted the *petit Breton* design include Knowles, Syracuse, and Southern Potteries. A curious situation involves the attribution of an American manufacturer to an easily identified *HB/Grande Maison* design. A *Della-Ware* plate by Stangl appeared on a 1999 Internet auction. It was described as made for the Philadelphia distributor, Fisher and Bruce, and found in a Stangl pottery book. The mark was *Della-Ware, Made in the USA, quimper, #33*. The same décor appeared on a plate marked *FBC HB Quimper (++.+) #179*.

HB is the manufacturer of this design replicated and marketed in the United States as *Della Ware* by Stangl Pottery. *Courtesy of Charlie and Donna Walker.*

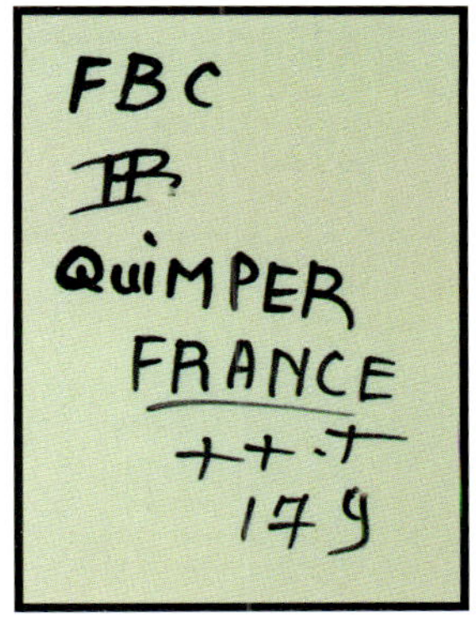

The signature on the HB plate has FBC, which was identified as a distributor in Philadelphia, Pennsylvania, by an Internet seller in 1999. *Courtesy of Charlie and Donna Walker.*

Angoulême in southwestern France was home to several faïenceries beginning the 1700s. In 1891, Alfred Renoleau opened one faïencerie, and then another 1895. In the early 20th century, Renoleau produced faïence with *petit Breton* motifs.

Boulogne-sur-Mer in northeastern France was home to Jules Verlingue's faïence factory, *Faïencerie de Madeleine,* before he purchased the *HB/Grande Maison* from the de la Hubudière family in 1917. The new owner at Boulogne was Henri Delcourt, who changed the mark from VJ to HD. The *petit Breton* figure appeared on faïence products from the Boulogne faïencerie also.

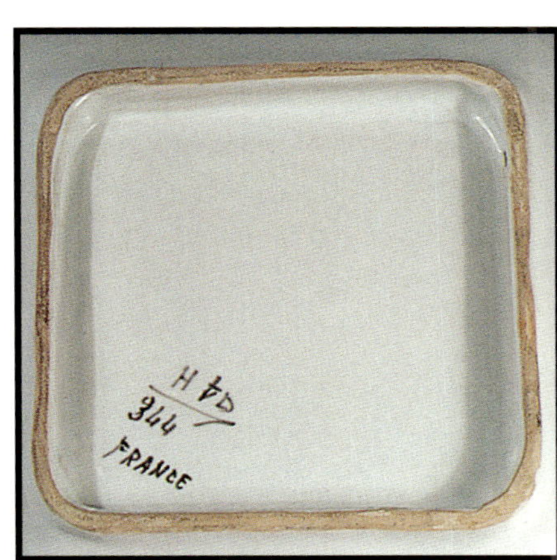

The signature, HD, with a downward-facing arrow between the letters, is the mark of the Boulogne-sur-Mer faïencerie of Henri Delcourt. *Courtesy of A.W. Styer.*

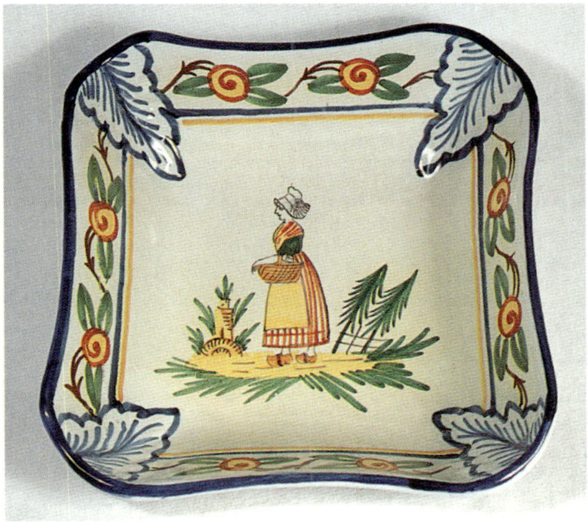

A nicely decorated square bowl features a lady in a *coiffe* of Normandy surrounded by an apple motif border with blue corner accents. Is it Quimper? *Courtesy of A.W. Styer.*

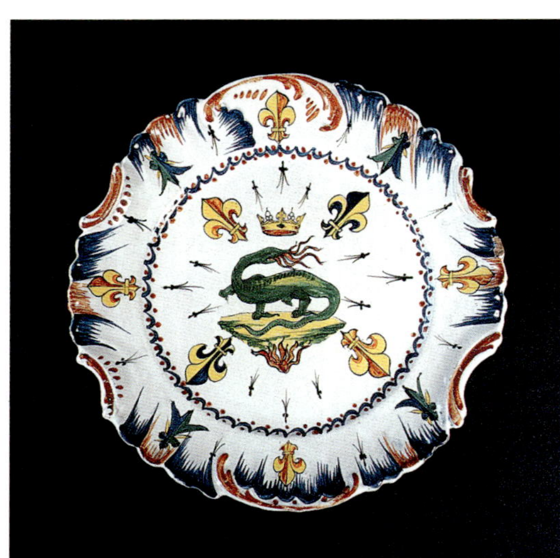

Is this 9.75" diameter plate, with the salamander emblem of François I, Quimper? No, it's CA faïence, form #381. *Courtesy of A.W. Styer.*

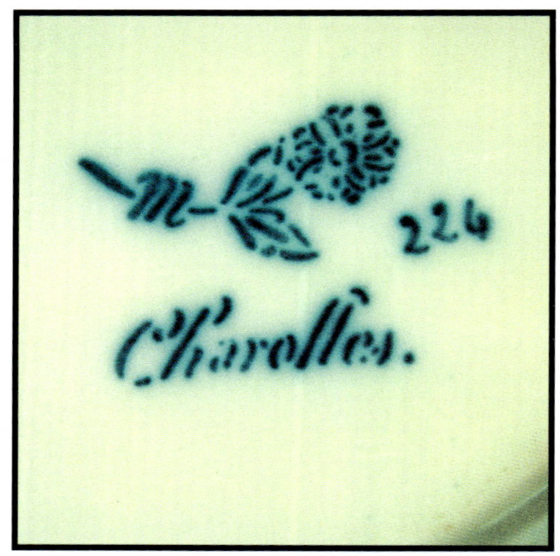

A look at the mark tells us it's from the Morin faïencerie in Charolles. *Private Collection.*

CA is the name of a previously unidentified French faïencerie in Paris. After 20 years of research, Millicent Mali named the elusive CA factory as belonging to the Chaumeil family. For more than three generations, the Chaumeils first produced porcelain, then faïence souvenirs and classic reproductions, and most recently noteworthy, original art pottery. Breton motifs appeared on CA faïence, in addition to Loire Valley and Canadian themes. *(Mali, CA, A French Faïence Breakthrough, p. 5.)*

Charolles is a potting center southeast of Paris, not far from Nevers.

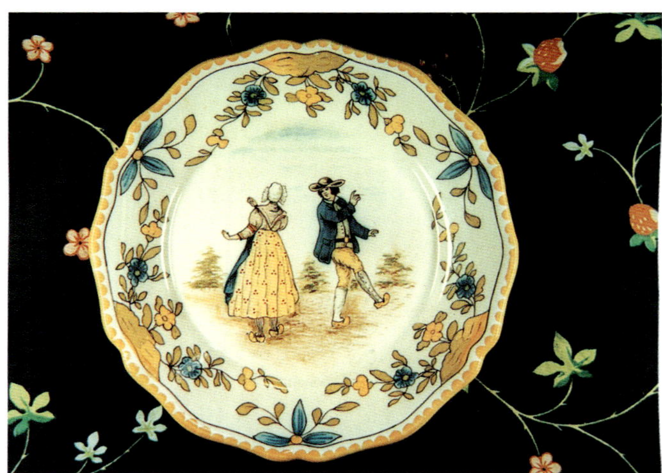

This 10" diameter plate contains a lovely rendition of peasants dancing in the countryside, a familiar Quimper theme. The costumes and colors don't seem to be Quimper. *Private Collection.*

China has even adopted the *petit Breton* on export wares.

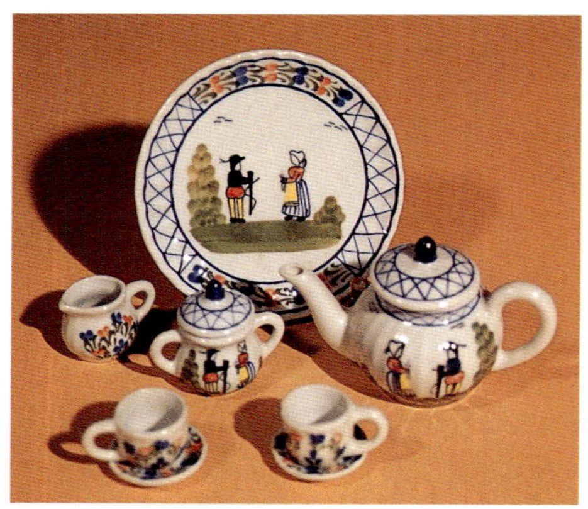

China exports this sweet tea set. We've seen several of these sets on Internet auctions and hope bidders aren't misled about the age and origin. *Authors' Collection.*

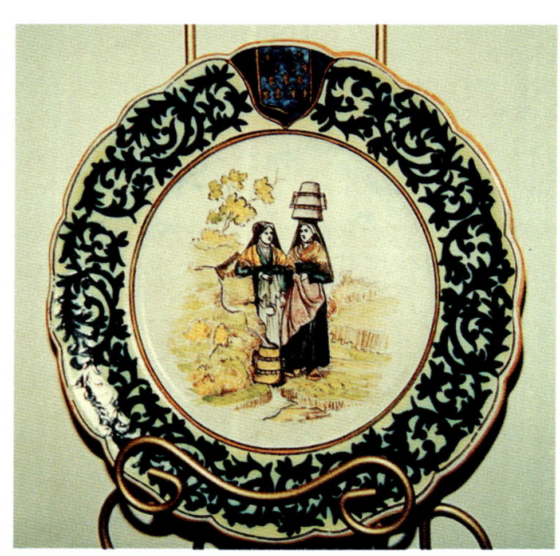

Desvres is in the northeastern section of France. The most easily recognized name in Desvres faience is Fourmaintreaux. *Fourmaintreaux-Courquin* and *Fourmaintreaux Frères* factory reproductions of earlier faïenceries' décors were marked with the combined FC and FF. After 1896, Emile Fourmanitreaux discovered the popularity of the *petit Breton* motifs and added them to his factory's products, signing them with FE. *(Piton, It's Desvres, p. 32.)* His son, Gabriel Fourmaintreaux, became a potter in 1906 and signed his wares with GF inside a wheel. *(Piton, p. 36.)*

The Desvres faïencerie of *Emile Fourmaintreaux* manufactured this Quimper-like plate. It contains a peasant scene similar to the Porquier-Beau *scène Bretonne* of *porteuse de panniers*. The plate also carries a *décor riche* border with an armorial, another Porquier-Beau device. *Courtesy of Christine T. Lindstrom.*

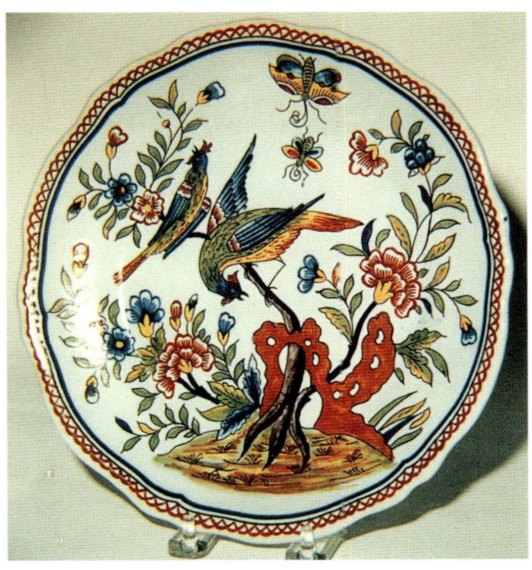

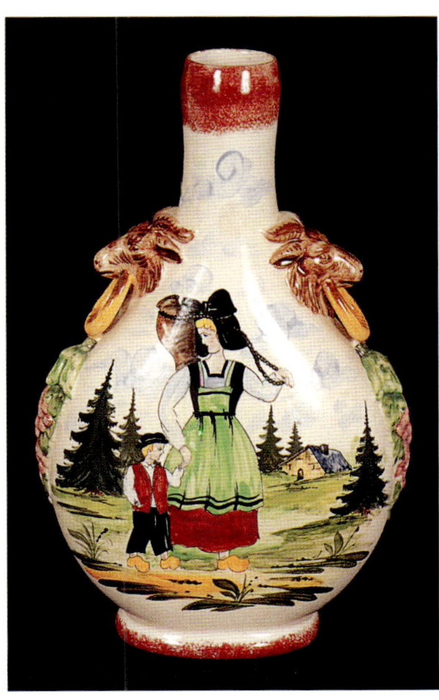

Left:
Another Desvres plate, signed only Rouen. Don't be fooled into thinking this is an 18th century plate. Rouen represents the design, or that it ws intended for sale in the town of Rouen. *Private Collection.*

Right:
This colorful vase is also from a Desvres faïencerie. It shows an Alsatian lass with a boy, both wearing *sabots*; the vase has ram's head handles. It's a product of Gabriel Fourmaintreaux.

Italian Quimper? An avid Quimper collector confirmed it for us.

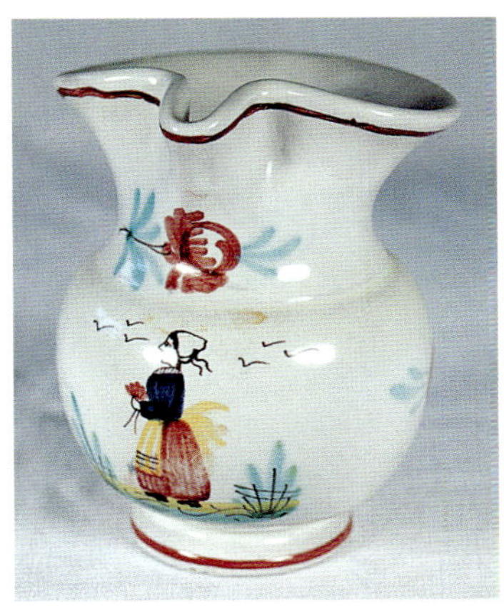

An Italian version of Quimper amused the buyer. *Courtesy of A.W. Styer.*

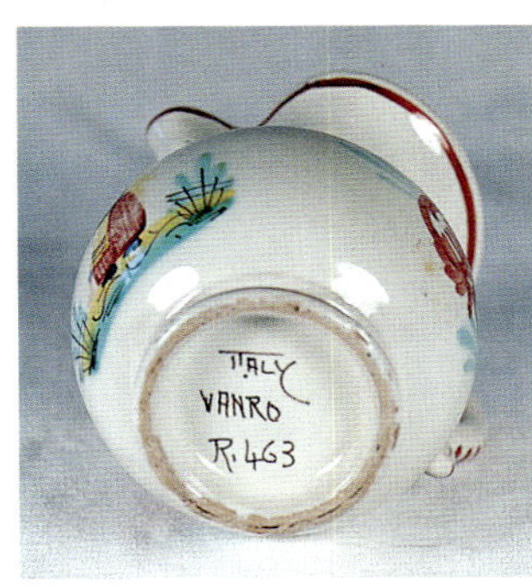

Yes, the proof was in the mark. *Courtesy of A.W. Styer.*

Japanese Quimper? Yes, the *petit Breton* traveled to Japan and returned on a variety of ceramic products made in Japan.

A basket in the *soleil* color is a Japanese interpretation of an HB design. The texture and weight didn't seem right for a Quimper product. *Authors' Collection.*

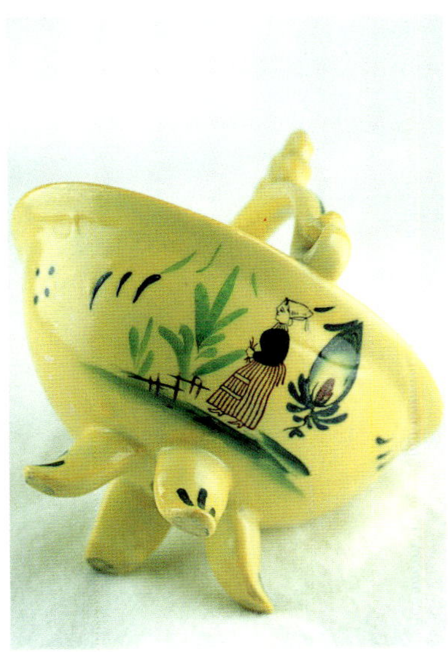

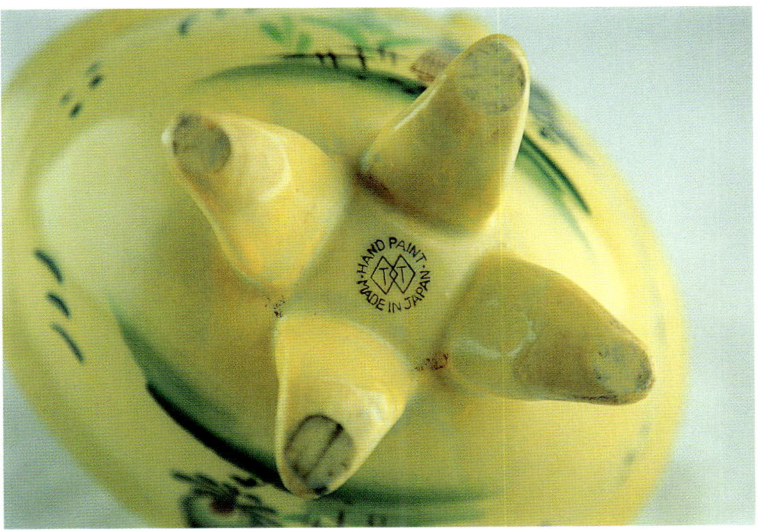

On the bottom of the basket was the proof! *Authors' Collection.*

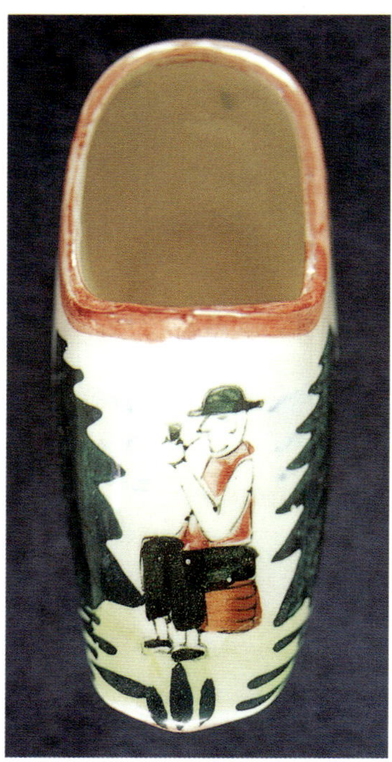

Another Japanese rendition, this time in a 5" long faïence *sabot*. Were you fooled? *Authors' Collection.*

Les Fils Duquenne is a faïencerie near Paris making Quimper reproductions since the 1970s. Items marked *quimper* from this faïencerie came to our attention in 1990s in the flea markets of Paris. Numerous faïence items appeared, such as the barber bowl illustrated in the Chapter *Paris*. The signature was the one word *quimper*, spelled with a lower case *q*. Any faïence marked Quimper is supposed to originate in the town of Quimper.

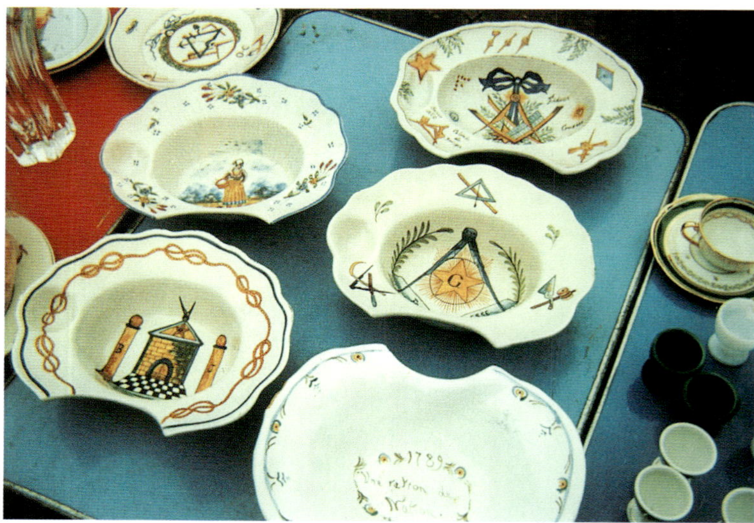

Les Fils Duquenne, a Paris faïencerie, flooded the market with items marked only *quimper*. These barber bowls were found at the Paris flea market in 1999.

Longchamps faïencerie, near Dijon in eastern France, developed its own line of the *petit Breton*.

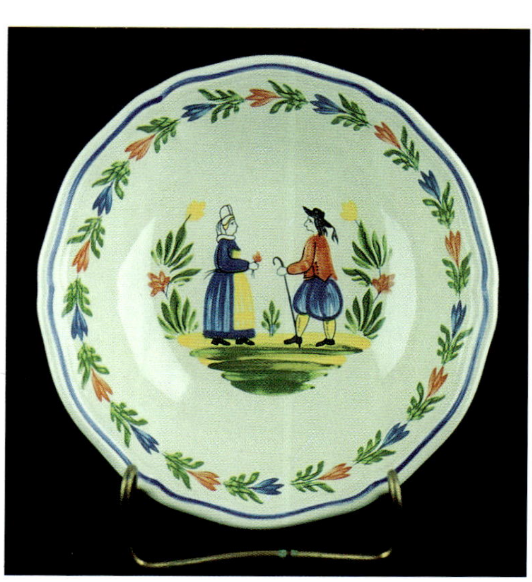

A 6" diameter bowl looks like Quimper. But a closer look tells us the two Bretons and the rim décor are just not Quimper. *Authors' Collection.*

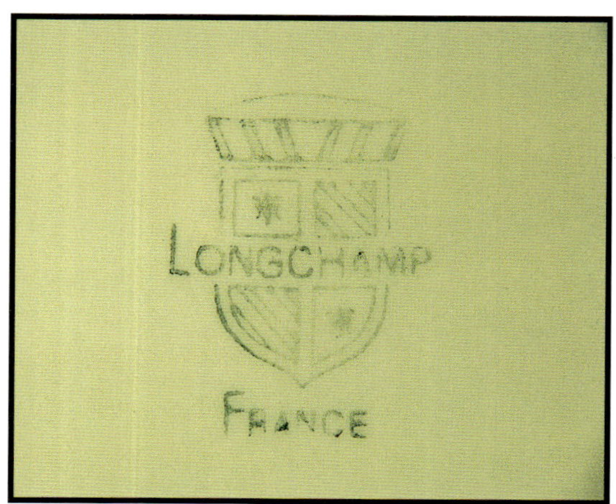

The signature, Longchamps. *Authors' Collection.*

Lunéville (commonly known as Lunéville-St. Clément) is a faïencerie in the Lorraine region of eastern France. Today it is called Lunéville-St.-Clément-Badonviller. *(Mali, p. 91.)* The *petit Breton* décor developed at Lunéville was edged with sponged diamond-shapes in blue. The Breton-type characters were portrayed between sponged trees rather than the *à la touche arbustes* (shrubs) of HB or floral sprays of Henriot design. *Manoirs* and churches were also popular designs of early 20th century Lunéville.

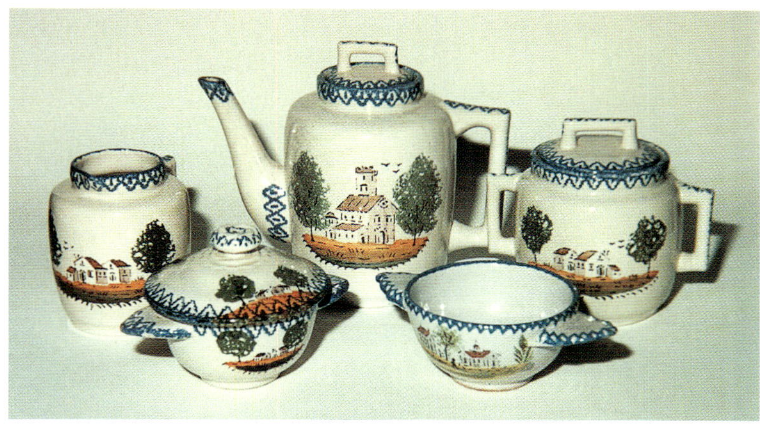

A tea set in the décor from Lunéville - St.Clément is eye-catching. There are buildings similar to Quimper themes, but the sponged décor and blue-diamond edging tell us it's not Quimper. *Private Collection.*

Malicorne is the name of a town nears LeMans, west of Paris, and is the name given to certain ceramic products manufactured there. The best-known Malicorne faïencerie is that of Léon Pouplard.

In 1888, Léon Pouplard married the daughter of Malicorne faïencerie owner Jules Beatrix. Within a few years Pouplard began copying designs by Alfred Beau. Pouplard developed the PB signature by combining his last initial and the last initial from his wife's maiden name. The earliest mark had the P backwards, and later ones had PB with an x, but all were meant to confuse the potential buyer about the faïence's origin.

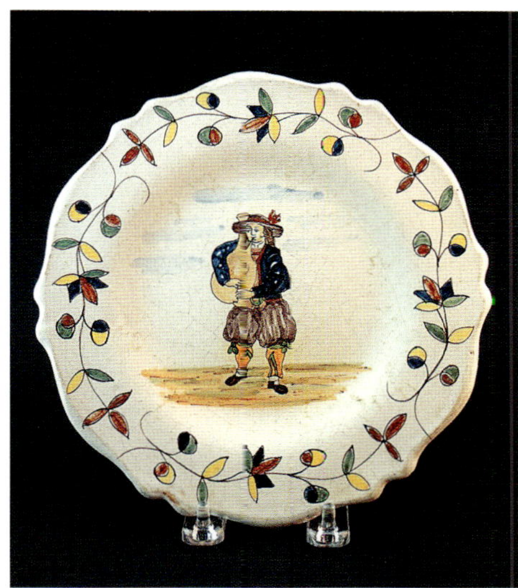

This 9.75" plate is an example of the Breton décor by the Pouplard faïencerie. The acorn border is an easily recognized Pouplard device. Many collectors prize Malicorne copies of Porquier-Beau products, and many times the prices are in the same range. *Courtesy of Ralph and Becky DeStefano.*

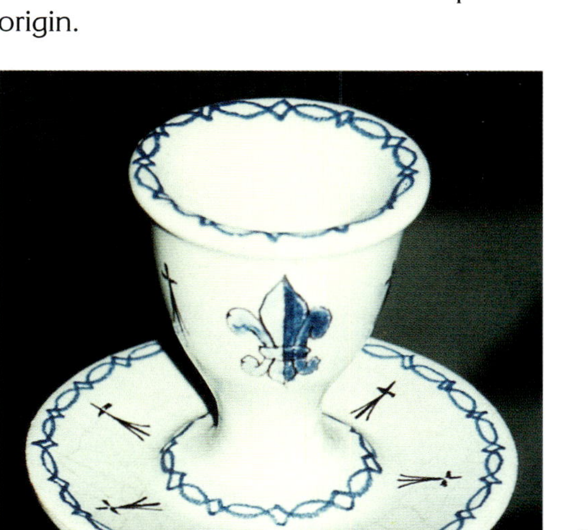

A two-toned blue *fleur-de-lys* egg cup has black ermine-tail accents and blue-chain rim décor. This is a typical design of the late 1800s, as rendered by the Pouplard faïencerie. *Private Collection.*

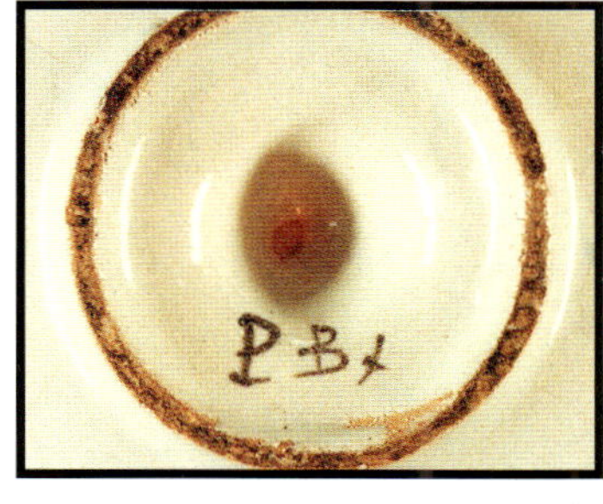

The PBx mark appears on the bottom of the *fleur-de-lys* eggcup, revealing it is a Pouplard faïencerie product, not Porquier-Beau! *Private Collection.*

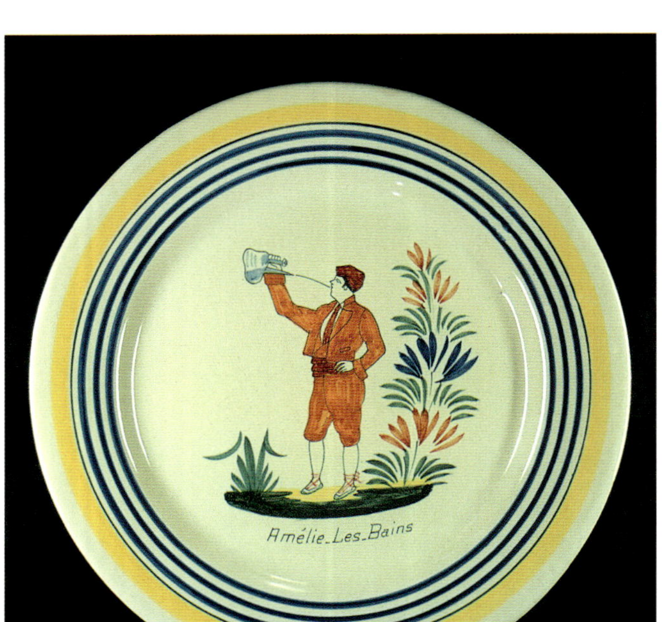

Looks like Quimper, but it's Malicorne. This 9.5" plate reads *Amélie Les Bains*, signifying it is a souvenir item. It's signed with a backward P and a B, similar to the Porquier-Beau mark, but TE appears too. *Authors' Collection.*

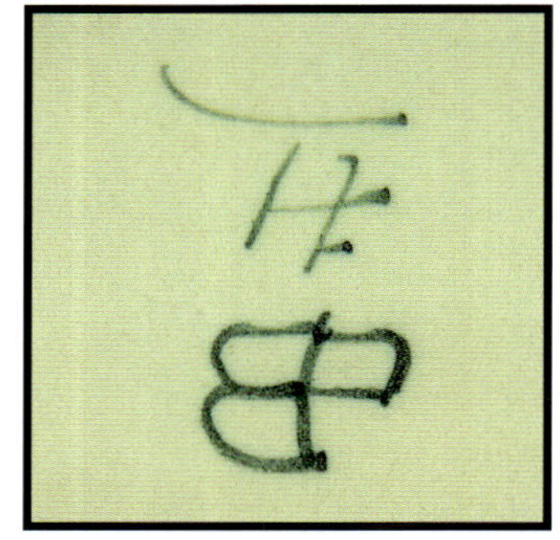

Just what is this curious signature meant to represent? Porquier-Beau, Pouplard, or Tessier/Deschang? The battle of the marks continues! *Authors' Collection.*

By copying the highly popular Breton décors of Porquier-Beau, the Pouplard factory gained some success. The unfair competition may have cut into Porquier-Beau profits and been one cause for its demise. A court case over this mark filed by the Porquier faïencerie in 1898 was found in Porquier's favor. The Pouplard faïencerie was told to destroy its stock so marked. Some pieces still may be found with the gouged-out mark on the back. Mali warns that this ruling applied to the imitations of the Breton themes, and that the PB signature may have continued on non-Breton designed products until 1952. Some collectors prize Quimper-like Malicorne products from the Pouplard faïencerie, and examples can command prices in the same range as similar Quimper products, despite the heavier reddish clay and less spectacular painting.

Another Malicorne-based faïencerie belonged to Emile Tessier. Tessier worked for Pouplard, but opened his own faïencerie in 1924. The Tessier faïencerie was purchased by Deshang in 1984 and continued to use the Tessier mark, a slanted T next to an upright E. It operates under the name *Faïenceries d'Art de Malicorne. (Mali, pp. 67-72.)*

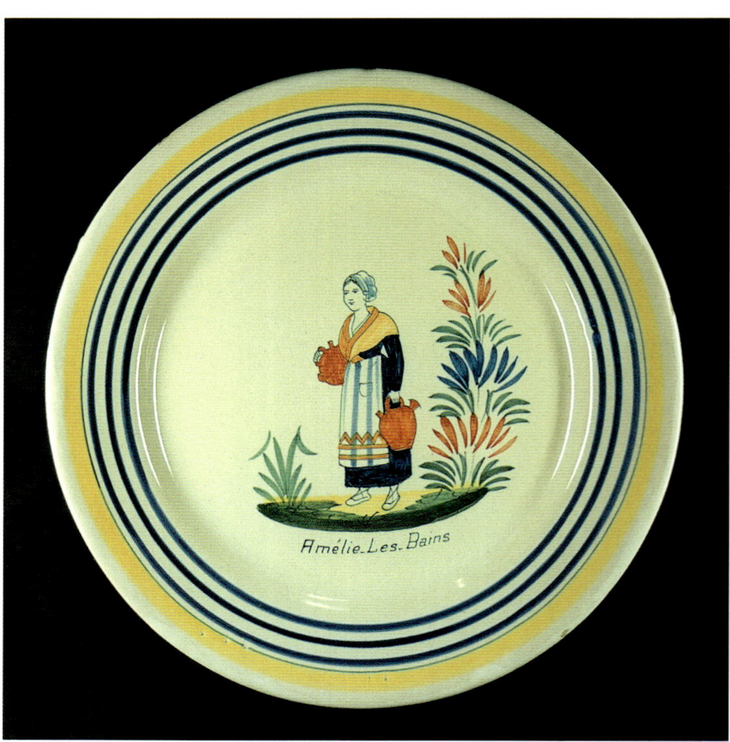

The 9.5" plate's mate also is signed with a backward PB and TE, identifying these plates as from the Tessier/Deschang factory, or *Faïenceries d'Art de Malicorne. Authors' Collection.*

Still another Malicorne faïencerie, Bourg-Joly, was sold to Gustave Leroy-Dubois. The Leroy-Dubois mark was a transposed L integrated with a D, leading some to think it was a JD. This faïencerie produced a wide variety of products, including Quimper-like designs. It was critiqued as not having the painters' skills of the Quimper faïenceries, resulting in figures that were out of proportion. In 1918 it was sold to Mme. Moreau and remained in her family until 1993, and since has been managed by M. Fouquet. *(Malicorne, Terre de Faïence, Extract.)* Another example of the Leroy-Dubois faïencerie mark appears in the Chapter: *Rennes and Environs.*

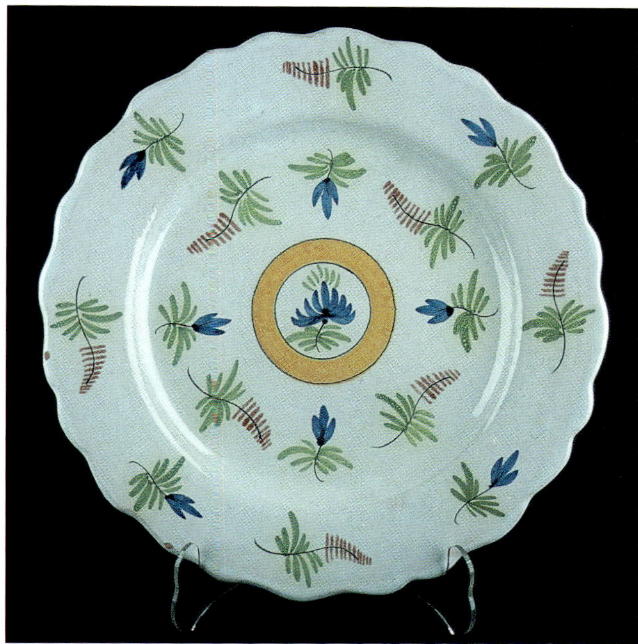

Left:
This 9.5" plate is from the Malicorne faïencerie of Gustave Leroy-Dubois. It features reddish clay, covered with a gray-blue glaze, floral motif, and yellow circle in the center. *Authors' Collection.*

Below:
The plate is signed with what appears to be a JD, but it's really a transposed L connected to a D. This Leroy-Dubois mark was used from 1899 to 1918, when the faïencerie was sold to Madame Moreau. *Authors' Collection.*

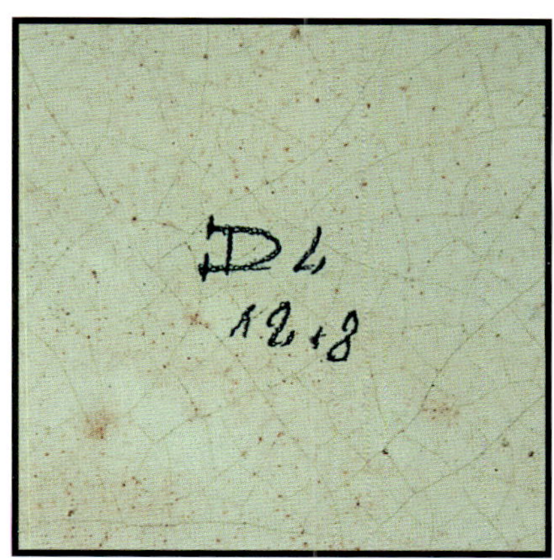

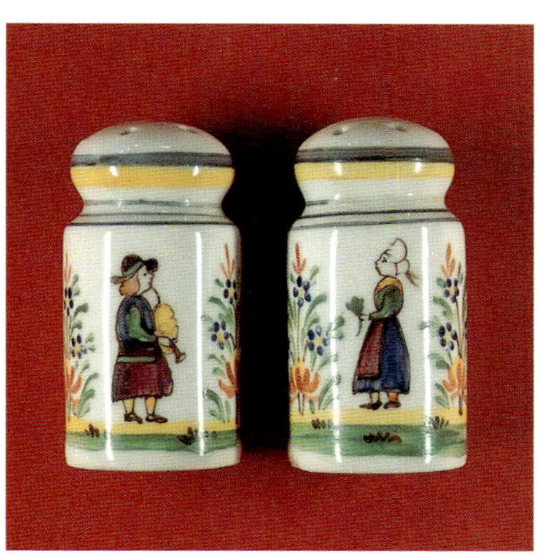

These salt and pepper shakers are un-marked, but something about the colors and the execution of the *petit Bretons* says, *Pas Quimper! Courtesy of Charlie and Donna Walker.*

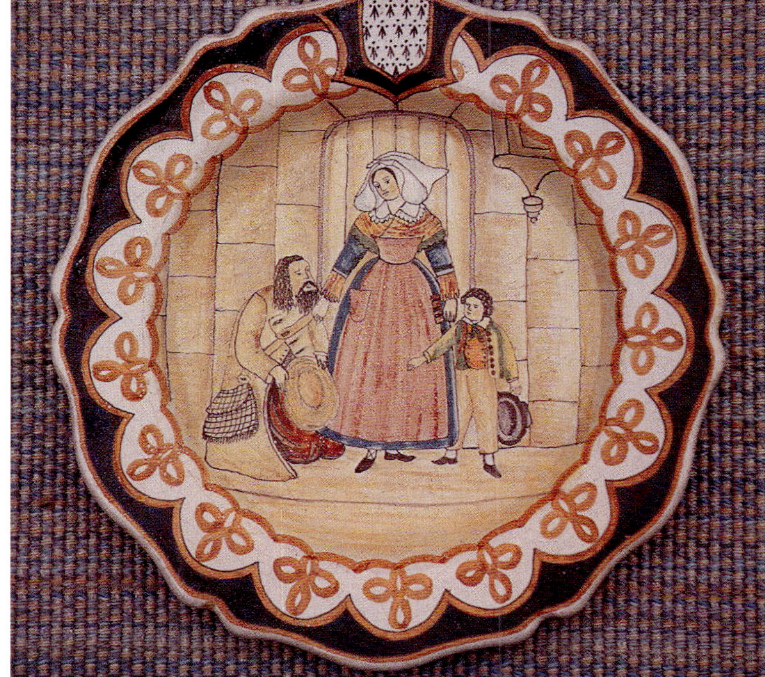

A rendition of a Porquier-Beau décor is shown on this stellar Pouplard faïencerie plate, signed PBx. The interior scene shows a *mendiant* begging for charity at the door, while a Bretonne and her daughter emerge. The most interesting element is the border. The Italian décor with blue, white, and yellow coloration encircles the scene in a rare duplication of Porquier designs. *Authors' Collection.*

Part V Quimper Faïenceries Timelines, Marks, and Histories
◈ Quimper Faïenceries: Timelines and Marks

Poterie production does not always have a serialized identification system. Quimper researchers have had to rely on journals, registration records, intra-company correspondence, and court rulings to determine when certain pieces were made. As new information is uncovered, the date of the marks and even the dates of faïencerie origins are questioned.

We propose that a timeline of approximate years of faïencerie operations and marks is the most valuable tool for a collector. Because many marks look similar, we recommend close inspection to determine which faïencerie produced the piece, and when. Remember, individual painters have signed faïencerie marks with their own interpretation or flair. This does not indicate a separate period of time, as some researchers may have thought. Also, dates can depend on the resource used by the researcher, and resources vary.

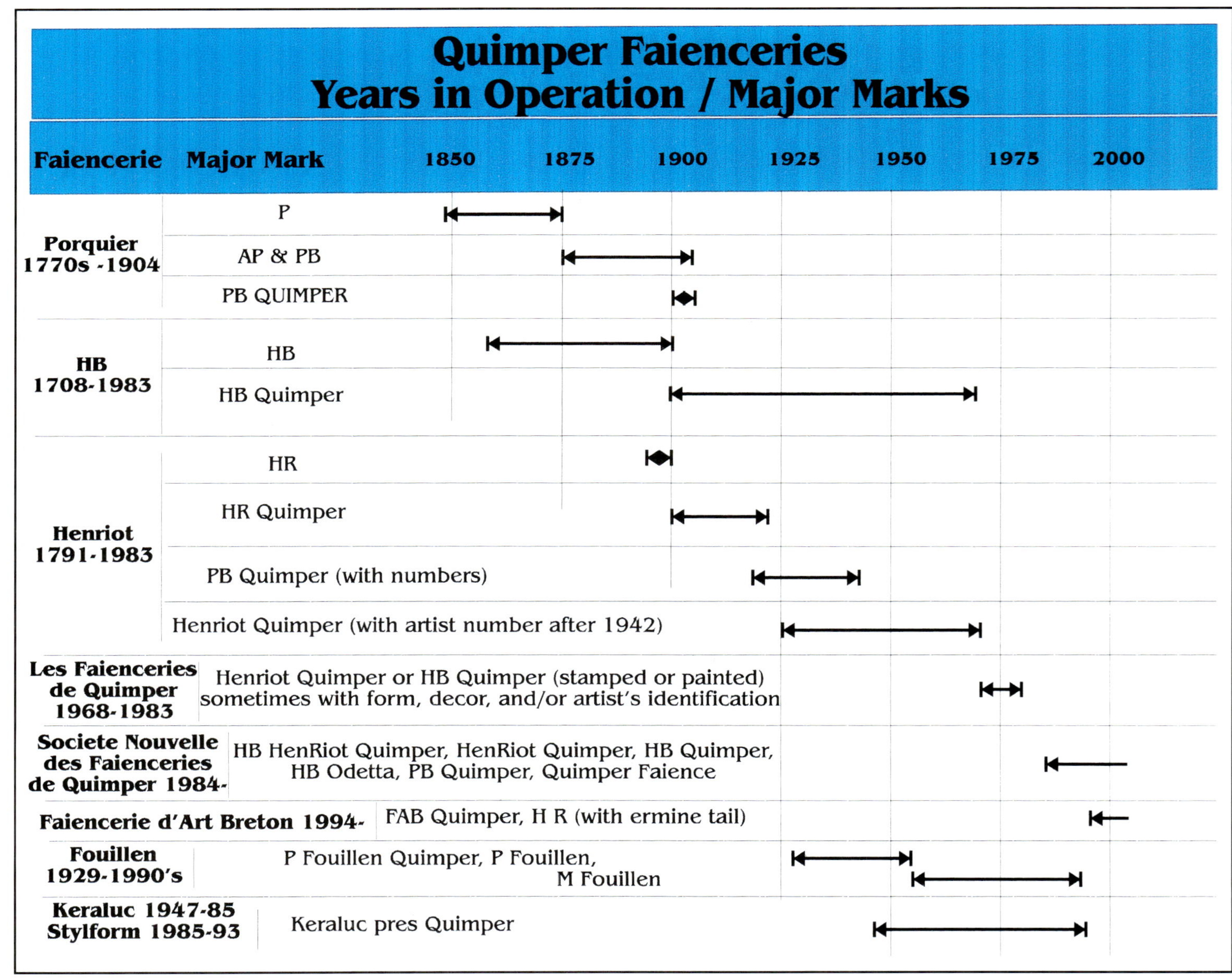

What's in a Mark?

Early Quimper marks merely identified the faiencerie. Over the years, various additions were made to indicate the form, the decor, and sometimes even the design artist or painter.

Examine the mark below to see the various

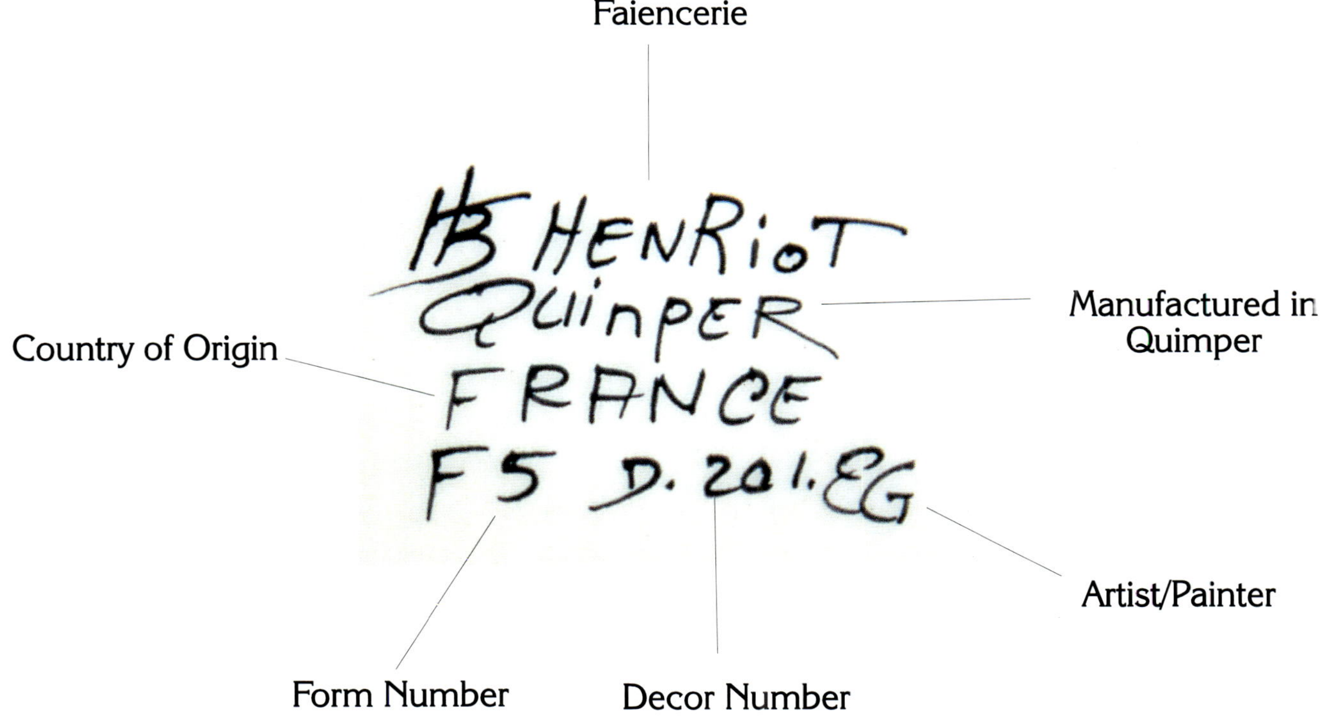

This example is from a plate from the current faiencerie Societe Nouvelle des Faienceries de Quimper...known by most as HB/HENRIOT.

Quimper Faiencerie Marks

	Porquier 1770's-1904	Hubaudiere 1708-1983	Henriot 1791-1983
19th C	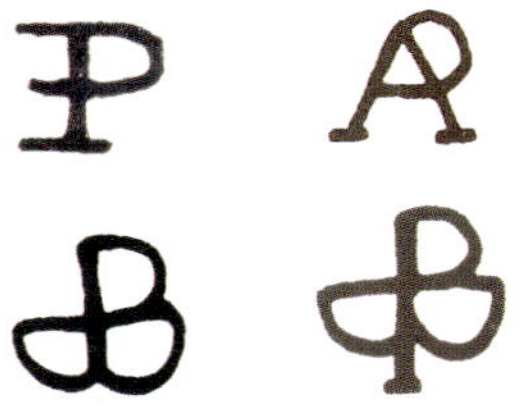	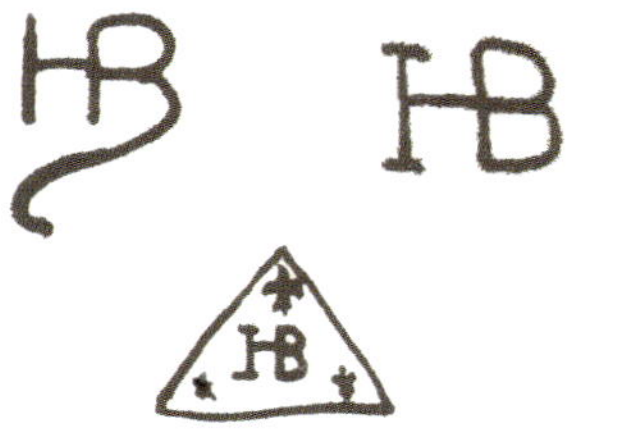	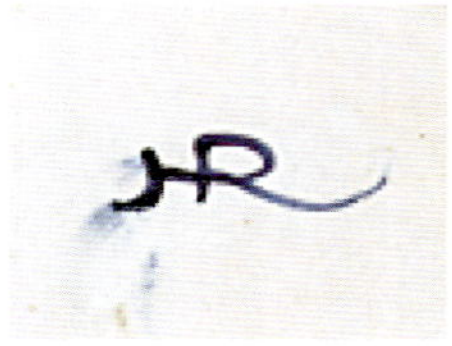
20th C	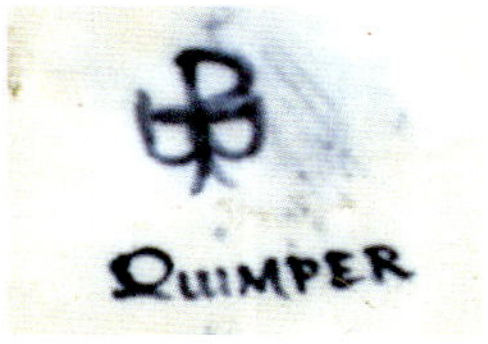 Founded 1770's under Eloury. Early mark (P) appeared mid 19th C; followed by (AP) and (PB) in last quarter 19th C. (PB Quimper) about 1900-1903. Ceased production by 1905.	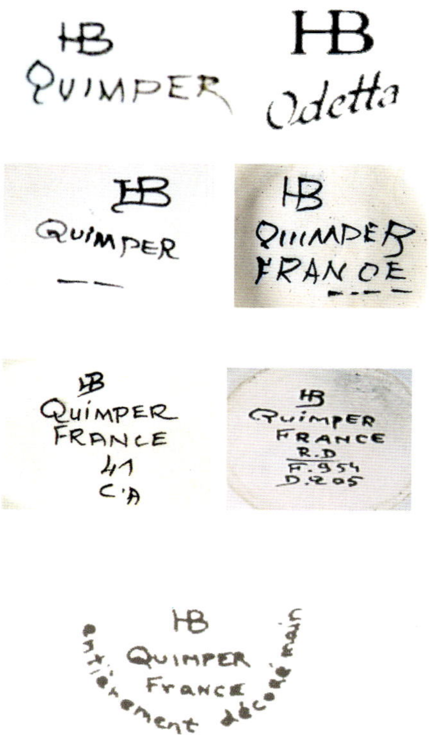 Founded 1708 by Pierre Bousquet. Early marks from mid 19th C: HB with/without tail; impressed triangle; HBQ from 1900; HBQ Odetta from 1922; HBQ + Morse Code Marks in 1920's-30's; HBQ with initials for atelier & artist - post WWII; HBQ with form & decor numbers and HBQ stamped between 1968-83. HB & Henriot faienceries were combined under Les Faienceries de Quimper from 1968-1983.	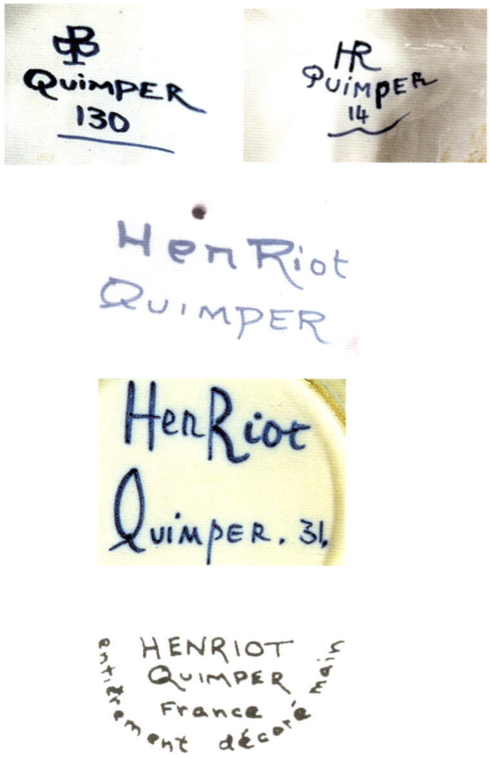 Founded 1791 by Dumaine, first mark (HR) early 1890's; HR Quimper 1900-1922; PB Quimper with number from 1919; HenRiot Quimper after 1922; Henriot Quimper after 1925; Henriot Quimper with artist's number after 1942; Henriot Quimper with form and decor numbers after 1968. Henriot & HB Faienceries combined under Les Faienceries de Quimper from 1968-1983.

Quimper Faiencerie Marks

Fouillen 1929 - 1980's	Keraluc 1947 - 1993	HB/HenRiot 1984 -	FAB 1994 -	
				19th C
				20th C

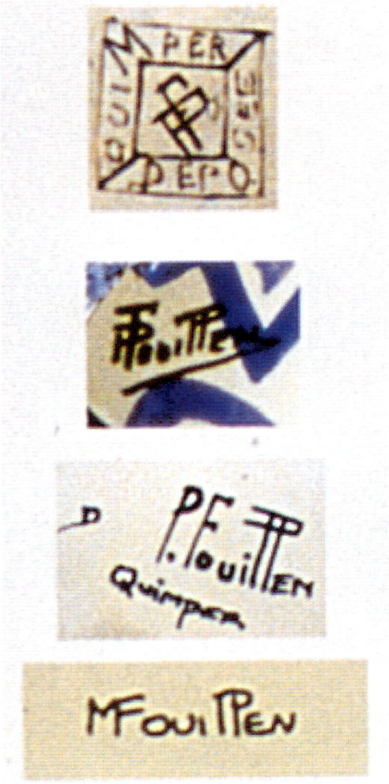

Paul Fouillen, famed artist of HB, started his own business in 1929, specializing in pyrogravure woodenware, creating marks for for both wood and poterie. After Paul's passing in 1958, Maurice, his son, continued the firm until the mid

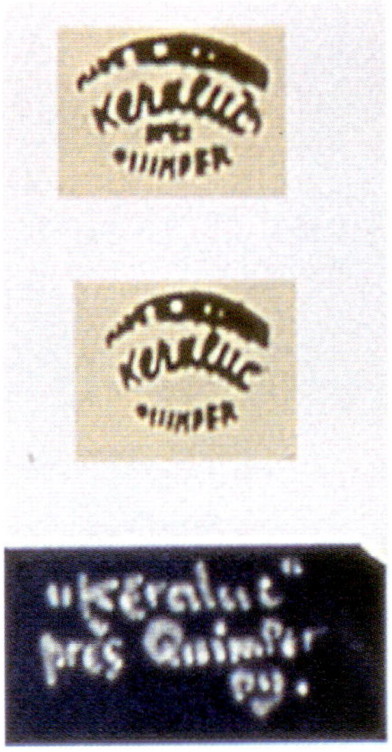

Victor Lucas, having worked for both HB and Henriot, began his own enterprise in 1946-47. In 1985 the firm declared bankruptcy and was purchased by Stylform, which in turn sold to Societe Nouvelle des Faienceries de Quimper in 1993.

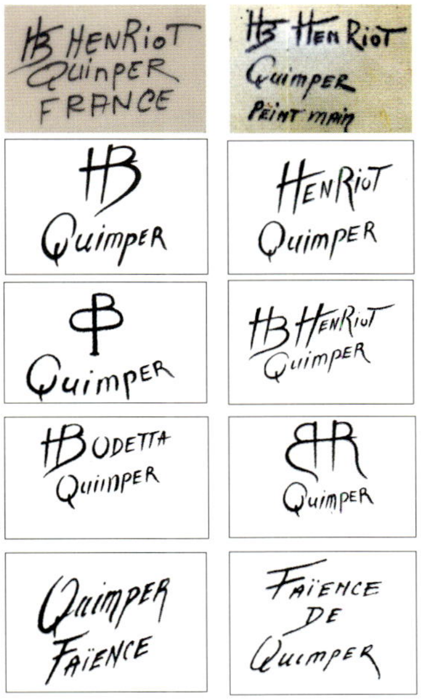

In 1984, newly formed Societe Nouvelle des Faienceries de Quimper acquired the business and marks from Les Faienceries de Quimper which closed in 1983. Marks were modified to avoid duplication. HB/HenRiot became the most widely recognized signature of the Societe.

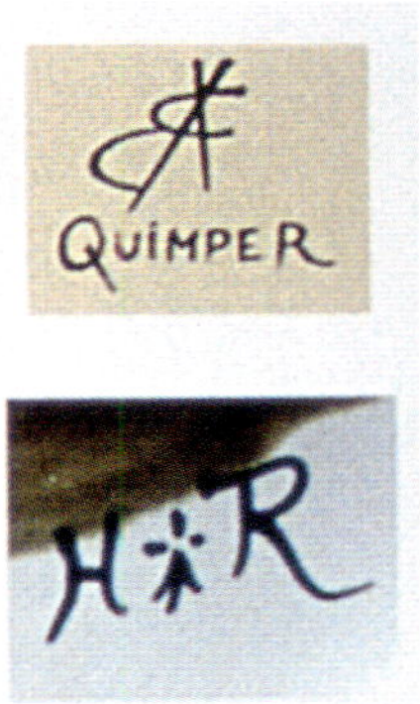

In 1994, a group of investors, including members of the Verlingue and Henriot families, started a new faiencerie in Quimper named Faiencerie d'Art Breton, better known by the acronym FAB.

Examples of Commissioned Marks

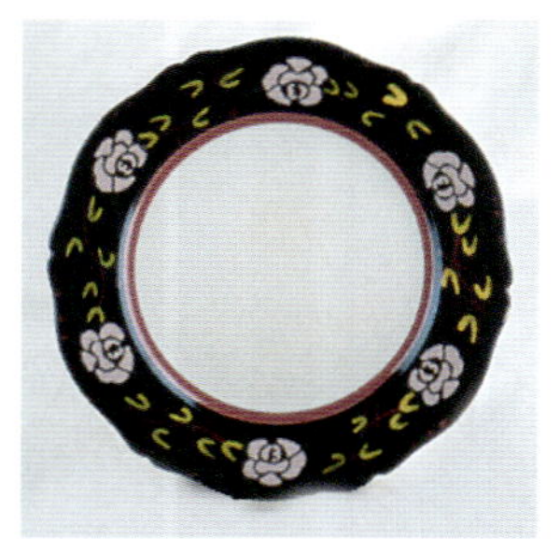

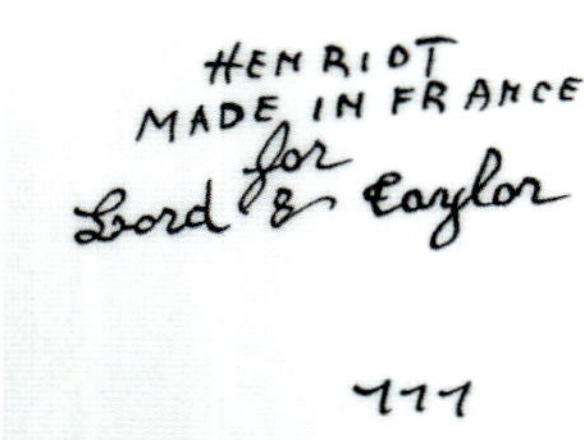

For Lord & Taylor by Henriot Quimper

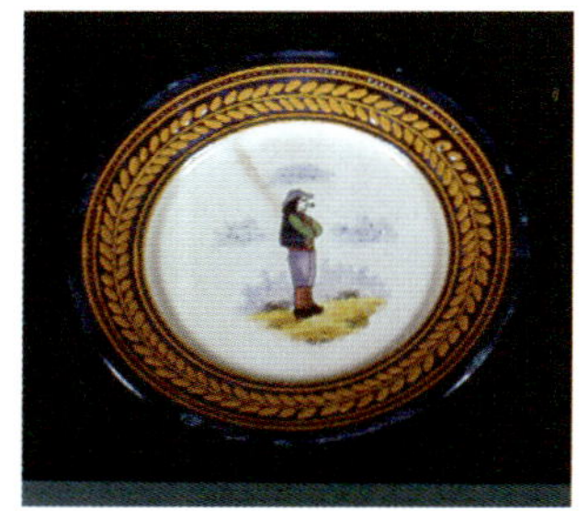

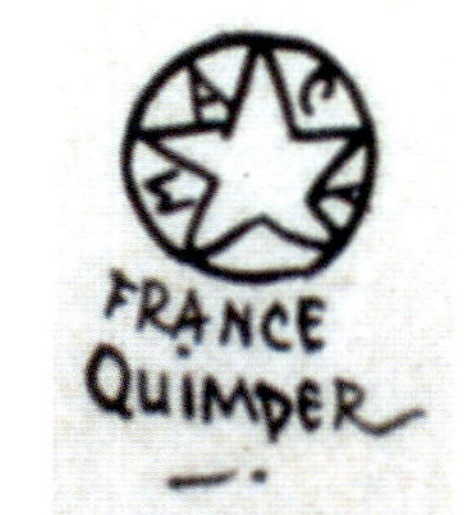

Broderie made by HB Quimper for Macy's Department Store
(Note artist's signature _.)

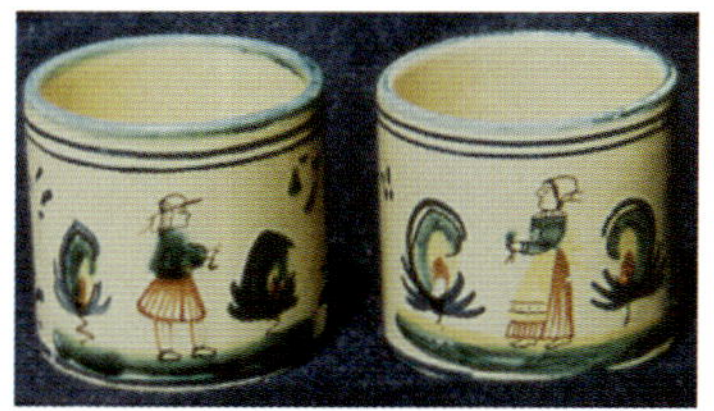

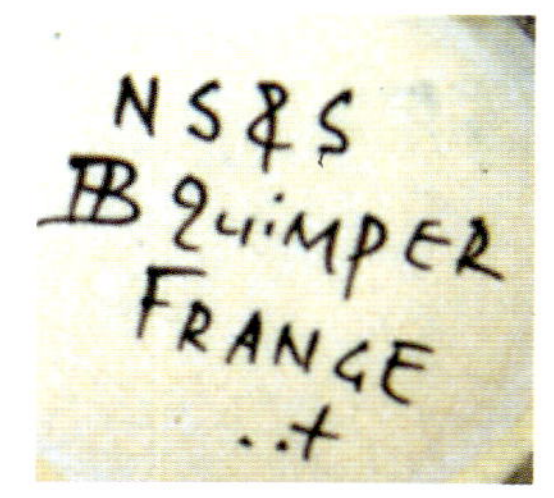

Pieces made for N S & S Department Store by HB Quimper
(Note artist's signature ..+)

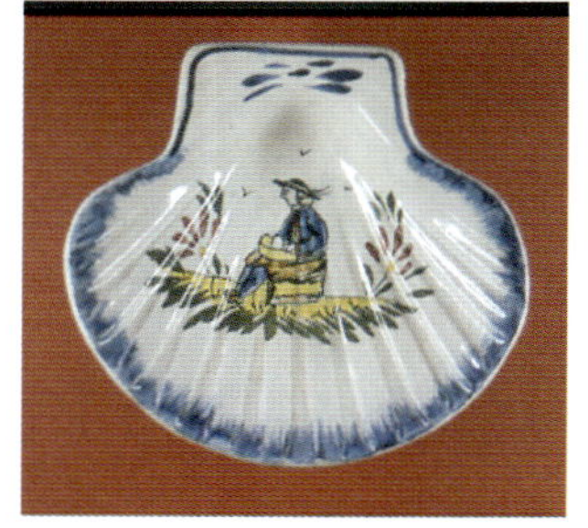

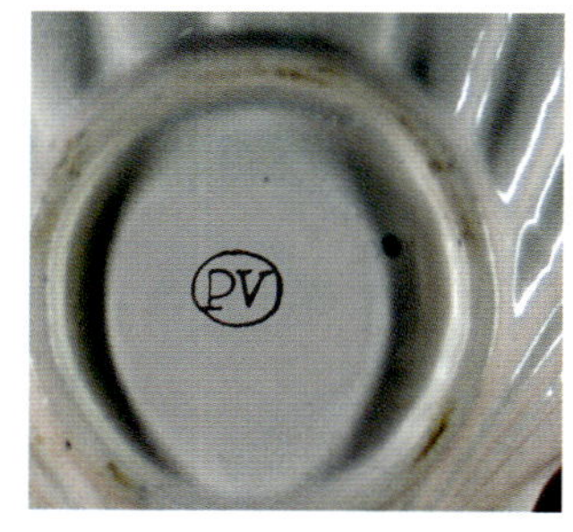

PV is the mark of Mitteldorfer Straus of New York.

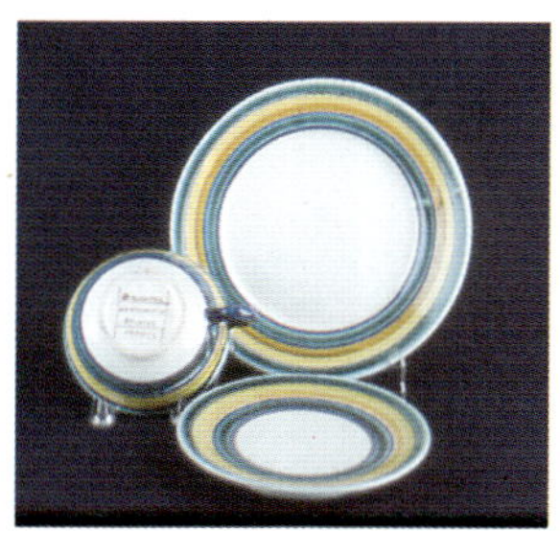

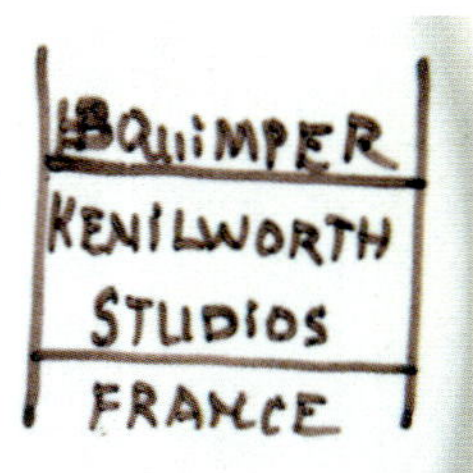

Kenilworth Studios is a copyright of Marshall Field & Company, Chicago, Illinois. HB Quimper was commissioned to make this private label.

HB/Grande Maison

The HB faïencerie or *Grande Maison*, as it became known due to the large building it occupied on the Place Styvel overlooking the port of Quimper, is considered to be the oldest continuing Quimper poterie establishment. Many researchers believed Jean-Baptist Bousquet began the family faïencerie in Locmaria about 1685 or 1690. The latter date was used as the basis for the 300th Anniversary of Faïence celebration held in Quimper in 1990. But there is some compelling evidence that the HB establishment began later. A 1996 publication by Christian de la Hubaudière, entitled *Quel Tricentenaire?*, calls the date into question.

De la Hubaudière, a descendent of the family that eventually took charge of the Bousquet firm in 1771, has a passion for genealogy. His research shows the founder of the family faïencerie in Locmaria was Jean-Baptiste Bousquet's son, Pierre, who opened the poterie in 1708. Pierre Bousquet married Elisabeth Elet and their daughter, Marie-Jeanne Bousquet, was born in Quimper in 1709. Marie-Jeanne married Pierre Bellevaux, a potter from the Nevers area in 1731. Bellevaux is credited with introducing several Nevers motifs and the *à la touche* technique to the Bousquet factory in Locmaria.

The Bellevaux's daughter, Marie-Jean Bellevaux, married Pierre-Clément Caussy in 1749. Caussy was a faïencerie director of note from the Rouen area. He brought many techniques, ideas, *poncifs* (design outlines), and some important artists with him to Quimper. Thus the family business grew due to propitious alliances through marriage.

The Caussy's daughter, Marie-Elizabeth Perrine Caussy, married Antoine Joseph Jean de la Hubaudière in 1771. Although not experienced in the faïence business, de la Hubaudière became the head of the factory in 1782. He was assassinated for his political beliefs in 1794, leaving his wife as the owner/manager of the firm.

After a period of joint-family leadership of the faïencerie, Félix de la Hubaudière, grandson of Antoine and Marie-Elizabeth, became the director of the firm. Upon his death in 1881, his second wife, Alix-Leonie Malherbe de la Bouëxière, became the faïencerie director. She formed a corporation, *Faïencerie Bretonne de la Grande Maison de Locmaria Quimper Corentin.*

Bouëxière remarried in 1889, to Count Lecourt de Béru. Upon her death in 1906, her son by her first marriage, Guy de la Hubaudière, became the head of the faïencerie. He was killed at Verdun in 1916 during World War I, and Jules Verlingue, who had a faïencerie in Boulogne-sur-Mer, completed the purchase of the *HB/Grande Maison* establishment in 1917.

Verlingue brought design concepts and artists such as Poulain and Soudane with him to Quimper. In 1922, he took on a new partner, Louis Bolloré, and the firm was renamed *Société Jules Verlingue, Bolloré et Cie, Etablissement de la Grande Maison, HB*. The firm soon moved to a new location closer to the church in Locmaria.

Major accomplishments under Verlingue's direction include: the development of the *Broderie* and *Keltia* décors, and Odetta, a heavier *grès* ware art pottery; hiring important artists such as René Quillivic and Paul Fouillen; the encouragement of *Ar Seiz Breur* (Seven Brothers), a group of artists supporting the revival of Brittany's Celtic heritage; and participation in important exhibitions where HB artists received national recognition.

Jules Verlingue relinquished controlling shares in the firm to Bolloré, but Jules' son, Jean-Yves Verlingue, bought the shares back in 1956. The factory's manufacturing methods were modernized under Jean-Yves' direction, and the business flourished. After absorbing Henriot faïencerie in 1968, the newly organized firm became known as the *Société des Faïenceries de Quimper*, also known as *Les Faïenceries de Quimper*. In 1983, this business closed. In 1984, the firm was purchased by a limited company of approximately 25 investors, headed by Paul and Sarah Janssens, and was renamed the *Société Nouvelles des Faïenceries de Quimper*.

The Verlingue history with Quimper faïence does not end here. The *Musée de la Faïence, Jules Verlingue*, opened in 1991, on the former site of an early Eloury poterie in Locmaria. Jean-Yves' son, Bernard, is the museum's *conservateur*, and another son, Laurant, works at the museum. The museum's collection numbers over 3,000 pieces of faïence, 500 to 600 of which may be on display at one time. Special events are held annually, keeping the spirit and history of Quimper faïence alive. Bernard has co-authored several books on Quimper faïence, is registered by the *Union Française des Experts*, or *UFE*, and serves as the faïence expert for Thierry & Lannon auctions in Douarnenez and Brest. He also is an active advisor to the *Faïencerie d'Art Breton* (*FAB*), and Verlingue supports artists' efforts to create new and exciting examples in faïence.

(De la Hubaudière, pp. 9-66; Mali, pp. 37-8, 44; Mali, Old Quimper Review, October 1990; Verlingue and Lecossois, pp.14 and 32; Verlingue and Mannoni, pp. 87-91; Verlingue et al, Mes Plus Beaux Quimper, pp. 3-14.)

Henriot Faïencerie

The roots of the Henriot faïencerie date back to the late 1700s. Guillaume Dumaine, a potter from Normandy, arrived in Quimper about 1780. Dumaine worked for the HB firm until 1783, when he opened his own poterie in Quimperlé. His business did not do well, and he returned to Quimper. In 1790, he tried to open a poterie, but he was unable to obtain the funding until 1791. Starting as a relatively small establishment, his poterie steadily grew.

When Dumaine died in 1821, his son, Guillaume-Marie, became manager. Guillaume's sister, Louise-Marie-Renée Dumaine, married Jean-Baptiste Tanquerey in 1821. By 1842, Guillaume Dumaine was incapacitated from the toxic lead used in potting, and his sister and brother-in-law Tanquerey acquired the firm. They renamed it *La Manufacture Tanquerey*.

After Tanquerey's death in 1869, one of his children, a daughter, Marie-Augustine Tanquerey, came into the business. In 1864, she and Pierre-Jules Henriot married. Henriot left a career in the military to participate in the firm, changing its name to *Tanquerey-Henriot*.

The son of Marie-Augustine and Pierre-Jules Henriot, Jules Henriot, was born in 1866. When his father died in 1884, Jules took over the family business at the age of 18. He immersed himself in the poterie firm, and helped create a viable active faïencerie, which he renamed *La Faïencerie d'Art Breton, Jules Henriot.*

Jules Henriot's contributions include: The purchase of the defunct Porquier factory models and marks for reproduction by his firm; hiring additional artists and encouragement of creativity in décor and design; improved production techniques; and Henriot participation in regional and national expositions. Rocuet's *l'ajonc and bruyère* (gorse and heather) décor, the series of saints plates by Pohier, and the rococo, *biniou* (bagpipe), and swirled forms of Le Borgne were some of the artistic innovations under Jules Henriot. While Mathurin Méheut was not an actual employee, his association with the firm attracted other noteworthy artists such as Bachelet, Creston, and Nicot, and brought new life to the Henriot products.

Jules Henriot also waged war on the competing firms outside of Quimper copying Quimper faïence products. In 1904, the *Tribunal de Commerce de Quimper* ruled that a souvenir from Quimper must carry the name of the location where it was made. (Some researchers use this date as the starting point for the name Quimper first being added to factory marks.) Despite the Tribunal's ruling, the practice continued. The *petit Breton* had captured the imagination of tourists and these outside poteries still were imitating the various motifs. In 1908, Henriot wrote a scathing tract, *De la protection de faïences Bretonnes ou Faïence de Quimper,* in which he attacked the other poteries copying Quimper designs.

In June 1893, Jules Henriot married Anne-Marie Riou. Their union is thought to be the origin of the mark for Henriot products, HR. It was a combination of the first two letters of their last names, Henriot and Riou. Two sons were born to the Henriots, Joseph and Robert. When Jules Henriot retired in 1927, these two sons took over the family business as co-directors. They had worked with their father, and the business continued to thrive. The brothers retired in the late 1950s and Alain, Robert's son, and Yves, Joseph's son, took over the business.

Beset by financial problems, the Henriot establishment merged with the *HB/Grande Maison* in 1968. The *Société des Faïenceries de Quimper,* also called *Les Faïenceries de Quimper,* was created by Jean-Yves Verlingue. This was the company that closed in 1983 and was purchased in 1984 by a limited company of investors headed by Sarah and Paul Janssens. The new company became the *Société Nouvelle des Faïenceries de Quimper.*

Alain's son, Pierre-Jules Henriot, worked for both the Henriot firm prior to 1968 and the combined firm until 1983. He was hired by the new management in 1984 and worked for the *Société Nouvelle des Faïenceries de Quimper* until 1987.

In 1994, a new faïencerie was born in Quimper. *Faïencerie d'Art Breton,* or *FAB,* is directed by Pierre-Jules Henriot, great-grandson of Jules Henriot. Pierre's brother, Philippe Henriot, is the sales manager, and the Verlingue family also has an interest in the new firm. These families of faïence, who trace their roots back to the 1700s, continue their presence in the Quimper faïence business in the 21st century.

(Henriot, Memoires d'un Faïencier Quimperois, pp. 1-18; Mali, Old Quimper Review, March, 1991; Mali, pp. 41-54; Verlingue et al, pp. 18-23; Verlingue and Mannoni, pp. 89-91.)

PORQUIER FAÏENCERIE

The Porquier faïencerie began in Locmaria in the 18th century. François Eloury, who had been employed by the HB firm, branched out and opened a poterie of his own in a neighboring suburb of Locmaria in the early 1770s. After his death in 1779, his widow took over the firm and moved the factory back to Locmaria, on the street closest to the Odet River.

By 1790, François' son, Guillaume Eloury, took over management of the growing poterie. Guillaume's daughter, Thérèse, married Charles Porquier in 1809. When Guillaume Eloury died in 1825, Porquier became a partner in the business, renaming it Eloury-Porquier. After Porquier's death in 1837, his older son, Guillaume Porquier, managed the factory, and by 1843 he bought out both of his uncles' interest in the faïencerie.

In 1845, Guillaume's younger brother, Clet-Adolph Porquier, bought into the business. The firm became known as *La Faïencerie Porquier Frères*. After Guillaume's death in 1853 and Clet-Adolph's death in 1869, the business, which had grown considerably, became the property of Clet-Adolph's widow, Marie-Augustine Caroff Porquier.

Enter Alfred Beau. As with the other factories in Quimper at the time, the products of the Porquier firm were utilitarian in nature. This saved them in times when faïenceries producing higher-dollar, higher-style wares went out of business. Beau was a professional photographer and accomplished artist. Apparently he was influenced by the work of Michel Bouquet, a painter of fine art on faïence. Bouquet had a studio near Morlaix, where Beau lived, and a career combining all of Beau's talents was in the offing.

Beau married Adah-Anna Souvestre, the daughter of author Emile Souvestre, who wrote *Les Derniers Bretons* and *Foyer Bretons*. The couple moved to Quimper about 1870. Some researchers believe Beau had an unsatisfactory stint with the HB faïencerie in the early 1870s and left the firm because he was not allowed to sign his works. This theory is based on plates bearing the HB signature as well as Alfred Beau's. Others say these plates were only demonstration examples Beau presented to HB director Fougeray as a testament to his skills. Beau's requirement that he sign his works prevented him from being hired.

It is known that Beau approached the widow Porquier about employment and an arrangement was made. Beau joined her firm as a designer-creator whose works, when executed by others, would be signed with the PB (Porquier-Beau) mark. On items he personally painted he signed his name A., Alf., or Alfred Beau. About 1875, to honor the revitalization of the Porquier factory with the addition of Beau-inspired artistic faïence, Mme. Porquier officially renamed the establishment Porquier-Beau.

This was a gracious period for Quimper faïence. True works of art were painted in a detailed fashion on faïence. Beau developed the *botanique* series, finely executed paintings of birds, flowers, insects, reptiles, fish, fruits, and small animals, painted in the English style of Chelsea faïence, with a Japanese flavor. These examples are highly sought by collectors.

Other Beau designs include terra cotta bas-relief plaques featuring peasants, saints, churches, towns, and country scenes. Stellar musical instruments, such as the full-sized viola in faïence displayed at the *Manoir de Kérazan*, were literally major productions.

A particularly poignant innovation was Beau's recreation of the past on faïence. A series called *scènes Bretonnes* featured regional costumes and pastoral, yet very human scenes from an earlier life in *Bretagne*. Based on works by Perrin and Lalaisse, these scenes carried the *petit Breton* image to a much more sophisticated level, and depicted the history of a culture on faïence. Beau even used his talent as a photographer to capture factory employees and their offspring as models for some of his *scènes Bretonnes*. The photographs could be manipulated for use on any size piece of faïence. Beau also created a border to encircle the scenes, which today we call *décor riche*. The border design included an armorial and an arabesque or scrolling foliage motif. Beau simplified earlier Nevers and Rouen décors to create this border, which was registered officially as a Porquier design.

Additionally, Beau illustrated some of the folklore and superstitions from his father-in-law's work. Souvestre's stories combined fact and myth and the *légendes Bretonnes* series by Beau depicts devils and beasts taunting the Bretons.

Alfred Beau's tenure at the Porquier firm was as an employee, never an actual partner, as the firm's name might lead one to believe. Therefore his designs and even the PB signature were not his own, but rather the property of the faïencerie. But he achieved his goal of being recognized as an artist, and what artistry he displayed! Unfortunately, other faïenceries capitalized on his designs and copies flooded the market, perhaps causing irreparable harm to the financial health of the Porquier-Beau factory. The Porquier-Beau relationship was dissolved in 1894, and Beau moved on to an active life of civic duties. He became the first *conservateur* of the *Musée des Beaux Arts* in Quimper. He died in Quimper in 1907, but the faïence world in Quimper had changed drastically, thanks to Alfred Beau.

Arthur Porquier, Mme. Porquier's son, took over the leadership of the Porquier firm and renewed the registration for the AP signature originally filed by his father, Adolph Porquier, in the third quarter of the 19th century. He continued the production of charming faïence products painted in a naïve fashion, but none carried the same artistic impact as an Alfred Beau work. The Porquier faïencerie closed in 1904, but Jules Henriot agreed to hire some of the Porquier employees and buy materials and stock. By 1913, Henriot also purchased the models and rights to the PB mark from the defunct enterprise. The Henriot firm achieved great success with re-issued PB pieces after World War I.

(Mali, Old Quimper Review, October 1990; Mali, pp. 38-43; Meadows, p. 65; Ruzette, pp. 4-5 and 98; Verlingue et al, pp. 14-19; Verlingue and Lecossois, pp. 25-30; Verlingue and Mannoni, pp. 29-47 and 88-91.)

For additional Quimper faïenceries histories, see Chapter *On to Quimper,* for *Société Nouvelle des Faïenceries de Quimper* and *Faïencerie d'Art Breton,* and Chapter *Quimper Sampler A to Z* for Fouillen and *Keraluc* faïenceries.

Internet vs. Being There

Nothing is forever, or so we've been told. The Internet has and will continue to alter the way people shop. It is here to stay, at least for a time, but we don't believe it will replace all other avenues of purchasing.

We have been buying and selling on the Internet for several years, have built our own Web sites, and enjoy the benefits of this new age. But there is still much to be said about physically touching and closely examining an item, as well as conversing face-to-face with the seller or expert. We can read or look at pictures on the monitor until our eyes burn, but nothing takes the place of being there. We feel this way about our quest for Quimper. Without traveling to France, to Paris, to Brittany, to Quimper, we never would have tasted the farmer's fresh cheese in Rennes, sipped that special local wine in Morlaix, or enjoyed the banter with merchants, museum and faïencerie personnel, and touched the many Quimper treasures throughout Brittany.

So when we ask ourselves, *Is the view worth the climb?* Our answer is *YES!* Our quest for Quimper gave us Brittany, and *Belle Bretagne* showered us with Quimper.

The people of Brittany were captured on faïence as well as canvas. The scene on this Henriot charger is *après Abel Villard*, after Abel Villard, well-known artist and head of a fine art school. The scene was rendered on faïence by Pierre-Marie Rocuet, signed HR Quimper, and dated 1907. Rocuet worked for the Porquier establishment until its demise in 1904. He then joined the Henriot firm and produced unique pieces such as this magnificent charger. *Courtesy of Musée de la Faïence, Quimper.*

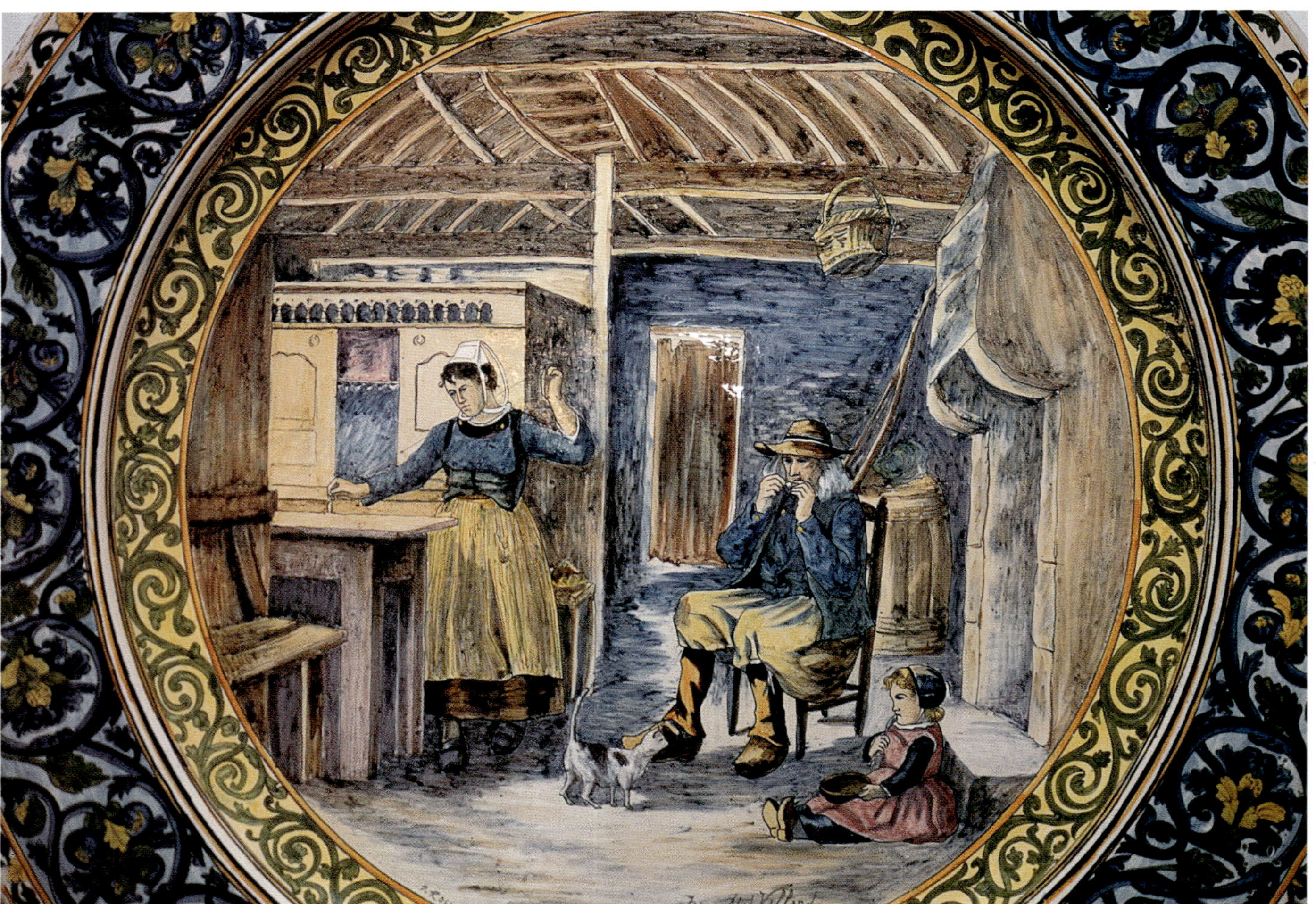

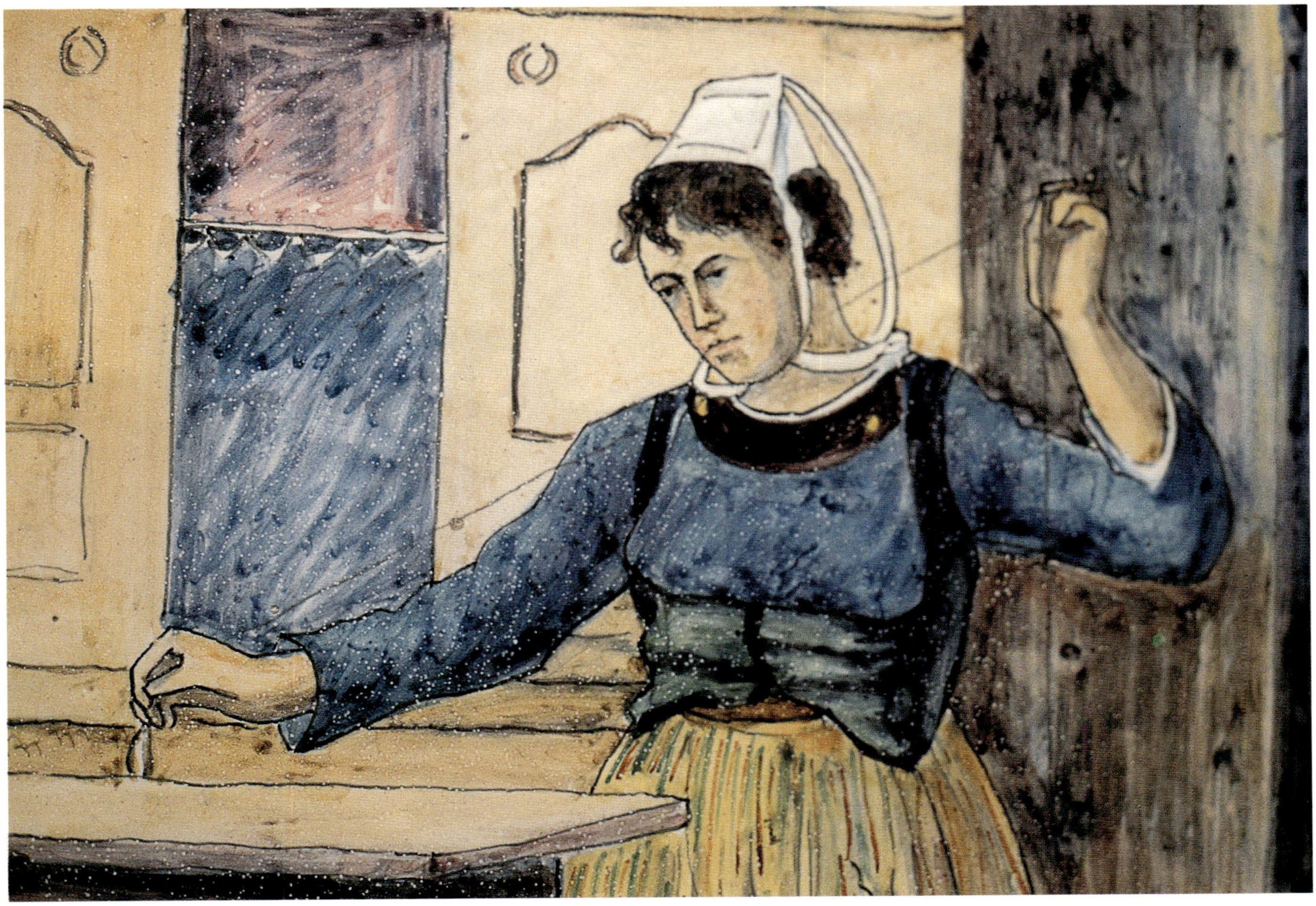

A closer view of the interior scene in a home in 19th century Brittany shows a Bretonne standing in front of the *lit clos* … *Courtesy of Musée de la Faïence, Quimper.*
… And a Breton seated and smoking his pipe. *Courtesy of Musée de la Faïence, Quimper.*

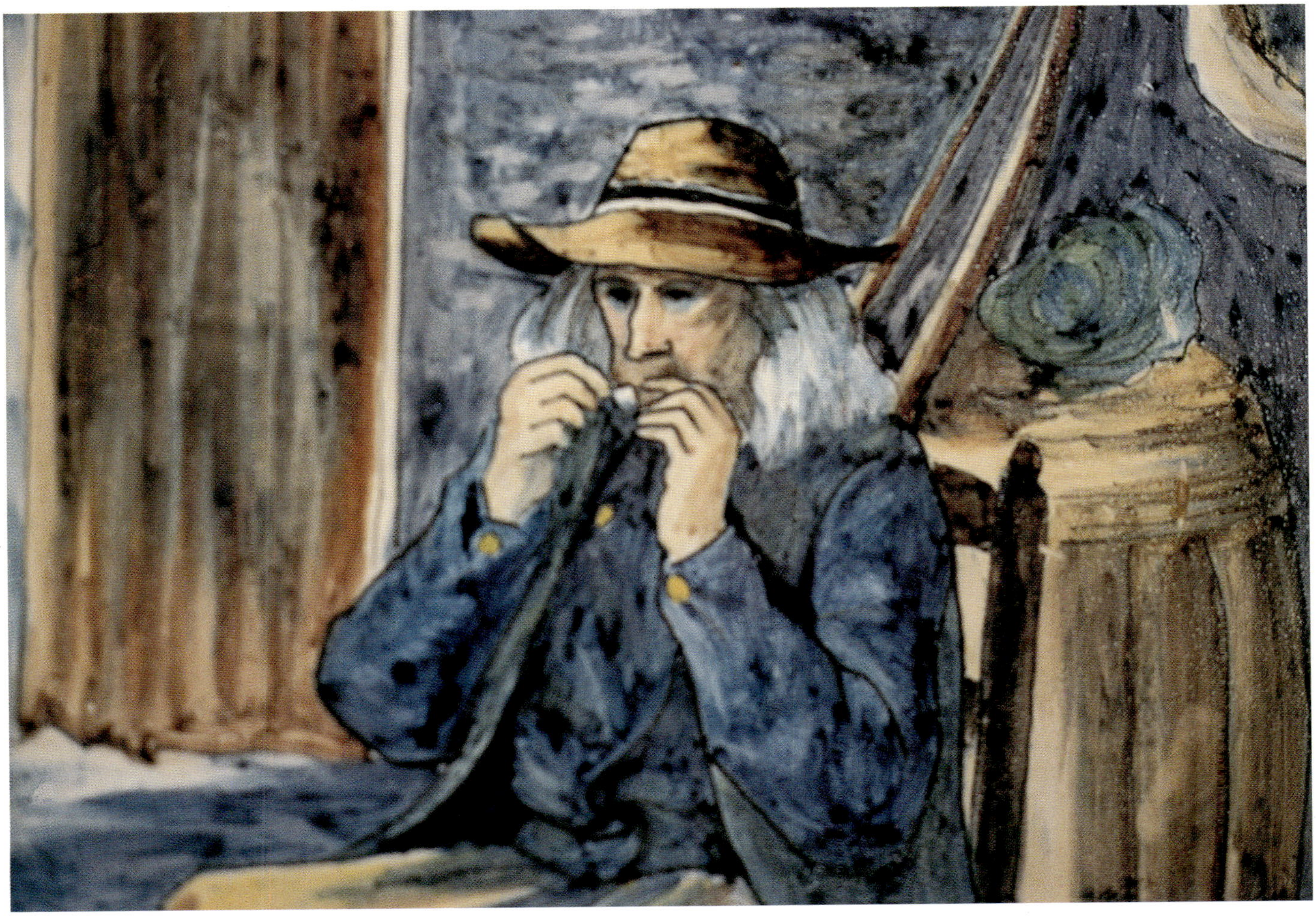

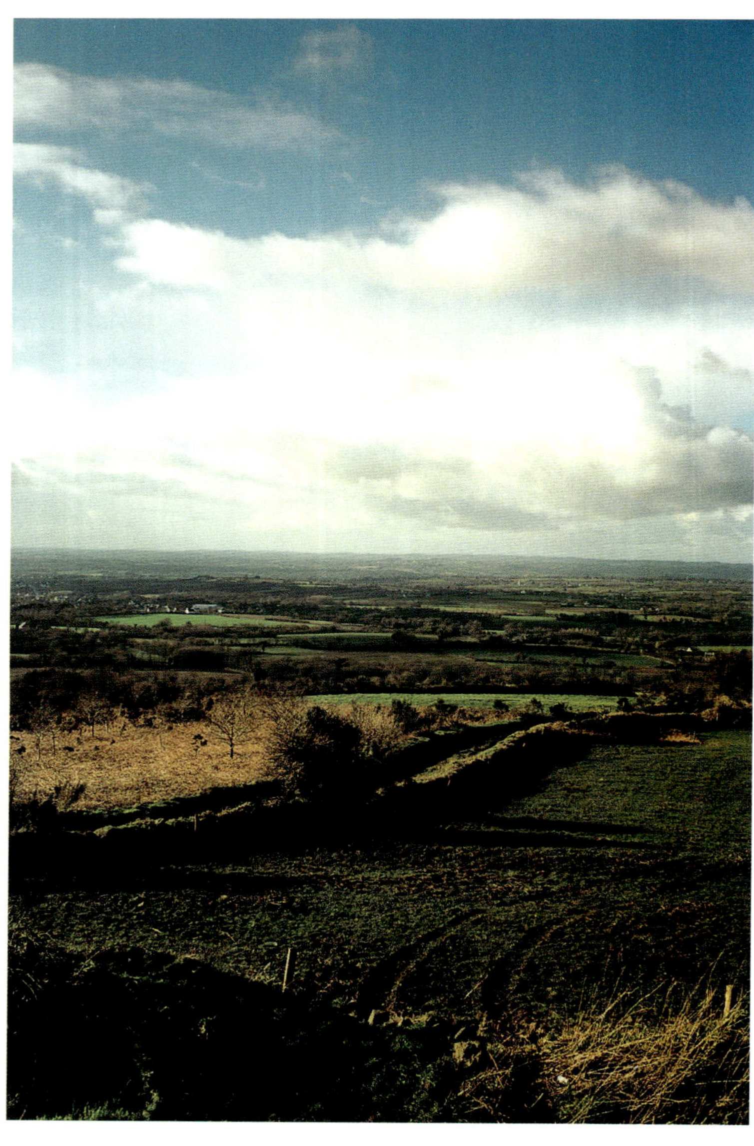

Whether it be the expansive interior of *Argoat* …

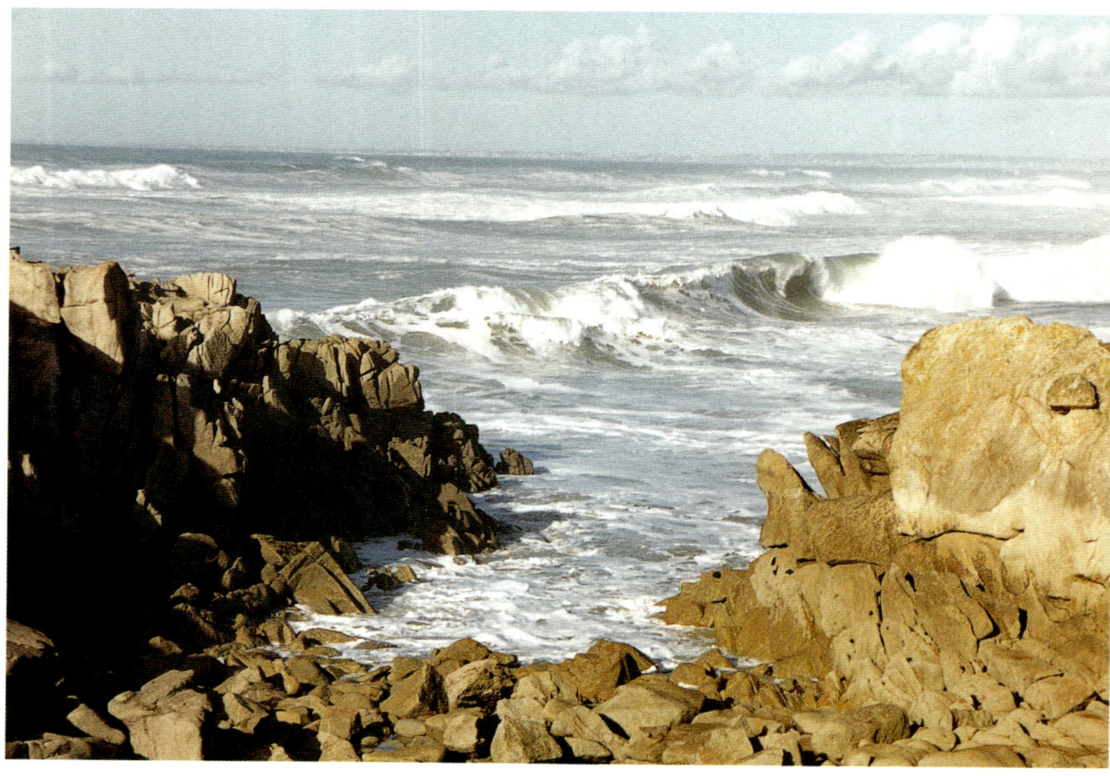

… Or the rugged coasts of Brittany, we found *Bretagne* a most enchanting journey. The view was worth the climb!

✤ Bibliography

Books

Algoud, LeClerc, and Baneat. *Authentic French Provencial Furniture from Provence, Normandy and Brittany*. New York: Dover Publications, Inc., 1993.

Aubert, O. *Celtic Legends of Brittany*, Spézet, Coop Breizh, 1993.

Bell, Brian, Ed. *Brittany*. Singapore Höfer Media (Pte) Ltd., 1989.

Boger, Louise A. *The Dictionary of World Pottery and Porcelain*. New York: Charles Scribner's Sons, 1977.

Bondhus, Sandra V. *Quimper Pottery: A French Folk Art Faïence*. Self-published, 1981.

Briard, Jacques. *The Megaliths of Brittany*. Editions Gisserot, 1997.

Cahn, Laurent. *Vierges et Saints. Les Statuettes Faïence de Quimper*. Quimper 1990.

Campbell, Joseph. *The Power of Myth*. New York: Doubleday, 1988.

Carnegy, Daphne. *Tin-Glazed Earthenware*. London: A & C Black, 1993.

Carrick, Alice Van Leer. *Collector's Luck in France*. Boston: The Atlantic Monthly Press, 1924.

Charleston, Robert J. *World Ceramics: An Illustrated History*. London: Hamlyn, 1968.

Cox, Warren E. *The Book of Pottery and Porcelain*. New York: Crown Publishers. 1956.

Creston, René-Yves. *Modes et Costumes Traditionnels de Bretagne*. Saint-Thonan: Éditions Kendalc'h de Cloitre, 1999.

Curtil, Henri. *Marques et Signatures de la Faïence Français*. Paris: Charles Massin, 1969.

Dantec, Dominique. *Rennes*. Editions Jos, 1996.

Datesman, Joan. *Collecting Quimper - Quimper Collections*. Newtown, PA: Merry Walk, 1987.

Dawes. Frank V. *Brittany*. Chicago: NTC Publishing Group, 1990.

De la Hubaudière, Christian. *Quel tricentenaire?*. Argentan: Graph 2000, 1996.

De Mauny, Michel. *Brocéliande, The Enchanted Forest*. Editions Jos, 1997.

Denieul, Patrick. *Bretagne L'histoire des faïenceries de Quimper*. Montreuil-Bellay: Editions C.M.D., 1998.

Duchesne, Louis-Claude. *Côte de Granit Rose*. Éditions Ouest-France, 1994.

Duigou, Serge. *Voyage En Bretagne*. Éditions D'Art Jos Le Doaré.

Durand, Alain. *La Roche Aux Fées*. Chateaulin: Éditions Jos., 1983.

Fenn, Patricia. *French Entrée 5 Brittany*, London: Quiller Press. 1991

Fodor's. *Exploring Brittany*, New York: Fodor's Travel Publications, Inc. 1999.

Fouillen, M., C. Sévère, and P. Théallet, *PFouillen*. Quimper: Association des amis de Paul Fouillen, 1999

Frelaut, Bertrand. *Il y a un siècle…la Bretagne*. Éditions Ouest-France, 1999.

Ganachaud, Guy. *Les Traditions Bretonnes*. Éditions Ouest-France, 1995.

Giot, P. R. *Brittany, Ancient Peoples and Places*. New York: Praeger Publishers, 1960.

Giot, P. R. *Prehistory In Brittany, Menhirs and Dolmens*. Chateaulin: Éditions d'Art, 1998.

Giot, Pierre-Roland. *The Carnac Alignments*. Éditions Ouest-France, 1993.

Gostling, Frances M. *The Bretons at Home*. Chicago: McCurg & Co., 1909.

Goven, Yann. *Brocéliande Un Pays Né De La Forêt*. Éditions Ouest-France, 1997.

Hélias, Pierre-Jakez. *Coiffes Et Costumes De Bretagne*. Chateaulin: Éditions Jos., 1986.

Hélias, Pierre-Jakez and Serge Digou. *Images of Brittany*. Chateaulin: Éditions d'art Jos Le Doaré, 1994.

Hélias, Pierre-Jakez. *Horse of Pride*. New Haven and London: Yale University Press, 1975.

Henriot, Joseph. *Mémoires d'un Faïencier Quimperois*. Quimper: Edition Frimset, 1990.

Hillion, D., and D. Mingant. *Île De Batz*. Rennes: Éditions Ouest-France, 1995.

Honey, William B. *European Ceramic Art-Illustrated Historical Survey from the End of the Middle Ages to about 1815*. London: Faber & Faber Limited, 1949.

Insight Guides. *Brittany*. Singapore: APA Publications. 1999.

Institut de France, *Le Manoir de Kérazan*, Hors Serie, 1999.

Jacob, Alain, Ed. *Le Nouveau Tardy: Poteries Grès Faïences*. Paris: ABC Collection, 1990.

Jehl, Colette, and Philippe Malot. *Quimper Hier & Aujourd'hui*. Éditions Ouest-France. 1998.

Jude, Patrick. *Mathurin Mehuet richesse & diversité*. Rennes: Editions Ouest-France, 1997.

Laffont, Robert, Ed. *The Illustrated History of Paris and the Parisians*. NY: Doubleday & Co. Inc. 1958.

Lane, Arthur. *French Faïence*. New York: Praeger Publishers, 1970.

Lehner, Lois. *Lehner's Encyclopedia of U.S. Marks on Pottery, Porcelain, and Clay.* Schroeder Publishing Co., Inc., 1998.

Le Cam, Gabriel. *Le Guide des Mégalithes du Morbihan.* Spézet: Coop Breizh, 1999.

Le Cunff, Louis. *Wonderful Brittany.* Rennes: Éditions Ouest-France. 1988.

Le Paul, Judy, and Charles-Guy. *Gauguin and the Impressionists at Pont Aven.* New York: Abbeville, 1987.

LeStum, Philippe. *Arts Populaires de Bretagne.* Rennes: Editions Ouest-France, 1995.

Mali, Millicent S. *CA, A French Faïence Breakthrough.* Harbor Springs, MI: Carpenter Printing, 2000.

Mali, Millicent S. *French Faïence Fantasie et Populaire of the 19th and 20th Centuries.* Self-published, 1986.

Meadows, Adela. *Quimper Pottery, A Guide to Origins, Styles, and Values.* Atglen, PA: Schiffer Publishing Ltd., 1998

O'Neill, Ann Marie. *Popular Quimper.* Atglen, PA: Schiffer Publishing Ltd., 2000.

Piton, François. *It's Desvres.* Self-published, 1999.

Renouard, Michel. *Brittany.* Rennes: Éditions Ouest-France, 1996.

Rotté, Jean. *Ar Seiz Breurs.* Elven: Breizh Hor Bro, 1987.

Roullet, Michel J. *Les Faïences Artistiques de Quimper aux XVIIIe Faïences et XIXe Siècles.* Lorient: Art-Media, 1980.

Ruaux, Jean-Yves. *Côte D' Emeraude.* Éditions Ouest-France, 1994.

Savage, George and Harold Newman. *An Illustrated Dictionary of Ceramics.* London: Thames and Hudson Ltd., 1989.

Taburet, Marjatta. *La Faïence de Quimper, Le Guide du Collectioneur.* Paris: Sous le Vent, 1990.

Verlingue, Bernard Jules. *Odetta,* 1999.

Verlingue, Bernard-Jules, and Lécossois, André. *Faïences de Quimper.* Uhel Izel Editions.

Verlingue, Bernard-Jules, and Edith Mannoni. *Les Faïences de Quimper.* Paris: Editions Charles Massin.

Whiteman, Kate. *Brittany Gastronomique.* New York: Abbeyville Press, 1996.

Zaczek, Iain. *Celtic Design.* London: Crescent Books, 1995.

Exposition Catalogs

Exposition au Château de Quintin. *Les Faïences Porquier-Beau à Quimper,* 1999.

Musée des Beaux-Arts de Quimper. Quimper: *Trois Siècles de Faïences.* Quimper: Editions Ouest-France, 1990.

Musée de Bretagne, Rennes. *Ar Seiz Breur.* LeCouédic ande Veillard, 2000.

Musée des Jacobins, Morlaix. *Yvonne Jean-Haffen, Finistère,* 1997.

Verlingue, Bernard-Jules, and C. R. Trognée. *Berthe Savigny,* 2000.

Verlingue, Bernard-Jules. *Mes Plus Beaux Quimper,* 1999.

Verlingue, Bernard-Jules, and Jean Rotté. *Quimper à L'Exposition Coloniale,* 1996.

Newsletters / Articles

Bulletin d'information de l'Association Les Amis du Musée de la Faïence, No. 1 – 14.

"Happy Birthday Quimper Ware, Quimper Style 300 Years, Faïence for all Time." *Country Living,* September 1990.

Harris, Frann. "From the Good Earth." *Art & Antiques,* January 1991.

Layec, Rozenn. "La Broderie Bigoudène." *ArMen,* July 1998.

Mali, Millicent S. *Old Quimper Review,* Vol. I – Vol. XII.

Quimper Club International Newsletter, Vol. 1 – 2.

Riding, Alan. "Celts and Proud of It (Even if They are French.)" *New York Times,* August 1991.

Young, Eric. "Not a Pretty Picture." *The Industry Standard,* March 2001.

Index

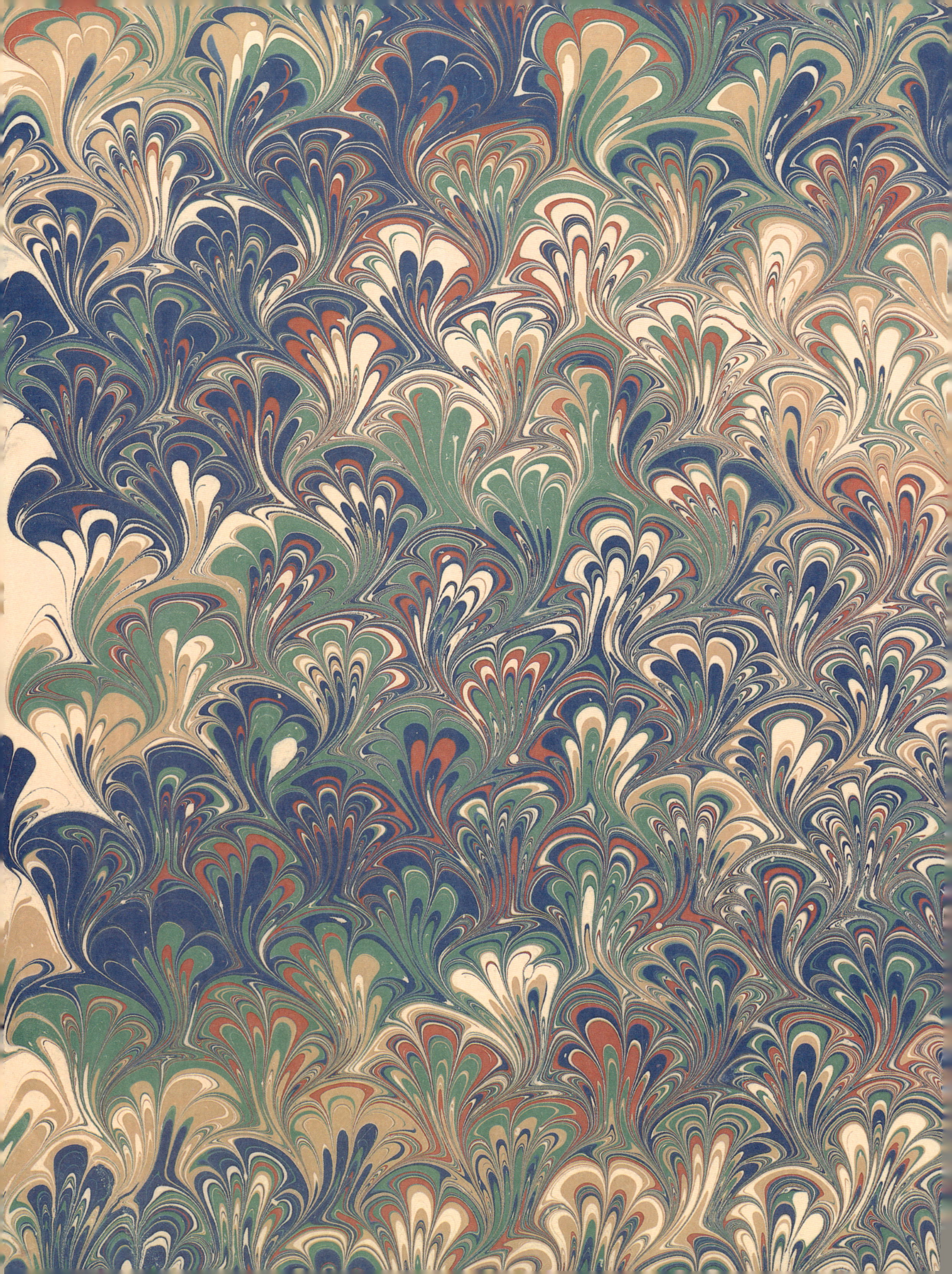